Villa Borghese

Via Salaria

Viale Regina Margherita

V. Dalmazia

Via Po

V. Isonzo

Via Nizza

Via Nomentana

Corso d'Italia

Via Piave

Policlinico
Universita

V. Veneto

Via Boncompagni

Viale Regina Elena

V. Ludovisi

panish
teps

XX Settembre

Biblioteca
Nazionale

Via Palestro

Via dell'Università

V. del due
Macelli

Via
Sistina

Via Barberini

Via

SALARIO
Museo
Nazionale
Romano
PIAZZA DEL
CINQUECENTO

Via Castro Pretorio

Via del Policlinico

Via del Tritone

V. d. Quattro Fontane

PIAZZA
DELLA
REPUBBLICA

A
revi
untain

Palazzo dei
Quirinale

Stazione
Termini

Via Marsala

ZA
ZIA

Via Nazionale

Via Panisperna

Via Cavour

Via Giovanni Giolitti

Via Tiburtina

glio

V. dei Fori Imperiali

Via Cavour

Via Giovanni Lanza

Via Merulana

PIAZZA
VITTORIO
EMANUELE

Forum

PIAZZA DEL
COLOSSEO

Via Labicana

Colosseum

Via Emanuele Fiberto

Viale Manzoni

V. S. Croce in Gerusalemme

PIAZZA
DI PTA.
MAGGIORE

MONTE
PALATINO

Via di S. Gregorio

Via Claudia

Parco del
Celio

Via di S. Stefano Rotondo

P. DI SAN
GIOVANNI
IN LATERANO

San Giovanni in
Laterano

Via dei Cerchi
Circo Massimo
(Circus Maximus)
a del Circo Massimo

CELIO

Via dell'Amba Aradam

Via d. Laterani

Via Appia

Via di

Via delle Terme

Via delle
Navicella

Via Druso

Via Gallia

P. DEI RE
DI ROMA

Viale Aventino

Via Cerveteri

Nuova

Terme di
Caracalla

Viale Metronio

Via Etruria

ale d.
Piramide Cestia

TINO

Via Aventina

Viale di Terme di Caracalla

Via Sacrico

Via Concordia

Viale Guido Baccelli

Via di Porta Latina

Via di Pora Sebastiano

Via Vetulonia

Via Siria

Viale Giotto

Rome Transport

TO YOUTH HOSTEL

FLAMINIO

F-LINE

A-LINE

Via G. Ferrari

Via Flaminia

•628•

•490•628•

•490•

•490•

•628•

Via Leptina

Via Angelico

Via Triomfale

Circ. Triomfale

Via Andrea Doria

Viale delle Medaglie d'Oro

•23•70•

•32•

•70•490•

Viale delle Milizie

LEPANTO

Viale Giulio Cesare

A-LINE

•70•

Via Marcanti Colonna

PIAZZA DEL POPOLO

•490•

OTTAVIANO

V. Ottaviano

Via Leone IV

Via Cola di Rienzo

•32•81•

Via Cicerone

Via del Babuino

Via di Ripetta

•81•

•269•

Via del Corso

•117•628•

Via Cipro

MOSCA

81 492

•23•492•

Via Crescenzio

•34•492•

•70•32•

PIAZZA CAVOUR

34

32

Via Condi

PIAZZA SILV

•23•492•

PIAZZA RISORGIMENTO

•23•492•

•81•

Via del Corso

64

Castel Sant'Angelo

•70•81•628•

•116•

St. Peter's Basilica

Via d. Conciliazione

Tiber

PIAZZA COLONNA

Viale Vaticano

•34•46•

•46•64•

870

Viale dei Coronari

PIAZZA NAVONA

•70•81•116•492•628•

•116•

Pantheon

Corso Vittorio Emanuele II

•23•870•

•23•870•

Via Giulia

•870•

CAMPO DEI FIORI

•44•46•60•64•70•81•170•492•628•

V. d. Plebescito

Stazione S. Pietro

34

Viale Gregorio VII

116

LARGO ARGENTINA

•44•46•

Via Aracelia

•870•

MONTE DEL GIANICOLO

Teatro Marcello

Via Teatro Marcello

Isola Tiberina

Via Aurelia Antica

60

TRASTEVERE

PIAZZA SONNINO

•44•170•

Via di S. Pancrazio

•44•870•

Viale Glorioso

V. Nicola Fabrizi

Porta Portese

•23•

AV

•23•715•

•44•870•

Via Giacinto Carini

Via Dandolo

•44•

Viale di Trastevere

Via Marmorea

•870•

Via Fontelana

Via di Villa Pamphili

•13•170•

•23•23•715•

Via Vitella

Viale dei Quattro Venti

Via G. Barrilli

Via Alessandro Poerio

Via Giovanni Branca

Via Nicola Zabella

•673•

•673•

Galvani

•44•

Via F. Oranam

13

Via di Donna Olimpia

Via

Parco Testaccio

PIRAMIDE

•13•

TESTACCIO

N

Stazione Trastevere

Circonvallazione

Gianicolense

•23•

Via Ostiense

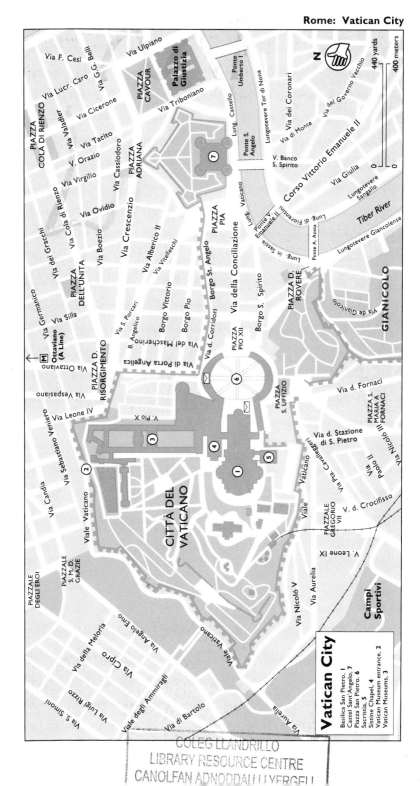

Vatican City

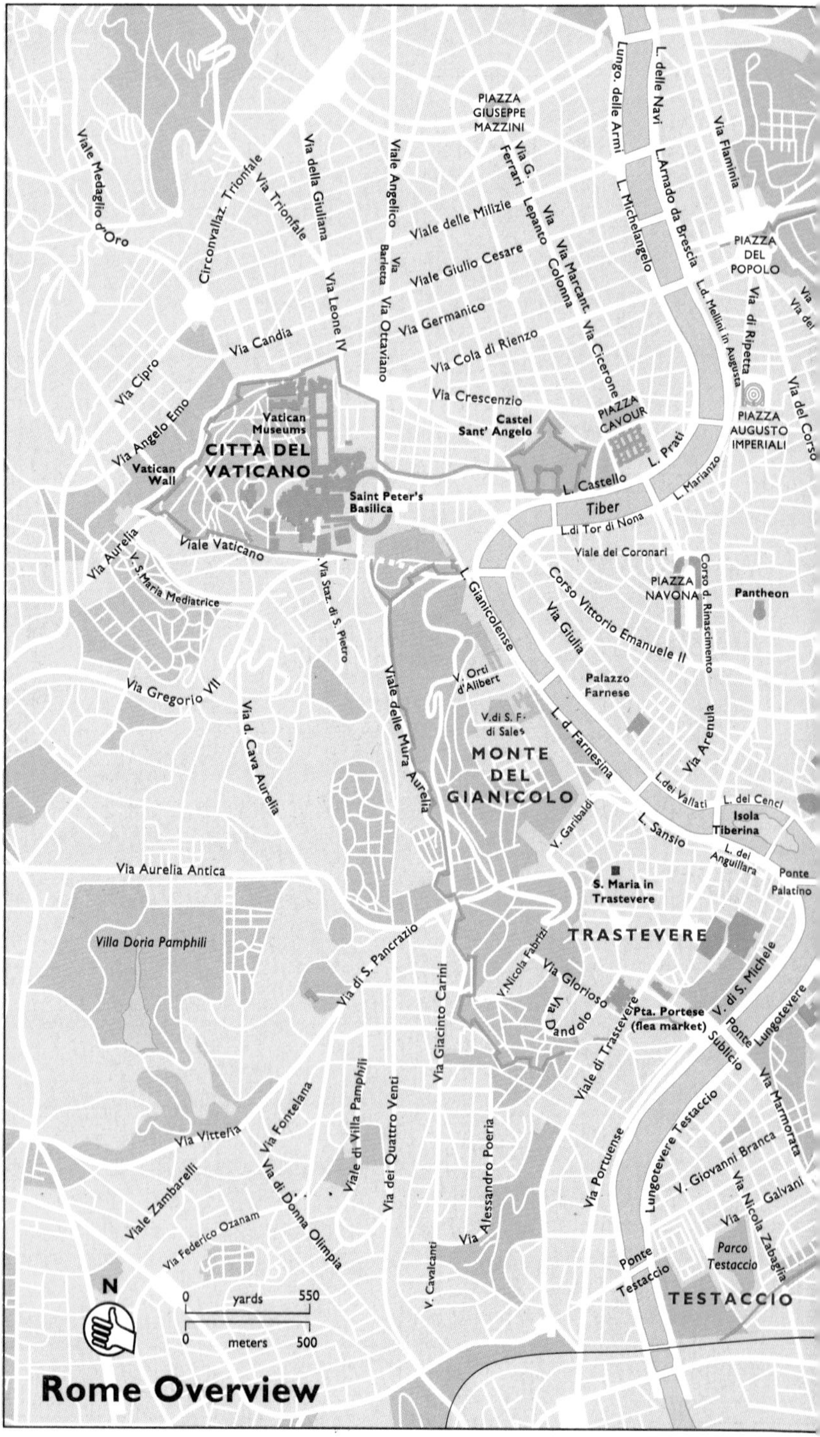
PIAZZA
GIUSEPPE
MAZZINI
Lungo. delle Armi
L. delle Navi
Via Flaminia
Viale Medaglio d'Oro
Circonvallaz. Trionfale
Via Trionfale
Via della Giuliana
Viale Angelico
Via G. Ferrari
Via Lepanto
L. Michelangelo
L.Arnaldo da Brescia
Viale delle Milizie
Via Barletta
Viale Giulio Cesare
Via Marcant. Colonna
PIAZZA
DEL
POPOLO
Via Leone IV
Via Ottaviano
Via Germanico
L.d. Mellini in Augusta
Via di Ripetta
Via del
Via Candia
Via Cola di Rienzo
Via Cicerone
Via Cipro
Via Crescenzio
PIAZZA
AUGUSTO
IMPERIALI
Via del Corso
Via Angelo Emo
Vatican
Museums
Castel
Sant' Angelo
PIAZZA
CAVOUR
CITTÀ DEL
VATICANO
L. Prati
Vatican
Wall
L. Castello
L. Marianzo
Saint Peter's
Basilica
Tiber
L.di Tor di Nona
Via Aurelia
Viale Vaticano
Viale dei Coronari
V. S.Maria Mediatrice
Via Staz. di S. Pietro
L. Gianicolense
Corso Vittorio Emanuele II
PIAZZA
NAVONA
Corso d. Rinascimento
Pantheon
Via Giulia
Via Gregorio VII
Viale delle Mura Aurelia
V. Orti
d'Alibert
Palazzo
Farnese
Via d. Cava Aurelia
V.di S. F-
di Sales
MONTE
DEL
GIANICOLO
L. d. Farnesina
Via Arenula
L.dei Vallati
L. del Cenci
Isola
Tiberina
V. Garibaldi
L. Sansio
L. dei
Anguillara
Via Aurelia Antica
Ponte
Palatino
S. Maria in
Trastevere
Villa Doria Pamphili
TRASTEVERE
Via di S. Pancrazio
V.Nicola Fabrizi
Via Glorioso
V. di S. Michele
Via Dandolo
Pta. Portese
(flea market)
Ponte Lungotevere
Via Giacinto Carini
Viale di Trastevere
Ponte Sublicio
Via Marmorata
Viale di Villa Pamphili
Lungotevere Testaccio
Via Fontelana
Via Vitellia
Viale dei Quattro Venti
Via Portuense
V. Giovanni Branca
Via Galvani
Via di Donna Olimpia
Via Alessandro Poeria
Viale Zambarelli
Via Nicola Zabaglia
Via Federico Ozanam
V. Cavalcanti
Ponte
Testaccio
Parco
Testaccio
TESTACCIO
N
0 yards 550
0 meters 500
Rome Overview

VILLA BORGHESE

BOLOGNA

Via Po

Via Salaria

Via Nizza

Viale Regina Margherita

•60•

Corso d'Italia •490•

Via Piave

Via Nomentana

Viale del Policlinico •490•

POLICLINICO

olo del Brasile

116

GNA

Via V. Veneto

Via Boncompagni

Via Piemonte

Via XX Settembre

N. Castro Pretoria

Viale Regina Elena

Via Sistina

•60•492•

SALARIO
CASTRO PRETORIO

•60•492•

Via Barberini

V. Goito

•492•

BARBERINI

V. d. Quattro Fontane

REPUBBLICA

P. D.
CINQUECENTO

V. Volturno

B-LINE

Via Presotoriano

Via Lollis

ain

P. D. A-LINE
REPUBBLICA

64
170 714

110

Stazione
Termini

•492•

•70•

TERMINI

Via Marsala

Via Tiburtino

embre

•64•70•170•

Via Nazionale

Via Giovanni Giolitti

Via Cavour

B-LINE

•70•

70

IA

•117•

Via Giov. Lanza

doglio

Via Cavour

CAVOUR

P. VITT.
EMANUELE

VITTORIO

Viale Manzoni

P. PORTA
MAGGIORE

•13•

Roman
Forum

COLOSSEO

Via Labicana

•714•

Via Merulana

MANZONI

Via Statilia

PALATINO

V. di S. Gregorio

Colosseum

•13•

Via di S. Giovanni in Laterano

S. Giovanni
in Laterano

Via Emanuele Filiberto

•13•

A-LINE

•81•

V. Claudia

117

Via di S. Stefano Rotondo

218

S. GIOVANNI

Via la Spezia

•81•628•

•13•81•673•

B-LINE

CELIO

Via della Navicella

Via dell'Amba Aradam

•81•673•714•

Via d. Laterani

Via Appia Nuova

Via Acosta

Via Monza

Via Taranto

RE DI ROMA

dei Cerchi

Circo Massimo

•628•

CIRCO MASSIMO

v. delle Terme

•673•

•218•673•

Via Gallia

Via Magna Grecia

Via Cerveteri

ale Aventino

Via Aventina

Terme Di
Caracalla

Viale Druso

Viale Metronio

•673•

Via Satrico •628•

Via Concordia

Via Etruria

PONTE LUNGO

Via Ivrea

Viale Guido Baccelli

Viale di Terme di Caracalla

•714•

Via di Porta Latina

Via di Porta Sebastiano

•218•

•218•

Via Vetulonia

Via Latina

V. Vescia

673

•628•

Stazione
Ustiense

•715•

Porta
S. Sebastiano

TO
CATACOMBS

Via Appia Antica

TO LAURENTINA

0   1/2 mile

0   500 meters

Central Rome

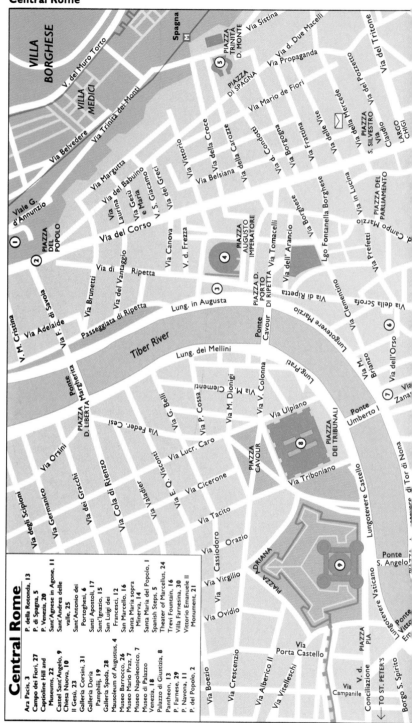

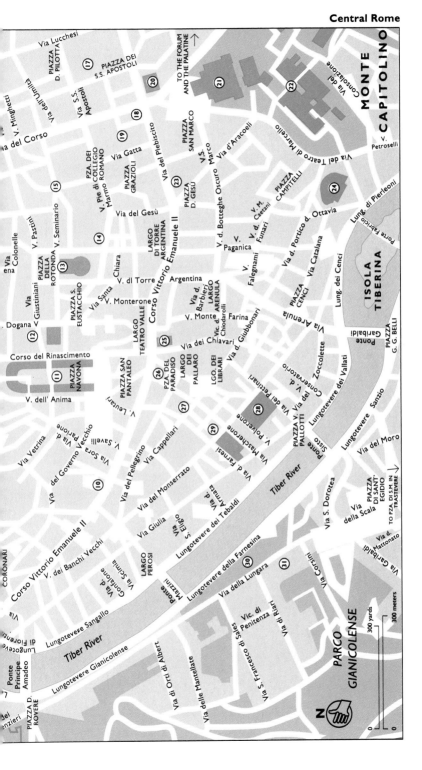

MONTE
CAPITOLINO

Via Lucchesi

PIAZZA D. PILOTTA

⑰ PIAZZA DEI S.S. APOSTOLI

TO THE FORUM AND THE PALATINE ↑

㉑

㉒

Via del Consolazione

S.S. Apostoli

⑳

Via del Corso

Via dei Pastini

Via della Umiltà

V. Minghetti

Via del Corso

⑱

⑲ Via Gatta

PIAZZA GRAZIOLI

V. Pie di COLLEGIO Marmo ROMANO

PIAZZA SAN MARCO

V.S. Marco

Via d'Aracoeli

V. del Plebiscito

㉓ PIAZZA D. GESÙ

Via del Gesù

V. Petroselli

⑮

V. Seminario

V. Pastini

Via Colonnelle

Via ena

LARGO DI TORRE ARGENTINA

Corso Vittorio Emanuele II

V. d. Botteghe Oscuro

V. M. Caetani

V. d. Funari

PIAZZA CAMPITELLI

㉔

Via del Teatro di Marcello

⑭

PIAZZA DELLA ROTONDA

⑬

Via Santa Chiara

V. dl Torre Argentina

V. Paganica

V. Falegnami

Via d. Portico d. Ottavia

Lung. di Pierleoni

Porta Fabricio

V. Giustiniani

PIAZZA S. EUSTACCHIO

V. Monterone

V. d. Barbieri

LARGO ARENULA

Via d. Chiodaroli

Via Catalana

ISOLA TIBERINA

. Dogana ⑫

Corso del Rinascimento

LARGO TEATRO VALLE

V. Monte Farina

PIAZZA CENCI

Via Arenula

Lung. dei Cenci

⑪ PIAZZA NAVONA

V. dell' Anima

PIAZZA SAN PANTALEO

㉕

Via dei Chiavari

LARGO DEI LIBRARI

V. d. Giubbonari

V. d. Zoccolette

Ponte Garibaldi

PIAZZA G. G. BELLI

㉖ PZA. DEL PARADISO

LARGO DEI PALLARO

㉗

V. Leutari

V. Savelli

V. d. Parione

Via del Pellegrino

Via Cappellari

㉙ Via delle Maschere

V. Polverone

㉘ V. dei Pettinari

Lungotevere dei Vallati

Lungotevere Sanzio

Via Verina

Via Sora

Via del Governo Vecchio

Via del Monserrato

Via d. Farnesi

PIAZZA V. PALLOTTI

Ponte Sisto

Lungotevere dei Tebaldi

Via del Moro

⑩

CORONARI

Corso Vittorio Emanuele II

V. dei Banchi Vecchi

V. Scimia

Gonfalone

Via Giulia

Via S. Eligio

Via d. Armata

Via S. Dorotea

Via della Scala

PIAZZA DI SANT' EGIDIO

TO PZA. DI S.M. IN TRASTEVERE →

Via di Fiorenzi

Lungotevere Sangallo

LARGO PEROSI

Monte Mazzini

Lungotevere della Farnesina

Via della Lungara

Via Corsini

Via d. Mattonsato

Via Garibaldi

Ponte Principe Amadeo

PIAZZA D. ROVERE

Lungotevere Gianicolense

Via di Orti di Albert

Via delle Mantellate

Tiber River

Vic. di Penitenza

Via S. Francesco di Sales

Via di Riari

PARCO GIANICOLENSE

N

300 yards

300 meters

Rome: Villa Borghese

V. Giovannelli

Via di S. Teresa

Via Po

V. Puglia

V. Romagna

Corso d'Italia

Giovanni Paisiello

PIAZZALE DEI RAIMONDI

Galleria Borghese

Via Boncompagni

Via Quintina

Via Sardegna

Via Sicilia

Via Piemonte

Via S. Mercadante

Via P. Raimondi

Via del Daini

Via dell'Uccelliera

V. Puccini

Via Museo Borghese

Viale Museo Borghese

PIAZZA E. SIENKIEWICZ

Via Pinciana

Via Toscana

Via Marche

Viale del Giardino

GIARDINO ZOOLOGICO

Zoologico

Viale dell'Uccelliera

Viale dei Cavalli Marini

Pineta

Viale d. Goethe

PIAZZALE BRASILE

Porta Pinciana

Via Vittorio Veneto

Via Emilia

Via Ludovisi

Via Liguria

VILLA BORGHESE

Viale P. Canonica

PIAZZA DI SIENA

Viale Casina di Raffaello

V. di S. Paolo del Brasile

Via Aurora

Via Porta Pinciana

Via Ulisse Aldrovandi

PIAZZALE D. CANESTRE

V. dell'Aranciera

V. Magnolie

GALOPPATOIO

Galleria Naz. d'Arte Moderne

Via Omero

V. F. Laguardia

Via Bernadotte

PIAZZALE DEL FIOCCO

Viale Galoppatoio

V. del Muro Torto

VILLA MEDICI

Via del Babuino

Spagna

A LINE

Viale delle Belle Arti

PIAZZALE PAOLA BORGHESE

Via Madama

Viale Madama

V. Washington

PIAZZALE DEI MARTIRI

Viale Valadier

Viale d. Belvedere

Viale Trinità dei Monti

Via del Babuino

Via della Croce

Via Vittoria

Museo Naz. di Villa Giulia

VILLA STROHL FERN

VILLA RUFFO

Flaminio

PIAZZALE FLAMINIO

PIAZZA DEL POPOLO

Via del Corso

Via Brunetti

Via del Vantaggio

V. A. Canova

PIAZZA AUGUSTO IMPERATORE

Via Ripetta

Via di Villa Giulia

V. di S. Eugenio

Via Flaminia

Via Flaminia

PIAZZA DELLA MARINA

V. D. A. Azuni

V. G. Pisanelli

V. Romanosi

V. Disavoia

PIAZZA SAVOIA DEL POPOLO

Lungo. in Augusta

Lungotevere delle Navi

Lungo. Arnaldo da Brescia

Ponte Nenni

Ponte Margherita

Lungo. d. Mellini

Ponte d. Risorg

Ponte G. Matteoti

Fiume Tevere

Lungo. Michelangelo

Via Fed. Cesi

Via E. Q. Visconte

Via G. Belli

PIAZZA MONTE GRAPPA

Lungotevere delle Armi

PIAZZA DELLE CINQUE GIORNATE

Via Giulio Cesare

A LINE

Via degli Scipioni

Via Pompeo Magno

Via dei Gracchi

PIAZZA D. LIBERTA

Via Valadier

PIAZZA COLA DI RIENZO

Via Giuseppe Mazzini

Viale della Milizie

Via Settembrini

Lepanto

Via Marc. Colonna

Via Ezio

Via Boezio

N

Villa Borghese

200 yards

200 meters

Let's Go writers travel on your budget.

"Guides that penetrate the veneer of the holiday brochures and mine the grit of real life."

—The Economist

"The writers seem to have experienced every rooster-packed bus and lunar-surfaced mattress about which they write."

—The New York Times

"All the dirt, dirt cheap."

—People

Great for independent travelers.

"The guides are aimed not only at young budget travelers but at the independent traveler; a sort of streetwise cookbook for traveling alone."

—The New York Times

"Flush with candor and irreverence, chock full of budget travel advice."

—The Des Moines Register

"An indispensible resource, *Let's Go*'s practical information can be used by every traveler."

—The Chattanooga Free Press

Let's Go is completely revised each year.

"Only *Let's Go* has the zeal to annually update every title on its list."

—The Boston Globe

"Unbeatable: good sightseeing advice; up-to-date info on restaurants, hotels, and inns; a commitment to money-saving travel; and a wry style that brightens nearly every page."

—The Washington Post

All the important information you need.

"*Let's Go* authors provide a comedic element while still providing concise information and thorough coverage of the country. Anything you need to know about budget traveling is detailed in this book."

—The Chicago Sun-Times

"Value-packed, unbeatable, accurate, and comprehensive."

—Los Angeles Times

Let's Go Publications

Let's Go: Alaska & the Pacific Northwest 2001
Let's Go: Australia 2001
Let's Go: Austria & Switzerland 2001
Let's Go: Boston 2001 **New Title!**
Let's Go: Britain & Ireland 2001
Let's Go: California 2001
Let's Go: Central America 2001
Let's Go: China 2001
Let's Go: Eastern Europe 2001
Let's Go: Europe 2001
Let's Go: France 2001
Let's Go: Germany 2001
Let's Go: Greece 2001
Let's Go: India & Nepal 2001
Let's Go: Ireland 2001
Let's Go: Israel 2001
Let's Go: Italy 2001
Let's Go: London 2001
Let's Go: Mexico 2001
Let's Go: Middle East 2001
Let's Go: New York City 2001
Let's Go: New Zealand 2001
Let's Go: Paris 2001
Let's Go: Peru, Bolivia & Ecuador 2001 **New Title!**
Let's Go: Rome 2001
Let's Go: San Francisco 2001 **New Title!**
Let's Go: South Africa 2001
Let's Go: Southeast Asia 2001
Let's Go: Spain & Portugal 2001
Let's Go: Turkey 2001
Let's Go: USA 2001
Let's Go: Washington, D.C. 2001
Let's Go: Western Europe 2001 **New Title!**

Let's Go *Map Guides*

Amsterdam	New Orleans
Berlin	New York City
Boston	Paris
Chicago	Prague
Florence	Rome
Hong Kong	San Francisco
London	Seattle
Los Angeles	Sydney
Madrid	Washington, D.C.

Coming Soon: *Dublin* and *Venice*

Let's Go

Rome

2001

Brady R. Dewar editor

researcher-writers
Adriane Noel Giebel
Charles R. Scott
Jeff Zinsmeister

Mike Durcak map editor
Luke Marion photographer

Macmillan

Published in Great Britain 2001 by Macmillan, an imprint of Macmillan Publishers Ltd, 25 Eccleston Place, London, SW1W 9NF, Basingstoke and Oxford.
Associated companies throughout the world
www.macmillan.com

Maps by David Lindroth copyright © 2001, 2000, 1999, 1998, 1997, 1996, 1995, 1994, 1993, 1992, 1991, 1990, 1989, 1988 by St. Martin's Press.

Published in the United States of America by St. Martin's Press.

ISBN: 0-333-90152-5
First edition
10 9 8 7 6 5 4 3 2 1

Let's Go: Rome is written by Let's Go Publications, 67 Mount Auburn Street, Cambridge, MA 02138, USA.

Let's Go® and the thumb logo are trademarks of Let's Go, Inc.
Printed in the USA on recycled paper with biodegradable soy ink.

Contents

🖐 daytripping 213

✈ planning your trip 245

🔨 accommodations 269

📲 living in rome 281

🔧 service directory 293

🔢 index 301

maps 312

➕ Hospital	✈ Airport	🏛 Museum	▲ Mountain		
✪ Police	🚌 Bus Station	🏨 Hotel/Hostel		Park	
✉ Post Office	☎ Train Station	⛺ Camping			
ⓘ Tourist Office	Ⓜ METRO STATION	🍎 Food & Drink		Beach	
$ Bank	⚓ Ferry Landing	🛍 Shopping			
⚑ Embassy/Consulate	✝ Church	♪ Arts & Entertainment		Water	
▪ Site or Point of Interest	✡ Synagogue	Nightlife			
☎ Telephone Office	🕌 Mosque	💻 Internet Café	N		
♨ Theater	🏰 Castle	Pedestrian Zone	👍 The Let's Go thumb always points N O R T H.		

RESEARCHER-WRITERS

*Adriane Noel Giebel   *Principal Collections, Vatican City*

Adriane, the consummate *Let's Go* veteran, must have thought she could sleep through Rome after such past itineraries as treks through rural Scotland and France and an assignment in Greece that culminated in some hillside surgical work—sans anesthesia. We have to hand it to her for staying awake through miles of sculpture galleries and hours spent studying art history. When each day's work was over, Adriane headed to Tazza d'Oro for her caffeine fix, then was off to Testaccio for some stellar nightlife research. After that, Adriane was able to zip through the rest of her itinerary, recapturing the title of bionic R-W. Adriane's goal in life is to someday visit the Vatican Museums and find ALL the galleries open.

Charles R. Scott   *Ancient City, Centro Storico, Termini and San Lorenzo*

Heading to Rome was something of a homecoming for Charley, who spent the first ten years of his life there with his archaeologist parents. Charley, a veteran of *Let's Go: Italy*, put his Classics education to work—while scouring the ruins of the Roman Forum, he not only reorganized our Sights chapter into a informative, pithy, and amusing read, but he discovered Julius Caesar's tomb, learned the meaning of life, and found Elvis. Charley kept us shocked and amused back home with tales of frightening underwear-clad hotel owners, gaudy American tourists, and papal scandals of biblical proportion. When he was not shredding lions in the Colosseum or worshipping Jupiter in the Pantheon, Charley found time to explore pasta museums, wax model galleries, and other repositories of fine art.

Jeff Zinsmeister   *Trastevere, Piazza di Spagna, Southern Rome*

Jeff managed to survive his stay in Rome without any major physical injury, unlike his misadventures in times past. In a strange coincidence, he also managed to survive without the assistance of a *motorino*, but just barely. Jeff adjusted quite well to the Mediterranean lifestyle: when not engaged in serious loitering or basket weaving, he could be found researching the far-flung suburbs that made up his itinerary, scouting out adult entertainment options, or poring over his copy over *caffè strettos* in Rome's finer coffee bars. Though at times Jeff was resigned to the outer reaches of the Eternal City, his editor was gracious enough to send him cliff-diving in the Pontine Islands. Jeff also had the honor of eating in Rome's worst restaurant, which he assures us is not in this book.

Charles DeSimone	*Pompeii, Herculaneum, Paestum*
Sam Spital	*Orvieto and Assisi*
Marc A. Wallenstein	*Editor, Italy*
Matthew S. Ryan	*Associate Editor, Italy*
Fiona McKinnon	*Associate Editor, Italy*

ACKNOWLEDGMENTS

BRD THANKS: Pierluigi and Fulvia, for correcting my Italian and introducing me to one of the world's greatest cities—and, for joining me there, Don, Bettye, Michael and Mom (who you can all thank—or not!—for my copy editing skills; this one's for her). Dad and Chris, Josh, Jay, and Kiersten. Jamie and Missy—if only everyone had siblings so cool. And of course, the cutest nephew in the entire world, Conor (he's made of love). Lani Johnson and other teachers who've helped me along my way. Jordan for all the nasty emails, and his mother, Susan, for teaching me that a little neuro-ego-materio-romanto-idealism is never a bad thing. Ugly, my most beautiful best friend, for the late night phone calls and cutting me down to size. Shana, for being himself. Meyeon, for always managing to win with me, and Sarah, for convincing me to apply at the Go and always speaking her mind. Ankur (half the reason this book is so good, and if you disagree, more than half the reason for that): I couldn't have asked for a more entertaining manager and partner. Charley, for all the last-minute mapping and incredible marginalia, and Jeff, for the most complete copy a guy could ask for. Miz Lucy and the other patrons (regular and irregular) of the Café de la Cité, for making life in this office seem like more than just work. Bede, for many lessons. And Alex, for putting up with all the late nights and countless other shenanigans. If there's anyone I've forgotten—I haven't.

ROMA 2001 THANKS: Pierluigi and Fulvia: words truly cannot express. Ankur, Kate, the Melissas, and the 2001 City Guides for turning this book inside out. Dara and Luke for some kick-ass photo work and John and Mike for their bad-ass mapping. Anne, for keeping the wheels greased. ANG thanks her private Michelangelo expert, Nitzan, and Yuh-Shioh, her clubbing partner. JZ thanks Fabiana, and CRS thanks god for the Roma soccer win. And, of course, we all thank our family, friends, roommates, and lovers….

Editor
Brady R. Dewar
Managing Editor
Ankur Ghosh
Map Editor
Mike Durcak

Publishing Director
Kaya Stone
Editor-in-Chief
Kate McCarthy
Production Manager
Melissa Rudolph
Cartography Manager
John Fiore
Editorial Managers
Alice Farmer, Ankur Ghosh,
Aarup Kubal, Anup Kubal
Financial Manager
Bede Sheppard
Low-Season Manager
Melissa Gibson
Marketing & Publicity Managers
Olivia L. Cowley, Esti Iturralde
New Media Manager
Jonathan Dawid
Personnel Manager
Nicholas Grossman
Photo Editor
Dara Cho
Production Associates
Sanjay Mavinkurve, Nicholas
Murphy, Rosa Rosalez,
Matthew Daniels, Rachel Mason,
Daniel Visel
(re)Designer
Matthew Daniels
Office Coordinators
Sarah Jacoby, Chris Russell

Director of Advertising Sales
Cindy Rodriguez
Senior Advertising Associates
Adam Grant, Rebecca Rendell
Advertising Artwork Editor
Palmer Truelson

President
Andrew M. Murphy
General Manager
Robert B. Rombauer
Assistant General Manager
Anne E. Chisholm

HOW TO USE THIS BOOK

How to use this book? Ideally, you should read it cover to cover and memorize everything. In reality, we know this **brand-new, redesigned** (complete with **photos!**) guide to Rome is just too irresistible to put down. So go ahead, bring it with you and join in-the-know tourists exploring the mesmerizing streets and sights of Rome. Know, however, that you are carrying the savviest guide available to all that is hip, cutting-edge, and not-to-be-missed in the Eternal City.

Start planning your big city escapade with **Discover Rome,** which breaks down the city's top 25 sights, annual festivals, **suggested itineraries,** and **Let's Go Picks,** the best (and weirdest) of Rome. Discover is also home to our two **half-day walking tours,** which will take you through some of Rome's most picturesque neighborhoods and past its most famous attractions. If you're in a hurry, walk straight through, and simply admire some of Rome's greatest sights from a distance, but if you have more time, use the cross-references and stop by some of the sights and museums along the way. For an after-dinner walking tour, flip to **Nightlife.**

The **Life and Times** chapter is like Cliff's Notes to three thousand years of Roman history and culture, condensing everyone from St. Peter to Michelangelo to Mussolini into an oh-so-witty survey course. Before you completely lose yourself in the city's wonders, however, read through **Planning Your Trip,** which has info on everything you need to plan your urban sojourn, from visas and plane tickets to bank cards and insurance. For those spending months (or even years) in Rome, **Living in Rome** breaks down everything from finding housing and procuring long-term visas to community centers and where to work out.

Once in Rome, **When in Rome** will be your best friend, dishing the dirt on the city's neighborhoods, public transport, and even how to act like a true Roman. The neighborhood breakdown here mirrors that of the rest of the book. **Sights, Food and Wine, Nightlife,** and **Accommodations** are all organized in the same geographical order: the Ancient City is listed first, followed by the Centro Storico, the region near the Spanish Steps, the Villa Borghese, the Vatican City, Trastevere, the area near Termini, and Southern Rome. All neighborhoods—complete with most hotels, museums, monuments, restaurants, bars, and shopping highlights—are plotted in the **map appendix** at the end of the book. Finally, the **Service Directory** is a quick reference to any phone number that you could possibly need; if you need to visit an embassy, find a hotline, rent a car, take a tour, or call a taxi, find that info here. Should you, for some reason, want you leave the city, **Daytripping** suggests some great spots to visit in South-Central Italy, and includes all the advice and information you'll need.

Scattered throughout this guide are tips on how best to explore Rome. Entries with a ◪ are our favorite favorites; they're either super cheap, super hip, or just plain super duper. Look for **On the Cheap** sidebars that highlight the best deals in the city. Or, if you want to live large, seek out **The Big Splurge** sidebars. Absolute essentials—such as using those scary European ATMs—are highlighted in white **Read Me!** boxes. Plain old **black sidebars** give the low-down on all that is quirky, interesting, and fab about Rome. Whether you want to know about gladiators or just how to look and act like a Prada-wearing, Invicta-toting, cell-phone-talking Roman, you'll find the details here.

And remember, anything you can't find is probably in the **Index.**

Discover Rome

Italy will return to the splendors of Rome, said the major. I don't like Rome, I said. It is hot and full of fleas. You don't like Rome? Yes, I love Rome. Rome is the mother of nations. I will never forget Romulus suckling the Tiber. What? Nothing. Let's all go to Rome to-night and never come back. Rome is a beautiful city, said the major.
—Ernest Hemingway, *A Farewell to Arms*

Rome is a sensory overload, rushing down the hills of the Lazio to knock you flat on your back, gasping for air and dying for more. It will exhaust any term you throw at it: tantalizing, intimidating, glorious, excruciating.... A contradiction in terms, Rome is all these and more: it is the capital of kingdoms and republics, the birthplace of Christianity, and the seat of modern Catholicism. Its system of government is still imitated today, its architectural feats have defined the course of modern building, its art is unparalleled, and its most recent contribution to world culture, its cinema, is revered. Rome is better than you; expect no excuses for how overwhelming it is.

Rome is a city of death and a city of life. Concerts animate the crumbling ruins, kids play soccer in the Circus Maximus, and august *palazzi* now serve as movie houses. In *bella Roma*, everything is beautiful and everything tastes good. Excise your senses from the crush of smog, Fiats, and maniacal mopeds that surge through its streets. Enjoy the dizzying paradox that is the *Caput Mundi*, is the Eternal City, is Rome.

WHEN TO GO

Few would disagree that a Roman **spring** is nothing less than heaven. The weather is pleasantly balmy (hovering around 50 to 70°F), but the tourists haven't yet caught on. Rome's gardens and green spaces catch fire, and Lazio's freshest produce fills the

1

ROME BY THE NUMBERS

Area: 577 mi². In that space are crammed 981 churches and 280 fountains.

Distance from the Mediterranean: 17 mi.

Official Age of the City: 2754 years. In That Time, there have been 168 popes, 73 emperors, and 9.3 million pairs of tight leather pants.

Population: 2.8 million (Metro Rome is home to over 4.5 million). Of those, 94% have their children baptized Catholic; 12% go to mass and confession weekly; and 37% believe they've been afflicted with the "evil eye."

Tourists: 15 million per year. (That's more than five tourists per Roman per year—but who's counting?)

Cars on Rome's Streets: 2 million daily.

Cats on Rome's Streets: do you *really* want to know?

Passengers on Rome's Metro: 3 million daily.

Ticket Inspectors: 120.

Gallons of Water Delivered Per Hour by Ancient Aqueducts: 312,000.

"Egyptian" Obelisks: 13.

Egyptian Obelisks: 7.

Egyptian Obelisks in Egypt: Fewer than that.

Pyramids in Rome: 1.

Pyramids in Egypt: 4.

streets. By June, the rains have ceased and hotels are booming. A Roman **summer** is sweltering (65-85°F) and congested, but you can catch major exhibitions, exciting festivals, and concerts under the stars. When the city gets too thick, cool off in the Mediterranean or in cold volcanic lakes. In August, the Romans leave town; you may not find as many hole-in-the-wall *trattorie* open, but the crowds will subside a bit. The trend continues into the **fall**, when the temperatures drop (45-60°F) and the prices do, too. **Winter** brings cold (expect temperatures between 40°F and 55°F), rain, and some of the lowest prices of the year, but it also brings the holidays, which are a major to-do in the city of St. Peter.

ROME'S MULTIPLE PERSONALITIES

CATHOLIC ROME. "Jesus, Mary, and Joseph! This city's churches are just divine. **St. Peter's Basilica** (p. 115) wins out for sheer grandeur, but even it can't touch **San Giovanni in Laterano** (p. 131), which gives new meaning to the term *Caput Mundi* ("Head of the World")—it holds the heads of both Peter and Paul. **San Clemente** (p. 129) wins the versatility award: it's a 12th-century church on top of a 4th-century church on top of a 2nd-century *mithraeum*, all on top of still-working Roman sewers. Just don't spend too long in the pagan lower levels. Speaking of heathens, those pesky Jesuits have put down roots at **Il Gesù** (p. 95), but between you, me, and J.P., it's a little gaudy for my taste. We're still not sure how those 2nd-century heathens built the **Pantheon** (p. 97), but that didn't stop us from turning it into a church, or from covering the nearby Temple to Wisdom with **Santa Maria Sopra Minerva** (p. 98), home to the remains of my favorite saint, Catherine (Cathy to her friends). The beauty of these churches was truly awe-inspiring, but the thing that nearly sent me into an ecstatic fit was seeing and hearing the **pope** himself (p. 115)."

MACABRE ROME. "Never have I felt nearer the glorious pits of Hell and the doors to the other side than on my sojourn in Rome. Don't miss the thousands of skeletons at the **Capuchin Crypt** (p. 110) or in the **catacombs** (p. 133), which once held the remains of thousands of Christians. I nearly went to pieces over the churches of Rome, which are chock-full of the **heads** (see p. 131) and **fingers** (see p. 127) of saints. (Then there's the **Rostra** (p. 73), where Cicero's hands and feet were put on display in ancient Roman times.) For a perfect picnic, I'd recommend the dungeons of the **Mamertine Prison** (p. 91). No dark day in Rome is complete without a spooky brew or two at **Pub Hallo'Ween** (p. 208)."

TACKY ROME. "Ohmigosh, so, like, me and my friend Traci wanted to go to Cancún, but I won a trip to Rome instead. So once we got to France, we saw some churches and ruins and stuff, but the best part was definitely P. Barberini (p. 111)—they had a **Planet Hollywood** and everything! We got some great **cheap plastic designer knock-offs** at one of the street markets. We had so much fun riding the Gravitron at **LunEUR** that I almost lost the **popesicles** (p. 167) I had after lunch (they look like some famous old dude or something). One of the best places for dinner is definitely the **McDonald's** (p. 188) in P. di Spagna—it's made out of marble! Oh yeah, the best bar in town has got to be **The Drunken Ship** (p. 205); there are lots of Americans there—Roman sounds funny anyways!"

TORTURED INTELLECTUAL ROME. "My soul brims with ennui, but Rome—city of dark romance, abode of Bertolucci—brings life to my mundane existence. They wouldn't let me smoke my cloves in the Vatican (religion is so bourgeois anyway), so yesterday, after spending hours studying history in the **Museo della Civiltà Romana** (p. 157), I caught a *film noir* festival at the **Palazzo delle Esposizioni** (p. 161) and dug some blues over straight vodka (on the rocks) at **Alexanderplatz Jazz Club** (p. 177). Tonight, I'll probably dance with vegans and golf-clap for avant garde performance artists at **C.S.I.O.A. Villaggio Globale** (p. 210), but not before I stop in at **Diesel** (p. 164). White is the new black, you know."

LITERARY ROME. "Do as the expats did and hit your creative peak over espresso at **Caffè Greco** (p. 196). Sit on the nearby **Spanish Steps** (p. 107) rereading *Daisy Miller*, then drop by the **Keats-Shelley Memorial House** (see p. 159) for inspiration. If you really need to commune with the literary greats, head for **Cimitero Acattolico per gli Stanieri** (see p. 135), resting place of many of them. Finally, make like Ernest Hemingway, and drink the night away at one of Rome's fine **wine bars** (p. 196)."

HIGHBROW ROME. "God knows why you would use a budget guide in such a marvelous city, but make the best with what you have. A *Let's Go* rule to live by: never eat or sleep anywhere unless it's listed as a **Big Splurge** establishment. My favorite Grand Tour sights are the masterpieces—Bernini's *baldacchino* in **St. Peter's** (p. 115), **The Last Judgement** (p. 147), the **Pietà** (p. 116), the **Trevi Fountain** (p. 109)—and, of course, **Gucci** (p. 164). When you go, do take a **taxi** (p. 25)."

ROME ON FILM

So you're going to Rome. Learn from the mistakes of those who came before you—Gregory Peck (don't fall in love with a stranger), Spartacus (crucifixion sucks), Matt Damon (despite the face, Jude Law is not divine), etc.—and rent these flicks:

Gladiator. So Rome's hills aren't that big, Marcus Aurelius was no altruistic Republican, and gladiators weren't as hot as Russell Crowe. Plus, the fake blood was really awesome.

The Talented Mr. Ripley. More hotness, and in a big way! Learn all about how to dispose of bodies in the Eternal City. Once you get past the inordinate amount of time the film spends in those boring *northern* Italian towns, it's a pretty good psychological thriller.

Rome, Open City is a Rossellini classic about the city during WWII, covertly filmed while the city was still occupied by the Nazis.

La Dolce Vita, by Fellini, is just plain good. That's all there is to it. Actually, what makes it really good is the sea monster at the end.

Nights of Cabiria, another Fellini flick. Everyone should familiarize themselves with the wily ways of Roman prostitutes, especially those played by Fellini's wife. Devastatingly beautiful.

Spartacus. It's Kubrick and it's flawed, but it's got a young Kirk Douglas. What a man he was.

Roman Holiday is cute and features Audrey Hepburn and Gregory Peck. Watch out for that pesky Bocca della Verità!

Belly of An Architect. Peter Greenaway's amazing camera work and fascinatingly visceral imagery will make an enduring impression on your inner eye, whether you want it to or not.

Caligula is Bob Guccione's infamous sex-fest. See p. 46 for an ancient Rome that is just as exciting and not nearly as painful.

TOP 25 SIGHTS...

1. Musei Vaticano (p. 140). Rome's largest collection, the Vatican holds an ungodly percentage of the world's high art, representing the personal picks of Popes (of varying taste) since 1506. While you can't miss the Sistine Chapel or Raphael Rooms, other treasures, such as the collection of modern art, shouldn't be overlooked.

2. Basilica San Pietro (p. 115). Dwarfing cathedrals the world over, the house that Bernini built offers the delicate beauty of Michelangelo's *Pietà*, the breathtaking beauty of the best birds' eye view of Rome, and the bizarre beauty of six-inch popesicles—on sale in Vatican giftshops and personally approved by the Holy See.

3. Church of San Clemente (p. 129). Two churches older than Methuselah, a mithraeum older than that, walkways through ancient sewers—is there anything this church doesn't have? Well, yes, but you can buy booze at St. Paul's Outside the Walls (see p. 136).

4. Colosseum (p. 82). Too many tourists? Yes. Still mind-blowing? Definitely.

Roman Forum

5. Galleria Borghese (p. 149). A lovely 17th-century villa in a lovely wooded park houses this lovely museum. Highlights: lovely Caravaggios and a very lovely nude of Napoleon's sister.

6. Capuchin Crypt (p. 110). 4000 dead friars. Wow. The Capuchin Crypt will satisfy anyone's desire to see molding made out of femur and tibia. The Counter-Reformation facade is neat, too.

7. The Spanish Steps (p. 107). The eternal paradox of the Eternal City: it's only when you're relaxing on the Spanish Steps (a gift from France, no less) that you know you're in Rome.

8. Piazza Campidoglio (p. 89). Climb Michelangelo's stairway to this blindingly white square for a stunning view of the Forum. Admire the copy of the famous Aurelian statue, then see the real thing in the Capitoline Museums next door (p. 152).

9. Trevi Fountain (p. 109). This new (1762) addition to the Roman tourist circuit is well worth a look. Neptune and his tritons are pretty inviting, but, please, try not to jump in.

10. Palatine Hill (p. 84). If I were a first-century Roman emperor, this is certainly where I'd want to live. The suckling site of Remus and Romulus, the hill has some of Rome's best ruins.

Vittorio Emanuele II

11. Piazza Navona (p. 99). The buildings circling this oblong *piazza* rest on the ruins of an ancient stadium. Dine outside at some of Rome's poshest eateries to the sounds of Rome's finest collection of fountains, or simply stroll the area's narrow medieval streets.

12. Basilica Santa Maria Maggiore (p. 127). After its grand Baroque facade, Maggiore's striking classical interior is a surprise. Don't miss the apse's 13th-century mosaics of Mary dressed as a Byzantine Empress.

13. Church of Santa Maria in Trastevere (p. 123). The first of many Roman churches dedicated to Mary, this 12th-century specimen dominates a lively Trastevere *piazza*. The images of Mary and other female saints outside are a bit deceptive; inside are lots and lots of mosaics of men.

14. Museo Nazionale Etrusco di Villa Giulia (p. 151). You can go to Etruria (p. 229) and see the ruins of this ancient people's civilization, or you can come here and see all the artifacts plundered from them. Or you can do both.

Chiesa Nuova

15. The Pantheon (p. 97). The huge dome of this pagan temple-turned-church still puzzles architects, who can't figure out how it was erected using 2nd-century building techniques.

16. Il Gesù (p. 95). Worldy and gold-encrusted, this 16th-century church was headquarters of the Jesuit order, the hardcore priests who brought us the Counter-Reformation and the Hoyas.

17. Church of San Giovanni in Laterano (p. 131). Former home of the Pope, resting place of the noggins of Peter and Paul, and a bad-ass *baldacchino*.

18. Church of Santa Maria in Cosmedin (p. 92). Of course, the stonework of this 6th-century church is worth a look, but we all know why you're here. Go ahead, stick your hand in the mouth of the Bocca della Verità and tell a lie. We dare you.

19. Aventine Hill (p. 132). One of Rome's most elegant residential areas, the Aventine offers a respite from the city bustle and attractions such as the famous keyhole view of St. Peter's.

20. The Catacombs (p. 133). This spooky, kilometer-long network of tunnels (and the burial site of persecuted Christians) winds beneath the property of well-to-do Roman persecutors.

21. The Janiculum Hill (p. 123). Widely regarded as having the best view of the city, this hill near Trastevere is capped by a vast park and botanical gardens and exclusive residential streets.

22. Basilica of Santa Cecilia in Trastevere (p. 122). Go for the quiet Trastevere *piazza*, but stay for the statue of the martyred saint's 1200-year-old corpse.

23. Castel Sant'Angelo (p. 119). Hadrian designed this hulking castle as a mausoleum for himself and his family in the 2nd century AD. Then the Church took it over and hired Raphael to do some redecorating. With such tasteful appointments by Renaissance popes, what could the Church administration under John Paul II possibly add? A cappuccino bar, of course!

24. Villa Farnesina (p. 154). Head on over to Chigi's place to find out just what being the wealthiest man in Europe meant in the early 16th century...the ability to commission dozens of incredible frescoes.

25. Ara Pacis and the Mausoleum of Augustus (p. 113). Well, after seeing Hadrian's grand tomb, it's only fair that you look at Augustus's, Hadrian's inspiration. If it's open, take a look at Augustus's Altar of Peace, decorated with oh-so-modest depictions of the Emperor and his family.

...AND OTHER PICKS

▨**WHERE TO GO FIRST, LAST, AND WHENEVER CONFUSED.** Pierluigi and Fulvia, proprietors of **Enjoy Rome** (p. 27), dish all the dirt on Rome, tell you what to do with it, and make all the necessary arrangements. Small miracles performed on request.

▨**BEST CHURCH IN WHICH TO BUY LIQUOR. Basilica San Paulo Fuori la Mura** (p. 136), where monks sell homemade benedictine to thirsty believers and passersby. Eminently tastier than the eucalyptine available at the **Abbey of the Three Fountains** (p. 137).

▨**BEST BATHROOM. Jonathan's Angels,** without a doubt (p. 205). Though **Termini's** (p. 257) aren't too shabby, either.

▨**HANDS DOWN BEST ITALIAN BEER. Peroni.** Or is it **Astro Nazurro?** No, Peroni. No, Astro Nazurro. Just a minute.

▨**MOST DESIRABLE JOB.** Working in the **Avvocato del Diavolo** (The Devil's Advocate), the Vatican office dedicated to finding the skeletons in the closets of would-be saints.

▨**BEST PERSON TO DEFEND THE HONOR OF ITALY SHOULD THE HONOR OF ITALY BE THREATENED.** Vasco Rossi, the King of Italian Pop.

SUGGESTED ITINERARIES

ONE DAY

Trying to cram the Eternal City into a day is going to be difficult, but you can try. In the morning, take our half-day **walking tour** through the medieval Centro Storico (p. 9), which begins and ends at P. Navona. After lunch nearby at one of the fantastic restaurants along V. del Governo Vecchio (p. 185), hop a bus to P. Venezia, and take our other half-day **walking tour** of the best of the rest of Rome, ending at St. Peter's Basilica in Vatican City. Head south and finish up with dinner at a busy pizzeria in Trastevere (p. 189), then head back across the Tiber for some nighttime fun (p. 201).

THREE DAYS

DAY ONE: GETTING ORIENTED. Begin with our **Best of Rome** walking tour (p. 8). Take your time touring the sights, stopping off in the **Roman Forum** (see p. 73) and the **Church of Santa Maria in Cosmedin** (see p. 92). When you're through, walk down the Tiber to Trastevere, and head for a rowdy outdoor pizzeria (see p. 189). Finish up by heading back up to the Borgo to catch some jazz at **Alexanderplatz Jazz Club** (p. 177).

DAY TWO: VATICAN CITY. Wake up early, go to the **Vatican Museums,** get in line, and race through the galleries to get to the Sistine Chapel before the crowds (p. 140). After you've caught your breath and had your fill of Michelangelo, spend a few hours in the rest of the museum. Be sure to spend some time at **St. Peter's** (p. 115), and make the climb to the top of the dome. Before heading off to dinner, explore Hadrian's mausoleum, better known as **Castel Sant'Angelo** (p. 119).

DAY THREE: BORGHESE AND THE SPANISH STEPS. Your first stop is the **Galleria Borghese** for the most concentrated two hours of art you've ever experienced in your life (p. 149). Relax afterward by wandering through the gardens of the Villa Borghese until you find yourself at the top of the Spanish Steps (p. 107). Catch lunch and do some shopping (p. 163), then take in the big sights in the area—don't miss the ancient Roman monuments (p. 113) or the **Trevi Fountain** (p. 109). Grab dinner near P. del Popolo (p. 187), then head back to the Spanish Steps to take the relaxing **after-dinner walking tour** (p. 201).

FIVE DAYS

In addition to the previous three-day tour, try the following:

DAY FOUR: POMPEII. Take the train or Enjoy Rome's phenomenally convenient bus trip (p. 27), but whatever you do, get there. Nothing has been built in Pompeii (p. 232) since the eruption of Mt. Vesuvius buried the town in AD 79.

DAY FIVE: SOUTHERN ROME. Spend some time examining the Colosseum up close, then head toward the grand **Church of San Giovanni in Laterano** (p. 131), stopping by the odd little **Church of San Clemente** (p. 129) along the way. From San Giovanni, take bus #218 to south to explore the **catacombs** and other sights along the **Appian Way** (p. 133).

SEVEN DAYS

So you wanted a tropical vacation, but got the hustle and bustle of Rome instead? Not to worry. After five days in Rome, take a two-day sojourn in the **Pontine Islands** (p. 226), just three hours from Rome by public transit. The islands offer pristine shoreline, fantastic seafood, and a little relaxation. You deserve it; this vacation has been hard work.

Foro Borario

View from Aventine Hill

Church of Sant'Agnese in Agone

WALKING TOURS

For an after-dinner walk, see p. 201—after dinner, of course.

BEST OF ROME—VITTORIO TO THE VATICAN

P. Venezia to St. Peter's Basilica. This walk explores the beautiful old residential district of Trastevere, as well as introducing the Forum, Campidoglio, and Vatican City. 4-6hr.

From the front of the mammoth **Vittorio Emanuelle II monument,** erected to honor the first king of united Italy and known variously as the giant wedding cake and Mussolini's typewriter (p. 94), turn right and proceed along its side to the huge staircase leading up to P. del Campidoglio (p. 89). This Michelangelo-designed *piazza* contains the **Capitoline Museums** (p. 152), home to one of Rome's finest ancient and Renaissance sculpture collections. For a marvelous view of the **Roman Forum,** the marketplace of Republican Rome and the early Empire (p. 73), continue onward between the **Palazzo dei Conservatori** (on the right) and the museums' central building; you'll find a small balcony with a big vista of the ancient marketplace.

Once you've had your fill of the Campidoglio and the Forum, go back down the stairs and turn left, following V. del Teatro di Marcello. On your left, admire the **Teatro di Marcello,** which inspired the Colosseum (p. 93). Turn right after the theater and cross the Tiber on the Ponte Fabricio. Explore the **Isola Tiberina** (p. 121), which has long been associated with the Aesclepius, the Greek god of healing; ancient inscriptions of the caduceus are visible along the island's embankments. The Tiber Island is still home to Rome's most fashionable hospital.

When you're done exploring the little island, head on over to the other bank to find yourself in Trastevere, the independent-minded community of artists and workers that offers a taste of truly Roman local life just steps from the most touristed areas of the city.

Follow V. Anicia south; turn left on V. dei Genovesi, then go right to the **Chuch of Santa Cecilia in Trastevere** (p. 122). Pay your tributes to the patron saint of music, then head back to V. dei Genovesi and follow it to V. Trastevere. Take a left, then a right on V. di San Francesco, which leads into P. Calisto and P. S. Maria in Trastevere. Enjoy the gold mosaics on the facade of the **Church of Santa Maria in Trastevere** (p. 123), and take a moment to admire the wares of artisans and olive-oil vendors who often set up shop in the little square.

Turn right as you face the church, and exit through P. San Egidio. Continue north, following V. di Bologna to P. Malva, and follow signs to the **Villa Farnesina** (p. 154). If time permits, visit the museum, which contains wonderful frescoes by Raphael and Il Sodoma. After a walk through the Villa's grounds, follow V. della Lungara around them, and double back along the Lungotevere della Farnesina until you come to the Ponte Sisto. Cross at this bridge and follow V. dei Pettinari inland until you reach Capo di Ferro; turn left, and walk to P. Farnese and the beautiful **Palazzo Farnese** (p. 103). Take any of the alleyways opposite the *palazzo*'s facade to reach **Campo dei Fiori,** one of Rome's liveliest *piazze*. It's home to a wonderful flower market in the mornings and buzzes with cafe- and bar-goers through the night (p. 204).

Take V. del Pellegrino to leave the Campo. Take a right on V. dei Cartari to C. V. Emanuele II; you'll come out opposite the huge **Chiesa Nuova** (p. 102). Take a right onto V. S. Spirito. Cross the ornate Ponte Sant'Angelo, which leads to the entrance of **Castel Sant'Angelo** (p. 119). Built in the 2nd century AD as a mausoleum for Emperor Hadrian, it was taken over by the Catholic Church and fixed up by a series of decadent popes. After a quick trip through the fortress, stand with your back to the entrance and turn right onto V. del Conciliazione, which leads into the Vatican. Visit **St. Peter's Basilica** if it is still open, or just enjoy the beautifully lit facade by night (p. 115).

CENTRO STORICO—THE MEDIEVAL CITY

⚑ *This is a loop through the medieval city, beginning and ending at P. Navona. 2½-5½hr.*

The walk begins in **Piazza Navona** (p. 99), an elliptical *piazza* built on the site of a stadium constructed by Emperor Domitian in the first century AD. Take a moment to shoo off pushy vendors and take in the *piazza*'s fountains, which include Bernini's **Fountain of the Four Rivers.** The **Church of Sant'Agnese in Agone** is also worth a look—the dead saint's skull is prominently displayed.

From the southeast corner of P. Navona—with the three fountains to your left and the church looming behind you—walk down V. di Canestrari (V. Sediari) to P. San Eustachio. Take V. Santa Chiara to P. della Minerva, where you can take in Michelangelo's *Risen Christ* at the **Church of Santa Maria Sopra Minerva** (p. 98). Take V. Minerva to P. della Rotonda and pay a visit to the hulking **Pantheon** (p. 97).

Living in Rome

From there, take V. del Seminario east, then turn right onto V. Sant'Ignazio into **Piazza Collegio Romano** (p. 95). Take in the **Galleria Doria Pamphilj** (p. 158) or continue on. Turn left, crossing the Corso, and turn left again onto V. di San Marcello, then right at the dead end onto V. dell'Umilta'. Take your next left onto V. dei Vergini. A right on V. delle Murate will lead you directly to the **Trevi Fountain** (p. 109).

Continuing east from the P. di Trevi, take V. del Lavoratore, stopping briefly at ▧**San Crispino** for the world's best *gelato* (p. 194). Take V. della Scuderie, cross V. del Traforo, and walk up V. Rassella. At V. delle Quattro Fontane, go left into **Piazza Barberini** (p. 111). Go up V. Veneto 50m to see the **Capuchin Crypt** in Chiesa Santa Maria della Concezione, then double back and take V. Sistina up the hill to the busy **Spanish Steps** (p. 107).

Pompeii

From the top of the Steps, take V. Trinita' dei Monti (V. G. D'Annunzio) to the left-hand turn-off onto P. del Popolo. Admire the Raphael chapel and the Caravaggios in the **Church of Santa Maria del Popolo** at the north end of the *piazza* (p. 111), then take V. di Ripetta from the southern side. Grab a bite at ▧**Pizza Re',** a block down on the left (p. 187).

V. di Ripetta runs into the **Ara Pacis** and **Mausoleum of Augustus** (p. 113). Continue down and take a left onto V. Borghese. Follow it and V. Divino Amore to P. Firenze, passing the **Palazzo Borghese** along the way (p. 149). Continue down V. d. Maddalena, pull back into P. della Rotonda, and rejuvenate at **Tazza d'Oro** (p. 196). From P. della Rotonda, take V. Giustiniani and go right through P. San Luigi dei Francesi onto Via della Scrofa, stopping by **Chiesa San Luigi dei Francesi** (p. 98) for a glimpse at three more Caravaggios. From V. della Scrofa, go left onto V. S. Agostino, stopping into **Chiesa Sant'Agostino** to see Caravaggio's *Madonna* and Raphael's *Isaiah.* From there, P. Cinque Lune spills into V. Angolare on the west, which runs back into the top end of P. Navona.

Castel Sant'Angelo

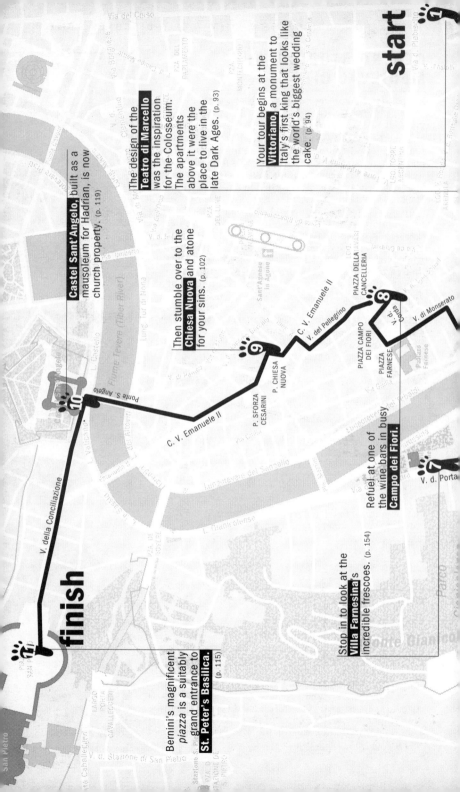

start

1

Your tour begins at the **Vittoriano,** a monument to Italy's first king that looks like the world's biggest wedding cake. (p. 94)

The design of the **Teatro di Marcello** was the inspiration for the Colosseum. The apartments above it were the place to live in the late Dark Ages. (p. 93)

Castel Sant'Angelo, built as a mausoleum for Hadrian, is now church property. (p. 119)

Then stumble over to the **Chiesa Nuova** and atone for your sins. (p. 102)

9

8

Refuel at one of the wine bars in busy **Campo dei Fiori.**

7

Stop in to look at the **Villa Farnesina's** incredible frescoes. (p. 154)

10

finish

11

Bernini's magnificent *piazza* is a suitably grand entrance to **St. Peter's Basilica.** (p. 115)

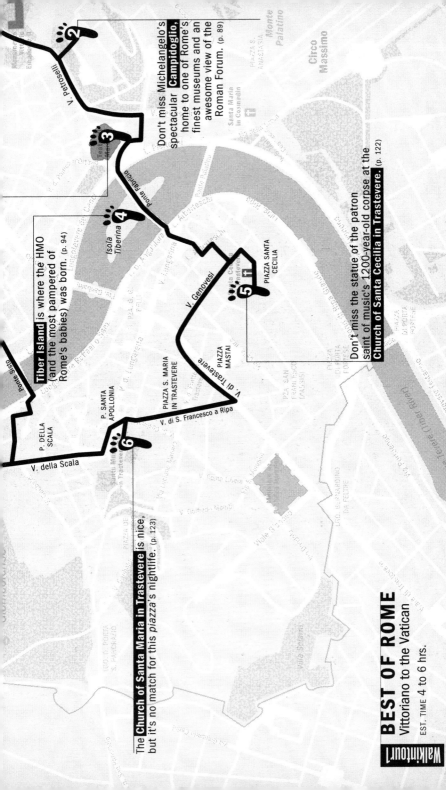

Don't miss Michelangelo's spectacular **Campidoglio,** home to one of Rome's finest museums and an awesome view of the Roman Forum. (p. 89)

Tiber Island is where the HMO (and the most pampered of Rome's babies) was born. (p. 94)

Don't miss the statue of the patron saint of music's 1200-year-old corpse at the **Church of Santa Cecilia in Trastevere.** (p. 122)

The **Church of Santa Maria in Trastevere** is nice, but it's no match for this *piazza's* nightlife. (p. 123)

BEST OF ROME
Vittoriano to the Vatican

EST. TIME 4 to 6 hrs.

Walkintour!

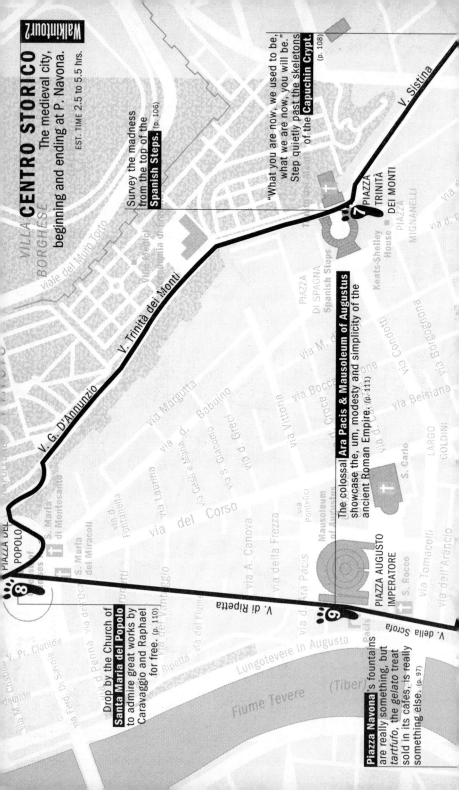

CENTRO STORICO

VILLA BORGHESE

The medieval city, beginning and ending at P. Navona.

EST. TIME 2.5 to 5.5 hrs.

Survey the madness from the top of the **Spanish Steps.** (p. 106)

"What you are now, we used to be, what we are now, you will be." Step quietly past the skeletons of the **Capuchin Crypt.** (p. 108)

7 PIAZZA TRINITÀ DEI MONTI

PIAZZA MIGNANELLI

Keats-Shelley House

PIAZZA DI SPAGNA
Spanish Steps

The colossal **Ara Pacis & Mausoleum of Augustus** showcase the, um, modesty and simplicity of the ancient Roman Empire. (p. 111)

PIAZZA AUGUSTO IMPERATORE

Mausoleum of Augustus

8 PIAZZA DEL POPOLO

Drop by the Church of **Santa Maria del Popolo** to admire great works by Caravaggio and Raphael for free. (p. 110)

S. Maria di Montesanto

S. Maria dei Miracoli

9

Piazza Navona's fountains are really something, but *tartufo*, the *gelato* treat sold in its cafés, is really something else. (p. 97)

Fiume Tevere (Tiber)

Lungotevere In Augusta

V. della Scrofa

V. di Ripetta

S. Rocco

S. Carlo

LARGO GOLDINI

via del Corso

via Tomacelli

via dell'Arancio

via Belsiana

via Borgognona

via Condotti

via della Croce

via M. de' Fiori

via Bocca di Leone

via Vittoria

via Mario de' Fiori

via della Frezza

via A. Canova

via Ara Pacis

via del Fiume

via di Ripetta

via d. Gesù e Maria

via Laurina

via d. — Babuino

via d. Greci

via S. Giacomo

via Margutta

V. Trinità dei Monti

V. G. D'Annunzio

Viale del Muro Torto

V. della Fontanella

d. Pennà

via dei Greci

Fiume Tevere

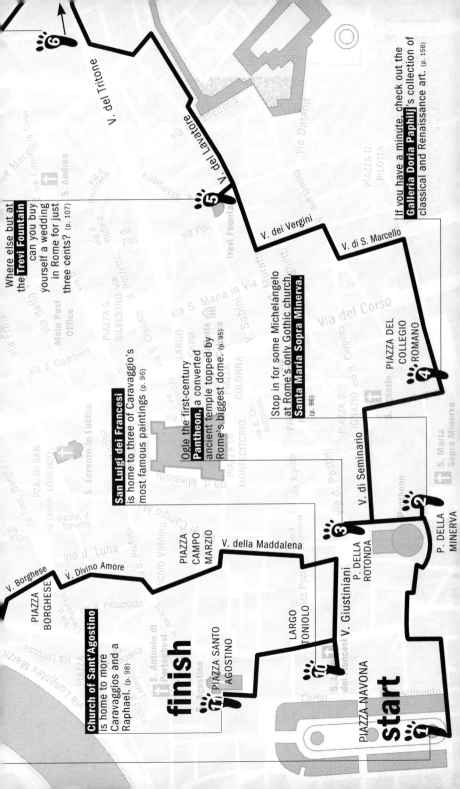

start

PIAZZA NAVONA

finish

Church of Sant'Agostino is home to more Caravaggios and a Raphael. (p. 98)

PIAZZA SANTO AGOSTINO

S. Antonio di Portoghesi

PIAZZA BORGHESE

V. Borghese

V. Divino Amore

V. della Maddalena

PIAZZA CAMPO MARZIO

San Luigi dei Francesi is home to three of Caravaggio's most famous paintings (p. 96)

S. Lorenzo in Lucina

LARGO TONIOLO

V. Giustiniani

P. DELLA ROTONDA

Ogle the first-century Pantheon, a converted ancient temple topped by Rome's biggest dome. (p. 95)

COLONNA

PIAZZA S. SILVESTRO

Where else but at the Trevi Fountain can you buy yourself a wedding in Rome for just three cents? (p. 107)

Main Post Office

V. del Tritone

V. di Gambero

V. del Tritone

S. Andrea

Trevi Fountain

V. del Lavatore

V. dei Vergini

V. di S. Marcello

Via del Corso

MONTECITORIO

V. di Seminario

V. di Pastini

P. DELLA MINERVA

S. Maria Sopra Minerva

Stop in for some Michelangelo at Rome's only Gothic church, Santa Maria Sopra Minerva. (p. 96)

PIAZZA DEL COLLEGIO ROMANO

If you have a minute, check out the Galleria Doria Pamphilj's collection of classical and Renaissance art. (p. 156)

TOUR COMPANIES

In Rome, a city with thousands of nooks and crannies, each with a story and a dozen tourists raring to hear it, guided tours have become a cottage industry. From day-long bus excursions to Pompeii and chats with art students in the Vatican Museums to break-neck bike treks and meandering strolls through Trastevere, there is something for everyone. However, many tours are unlicensed, some are illegal, and most charge much more than they're worth. For a list of *Let's Go*'s favorites, see **Service Directory**, p. 298.

ROME BY SEASON

SPRING

As soon as the azaleas bloom at the end of March, piles of their pink blossoms are brought to the Spanish Steps to celebrate **La Festa di Primavera,** the coming of spring. The exhibition lasts until the flowers die, usually a week or two. **Good Friday** brings the Pope's **Procession of the Cross** from the Colosseum to the Palatine and a week of services in basilicas across the city, culminating in the Pope's Easter **Urbi et Orbi** blessing in 50 languages. Don't miss **Rome's birthday;** April 21 sees the Capitoline Hill alive with partyers, Latin poetry, a concert, and fireworks set off from the Circus Maximus. The **Rose Show** arrives in early May at Valle Murcia, on the Aventine above the Circus Maximus, and lasts through June. Also, the **Italian International Tennis Tournament** brings excitement to the Foro Italico during the first two weeks of May.

SUMMER

Festivals and concerts abound, so be sure to check *Roma C'è* for current listings. On June 23, the **Church of San Giovanni in Laterano** sponsors a gluttonous banquet of snails and roast pork. **Festa dei Santi Pietro e Paolo,** June 29, is an awe-inspiring religious ceremony for Rome's patron saints, taking place in the Basilica dei Santi Pietro e Paolo. The 3rd Sunday in July brings **Noantri,** a 10-day celebration of the planet called Trastevere, complete with midway rides and grand religious processions. Finally, on August 5, the **Festa della Madonna della Neve** is a blizzard of white flower petals representing the legendary out-of-season snow at the **Church of Santa Maria Maggiore.**

FALL

In September, watch out for the **art festival** featuring the works of over 100 painters along V. Margutta. Vats of wine make for hazy evenings at the **Sagra delle Uva** in the Forum's Basilica of Maxentius, and a torch-lit **medieval crafts fair** (late September to early October) on V. dell'Orso complements the V. dei Coronari **antique fair** (last two weeks of October).

WINTER

Christmas sees P. Navona full of crêche figures for sale and children begging for toys and candy and reciting poems and speeches. It's hopelessly cute. On December 8, the Pope and other worshipers leave elaborate floral tributes to the statue of the virgin in P. di Spagna for the **Festa dell'Immacolata Connezione.** **Capodanno** (New Year's) merrymaking includes sparklers, throwing old dishes (or clothes, or old bathtubs) from windows, eating *cotecchino* (pig's feet), and washing it all down with *spumante* and an amazing fireworks display. On the first, the faithful light candles and make their way through the catacombs of Santa Priscilla, while the pope gives a solemn High Mass at St. Peter's. On January 17, during the **Festa di Sant'Antonio,** pet cats, dogs, and canaries are blessed after mass on the steps of the Church of Sant'Eusebio all'Esquilino. The **Carnevale** parade (the day before Ash Wednesday) down the Corso is a sight to be seen. Throw on a fancy costume and bring some silly string.

When in Rome

The best way to inspect the streets of Rome, if you wish to study as well as see them, is to break your pocket-compass and burn your maps and guidebooks...take Chance for a mentor and lose yourself.
　　—George Sala, 1866

In his *History of Rome*, Livy concluded that "the layout of Rome is more like a squatter's settlement than a properly planned city." Two thousand years of city planning later, Rome still seems like an unnavigable sea of one-way streets, dead ends, clandestine *piazze*, incongruous monuments, and incurable traffic. The following pages will help you get your footing the minute your plane touches down in the Eternal City. Chances are you're still going to get lost—even Roman residents lose their way in Rome's sprawling streets. And when in Rome....

UPON ARRIVAL

Most international flights touch down at Leonardo da Vinci International Airport (☎ 06 65951), referred to as **Fiumicino** for the coastal village in which it is located. Up-to-the-minute information on both of Rome's airports is online at www.adr.it. Services at Fiumicino's international terminal include:

EPT (Rome Tourist Authority) (☎ 06 65956074), directly in front of the customs exit of Terminal C. Hotel reservations and brochures. English spoken. Open daily 8:15am-7pm.

Banca di Roma, a small branch sits immediately to the right of customs; go right from customs to the end of the hallway to find the large office. Decent exchange rates. Open M-F 8:25am-1:25pm and 2:30-3:40pm, Sa. 8:25-11:55am. **ATM** at both locations accepts AmEx, Cirrus, MC, and V cards. Its **currency exchange** office is found to the right of customs. Open daily 6am-midnight.

Luggage Storage, on the right at the end of the hall as you exit customs. Open 24hr. L4100 per bag per day ending at midnight.

Post Office, next to luggage storage and the large Banca di Roma office. Services include fax and telegrams. Open M-F 8:30am-3:15pm, Sa 8:30pm-1:45pm.

Rent-A-Car/Autonoleggi, two conveyer belts away from the train depot.

CIAMPINO. Most charter and a few domestic flights arrive at Ciampino airport (☎06 794941). To get to Ciampino from Rome, take the COTRAL bus (every 30min. or so, 6:10am-11pm, L2000) to Anagnina station on Metro Linea A (see p. 25). To get to Ciampino, reverse these directions. Another option is taking a train from Termini to Ciampino station and a bus to the airport; check with FS (☎1478 88088; www.fs-on-line.com) for details. After 11pm, you'll have to take a cab to and from Ciampino. Although Ciampino is inside the Rome city limits, there is a supplemental charge of L10,000.

TO AND FROM THE AIRPORT BY TRAIN

Upon seeing the dozens of people crowded outside customs waiting for loved ones, you may feel compelled to pretend to be related to one of these people and convince them to take you to their Italian home, where you'll enjoy home-cooked meals and a warm bed. Resist this urge. Instead, follow the signs to your left for **Stazione FS/Railway Station.** Take the elevator or escalators up two floors to the pedestrian bridge to the airport train station. From here you can take one of the two trains to the center of Rome.

TERMINI STATION. The Termini line runs nonstop to Rome's main train station and transportation hub, Termini Station (30 min.; twice hourly 12 and 37min. past the hour 7:37am-10:37pm, extra trains 7:37am, 6:37, and 8:37pm; L16,000, L40,000 on board). Buy a ticket *"Per Termini"* at the FS ticket counter, the *tabacchi* on the right, or from one of the machines in the station.

A train leaves Termini for Fiumicino from track #22 or #23, which is at the very end of #22 and a bit of a walk (40 min.; houly at 20min. past the hour 7:20am-9:20pm; extra trains 6:50am, 3:50, 5:50, and 7:50pm; L16,000). Buy tickets at the Alitalia office at track #22 at the window marked *"Biglietti Per Fiumicino"* or from other designated areas and machines in the station. Validate (and retain) your ticket before boarding.

TIBURTINA STATION. The Tiburtina/Orte/Fara Sabina train stops at many of the minor train stations (but NOT Termini) on the outskirts of the city center, all of which are, in turn, connected to the city center by bus or Metro. Service is erratic on Sundays and in August, and trains may arrive at Tiburtina after the Metro closes (40min.; every 15min. 6:27am-9:27pm; extra trains 5:37am, 9:57, 10:27, 10:57, and 11:27pm; L8000). Buy tickets *"Per Tiburtina"* on the right, or from the machines in the station, or on the train after hours. Note that the final destination of this train may be indicated on the signs by "Orte (6th stop)," "Tiburtina (8th stop)," or "Fara Sabina (15th stop)." Validate and retain your ticket for the entire trip.

The most convenient way to reach the city center when using this line is to get off at the Tiburtina station, which is connected to the Metro stop "Tiburtina" (Linea B). When you get off the train (track #1), go down the stairs, following the signs for the *Metropolitana.* Buy a ticket (L1500), validate it, and take Metro Linea B (dir: "Laurentina").

A train leaves Tiburtina for Fiumicino from track #4 or #5 (40min., every 15 to 60min. 5:04am-10:33pm, L8000). Buy tickets at the ticket booths.

EARLY AND LATE FLIGHTS

If your flight arrives at Fiumicino after 10pm or leaves before 8am, you may have transportation difficulties. The most reliable, albeit expensive, option is to take a **cab,** which should cost between L65,000 and 85,000. (Request one at the kiosk in the airport or call 06 3570, 06 4994, or 06 6645.) In the wee hours, the cheapest option is to take the blue **COTRAL bus** to Tiburtina from the ground floor outside the main exit doors after customs (1:15, 2:15, 3:30, and 5am; L8000, pay on board). From Tiburtina, take bus #40N to Termini. Reserve a room in the area ahead of time to avoid setting up camp in Termini.

To get to Fiumicino from Rome late at night or early in the morning, take bus #40N from Termini to Tiburtina (every 20-30min.), then catch the blue COTRAL bus to Fiumicino from the plaza outside (12:30, 1:15, 2:30, and 3:45am; L8000, buy on board).

LET'S GET ORIENTED

Most sights and establishments listed in *Let's Go: Rome 2001* are grouped by location and then ranked by interest and quality. Each neighborhood corresponds to a map at the back of this book (on which most sights and establishments are plotted). Street names change often in Rome; in directions to establishments, this is denoted by placing another street name in parentheses after the initial name. For instance, Via del Quirinale turning into Via XX Settembre would be denoted as "V. del Quirinale (V. XX Settembre)."

Abbreviations used include: V. for Via and Viale, P. for Piazza and Piazzale, and C. for Corso. First names (as in C. V. Emanuele II) and San/Santa are abbreviated in addresses.

ROME BY NEIGHBORHOOD

No longer defined by the Seven Hills, modern Rome is huge, sprawling over a large area between the hills of the Castelli Romani to the north, the beach at Ostia to the west, and Lake Albano to the south, counting within its boundaries such memorable eyesores as Anagnina, Spinaceto, and Infernetto ("little Hell"). Encircling it all is a broad highway, the Grande Raccordo Anulare (GRA), whose name loosely translates as "traffic jams of Biblical proportions." Luckily for you, though, most major sights lie within a comparatively small radius, which can be neatly divided into eight areas.

ANCIENT CITY

◪ *Accessible by Metro (Linea B) and buses serving P. Venezia. For sights, see p. 73.*

The Ancient City begins directly south of **Piazza Venezia** (the center of the city and home to the huge Vittorio Emanuele II monument; see p. 94). Directly behind the monument, the **Capitoline Hill,** capped by Michelangelo's Piazza di Campidoglio, is accessible by **Via di Teatro di Marcello,** which runs southwest toward the Velabrum and the Tiber. On the other side of the monument, **Via dei For Imperiali** runs southeast all the way to the **Colosseum.** Off Via dei Fori Imperiali are the **Imperial Fora** and the **Roman Forum** itself. Behind the Forum looms the imposing **Palatine Hill** and, beyond that, the **Circus Maximus.**

CENTRO STORICO

◪ *Accessible by buses #60 and #117 on the Corso, as well as a number of buses along C. Vittorio Emanuel II. For sights, see p. 94.*

The medieval neighborhood of Rome spreads north and West from **Piazza Venezia,** bordered by Via del Corso on the East and the Tiber to the west. **Corso Vittorio Emanule II** runs northwest from Piazza Venezia toward the Vatican; much of the third of the Centro south of this thourougfare is taken up by the **Jewish Ghetto.**

PIAZZA DI SPAGNA AND THE CORSO

◪ *Accessible via Metro Linea A and many buses, including #60 and #492 to P. Barberini and #117 to the P. di Spagna. For sights, see p. 107.*

East of the Corso, stretching from Piazza Venezia up toward Villa Borghese, is the area around the **Spanish Steps.** The famous steps themselves, which climb from **Piazza di Spagna** up to **Piazza Trinità dei Monti,** are four blocks from the Corso along Rome's most exclusive shopping area, **Via Condotti.** On the western side of the Corso (north of the Centro Storico, near **Piazza del Popolo,** the northern terminus of the Corso) are the famous Mausoleum of Augustus and the Ara Pacis. South of the Spanish Steps is the über-crowded **Trevi Fountain.** East of the fountain is the **Quirinale,** headquarters of Italian government. **Via del Tritone** runs east from the Corso to **Piazza Barberini,** home to a Bernini fountain and Planet Hollywood, and continues on toward Termini as **Via Barberini.**

VILLA BORGHESE

◪ M:A-Flaminio or M:A-Spagna. Bus #490 runs through the park. For sights, see p. 114.

Northeast of Piazza del Popolo and the Spanish Steps is the **Villa Borghese**, a vast park that is home to the **zoo** and several prominent museums. Since it is park, there are kilometers of verdant paths. The neighborhood of the Villa Borghese stretches around Piazza del Popolo east to cover the environs north of Termini and **Via XX Settembre**.

BORGO, PRATI, AND THE VATICAN CITY

◪ Accessible via Metro Linea A and many buses, including #64, #492, and #490, which serves northern Prati. For sights, see p. 115.

Across the Tiber to the northwest from the Centro Storico is the **Vatican City**. Crossing the Ponte Vittorio Emanuele II from C. Vittorio Emanuele II leads you directly to **Via della Conciliazione**, the stately avenue that leads west directly to P. San Pietro and **Saint Peter's Basilica**. The **Vatican Museums** are just next door. At the eastern end of Via della Conciliazione, **Castel Sant'Angelo**, the Pope's historical fortified residence, overlooks the Tiber. Between Castel Sant'Angelo and the Vatican is the quiet **Borgo** neighborhood. To the north is less quiet **Prati**, home to scattered hotels, restaurants, and pubs. **Via Cola di Rienzo** runs through Prati from **Piazza del Risorgimento**, next to the Vatican, across Ponte Regina Margherita to **Piazza del Popolo; Via Giulio Cesare** is the major street through central Prati.

TRASTEVERE

◪ Tram #13 runs the length of Viale di Trastevere from Largo Argentina in the Centro Storico south past Stazione Trastevere. Among others, buses #23 and #170 provide service to southern Trastevere and bus #870 serves the Gianicolo. For sights, see p. 120.

Trastevere, easily Rome's most picturesque neighborhood, and certainly its most entertaining to navigate, is south of the Vatican and west, across the Tiber, from the Centro Storico. Viale Trastevere runs across Ponte Garibaldi all the way to Largo Argentina and C. Vittorio Emanuele II and is the main drag of the neighborhood. Most of Trastevere's points of interest lie near this street, and not far from the river. Between Trastevere and the Vatican is the exclusive and park-like Janiculum Hill, or the Gianicolo.

TERMINI AND SAN LORENZO

◪ Termini is the transfer point between the two Metro lines and is served by countless buses. San Lorenzo is served by bus #492, Esquilino is accessible by buses #70 and #714, and bus #60 runs out of the city along V. XX Settembre (V. Nomentana). For sights, see p. 124.

Located east of the center of town, this is the area most people see first when arriving in Rome. Get used to it, because it's also where most budget travelers stay. The neighborhood immediately northeast of **Stazione Termini** is jam-packed with hotels, hostels, restaurants, and Internet cafes. East of the station is the **Città Universitaria,** home to Rome's La Sapienza university. South of that is **San Lorenzo**, the student neighborhood, which is home to many cheap and delicious restaurants, as well a healthy dose of left-wing student spirit. South of Termini, along V. Giovanni Giolitti and V. Merulana, is the **Esquilino** neighborhood. San Lorenzo is connected to Esquilino by **Via Tiburtina**. **Via XX Settembre (Via Nomentana)** cuts through the quieter area northwest of the station. In front of the station, **Via Nazionale** runs from **Piazza della Repubblica** west toward the older center of town. **Via Cavour** runs southeast from the station to the Colosseum.

SOUTHERN ROME

◪ Testaccio, the Aventine, and EUR are served by Metro Linea B and buses including #23 and #673. Metro Linea A and buses #673 and #714 run to the Caelian and southeast Rome. For sights, see p. 129.

Across the river from Trastevere and south of the Jewish Ghetto and the Ancient City are the posh **Aventine Hill** and the working-class **Testaccio** district. The former home to Rome's slaughterhouses is named after a hill of ancient amphora shards and has many of Rome's most popular nightclubs (not to mention its only pyramid). Further south are

Ostiense and **EUR**, Mussolini's prototype neighborhood of wide boulevards, nationalistic slogans, and museums. Further east from the Tiber are the **Caelian Hill,** southeast of the Colosseum and home to the San Giovanni neighborhood, and further south, the **Appian Way.**

MAPS

It's impossible to navigate the winding streets of Rome without a map, and using the free and omnipresent **McDonald's** map will probably get you lost (though you're likely to find at least one of the 35 McDonald's locations gracing the Eternal City). Instead, pick up the concise and detailed **Charta Roma** map (at EPT or PIT kiosks) or the one published by Enjoy Rome. *Let's Go* publishes a **map guide** to Rome, a pocket-sized map of transportation, sights, etc., with 32 pages of advice on where to sleep, eat, and dance in Rome.

The compact Bus/Tram/Metro map available for free at Termini is little more than a hallucinogenic swirl of pretty colors, so buy a **Roma Metro-Bus** map at a newsstand (L8000), complete with all bus and tram routes. **Rome A to Z** (sold with **Lazio A to Z**) includes a pocket guide of 20 bike routes (available at newsstands, L12,000). **Tuttocittà,** distributed yearly with Roman phone books, is the best atlas, but is not sold in stores; ask Roman friends or store owners if you can look at it.

Piazza Garibaldi

LET'S USE PUBLIC TRANSPORTATION

Bus and subway tickets (L1500) are one and the same and can be bought at *tabacchi*, newsstands, some bars, and vending machines (in stations, on occasional street corners, and at major bus stops). Look for the ATAC label. Each ticket is valid for either one ride on the Metro or for unlimited bus travel within 75 minutes of validation. A BIG **daily ticket** costs L8000 and allows for unlimited bus or train travel everywhere in the *Comune di Roma*, including Ostia but not Fiumicino; a CIS **weekly ticket** costs L32,000. If you'll be in Rome for more than a few weeks, consider purchasing the *abbonamento mensile*, which allows one month (beginning the first of the month) of unlimited transport for L50,000. Ask for the pass anywhere tickets are sold. Student passes are cheaper, but are only for Italian students or foreign students at Italian universities.

Subway

BUSES

Though the network of routes may seem daunting at first, Rome's bus system is very efficient and inexpensive. Buses also cover far more area than the rather scanty metro system. The **ATAC** (*Aziende Tramvie Autobus Communali;* ☎800 555666, 8am-8pm) intracity bus company has a myriad of **information booths,** including one in Termini. The invaluable **Roma Metro-Bus map,** published by Lozzi, is available at newsstands for L8000. Ask at the tourist office (see p. 28) for a useful Bus/Tram/Metro map of central Rome.

On the Street

Rome Transport

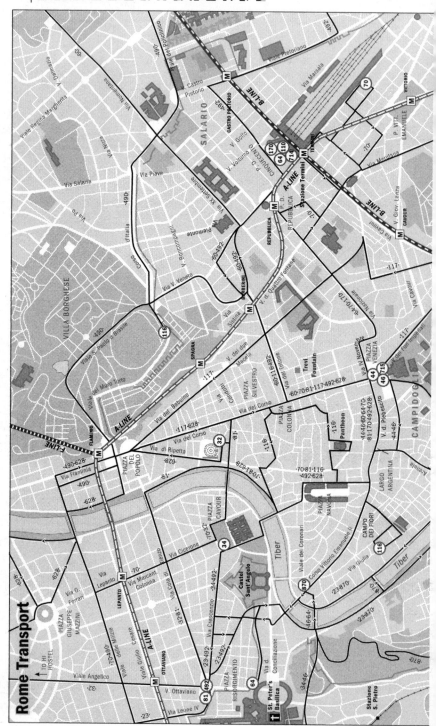

Each bus stop (*fermata*) is marked by yellow signs listing routes that stop there and key streets and stops on those routes. The name of the stop at which you are standing is boxed; the bus will take you to any of the places listed below the boxed stop. **To go to a stop listed above the box,** cross the street to catch the same bus in the opposite direction.

Temporary bus signs are simple yellow poles with the route marked in cursive; you'll need to check a map to know all the stops. Some buses run only on weekdays (*feriali*) or weekends (*festivi*), while others may have different routes, depending on the day of the week. Hours vary, but most buses begin around 6am and stop around midnight.

Board buses from the front or back doors, not from the middle, then stamp your ticket in the orange machine at the back; exit only through the middle, helpfully marked *uscita*. The ticket is then good for any number of transfers over the next 75min. Stamp the other end of the ticket after your first transfer. If you exceed 1¼hr., you must stamp a new ticket. There is a **L100,000 fine** for not carrying a validated ticket or bus pass, and inspections are becoming more common. Playing dumb tourist won't help. Buy several tickets and keep them on you: at night and on weekends they can be hard to find.

Night routes are indicated on signs by black shields, owls, and the letter N following the route number. Below the bus itinerary should be listed the approximate time that the bus will pass. Signal a night bus to stop by standing right under its sign and flailing wildly. They run infrequently, and you may have to transfer several times to get where you want to go. Don't depend too heavily on *notturno* buses, as they are often unreliable.

ATAC offers *Giro Turistico*, a no-frills, 3-hour circuit of the city. (Bus #110; leaves Termini 10:30am, 2, 3, 5, and 6pm; L15,000.) They provide a map and some explanation in Italian and quasi-English, whirling you around the city for a comprehensive peek at the city's more visible monuments.

A word on **bus etiquette:** If you are a young person, you really should give your seat to elderly people. Inexplicably, Romans on the bus like to prepare for their grand descent several stops in advance by crowding around the exit doors. If you are standing in their way near the exit, you will be asked repeatedly, "*Scende (la prossima)?*" which means, "Are you getting off at the next stop?" Answer appropriately.

POPULAR ATAC BUS ROUTES

Rome is always revamping its transportation system. Be sure to check a map for the most up-to-date route information.

DAY BUSES

46: Vatican, C. V. Emanuele II, Largo Argentina, P. Venezia.

60: V. Nomentana, V. XX Settembre, P. Barberini, San Silvestro, V. del Corso, P. Venezia, Largo Torre Argentina, P. Venezia, Teatro Marcello.

64: Termini, V. Nazionale, P. Venezia, Largo Argentina, C. V. Emanuele II, Vatican (known as the "wallet-eater." AVOID THIS BUS!)

81: P. Malatesta, San Giovanni, Colosseo, Bocca della Verita, P. Venezia, Largo Argentina, P. Cavour, V. Cola di Rienzo, Vatican.

117: San Giovanni, Colosseum, Largo Tritone, P. di Spagna, P. del Popolo, V. del Corso, P. Venezia, Colosseum. Weekdays only, from 8am-9pm.

170: Termini, V. Nazionale, P. Venezia, Largo Argentina, V. Marmorata, southern Trastevere, San Paolo Basilica, P. Agricoltura (EUR).

492: Tiburtina, Termini, P. Barberini, P. Venezia, C. Rinascimento, P. Cavour, P. Risorgimento.

TRAMS

8: Largo Argentino, Porta Portese, Trastevere, Gianicolum.

19: San Lorenzo, Villa Borghese, V. Ottaviano, P. Risorgimento (Vatican).

30B: Porta San Paolo, Colosseo, San Giovanni, San Lorenzo, Villa Borghese. Stops at 10pm.

NIGHT (NOTTURNO) BUSES

You must signal a night bus to stop for you. Buses are supposed to come at 30min.-1hr. intervals, but can be unreliable; try to avoid waiting alone.

20N: P. Flaminio, P. Cavour (near Vatican), Porta San Paolo, Colosseo, S. Maria Maggiore, Termini, P. Indipendenza, P. Flaminio. Leaves Flaminio 12:12, 1:08, 2:10, 3:10, 4:10, and 5:10am.

21N: Same as 20N, in reverse order. Leaves Flaminio at 12:45, 1:45, 2:45, 3:45, and 4:45am.

29N: Testaccio, Lungotevere de' Cenci, V. Crescenzio (Vatican), V. Belle Arti, V. Regina Marherita, San Lorenzo, Colosseum.

40N: Approximately the same route as Metro B, from Termini to Tiburtina. Runs every 30min.

45N: P. Capecelatro, P. della Rovere (Vatican), C. Vittorio Emanuele, Largo Argentina, P. Venezia, V. del Corso, P. San Silvestro. Leaves Capecelatro 12:51, 1:50, and 4:50am; leaves Silvestro 12:23, 1:22, 2:21, and 4:22am.

55N: Approximately the same route as Metro A, from Termini to Cinecittà. Runs every 30min.

60N: P. Vimercati, V. Nomentana, V. Veneto, P. Venezia, Largo Argentina, P. Sonnino (Trastevere). Leaves Vimercati 12:08, 12:38, 1:38, 2:08, 3:08, 3:38, and 4:38am. Leaves Sonnino 12:45, 2:15, 2:45, 3:45, and 4:50am.

78N: P. Clodio, Vatican, V. Flaminia, P. Cavour, C. Rinascimento, P. Venezia, Termini. Leaves Clodio 12:30, 1:30, 3, 4, 5, and 5:30am. Leaves Termini 1, 3:30, 4:30, and 5:30am.

BUSES TO RURAL LAZIO

COTRAL buses between Rome and the province of Lazio (☎ 06 5915551) now leave from outside the city center; you must take the subway to an outlying area and catch a bus from there: M:A-Anagnina for Frascati and the Colli Albani; M:B-Rebibbia for Tivoli and Subiaco; M:A-Lepanto for Cerveteri, Tarquinia, Bracciano, Lago Vico, and Civitavecchia. *Let's Go* lists transportation information in the Daytrips chapter (see p. 213). For more information, contact COTRAL (☎ 06 5915551) or a tourist agency (see p. 298).

METRO

Every time they tried to dig more tracks for their subway system, the Romans discovered more ancient ruins. As a result, Rome's subway system is sparse. Many of Rome's sights are a trek from the nearest stop, but for covering large distances quickly, the subway beats the bus—it's comparatively fast and reliable. The two lines (A and B) of the *Metropolitana* intersect at Termini and can be reached by several entrances, including the stairway between the station and Piazza del Cinquecento. Entrances to Metro stations elsewhere are marked by poles with a white "M" on a red square. **The subway runs daily from 5:30am to 11:30pm.**

You don't actually have to validate your ticket to pass through the turnstiles on the subway; however, ATAC's ticket inspectors prowl trains and stations and, as on the buses, checks are becoming much more common.

TAXIS AND RADIO TAXIS

Taxis in Rome are convenient but expensive (though less so than in other major cities). You can flag them down in the street, but they are easily found at stands near Termini and in major *piazze*. Ride only in yellow or white taxis, and make sure your taxi has a meter (if not, settle on a price before you get in the car). The meter starts at L4500. Surcharges are levied at night (L5000), on Sunday (L2000), and when heading to or from Fiumicino (L14,000) and Ciampino (L10,000), with a charge per suitcase of L2000. Standard tip is 15%. Expect to pay about L15,000 for a ride from Termini to the Vatican. Taxis between the city center and Fiumicino cost around L70,000.

Radio taxis will pick you up at a given location within a few minutes of your call. Beware: radio taxis start the meter the moment your call is answered! See the **Service Directory,** p. 298, for a listing of taxi and radio taxis.

LET'S DRIVE

CARS

Driving in Rome is a bad idea. Roman drivers are aggressive, and those who drive mopeds appear not to care whether they live or die. Parking is expensive and very difficult to find, and if you don't keep your eyes peeled, you may drive into a car-free zone (certain streets are reserved for public transportation and the police) and incur a fine. Car theft and robberies on cars are rampant, even during the day in busy areas. As if that weren't enough, gas (**benzina** in Italian) is exorbitantly priced (approximately L2000 per liter). Luckily, most gas stations accept credit cards.

Rome is linked to the north and south of Italy by a great north-south highway called the **A1**, which feeds into the **Grande Raccordo Anulare (GRA)**, the beltway that encircles Rome. Tolls on these roads are high; a trip to Florence can cost around L20,000. Besides the highway, there are several good *strade statale* that lead into Rome. From the north, enter on V. Flaminia, V. Salaria, or V. Nomentana. Avoid V. Cassia, V. Tiburtina, and V. del Mare at all costs; the ancient two-chariot lanes can't cope with modern-day traffic.

When leaving the city, don't try to follow the green *Autostrada per Firenze* signs— get on the GRA instead and follow it around; it's longer but faster. To get to the Adriatic coast, take highway A24. To reach beaches and port towns, try V. Pontina, which sticks close to the sea and connects you to most coastal spots.

INTERNATIONAL DRIVING PERMITS (IDP)

If you plan to drive a car while in Italy, you should obtain an **International Driving Permit (IDP)**. Although most car rental agencies don't require the permit, it is required for legal reasons if you drive for more than a month. Your IDP, valid for one year, must be issued in your own country before you depart and must be accompanied by a valid driver's license. You must be 18 years old to receive the IDP. Applications usually need to include one or two photos, a current local license, an additional form of identification, and a fee. Those driving in Italy for more than one year must obtain an Italian license (L70,000).

Australia: Contact your local **Royal Automobile Club (RAC)** or **National Royal Motorist Association (NRMA)** in NSW or the ACT (☎ (08) 9421 4444; www.rac.com.au/travel). AUS$15.

Canada: Contact any **Canadian Automobile Association (CAA)** branch office or write to CAA, 1145 Hunt Club Rd., #200, K1V 0Y3. (☎ (613) 247-0117; www.caa.ca/CAAInternet/travelservices/internationaldocumentation/idptravel.htm.) Permits CDN$10.

Ireland: Contact the nearest **Automobile Association (AA)** office or write to the UK address below. Permits IR£4. The Irish Automobile Association, 23 Suffolk St., Rockhill, Blackrock, Co. Dublin (☎ (01) 677 9481), honors most foreign automobile memberships (24hr. breakdown and road service ☎ (800) 667 788; toll-free in Ireland).

New Zealand: Contact your local **Automobile Association (AA)** or their main office at Auckland Central, 99 Albert St. (☎ (9) 377 4660; www.nzaa.co.nz). Permits NZ$8.

South Africa: Contact the Travel Services Department of the Automobile Association of South Africa at P.O. Box 596, 2000 Johannesburg (☎ (11) 799 1400; fax 799 1410; http://aasa.co.za). Permits SAR28.50.

UK: Contact your local AA or the **AA Headquarters** (☎ (0990) 44 88 66), or write to: The Automobile Association, International Documents, Fanum House, Erskine, Renfrewshire PA8 6BW. To find the location nearest you that issues the IDP, call (0990) 50 06 00 or (0990) 44 88 66. For more info, see www.theaa.co.uk/motoringandtravel/idp/index.asp. Permits UK£4.

US: Visit any **American Automobile Association (AAA)** office or write to AAA Florida, Travel Related Services, 1000 AAA Drive (mail stop 100), Heathrow, FL 32746 (☎ (407) 444-7000; fax 444-7380). You don't have to be a member to buy an IDP (US$10). AAA Travel Related Services (☎ (800) 222-4357) provides road maps, travel guides, emergency road services, travel services, and auto insurance.

CAR RENTALS

Economy cars are around L500,000 per week (L90,000-180,000 per day), though you may be able to find deals (without radio or A/C) as low as L300,000. By reserving in advance, non-residents of Italy are eligible for discounts of up to 60%. Insurance is required, augmenting the rates by as much as L100,000 a week. Paying by credit card may give you free insurance on rentals; check with your credit card company. All agencies require either a credit card or a cash deposit of at least L300,000, and most take only plastic. You must be 21 and have a valid driver's license, and preferably an International Driver's Permit (see above); the IDP is required for those who drive for more than one month.

You can make arrangements to pick up cars at Termini, the airports, or in the city offices. You may return your car at any rental location in Italy (with an additional charge of roughly L50,000 north of Rome and a monumental L300,000 or more to the south). Before making a reservation, ask your airline or travel agent about special deals. For listings of car rental agencies in Rome, see the **Service Directory,** p. 294.

HITCHHIKING

Let's Go does not recommend getting around by thumb as a safe means of transportation, and none of the following is intended to imply otherwise. Never get in the back of a two-door car. Never let go of your bag, and don't put anything in the trunk. If you feel threatened, experienced hitchers recommend you insist on being let out immediately, regardless of where you are. If the driver refuses, many people act as though they're going to open the door or vomit on the upholstery.

BIKES AND MOPEDS

Rome's hilly cobblestone streets, dense traffic, and *pazzo* drivers make the city a challenge for bikes and mopeds. Bikes cost around L5000 per hour or L15,000 per day, but the length of that "day" varies according to the shop's closing time. In summer, try the stands on V. del Corso at P. di San Lorenzo and V. di Pontifici. (Open daily 10am-7pm or so.) You need to be at least 16 years old to rent. Helmets are required by a strictly enforced law, and should be included with your rental. Prices do not include 20% sales tax. For those just interested in an afternoon on a bike, Enjoy Rome (p. 27) offers an informative, albeit harrowing, tour of the city's best sights. For a list of bike and moped rental agencies in the city, see the **Service Directory,** p. 294.

LET'S GET INFORMED

TOURIST OFFICES

■ **Enjoy Rome,** V. Marghera, 8a (☎06 4451843 or 06 4456890; fax 06 4450734; www.enjoyrome.com). From the middle concourse of Termini (between the trains and the ticket booths), exit right, with the trains behind you. Cross V. Marsala. The office is on the 3rd block down V. Marghera. Owners Fulvia and Pierluigi answer questions and offer useful tidbits about the city free of charge and in perfect English. Enjoy Rome arranges hotel accommodations (as well as short-term apartments), walking and bicycle tours (see p. 298), and bus service to Pompeii (see p. 232). Additionally, Enjoy Rome offers Internet access and a full-service travel agency, booking transportation worldwide and lodgings throughout Italy. Branch office at V. Varese, 39 (walk down V. Marghera another block and turn right). Open M-F 8:30am-2pm and 3:30-6:30pm, Sa 8:30am-2pm.

PIT (Tourist Information Point) (☎06 48906300), at track #4 in Termini. Run by the city, this English-speaking office provides limited information on events, hotels, restaurants, and transportation, as well as countless brochures and a serviceable map of Rome with sights listed on the back. Open daily 8am-8pm. **PIT kiosks** offer the same services at various spots around Rome. **Castel Sant'Angelo** (P. Pia; ☎06 68809707), **Fori Imperiali** (V. del Tempio della Pace; ☎06 69924307), **Piazza di Spagna** (Largo Goldoni; ☎06 68136061), **Piazza Navona** (P. delle

Cinque Lune; ☎06 68809240), **Trastevere** (P. Sonnino; ☎06 58333457), **San Giovanni** (P. S. Giovanni in Laterano; ☎06 77203535), **Santa Maria Maggiore** (V. dell'Olmata; ☎06 47880294), **V. del Corso** (V. Minghetti; ☎06 6782988), **V. Nazionale** (Palazzo delle Espozioni; ☎06 47824525), **Termini** (P. dei Cinquecento; ☎06 47825194), and **Fiumicino** (international arrivals area; ☎06 65956074). All kiosks except Fiumicino open daily 9am-6pm. Fiumicino open daily 8:15am-7:15pm. You can get the same info from the **Call Center Comune di Roma** (☎06 36004399), which operates daily 9am-7pm.

EPT, V. Parigi, 5 (☎06 48899255 or 06 48899253; fax 06 48899228) generally has the same information as PIT. Walk from the station diagonally to the left across P. del Cinquecento (filled with buses) and go straight across P. della Repubblica. Turn right onto V. Parigi, which starts on the other side of the church, at the Grand Hotel. English spoken, but not very well. *Alberghi di Roma e Provincia* lists all hotels and *pensioni* around Rome registered with the EPT. Open M-F 8:15am-7:15pm, Sa 8:15am-1:45pm.

USEFUL PUBLICATIONS

BROCHURES AND PAMPHLETS. The PIT offices and Enjoy Rome have free brochures and maps of downtown Rome. Enjoy Rome's aptly titled booklet, **Enjoy Rome,** is packed with information geared toward the English-speaking budget traveler. The EPT (via Parigi, 5) publishes **Un Ospite a Roma** (A Guest in Rome), a free pamphlet updated bi-weekly, listing events, exhibits, and concerts, as well as vital phone numbers for museums, galleries, and emergency services. It is also available at "finer hotels."

MAGAZINES. Roma C'è (L2000) is the comprehensive, tried-and-true guide to everything from restaurants to church services to discos. It is written in (easily decipherable) Italian with a small English language section at the end. **Time Out: Rome** (L2000), a flashy up-and-comer in the market of entertainment and culture mags, has plenty of useful information (entirely in Italian), including special info for women and gays. Both magazines are available on Thursdays. Also on Thursdays, **La Reppublica** publishes *Trovaroma* (L1500), which lists events and recreational possibilities. The daily **Il Messaggero** has some of the best entertainment listings, but is written in hard-to-decipher Italian.

LET'S KEEP IN TOUCH

BY TELEPHONE

CALLING ROME FROM ABROAD. Phone numbers range from five to eight digits in length. Rome is changing all numbers to seven or eight digits. Many changes are expected in 2001; if a number listed does not work, dial 12 or 170 for information. In Italy it is necessary to dial the city code for all numbers, even if you are calling from within the same city. Calls to Italy must begin with your country's **international access code** (011 in the US), then Italy's counry code (39), and the **city code** without the initial zero (06 becomes 6). **Toll-Free numbers:** *numero verde* numbers begin with 800 or 167.

CALLING ABROAD FROM ROME. To dial direct internationally, dial **two zeros** and the **country code** (Australia 61, Ireland 353, New Zealand 64, South Africa 27, United Kingdom 44, US and Canada 1), then the area/city code and number. If you normally dial a zero before the area/city code when calling within your country, do not do so when calling to your home country from Italy.

Miraculously, **rates** have actually dropped lately for international calls from Italy. At their most expensive, rates to the US are L2127 for the first minute and L1675 for each additional minute. Rates are highest on weekdays from 8am to 8pm. Lowest rates are from 11pm to 8am, on holidays, and between 2:30pm on Saturday and 8am on Mondays.

The easiest way to call home is with a pay phone and pre-paid phone card (see **Pay Phones,** below), but a call of any length may require several cards. The English-speaking operator in Italy can put through **collect calls** (☎170), though it's cheaper to find a pay phone and deposit just enough money to be able to say "Call me" and give your number (though some pay phones can't receive calls). Some companies have created callback phone services: you call a specified number, let it ring once, and hang up. The company's computer calls back and gives you a dial tone. You can then make as many calls as you want, at rates 20-60% lower than many phone cards. This option is most economical for loquacious travelers, as there may be a monthly minimum of US$10-25. For info, call **Telegroup** in the US (☎ (800) 338-0225).

Depending on your calling plan, a **calling card** may be your best and cheapest bet; your long distance provider has an international access number (billed as a toll-free or local call) you can dial from Italy to make collect or calling card calls: **AT&T** (☎1721011), **MCI** (☎1721022), **Sprint** (☎1721877), **Bell Canada Direct** (☎1721001), **British Telecom Direct** (☎1720044), **Telecom Éireann Ireland Direct** (☎1720353), **Telstra Australia Direct** (☎1721161), **Telecom New Zealand** (☎1721064), and **Telkom South Africa** (☎1721027). Call your long distance provider before your trip and do some research.

Italy is in the Western European **time zone,** six hours ahead of Eastern time in North America, one hour ahead of Britain and Ireland, one hour behind South Africa, nine hours behind Australia, and 11 hours behind New Zealand. Italy participates Daylight Savings but doesn't necessarily change on the same weekend as your home country.

PAY PHONES. Orange pay phones are all over the city, although ubiquitous cell phones *(telefonini)* are gradually driving them out. Some still take change (L100, L200, and L500 coins), but it is far more convenient to use pre-paid phone cards *(schede telefoniche)*. They come in denominations of L5000, L10,000, and L15,000, and are available at bars, *tabacchi*, and vending machines. As these cards will only pay for a 3min. call to the US during peak hours, some *tabacchi* now carry cards in denominations up to L50,000. Once you have purchased the card, break off the perforated corner and insert it into the machine with the magnetic strip facing up. The amount left on the card will be displayed on the screen. Dial away. An initial L100 will be taken when your call goes through. It costs L200 to connect to mobile phones; all have the area codes 0337, 0338, or 0339. A clicking noise warns you that you're about to run out of money; you can insert another card (or some coinage). Once you have hung up, wait around and savor *la dolce vita* until the phone spits your card back. Don't even think of coming back to look for your card if you forget it: criminal masterminds disguised as kindly old gentlemen and playful children will swoop down on the phone looking for *schede* the instant you leave.

BY MAIL

Although the Italian postal system has justly drawn snickers from the rest of Western Europe, things are getting better, partly thanks to new EU standards. Airmail from Italy takes anywhere from one to three weeks to arrive in the US, while much less expensive surface mail takes a month or longer. Letters and small parcels rarely get lost if they are *raccomandata* (registered), *espresso* (express), or *via aerea* (air mail).

HELP!

Carabinieri: ☎112.

Police/Fire/Ambulance: ☎113.

Police Foreigner's Office: ☎06 46862876.

Police Headquarters: ☎06 46861.

Medical Emergencies: ☎118.

Fire Service: ☎115.

TELEPHONIC FACTS

To call abroad when in Rome, dial:

1. **00 + the country code** (Australia 61, Ireland 353, NZ 64, S. Africa 27, UK 44, US/Canada 1)

2. **area/city code**

3. **phone number**

Telephone codes

Italy's country code: 39

Rome's city code: 06

Directory Assistance

Italy: ☎12 (L2000 to connect, but you'll get it back when you hang up)

Europe and Mediterranean: ☎176 (L1200).

Intercontinental: ☎17 90 (L1200).

English-speaking operator: ☎170.

Stamps are available at face value in *tabacchi* (they're everywhere; look for the big, white T), but mail letters from a post office to be sure they are stamped correctly.

POST OFFICES. Rome's main post offce is at P. San Silvestro, 19, south of P. di Spagna (take bus #62, 80, 116, or 492). Stamps are at booths #23-25. Currency exchange is available at booth #19. Fax and telegram service is also available; see p. 31. (☎ 06 679 8495; fax 06 6786618. Open M-F 9am-6pm, Sa 9am-2pm.) Come to San Silvestro with especially large packages, or if you need to insure your mail. Another large post office is at V. delle Terme di Diocleziano, 30, near Termini. (☎ 06 4745602; fax 06 4743536. Same hours as San Silvestro branch.)

RECEIVING MAIL IN ROME

Those sending you mail in Rome from North America should plan on it taking up to two weeks. Mail can usually be sent to your hotel, though you should let the proprietor know something is coming. The **American Express** office (see **Service Directory**, p. 295) will hold mail for up to 30 days for AmEx cardmembers or traveler's check holders. Have the sender write "client mail" on the envelope, as well as your name, with surname capitalized and underlined. Letters addressed to the main downtown post office should be labeled **Fermo Posta** (held mail) and look like this: LAST NAME, first name; *Fermo Posta;* Piazza San Silvestro, 19; 00187 Roma. You must claim your mail in person at booth #72 at the P. San Silvestro post office (see below) with your passport as ID. The fee is L3000 per piece of mail.

SENDING MAIL FROM ROME

EXPRESS MAIL, OVERNIGHT MAIL, AND PARCELS. Priority mail through the Italian Postal Service is called *Posta Prioriaria*. It's faster and more reliable than regular mail. Packages of up to 2kg are accepted starting at L1200. (Info ☎ 800 222666.) *Posta Celere* guarantees 24hr. delivery to most locations within Italy for packages up to 30kg. Rates start at L12,000. (Info ☎ 800 009966.) Parcels, and unsealed packages under 1kg (500g for Australia) may be mailed from the San Silvestro post office. Sealed packages of up to 20kg and 200cm total outside dimensions (length plus width and height) may be shipped, provided they are wrapped in brown paper, available at any *tabacchi*.

COURIERS. The quickest, most reliable service is available through private couriers. Service and rates are the same between companies. It L60,000 to send documents abroad (up to 500g) with guaranteed 48hr. delivery. Mailboxes, Etc. (see p. 31) will accept courier packages at its many locations, or you can visit the following offices. See the **Service Directory (p. 296)** for a list of courier services available in Rome.

PAPAL MAIL. The Vatican administers its own postal service, which is supposedly faster and more reliable than Italy's yet costs the same. What's the secret? They're not telling, but we think it may have something to do with their secret alliance with the Swiss postal service. Visit the locations in P. San Pietro: one on the left, near the tourist office and another on the right, near the center of the colonnade. There is a branch office on the 2nd floor of the Vatican Museum (open during museum hours, but with no *Fermo Posta*). Packages up to 2kg and 90 cm^3 are accepted. (☎ 06 69883406. Open M-F 8:30am-7pm, Sa 8:30am-6pm.)

BY EMAIL

With the increasingly ubiquitous presence of ATMs in Rome, money exchange shops are becoming a thing of the past. Don't shed a tear for their former owners, though: they're busy opening Internet access points in order to be able to take your money in other ways. Internet points, Internet cafes, and even Internet laundromats (see p. 296), are breeding like rats; in fact, there's probably one around the corner from your hotel (or even inside), especially if you're staying near Termini. *Let's Go* lists a few with good rates or other attractions. If you plan to bring a computer to Rome, obtain the necessary hardware before you go (see **Packing,** p. 256). Contact your local Internet service provider for information before arriving in Rome. To set up a new account, check the Yellow Pages under "Internet." Be sure to turn off your modem's "Detect Dial Tone" setting in order to be able to connect.

▨ **Marco's Bar,** V. Varese, 54 (☎06 44703591). Three blocks north of Termini, across the street from the Enjoy Rome tourist office (see p. 298). Completely renovated for 2001, Marco's boasts a cool, laid-back atmosphere, with music, a well-stocked bar, friendly staff, and cheap Internet access (L8000 per hr., with *Let's Go* L5000). Open daily 5:30am-2am.

▨ **Trevi Tourist Service: Trevi Internet,** V. dei Lucchesi, 31-32 (☎/fax 06 6920 0799). One block from the Trevi Fountain (toward P. Venezia on the road that becomes V. della Pilotta). Central location, fast connection, and great rates (L5000 for 30 min., L10,000 for 90 min.; if you don't use all your time up, you can come back again at a later date to do so). You want more? How about printing (L200 per page b/w, L2000 per page color), scanning (L2000 per page), video conferencing, photocopying, fax service (see below), Western Union money transfers, money exchange, newfangled cheap international calls on a newfangled phone system, and scooter rentals, all in A/C comfort. Open daily 9am-10pm.

Internet Café, V. dei Marrucini, 12 (☎/fax 06 4454953; www.Internetcafe.it; email info@Internet-cafe.it.) In San Lorenzo. Bus #492 bus from Termini or take a 15min. walk. Swank Internet cafe with fully stocked bar, fast connections, and A/C. 30min. L5000, 1hr. L8000; after 9pm 30min. L6000, 1 hr. L10,000. Special lunch deal 11am-3pm gets you a sandwich, a drink, and an hour of Internet access for L10,000. Between 7pm and 9pm, the same deal's L12,000. Open M-F 9am-2am, Sa-Su 5pm-2am.

Freedom Traveller, V. Gaeta, 25 (☎06 4782 3682; www.freedom-traveller.it). North of P. del Cinquecento. Run by a youth hostel, Freedom's just another word for Internet café with full bar and couchful common room featuring movies in English. L10,000 per hr., students L8000. 8hrs. L50,000. Open M-Sa 9am-midnight.

Internet Café, V. Cavour, 213 (☎06 4782 3051). Just south of the Cavour (B) Metro stop on the right. While there's nothing particularly exciting about this place, it gets the job done nicely. Also offers game machines should you not feel particularly communicative. L10,000 per hr., 10hr. pass L60,000. Open daily 9am-1am.

The Netgate Internet Point, P. Firenze, 25 (☎06 6893445). Down P. di Parlamento from V. del Corso. Large (40 computers) and A/C with webcams and microphones. W and S free Internet access during "Happy Time" (8pm-8:30pm); otherwise L10,000 per hr., 16 hrs. L100,000, 35 hrs. L200,000. Unused time can be used here or at the Florence location.

X-plore, V. dei Gracchi, 83-85 (☎06 50797474; www.xplore.it). Off P. del Risorgimento north of the Vatican. Space-age cafe with bar in the back. Internet L10,000 per hr.; afternoon special gets you a free beer with an hour's use. Open M-Th 10-1am, F-Sa 10-3am.

BY FAX

Fax service is quite common at *tabacchi* and photocopy shops. Public fax service is available at the main post office in P. S. Silvestro 9am-6pm at booths #73-76. (Faxes can be received 24hrs. a day, although they can only be picked up during business hours; see p. 30.) Also try the following:

Trevi Tourist Service, V. dei Lucchesi, 31-32 (☎/fax 06 69200799). One block from the Trevi Fountain (toward P. Venezia on the road that becomes V. della Pilotta). Sending L1000 per page plus cost of phone call. Receiving L1000 per page. Also Internet access (see above), printing, scanning, photocopying, Western Union money transfer, money exchange, phone service, and scooter rental. Open daily 9am-10pm.

Mailboxes, Etc., V. dei Mille, 38-40 (☎06 4461945; fax 06 4461338). South of P. Indipendenza near Termini. Sending: to US L5000 first page, L2000 each additional page (varies according to destination). Receiving: L2000 per page Open M-Sa 9am-2pm and 3-7pm. AmEx, MC, V.

XeroMania, V. S. Francesco a Ripa, 109 (☎06 5814433; fax 06 5817507). Off V. di Trastevere. Sending: L3000 first page, L1000 each additional page plus cost of phone call. Receiving: L2000 first page, L1800 each additional page (24hr. receiving services). Open M-F 9am-1pm and 3:30-7:30pm, Sa 9am-1pm.

LET'S SPEAK ITALIAN

If you don't speak Italian, you'll probably be able to manage with English in Rome. Most Romans who interact with tourists regularly know some English, and cognates often help French and Spanish speakers. Knowing some of the language can't hurt, though.

VOWELS

There are seven vowel sounds in standard Italian. **A**, **I**, and **U** are always pronounced the same way; **E** and **O** have two possible pronunciations, either tense or lax, depending on where the vowel appears in the word, whether it's stressed or not, and regional accent. It's difficult for non-native speakers to predict the quality of vowels. We illustrate the *approximate* pronunciation of the vowels below; don't worry too much about **E** and **O**.

a	*a* as in f*a*ther *(casa)*	**o** (tense)	*o* as in b*o*ne *(sono)*
e (tense)	*ay* as in b*a*y *(sete)*	**o** (lax)	between *o* of bone and *au* of c*au*ght *(zona)*
e (lax)	*eh* as in s*e*t *(bella)*		
i	*ee* as in ch*ee*se *(vino)*	**u**	*oo* as in dr*oo*p *(gusto)*

CONSONANTS

But for a few quirks, consonants won't be a problem. **H** is always silent and **R** is trilled.

C and G: before **a**, **o**, or **u**, **c** and **g** are hard, as in *cat* and *goose* or as in the Italian word *colore* (*koh*-LOHR-eh), "color," or *gatto* (GAHT-toh), "cat." They soften into "ch" and "j" sounds, respectively, when followed by i or e, as in the English *cheese* and *jeep* or the Italian *ciao* (CHOW), "good-bye," and *gelato* (jeh-LAH-toh), "ice cream."

CH and GH: h returns **c** and **g** to their "hard" sounds in front of **i** or **e** (see above); making words like *chiave* (key-AH-vay), "keys," and *tartarughe* (tahr-tah-RU-geh), "tortoises."

GN and GLI: pronounce **gn** like the **ni** in o*ni*on, thus *bagno* ("bath") is "BAHN-yo." **Gli** is like the **lli** in *million*, so *sbagliato* ("wrong") is said "zbal-YAH-toh."

S and Z: An **s** between two vowels or followed by the letters **b, d, g, l, m, n r,** and **v** is pronounced as a **z**; thus *casa* ("house") sounds like "KAH-zah" and *smarrito* ("lost") like "zmahr-REE-toh." A double **s** or an **s** followed by any other letter has the same sound as English initial **s**, so *sacco* ("bag") is SAHK-koh. **Z** has a **ts** or **dz** sound; thus *stazione* ("station") is pronounced "staht-see-YOH-nay," while *zoo* ("zoo") is pronounced "dzoh" and *mezzo* ("half") is "MEH-dzoh."

SC and SCH: when followed by **a**, **o**, or **u**, **sc** is pronounced as **sk**, so *scusi* ("excuse me") yields "SKOO-zee." When followed by an **e** or **i**, the combination is pronounced "**sh**" as in *sciopero* (SHOH-pair-oh), "strike." **H** returns **c** to its hard sound **(sk)** in front of **i** or **e**, as in *pesche* (PEH-skeh), "peaches," not to be confused with *pesce* (PEH-sheh), "fish."

Double consonants: The difference between double and single consonants in Italian is likely to cause problems for English speakers. When you see a double consonant, think about actually pronouncing it twice or holding it for a long time. English phrases like "bad dog" approximate the sound of a double consonant. Failing to make the distinction can lead to confusion; for example, *pen**ne** all'arrabbiata* is "short pasta in a spicy red sauce," whereas *pe**ne** all'arrabbiata* means "penis in a spicy red sauce." How long you hold the consonant here is a matter of taste.

STRESS

In many Italian words, stress falls on the next-to-last syllable. When stress falls on the last syllable, an accent indicates where stress should fall: *cit**tà*** (cheet-TAH) or *per**ché*** (pair-KAY). Stress can fall on the third-to-last syllable as well. It's not easy to predict stress, so you'll have to pick this up by listening to Italian speech.

PLURALS

Italians words form their plurals by changing the last vowel. Words that end in an **a** in the singular (usually feminine), end with an **e** in the plural; thus *mela* (MAY-lah), "apple," becomes *mele* (MAY-lay). Words that end with **o** or **e** in the singular take an **i** in the plural: *conto* (COHN-toh), "bill," is *conti* (COHN-tee) and *cane* (KAH-neh), "dog," becomes *cani* (KAH-nee). There are several exceptions to these rules; for example, *braccio* becomes *braccia* in the plural. Words with final accent, like *città* and *caffè*, and foreign words like *bar* and *sport* do not change in the plural.

PHRASEBOOK

DAYS OF THE WEEK		
ENGLISH	ITALIAN	PRONOUNCIATION
Monday	*lunedì*	loo-nay-DEE
Tuesday	*martedì*	mahr-tay-DEE
Wednesday	*mercoledì*	mair-coh-leh-DEE
Thursday	*giovedì*	joh-veh-DEE
Friday	*venerdì*	veh-nair-DEE
Saturday	*sabato*	SAH-bah-toh
Sunday	*domenica*	doh-MEH-nee-kah

MONTHS		
ENGLISH	ITALIAN	PRONOUNCIATION
January	gennaio	jehn-NAH-yoh
February	febbraio	Fehb-BRAH-yoh
March	marzo	MAHRT-soh
April	aprile	ah-PREE-lay
May	maggio	MAHJ-joh
June	giugno	JOON-yoh
July	luglio	LOOL-yoh
August	agosto	ah-GOH-stoh
September	settembre	seht-TEHM-bray
October	ottobre	oht-TOH-bray
November	novembre	noh-VEHM-bray
December	dicembre	dee-CHEM-bray

TIME		
ENGLISH	ITALIAN	PRONOUNCIATION
At what time...?	*A che ora...?*	ah kay OHR-ah
What time is it?	*Che ore sono?*	kay OHR-ay SOH-noh
It's 3:30.	*Sono le tre e mezzo.*	SOH-noh lay tray ay MEHD-zoh
It's noon.	*È mezzogiorno.*	eh MEHD-zoh-JOHR-noh
now	*adesso/ora*	ah-DEHS-so/OH-rah
tomorrow	*domani*	doh-MAH-nee
today	*oggi*	OHJ-jee
yesterday	*ieri*	YAIR-ee
right away	*subito*	SU-bee-toh
soon	*fra poco*	frah POH-koh
already	*già*	jah
after(wards)	*dopo*	DOH-poh
before	*prima*	PREE-mah
early/earlier	*presto/più presto*	PREHS-toh/pyoo PREHS-toh
late/later	*tardi/più tardi*	TAHR-dee/pyoo TAHRdee
early (before scheduled arrival time)	*in anticipo*	een ahn-TEE-chee-poh
late (after scheduled arrival time)	*in ritardo*	een ree-TAHR-doh

TIME

ENGLISH	ITALIAN	PRONOUNCIATION
daily	*quotidiano*	kwoh-tee-dee-AH-no
weekly	*settimanale*	seht-tee-mah-NAH-leh
monthly	*mensile*	mehn-SEE-leh
vacation	*le ferie*	lay FEH-ree-eh
weekdays	*i giorni feriali*	ee JOHR-nee feh-ree-AH-lee
Sundays and holidays	*i giorni festivi*	ee JOHR-nee fehs-TEE-vee
day off (at store, restaurant, etc.)	*riposo*	ree-POH-zo
a strike	*uno sciopero*	SHOH-peh-roh
a protest	*una manifestazione*	mah-nee-fehs-taht-see-OH-neh

PHRASES

ENGLISH	ITALIAN	PRONOUNCIATION
Hi!/So long! (informal)	*Ciao!*	chaow
Good day./Hello.	*Buongiorno.*	bwohn JOHR-noh
Good evening.	*Buona sera.*	BWOH-nah SEH-rah
My name is...	*Mi chiamo...*	mee Key-YAH-moh
What is your name...?	*Come ti chiami? (informal)/Come si chiama Lei? (formal)*	KOH-may tee key-YAH-mee/KOH-may see key-YAH-mah lay
I'm/We're from . . .	*Vengo/Veniamo dal/dalla. . .*	VAIN-goh/VAIN-ee-Am-oh doll
How are you?	*Come sta/state?*	KOH-may STAH/STAH-tay
Good night.	*Buona notte.*	BWOH-nah NOHT-tay
Goodbye.	*Arrivederci./ArrivederLa.*	ah-ree-veh-DAIR-chee/ ah-ree-veh-DAIR-lah
please	*per favore/per cortesia/ per piacere*	pair fah-VOH-ray/ pair kohr-teh-ZEE-ah/ pair pyah-CHEH-reh
Thank you.	*Grazie.*	GRAHT-see-yeh
You're welcome. May I help you? Go right ahead.	*Prego.*	PRAY-goh
Pardon me.	*Scusi.*	SKOO-zee
I'm sorry.	*Mi dispiace.*	mee dees-PYAH-cheh
Yes./No./Maybe.	*Sì./No./Forse.*	see/no/FOHR-say
I don't know.	*Non lo so.*	nohn loh soh
I have no idea.	*Boh...*	boh
Let's Go! (our favorite)	*Andiamo*	ahnd-ee-AH-moh
Could you repeat that?	*Potrebbe ripetere?*	poh-TREHB-beh ree-PEH-teh-reh
What does this mean?	*Che vuol dire questo?*	kay vwohl DEE-reh KWEH-stoh
Okay./I understand.	*Ho capito.*	Oh kah-PEE-toh
I don't understand.	*Non capisco.*	nohn kah-PEES-koh
I don't speak Italian.	*Non parlo italiano.*	nohn PAR-loh ee-tahl-YAH-noh
I'm an artist	*Sono artista*	SOH-noh ahrt-EE-stah
Is there someone who speaks English?	*C'è qualcuno che parla inglese?*	cheh kwahl-KO-noh kay PAR-lah een-GLAY-zay
Could you help me?	*Potrebbe aiutarmi?*	poh-TREHB-beh ah-yoo-TAHR-mee
How do you say...?	*Come si dice...?*	KOH-may see DEE-chay
What do you call this in Italian?	*Come si chiama questo in italiano?*	KOH-may see key-YAH-mah KWEH-stoh een ee-tahl-YAH-no
this/that	*questo/quello*	KWEH-sto/KWEHL-loh
who	*chi*	kee

PHRASES		
ENGLISH	**ITALIAN**	**PRONOUNCIATION**
where	dove	DOH-vay
which	quale	KWAH-lay
when	quando	KWAN-doh
what	che/cosa/che cosa	kay/KOH-za/kay KOH-za
why/because	perchè	pair-KEH
more/less	più/meno	pyoo/MEH-noh

DIRECTIONS AND TRANSPORTATION		
ENGLISH	**ITALIAN**	**PRONOUNCIATION**
Where is...?	Dov'è...?	doh-VEH
How do you get to...?	Come si arriva a...	KOH-meh see ahr-REE-vah
Do you stop at...?	Ferma a...?	FAIR-mah ah
...the beach	la spiaggia	lah spee-AH-jah
...the building	il palazzo/l'edificio	eel pah-LAHT-so/leh-dee-FEE-choh
...the bus stop	la fermata d'autobus	lah fair-MAH-tah DAOW-toh-boos
...the center of town	il centro	eel CHEN-troh
...the church	la chiesa	lah kee-AY-zah
...the consulate	il consolato	eel kohn-so-LAH-toh
...the grocery store	l'alimentari	lah-lee-men-TAH-ree
...the hospital	l'ospedale	los-peh-DAH-lay
...the market	il mercato	eel mair-KAH-toh
...the office	l'ufficio	loo-FEE-choh
...the post office	l'ufficio postale	loo-FEE-choh poh-STAH-lay
...the station	la stazione	lah staht-see-YOH-nay
near/far	vicino/lontano	vee-CHEE-noh/lohn-TAH-noh
Turn left/right	Gira a sinistra/destra	JEE-rah ah see-NEE-strah/DEH-strah
straight ahead	sempre diritto	SEHM-pray DREET-toh
here	qui/qua	kwee/kwah
there	lì/là	lee/lah
the street address	l'indirizzo	leen-dee-REET-soh
the telephone	il telefono	eel teh-LAY-foh-noh
street	strada, via, viale, vico, vicolo, corso	STRAH-dah, VEE-ah, vee-AH-lay, VEE-koh, VEE-koh-loh, KOHR-soh
Take the bus from... to...	Prenda l'autobus da... a...	PREN-dah LAOW-toh-boos dah... ah...
Do you believe in UFOs?	Credi negli UFO?	CRAY-dee nay-lyee ooh-eff-oh
What time does the... leave?	A che ora parte...?	ah kay OHR-ah PAHR-tay
...the (city) bus	l'autobus	LAOW-toh-boos
...the (intercity) bus	il pullman	eel POOL-mahn
...the ferry	il traghetto	eel tra-GHEHT-toh
...the plane	l'aereo	lah-EHR-reh–oh
...the train	il treno	eel TRAY-no
I would like a ticket for...	Vorrei un biglietto per...	vohr-RAY oon beel-YET-toh pair
How much does it cost?	Quanto costa?	KWAN-toh CO-stah
How much does... cost?	Quanto costa...?	KWAN-toh CO-stah
I would like...	Vorrei...	voh-RAY

DIRECTIONS AND TRANSPORTATION

ENGLISH	ITALIAN	PRONOUNCIATION
...a ticket	un biglietto	oon beel-YEHT-toh
...a pass (bus, etc.)	una tessera	OO-nah TEHS-seh-rah
one way	solo andata	SO-lo ahn-DAH-tah
round-trip	andata e ritorno	ahn-DAH-tah ey ree-TOHR-noh
reduced price	ridotto	ree-DOHT-toh
student discount	sconto studentesco	SKOHN-toh stoo-dehn-TEHS-koh
What time does the train for... leave?	A che ora parte il treno per...?	ah kay OH-rah PAHR-tay eel TRAY-noh pair
What platform for...?	Che binario per...?	kay bee-NAH-ree-oh pair
Where does the bus leave from...?	Da dove parte l'autobus per...?	dah DOH-vay PAHR-tay LAU-toh-boos pair
Is the train late?	È in ritardo il treno?	eh een ree-TAHR-doh eel TRAY-no
When will the strike be over?	Quando finisce lo sciopero?	KWAN-doh fee-NEE-shay eel SHOH-peh-roh
the arrival	l'arrivo	la-REE-voh
the departure	la partenza	la par-TENT-sah
the track	il binario	eel bee-NAH-ree-oh
the terminus (of a bus)	il capolinea	eel kah-poh-LEE-neh-ah
the flight	il volo	eel VOH-loh
the reservation	la prenotazione	la pray-no-taht-see-YOH-neh
the entrance/the exit	l'ingresso/l'uscita	leen-GREH-so/loo-SHEE-tah

HOTEL RESERVATIONS

ENGLISH	ITALIAN	PRONOUNCIATION
Hello? (used when answering the phone)	Pronto!	PROHN-toh
Do you speak English?	Parla inglese?	PAHR-lah een-GLAY-zay
Could I reserve a single/double room for the second of August?	Potrei prenotare una camera singola/doppia per il due agosto?	POH-tray pray-noh-TAH-ray OO-nah CAH-meh-rah SEEN-goh-lah/DOH-pee-yah pair eel DOO-ay ah-GOH-stoh?
with bath/shower	con bagno/doccia	kohn BAHN-yo/DOH-cha
with bathroom	con un gabinetto/un bagno/una toletta	eel gah-bee-NEHT-toh/eel BAHN-yoh/ lah toh-LEHT-toh
open/closed	aperto/chiuso	ah-PAIR-toh/KYOO-zoh
a towel	un asciugamano	oon ah-shoo-gah-MAH-noh
sheets	le lenzuola	lay lehn-SUO-lah
a blanket	una coperta	OO-nah koh-PAIR-tah
heating	il riscaldamento	eel ree-skahl-dah-MEHN-toh
How much is the room?	Quanto costa la camera?	KWAHN-toh KOHS-ta lah KAM-eh-rah
My name is...	Mi chiamo...	mee key-YAH-moh..
I will arrive at 2:30pm.	Arriverò alle quattordici e mezzo.	ah-ree-vair-OH ah-lay kwah-TOHR-dee-chee eh MED-zoh
Certainly!	Certo!	CHAIR-toh
I'm sorry but...	Mi dispiace, ma...	mee dis-pee-YAH-chay, mah...
We're closed during August.	Chiudiamo ad agosto.	kyu-dee-AH-moh ahd ah-GOH-stoh
No, we're full.	No, siamo al completo.	no, see-YAH-moh ahl cohm-PLAY-toh

HOTEL RESERVATIONS

ENGLISH	ITALIAN	PRONOUNCIATION
We don't take telephone reservations.	*Non si fanno le prenotazioni per telefono.*	nohn see FAHN-noh lay pray-noh-tat-see-YOH-nee pair tay-LAY-foh-noh
You'll have to send a deposit/check.	*Bisogna mandare un acconto/un anticipo/un assegno.*	bee-ZOHN-yah mahn-DAH-reh oon ahk-KOHN-toh/oon ahn-TEE-chee-poh/oon ahs-SAY-nyoh
You must arrive before 2pm.	*Deve arrivare primo delle quattordici.*	DAY-vay ah-ree-VAH-ray PREE-moh day-lay kwah-TOHR-dee-chee
Okay, I'll take it.	*Va bene. La prendo.*	vah BEHN-eh. lah PREHN-doh

RESTAURANTS

ENGLISH	ITALIAN	PRONOUNCIATION
the breakfast	*la (prima) colazione*	lah (PREE-mah) coh-laht-see-YO-nay
the lunch	*il pranzo*	eel PRAHND-zoh
the dinner	*la cena*	lah CHEH-nah
the appetizer	*l'antipasto*	lahn-tee-PAH-stoh
the first course	*il primo (piatto)*	eel PREE-moh pee-YAH-toh
the second course	*il secondo (piatto)*	eel seh-COHN-doh pee-YAH-toh
the side dish	*il contorno*	eel cohn-TOHR-noh
the dessert	*il dolce*	eel DOHL-chay
the fork	*la forchetta*	lah fohr-KEH-tah
the knife	*il coltello*	eel cohl-TEHL-loh
the spoon	*il cucchiaio*	eel koo-kee-EYE-yoh
the bottle	*la bottiglia*	lah boh-TEEL-yah
the glass	*il bicchiere*	eel bee-kee-YAIR-eh
the napkin	*il tovagliolo*	eel toh-vahl-YOH-loh
the plate	*il piatto*	eel pee-YAH-toh
the waiter/waitress	*il/la cameriere/a*	eel/lah kah-meh-ree-AIR-ray/rah
the bill	*il conto*	eel COHN-toh
the cover charge	*il coperto*	eel koh-PAIR-toh
the service charge/tip	*il servizio*	eel sair-VEET-see-oh
included	*compreso/a*	KOHM-pray-zoh/ah

MEDICAL

ENGLISH	ITALIAN	PRONOUNCIATION
I have...	*Ho...*	OH
...allergies	*delle allergie*	lay ahl-lair-JEE-eh
...a blister	*una bolla*	lah BOH-lah
...a cold	*un raffreddore*	oon rahf-freh-DOH-reh
...a cough	*una tosse*	OO-nah TOHS-seh
...the flu	*l'influenza*	lenn-floo-ENT-sah
...a fever	*una febbre*	OO-nah FEHB-breh
...a headache	*un mal di testa*	oon mahl dee TEHS-tah
...a lump (on the head)	*un bernoccolo*	eel bear-NOH-koh-loh
...a rash	*un'esantema /un sfogo/ un'eruzione*	leh-zahn-TAY-mah/ eel SFOH-goh/ leh-root-see-OHN-eh
...a stomach ache	*un mal di stomaco*	oon mahl dee STOH-mah-koh
...a swelling/growth	*un gonfiore*	eel gohn-fee-OR-ay

MEDICAL

ENGLISH	ITALIAN	PRONOUNCIATION
...a venereal disease	*una malattia venerea*	lah mah-lah-TEE-ah veh-NAIR-ee-ah
...a vaginal infection	*un'infezione vaginale*	leen-feht-see-OH-nay vah-jee-NAH-lay
My foot hurts.	*Mi fa male il piede.*	mee fah MAH-le eel PYEHD-deh
I'm on the pill.	*Prendo la pillola.*	PREHN-doh lah PEE-loh-lah
I haven't had my period for (2) months.	*Non ho le mestruazioni da (due) mesi.*	nohn oh lay meh-stroo-aht-see-OH-nee dah (DOO-ay) may-zee
I'm (3 months) pregnant.	*Sono incinta (da tre mesi).*	SOH-noh een-CHEEN-tah (dah tray MAY-zee)
You're (a month) pregnant.	*Lei è incinta (da un mese).*	lay ay een-CHEEN-tah (dah oon MAY-zay)
blood	*il sangue*	eel SAHN-gweh
a gynecologist	*un ginecologo*	jee-neh-KOH-loh-goh
the skin	*la pelle*	lah PEHL-lay

EMERGENCIES

ENGLISH	ITALIAN	PRONOUNCIATION
I lost my passport.	*Ho perso il passaporto.*	oh PAIR-soh eel pahs-sah-POHR-toh
I've been robbed.	*Sono stato derubato.*	SOH-noh STAH-toh deh-roo-BAH-toh
The ATM has eaten my credit card	*Il Bancomat ha trattenuto la mia carta.*	eel BAHN-koh-maht ah trah-tehn-OO-toh lah MEE-ah CAHR-tah
Wait!	*Aspetta!*	ahs-PEHT-tah
Stop!	*Ferma!*	FAIR-mah
Help!	*Aiuto!*	ah-YOO-toh
Leave me alone!	*Lasciami in pace!*	LAH-shah-mee een PAH-cheh
Don't touch me!	*Non mi toccare!*	NOHN mee tohk-KAH-reh
I'm calling the police!	*Telefono alla polizia!*	tehl-LAY-foh-noh ah-lah poh-leet-SEE-ah
Go away!	*Vai via!*	VY VEE-ah
Go away, cretin!	*Vattene, cretino!*	VAH-teh-neh creh-TEE-noh

LOVE

ENGLISH	ITALIAN	PRONOUNCIATION
May I buy you a drink?	*Posso offrirle qualcosa da bere?*	POHS-soh ohf-FREER-lay kwahl-COH-zah dah BAY-ray
Would you buy me a drink?	*Può offrirmi qualcosa da bere?*	pwoh ohf-FREER-mi kwahl-COH-zah dah BAY-ray
I'm drunk.	*Sono ubriaco.*	SOH-noh oo-BRYAH-coh
Are you drunk?	*È lei ubriaco?*	ay LAY-ee oo-BRYAH-coh
You're cute.	*Lei è bello.*	LAY-ee ay BEHL-loh
I'm an anarchist.	*Sono un'anarchica.*	Soh-noh uhn ann-AHR-key-cuh
Your friend is cute.	*Il suo amico è bello.*	eel SOO-oh ah-MEE-cah ay BEHL-loh
I have a boyfriend/ a girlfriend.	*Ho un ragazzo/una ragazza*	oh oon rah-GAHT-soh/ oo-nah rah-GAHT-sah
I love you, I swear.	*Ti amo, te lo giuro.*	tee AH-moh, tee loh JOO-roh

GLOSSARY

abbazia	also badia, an abbey
anfiteatro	ampitheater
arco	arch
apse	a semicircular, domed niche projecting from the altar end of a church.
atrium	an open central court, usually to an ancient Roman house.
baldacchino	stone or bronze canopy supported by columns over the altar of a church
basilica	a rectangular building with aisle and apse; no transepts. Used by ancient Romans for public adminstration. The Christians later adopted the style for their churches.
battistero	a baptistry, usually a separate building near the town's duomo, where the town's baptisms were performed.
borgo	ancient town or village
campanile	a bell tower, usually freestanding.
cappella	chapel
cartoon	full-sized drawing used to transfer a preparatory design to the final work, especially to a wall for a fresco.
castrum	the ancient Roman military camp. Many Italian cities were originally built on this plan: a rectilinear city with straight streets, the chief of which was called the decumanus maximus.
cenacolo	"Last Supper"; A depiction of Christ at dinner on the evening before his crucifixion, often found in the refectory of an abbey or convent.
chancel	the space around the altar reserved for clergy and choir.
chiaroscuro	the balance between light and dark in a painting, and the painter's ability to show the contrast between them.
chiesa	church
cloister/chiostro	a courtyard; generally a quadrangle with covered walkways along its edges, often with a central garden, forming part of a church or monastery.
comune	the government of a free city of the Middle Ages.
corso	a principal street or avenue
cosmati work	mosaic on marble, found in early Christian churches around Rome
cupola	a dome
diptych	a painting in two parts or panels.
duomo	cathedral; the official seat of a diocesan bishop, and usually the central church of an Italian town.
facade	the front of a building, or any wall given special architectural treatment.
fiume	a river
forum	in an ancient Roman town, a square containing municipal buildings and/or market space. Smaller towns usually have only one central forum, while large cities, such as Rome, can have several.
fresco	affresco, a painting made on wet plaster. When it dries, the painting becomes part of the wall.
frieze	a band of decoration in any medium. Architecturally, can also refer to the middle part of an entablature (everything above the columns of a building) between the architrave and the cornice.
giardino	garden
gabinetto	Toilet, WC
Greek Cross	a cross whose arms are of equal length.
grotesque	painted, carved, or stucco decorations of fantastic, distorted human or animal figures, named for the grotto work found in Nero's buried Golden House.
in restuaro	under restoration; a key concept in Rome.
Intarsia	inlay work, usually of marble, metal, or wood.
Latin Cross	a cross whose vertical arm is longer than its horizontal arm.
loggia	a covered gallery or balcony.

lungo, lung	literally "along," so that a lungomare is a boardwalk or promenade alongside the mare (ocean).
lunette	a semi-circular frame in the ceiling or vault of a building that holds a painting or sculpture.
mausoleum	a large tomb or building with places to entomb the dead above ground.
nave	the central body of a church.
necropolis	ancient burial site; definitely spooky
palazzo	an important building of any type, not just a palace. Many were built as townhouses for wealthy families.
Pietà	a scene of the Virgin mourning the dead Christ.
polyptych	altarpiece with more than three panels
ponte	bridge
presepio	nativity scene
putto	(pl. putti) the little nude babies that flit around Renaissance art occasionally, and Baroque art incessantly.
reliquary	holding place for a saint's relics, which usually consist of bones, but are often much much stranger.
sinopia drawing	a red pigment sketch made on a wall as a preliminary study for a fresco.
scalinata	stairway
spiaggia	beach
stigmata	miraculous body pains or bleeding that resemble the wounds of the crucified Christ.
thermae	(terme in Italian) ancient Roman baths and, consequently, social centers.
telamoni	large, often sensual, statues of men used as columns in temples.
transept	in a cruciform church, the arm of the church that intersects the nave or central aisle (i.e. the cross-bar of the T).
travertine	a light colored marble or limestone used in many of the buildings in Rome.
triptych	a painting in three panels or parts.
trompe l'oeil	literally, "to fool the eye," a painting or other piece or art whose purpose is to trick the viewer, as in a flat ceiling painted so as to appear domed.
tufa	a soft stone composed of volcanic ash (tufo in Italian).
villa	a country house, usually a large estate with a formal garden. In Rome, villa refers to the area surrounding the estates that have become public parks.

THOSE CRAZY ROMANS

No book could possibly list all of Rome and Italy's cultural idiosyncrasies; the following tips, however, might save the well-meaning tourist some confusion and frustration.

HOURS. Roman **business hours,** or lack thereof, can be aggravating for tourists. Schedules and timetables are often unreliable. Most **shops** are open in the morning from 8 or 9am to 1pm and in the afternoon from 4 to 8pm. A few stores stay open during the lunch break, *all'americana;* look for signs reading *orario non-stop.* Most businesses, less touristy restaurants, and some cafes shut down on Sundays and Monday mornings, and some close on Saturday afternoons. **Food shops** *(alimentari)* are frequently closed on Thursday afternoons, although a few on V. del Corso have reduced hours for desperate weekend consumers. For all listings and attractions, *Let's Go* provides the most current hours—keep in mind that, even if these haven't changed, they may not be honored.

Rome shuts down at the beginning of August, and by **Ferragosto** (The Feast of the Assumption, Aug. 15, 2001), Italy's big summer holiday, you'll be hard-pressed to find a Roman in the city. Although museums and sights remain open, most offices and restaurants close down completely. You won't starve, though; a humanitarian law bars bread shops from closing for more than one day at a time. *La Repubblica* and *Il Messaggero* publish daily lists of open pharmacies and other essential services.

TIPPING. Italians tip with style, and even mandate it with an automatic service charge. While restaurants usually tack on 15%, it is customary to add 10% or so for good service. Also tipped: taxi drivers (15%); doormen (L1000 for calling cabs); chambermaids (L2000 per day); porters (L2000 per day); and cafes and bars (15%). Finally, tour guides work hard for little pay; if you learn something, give them a few thousand *lire*.

BARGAINING. Bargaining is common in Rome only at outdoor markets and over unmetered cab fares. Hotel haggling is successful only in uncrowded, smaller *pensioni*. If you don't speak Italian, at least memorize the numbers. Let the merchant make the first offer and counter with roughly two-thirds of his bid. The merchant will probably act mildly offended by your offer, even if the context warrants bargaining, but stand firm. Never offer anything you are unwilling to pay—you are expected to buy if the merchant accepts your price. It's as bad as Priceline.

PERSONAL SPACE. All travelers to Italy should be aware that the Italian conception of personal space might be different from that to which they are accustomed. The guy crowded next to you on the bus or the woman gesticulating madly in your face is not necessarily threatening you or being rude; it is fairly normal in Italian culture to stand close to the person you're addressing and to gesture wildly.

CASHIERS WHO WON'T MAKE CHANGE. You may notice that Italians never seem to have change; even after hours of doing business, they will refuse to break the L50,000 notes ATMs spit out. Cashiers will often ask you if you have coins to cover the hundreds of *lire* in your total *(Ce l'hai due cento?)*, claiming that they have no coins themselves. You have two options; either rummage through your pockets or smile sweetly and sadly, forcing them to make change.

FONTANELLAS. The streets of Rome are dotted with free-flowing spigots, often with marble basins. Don't be afraid to drink from them. Unless the words *"non potabile"* are written nearby, they are entirely safe (thanks to the still-excellent ancient aqueduct and sewer systems) and usually quite cold. Don't drink from or dip your hands in the decorative fountains found in *piazze*; Anita Eckberg may have been able to pull it off, but those who try and live *La Dolce Vita* in the Trevi Fountain (or any other public *fontana*) face a L1,000,000 fine and a stern talking-to in Italian (see **Sights,** p. 109, for a full explanation). Also, the *piazza* fountains' filthy water is recycled through again and again.

FLOORS. Europeans count floors differently than North Americans. Street-level floors are the *piano terra*, abbreviated "T" or "0." The North American 2nd floor is Italy's first.

Life & Times

HISTORY

VARIOUS BEGINNINGS

Once upon a time, **Aeneas** (variously the son of Anchises and the goddess Aphrodite or a distant descendent of Noah) left his crumbling Troy with his aged father on his back and, after a series of trials and tribulations, landed in the land of the Latins. Deciding that the Latins were reasonably friendly, he endeared himself to them by marrying Lavinia, their princess. He then crowned himself king and called his kingdom Lavinium. This is the charming story as Virgil's *Aeneid* tells it (see **Latin is Your Friend,** p. 59), but it isn't nearly all there is to say on the matter.

Shortly after all this happened, according to Livy, the ancient Roman historian, a Vestal Virgin named Rhea Silvia went bad and had a bouncing pair of twin sons. Their father, as she told anyone who cared to ask, was the god Mars. The establishment, alas, wouldn't stand for this sort of nonsense, and the kids were set adrift in a basket on the Tiber River. However, the basket and its contents were found by a motherly she-wolf; the she-wolf, it turns out, was puppyless and found the brothers an acceptable substitute. So the twin brothers, **Romulus** and **Remus,** were raised in a caring (if lupine) home until a kindly shepherd came along and rescued the boys from this domestic disarray.

In spite of their confused past, the twins grew up to make their mother(s) proud by founding a city on the Palatine Hill, **Rome,** on April 21, 753 BC. Remus was not terribly happy about the name of the city, and Romulus thought Remus quite extraneous, so he killed Remus and made himself king. Thus was the glorious city of Rome founded, kicking off a grand tradition of ruthlessly bloody Italian politics.

44

753 BC Livy's date for the founding of Rome by Romulus and Remus.

715-672 Sabines rule Rome.

616-509 Three Etruscan kings rule Rome

509 Romans rebel against Etruscan rule, found Republic, and just generally act like rebels.

493 Plebeians, unhappy with the patricians, refuse to be plebeians.

450 Plebeians are represented in the government by 10 tribunes.

440 Republican laws codified into Twelve Tables.

390 Quacking geese save the day, alerting Romans of the invading Gauls.

275 Romans defeat Pyrrhus, last defender of the Greeks, seizing control of the entire peninsula.

While Livy's story is nice, it's probably not all that accurate. A shadow of a doubt appears when one notes the striking similarity in the etymology of "she-wolf" and "prostitute." But you can't found a city as grand as Rome with two babies and a hooker. Starting off a city with the descendents of the goddess of love and the god of war is much more suitable.

What was really happening at the time is unclear. Pottery dating from as far back as 1200 BC has been found, suggesting older origins. Remains of villages in the area date from about 800 BC; the people who first ruled Rome were the **Sabines.** Three Sabine kings ruled Rome: Numa Pompilius, who took charge in 715 BC, Tullus Hostilius, and Ancus Martius.

The Sabines were soon deposed, however, by the **Etruscans,** a tribe from the North. (See **Cerveteri,** p. 230, and **Tarquinia,** p. 230, for more information on Etruscan villages.) Responsible for the adaptation of the Latin language and the Latinization of the Greek gods, Etruscan kings controlled Rome starting in 616 BC. Some remains of their civilization can still be seen: most notably, the Etruscans built the Cloaca Maxima, the pride and joy of the Roman sewer system. Their rule came to an end in 509 BC, when the son of King **Tarquinius Superbus** raped the virtuous Roman matron **Lucretia.** She publicly committed suicide, and her outraged family led the Roman populace in overthrowing the Tarquin dynasty in 509 BC. The next day, the first Roman republic was founded.

Free from Etruscan rule, the Romans set about figuring out exactly what this republic that they had founded would be. Originally, the government was an oligarchy in which landowning patricians (and after 450 BC, wealthy plebeians) gathered in the Senate to make laws, hear trials, and declare war.

A complex bureaucracy made up of *praetores* (judicial officer), *quaestores* (tax collectors), *aediles* (magistrate), and *tribunes* oversaw the city's burgeoning infrastructure, and Rome strutted its stuff with loads of new temples, roads, bridges, and aqueducts.

From its power base in the Tiber valley, the city expanded, conquering neighbors with astounding efficiency and generally rabble-rousing in the surrounding countryside. In 395 BC, the Etruscans were put down for good when the Romans captured Veia, their capital. Southern Italy was made safe for Romans in 275 BC, when **Pyrrhus,** the Greek ruler of Tarentum, was defeated at the Battle of Beneventum.

THE REPUBLIC GROWS...

What did Caesar really whisper to his protégé as he fell? *Et tu*, Brute, the official lie, is about what you'd expect to get from them—it says exactly nothing.... When one speaks to the other then it is not to pass the time of day with et-tu-Brutes. What passes is a truth so terrible that history—at best a conspiracy...to defraud—will never admit it. The truth will be repressed or in ages of particular elegance be disguised as something else.

—Thomas Pynchon, *Gravity's Rainbow*

264-241 First Punic War accomplishes very little.

After the conquest of Italy, the most important battles of the Republic were the three **Punic Wars** (264-146 BC), waged against Carthage (in modern-day Tunisia) for control of important Mediterranean trade routes, Spanish and Sicilian territory, and all-important "bragging rights."

During the second of these wars, the Carthaginian general **Hannibal** marched his army—elephants and all—up through Spain and across the Alps. He swooped down the peninsula, surprising a series of Roman generals, and made it all the way to the walls of Rome, but failed to breach them. His campaign devolved into a cat-and-mouse game with **Fabius Maximus,** who eluded the overeager Hannibal for several years until the starving Carthaginians dragged their tired elephants home. Carthage was decisively defeated at Zama, in Africa, in 202 BC by another great Roman general, **Scipio Africanus.** Pressing the advantage, **Cato the Censor** egged on his fellow Romans to utterly raze the powerless Carthage in the Third Punic War of 146 BC. Rumor has it that Roman soldiers sowed Carthaginian fields with salt to keep the city from causing trouble again.

Traditional Roman society had been austere and pious, but, drowning in riches from such successful conquests, it became a festering swamp of greed and corruption. Yeoman farmers were pushed off their land by avaricious landowners and driven into slavery or starvation. Less than grateful, the yeomen protested; by 131 BC, popular demands for land redistribution led to riots against the corrupt patricians, culminating in the **Social War** (91-87 BC). Tribes throughout the peninsula fought successfully for the extension of Roman citizenship.

Fed up, **Sulla,** the general who had led Roman troops during the conflict, marched on Rome (traditionally a demilitarized zone), seizing control of the city in a bloody military coup. Over 1600 nobles and senators were executed without benefit of trial. Sulla's strong-arm tactics set a dangerous precedent for the Republic as generals began to amass private armies funded by huge personal fortunes. In 73 BC, **Spartacus,** a rebellious gladiatorial slave, led a 70,000-man army of slaves and farmers in a two-year rampage down the peninsula. When the dust cleared, 6000 slaves had been crucified, and **Pompey the Great,** an associate of Sulla, took de facto control of Rome.

Disallowed by the Senate from ruling alone, Pompey ran the city with **Julius Caesar** and **Crassus,** forming the **First Triumvirate.** The threesome quickly went sour, and Caesar, the charismatic conqueror of the Gauls, emerged victorious, having poor Pompey assassinated in 48 BC. Caesar's reign was not to last long: a small senatorial faction, fearful of his growing power, assassinated him on the Ides (15th) of March in 44 BC. In the ensuing power vacuum, a **Second Triumvirate** was formed. The big three were Caesar's grand-nephew and adopted son, Octavian, Marc Antony (soon to be tangled up with Cleopatra and off to Africa), and Lepidus, a no-account rascal. Octavian soon declared war on Marc Antony and Cleopatra (otherwise known as the young Liz Taylor), and spanked them soundly—so soundly, in fact, that they killed themselves in 30 BC. And Lepidus? Nobody remembers what happened to him.

...AND BECOMES AN EMPIRE

Under the name **Augustus,** Octavian consolidated power and began assembling an imperial government in 27 BC. His reign (27 BC-AD 14) is considered the golden age of Rome, a flourishing of culture ushering in the 200 years of the **Pax Romana**

218-202 Second Punic War. Hannibal crosses the Alps.

148-146 Third Punic War takes care of Carthage for good. *Carthago delenda est!*

91-87 Commoners win such benefits as domestic partner insurance and dental coverage in Social War.

82-79 Sulla is dictator.

73 Slave rebellion led by Spartacus, put down by Pompey. Steamy bath scene ensues.

60-50 First Triumvirate rules Rome: Caesar, Pompey, and Crassus.

44 Caesar learns, thanks to Brutus *et al,* that he can't live with multiple stab wounds.

43 Second Triumvirate rules Rome: Octavian, Marc Antony, and, um, Lepidus.

27 Caesar's nephew Octavian calls himself Emperor, takes the title "Caesar Augustus," and initiates the *Pax Romana.*

(Roman Peace). Augustus's power was not only political: he declared himself a god, paving the way for all sorts of mischief among future emperors. Nonetheless, Rome benefited from a huge building boom including a new forum and the first Pantheon. However, the peace was not extended to those who wouldn't consent to be ruled by Augustus; the good emperor's generals busied themselves hacking up Germans.

SONS & LOVERS: JULIO-CLAUDIANS

The descendants of Augustus proved unequal to the task of world government, as their minds, drunk with megalomania, slipped into fevers of cruelty, debauchery, and insanity. **Tiberius** (AD 14-37), who allegedly conducted sexual experiments on goldfish, ushered in an era of decadence. Deranged **Caligula** (who once made his horse *consul*), drooling **Claudius** (41-54), and sadistically wacky **Nero** (54-68; see **Less Than Nero**, p. 86) drained the treasury to support their decadent lifestyles. Much of Rome was burned in the great fire of 64. Nero may or may not have been responsible for the blaze, but certainly took advantage of the situation, building himself a gigantic new house, the **Domus Aurea** (see p. 86).

Nero found a fine set of scapegoats for the fire in the early Christians. Common Romans were entertained and appeased watching Christians dressed in the hides of animals torn to shreds by savage beasts. The Christians who died came to be known as "martyrs," from the Greek "witnesses," an apt term for those who saw firsthand the extent of Roman cruelty.

FLAVIANS & ANTONINES

Tired of his inanities, the Senate forced Nero to commit suicide in AD 68. **Vespatian** (69-79) cleaned up Nero's mess, tearing down the Domus Aurea and erecting the Colosseum (see p. 82). His sons **Titus** (79-81) and **Domitian** (81-96) continued in Vespatian's footsteps

The **Antonine** emperors, starting with **Nerva** (96-98), marked the apex of the Empire. Spanish emperor **Trajan** (98-117) grew the Empire to its greatest size, conquering Dacia (modern Romania) and the Danube region with feats of engineering and tactical brilliance. Trajan died while conquering Persia and the general **Hadrian** (118-138) seized the moment and the title. Hadrian preferred philosophy to war and concentrated on decorating Rome with his own architectural designs, including another **Pantheon** (see p. 97) and his colossal mausoleum, now **Castel Sant'Angelo** (see p. 119).

It was all downhill after Hadrian. The city clung to its status as *Caput Mundi* (head of the world) until the death of **Marcus Aurelius** in 180. By then, the Empire had grown too large to defend. Emperors, forced to relegate power and money to generals in the field, lay vulnerable to military coups. The tumultuous 3rd century saw no fewer than 30 emperors—only one of them lucky enough to die of natural causes. Despite occasionally enlightened administrations, the brutality and depravity of despots like the unfortunately named **Commodus**, Caracalla (see **Baths of Caracalla**, p. 91), and the confused Elagabalus, who believed he was the sun, did much to undermine the stability of the Empire.

RISE OF CHRISTIANITY AND FALL OF ROME

By the 3rd century, Rome was in poor shape. **Aurelian** (270-275) thought that the surest way to solve the city's military and economic crises was to build a wall around it. **Diocletian** (284-305) secured control of the fragmented Empire in 284, established order, and subdivided the Empire into four manageable parts. He also intensified the persecution of Christians. Nonetheless, by the end of Diocletian's reign, approximately 30,000 Christians lived in Rome.

After Diocletian, the fortunes of Christianity took a turn for the better. Gallerius, ruling the western part of the Empire, granted freedom of worship to Christians in 311. In 312, while battling it out with Maxentius for the imperial throne at the Milvian Bridge (which now lies near Rome's Olympic Stadium), **Constantine** (312-337) saw a huge cross in the sky along with the phrase, *In hoc signo vinces* (By this sign you shall conquer). Sure enough, victory followed, and the next year Constantine's **Edict of Milan** made Christianity the official religion of the Empire, with freedom of worship for all. Despite the attempts of **Julian the Apostate** (361-363) to revive old Roman rituals, Christianity became the dominant religion. In 391, **Theodosius** (379-395) issued an edict against paganism.

Constantine hastened the end of Rome's supremacy by moving the capital east to Byzantium (which he modestly renamed **Constantinople**) in 330. Right on cue, armies of northern barbarians knocked politely on Rome's crumbling fortifications, asking if they could please be let in to steal anything not nailed down. First came the pre-Attila **Huns,** who showed up in 375. In 410, **Alaric,** king of the Visigoths, sacked the city. Sacker-extraordinaire **Attila the Hun** arrived on tour in 452, but fast-talking Pope Leo I convinced him to pillage elsewhere. Three years later, however, Genseric the Vandal batted clean-up.

In 476, the Western Roman Empire was finally done in when **Odoacer the Goth** ousted Romulus Augustulus. The Roman Empire was through. Gothic rule wasn't such a bad thing: under Odoacer and his son Theodoric, Roman life proceeded peacefully, perhaps because of the novelty of being ruled from outside (Ravenna, to be precise).

MIDDLE AGES

The Byzantine emperor **Justinian** brutally conquered much of the western division between 535 and 554, and imposed the *corpus juris,* or codified law of the Empire, which served as Europe's legal model for 500 years. By the 6th century, the Eternal City, once home to nearly a million people, supported only several thousand. When King Totila of the Goths pillaged the aqueducts in 546, the city's fate was sealed. The hills of Rome, once *the* place for Roman domiciles, gave way to the suddenly more appealing neighborhoods on the Tiber. It was in these days that some of the most famous neighborhoods of Rome—Trastevere, Campo de' Fiori, and the area around Piazza Navona—were settled. Starvation and plague ran rampant in the ramshackle alleyways near the river, while periodic invasions by barbarians further lowered property values.

202 Septimius Severus bans conversion to Christianity.

247 Rome celebrates its 1000th year: bacchanalia in the streets of the crumbling Empire.

313 Constantine makes Christianity the official religion.

330 Constantine moves capital of Empire from Rome to Byzantium-cum-Constantinople-cum-Istanbul.

375 Huns pop in to invade Rome.

410 Rome taken by the Alaric's Goths.

452 Pope Leo I outwits sacker extraordinaire Attila the Hun.

455 Rome sacked by the Vandals.

476 Odoacer the Goth brings about the end of the Empire and sets himself to running the place.

535-554 Byzantine emperor Justinian conquers much of the West, kicks out the Goths, and imposes *corpus juris*.

546 Totila takes out the aqueducts.

Rome owed its salvation from the turbulence of the Dark Ages in large part to wealthy popes who attracted cash-laden pilgrims and invoked the wrath of God to intimidate would-be invaders. Pope **Gregory the Great** (590-604) devised efficient strategies for distributing food and spreading the word of God across Europe via missionaries. His actions laid the framework for the temporal power subsequent popes would wield.

MEDIEVAL CHAOS, PART I

Faced again with the threat of invasion from the German Lombards in 752, Pope Stephen II was forced to ask for help from the Frankish warlord Pepin the Short. Pepin's forces prevailed and he gave the city to the "Republic of the Holy Church of God" instead of the Byzantine emperor. Pepin's **Gift of Quiersy-Sur-Oise** effectively set up the papal states.

Pepin pushed the fledgling republic along for a bit until God took over. Under the short one's benevolent protection, **Pope Adrian I** repaired the city's aqueducts and restored its churches. Adrian's successor, **Pope Leo III**, slipped a crown on the head of Pepin's son **Charlemagne** on Christmas Day, 800, declaring him "Emperor of the Romans." The relationship between the popes and the Holy Roman Emperors, however, was difficult to maintain. Charlemagne's death in 814 set off another 200 years of near-anarchy as his descendants killed each other in the fight to rule Europe.

In 846, Muslim **Saracens** rowed up the Tiber and plundered several basilicas. Many felt this was God's retribution for clerical misbehavior; indeed, all manner of licentiousness was going on. The most bizarre tale from these years is the posthumous trial of **Pope Formosus**. Formosus's successor **Pope Stephen VI** dug up Formosus and dressed him in ecclesiastical robes to attend a "cadaver synod." After a poor defense, the corpse was convicted on all counts, including coveting the papacy, and, confusingly, perjury. Its three blessing fingers were severed (one can never be too careful), and the corpse formerly known as Formosus was chucked into the Tiber. Pope Stephen himself was later murdered, the next pope was overthrown, and the pope after that was murdered as well.

Around the turn of the 10th century, eight popes took the throne in eight years; nine popes were murdered during the 1100s. It was not a good time to be pope.

With the papacy in disarray, power was seized in 880 by a woman named **Theodora**. Calling herself Senatrix, Theodora and her family—most notably, her daughter **Marozia**—set up a secular dominion over Rome. Starting with Anastasius III in 911, the family managed to choose eleven popes, many of them lovers and children of Marozia. Unfortunately, they never seemed to last very long. A slightly better fate was that of Marozia's son **Alberic the Younger,** who came to power in 932. Alberic attempted to wrest temporal control of Rome away from the Church. Alberic had no idea how mammoth this task was; the Vatican wouldn't officially excise itself from Roman politics for nearly a millennium.

In 954, Alberic appointed his degenerate teenage son **John XII** as pope. Getting his priorities straight, John installed a harem at the Vatican shortly after his father's death. Before he stroked out while in bed with a married woman in 964, John crowned German monarch **Otto I** Holy Roman Emperor, largely for protection against the Northern Italian **Berengar.** Panicked by thoughts that he had allied himself with the weaker leader, John asked Berengar for similar protection. Otto emerged victorious and took the city and the papacy. For the next century, the pope was picked by the Emperor.

The next century of Roman history was dominated by a gruesome tit-for-tat as Romans revolted against imperialist papal appointments and popes imposed punishments on the rebels (e.g. grounding them in their *palazzi*). Around the turn of the 11th century, **Otto III** developed a penchant for ripping out the eyes of members of the **Crescenzi** family, the persistent and powerful nobility who periodically stormed the papal fortress, Castel Sant'Angelo, to declare themselves "Consuls."

In 1075, Pope **Hildebrand** demanded an end to the Holy Roman Emperor's interference with the Church, forcing Emperor Henry VI, whom he had excommunicated, to beg in the snow for forgiveness. It all turned out to be a trick, however: the second time the emperor was excommunicated he laid siege to Rome, and Hildebrand's followers jumped ship. In 1084, the Norman conqueror **Robert Guiscard** remembered—a little ahead of schedule—that Rome was due for its tercentennial sacking and made very convincing work of it.

MEDIEVAL CHAOS, PART II

Around the same time that King John was buying time with the Magna Carta in England, Romans received a measure of self-rule. The 1122 **Concordat of Worms** transferred the balance of power from the Emperor to the Church. Tipsy on its gains, the Church soon predictably arrived in an advanced state of corruption. A secular senate was formed in 1143, but a few hangings later, in 1155, power over the city returned to the pope, Adrian IV, the only English pope.

Unhappy with the popes, Romans kicked them out of the city in 1181. In 1188, during the papacy of **Clement III** (a Roman by birth) the rebels and the Church struck a bargain. The papacy's (super)powers were accepted, and members of the senate swore their loyalty to the pope. In exchange, the Church agreed to recognize the city of Rome as a *comune*, with the power to declare war or peace. This agreement paved the way for the unprecedented power of **Pope Innocent III.** Innocent excommunicated England's King John, declared the Magna Carta null and void, and fought heresy with a vengeance. Innocent declared the Pope to be Vicar of Christ on Earth, "set midway between God and Man," in charge of "the whole world." Innocent's power over the city itself, however, was weak: the citizens maintained earlier reforms, leading to a period of widespread prosperity, if not peace.

Boniface VIII, elected in 1294, antagonized nearly every ruler in Europe with a string of excommunications and the papal edict **Unam Sanctam,** which decreed that it was necessary for salvation that every living thing be subject to the Pope. Fed up, the French assaulted Boniface in his home and accused him of such crimes as sodomy and keeping a pet demon. Poor Boniface died of shock. His successor, the Frenchman Clement V, moved the papacy to Avignon, France, beginning the **Babylonian Captivity** in 1309. For most of the 14th century, popes

954 Pope John XII brings a harem to the papal palace. Wonder how *he* felt about birth control.

962 John XII gives control of the church to Otto I.

1054 The eastern church splits from Rome in the Great Schism (see p. 58).

1075 Pope Gregory VII tells Holy Roman Emperor to get lost.

1084 Rome is sacked by erstwhile Hildebrand supporter Robert Guiscard.

1122 Concordat of Worms: emperor gives up rights of investiture.

1130-1155 Valiant monk Arnaldo da Brescia tries to make Rome into a republic.

1153 Frederick Barbarossa protects the popes.

1155 Valiant monk Arnaldo da Brescia hanged.

1181 Pope kicked out of Rome.

1188 Pope comes back to Rome.

1209 Innocent III excommunicates King John.

1232 Pope Gregory II bored; first Inquisition ensues (see p. 58).

1290 Dante begins his Divine Comedy in the vulgar (see p. 60).

would conduct their business from Avignon under the watchful eyes of the French kings.

Freed from the Church, the city struggled to find peace, but feuding between the Orsini and Colonna families and the outbreak of the **Black Death** in 1348 kept Rome exciting.

At the behest of St. Catherine of Siena, **Pope Gregory XI** agreed to return the papacy to Rome in 1377, restoring the city's greatest source of income. The **Great Western Schism** (1378-1417), the period during which there were two (and occasionally three) popes, however, jeopardized the power of the papacy, and war was widespread. The **Council of Pisa** (1409-1417) resolved the situation to Rome's satisfaction.

RENAISSANCE AND BAROQUE

UP COME THE PROTESTANTS

Taking charge in 1417, **Pope Martin V** initiated a period of Renaissance urbanity and absolute rule in Rome that lasted until 1870. No-nonsense Martin widened and paved roads, and buildings in new Renaissance styles went up. **Julius II** (1503-13) began an ambitious building program, setting out plans for Rome in general and for St. Peter's dome in particular (see p. 115). He hired the architect Bramante (see p. 66), who demolished medieval Rome with such enthusiasm and intent that Raphael nicknamed him *Ruinante*.

When Protestant upstart **Martin Luther** returned to Rome in 1510, he was sorely disappointed by the city's aesthetic indulgence and spiritual dissolution. He was revolted by the sight of Raphael's ornate *Stanze* in the Vatican, in which Christian and pagan symbols mingled—in the buff, no less. While the pope went "triumphing about with fair-decked stallions, the priests gabbled Mass," Luther went about writing the *95 Theses* that kicked off the **Protestant Reformation.**

After excommunicating Luther, **Pope Leo X** (1513-1521) asserted his interest in the humanities, drawing up plans for a new St. Peter's dome and commissioning artists Michelangelo and Raphael. To support their caviar taste, Renaissance popes taxed Romans and their country cousins. Lazio and Umbria soon filed for bankruptcy, and much of the distressed agricultural population up and left. The popes also curried favor with and extracted money from whichever foreign nations suited them best at the time. Fragmented alliances left Rome vulnerable to invasion, and soon proved fatal.

SACK OF ROME

The **Sack of Rome,** an intense eight-day pillage by German warriors, Spanish marauders, and 15,000 angry Lutherans, came in May 1527. The city fell to bloodthirsty imperialist troops, who stormed through the Borgo, destroying everyone and everything in sight. Little respect was shown for religious artifacts, artistic or otherwise. One priest was murdered because he refused to kneel and give the Holy Communion to a donkey. The pope, Clement VII, escaped by holing himself up for six months in Castel Sant'Angelo, besieged by the troops of the French King Charles V.

Pope Paul III, disappointed by the sack, set up the **Inquisition** in 1542. It took hold remarkably well (with even more voracity than in Spain), and the burning of books, infidels, and free-thinkers carried on until 1610 when all of Rome was clearly in line and behaving. Powerful families and the papacy were still hopelessly corrupt, but they didn't seem to be hurting anyone. Having created such havoc, the popes lost much of their political credibility and relevance in the play among European powers during the Thirty Years's War. Most of the 17th and 18th centuries were relatively quiet for Rome.

19TH CENTURY

Pius VI amiably mishandled conflicts between the church and the Revolutionary French government, inducing anti-clerical sentiment to explode in Paris. Effigies of Pius were set on fire and a severed head landed in the lap of the Papal Nuncio as he was traveling in his coach. Romans, roused from their usual complacency, attacked a French delegation on the Corso in 1793. Homes of French sympathizers were vandalized and the French Academy was set on fire with shouts of "Long live the Catholic religion."

Napoleon Bonaparte arrived on the scene in 1796 to deal with the problem and to refill French coffers with the treasures of Italy. Napoleon refused to depose the pope for strategic reasons, but he brought the Church to its knees, extorting millions in tribute and carrying off precious works of art. Romans watched 500 wagons leave the city loaded with booty; some of the most important pieces of Italian and Roman art are still found in Parisian museums. In 1798, French **General Berthier** stormed the Vatican, kidnapped the pope, and established yet another **Roman Republic.** When Napoleon's empire crumbled, however, the 1815 Congress of Vienna returned the papacy to temporal power in Rome.

In 1849, with the liberal **Risorgimento** raging, Rome voted to abolish the papal state and establish, you guessed it, another **Roman Republic. Pope Pius IX** appealed to Catholic heads of state with great success; Rome was once again besieged by a meddling Bonaparte, Napoleon III. The resistance was led by **Giuseppe Mazzini** and **Giuseppe Garibaldi.** The former preached with revolutionary fervor, and the latter led Rome against the French, who still triumphed and reinstated Pope Pius IX.

Nonetheless, regional Italian rulers united all of the country (except Rome and Venice), declared Rome the capital, and crowned the first Italian king, **Vittorio Emanuele II.** In 1870, when the French left for war with Prussia, there was no one to stop the Italian forces (led in part by the resurgent Garibaldi) from crashing through the Vatican. The pope, who had just declared the doctrine of Papal Infallibility, "imprisoned" himself, refused to give up, and urged all Italians to support him; he died alone in 1878.

20TH CENTURY

Rome's recent history may sound vaguely familiar. In a century marked by immense political unrest, public debate between the classes, and a resurgence in new forms of art and

1542 Pope Paul III decides that it's time for another Inquisition.

1600 Once again a cosmopolitan city, Rome's population reaches 100,000 for the first time since 250.

1610 Pope Paul V decides that he's gotten bored with the Inquisition.

1626 Consecration of St. Peter's.

17th and 18th centuries Just about nothing happens.

1797 Napoleon captures Rome.

1798 French kidnap the pope. Can't we all just get along?

1815 Thanks to the Congress of Vienna, Pope becomes hip priest once again.

1820 John Keats briefly sets up shop in town (see p. 61).

1849 Yet another Roman Republic formed.

1849-1866 French rule Rome.

1869 First Vatican Council (see p. 58).

1870 Italian troops enter Rome. City made capital of a recently united Italy.

1881 American novelist and Italophile Henry James sets his *Portrait of a Lady* in the Eternal City.

culture, citizens are taking part in Caesar's grand Roman tradition. Political fights have moved from the *rostra* to the capitol, although the arguments remain just as heated. Even the *fascisti* of the 1920s took their name from the symbol of authority in ancient Rome, the *fasces*, a bundle of sticks tightly wound around an axe-blade. Today, the Italians (divided principally into northern and southern alliances) are seriously rethinking the formation of a single state.

1914-1918 First World War.

IL DUCE

The life of **Benito Mussolini** is a tribute to the bigness of which even the littlest man is capable. After stints as a schoolteacher, a journalist, and, improbably, a pacifist, Mussolini (or *Il Duce*, "the Leader") started his political career with the militant left, but soon abandoned Marx and socialism for Nationalism. At the tender age of 25, Mussolini called for the appointment of a "ruthless and energetic" dictator to clean up Italy. Three months later, he conceded that he might, in fact, be the man needed for the job.

"Everybody wants to be a fascist," Fèlix Guattari once remarked, and nowhere was this more true than in Italy after World War I, when Mussolini's ideology proved to be spectacularly popular. In 1919, Mussolini assembled paramilitary combat groups (the *fasci di combattimenti*), also known as the **Blackshirts.** These militant right-wing squadrons (*squadristi*) waged a fierce, anti-leftist campaign for power shaped by Mussolini's taste for the theatrical. Shouting patriotic slogans, they broke labor strikes for industrialists, raided newspapers soft on Bolshevism, and established mini-dictatorships in small cities. If nothing else, the Blackshirts were more efficient than any government to have graced Roma since. Mussolini had grown so powerful in Italy that the 1922 **March on Rome** was just for show, as were the reports that 3000 Fascist martyrs had died in the attempt.

1919 Mussolini organizes the Blackshirts.

When Vittorio Emanuele III named him Prime Minister, Mussolini forged a totalitarian state, suppressing opposition parties, regulating the press, and demolishing labor unions. His few pieces of constructive legislation include his proverbial revamping of the train system to increase efficiency and the **Lateran Pact of 1929,** regulating Vatican-Italian relations.

1922 *Il Duce* leads Fascist March on Rome and becomes Prime Minister.

In 1929, Mussolini moved his office to **Palazzo Venezia,** where he delivered his imperial orations. Mussolini fancied himself an emperor in the grandest tradition and was determined to mark his territory by a series of unfinished, gargantuan architectural schemes. Under his aegis, the government spent more than 33 billion lire on public works; he plowed down medieval, Renaissance, as well as over three-quarters of the ruins he claimed to be preserving, to create a wide processional street, **via dei Fori Imperiali.** Ironically, the pollution-belching traffic along this street is now the major cause of the rapid deterioration of the Colosseum. To symbolize Fascist achievement, Mussolini envisioned a huge forum that would make St. Peter's and the Colosseum look like Legoland. For the centerpiece of his Foro Mussoliano, he commissioned a 263ft. statue of himself as Hercules. One hundred tons of metal later, with only an enormous foot and head to show for it, the project lost its balance and collapsed.

1929 Lateran Pact sets up Vatican City, ending the Church's official temporal power.

1934 Celluloid sex goddess Sophia Loren born Sofia Scicolone in Roma.

Impressed by German efficiency, Mussolini entered World War II with Hitler in 1939. Used to relying on propaganda rather than strength, Mussolini squandered his army in France, Russia, and Greece until a coup and the Allied forces deposed *Il Duce,* who was ingloriously hanged.

Rome's sizable resistance movement made up for Italy's dreadful military performance, protecting Jews and anti-Fascists from the occupying Germans. Serious damage to the city was averted; Hitler had the sense to declare Rome an "open city" as the liberating Allies approached in June 1944.

The dreary **EUR** area (see p. 136) is a reminder of Mussolini's unsettling vision and his ultimate failure. His legacy lives on in his granddaughter, **Alessandra Mussolini,** who is trying to revive Italian Fascism. Elected to Parliament, she made an unsuccessful bid for mayor of Naples in 1993.

THE BABY NATION GETS COLIC

The end of World War II led to sweeping changes in Italian government. The **Italian Constitution** of 1948 established a **Republic** with a president, a parliament with a 315-member Senate and 630-member Chamber of Deputies, and an independent judiciary. Within this framework, the **Christian Democratic Party,** bolstered by American aid (and rumored Mafia collusion), bested the Socialists. Domination by a single party did not stabilize the country; political turmoil has reigned, along with over 50 different governments since World War II.

Postwar instability and industrialization led to violence in the 1970s. The *autunno caldo* (hot autumn) of 1969, a season of strikes, demonstrations, and riots, opened a decade of unrest. The most disturbing event was the 1978 murder of ex-Prime Minister Aldo Moro, who is remembered by a plaque in the Jewish Ghetto where his body was dumped by the leftist Brigade Rosse.

Because the nation is still young, city and regional bonds often prove stronger than nationalist sentiment. The most pronounced split exists between the north's wealthy industrial areas and the south's agrarian territories. Regional governments have been granted more autonomy, but some northerners want more: the right-wing Lombard League seeks to unite the fattest part of the north and rejects the especially unproductive Rome and the rest of the south.

RECENT EVENTS

The daily minutiae of Italian politics are like a soap opera that, taken *cum grano salis* (with a grain of salt), is more amusing than disturbing. In 1992, **Oscar Luigi Scalfaro** was elected president on a platform of governmental reform, including streamlining of the cabinet. Since then, politics have been characterized by the slow process of electoral law reform, resulting in **"Tangentopoli"** ("Kickback City"); over 2600 politicians have been implicated in corruption scandals.

Reaction to the crackdown on corruption and the Mafia in politics has included such acts of violence as the 1993 bombings of the Uffizi, Florence's premier art museum, and several sites in Rome, including the Church of San Giorgio in Velabro (see p. 92), the "suicides" of 10 indicted officials over the past four years, and open Mafia retaliation against judges.

1939 Under Mussolini, Italy enters WWII on the side of Hitler. Bad idea.

1944 Allies liberate Rome.

1960 Fellini's *La Dolce Vita* premieres (see p. 170).

1960 Rome hosts the Olympic Games.

1962 Vatican II—this time it's personal (see p. 59).

1978 Christian Democratic presidential candidate Aldo Moro murdered by Red Brigade.

1981 Pope John Paul II shot and wounded in St. Peter's Square. The bulletproof "Pope Mobile" is invented.

1990 World Cup mania seizes Rome, much like the Black Death of 1348.

2000 Papal Jubilee Year. J.P. also makes a visit to The Holy Land.

May 2000 Giuliano Amato takes the helm of Italy's 58th government since WWII.

FINDING GOD
THE PANTHEON SUPER-POWER CHECKLIST

More than you ever wanted to know about the ancient Roman gods. Impress your friends!

Jupiter: King of the gods; sexual gymnast; law-maker; kept order with handy thunderbolt.

Juno: Queen of heaven; goddess of women and marriage; Jupiter's wife...and sister.

Mars: God of war and the spirit of battle; represented the gruesome aspects of fighting.

Vulcan: God of fire; divine smith and patron of all craftsman; Venus's hubby; ugly.

Ceres: Goddess of the Earth and fertility. Talk about responsibility!

Venus: Goddess of love and lust; patron of prostitutes; wife of Vulcan; noted philanderer (especially with Mars).

Vesta: Goddess of the family hearth (and the city hearth on a larger scale); forever a virgin.

Minerva: Goddess of war, handicraft, and reason; born fully grown from Jupiter's head.

Neptune: God of the sea and water; Jupiter's brother; always on the prowl for dry real estate.

Apollo: God of the sun, music, and song; Diana's twin; the most revered and feared god.

Diana: Goddess of the moon, wild animals, hunting, vegetation, chastity, and childbirth.

Mercury: God of animals, wealth, commerce, shrewdness, persuasion, and travelers (yeah!).

Until 1994, former Prime Minister **Silvio Berlusconi** (who moonlights as a billionaire publishing tycoon and owner of three national TV channels) presided over a tenuous "Freedom Alliance" of three right-wing parties: his conservative **Forza Italia,** the reactionary **Lega Nord,** and the formerly neo-fascist **Alleanza Nazionale.** When the Lega Nord pulled out, Berlusconi lost his Parliamentary majority and was forced to resign as Prime Minister.

The elections of 1996 brought the center left-coalition, the **Olive Tree** (L'Ulivo), to power, and **Romano Prodi** was elected Prime Minister. Prodi's major designs were balancing the budget and the stabilization of Italian politics. He now serves as president of the European Union Commission. Despite his removal to Brussels, however, Prodi's voice still carries weight: he's in the odd position of having left the presidency without horribly disgracing himself.

In 1998, **Massimo D'Alema** came to power also representing the center-left, but not the same center-left as Prodi. His policy, however, is largely similar to Prodi's. In June 1999, a government bureaucrat was found assassinated in the streets of Rome; the same night, a 19-page manifesto was found in trash cans across the city. It was feared that this might mark a resurgence of the anarchic Italy of the 1970s, and carabinieri in the city were on full alert. Though the incident seems to have been an isolated one, D'Alema saw his support crumble at the end of the year as he failed to push through welfare reforms and alienated unions in trying to do so.

D'Alema resigned at the end of April 2000, after parliament all but told him to do so. The battered center-left managed to elect **Giuliano Amato,** a Socialist respected for his economic expertise. However, given the vicissitudes of Italian politics and the fact that combatting such problems as southern Italy's 20% unemployment rate will prove difficult, it is entirely possible that Amato will no longer be at the helm when you read this text. Waiting in the wings is the conservative Berlusconi, who told Amato in a pre-election debate, "No one, not even you, can save the center-left. The day is not far when voters you so fear will take back the power to decide that you have kidnapped for so long."

Currently, the city of Rome is being run by center-leftist Mayor Francesco Rutelli, now in his last term. Having endured criticism over his handling of preparations for the **Jubilee,** Rutelli is now faced with resentment for prioritizing his future in the European parliament over city issues.

JUBILEE. Every 25 years since 1675, the Pope has declared a Holy Year of Jubilee. Though it did not attract the crowds that were hoped for, the 2000 Jubilee saw not only a Pope apologizing for centuries of Church wrongdoings, but a city cleaner, more put-together and more welcoming to visitors than at any

WORLDWIDE CALLING MADE EASY

The MCI WorldCom Card, designed specifically to keep you in touch with the people that matter the most to you.

MCI WORLDCOM — WORLDPHONE

1·800·888·8000

J. L. SMITH

www.wcom.com/worldphone

Please tear off this card and keep it in your wallet as a reference guide for convenient U.S. and worldwide calling with the MCI WorldCom Card. ✂----

---

HOW TO MAKE CALLS USING YOUR MCI WORLDCOM CARD

> **When calling from the U.S., Puerto Rico, the U.S. Virgin Islands or Canada** to virtually anywhere in the world:
1. Dial 1-800-888-8000
2. Enter your card number + PIN, listen for the dial tone
3. Dial the number you are calling :
   Domestic Calls: Area Code + Phone number
   International Calls:
   011+ Country Code + City Code + Phone Number

> **When calling from outside the U.S.,** use WorldPhone from over 125 countries and places worldwide:
1. Dial the WorldPhone toll-free access number of the country you are calling from.
2. Follow the voice instructions or hold for a WorldPhone operator to complete the call.

> **For calls from your hotel:**
1. Obtain an outside line.
2. Follow the instructions above on how to place a call.
   Note: If your hotel blocks the use of your MCI WorldCom Card, you may have to use an alternative location to place your call.

RECEIVING INTERNATIONAL COLLECT CALLS*

Have family and friends call you collect at home using WorldPhone Service and pay the same low rate as if you called them.
1. Provide them with the WorldPhone access number for the country they are calling from (in the U.S., 1-800-888-8000; for international access numbers see reverse side).
2. Have them dial that access number, wait for an operator, and ask to call you collect at your home number.

* For U.S. based customers only.

START USING YOUR MCI WORLDCOM CARD TODAY. MCI WORLDCOM STEPSAVERS℠

Get the same low rate per country as on calls from home, when you:

1. **Receive international collect calls to your home** using WorldPhone access numbers

2. **Make international calls with your MCI WorldCom Card** from the U.S.*

3. **Call back to anywhere in the U.S. from Abroad** using your MCI WorldCom Card and WorldPhone access numbers.

* An additional charge applies to calls from U.S. pay phones.

WorldPhone Overseas Laptop Connection Tips — Visit our website, www.wcom.com/worldphone, to learn how to access the Internet and email via your laptop when traveling abroad using the MCI WorldCom Card and WorldPhone access numbers.

   Travelers Assist® — When you are overseas, get emergency interpretation assistance and local medical, legal, and entertainment referrals. Simply dial the country's toll-free access number.

   Planning a Trip?—Call the WorldPhone customer service hotline at 1-800-736-1828 for new and updated country access availability or visit our website:

   ## www.wcom.com/worldphone

MCI WorldCom Worldphone Access Numbers

Easy Worldwide Calling

MCI WORLDCOM — WORLDPHONE
1-800-888-8000
J. L. SMITH

MCI WORLDCOM™

The MCI WorldCom Card.
The easy way to call when traveling worldwide.

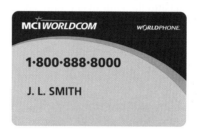

The MCI WorldCom Card gives you...

- Access to the US and other countries worldwide.
- Customer Service 24 hours a day
- Operators who speak your language
- Great MCI WorldCom rates and no sign-up fees

For more information or to apply for a Card call:
1-800-955-0925

Outside the U.S., call MCI WorldCom collect (reverse charge) at:
1-712-943-6839

COUNTRY — WORLDPHONE TOLL-FREE ACCESS #	
Argentina (CC)	
Using Telefonica	0800-222-6249
Using Telecom	0800-555-1002
Australia (CC) ♦	
Using OPTUS	1-800-551-111
Using TELSTRA	1-800-881-100
Austria (CC) ♦	0800-200-235
Bahamas (CC) +	1-800-888-8000
Belgium (CC) ♦	0800-10012
Bermuda (CC) +	1-800-888-8000
Bolivia (CC) ♦	0-800-2222
Brazil (CC)	000-8012
British Virgin Islands +	1-800-888-8000
Canada (CC)	1-800-888-8000
Cayman Islands +	1-800-888-8000
Chile (CC)	
Using CTC	800-207-300
Using ENTEL	800-360-180
China ♦	108-12
Mandarin Speaking Operator	108-17
Colombia (CC) ♦	980-9-16-0001
Collect Access in Spanish	980-9-16-1111
Costa Rica ♦	0800-012-2222
Czech Republic (CC) ♦	00-42-000112
Denmark (CC) ♦	8001-0022
Dominica+	1-800-888-8000
Dominican Republic (CC) +	
Collect Access	1-800-888-8000
Collect Access in Spanish	1121

COUNTRY	ACCESS #
Ecuador (CC) +	999-170
El Salvador (CC)	800-1767
Finland (CC) ♦	08001-102-80
France (CC) ♦	0-800-99-0019
French Guiana (CC)	0-800-99-0019
Germany (CC)	0800-888-8000
Greece (CC) ♦	00-800-1211
Guam (CC)	1-800-888-8000
Guatemala (CC) ♦	99-99-189
Haiti +	
Collect Access	193
Collect access in Creole	190
Honduras +	8000-122
Hong Kong (CC)	800-96-1121
Hungary (CC) ♦	06*-800-01411
India (CC)	000-127
Collect access	000-126
Ireland (CC)	1-800-55-1001
Israel (CC)	1-800-920-2727
Italy (CC) ♦	172-1022
Jamaica +	
Collect Access	1-800-888-8000
From pay phones	#2
Japan (CC) ♦	
Using KDD	00539-121 ▶
Using IDC	0066-55-121
Using JT	0044-11-121

COUNTRY	ACCESS #
Korea (CC)	
To call using KT	00729-14
Using DACOM	00309-12
Phone Booths +	
Press red button ,03,then*	
Military Bases	550-2255
Luxembourg (CC)	8002-0112
Malaysia (CC) ♦	1-800-80-0012
Mexico (CC)	01-800-021-8000
Monaco (CC) ♦	800-90-019
Netherlands (CC) ♦	0800-022-91-22
New Zealand (CC)	000-912
Nicaragua (CC)	166
Norway (CC) ♦	800-19912
Panama	00800-001-0108
Philippines (CC) ♦	
Using PLDT	105-14
Filipino speaking operator	105-15
Using Bayantel	1237-14
Using Bayantel (Filipino)	1237-77
Using ETPI (English)	1066-14
Poland (CC) +	800-111-21-22
Portugal (CC) +	800-800-123
Romania (CC) +	01-800-1800
Russia (CC) + ♦	
Russian speaking operator	
	747-3320
Using Rostelcom	747-3322
Using Sovintel	960-2222
Saudi Arabia (CC)	1-800-11

COUNTRY — WORLDPHONE TOLL-FREE ACCESS #	
Singapore (CC)	8000-112-112
Slovak Republic (CC)	08000-00112
South Africa (CC)	0800-99-0011
Spain (CC)	900-99-0014
St. Lucia ♦	1-800-888-8000
Sweden (CC) ♦	020-795-922
Switzerland (CC) ♦	0800-89-0222
Taiwan (CC) ♦	0080-13-4567
Thailand (CC)	001-999-1-2001
Turkey (CC) ♦	00-8001-1177
United Kingdom (CC)	
Using BT	0800-89-0222
Using C & W	0500-89-0222
Venezuela (CC) + ♦	800-1114-0
Vietnam + ●	1201-1022

KEY
Note: Automation available from most locations. Countries where automation is not yet available are shown in *Italic*.

(CC) Country-to-country calling available.

+ Limited availability.

✱ Not available from public pay phones.

♦ Public phones may require deposit of coin or phone card for dial tone.

● Local service fee in U.S. currency required to complete call.

▶ Regulation does not permit Intra-Japan Calls.

* Wait for second dial tone.

■ Local surcharge may apply.

Hint: For Puerto Rico and Caribbean Islands not listed above, you can use 1-800-888-8000 as the WorldPhone access number.

time in recent memory. Over 700 projects included Metro expansions, restoration of the Colosseum, better roads to the airport, and a scrub-down of everything in sight.

RELIGION

Religion has been a major force in the shaping of Roman history, politically as much as socially. From the Pantheon to St. Peter's, the majority of sights in Rome are or were connected with religion. This section aims to be a history of belief: for information on religion and politics, see **History** above.

GODS OF THE ROMANS

Early Roman religion is difficult to piece together, mostly because the ancient Romans themselves were involved in forgetting it by the first century BC. All that can be certain is that the Romans had the typical Indo-European *paterfamilias* structure of a male head of household who bore sacral life-and-death power over the rest of the family. The **lares** were gods attached to a particular household and worshiped by the family and its slaves. The **penates** were also household gods, but they were associated more with the storage cupboards of the household and the care of the hearth. Along with war rituals, the hearth was an area of strong religious importance, and the cult of **Vesta** (with her league of Vestal Virgins; see **House of the Vestal Virgins,** p. 80) was one of the most fundamental elements of early Roman religious practice.

Piazza Farnese

Like the vast majority of inhabitants of the ancient world, the Romans practiced animal sacrifice, believing it important to achieve a state of *pax deorum* (peace of the gods) instead of *ira deorum* (the wrath of heaven.) War rites of the Romans were even known to include human sacrifice in cases of dire crisis, though this was outlawed by the more refined citizenry of later centuries.

Romans were introduced to the entire package of Greek gods and goddesses by the Etruscans. The awed Romans soon adopted most of the Greek religious cast, simply transposing Hellenic names into Latinate versions for use at home. As the god of war, **Mars** was declared patron of belligerent Rome.

Trevi Fountain

Roman polytheism was of a tolerant sort; religion was seen as a local practice, and foreign gods were frequently "interpreted" as versions of the Greco-Roman gods under other names. The Romans didn't impose their religion on anyone, and even the notorious "cult of the emperor"—which began with Julius Caesar and Augustus, who were deified posthumously—actually began by popular demand in one of the eastern provinces, where local inhabitants had a custom of deifying their rulers. Many of the more educated Romans were non-religious, having absorbed the Stoic, Epicurean, and Platonic teachings of Greek philosophy.

Toward the end of the Empire, Roman territory sheltered a variety of assorted cults and sects: the Egyptian gods Isis and Osiris were integrated into the Roman pantheon by some, while Mithraism (see p. 56) spread through the army. Temples were erected to Cybele, a fertility goddess of Eastern origin. Christians were persecuted anomalously in the Roman Empire

Horse Carriage

A FIELD GUIDE TO HERETICS

In the early days of Christianity, there were plenty of heretics. A brief guide to major credences:

Arianism: Following Arius (250-336), Arianism argued that Christ was not eternal, having been created by God the Father. While Arianism was supported by Emperors Constantius II and Valens, the First Council of Nicaea in 325 denounced it.

Docetism: The Docetists (2nd century) argued that Christ's divine nature was incompatible with human suffering and that Christ was not human.

Donatism: The Donatists, a North African sect, split from the church in 312 and survived until the 7th century, when Islam arrived. They believed that the Church should not be tainted with the political and valued personal holiness.

Eunomianism: The Eunomians believed that the only proper name for God the Father, an incomprehensible concept, was "Ungenerated;" everything else, including Christ, had been generated. They were denounced as being too philosophical.

Gnosticism: Gnosticism denotes a wide variety of beliefs. In most Gnostic cosmogonies, a creator god was the supreme being; from the creator came a demiurge, a flawed figure who created a flawed world. The world was thus an evil place; salvation could be attained through knowledge, called *gnosis*, of the divine spark of god.

because they were regarded as a renegade sect, people who had withdrawn from the local community. It didn't help that they refused to worship Julius or Augustus Caesar on demand, either.

MITHRAISM

> Mithras?...It didn't fail because it was bad.
> Mithraism almost triumphed over Christianity. It failed because it was so nearly good.
> William Gaddis, *The Recognitions*

Mithraism, a religion with strong similarities to Christianity that flourished in the first few centuries AD, was the first successful monotheistic religion in the Empire. Imported from Persia, it centered around the god **Mitras,** who created the world by killing a sacred bull. Mithraism remains shrouded in mystery, mainly because it was a secretive cult based on the celebration of **mysteries** known only to initiates. The vast majority of our knowledge about the religion comes from archaeological remains. Their place of worship, the **mithraeum,** was usually built underground, and several Christian churches, notably the **Basilicas of San Clemente** (see p. 129) and **Santa Prisca,** were constructed on top of them. Although only eight mithraea have been excavated in Rome, there may have been over 700 at the height of the movement. Several mithrae have also been excavated in Ostia Antica (see **Daytrips,** p. 216).

The mithraeum was usually an artificial cave with stone benches facing a depiction of Mithras killing the sacred bull. Several other minor figures were present in the scene, including a scorpion, a dog, a snake, the sun, the moon, and a male figure named Cautopates holding a torch. The best-preserved artifact of the scene is the bull sculpture in the Room of the Animals at the Vatican Museums (see p. 140).

Mithras, the central figure in the religion, originated as a minor Zoroastrian and Hindu deity. An Apollo-like figure, he was the god of the sky, the sun's light, contracts, and mediation. The cult's Roman popularity began around AD 100. Historians speculate that Mithraism was a social religion for bourgeois Roman military veterans. With nothing but artificial ties to its Zoroastrian roots, it was a sort of Roman New Age religion.

Mithraism was widespread by the 2nd century, gradually moving from the army to the upper class. However, its potential was seriously hindered by its exclusion of women. With the ban on paganism in 391, the death knell was sounded for Mithraism, though some isolated believers may have kept the faith in the outskirts of the Empire. In fact, some claim that the Masons represent, in concept and descent, a late outcropping of Mithraism. Other remnants of Mithraism linger on: December 25, now celebrated as Christmas, was once celebrated as the birthday of Mithras.

CHRISTIANITY & CATHOLICISM

> Suppressed for the moment, the deadly
> superstition broke out again, not only in Judea,
> the land which originated this evil, but also in
> the city of Rome, where all sorts of horrendous
> and shameful practices from every part of the
> world converge and are fervently cultivated.
>> Tacitus, *Annals* 15:44

Since Peter and Paul arrived shortly after Christ's death, Christianity has been big in Rome. Christ said to give unto Caesar what is Caesar's and unto God what is God's; in reality, separating politics and religion hasn't been quite so simple.

As early as AD 35, the Senate declared Christianity to be "strange and unlawful." Nonetheless, in 42, **Saint Peter,** the first Bishop of Rome, set up shop in the city. **Saint Paul,** the codifier of Christian thought, dropped by often. In 62, he was beheaded near EUR. Peter, responsible for the structure of the church, met his end when he was crucified upside down near the site of the Vatican in 67. Besides having fathered Catholicism, the duo are recognized as Rome's patron saints.

Persecution of Christianity began in earnest after the Great Fire of Rome in 64. It continued sporadically for the next 240 years. From 200 to 500, the **catacombs** outside of the center of Rome were used as cemeteries by Christians (see p. 133). Although the Christians did not live there, as commonly assumed, much has been learned about the early church from decorations found therein. Early Christian symbols includes the fish, the dove, the shepherd, and the anchor. This iconography is shared by the earliest Christian churches in Rome, dating from 230.

Fragmentation of the church started early. Various gnostic movements were popular in these early times. By about 100, the movement nominally headed by **Marcion** had gained a following. Marcion believed that Christ was not of the same substance as the God portrayed in the Hebrew Bible; he conceived the creator of the world as being a **demiurge,** a narcissist removed from the true God. Marcion thought that only the Gospel of Luke and the Pauline Epistles had merit as religious texts. In opposition to gnostic conceptions such as this, orthodox (or **Pistic**) Christianity was created. **Irenaeus**'s *Against Heresies*, published around 190, refutes prominent heresies, defining Pistic Christianity as what is not heretical.

The persecution of Christians in Rome ended just before Christianity was made the state religion in 315. Free from outside persecution, the church struggled to find its feet. The **Nicaean Creed** of 325 was the first cohesive statement of belief by the Pistic church, nailing down the basics of Christianity. Soon,

A FIELD GUIDE TO HERETICS (CONT.)

Marcionism: Marcion (84-160) denounced the Jewish scriptures as being written in honor of the evil demiurge (see Gnosticism, above) in favor of the Gospel of Luke and the Pauline Epistles. The movement lasted until the 5th century.

Monarchianism: Monarchianism, beginning in the 2nd century, denied the trinity in favor of one godhead. This marked the beginning of tensions between the Eastern and Western churches.

Monophysitism: The Monophysites of the 5th century believed that Christ was of divine and not human nature.

Nestorianism: Nestor (c.381-c.451) argued that Christ was of two persons—one human and one divine. As Mary had given birth only to the human Christ, she could not be called the Mother of God. Nestorianism survives today in Iran, Iraq, and Syria.

Pelagianism: Pelagianism, a heresy which arose in the 5th century, denied the concepts of original sin and Christian grace.

POPE JOAN

Canonical history holds that Nicholas Breakspear, Pope Adrian IV, was the only English Pope. Popular tradition, however, has it that John VIII (853-855), elected for his saintliness and Greek learning, was not only of English descent but also, to add insult to injury, a woman. "Joan" was found out when she gave birth during a procession; the enraged citizens of Rome promptly stoned her and the baby to death. The truth of the story of Pope Joan is unclear: historical records are hazy, and the tale has been used polemically to support anti-Catholic, feminist, anti-feminist, and Catholic-reformist agendas. Joan's story gave birth to a tradition in which the elected heir of St. Peter's apostolic seat was required to sit in a special chair with a carved slot for the purpose of having his testicles touched by a young cardinal to verify his gender. In popular culture, Pope Joan inspired the Popess card in the Tarot deck. Bernini may have memorialized her end in some half-hidden sculpting on the famous *baldacchino* in St. Peter's cathedral (see p. 115).

with the banning of paganism, Christianity found itself a majority with few competitors. A flurry of theological writing went on: **St. Jerome**'s Latin translation of the Bible standardized the work, while Rome's own **St. Augustine** wrote the *City of God* and *Confessions*, the framework of most Christian theology.

During this period of ascendancy, most of the major basilicas of Rome were begun, though in forms vastly different from their present states. The **crucifix**, today the ubiquitous symbol of Christianity, only became widely used around 550. In 490, the Council of Chalcedon declared that Jesus was of both human and divine nature, answering a question that had spawned innumerable heretic sects.

In 787, the Second Council of Nicaea declared that the Holy Spirit proceeds from the Father and the Son. As a result, the first major break in the church began to form: in 1054, the Eastern and Western halves of the church separated in an event known as the **Great Schism.** Rome and Constantinople were too far apart for effective government, and Roman religious rule grated on the Byzantines. In addition, there was theological dissent: the Eastern church believed that icons had special religious significance, while the Western church did not.

The (Western) Church's history during the Middle Ages was tumultuous. Papal succession was largely political, and, although good Popes did come along occasionally, greed and corruption were rampant. Pope Urban II kicked off the **First Crusade** in 1047 in order to unify the Church and squelch partisanship. While this crusade, like those that followed, failed to retake the Holy Land and created all manner of havoc in the Middle East, it succeeded in bringing something of a rebirth to a religion in danger of becoming stagnant. For somewhat similar reasons, Pope Gregory II initiated the first incarnation of the **Inquisition** in 1232.

The 14th century, during which the papacy jumped borders and duplicated and even triplicated itself (see **History,** p. 49), was only dress rehearsal for the confusion that would come with the **Protestant Reformation** of the 1500s. In 1517, Martin Luther's accusatory *95 Theses* significantly threatened Rome's religious power. Ignatius of Loyola founded the Jesuits in 1534 to combat the Protestant menace; from 1534-1563, the Council of Trent met to plan the **Counter Reformation** and further define what had become known as Roman Catholicism.

The Catholic Church's influence on the world, while not inconsequential, has declined tremendously since the Reformation. The biggest news: Pius IX's **First Vatican Council** of 1869 resulted in the somewhat archaic doctrine of papal infallibility.

Since World War II, however, the Church has spread its message globally with renewed strength and vigor, particularly in Eastern Europe and the developing world. However, in Rome, the Church has lost much of its following: less than 10% of Romans attend mass regularly. The Church's responses to public affairs during this century have been contradictory. While Pope Pius XII insisted that the Church would stay out of politics, a 1950s papal decree forbade Catholics from associating with the Communist party. Ironically, in many other Western European countries at the time, the Church was directly affiliated with Socialist parties.

During the 1960s, in an effort to transform the church into a 20th-century institution, the much-loved Pope John XXII agreed to open dialogue with the Communist Party, showing a new commitment to compromising with non-believers. Before his death, he convened the **Second Vatican Council** in 1962. The aim of the council was to improve relations with other religions and to make the Church more accessible to the layperson. The most visible results of the Council, which concluded under Paul VI in 1965, included the replacement of Latin with the vernacular in the mass, the increased role of local clergy and bishops in church administration, and the re-evaluation of the place of scripture with regard to belief.

Since 1981, Pope John Paul II's international approach to papacy—including his overt use of the media and his constant traveling—has reflected the Church's intention to establish a more direct relationship with believers without the interference of politics. The fact that the current pope is Polish (Italian newspapers don't call him Giovanni Paolo II but Wojtyla, his last name) has somewhat removed the Pope from Italian politics, and the papacy has concerned itself with global issues. While the pope has been suggested to have played a part in the fall of Communism, he has also denounced the excesses of capitalism. Elsewhere, John Paul II's papacy has displayed a conservative slant. Though his endorsements of social justice have been perceived as carrying forward the measures of Vatican II, his rigid stance on social and moral issues has alienated many liberal Catholics.

LITERATURE

SUM, ES, EST, SUMUS, ESTIS, SUNT

Anyone who has experienced the joy of memorizing Latin verb conjugations will recall the heavy hitters of Latin literature, most of them coming out of Augustus's golden age (see **History,** p. 45). **Plautus** (220-184 BC) wrote popular farces that entertained the masses. (His comedy *Pseudolus* was the basis for the Broadway musical *A Funny Thing Happened on the Way to the Forum.*)

The poetry of **Catullus** (84-54 BC) set a high standard for passion and provided a great source of Latin obscenities for future generations of Latin students. **Livy** (c. 59 BC-AD 17) wrote Rome's official history, while **Julius Caesar** (100-44 BC) gave a first-hand account of the shredding of the Republic in *De Bello Civili.* Caesar's contemporary, the philosopher **Cicero** (106-43 BC), penned works notable for their carefully crafted Latin, including the political speech *In Catilinam* ("O tempora, O mores!").

Virgil (70-19 BC) wrote the **Aeneid**, linking the founding of Rome to the fall of Troy via the wanderings of Aeneas. **Horace**'s (65-8 BC) verse (*Odes, Epodes, Satires,* and *Epistles*) was more autobiographical. Fed up with the squalor and chaos of first-century BC Rome, both Virgil and Horace praised the simple life of the country dweller. City-lover **Ovid** (43 BC-AD 17), though originally employed by Augustus, was later banished to the Black Sea for his involvement in the escapades of Augustus's rebellious and promiscuous daughter and grand-daughter, both named Julia. His poems—among them the *Amores,* the *Metamorphoses,* and the *Ars Amatoria* (a tongue-in-cheek guide to love)—are much more light-hearted than those of his contemporaries and surprisingly relevant today.

Post-Augustan literature included **Petronius**'s first-century AD *Satyricon,* a blunt look at the Nero's decadence, while **Tacitus**'s *Histories* summarizes the war, politics, and scandals in the years after Nero's death. **Suetonius** (AD 69-c. 130), the Robin Leach of the era, dished the dirt on the first 12 Roman emperors in *The Lives of the Caesars.* **Marcus Aurelius**'s (121-180) *Meditations* recount the musings of a philosopher-king during the final hours of Rome's glorious imperial era.

EARLY CHRISTIAN LITERATURE

The early Christian church wasted no time in building itself up a body of work. Much of the New Testament, as well as other important theological books, were written in Rome. Among the latter are the *Epistles of St. Clement of Rome*, which were actually forged well after the death of **St. Clement,** the fourth Bishop of Rome. The work is an argument for headquartering the Church in Rome, instead of Alexandria, an early rival of the Eternal City. Another forgery attributed to Clement is the so-called Clementine *Recognitions*. Called the first Christian novel, it tells the tale of a wanderer who finds meaning in life when he happens to run into St. Peter and his merry band of Christians. Naturally.

Other major works by the early Christians include St. Jerome's Latin translation of the Bible, or the **Vulgate,** in 405, and **Tertullian**'s defenses of orthodox Christianity from Gnostic thought. Tertullian's work went a long way toward defining Christian thought. His style also set the tone for many future works, including *The Confessions* of **Saint Augustine,** a 4th-century Roman native.

TALES OF HEAVEN, HELL, & NAUGHTY NUNS

After the fall of the Roman Empire, the focus of Italian literature moved (permanently, it would seem) away from Rome. The influence of Rome was still felt, however: during the Middle Ages, the literary language of choice remained Latin, in spite of the fact that the Latin of Caesar and Cicero hadn't been spoken by the people since the days of the early Empire. This gap between the written language and the vernacular, or *volgare*, eventually led to a rejection of Latin among writers and poets throughout the Romance language-speaking parts of Europe. Tuscan **Dante Alighieri** (1265-1321), considered as much the father of the modern Italian language as of its literature, was one of the first European poets to eschew Latin. After the death of his young love Beatrice in 1290, Dante began his masterpiece, *La Divina Commedia.* Dante's allegorical journey through the afterlife is guided by his ancient Roman counterpart, Virgil. Among the *Commedia*'s charms are Dante's acrid descriptions of Italian cities and their inhabitants; he skewers Rome and many of the popes like few had ever dared.

Although he preferred to write in Latin, **Petrarch** (1304-1374) was perhaps more influential than Dante in establishing a model for future Tuscan poets. **Giovanni Boccaccio**'s (1313-1375) *Decameron,* a collection of 100 stories told by 10 young Florentines fleeing their plague-ridden city, ranges in tone from cheeky to downright bawdy; in one story, a hard-working gardener fertilizes an entire convent. Boccaccio also knocked the "wicked behavior" of the churchmen in Rome.

RENAISSANCE LITERATURE

Florence continued to dominate Italian culture and literature through the Renaissance, leaving Rome in its shadow. Most of the best known Renaissance thinkers and artists, including Nicolò Macchiavelli, Michelango, and Leonardo da Vinci, lived and worked in Florence. While arguments about the Italian language, the nature of love, and the place of women erupted throughout Northern Italy, Rome remained largely silent. Commissions by the Church lured many artists to Rome, but most authors chose to write about the city rather than live there.

Among those who wrote about Rome was **Benevenuto Cellini** (1500-1571), a Florentine sculptor and goldsmith, remembered for his autobiographical *Vita*. The somewhat paranoid Cellini presents himself as a model of bravery and determination. Among other exploits, he recounts in livid detail his successful defense of Castel Sant'Angelo (see p. 119) against Imperial forces and his daring escape from imprisonment in the same in 1538. Also chronicled in *Vita* are Cellini's memories of a number of famous Romans, including Pope Clement VII.

The scathing **Pietro Aretino** created new possibilities for literature, accepting bribes to not skewer notable targets. Aretino found ample subjects for satire in the Roman court.

The Church, however, was not amused by his coarse humor and was unimpressed by his innovative prose, so Aretino left for Mantua and then Venice.

A number of Renaissance writers, including Leon Battista Alberti, Baldassare Castiglione, and Giorgio Vasari, passed through and worked in Rome. The philosopher **Giordano Bruno** (1548-1600) never managed to leave, as he was burned at the stake for his humanist thought, which contradicted the ideas of the Church.

ROMAN ROMANTICISM

After the brightness of the Renaissance, Italian literature stagnated in the 17th century. But although few notable *literati* emerged, a number of new literary forms appeared, including the novel, the opera, and *commedia dell'arte*.

Italian theater came into its own in the 18th century. Roman dramatist **Metastasio** wrote popular melodramas while **Carlo Goldoni** transformed *commedia dell'arte* by replacing its stock figures with unpredictable characters in such works as *Il Ventaglio*. By the late 19th century, the written and spoken language had again drifted apart, causing another vernacular movement in literature. **Alessandro Manzoni** promoted the use of the "living and true" tongue with his hugely popular novel *I Promessi Sposi*.

Piazza Farnese

Rome's unique contribution to 19th- and 20th-century writing came in the form its **dialect poetry.** One of the greatest dialect poets was **G.G. Belli** (1791-1863), An imaginary explanation by Belli of the advantages of dialects over national languages appeared in Anthony Burgess's *ABBA ABBA*: "A language waves a flag and is blown up by politicians. A dialect keeps to things, things, things, street smells and street noises, life." Author of nearly 3000 sonnets, Belli was known for his vulgar caricatures of important Risorgimento figures.

Meanwhile, Rome was a favorite destination of expatriate European artists. Rome was the "paradise of exiles," according to Percy Bysshe Shelley. **Goethe**, arriving in Rome in 1787, gushed, "Only now do I begin to live." **Emile Zola** wrote of the wondrous squalor in *Rome*. The histrionic protagonist in **Lord Byron**'s wildly popular *Childe Harold's Pilgrimage* exclaims, "Oh Rome! my country! city of the soul! The orphans of the heart must turn to thee, Lone mother of dead empires." **Frederick Jackson Turner** would later use excerpts from *Childe Harold* as inspiration for a series of Roman paintings.

Piazza Navona

No discussion of expats in Rome would be complete without mentioning **John Keats,** who came to Rome in 1820 to improve his health. Despite a posh *pensione* with a to-die-for view of the Spanish Steps (now the Keats-Shelley Memorial House, see p. 159), Rome didn't do much for Keats's tuberculosis; he died three months later, at the age of 25.

Sigmund Freud, on whom it wasn't lost that "Roma" is "Amor" spelled backwards, writes of being aroused by the city in *The Interpretation of Dreams*. **Nathaniel Hawthorne** was disturbed enough by the confusion of peoples, historical periods, and art in Rome to write his classic novel *The Marble Faun* after a visit here. The **Brownings,** both Robert and Elizabeth Barrett, found Rome an inexhaustible source of inspira-

Filetti di Baccala

tion and refuge. Perhaps Rome's greatest popularizer in the 19th century was American expat **Henry James,** who made 14 visits to Italy, beginning in 1869 and ending in 1907. James's *Italian Hours* records one of his longest visits to Rome. In addition, his novel *Portrait of a Lady* is mostly set there, and the novella *Daisy Miller* chronicles the follies of expat society in Rome. If *you* are an aspiring expat seeking extended inspiration in Rome, see **Living in Rome,** p. 281.

20TH-CENTURY LITERATURE

As Communism, Socialism, and Fascism gave rise to anti-traditional literary movements, Italy became a center of Modernist poetry. The most flamboyant and controversial of Modernism's poets was **Gabriele d'Annunzio,** whose cavalier heroics and sexual escapades earned him as much fame as his eccentric, over-the-top, and often nationalistic verse (exemplified by his novel, *Il Piacere,* set in Rome).

The 1930s saw the rise of young Italian writers influenced by the experimental narratives and themes of social alienation found in the works of American writers such as Ernest Hemingway and John Steinbeck. These included Cesare Pavese, Ignazio Silone, and Elio Vittorini. The most prolific of these writers, Roman-born **Alberto Moravia,** wrote the ground-breaking—and promptly banned—*The Time of Indifference,* attacking the Fascist regime. To evade government censors, Moravia employed experimental surreal forms in his subsequent works. *La Romana* is the story of a Roman who slowly finds herself becoming a prostitute. Oops, how'd that happen! Two of Moravia's works became important films: *Il Disprezzo* formed the basis for Jean-Luc Godard's superb *Le Mépris,* and Bernardo Bertolucci's *The Conformist* was based on Moravia's novel of the same name.

The concept of the Modernist Italian novel was largely formed by Rome-born **Carlo Emilio Gadda's** *That Awful Mess on Via Merulana,* a novel described as the Italian analogue to James Joyce's *Ulysses.* Gadda makes extensive use of Roman dialect, expanding what starts out as a simple detective story into a broad portrait of life under Fascism. Among Gadda's followers were **Elsa Morante,** who wrote about the Jewish experience in Rome in such novels as *Menzogna e Sortilegio.*

The other major contemporary Italian author writing in and about Rome is **Natalia Ginzburg,** author of several psychological novels centered on the interiors of the self and the family. Many, such as *Famiglia* and *Borghesia,* are set in Rome and betray a deep understanding of its streets and its mores. While most of the best known Italian writers of the 20th century hail from outside Rome, the city continues to contribute to Italian literature. **Pier Paolo Pasolini,** better known as a director (see **Entertainment,** p. 171), also wrote a significant amount of poetry. In 1997, the unlikely candidate **Dario Fo,** a *commedia dell'arte*-inspired Italian playwright and actor denounced by the Catholic church, won the Nobel Prize for literature, in honor of his comic plays and his dramatic satires of post-war Italian texts. Fo's most popular works are *The Accidental Death of an Anarchist* (1970) and *We Won't Pay! We Won't Pay!* (1974).

ART AND ARCHITECTURE

Before Rome was Rome, Etruscans lived, worked, and made art that influenced the Roman conquerors who would later take over their territory. They are most famous for their subtle, reddish pottery, which took heavy inspiration both from the Greeks and from Oriental, Phoenician, and Hittite sources. Their earliest pottery (9th century BC) took the form of funerary urns, mostly decorated with stippled or incised patterns. In the 7th century, the **bucchero** style—shiny black or grey funeral pottery that looks an awful lot like metal—came into style, a must-have for every Etruscan lady who lunched. Just as typical, however, are the earthy **terra-cotta** bas reliefs that the Etruscans introduced and the Romans went on to claim. Nationalistic Roman orator Cato even had the nerve to announce, several hundred years later: "I hear too many people praising the knickknacks of Corinth and Athens, and laughing at the terra-cotta antefixes of our Roman gods." Etruscans liked bright colors and fluid lines, even in their still plentiful necropoloi, tomb paintings, and funerary statues, a taste which prompted D.H. Lawrence to wax ecstatic about the sensuality of Etruscan art: "so alive…flexible." (Mr. Lawrence, there are children present!) Etruscans ruled Rome until the last of their dynasty, Tarquinius Superbus, was kicked out by the Latins (see **History**, p. 44). Ruins of Etruscan buildings coexist with and lie just beneath the classical Roman ruins, showing traces of their former gaudy terra-cotta decorations and the **gargoyles of Greek deities** that once adorned their gables and gutters. Etruscan influence persisted beyond their political fade-out, most notably in Roman religious and domestic art.

CLASSICAL ROME

The emerging Roman styles in art fall mainly into two large categories—art in service of the state and private household art, which finds its origins in the votive statues of household gods (the *lares* and *penates*) created by ancient Roman tribes. Household art was a democratic form, splashed across the interiors of houses, courtyards, and shops, and taking everything from scenes of the gods and goddesses at play to illusionary woodland landscapes as its subject. Most private Roman art took the form of **frescoes**, Greek-influenced paintings that were daubed onto wet plaster so that both plaster and paint would dry together, forming a lasting and time-resistant patina. (Da Vinci's *The Last Supper* is probably the most famous fresco.) Proud household owners often embellished their abodes with sneaky **trompe l'oeil** doors or columns to make the place look bigger. **Mosaic** (painting with tiles) was another popular genre from the Hellenistic period onward; a favorite subject was the watchdog, often executed on the vestibule floor, with the helpful inscription *cave canem* ("beware of dog"). Craftsmen-artists fashioned these mosaics by painting scenes into the floor (or occasionally wall) of a building, pressing finely shaded **tesserae** (bits of colored stone and glass) onto the painting's surface, and squeezing a soft bed of mortar in between the cracks to cement everything in place. An even more personalized art form of sorts—graffiti—was also widely practiced by citizens of the ancient Roman Empire. Look out for walls in Pompeii or excavated buried buildings to see the full range of uninhibited ancient self-expression—everything from love declarations to denunciations of Christianity as a cannibal religion, as well as such judiciously weighed sentiments as "Marcus Lucius is a very large ass."

Public art in Rome was commissioned by the Roman government and usually reflected the tastes and victories of whoever was in power at the time. At first the Romans simply exploited Greek design features for their buildings, but soon they developed the revolutionary technology of the **arch** from earlier Etruscan vaults. This, along with the happy invention of **concrete**, revolutionized their conceptions of architecture and made possible such monuments as the Colosseum (p. 82), triumphal arches celebrating military victories, aqueducts, amphitheaters, basilicas, and much more. The Romans then finessed the arch, lengthening it into a **barrel vault,** crossing two arches to make a **groin vault,** or rotating it in a tight circle to build **domes.** Monumental public buildings either reminded the spectator of a particular emperor's exploits in battle (like the artistically sublimated propaganda of Trajan's Column) or functioned as frenzied arenas of mass entertainment intended to pacify an unruly populace. Some of the most famous building occurred around AD 80, when the normally affable ex-plebe emperor Vespatian built the blood-soaked arches and columns of the **Colosseum** (see **Pacifying the Populace,** p. 82), and when Titus had his triumphal **Arch of Titus** constructed to provide a suitable backdrop for him to parade his booty and slaves.

Religion, Marx noticed, keeps the people busy and out of trouble. The Roman government scooped him on this, making sure to spend money on the construction of religious temples and on festivals and rites to calm and patriotically inspire the populace by offering it a spectacle of spiritual unity and power. Temples were usually constructed along the Greek model, with a triangular portico supported by the classical row of columns and decorated with strips of friezes on strategic flat surfaces. In capitals (the decorative upper portion of a column), Romans used the Greek orders of Doric, Ionic, and Corinthian, making the latter more elaborate than ever by supplementing its crown of acanthus leaves with all manner of ornate curlicues. Later on, the Romans would begin to transfer column style and the full panoply of Greek architecture to almost any building.

The earliest and most sacred man-made monument in Rome was probably the Temple to Vesta, although its white simplicity was soon overshadowed by more pragmatic temples (such as those devoted to the deified Augustus and Julius Caesar). Rome's most important architect was **Vitruvius,** who originated the idea that harmonious buildings would base their measurements and proportions on the human body—a.k.a. the "measure of man." (Cement modernist Le Corbusier, among others, picked up on Vitruvius's graceful building philosophies.) Later on, Romans became more interested in theaters and basilicas for distraction and contemplation. At this point, basilicas were still used in as courthouses and shopping arcades, although the cool and climate-adapted design of a long rectangle with arch-and-column supports would be recycled by later Christian and Byzantine emperors as the first floorplan for early churches.

BYZANTINE DECADENCE

When Constantine transferred the capital of the Roman Empire in AD 330 from Rome to **Constantinople** (then known as Byzantium, and now reincarnated as modern-day Istanbul), artistic influences in Rome took a decidedly Asiatic twist. Born from the aesthetic traditions of the Christian catacombs and the Greek and Oriental styles, Byzantine art favored immobile, mystical, slender-fingered figures against flat gold or midnight blue backgrounds, shadowy domes, and an atmosphere of enigmatic and flooding holiness. Spread the world over by the Emperor Justinian and his powerful wife Theodora, the Byzantine style reveled in gorgeously ornate mosaics, some of which can still be seen in the churches of Santa Cecilia in Trastevere, Santa Prassede, and Santa Maria in Domenica, although the best examples of this style in Italy are all in Ravenna. Despite the fact that the deeply religious Byzantine emperors erected countless costly Byzantine palaces, only their religious buildings have survived subsequent sackings, medieval recycling, and modernization. These buildings were all built on the model of Roman **basilicas** (law courts); instead of having a cathedral shape, they are rectangular and frequently domed, with stony cold sarcophagi and the dim gold glare of far-off mosaics and anemic saints.

A TOUCH OF ROMANESQUE

Given the chaos of the 3rd and 4th centuries, emperors' minds tended to focus on making war, not art. The gaze of the Christian art that eventually emerged in the Middle Ages was fixed firmly on heaven. From roughly AD 500 to 1200, Romanesque-style churches dominated Europe. In Rome, these Romanesque fashions slowly and incrementally overtook the older Byzantine style, retaining the basilica floorplan but updating it with rows of pillared round arches, low ceilings, oriel windows, peeling wooden statues of saints, and an elaborate and arcane bestiary of symbolic men and beasts cavorting in the caps of pillars and the reliefs above doorways. Wall frescoes and mosaics from this period abound in Rome, particularly in **San Paolo fuori le Mura** (which also hoards mosaics imported *in toto* from Byzantium), **Santa Maria Maggiore,** and **Santa Prassede.**

GOTHIC: NO THANKS

The Romans never approved of the Teutonic barbarian hordes living to their north, and when somebody in the Renaissance wanted to find a disparaging name for the bad old Dark Ages style that Europe was recovering from back then, "Gothic" seemed made to order. Gothic never really caught on in the Holy Roman Empire; not only is there just one Gothic church in all of Rome—Santa Maria sopra Minerva—it's more famous for an ancient altar to the owl-loving Roman goddess of Wisdom (razed by Christians) than for its current dedication to the Blessed Virgin.

RENAISSANCE IN ROME

> …if cleanliness is next to godliness, it is a very distant
> neighbor to chiaroscuro.
> —Henry James

The succession of wealthy Renaissance popes eager to leave
their mark on the city in the form of new buildings, paintings,
and sculpture gave a sagging Rome its most striking stylistic
tummy-tuck since its ancient days. This age heralded the split
between science and faith, and the Church condemned both
Galileo and Giordano Bruno for their astronomical assertions
that the earth was not the center of the universe. Painters,
sculptors, and architects relied heavily on subjective experience while at the same time employing the technical discoveries of the Age of Science, such as the newly reinvented trick of
creating **perspective.** Although Rome was certainly not the center of the Italian Renaissance, it did manage to lure many of
the most famous Florentine artists to come refurbish the
imperial city's image, including Michelangelo, Brunelleschi,
and Rafael. It is also home to one of the period's trendiest
churches, the Mannerist Jesuit headquarters, **Il Gesù.**

Piazza Navona

The supreme artist with the supremely tortured soul, **Michelangelo Buonarroti** (1475-1564), grew up among the stonema-
sons of Tuscany; as the man later said: "with my wet-nurse's
milk, I sucked in the hammer and chisels I use for my statues."
During this period, Michelangelo honed his knowledge of the
human body after he swapped his crucifix for the privilege of
dissecting corpses in the Cloisters of Santo Spirito. At the age
of 21, he headed to the already ancient capital city to seek his
fortune. Originally commissioned by the pope for some minor
works, Michelangelo was deluged with requests for work once
he became well known in Rome. It is for one of these commissions that he created the profoundly sorrowful and career-
making **Pietà** in St. Peter's (p. 116).

In 1502, Pope Julius II sent for Michelangelo, now almost 30
and at the height of his career, to return once more to Rome to
build the pope's **tomb** (in San Pietro in Vincoli). The relationship that was to last 10 years between the overbearing, irasci-
ble, and demanding Julius II and the introverted and
temperamental Michelangelo was hardly a meeting of like
minds. The colossal tomb was left unfinished when Julius got
carried away instead with plans for St. Peter's. Irritated, Michelangelo abandoned Rome in 1504, but Julius managed to
sweet-talk the moody artist into returning to Rome to paint the
Sistine Chapel ceiling. Mikey spent the next four years slaving
over—or rather under—the problem-ridden project, beginning
by learning how to paint frescoes. In the following years, he
threw away the his original pictorial design, redesigned his
plans, fired his assistants, and ended up doing the whole job
himself. The ceiling was finished in 1512, four months before
Julius's death, and Michelangelo escaped to Florence. Thirty
years later, Michelangelo returned to Rome, greeted by the
new Pope Paul II, who called the aged Michelangelo back to
the Sistine Chapel for arguably his most important work, **The
Last Judgment** (p. 147). Michelangelo would continue his architectural designs, but he would never paint again. Before his
death at the age of 89, he expressed his wish to be buried in

Piazza Barberini

Trevi Fountain

Florence. To circumvent the Romans, who would certainly want to claim Michelangelo's body, his casket was smuggled to Florence and interred.

Michelangelo's Florentine contemporary **Raphael** (Raffaello Sanzio) also made the obligatory pilgrimage to Rome for prestige and generous papal commissions. Julius had him fresco his private rooms, now world-famous as the **Raphael Stanze.** Raphael profited from his stay in the Vatican to covertly learn some of Michelangelo's techniques for creating realistic and dynamic art, much to Michelangelo's annoyance.

BERNINI + BORROMINI = BAROQUE

The Baroque in Rome can be summed up in the work of two heavily lionized artists: **Gian Lorenzo Bernini** and **Francesco Castelli Borromini.** The personality differences between effervescent, cavalier boy-genius Bernini and dark, temperamental Borromini are abundantly clear in their works. Known as the "greatest European" in his day, the architect, sculptor, painter, and dandy Bernini more than set the standard for the Baroque during his prolific career. Bernini's father, a Florentine sculptor, brought his son to Rome to start work; he was immediately signed on for training and didn't stop working until the age of 80. He died having worked for every pope that was in power during his lifetime.

Along with his charged **St. Teresa in Ecstasy** (in Santa Maria della Vittoria), Bernini's Hellenistic **David** (in the Galleria Borghese, p. 149) stands in great contrast to Michelangelo's classical version. Although sculpture was only one facet of Bernini's career, he made great contributions to Rome in the architecture department. The oval of the *piazza* of St. Peter's was the culmination of a life's work; he personally supervised the construction of each and every one of the 284 Doric columns of travertine marble. Bernini's churches and monuments (including the grand **baldacchino** at St. Peter's and his own favorite, the **church of Sant'Andrea al Quirinale**) exemplify the exuberantly showy, theatrical, illusory style that came to define the Baroque.

The non-conformist Swiss **Borromini** spent much of his career fitfully working against the gaudy showiness of the Baroque. Borromini was commissioned to design some of the details on Bernini's *baldacchino,* but it became increasingly apparent that Bernini and Borromini's styles were wholly incompatible. In works like the **church of San Carlo alle Quattro Fontane,** Borromini created an entirely new architectural vocabulary that fused sculpture and architecture. Eventually the complexity of Borromini's work caught up with him; he became obsessed with his calculations and machinations and withdrew completely from society. A few days after burning a final series of architectural plans, he impaled himself on a sword.

NEOCLASSICAL RE-REVIVAL

In the late 1700s, southern Italy would provide the long-awaited reaction to the Baroque in the form of **Neoclassicism.** Morbidly infected by the excitement surrounding the excavations in Pompeii, Herculaneum, and Paestum, Neoclassical artists reasserted the values of Greco-Roman art that the Renaissance already had taken a shot at imitating. The greatest artists of this period weren't Roman but they soon immigrated to Rome, where they found the world's unrivaled source of antiquities. Foremost among the Neoclassicists was **Jacques-Louis David** (1748-1825), who studied in Rome at the French Academy. In sculpture, the coldly pure lines of **Antonio Canova** also found fans, leading the Borghese to install some of his marble statues in their gardens.

Pope Benedict XIV preferred restoring Rome for tourists over conducting church business; street signs and historical markers appeared for the first time. He commissioned paintings for St. Peter's and mosaics for Santa Maria Maggiore (redesigned by prominent architect **Fernando Fuga**). Baroque artists mostly managed to resist the tide of Neoclassicism, as **Nicola Salvi**'s decidedly Baroque Trevi Fountain (p. 109)—completed in 1762—testifies. The tumultuous Risorgimento put a damper on construction in the mid-1800s; once the country was unified, however, large-scale building began, to accommodate the new government. The previously undeveloped area east, southeast, and northeast of Termini was soon crowded with apartment buildings. A number of beautiful buildings were lost to this expansion, including Henry James's favorite, the Villa Ludovisi.

FASCIST ART

Mussolini was one of the biggest builders of public works since the cadre of popes who built St. Peter's and the rest of the Vatican complex. Unfortunately, most of the monuments he erected, like the philosophy he founded, are pompous, rigid, unimaginatively geometrical, and based on an artistic model that subjugates the individual to the public masses. Much of the Fascist legacy in Roman architecture can be found in the **EUR** neighborhood on the outskirts of Rome (p. 136), including one building (the Palace of Labor) that architect **Marcello Piancentini** described proudly as a "square Colosseum." The **Foro Italico,** meant to be the monumental symbolic center for a heroic nation, is also a prime example of the Fascist notion of artistic expression—not too different from their notion of political expression. Note the excessive use of "DUCE A NOI" in the tilework, as well as the heroic nude figures wrestling, swimming, laboring, and piloting biplanes.

POST-FASCIST ART

Things got a little more complicated and a lot less megalomaniacal after Mussolini was out of the picture. Although Italy and Rome are perhaps best known in modern times for their celluloid art (see p. 174 for more info on Italian cinema), Italian visual artists had some degree of fame. Several turned to more traditional forms for less than traditional purposes: neo-*neo*-Classicist Felice Casarotti kicked it with the old *old* school, while **Giorgio di Chirico** painted surrealist landscapes that combined ancient Roman architecture with signs of Italian modernity like trains and cars—Vespa meets Vespatian, so to speak. Textures and artistic materials also became more important, with Lucio Fontana exploring the aesthetics of the disgusting in sculpture and painting, and multimedia sculptor **Alberto Burri** melding masterpieces out of scraps of plastic, fabric, and cellophane. No tour of Roman museums is complete without ogling **Amedeo Modigliani**'s paintings of voluptuously sexy nude women—they're always lurking around the corner in Roman museums.

Sights

Turn all the pages of history, but Fortune never produced a greater example of her own fickleness than the city of Rome, once the most beautiful and magnificent of all that ever was or will be...not a city in truth, but a certain part of heaven.
   —Poggio Bracciolini

Rome wasn't built in a day, and you won't see any substantial portion of it in 24 hours, (although you can try, using our one-day tour of Rome, p. 6). Ancient temples and forums, medieval churches, Renaissance basilicas, Baroque fountains, 19th-century museums, and Fascist architecture all cluster together in a city bursting with masterpieces from every era of Western civilization.

Whichever of the thousands of sights you choose to see, there are a few pieces of advice that pertain to almost all of them. First and foremost, most sights are best visited in the morning—the earlier, the better. Not only do you avoid the crowds (the Trevi fountain is sheer madness in the afternoon), but in the summer you miss the crushing heat that descends upon the city. Second, remember that most churches are only open from 8:30am to 12:30pm and from 4 to 7pm, so plan accordingly.

Finally...have one hell of a time! Rome is possibly the greatest exposition of human endeavor on the planet. Let its glory overwhelm you, whether it be from the immense magnificence of the Colosseum, the silent, piercing beauty of Caravaggio's *The Calling of St. Matthew*, the glittering splendor of St. Peter's, or the supremely elegant Trevi Fountain. Western civilization is spread out before your eyes—drink it up!

Rome Major Museums and Monuments

500 yards
500 meters

N

PIAZZALE
CLODIO

PIAZZA
GIUSEPPE
MAZZINI

Viale Medaglie d'Oro

Circ. Codia

Circ. Trionfale

Via delle Giuliana

Via Trionfale

Viale Angelico

Viale delle Milizie

Via G. Ferrari

Via L. Settembrini

Ponte G.
Margherita

L. delle Navi

L. Amaldo da Brescia

L. delle Armi

Viale di S. Eisenna

Via di S. Eisenna

Via Flaminia

LGO. TRIONFALE

Via Andrea Doria

Via Barletta

Via Leone IV

Via Ottaviano

Via Vespasiano

Viale Giulio Cesare

Via Marcant. Colonna

Via Germanico

Via Cola di Rienzo

Via Crescenzio

Via Cicerone

Ponte
Regina
Margherita

Ponte
P.
Nenni

Via di Ripetta

Via del Babuino

PIAZZA
DEL
POPOLO

Ld. Mellini in Augusta

Cd. Mellini

PIAZZALE
DEGLI
EROI

Via Candia

Via Cipro

Via Angelo Emo

Viale Vaticano

Via Calo Mario

Via F. Massimo

PIAZZA
CAVOUR

Ponte
Cavour

PIAZZA
AUGUSTO
IMPERATORIO

Via del Corso

Vatican
Wall

CITTÀ DEL
VATICANO

Saint Peter's
Basilica

Castel
Sant'Angelo

Via d. Conciliazione

L. Prati

River

Ld. Mariano

Via Aurelia

Via S. Maria Mediatrice

Viale Vaticano

Via d. Staz. di S. Pietro

Via Gregorio VII

In. Sassia

L. in Sassia

Ponte P. A.S. Aosta

Via d. Conciliazione

Ponte
S. Angelo

Ponte V.
Emanuele

L. di Tor di Nona

Tiber

Viale dei Coronari

corso Vittorio Emanuele II

L. del Sangallo

Via Giulia

PIAZZA
NAVONA

corso d. Rinascimento

Pantheon

Via d. Scrofa

Via d. Cestari

Via d.

Via delle Mura Aurelie

MONTE
DEL
GIANICOLO

Via Orti
d'Albert

Ponte
Mazzini

Via di S. F. di Sale

L. dei Tebaldi

Palazzo
Farnese

L. di Farnesina

L. dei Vallati

Via del

Via Botteghe

Via Gregorio VII

Via d. Cava Aurelia

Via Aurelia Antica

Via Garibaldi

Ponte
Sisto

L. Sanzio

Ponte
Garibaldi

Isola
Tiberina

Ponte
Cestio

Via Arenula

L. dei Cenci

Teatre
Marcelle

Ponte
Anguillara

PIAZZA
S. SONNINO

Via di S.
Pancrazio

Via Garibaldi

Via Nicola Fabrti

Via Glorioso

Via
D'Andolo

TRASTEVERE

Via di S. Michele

L. Ripa

Lungotevere

Ponte
Sublico

Via Giacinto Carini

Via di Trastevere

Lungotevere Testaccio

Via Marmorata

Via Alessandro Poeria

Via Portuense

Via Giovanni Branca

Via Nicola Zabaglia

Via Galvani

Parco
Testaccio

TESTACCIO

Ponte
Testaccio

Stazione
Magliana

Via d. Tre Fontane

TO CENTRAL
ROME (5 km)

Via C.
Colombo

PIAZZALE D.
NAZIONI

PIAZZA G.
MARCONI

Viale Europa

Viale America

Viale Civilta
Romana

v. Lincoln

Viale Asia

PIAZZA G.
AGNELLI

Via Cristoforo Colombo

Via d. C. Colombo

Palazzo dello Sport

EUR

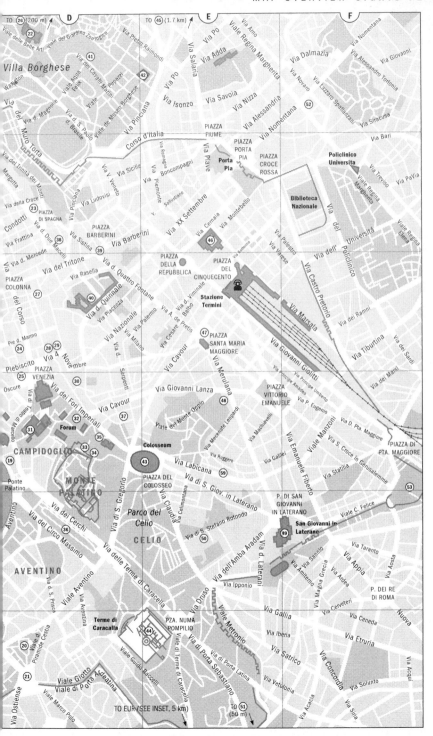

MUSEUMS

dell'Alto Medioevo, 56	A6
Antiquarium Palatino, 34	D4
d'Arte Ebraica, 17	C4
d'Arte Moderna, 22	D1
d'Arte Orientale, 48	E4
d'Arte e Tradizioni Populari, 54	A5
Barracco, 7	C3
Borghese, 42	E1
Campidoglio (Capitoline), 31	D4
Canonica, 41	D1
delle Cere (Waxworks), 28	D3
delle Civilatà Romana, 57	B6
Colonna, 29	D3
Communale d'Arte Moderna, 38	D2
Corsini, 4	C4
Doria Pamphilj, 24	D3
Keats-Shelley Memorial House, 23	D2
delle Mura, 51	E6
Mario Praz, 6	C3
Napoleonico, 6	C3
di Nazionale Etrusco, 15	C1
di Palazzo Venezia, 25	D4
Preistorico Etnografico, 55	A6
di Roma, 10	C3
Romano delle Terme, 46	E2
Spada, 8	E2
Degli Stumenti Musicali, 53	F4
Vatican Museums, 1	B2
Villa Farnesina, 5	C4

CHURCHES

Domine Quo Vadis, 51	E6
Il Gesù, 16	C4
Pantheon, 14	C3
S. Cecilia in Trastevere, 59	E4
S. Clemente, 58	C5
S. Giovanni in Laterano, 49	F5
S. Maria in Cosmedin, 19	D4
S. Maria Maggiore, 47	E3
S. Maria del Popolo, 12	C1
S. Maria in Trastevere, 11	C4
S. Pietro in Vincoli, 37	D4
S. Stefano Rotondo, 50	E5
S. Trinità dei Monti, 23	D2
Sinagoga Ashkenazita, 17	C4

ROMAN MONUMENTS

Ara Pacis, 13	C2
Basilica of Mazentius, 35	D4
Bocca della Verità, 19	D4
Campidoglio (Capitoline), 31	D4
Castel S. Angelo, 3	B3

Catacombs:

S. Agnese, 52	F1
S. Callisto, 51	E6
S. Domitilla, 51	E6
S. Priscilla, 45	E1
S. Sebastiano, 51	E6
Colosseo (Colosseum), 43	E4
Circus Maximus, 36	D5
Fori Imperiali, 30	D4
The Forum, 32	D4
Mausolueum of Augustus, 13	C2
Pyramid (of Gaius Cestius), 21	D6
Teatro Marcello, 18	C4
Baths of Caracalla, 44	E6
Baths of Diocletian, 46	E2
Via Appia Antica (The Appian Way), 51	E6

PARKS AND FOUNTAINS

Fontana dei Quattro Fiumi (Fountain of the Four Rivers), 9	C3
Fontana di Trevi, 27	D3
Fontana del Tritone, 39	D2
Giardino Zoologio, 26	D1
Orto Botanico, 2	B4
Protestant Cemetery, 20	D6

PIAZZE

Campo dei Fiori, 8	C4
Piazza di Spagna (Spanish Steps), 23	D2
Piazza Augusto Imperiali, 13	C2
Piazza Barberini, 39	D2
Piazza del Cinquecento, 46	E2
Piazza del Colosseo, 43	E4
Piazza Navona, 9	C3
Piazza del Popolo, 12	C1
Piazza della Rotonda, 14	C3
Piazza Venezia, 25	D4

ANCIENT CITY

see map p. 77

In the midst of the countless, scattered stones of the **Roman Forum** and the **Palatine** stands a small, truncated column. This spot was the **Umbilicus Urbis,** the "navel of the city," marking the geographical center of the ancient city. More than any other monument in Rome, it symbolizes what the Roman Forum used to be—the center of all the ancient West's political, economic, social, and religious life. Although on a summer day *il Foro* may begin to feel more like *il forno* (the oven), visiting the ancient city is an incredible experience. Despite the ravages of time, the glory of Rome's early history is still palpable. In a relatively small area, one can see the venues of Roman government, religion, entertainment, privilege, and even sanitation. The volume of camera-and-bottled-water-toting tourists speaking every language under the sun (except Latin) make it impossible to really recreate ancient Rome in your mind, but it's fun to try. Exploring the ancient city is time-consuming and involves a great deal of walking; **give yourself a full day to visit the Forum, Palatine, and Colosseum thoroughly.**

ROMAN FORUM

🚩 *Main entrance: V. dei Fori Imperiali (between P. Venezia and the Colosseum). Other entrances are opposite the Colosseum (from here, you can reach the Palatine Hill, too) and at the Clivus Capitolinus, near P. del Campidoglio.* **M:***B-Colosseo, or bus to P. Venezia.* **Open** *M-Sa 9am-7pm, Su 9am-1pm; in winter M-Sa 9am-1hr. before sunset, Su 9am-1hr. before sunset; sometimes closes M-F by 3pm, Su and holidays by noon. Free.* **Guided tour** *with archaeologist L6000; audioguide tour for Forum L7000 in English, French, German, Italian, Japanese, or Spanish; both available at main entrance.*

The Forum, once a marshland prone to flooding and eschewed by Rome's Iron Age (1000-900 BC) inhabitants, spreads from the Colosseum west toward the Capitoline Hill. Today, many of the Forum's structures are no more, and the locations of many sites are just hypotheses. Access is unpredictable, as you never know which areas will be fenced off because of excavation, restoration, or cruelty.

In the 7th and 8th centuries BC, Etruscans and Greeks used the Tiber Island as a crossing point for trade and the Forum as a market. Rome was founded as a market town for sober farmers who came to trade and perform religious rites; the Romans were peacefully dominated by the more advanced Etruscans until 510 BC, when the Republic was established. The **Curia,** the meeting place of the Senate; the **Comitium Well,** or assembly place; the **three sacred trees** of Rome; and the **Rostra,** the speaker's platform, were built here to serve the young government. The earliest **temples** (to Saturn and to Castor and Pollux) were dedicated in honor of the revolution. The already extant **Via Sacra,** Rome's oldest street, became the main thoroughfare of the young city. The conquest of Greece in the 2nd century BC brought new architectural forms to the city, including the lofty **Basilica Aemilia,** used as a center for business and judicial work before Christians co-opted the form for their churches.

ESSENTIAL
INFORMATION

CHURCH ETIQUETTE

It's not nice to walk into a church in the middle of mass unless you intend to participate. At all times, refrain from speaking loudly, parading directly in front of the altar, and taking flash photographs.

While some churches strictly adhere to established dress codes (no shorts, short skirts, bare midriffs, or tank tops), others may not be so adamant. Even in the latter case, however, grubbiness and bare skin will generally attract disapproving stares from pious Italians; wear modest clothing if you plan on going church-hopping. Another option is to keep a large scarf or sarong stashed in your backpack and to drape it over your immodestly bare flesh before entering houses of worship. Men may just have to suck it up and wear light cotton pants.

The Forum was never reserved for a single activity. Senators debated the fates of far-flung nations over the din of haggling traders. The **Vestal Virgins** kept the city's eternal flame burning in their house on a street full of prostitutes, who kept flames of a different sort burning. Elsewhere, priests offered sacrifices in the temples, generals led triumphal processions up to the Capitoline, and pickpockets pickpocketed tourists without the aid of bus #64.

The Forum witnessed political turbulence in the Republic in the first century BC. **Cicero**'s orations against the antics of corrupt young aristocrats echoed off the temple walls and **Julius Caesar**'s dead body was cremated, amid rioting crowds, in the small temple that bears his name. Augustus, Caesar's great-nephew and adopted son, exploited the Forum to support his new government, closing off the old town square with a temple to the newly deified Caesar and building a triumphal arch honoring himself. His successors followed suit, clotting the old markets with successively grander tokens of their majesty (often looted from the monuments of their predecessors). The construction of the imperial palace on the Palatine in the first century AD, and of new *fora* on higher ground to the north, cleared out the old neighborhoods around the square.

By the 2nd century, the Forum, though packed with gleaming white monuments, had become a deserted ceremonial space. Barbarian invaders of the 5th century found the Forum offensive to their aesthetic sensibilities, burning and looting it. In the wake of Constantine, the Christian government of the city ordered the pagan temples closed.

In the Middle Ages, many buildings were converted to churches and alms houses; marble was stolen and the Forum gradually became Campo Vaccino, a cow pasture, with only the tallest columns peeking through the tall grass. The last bits of the Forum's accesible marble were quarried by Renaissance popes for their own monumental constructions. Excavations, begun in 1803, have uncovered a vast array of remnants large and small, but have also rendered the site extremely confusing—the ruins of structures built over and on top of each other for more than a thousand years are now exposed to a single view. For more on the Forum's past, see **History**, p. 45.

CIVIC CENTER

◪ *The Forum's main entrance ramp leads directly to V. Sacra. To the right, the Capitoline Hill and the Arch of Septimius Severus stand in the distance. V. Sacra cuts through the old market square and civic center; the **Basilica Aemilia** is to your immediate right, and the brick **Curia** building is just beyond.*

BASILICA AEMILIA. Completed in 179 BC, the Basilica Aemilia was the judicial center of ancient Rome. It also housed the guild of the *argentarii* (money-changers), who operated the city's first *cambiomat* and provided Roman *denarii* for traders and tourists (doubtless at the same great rates found today at Termini). The basilica was damaged several times by fire and rebuilt; in the pavement you can see bronze marks from the melted coins lost in these blazes. While money might have been able to buy love in some of the seedier parts of the Forum, it could not stop the destruction of the basilica by Alaric and his merry band of Goths in AD 410. The broken bases of columns are all that remain of the aisled interior. The foundations of the row of *tabernae* (shops) that once faced the Forum are still visible along the path. In the back right corner of the basilica are reliefs of the *Rape of the Sabine Women* and the *Death of Tarpeia*.

CURIA. To the left of Basilica Aemilia (as you face it) stands the Curia, or Senate House, one of the oldest buildings in the Forum. Its origins go back to Tullus Hostilius, the 3rd king of Rome, though the structure of the building dates only from the time of Diocletian (AD 283). It was converted to a church in 630 and only recently restored by Mussolini to reveal inlaid Egyptian marble pavement and the long steps where the senators placed their own chairs for meetings. The stone base shows where Augustus' legendary golden statue of Victory rested until the end of the 4th century, when Christian senators decided that they had had enough of paganism and got rid of it. The Curia also houses the **Plutei of Trajan,** two sculpted parapets that originally decorated the Rostrum, and that depict the burning of the tax registers and the distribution of food to poor children. To the left of the Curia stands the **Church of Santi Luca e Martina**, formerly the **Secretarium Senatus.** Further up the hill, below the **Church of San Giuseppe dei Falegnami**, is the 2nd-century BC **Mamertine Prison** (see p. 91), where St. Peter is said to have been

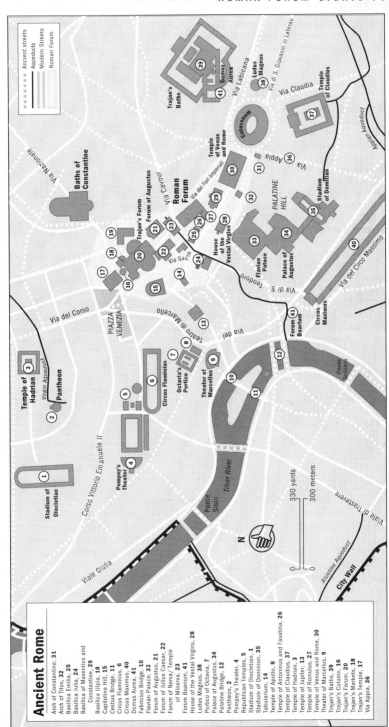

Ancient Rome

Arch of Constantine, **31**
Arch of Titus, **32**
Basilica Emilia, **25**
Basilica Julia, **24**
Basilica of Maxentius and Constantine, **29**
Basilica Ulpia, **18**
Capitoline Hill, **15**
Cestius Bridge, **11**
Circus Flaminius, **6**
Circus Maximus, **40**
Domus Aurea, **41**
Fabricius Bridge, **10**
Flavian Palace, **33**
Forum of Augustus, **21**
Forum of Julius Caesar, **22**
Forum of Nerva / Temple of Minerva, **23**
Forum Boarium, **41**
House of the Vestal Virgins, **28**
Ludus Magnus, **38**
Palace of Augustus, **34**
Palatine Bridge, **12**
Pantheon, **2**
Pompey's Theater, **4**
Portico of Octavia, **7**
Republican Temples, **5**
Stadium of Diocletian, **1**
Stadium of Dominion, **35**
Tabularium, **14**
Temple of Apollo, **8**
Temple of Antoninus and Faustina, **26**
Temple of Claudius, **37**
Temple of Hadrian, **3**
Temple of Jupiter, **13**
Temple of Romulus, **27**
Temple of Venus and Rome, **30**
Theater of Marcellus, **9**
Trajan's Baths, **39**
Trajan's Column, **16**
Trajan's Forum, **20**
Trajan's Markets, **18**
Trajan's Temple, **17**
Via Appia, **36**

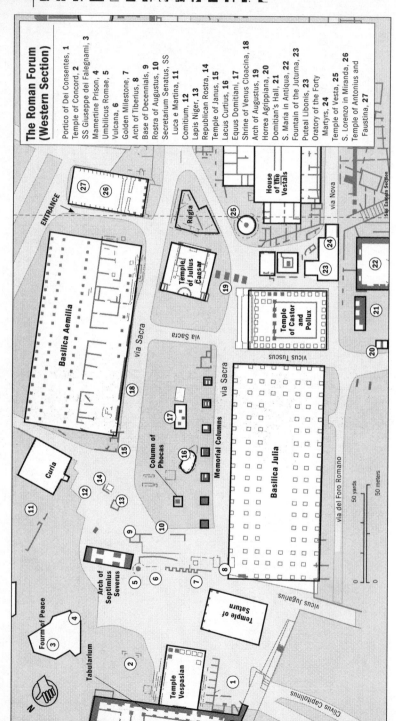

The Roman Forum (Western Section)

Portico of Dei Consentes, 1
Temple of Concord, 2
SS Giuseppe dei Falegnami, 3
Mamertine Prison, 4
Umbilicus Romae, 5
Vulcana, 6
Golden Milestone, 7
Arch of Tiberius, 8
Base of Decennials, 9
Rostra of Augustus, 10
Secretarium Senatus, SS
Luca e Martina, 11
Comitium, 12
Lapis Niger, 13
Republican Rostra, 14
Temple of Janus, 15
Lacus Curtius, 16
Equus Domitiani, 17
Shrine of Venus Cloacina, 18
Arch of Augustus, 19
Horrea Agrippiana, 20
Domitian's Hall, 21
S. Maria in Antiqua, 22
Fountain of the Juturna, 23
Puteal Libonis, 23
Oratory of the Forty
Martyrs, 24
Temple of Vesta, 25
S. Lorenzo in Miranda, 26
Temple of Antonius and
Faustina, 27

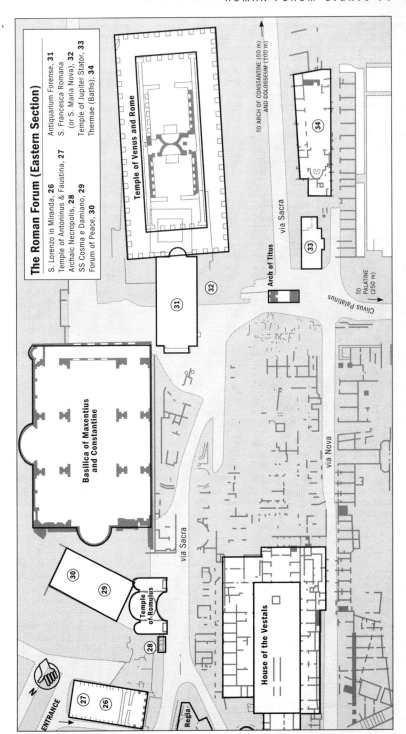

The Roman Forum (Eastern Section)

S. Lorenzo in Miranda, **26**
Temple of Antoninus & Faustina, **27**
Archaic Necropolis, **28**
SS Cosma e Damiano, **29**
Forum of Peace, **30**

Antiquarium Forense, **31**
S. Francesca Romana
(or S. Maria Nova), **32**
Temple of Jupiter Stator, **33**
Thermae (Baths), **34**

Temple of Venus and Rome

Basilica of Maxentius and Constantine

Temple of Romulus

House of the Vestals

Regia

Arch of Titus

via Sacra

via Nova

Clivus Palatinus

TO ARCH OF CONSTANTINE (50 m)
AND COLOSSEUM (100 m)

TO PALATINE (250 m)

ENTRANCE

N

BENITO MUSSOLINI: SAGE AND SEER

On one of the walls of the Ancient Forum, facing V. del Foro Imperiale, four large marble maps of Europe—from Northern Africa to Scandinavia, the Atlantic Ocean to the Caspian Sea—delineate Rome's dominance over the years. Roman territories are in white, the rest of the map is in black. The first one (on the left) is of Rome in its beginnings, 8th century BC, when only the city itself is white. The next three show Rome's expanded empire, from 146 BC (the end of the Punic Wars) to AD 14 (death of Augustus) to AD 117 (end of Trajan's reign). By the fourth map, two-thirds of Europe, North Africa, Mesopotamia, and Britannia are white. Very nice. Look at the wall directly to the right of the last map. Behind a tree, there's a large discolored space on the bricks. Apparently Mussolini had constructed a fifth map to hang there in 1937, celebrating Rome's imminent renewed dominion over Europe. After Mussolini died, the map disappeared, only to be uncovered in pieces in the attic of an American soldier three decades later. Now it's to be found in the Capitoline Museums (see p. 152).

imprisoned and miraculously made water appear with which to baptize his cellmates.

COMITIUM. The broad space in front of the Curia was the Comitium, where male citizens came to vote and representatives of the people gathered for public discussion. This space was also home to the famed **Twelve Tables,** bronze tablets upon which the first codified laws of the Republic were inscribed. To the left of the Arch of Septimius Severus is the large brick **Rostrum,** or speaker's platform, erected by Julius Caesar in 44 BC (just before his death). The term *rostra* refers to the metal ramrods on the bows of warships. *Rostra* from warships captured at Antium in 342 BC decorated the platform. The literal *rostrum* is gone, but the regularly spaced holes in its platform remain. Senators and consuls orated to the Roman plebes from here, and any citizen could mount to voice his opinion. After his assassination, Cicero's head and hands were put on display here. Augustus's rebellious daughter Julia is said to have voiced her disdain for her father's new legislation promoting family values by engaging in amorous activities with Augustus's enemies on the very spot where the laws had been announced.

ARCH OF SEPTIMIUS SEVERUS. The hefty Arch of Septimius Severus at the end of V. Sacra is an anachronism in this Republican square. Dedicated in AD 203 to celebrate that emperor's victories in the Middle East, the arch's reliefs depict the imperial family. Severus' classy son and successor, Caracalla, grabbed the throne by killing his brother Geta and then scraped his name and portrait off the arch. Behind the arch stand the grey tufa walls of the **Tabularium,** once the repository of Senate archives, now the basement of the Renaissance **Palazzo dei Senatori.**

MARKET SQUARE. The original market square (in front of the Curia) was graced by a number of shrines and sacred precincts. Immediately down the stairs from the Curia lies the **Lapis Niger** (Black Stone), surrounded by a circle of bricks. Republican Romans believed this is where the legendary founder of the city, Romulus, was murdered. Modern scholars now think the Lapis Niger was actually an early shrine to Vulcan. The shrine was considered passé even during the Republic, when its statuary and columns were covered by gray pavement. Below the Lapis Niger rest the underground ruins of a 6th-century BC altar, along with a pyramidal pillar where the oldest known Latin inscription in Rome warns the public against defiling the shrine. Across from the far side of the **Basilica Julia,** the **Three Sacred Trees** of Rome—olive, fig, and grape—have been replanted by the Italian state (never mind that grapes grow on vines). On the other side, across from the Basilica Julia, lies a circular tufa basin (sometimes covered by a low tin roof, the purpose of which could only be to block your view of it), the **Lacus Curtius,** commemorating the swamp that had been there before. It received its name from the story of either Marcus Curtius, who sacrificed himself on the spot to save the city, or the less exciting Gaius Curtius (no relation), who once saw a lightning bolt hit it.

The newest part of the Forum is the **Column of Phocas,** erected in 608 to celebrate the visiting Byzantine emperor, Phocas—a sacrilege that would have probably made early Republican Romans roll in their graves. The marketplace area may also have been home to three important markers: the **Umbilicus Urbis,** the **Golden Milestone,** and the **Vulcanal.** Unfortunately, the locations of these, which marked the center not only of the city, but of the Roman world, are only hypotheses.

LOWER FORUM

🛈 *To the left and behind the Arch of Septimius Severus are Basilica Julia and the three great (somewhat) extant temples of the lower Forum.*

TEMPLE OF SATURN. Eight columns mark the Temple of Saturn, one of the first buildings constructed in Rome. The Romans believed that Saturn had taught them the art of agriculture, and customarily filled his statue inside the temple with fresh olive oil. Though actually built in the early 5th century BC, the temple has its mythological origins in an earlier Rome, one with no property, war, or slavery. The temple was the site of Saturnalia, the Roman winter bash that signified the end of the year. During this raucous party, class and social distinctions became null and void and masters served slaves.

Behind the temple are (left to right): the **Portico of the Dei Consentes,** the last pagan monument built in Rome; the three Corinthian columns of the **Temple of Vespatian,** completed by his son Domitian in AD 81; and the foundations of the **Temple of Concord,** which was built to celebrate the peace between patrician and plebeian Romans in 367 BC.

BASILICA JULIA. Around the corner to the left of the Temple of Saturn, rows of deserted column bases are the sole remains of the Basilica Julia. Begun by Julius Caesar in 54 BC, completed by Augustus, and restored by Diocletian, it followed the same plan as the Basilica Aemilia (see above) on a larger scale. The central hall, flanked by three rows of columns on each side, was used by tribunals of judges for laying down the law. Look for grids and circles in the steps where anxious Romans, waiting to go before the judge, played an ancient version of snakes and ladders. If you've had your fill of culture, at the end of the basilica opposite the Temple of Castor and Pollux you will see part of the **Cloaca Maxima,** the huge sewer which drained from the Forum directly into the Tiber. Do not try to avail yourself of this resource. Further down the Vicus Tuscus is the **Horrea Agrippiana,** where grain was stored.

TEMPLE OF CASTOR AND POLLUX. At the far end of the Basilica Julia, three white marble columns mark the massive podium of the **Temple of Castor and Pollux.** It was dedicated in 484 BC to celebrate the Roman rebellion against their Etruscan king, Tarquinius Superbus. The Romans attributed a subsequent victory over the Latins at Lake Regillus in 499 BC to

Circus Maximus

Piazza di Campidoglio

Bocca della Verita

the help of the twin gods Castor and Pollux (not the nefarious brothers of the movie *Face/Off*), who miraculously outflanked the mortal Etruscans.

Legend says that immediately after the battle the twins appeared in the Forum to water their horses at the nearby **Lacus Juturnae** (Basin of Juturna). Now marked by a reconstructed marble *aedicula* to the left of the gods' temple, the site was once the location of the ancient city's water company. Behind the temple, the **Church of Santa Maria Antiqua** is the oldest in the forum, dating to the sixth century.

TEMPLE OF THE DEIFIED JULIUS. Across from the Temple of Castor and Pollux is the rectangular base of the **Temple of the Deified Julius,** which Augustus built in 29 BC to honor his murdered adoptive father and to proclaim himself the son of a god. The circular pile of rocks inside housed an altar and likely marks the spot where Caesar's body was cremated in 44 BC after his assassination near largo Argentina. Wistful monarchists leave flowers here on the Ides of March. In his own modest glory, Augustus built the **Arch of Augustus,** a triple arch (only the bases are visible now) that straddled V. Sacra.

UPPER FORUM

TEMPLE OF VESTA. The circular building behind the Temple of the Deified Julius is the Temple of Vesta, originally built by the Etruscans but rebuilt on the same site by Septimius Severus in the end of the 2nd century AD. Built to imitate a Latin hut, the temple is where the Vestal Virgins tended the sacred fire of the city, keeping it continuously lit for more than a thousand years (until the 4th century). Within one of the temple's secret rooms, visited only by the Vestal Virgins, stood the **Palladium,** the small statue of Minerva that Aeneas was said to have brought from Troy to Italy. Behind the temple, between the House of Vestal Virgins and the Temple of Antoninus and Faustina, lies the triangular **Regia,** office of the Pontifex Maximus, Rome's high priest and titular ancestor of the Pope. Long before the first Pontifex (Numa Pompilius) took it over, as early as the 6th century BC, the Regia was the site of sacrifices to gods of agriculture (as well as to Mars, Jupiter, Juno, and Janus). One of the rites performed here was the October harvest ritual, in which the tail and genitalia of a slain horse were brought to the Regia in an offering to the god of vegetation. Sadly, this ceremony has been discontinued.

HOUSE OF THE VESTAL VIRGINS. The sprawling complex of rooms and courtyards behind the Temple of Vesta was the House of Vestal Virgins. Here, in spacious seclusion in the shade of the Palatine, lived the six virgins who officiated over Vesta's rites, chosen for their purity and physical perfection and ordained at the age of seven. As long as they kept their vows of chastity, the Vestal Virgins were among the most respected people in ancient Rome; they were the only women allowed to walk unaccompanied in the Forum and could protect or pardon anyone. This easy life had its price; if a virgin strayed from celibacy, she was buried alive with a loaf of bread and a candle, on the assumption that the sustenance that it provided would give her time to contemplate her sins during her prolonged death. Only a handful of women met this fate.

Off-and-on restoration often means that visitors can only peer through the iron gates surrounding the House of the Vestal Virgins. Still, there is a view (head up to the Palatine to get a really good view) of the central courtyard where statues of the priestesses who served between AD 291 and 364 reside, including one whose name was scraped away (8th on the left as you enter the courtyard). The erased priestess is thought to have been Claudia, the Vestal Virgin who, at the end of the 4th century, converted to that new-fangled religion from the south, Christianity.

TEMPLE OF ANTONINUS AND FAUSTINA. Back on V. Sacra is the Temple of Antoninus and Faustina (opposite the Temple of Vesta, to the immediate right as you face the entrance ramp), whose strong foundation, columns, and rigid lattice ceiling have preserved it unusually well over the ages. In the 7th and 8th centuries, the **Church of San Lorenzo in Miranda** was built in the interior of the abandoned temple. The temple's columns and frieze were incorporated into the Christian structure. This is not to say that the Christian rulers didn't try to destroy the pagan temple: the deep grooves at the top of the columns show where cables were tied in attempts to demolish this steadfast symbol of pagan worship. The original building was constructed by Emperor Antoninus and dedicated to his wife Faustina (his name was added after his death in AD 161).

In the shadow of the temple (to the right as you face it) is an archaic **necropolis**, with Iron Age graves dating to between the 10th and 8th centuries BC. This lends credence to Rome's legendary founding date of 753 BC. The bodies from the ancient graveyard were found in hollow tree trunks. The remains are visible in the Antiquarium (see **Velia**, below).

TEMPLE OF ROMULUS. Further up V. Sacra stands the round Temple of Romulus, which retains its original bronze doors, with a working lock, from the 4th century AD. The name of the structure, however, is misleading for two reasons. First, the "Romulus" in question here was probably the son of the 4th-century emperor, Maxentius, not the legendary founder of Rome. Second, the temple probably wasn't a temple at all but an office of the urban *praetor* during the Empire.

The temple now houses the **Church of Santi Cosma e Damiano.** Across V. Sacra from the structure, remains of fortifications from between 730 and 540 BC have been discovered. Behind the temple, recently excavated ruins of Vespatian's **Forum Pacis** (Forum of Peace) are visible along V. dei Fori Imperiali, beginning just past the main entrance.

Roman Forum

VELIA

▶ *Take V. Sacra out of the Forum proper, toward the Arch of Titus.*

BASILICA OF MAXENTIUS AND CONSTANTINE. The gargantuan Basilica of Maxentius and Constantine is on the left as you walk down V. Sacra. The three gaping arches that remain are only the side chapels for an enormous central hall, whose coffered ceiling covered the entire gravel court and three chapels on the other side. Emperor Maxentius began construction of the basilica in 308 but was forcefully deposed by Constantine at the Battle of the Milvian Bridge in 312. Constantine converted to Christianity during the battle, and although he oversaw completion of the basilica, some pagan reverence for the Forum kept him from ever dedicating it as a church. He built the basilica of San Giovanni in Laterano instead, with a similar plan (see p. 131). Constantine didn't let his piety get in the way of his ego, though. The middle apse of the basilica once contained a gigantic statue of him; the body was bronze, and the head, legs, and arms were marble. The remains that were found (on exhibit at the **Museo Capitolino;** see p. 152) include a 6½ ft. long foot. In the end, though, Christianity won out; all the bronze in the basilica was melted down in the 7th century to cover the first basilica of St. Peter's.

Church of Santa Maria in Cosmedin

The Baroque facade of the **Church of Santa Francesca Romana** is built over Hadrian's Temple to Venus and Rome *(Amor* and *Roma).* It hides the entrance to the **Antiquarium Forense,** a small museum that houses artifacts from the Forum. Among the items on display are skeletons from the necropolis. *(Antiquarium open daily 9am-1pm. Free.)*

ARCH OF TITUS. On the summit of the Velian hill, where V. Sacra intersects with the road down from the Palatine, is the Arch of Titus, built in AD 81 by Domitian to celebrate his brother Titus's destruction of Jerusalem 10 years earlier.

Arch of Janus

Though the paranoid Frangipane family turned it into a fortified tower in the Middle Ages, Pope Pius VII ordered it restored to its original state in 1821. On the interior of the arch is a famous frieze depicting Titus's victory and the treasure he took from the Great Temple (which appears subsequently to have been spent by Titus on the construction of the Colosseum).

THE COLOSSEUM

> As long the Colosseum stands, Rome shall stand. When the Colosseum falls, Rome shall fall. When Rome falls, the world shall end.
> —The Venerable Bede (c. 673-735)

🚇 *M:*B-Colosseo. **Open** *daily 9am-6:30pm; in winter daily 9am-1hr. before sunset.* **Admission** *L10,000, EU citizens under 18 and over 60 free, EU citizens 18-24 L5000. A* **six-day ticket book** *is good for the three Musei Nazionali Romani (see p. 156), the Colosseum, and the Palatine Hill (L30,000).* **Tours** *with archaeologist L6000; audioguide in English, French, German, Italian, Japanese, or Spanish L7000.*

The Colosseum is the enduring symbol of the Eternal City—a hollowed-out ghost of travertine marble dwarfing every other ruin in Rome. Recently completed renovations have cleaned the exterior and reconstructed several missing sections (in brick instead of marble, unfortunately) to give a better sense of what the ancient amphitheater looked like, but it is still pretty barren and empty inside. Use your imagination (or perhaps scenes from *Gladiator*) or pick up an audioguide (*telefonini* on steroids) to make the visit more interesting. The city of Rome does its part to make the Colosseum come alive by hiring poor souls to dress up as gladiators and centurions outside, as well the occasional historically inaccurate but provocatively dressed gladiatoress. They're amusing enough to look at, but what they really want is to have their picture taken with you for a cool L10,000 a pop. You enter on the lowest level of seating (the arena floor is off-limits) and can take stairs to the upper level.

The term "Colosseum" is actually a nickname for the *Amphitheatrum Flavium*, which Vespatian began building in AD 72 to block out the private lake that Nero had installed for his own seedy purposes. The nickname derives from the colossal bronze statue of Nero as sun-god that used to grace the area next to the amphitheater (see the **Domus Aurea,** p. 86). The Colosseum was completed in 80 by Titus, Vespatian's son, with spoils from the emperors' campaigns in Judaea. Titus allegedly threw a monster bash for its inauguration: a 100-day fête that saw 5000 wild beasts perish in the bloody arena (from the Latin for sand, *harena,* which was put on the floor to absorb blood). Though the maximum capacity is still debatable, feuding archaeologists have placed the number

PACIFYING THE POPULACE

When Juvenal wrote that "bread and circuses" were all that were necessary to keep the Roman populace happy, he was referring in part to the free snacks and wild spectacles staged in the 50,000-person Colosseo. In order to keep the large numbers of unemployed Romans occupied, emperors depended upon the distracting powers of ceremonial pageantry and calculated violence of gladiatorial combats. Fallen, injured gladiators could make a sign begging for mercy. While the emperor mulled over his decision, the blood-thirsty crowd howled for a thumbs-down, the death sentence. Most Romans, including the elite, saw nothing wrong with these savage spectacles. Another popular event at the Colosseum was the killing of wild animals. Lions and tigers and bears, crocodiles, giraffes, and camels were all released from an underground network of tunnels into a simulated forest. Professionals *(venatores)* would work the frightened animals into a feverish state and draw out their deaths.

at at least 50,000. Because the Colosseum events took place for the "public good," tickets to see the slaughter were always free.

Chances are that the house was packed for Trajan's celebration of his Dacian victories, when 10,000 gladiators and 11,000 beasts duked it out for a month. Over the centuries, it wasn't only gladiator fights that filled the arena: in the mornings, as a warm-up for the evening's battles, exotic animal hunts were a huge draw—the idea of two Romans stalking a hippopotamus was enough to get bloodthirsty teens out of bed and over to the Colosseum. It's also said that the elliptical interior was flooded for sea battles, although some archaeologists and native Romans insist that it wouldn't have been possible, citing the Circus Maximus as the more probable locale. Sadly, gladiatorial games were suspended in 438 by a Christian-dominated empry and Senate, and animal hunts soon bit the dust as well. The Colosseum was used briefly as a fortress in the Middle Ages and as a quarry in the Renaissance, when popes, beginning with Urban VIII, pillaged marble for use in their own grandiose enterprises, including St. Peter's Basilica (see p. 115) and Palazzo Barberini (see p. 153). The former pagan symbol became the site of Christian liturgical rites in the 17th and 18th centuries, and a chapel and rows of crosses were eventually built on the north end of the hollowed-out amphitheater. The crosses were removed in the 19th century when excavations started on the Colosseum, leaving the structure, with the exception of the ongoing exterior renovations, as it is today.

The outside of the arena, with the layers of Doric, Ionic, and Corinthian columns, was considered the ideal orchestration of the classical architectural orders, from the most staid to the most ornamental. On the outer side opposite the entrance, look for five marble posts on the edge of the pavement. These posts are remnants of anchors for a giant *velarium*, the retractable shade that once covered the amphitheater. During each game, 1000 naval troops operated the *velarium*. Inside, the tremendous wooden floor is now gone, revealing the brick cells, corridors, ramps, and elevators that were used to transport wild animals from their cages up to the arena level.

Note the large cross directly across from the side entrance. It symbolizes the Colosseum's escape from total destruction at the hands of pillagers by a lucky mistake. The Pope, in order to commemorate the martyrdom of the thousands of Christians supposedly killed in the amphitheater, declared the monument a sacred place and forbade any further demolition. It was later discovered that no Christians had been ever killed in the Colosseum. These days, in fact, the Pope holds occasional masses there. Additionally, in the summer of 2000, the Colosseum was used as a stage for several Italian TV variety show extravaganzas as well as Greek drama and classical music performances. Organizers bragged that it was the first time in 15 centuries that it had been used as an entertainment venue, though the maximum audience of 700 for these events paled by comparison to the arena's former glory.

ARCH OF CONSTANTINE

Between the Colosseum and the Palatine Hill, marking the tail end of the V. Sacra, is the Arch of Constantine, one of the latest and best-preserved imperial monuments to grace the area. The Senate dedicated the arch in 315 to commemorate Constantine's victory over his rival Maxentius at the Battle of the Milvian Bridge in 312 (see **History**, p. 47). The arch's friezes show how grateful that dedication actually was: one side's images depict life in Constantine's camps and images of war; on the other side, the images depict life after Constantine's victory and the virtues of peace and humanity. There are a few, rough 4th-century friezes, which inadvertently show how much Roman sculptural art declined from highs in the first centuries AD, but otherwise the triple arch is cobbled together almost entirely from sculptural fragments pilfered from earlier Roman monuments. The four sad-looking men near the top (two on each side), for example, are Dacian prisoners taken from one of Trajan's monuments; the medallions once belonged to a monument for Hadrian and include depictions of his lover, Antinous; and the rest of the scatterings celebrate the military prowess of Marcus Aurelius.

RUINING THE RUINS

When Mussolini created wide roads to circle the city's monuments, he also paved the way for their destruction. Today, the Colosseum faces serious damage due to the constant rush of polluting traffic around it. Thousands of cars, scooters, and buses race past the arena daily; when the subway rumbles by, the ground beneath it shakes. Restoration is a Sisyphian task: as workers slowly make their way around the Colosseum, pollution begins to tarnish the already cleaned exterior. For the past 25 years, the government has been considering designating the area from Piazza Venezia to beyond the Colosseum as an "archaeological park," closed to traffic. This would seriously aggravate the already horrible traffic that plagues the city, but it may be the only way to prevent complete collapse of the ancient monument.

PALATINE HILL

◈ *The Palatine rises to the south of the Forum. **Open** M-Sa 9:30am-7:15pm, Su 9am-1pm; in winter M-Sa 9:30am-1hr. before sunset, Su 9am-1pm; sometimes closes M-F by 3pm, Su and holidays by noon. Last entrance 45min. before closing. **Admission** L12,000, EU citizens between 18 and 24 L6000, EU citizens under 18 and over 60 free. A **six-day ticket book** is good for the three Musei Nazionali Romani (see p. 156), the Colosseum, and the Palatine Hill (L30,000). May be purchased at the booth beyond the Arch of Titus and on the left in the Forum (the recommended entrance), 100 yards down V. di San Gregorio from the Colosseum, or at the Forum's main entrance. **Visit the Palatine after the Forum;** it is more recently developed, and you will better appreciate the views of the Forum after having visited it.*

The Palatine boasts not only vast temples and imperial palaces, but also some of the best views of ancient Rome imaginable—these alone are worth the price of admission. The hill, a square plateau rising between the Tiber and the Forum, contains some of the oldest and "newest" Roman ruins.

The first and final chapters of the ancient Empire unfolded atop the Palatine's heights. The she-wolf that suckled Romulus and Remus had her den here, and it was here that Romulus built the first walls and houses of the city, a legend corroborated by the discovery of 9th-century BC huts on the southeastern side of the hill. During the Republic, the Palatine was the city's most fashionable residential quarter, where aristocrats and statesmen, including Cicero and Marc Antony, built their homes. Augustus lived on the hill in a relatively modest house, but later emperors capitalized on the hill's prestige by building progressively more gargantuan quarters for themselves and their courts. By the end of the first century AD, the imperial residence had swallowed up the entire hill, whose Latin name, Palatium, became synonymous with the palace that dominated it. After the fall of Rome, the hill suffered the same fate as the Forum, although Byzantine ambassadors and even popes sometimes set up house in the crumbling palace.

ORTI FARNESIANI

As you start up the hill from the Arch of Titus, take your first right past the 16th-century Uccelliere, commissioned by Cardinal Alessandro Farnese, to the Orti Farnesiani, which opened in 1625 as the first botanical gardens in the world. For incredible Forum views, follow the signs for the *"Affacciata sul Foro."* At the end opposite from the Forum, terraces look down on several structures that are currently being excavated (and will likely be off-limits until 2002). On the far right are the foundations of the Temple of Cybele, constructed in 204 BC on the orders of a prophecy from a Sibylline book. Immediately to its left are the remains of a 9th-century BC village, the **Casa di Romulo** (House of Romulus). The Iron Age inhabitants (who might indeed have included that legendary twin) built their oval huts out of wood; all that remains are the holes they sunk into the tufa bedrock for their roofposts.

Left of the temple is the **House of Livia**. Livia was Augustus's wife, the first Roman empress, and according to Robert Graves's *I, Claudius*, an "abominable grandmother." She had the house, with its vestibule, courtyard, and three vaulted living rooms, connected to the House of Augustus next door. Along the pathways between the House of Livia and the House of Augustus, excavation and restoration continues on rooms once lined with marble and gold. Frescoes, hidden from view, decorate the interior walls.

IMPERIAL COMPLEX

Descending the stairs from the terrace to the Domitian's (AD 81-96) imperial complex, you cross the long, spooky **Cryptoporticus**, a tunnel that connected Tiberius's palace with the buildings nearby. Used by slaves and imperial couriers as a secret passage, it was probably built by Nero in one of his more paranoid moments.

Colosseum

DOMUS FLAVIA. First is the sprawling Domus Flavia, site of a gigantic octagonal fountain that occupied almost the entire courtyard. The building was divided into three halls, and was used by the emperor for all sorts of social, political, and religious functions. It was also the site of a huge throne room where Domitian could preside over public audiences. He clearly had a thing for fountains, because the ruins of a smaller, elliptical one remain intact next to the sunken **Triclinium**, where imperial banquets were held between a set of twin oval fishponds. On the other side of the Triclinium, a walkway offers sweeping views of the grassy **Circus Maximus** (see p. 87) and, farther to the left, the **Baths of Caracalla** (see p. 91).

DOMUS AUGUSTANA. Next door, the solemn Domus Augustana was the emperors' private residence. The exterior walls that remain are so high that archaeologists are still unsure how they were roofed over. The palace was built on the side of the hill, and three floors descend below the level of the main hall, including a sunken courtyard with yet another fishpond. The emperor's quarters were in the maze of staircases and corridors behind the courtyard leading towards the side of the hill. Further down the hill were the **Paedagogium,** the servants' quarters, and the **Domus Praeconum,** which served as the palace's physical plant.

Palatine Hill

HIPPODROME. The most visible ruins on the Palatine are in the east wing of the palace, where the **Stadium Palatinum**, or Hippodrome, stands. Set below the level of the Domus Augustana, this curious stadium has at its southern end a sunken oval space, once surrounded by a colonnade, but now tastefully decorated by the Archaeological Superintendency with fragments of porticoes, statues, and fountains. Although it is fairly certain that this was not a racetrack for hippopotamuses, its exact nature remains uncertain. There are two prominent theories: first, that it was a private arena, where the imperial family would get their kicks watching the lesser classes fight for their lives; and second, that it was a private garden, where the imperial family would get their kicks watching plants photosynthesize. From the northern end of the

Baths of Caracalla

LESS THAN NERO

Nero, son of Claudius's 4th wife, began a sadistic reign of terror, torture, and debauchery at the tender age of 16, after his mother fed her ex-husband poisonous mushrooms. Nero started out mildly, guided by his overbearing but well-meaning mother; he was too timid even to sign the standard death warrants. Soon, though, he proved to be one of the most ill-adjusted teens in history. He transmogrified into a megalo-maniacal monster and ordered the cruel murders of his mother, Agrippina, and his 19-year-old wife, who was found tied up in a hot bath with her veins slashed. He made his best friend and advisor, famed philosopher and tragedian Seneca, cut his own wrists. Nero was haunted by paranoid visions—he often woke up screaming from nightmares of his mother—so he initiated a one-man witch-hunt, condemning senators, army officers, aristocrats, and others to be beheaded as traitors. Many blame Nero for the fire of 64 BC—guilty or not, he certainly took advantage of its destruction, commandeering acres of burnt-out land to construct the Domus Aurea. Ultimately, Nero pushed the patience and the coffers of his empire too far; the Senate sentenced him to death by flogging. Nero, in disguise, escaped on horseback to have a servant slit his throat, as he didn't have the guts to do so himself. The notoriously bad musician and actor did, however, have enough panache to utter in his last moments, "What an artist dies with me." That's style. Style for miles.

stadium, a winding path leads around to the **Domus Severiana,** a later addition to the imperial complex that boasted its own central heating system. The path then curves back around to the exit on V. di San Gregorio.

PALATINE ANTIQUARIUM. Built on the ruins of Domitian's imperial palace, this history museum's nine rooms hold pottery from as early as the 9th century BC, as well as frescoes and sculptures from the 5th century BC and later. *(Between the Domus Augustana and the Domus Flavia. 30 people admitted every 20min. starting at 9:10am. Free with entrance to Palatine.)*

DOMUS AUREA

◪ On the Oppian Hill, below Trajan's baths. From the Colosseum, walk through the gates up V. della Domus Aurea and make the first right. ☎06 39749907. Open Tu-Su 9am-8pm. Groups of 30 admitted every 15min. Admission L10,000. All visits are supervised by a guard who will give you a rather spartan tour in Italian or English. A better bet is the audioguide (L3000). Italian tour with archaeologist L6000. Reservations recommended for all visits: L2000 (L3000 for guided tour).

The recently re-opened Domus Aurea was only a small part of Emperor Nero's residence, which once took up fully one-third of Rome. "Golden House" is something of a misnomer, since this edifice was actually a series of banquet halls and galleries; Nero's private chambers were probably on the Palatine.

Having decided that he was a god, Nero had the architects Severus and Celer design a palace to suit divinity. "Using art and squandering the wealth of the Emperor," writes Tacitus, they created "eccentricities which went against the laws of nature." Between the Oppian and Palatine palaces was an enclosed lake, where the Colosseum now stands, and the Caelian Hill became private gardens. The Forum was reduced to a vestibule of the palace; Nero crowned it with a colossal statue of himself as the sun. Standing 35m tall, it was the largest bronze statue ever made and was justly called the Colossus.

The party didn't last long, however. Nero was forced to commit suicide only five years after building his gargantuan pleasure garden, and his memory was condemned by the Senate. Following suit, the Flavian emperors who succeeded Nero replaced all traces of the palace with monuments built for the public good. The Flavian Baths were built on top of the Caelian Hill, the lake was drained, and the Colosseum was erected. Trajan filled the Domus Aurea with dirt (so that it would make a stronger foundation) and built his baths on top of it in AD 115, and Hadrian covered the western end with his Temple of Venus and Rome in 135. The Domus Aurea itself was rediscovered in the 14th century.

The Domus Aurea was originally built around a large central courtyard, and designed so that the whole building was perpetually illuminated by

Call the USA

"feel free to call"

1-800-COLLECT

When in Ireland
Dial: 1-800-COLLECT (265 5328)

When in N. Ireland, UK & Europe
Dial: 00-800-COLLECT USA (265 5328 872)

sunlight that streamed through skylights and aligned corridors (after all, Nero did fancy himself the sun god). Thanks to Trajan, it's all pitch-black now, though artificial light streams in through aligned floodlights. The best-preserved frescoes are on the ceiling, and that is also where a number of signatures, made with candle-smoke or incised, can be seen. Trajan did not completely fill in the Domus Aurea, and many artists, including Raphael, lowered themselves down into the building with ropes in order to study its artwork. Early archaeologists removed many of the treasures Nero had accumulated during his year of "study" in Greece. Among others, the Laocoön sculpture group and *The Dying Gaul* (now in the **Capitoline Museums,** see p. 152) once graced the Domus Aurea.

The visit begins in a corridor of Trajan's baths, but quickly progresses into the palace itself, meandering through several small rooms before reaching the **Corridor of the Eagles,** notable for the splendid ceiling it once had. While time has taken its toll on the ceiling, fragments of friezes of eagles and vegetation can be made out, as can a central scene thought to be Ariadne after she was abandoned by Theseus.

The tour passes through the **Nymphaeum of Ulysses and Polyphemus,** which was supposed to resemble a natural grotto: fake stalactites and an artificial waterfall were installed. A statue of the Muse Terpsichore was found here, and there is still a pentagonal mosaic of Ulysses and Polyphemus on the ceiling. The next notable sight is the **Golden Vault,** once a sumptuous banquet hall covered in gold leaf. Traces of the precious metal are still visible, but this is also where you can see just how high dirt was piled in the Domus Aurea before its excavation, as there is a huge heap of it in an adjoining room.

Another highlight of the visit is the **Pentagonal Court.** Unfortunately (thanks to good old Trajan, again), only a sliver of it is open, but a fresco high in the upper right-hand corner as you enter the room hints at the majesty of the palace in its heyday. Exiting the Court eventually brings you to the **Room of Achilles at Scyros.** On the ceiling is an image of a cross-dressing Achilles (his father, who had received a prophecy that he would die in the Trojan War, ordered him into drag to avoid it) blowing his cover by eagerly grabbing a spear to amuse himself with instead of a makeup kit. Boys will be boys.

Further down the corridor is the most hyped room in the Domus Aurea, the **Octagonal Room.** Ancient authors had written that Nero's palace was so extravagant that he had a rotating banquet hall that turned throughout the day, and this might have been it. Unfortunately, there is no evidence of the equipment needed to achieve this effect, so a few modern scholars have posited that it was all an optical illusion: the room is, in fact, designed so that sunlight circles its walls throughout the day (sunlight still streams into the room, making it by far the brightest), and this may have made the room appear to spin (especially at the end of a drunken banquet).

Just off the Octagonal Room is the last stop on the tour, the **Room of Hector and Andromache,** notable for its elaborate friezes and vault.

CIRCUS MAXIMUS

🚩 *Walk down V. di San Gregorio from the Colosseum. Always open.*

Cradled in the valley between the Palatine and Aventine hills, the Circus Maximus is today only a grassy shadow of its former glory. This rather plain park was the sight of all the uproar depicted by Charlton Heston in *Ben Hur.* After its construction around 600 BC, more than 300,000 Romans often gathered here to watch the careening of chariots around the quarter-mile track. Obelisks in the arena's center served as distance markers, and the turning points of the track were perilously sharp to ensure enough thrills 'n' spills to keep the crowds happy. The excitement of the chariot races was interspersed with a variety of other competitions ranging from bareback horse-racing to more esoteric events like tent-pegging. Emperors watched from special terraces built onto the Palatine palaces. The Circus may also have been the site of the mythical sea battles that some have attributed to the Colosseum. Nowadays, dogs and toddlers perform great athletic feats such as chasing rubber balls down the grassy banks of the stadium, and you'll find many a game of pick-up soccer here during the warm months. Run the track if you want, but expect a lot of exhaust from the heavy traffic on V. Aventino. Rome's teenagers gathers here at night to bang on drums, smoke rather strange-smelling cigarettes, and generally worry the adults.

FORI IMPERIALI

The sprawling Fori Imperiali lie on either side of V. dei Fori Imperiali, stretching from the Forum to P. Venezia. Excavations that will proceed through summer 2001 mean that the area is closed off, but you can still get excellent, free views by peering over the railing from V. dei Fori Imperiali or V. Alessandrina, which runs diagonally off of V. dei Fori Imperiali. The large conglomeration of temples, basilicas, and public squares was constructed by emperors from the first century BC to the 2nd century AD, partly in response to increasing congestion in the old Forum. The area was excavated in the early 1930s.

FORUM OF CAESAR

On the left-hand side of V. dei Fori Imperiali, just past the Forum as you walk towards P. Venezia. Julius Caesar was the first Roman leader to expand the city center outside the Forum proper, constructing the Forum of Caesar in 46 BC. Caesar's motivations were political: the new forum and temple he built in honor of Venus, his supposed ancestress, seriously undercut the prestige of the Senate and its older precinct around the Curia. The remains of the **Temple of Venus Genetrix** are marked by three columns. Additions from the reign of Trajan include the brick **Basilica Argentaria,** an ancient bank, and the heated public bathroom—the semi-circular room with holes along the walls. Nearby, a replica of a bronze statue of Caesar from his forum has been placed on the sidewalk of V. dei Fori Imperiali for foreign tourists to have their pictures taken with and Italian teenagers to deface.

FORUM OF AUGUSTUS

The first ruins on the right as you walk up V. dei Fori Imperiali toward P. Venezia (although they are better seen from V. Alessandrina, if it is open) are those of the Forum of Augustus, completed in 2 BC. Dedicated by Augustus in honor of *Mars Ultor* (Mars the Avenger), the huge complex commemorated Augustus's vengeful victory over his adoptive father Julius Caesar's murderers, Brutus and Cassius, at the Battle of Philippi in 42 BC. Three columns remain of the **Temple of Mars Ultor,** which was centered upon a statue of Mars (oddly enough, it bore a striking resemblance to a certain avenging Emperor) and lined with statues of Roman history's most important figures. A later copy of the Mars statue can be seen at the Capitoline Museums (see p. 152).

The hefty wall behind the temple, built to protect the precious new monument from the seamy Subura slums that spread up the hill behind it, doesn't run exactly straight. Legend says that when the land was being prepared for construction, even Augustus couldn't convince one stubborn homeowner to give up his domicile, so the great wall was built at an angle around it.

The aptly named **Forum Transitorium** (also called the **Forum of Nerva**) was a narrow, rectangular space connecting Augustus's forum with the old Roman Forum and the forum of Vespatian (near present-day V. Cavour). Most of it now lies under the street, but new excavations have begun to uncover more of it. Although Domitian began it, Emperor Nerva inaugurated the forum in 97, displaying the wit that Roman emperors were known for: he dedicated the temple to "Minerva," the deity whose name was closest to his own. The nerva of some rulers. All that remains to view is a colossal doorway that once led into Vespatian's Forum; between two Corinthian columns is a relief of Minerva and a decorative frieze.

CHURCH OF SANTI COSMA E DAMIANO. The only remnant of **Vespatian's Forum** was built in 527 out of a library in Vespatian's complex. The interior displays a set of 6th-century mosaics including a multi-color Christ with his robes blowing in the wind, made with a realism and flexibility reminiscent of Hellenic skill. *(Near the entrance to the Roman Forum on V. Cavour. Open daily 9am-1pm and 3-7pm.)*

MARKETS OF TRAJAN. Across V. dei Fori Imperiali from the Vittorio Emanuele II monument stand the brick **Markets of Trajan.** The three-floor, semi-circular complex, built during the early 2nd century BC, provides a glimpse of the early Roman shopping malls. Built into the Quirinal Hill, the market had space for 150 shops, selling everything from imported fabrics to tasty Eastern spices. Part of the vast structure housed public administration offices and a stock exchange. The ground- and first-floor rooms of the markets are now home to an impressive, albeit crumbling display of sculpture and statuary from the imperial forum, including two colossal torsos of Nerva and Agrippa and part of a frieze of a griffin. *(Depending on how excavations proceed, it might be possible to visit them. Enter at V. IV Novembre, 94, up the steps in V. Magnanapoli, to the right of the two churches behind Trajan's column. ☎ 06 6790048.)*

FORUM OF TRAJAN

Marked by an imposing column, the Forum of Trajan, the largest, newest, and most impressive of the imperial *fora*, is hard to miss. Built between 107 and 113, the forum was a celebration of Trajan's campaigns in modern-day Romania. The complex included a colossal equestrian statue of Trajan and a triumphal arch. In the back of the forum, the enormous **Basilica Ulpia** once stood in judicial might. The largest basilica ever built in Rome (17m by 60m), the Ulpia is today just two rows of truncated columns and fragments of the friezes.

Pantheon

TRAJAN'S COLUMN. At one end of the decimated forum stands the almost perfectly preserved spiral of Trajan's Column, one of the greatest specimens of Roman relief sculpture ever found. At 40m, it is exactly the same height as the hill leveled in order to build Trajan's Forum. The continuous frieze that wraps around the column narrates the Emperor's campaigns. From the bottom, you can survey Roman legionnaires preparing supplies, building a stockaded camp, and loading boats to cross the Danube. Twenty-five hundred figures in all have been making their way up the column since 113. The statue of their Emperor that crowned the structure in ancient days was destroyed in the Middle Ages and replaced by the figure of St. Peter in 1588. The column survived the 6th and 7th centuries only because Pope Gregory I was so moved by some of the reliefs that he prayed for Trajan's acceptance into heaven. The Pope then claimed that God had come to him in a vision, ensuring Trajan's safe passage but refusing to admit any other pagans. The small holes in the column are actually windows that illuminate an internal staircase. In the column's base is a door that leads to the tomb of Trajan and his wife, where Trajan's ashes rested in a golden urn only to be stolen in the Middle Ages. For a look at a replica of the column, visit **Museo della Civiltà Romana** (see p. 157).

Piazza Colonna

CAPITOLINE HILL

PIAZZA DEL CAMPIDOGLIO

The Capitoline was the smallest of ancient Rome's seven hills, but also the most important and sacred. The highlight of the modern hill is the spectacular P. del Campidoglio, designed by Michelangelo in 1536 (to celebrate the visit of Emperor Charles V) to evoke the hill's ancient glory. To get to the *piazza* from P. Venezia, take **La Cordonata,** the second staircase down V. del Teatro di Marcello. Michelangelo set up the imposing statues of the twin warriors **Castor and Pollux** that flank the wide and gently-sloping staircase, as well as the two reclining river gods and the statue of the goddess Roma. In ancient times, the hill was the site of a gilded temple to Jupiter

Piazza Farnese

BABE *VS.* BAMBINO

Inside the Bufalini Chapel in the **Church of Santa Maria in Aracoeli** resides the world-renowned Santo Bambino, which has been revered for centuries for its mystical, religious healing powers. Letter after letter has come to Rome in prayers and thanks, addressed simply to "Bambino." New York Yankee George Herman Ruth, better known in the baseball world as "Babe," has also been revered for his mystical powers. But the similarities don't end there:

SANTO BAMBINO

Nickname: Bambino.

Born and raised: Jerusalem chapel.

How he got to major city: Tossed from ship in storm.

Appearance: Chubby baby decked out in majestic robes.

Wages: Gifts of gold come in thanks.

Healing powers: Brought to hospitals with promise of cures.

Drinking problem: No.

Saved from Napoleon's troops by large ransom: Yes, once.

What happened to it: Stolen in 1994 and replaced by a copy.

(dedicated in 509 BC); also based on the hill were the state mint, senatorial archives, and the Department of Throwing People off the Capitoline Hill. The northern peak of the hill was home to Juno's sacred geese, which saved the city from ambush by the Gauls in 390 BC by honking so loudly that they woke the populace.

The original form of the hill is almost completely obscured, but it is unlikely that it was as beautiful as Michelangelo's version. To the right and left of P. del Campidoglio stand **Palazzo dei Conservatori** and **Palazzo Nuovo,** home to the **Capitoline Museums** (see p. 152). At the far end, opposite the stairs, lies the turreted **Palazzo dei Senatori** (Rome's city hall).

In the center of the *piazza* stands the famous equestrian statue of **Marcus Aurelius,** brought here from the Lateran Palace. The gilded bronze was one of a handful of ancient bronzes to escape medieval meltdown, and then only because it was thought to be a portrait of Constantine, the first Christian emperor. Unfortunately, both man and steed succumbed to the assault of modern pollution and were removed for restoration in 1981, leaving behind only their pedestal. The Emperor now resides in climate-controlled comfort in the courtyard of the Palazzo Nuovo, and the statue you see now is a weatherproof copy. Across the way, in the courtyard of the Palazzo dei Conservatori, lie the gargantuan foot, head, arm, and kneecap of the statue of Constantine that once graced the Basilica of Maxentius.

On the open side of the *piazza,* rejoin *La Cordonata* to make the descent to P. Venezia. The staircase was designed so that Charles V, apparently penitent over his sack of the city a decade before, could ride his horse up the hill to meet Paul III during his triumphal visit. On the right-hand side of *La Cordonata* stands a dark statue of a hooded man, **Cola di Rienzo,** the leader of a popular revolt in 1347 that attempted to re-establish a Roman Republic. The statue marks the spot where the disgruntled populace tore him limb from limb shortly after electing him first consul.

SANTA MARIA IN ARACOELI. The 7th-century Church of Santa Maria in Aracoeli lies on the site of the Temple to Juno Moneta. "Aracoeli" comes from a medieval legend that Augustus once had a vision of the Virgin Mary, causing him to raise an altar to Heaven *(Ara Coeli)* on the spot she indicated; this explains the rather unusual fresco of Augustus and the Tiburtine Sibyl, in the company of saints and angels. The stunning **Bufalini Chapel** on the left is home to Pinturicchio's Renaissance frescoes of St. Bernardino of Siena. Across the aisle from St. Bernardino is a boarded-up chapel, once the home of the now-purloined **Santo Bambino.** The 3rd chapel on the left houses a beautiful fresco of St. Antonio of Padova, the only one left of a late 15th-century series by Benozzo Gozzoli. *(Climb 124 pilgrims' stairsteps up from the left side of* La Cordonata. *Open daily 9am-6pm.)*

MAMERTINE PRISON. The gloomy Mamertine Prison, consecrated as the **Church of San Pietro in Carcere**, once held St. Peter, who supposedly caused water to flood into his cell and used it to baptize his captors. Although a stairway now leads down to the dank lower chamber, a small hole used to be the only access to the dungeon. The Romans used the lightless lower chamber as a holding cell for prisoners and captives awaiting execution. Inmates were often tortured and occasionally strangled to death in the dark by order of the government. Among the more unfortunate residents were Jugurtha, King of Numidia; Vercingetorix, chieftain of the Gauls; and the accomplices of the dictator Catiline. The prisoners are long gone, but the oldest jail for political prisoners in Rome has kept that delicious musty odor. *(Downhill from Santa Maria in Aracoeli, away from the Campidoglio.* ☎ *06 6792902. Open daily 9am-noon and 2:30-6pm. Donation requested. Audioguide L5000.)*

BATHS OF CARACALLA

The Baths of Caracalla were used continuously from their construction in AD 212 until the Goths cut off the aqueducts that supplied them in the 6th century. They are the largest and best preserved baths in Rome. You might remember their builder, Caracalla, from such sagas as "I killed my brother Geta, took the throne from my father Severus, and scratched Geta's likeness off the arch of Janus and the arch of Septimius Severus."

Although Caracalla wasn't known for his kindly nature, his construction of this monumental complex did do the city some good—some 1500 muddy Romans could sponge themselves off here at the same time (men in the mornings, women in the afternoons, and slaves in the evenings). While the mosaic floors are beautiful, particularly in the *apodyteria* (dressing rooms), it's the sheer magnitude of this proto-health club that boggles the mind. The complex had a central hall opening onto a round, warm swimming pool on one side and a cold pool on the other. Romans would follow a particular regimen for cleaning, beginning with the warm bath, moving from hot *(caldarium)* to cold rooms (the lukewarm *tepidarium* and the cold *frigidarium*), finishing with a dip in the *natatio*, the cold, open-air pool.

The original colorful tile floors are reason enough for the walk around the gigantic *thermae*. Remains of a rectangular brick wall mark the boundary of the ancient gym where Romans played sports, sipped juices, and had their body-hair plucked by special servants. Rome's opera company used to stage Verdi's *Aïda* here, complete with horses and elephants, until it was discovered that, due either to the weight of the animals or the sopranos' voices (perhaps it was the other way around), the performances caused structural damage. *(From the eastern end of Circus Maximus walk up V. delle Terme di Caracalla. Open daily 9am-6pm; in winter 9am-1hr. before sunset. L8000.)*

BABE RUTH

Nickname: Bambino.

Born and raised: Maryland convent.

How he got to major city: Tossed from Red Sox for $100,000.

Appearance: Chubby Babe decked out in pinstripes.

Wages: In 1928, he earned more than the US President.

Healing powers: Brought to hospitals with promise of home runs.

Drinking problem: Oh yeah.

Saved from Napoleon's troops by large ransom: Yes, once.

What happened to him: Died in 1948; replaced as holder of home run record by Hank Aaron in 1974.

VELABRUM

The Velabrum is a low plain west of the Forum and south of the Jewish Ghetto in the shadow of the Capitoline and Palatine hills. The best way to access its sights is to walk down V. Teatro di Marcello (right of the Vittorio Emanuele II monument) from P. Venezia. This flat floodplain of the Tiber was a sacred area for the ancient Romans, and for that reason there are a number of ancient ruins there. It was believed that the mighty Hercules kept his cattle here, and it is also where Aeneas probably first set foot on what was to become Rome. It was also here where baby Romulus and Remus were found by a she-wolf with a ticking biological clock.

During the days of the Republic, the area's proximity to a port on the Tiber made it an ideal spot for the city's cattle and vegetable markets. Civic-minded merchants forested the riverbanks with temples, arches, and a grandiose theater, all dedicated to their gods of trade and commerce. Even after the empire fell, the area remained a busy market center, and medieval Romans continued the dutiful tradition of sacred building.

BOCCA DELLA VERITÀ

The **Church of Santa Maria in Cosmedin,** one of Rome's eternal tourist attractions, was built in the 6th century to serve the local Greek colony. The interior brims with intricate stonework, from the choir enclosure and pulpits to the geometric, marble-inlaid floor. In the walls, you can see embedded Roman columns, which were once part of the *Statio Annonae,* classical Rome's main food distribution center.

The church is interesting, but most people visit for the famous Bocca della Verità in the portico. Originally a drain cover carved as a river god's face, the circular relief was credited with supernatural powers in the Middle Ages, when it was claimed that the hoary face liked to chomp off the fingers of anyone who dared the gods by speaking an untruth while his hand was in its mouth. To keep the superstition alive, the caretaker-priest used to stick a scorpion in the back of the mouth to sting the fingers of suspected fibbers. The Bocca made a cameo in *Roman Holiday;* during the filming, Gregory Peck stuck his hand in the mouth and jokingly hid his hand in his sleeve when he yanked it out, causing Audrey Hepburn to yelp in shock. The scene wasn't scripted, but it worked so well that it was kept in the movie. For more wacky medieval fun, test the honesty of your friends at home with clay replicas of the Bocca that sell for L4000-70,000 in the church gift shop, which also has a 9th-century mosaic of the epiphany on display inside. *(Two blocks south of the Theater of Marcellus along V. Luigi Petroselli. Portico open daily 9am-7pm. Church open daily 10am-1pm and 3-7pm. Byzantine mass Su 10:30am.)*

FORO BOARIO

P. della Bocca della Verità is also the site of the ancient Foro Boario, or cattle market. Its two ancient **temples** are among the best-preserved in Rome. The rectangular **Temple of Portunus,** once known as the Temple of Fortuna Virilis, reveals both Greek and Etruscan influence. The present construction dates from the late 2nd century BC, although there was probably a temple on the site for years before. The **circular temple** next door, thought to be the Temple of Hercules Victor, was once believed to be dedicated to Vesta because of its similarities to the Temple of Vesta in the Forum (p. 80).

CHURCH OF SAN GIORGIO IN VELABRO. A block from Foro Boario, V. del Velabro climbs a short way toward the Capitoline Hill. Behind the hulking **Arch of Janus** (built in the 4th century as a covered market for cattle traders) once stood the little Church of San Giorgio in Velabro. A marvelous edifice, it boasted a 9th-century porch and pillars, a simple early Romanesque interior, and a brick and stone arch *campanile* (bell tower). A terrorist car bombing in 1993 reduced the church's famed portico to a single arch and part of a stone beam. Both the church and the arch are currently undergoing restoration. To the left of the church, the eroded **Arch of the Argentarii** was erected in the 3rd century AD by the *argentarii* (money changers) and cattle merchants who used the *piazza* as a market in honor of Emperor Septimius Severus. Caracalla, Severus' son and successor, rubbed out both his brother Geta's name from this arch (just like the arch next to the Curia in the Forum) and Geta himself.

CHURCH OF CONSOLATION. Here in P. della Consolazione, prisoners in ancient times were given a prayer, a pat on the back, and a "good luck out there," before they were put to death. The Church of Consolation, on the right side of the *piazza*, was once home to an order of monks (equipped humanely with smelling salts and liquor flasks) who were dedicated to giving succor to the condemned and accompanying them on their last mortal journey. *(From P. della Bocca della Verità, take V. G. Decollato one block uphill. Open M-Sa 8am-noon and 3-6pm.)*

THEATER OF MARCELLUS

The Teatro di Marcello was begun by Caesar and finished by Augustus in 13 BC. It is the short, stocky gray structure facing the Tiber, on the right where V. Teatro di Marcello bends to the left. You cannot enter the theater, but excellent views are available from the outside.

Piazza Mattei

The theater bears the name of Augustus's nephew, a potential successor whom he was particularly fond of, and whose early and sudden death remains a mystery. He may have been poisoned by Augustus's wife, Livia, who intended her own son from a previous marriage, Tiberius, to be the next emperor.

The arches and pilasters on the exterior of the theater served as a model for the Colosseum. It represents the classic arrangement of architectural orders, which grows more complex from the ground up: stocky Doric pilasters support the bottom floor, curved Ionic capitals hold up the middle, and elaborate Corinthian columns once crowned the top tier. Vitruvius and other ancient architects called this arrangement the most perfect possible for exterior decoration, inspiring Michelangelo, Bramante, and other Renaissance architects to copy the pattern. Sadly, the perfect exterior is all that remains of the theater, as a succession of medieval families used its seats and stage as the foundation for their fortified castles. The park around the theater is only open for classical concerts on summer nights. See **Entertainment,** p. 176, for more info.

SAN NICOLA IN CARCERE

Campo dei Fiori

The 12th-century church rests on the foundations of three Republican temples, which were originally built and dedicated to the gods Juno, Janus, and Spes (Hope) during the hairy times of the First Punic War. The ancient buildings were converted into a prison during the Middle Ages—hence the name *carcere*, meaning "prison." The only captives in the deserted interior today are well-labeled paintings and restored engravings, including part of the church's original dedication from May 12, 1128. On the right side of the church lies the most well-preserved temple, its Ionic columns scattered on the grass and embedded in the church's wall. The left wall preserves the Doric columns of another temple. The third temple lies buried beneath the little church. *(Across V. Olitorio from the Teatro di Marcello. ☎06 6869972. Call ahead to visit the interior. Open Sept.-July M-Sa 7:30am-noon and 4-7pm.)*

PORTICO D'OTTAVIA

At the bend of V. del Portico d'Ottavia in the Jewish Ghetto, a shattered pediment and five ivy-covered columns in the shadow of the Theater of Marcellus are all that remain of the

Church of Sant'Agnese in Agone

once magnificent Portico d'Ottavia, one of Augustus's grandest contributions to Rome's architecture. Built by Quintus Metellus in 149 BC, it was revamped and imperially restyled by Augustus, who dedicated it to his sister Octavia in 23 BC. The portico was a rectangular enclosure sheltering temples to Jupiter and Juno, some libraries, and public rooms adjunct to the Theater of Marcellus next door. The Romans stuck many of their imported Greek masterpieces here, including the famous Mèdici Venus, now in Florence's Uffizi. She was later rediscovered under the crumbling detritus and refuse that had accumulated on the site thanks to the ravages of a nearby fish market. In fact, a church was built into its wall in 755 (see p. 106)

TEMPLE OF APOLLO SOSIANUS. Through the fence to the right of the Portico are the polished white columns of the Temple of Apollo Sosianus. The area around the temple, behind the Theater of Marcellus, has been closed in recent years, but should be reopened by 2001. Although it dates back to 433 BC, the dilapidated temple needed a little nip and tuck after centuries of neglect. So in 34 BC, Gaius Sosius rebuilt the temple and attached his own name to it. The three Corinthian columns support a well-preserved frieze of bulls' skulls and floral garlands. The temple's ornate original 5th-century Greek pediment is visible in the Montemartini Museum (see p. 158).

CENTRO STORICO

This sprawling maze of ancient streets and alleys—the historic center of Rome—brims with dim Baroque churches, cramped picture galleries, ancient ruins, and vast *piazze*. V. del Corso, running from P. Venezia nearly a mile north to P. del Popolo, forms a rough eastern boundary of the Centro Storico; the Tiber is its boundary to the West.

see map p. 314–315

PIAZZA VENEZIA & VIA DEL CORSO

VITTORIO EMANUELE II MONUMENT. Also known as the *Vittoriano* or "Mussolini's typewriter," this colossal confection of gleaming white marble dominates both P. Venezia, and many views of the city. It is a memorial to king Vittorio Emanuele II of the House of Savoia (under whom Italy was first united) begun in 1885, the day after his death. Often dubbed "the wedding cake," this awesome monolith stands at the north face of the Capitoline Hill. At the top of the staircase on the exterior is the *Altare della Patria* (Altar of the Fatherland), which has an eternal flame guarded night and day by two members of the armed forces. Behind it is the **Tomb of the Unknown Soldier**, and above is an impressive equestrian bronze of the man of honor. The only part of the monument open to the public is its tiny military museum (see **Sacrario delle Bandiere,** p. 160).

PALAZZO DI VENEZIA. This building, on the left as you stand with your back to the *Vittoriano*, is the oldest extant example (begun in 1455) of a Renaissance Roman *palazzo*, as evidenced by its plain, battlemented facade, which shows a healthy attachment to the Middle Ages. It housed the embassy of the Venetian Republic from 1564 to 1797 and later the French and Austrian embassies. Mussolini later made the building his personal residence and seat of the Fascist Grand Council, and delivered some of his most famous speeches from its balcony. It is now home to the **Museo Nazionale del Palazzo Venezia,** which has temporary exhibits and a small permanent collection (see p. 161). Walk inside (around the corner, on V. del Plebiscito) to take a look at the garden.

BASILICA OF SAN MARCO. This church, whose *loggie* date from the Renaissance, is dedicated to the patron saint of Venice, and served as Palazzo Venezia's chapel. Parts of the foundation, however, can be traced to 336, when the church was founded by a Pope Mark quite fond of his namesake saint. Inside the dark church, Melazzo da Forli's *San Marco Evangelista* hangs in the chapel to the right of the altar. The 829 mosaic in the apse depicts Christ and Pope Gregory IV holding a model of the recently restored church. Historical note: Christ was not alive when this church was restored, and he never even met Pope Gregory IV, rendering this painting improbable. On the right wall of the beautiful Renaissance portico, you'll find the funerary inscription of Vannozza Cattanei, mistress of Borgia Pope Alexander VI and mother of his well-known and well-behaved children Cesare and Lucrezia. *(In the same building as Palazzo Venezia, in the end towards the Vittorio Emanuele II monument. Open daily 8:30am-noon and 4-7pm. Enter from P. di San Marco, toward the Vittorio Emanuele monument.)*

BASILICA DEI SANTI APOSTOLI. Tucked in the corner of the *piazza*, this church was built in the 15th century for Pope Martin V. It has an arcaded portico with sculptures both above and below. If you're brave enough to get past the lions guarding the entrance, you'll be able to marvel at the imperial eagle, a scary 2nd-century Roman relief, and the largest altarpiece in Rome. In the same block is the **Galleria Colona** (see p. 158). *(One block up V. C. Battisti toward Termini from P. Venezia in P. S. Apostoli. Open daily 7am-noon and 4-7pm.)*

IL GESÙ

🌓 *Two blocks down from P. Venezia on the left. Open daily 6am-12:30pm and 4-7:15pm. Private apartments: P. del Gesù, 45. Open M-Sa 4-6pm and Su 10am-noon.*

The imposing and sumptuous Il Gesù is the principal Jesuit church in Rome, and one of the richest in the city. Its construction was decreed in 1540 by St. Ignatius Loyola, founder of the Jesuit order. The hardest of the hardcore Catholics of the Counter Reformation, they were brought into existence under the papacy of Paul III to combat the growing influence of Protestantism. The objective of the Jesuits was more or less to go out and conquer the world (for Christ), with a complex battery of missionary expeditions, propaganda, and political influence. The church was begun in 1568 by Jacopo Barozzi and completed in 1577 by Giacomo della Porta (who drew from some of Michelangelo's designs for St. Peter's, including the paired pilasters).

Architecturally, Il Gesù became the standard for Baroque churches. It exemplifies the spirit of the Counter Reformation: the dour travertine facade was designed to create a wide single nave inside, the better to accommodate the hordes of faithful common folk and firmly direct their attention ahead to the altar and towering dome. This departure from the Greek-cross plan was deliberate; according to the Council of Trent, the churches of the Renaissance had subordinated the priest and his altar from their place at the "head" of the church.

The interior is lavishly ornate: on the ceiling of the nave, Il Baciccia's celebrated fresco, *Triumph in the Name of Jesus*, uses spectacular perspective to make it seem as if the figures are springing forth from the ceiling. The large monogram "IHS" in the apse is the Jesuits' device and represents the first three letters of Jesus' name in Greek. Be sure not to miss Bernini's statue of St. Robert Bellarmine.

Look to the left of the dome for the most gold you've ever seen, anywhere: the enormous **Cappella di Sant'Ignazio di Loyola** is dedicated to the founder of the order, who lies under the ornate altar of bronze, marble, and lapis lazuli. Next door to the church, St. Ignatius's old **apartments** contain artifacts and paintings.

PIAZZE DEL COLLEGIO ROMANO & SANT'IGNAZIO

🌓 *V. Lata, two blocks up V. del Corso from P. Venezia on the left, leads into P. del Collegio Romano. P. di Sant'Ignazio is one block off V. del Corso on V. del Caravita (four blocks up from P. Venezia).*

PALAZZO DORIA PAMPHILJ. P. del Collegio Romano's stalwart *palazzo* harbors the extensive art collection of the **Galleria Doria Pamphilj** (see p. 158). It was built in the late 15th century by the Doria-Pamphilj family, who inhabit it to this day. Although their part of the building is off-limits, you can get a good look at one of the *palazzo*'s former inhabitants in the museum, where a saint's body lies in a glass case in the chapel.

CHURCH OF SAN MARCELLO AL CORSO. This church is the site where the aggressive tribune Cola di Rienzo hung for two days and nights in 1345 before being taken to the Augusteum and burned. *(Across V. del Corso from Palazzo Doria Pamphilj, opposite V. Lata. Open M-Sa 7:15am-12:30pm and 4:30-7pm, Su 8:30am-noon and 4-7pm; Sept.-June closed Su.)*

CHURCH OF SANT'IGNAZIO DI LOYOLA. This Jesuit church (begun in 1582 and brought to its present state in 1685) contains Andrea Pozzo's *trompe l'oeil* fresco, *The Triumph of St. Ignatius*, along the vault of the great, aisle-less nave. Taking his inspiration from Michelangelo's Sistine ceiling and its intricate, logic-defying architecture, Pozzo went one step further. Instead of the Sistine's flat central scenes, the figures on Pozzo's ceiling exist in the same space as the architecture, and the painter's mastery of perspective makes their foreshortened forms seem to float in the air above the nave. The church was originally meant to have a grandiose dome, like the one in Il Gesù, Sant'Ignazio's sister church (see p. 95), but the Jesuits ran out of money during the initial construction. Pozzo saved the altar from domelessness by painting the deceptively realistic *trompe l'oeil* cupola on the flat ceiling of the unfinished drum. *(In P. Sant'Ignazio. Open daily 7:30am-12:30pm and 4-7:15pm.)*

PIAZZA COLONNA

COLUMN OF MARCUS AURELIUS. Another seven blocks up the Corso is P. Colonna, named for the massive column that dominates it. The monument was erected after Marcus Aurelius' death in AD 180 (contrary to *Gladiator*, he was not murdered by Commodus), and commemorates his victories over the barbarian tribes of the Danube, although the reliefs depict earlier wars against the Germans and Sarmatians. Unfortunately for poor old Marcus Aurelius, those earlier wars didn't really go all that well. Trajan, who had a column of his own set up in 113 (see p. 88) had expanded the Empire to its farthest boundaries, making it a little unmanageable; Aurelius had to spend much of his time fending off barbarian attacks. Things actually got so bad that one of his armies was defeated in battle—the first time a Roman army had been defeated in over 300 years. One can only assume that, if he had actually had a Spanish general named Maximus in his army, things would have gone better for old Marcus Aurelius. Unless you're 90 ft. tall or can fly, the best way to get a look at the column reliefs is to go see the plaster casts of them at the **Museo della Civiltà Romana,** in EUR (p. 157). By the way, the statue on top of the column is not Marcus Aurelius, but rather St. Paul. It was placed there by Pope Sixtus V in the 16th century.

PALAZZI. On the western side of the *piazza* (away from the Corso), **Palazzo Wedekind** (home to the newspaper *Il Tempo*) was built in 1838 with Roman columns from the Etruscan city of Veio. Check out the magnificent clock supported by four strange human figures. **Palazzo Chigi,** built in the 16th and 17th centuries and now the official residence of the Prime Minister, forms the north side of the *piazza.* Guards with really big guns prevent public entrance, but you can look through into the courtyard.

OTHER SIGHTS. Colonna's northwest corner flows into P. di Montecitorio, dominated by Bernini's **Palazzo Montecitorio,** seat of the Chamber of Deputies. The 6th-century BC obelisk in front of the *palazzo* was brought from Egypt to serve as a sundial in Augustus's *Ara Pacis* complex (see p. 88). Running just off P. Colonna to the south, V. Bergamaschi leads to **Piazza di Pietra,** where the remaining pieces of the **Temple of Hadrian** (dedicated to the emperor in 145 by his son, Antonius Pius) serve as part of the facade of the **Palazzo della Borsa** (the now-defunct stock exchange). Ah, progress.

PIAZZA DELLA ROTONDA

Simple, erect, severe, austere, sublime—
Shrine of all saints and temple of all gods,
From Jove to Jesus—spared and blessed by time;
Looking tranquillity, while falls or nods
Arch, empire, each thing round thee, and man plods
His way through thorns to ashes—glorious dome!
Shalt thou not last? Time's scythe and tyrants' rods
Shiver upon thee—sanctuary and home
Of art and piety—Pantheon!—pride of Rome!
    —George Gordon, Lord Byron, *Childe Harolde*

In the middle of P. della Rotunda, among the hordes of tourists and McDonald's patrons gawking at the Pantheon, Giacomo della Porta's late-Renaissance fountain supports an **Egyptian obelisk.** The phallic monolith was added in the 18th century, when obelisks—popular among ancient Romans—came back into fashion. Sometimes an obelisk is just an obelisk.

PANTHEON

⬤ *In P. della Rotonda. Open June M-Sa 9am-7pm, Su 9am-1pm; July-Aug. M-Sa 9am-7:30pm, Su 9am-1pm; Oct.-May M-Sa 9am-4pm, Su 9am-1pm. Free.*

Piazza del'Orlogio

Originally dedicated to all the gods (the name derives from the Greek *pan*—"all"—and *theos*—"god"), the Pantheon has stood for nearly 2000 years, with its granite columns, pediment, and soaring domed interior remarkably the same as the day it was erected, save superficial decorative alterations. Centuries of active Christian neglect toward other pagan monuments in Rome almost never affected the Pantheon. In fact, Emperor Phocas gave it to Pope Boniface IV in 606 and it was consecrated as the **Church of Santa Maria ad Martyres,** its official name to this day. Masses are held every Sunday. The Pantheon contains several important tombs: Raphael's final resting place, the 3rd chapel on the right, is decorated by Raphael's beautiful *Madonna del Sasso*, which was commissioned by Lorenzetto. Three members of the Italian royal family are also buried here: King Vittorio Emanuele II (2nd chapel on the right) and King Umberto I and his wife Margherita (2nd on the left). The real attraction, though, is the building itself.

HISTORY. Hadrian, who fancied himself some kind of mad genius, was responsible for its construction between AD 118 and 125 (on the site of a 26 BC temple that had served the same purpose); some argue that he designed the building himself—an uncertain and unlikely claim, even though he is credited with the revolutionary design of the Temple of Venus and Rome in the Forum (see p. 81), the sprawling Villa Adriana at Tivoli, and his own mausoleum (Castel Sant'Angelo; p. 119).

Bar da Benito

Following its transformation from pagan temple to Christian church in 606, the Pantheon weathered the Middle Ages with few losses, although it sometimes moonlighted as a fortress and even a fish market (the spotty low holes on the interior walls are marks from the wooden stands vendors built right into the structure). Later artists and architects adored and imitated the building. It served as the inspiration for countless Renaissance and Neoclassical edifices, including Washington, DC's Jefferson Memorial. Michelangelo, who used the Pantheon as a model for St. Peter's Basilica, is said to have designed his own dome about 2m shorter in diameter, out of respect for his ancient model. The 17th century wasn't quite so deferential: when Barberini Pope Urban VIII melted down the bronze door (which has since been replaced), the bronze eagle that adorned the tympanum, and other elements to make cannons for Castel Sant'Angelo (as well as the *Baldacchino* of St. Peter's), horrified Romans remonstrated: "What the barbarians didn't do, the Barberini did."

EXTERIOR. The traditional triangular pediment, inscribed dedication, and Corinthian columns of the exterior are all designed to deceive the first-time visitor into expecting an

Marcus Aurelius

equally traditional interior: in fact, the only purpose of the large rectangular brick element that rises behind the pediment is to hide the dome from the view of those approaching (this effect worked better in the days of the Roman Empire, when the level of the surrounding *piazza* was some seven meters lower and the temple had to be approached by a staircase). The inscription across the frieze on the facade is deceptive too: "M[arcus] Agrippa L[uci] f[ilius] co[n]s[ul] tertium fecit," meaning "Marcus Agrippa, son of Lucius, made this in his 3rd consulship." This refers to the earlier temple, which Hadrian tore down after a fire in AD 117. He presumably had the old inscription copied here to avoid accusations of overweaning pride.

DOME. All modesty was left at the door. Even if you have spotted the dome from outside, the central *oculus* (the big hole in the ceiling), comes as a shock. The dome itself has a radius and a height of 21.3m, making it a perfect half-sphere, and its base is 21.3m above the floor. The dome was constructed entirely out of poured concrete in a series of rings decreasing in thickness and weight, without supporting vaults, arches, or ribs. The dome is the largest ever covered in masonry, a fact that has perplexed centuries of archaeologists and architects, who still can't figure out how the thing was actually erected. The 9m *oculus* provides the only source of light. The sunlight that enters via the *oculus* was originally used to mark time on a sundial, but one of the most interesting times to visit the Pantheon is during a rainstorm, when water falls in the center of the floor in a perfect circle.

PIAZZA DELLA MINERVA

ELEFANTINO. A cute little monument marks the center of this tiny *piazza:* a statue of a baby elephant known as the Elefantino, or **Pulcin della Minerva.** Crafted by Bernini, it supports a 6th-century BC Egyptian obelisk. The monument was set up in 1667, in honor of Pope Alexander VI. The gist of the inscription is that it takes a strong mind (the elephant, which is symbolic of Alexander's mind) to support wisdom (the obelisk).

CHURCH OF SANTA MARIA SOPRA MINERVA. The gleaming white Church of Santa Maria Sopra Minerva was built on top of a temple incorrectly attributed to Minerva, Goddess of Wisdom. Begun by the Dominicans in 1280, this is the only Gothic church in all of Rome, although the simple exterior, which was redone in the 19th century, does not belie it. To the right of the entrance, six plaques mark the high-water levels of Tiber floods over the centuries. The interior is pure Gothic, and spangled with colored shadows from the beautiful stained glass windows. To the left of the high altar is Michelangelo's 1520 sculpture, **Christ the Redeemer.** The chapels on the right house a number of treasures as well, including (in the 5th) a panel of the *Annunciation* by Antoniazzo Romano, a pupil of Pinturicchio. The last chapel in the south transept is the **Carafa Chapel,** which is decorated by a brilliant fresco cycle depicting the life of St. Thomas Aquinas by Fra Filippo Lippi. The altar of many a church in Rome houses a holy relic, and Santa Maria Sopra Minerva has a great one—the body of St. Catherine of Siena, the famous 14th-century ascetic and church reformer who died in a house nearby. To the left of the altar, another medieval great, the painter-saint Fra Angelico, lies under a tomb surrounded by a bronze-leaved fence. *(Open M-Sa 7am-7pm, Su 7am-1pm and 3:30-7pm.)*

PIAZZA SAN LUIGI DEI FRANCESI

CHURCH OF SAN LUIGI DEI FRANCESI. The simple and sooty Church of San Luigi dei Francesi serves as the French National Church in Rome (Bastille Day is celebrated in the *piazza*) and is home to three of **Caravaggio**'s most famous ecclesiastical masterpieces. The flamboyant artist decorated the last chapel on the left, dedicated to the evangelist St. Matthew, between 1597 and 1602. The *Calling of St. Matthew*, to the left of the chapel's altar, is the most famous piece, but *St. Matthew and the Angel*, in the center, and the *Crucifixion of St. Matthew*, to the right, are also breathtaking. You must pay L200 to shed light on the works, or it'll be impossible to see anything. Note Caravaggio's revolutionary attention to everyday detail and his refusal to idealize what he saw: while his Baroque compatriots were busy painting saccharine Madonnas on pastel clouds, Caravaggio didn't hesitate to imbue even biblical scenes with the dark and dirty atmosphere of his own day. Not surprisingly, Caravaggio's warts-and-all portraiture wasn't always pleasing to his patrons. His first rendition of *St. Matthew and the Angel*, in which an angel helps the aged saint compose his Gospel, was an example of his relentless effort to make the most legendary scenes seem real to viewers. The chapel's patrons, on seeing the work, cried foul and demanded a more respectful treatment of the subject, which you can see hanging over the altar. *(One block down V. del Salvatore from C. Rinascimento as it passes P. Navona. Open F-W 7:30am-12:30pm and 3:30-7pm, Th 7:30am-12:30pm.)*

CHURCH OF SANT'IVO. The otherworldly Church of Sant'Ivo exhibits its famous corkscrew cupola over the Palazzo della Sapienza, the original home of the University of Rome. Founded by Pope Sixtus IV in the 15th century, the palace now houses a branch of the state archives. The entrance (around the corner at C. del Rinascimento, 40) provides the best view of Borromini's intricate facade and cupola, designed in 1660 and recently restored. *(One block down V. Dogana Vecchia from S. Luigi dei Francesi; turn right as you exit the church. Open daily 9am-noon.)*

PIAZZA NAVONA AND ENVIRONS

My Piazza Navona doesn't give a damn
about either St. Peter's or Piazza di Spagna.
This isn't a *piazza*, it's an open field,
a theater, a fair, a happy home.
—Giuseppe Giacomo Belli, *Piazza Navona*

This famous and fashionable *piazza* is north of C. Vittorio Emanuele II, best reached by walking three blocks up C. del Rinascimento from P. S. Andrea della Valle and turning left. The *piazza* was once a marketplace, and is still filled with merchants hawking their wares, although these days you're more likely to find caricaturists and tiny cherub lighters than produce and livestock. Artists and street performers descend on the area in the evenings, drawing eager crowds whose size is often quite out of proportion with the quality of the acts. Meanwhile, pickpockets ply their trade in the shadow of Navona's three fountains, while customers of the expensive *enoteche* and restaurants nearby do their best to look like jaded sophisticates, even while shooing away rose-selling *vu cumpràs*. It's hustle. It's bustle. For better or worse, it's Rome.

HISTORY. Navona's oblong shape is due to its past as a stadium built by Domitian in AD 86. You can still see some of the stadium's foundations in P. Tor Sanguigna, immediately outside the northern end of Piazza Navona. Contrary to popular belief, Domitian never used his 30,000-person venue to shred Christians; it was a racetrack—he had other *piazze* for shredding Christians. From its opening day, the stadium witnessed daily contests of strength and agility: wrestling matches, javelin and discus tosses, foot and chariot races, and even mock naval battles. For the sea-faring fracas, the stadium was flooded and filled with fleets of ships skippered by convicts. These days the only water is in the fountains, and the best shows you'll see are a guy who uses his fingers as dancing puppets. If seeing the ruins give you a craving for ancient sculpture, continue north to **Museo Nazionale Romano Palazzo Altemps** (p. 156).

As the Empire fell, real-life battles with marauding Goths replaced staged contests, the stadium fell into disuse, and resourceful Romans used its crumbling outer walls as foundations for new houses. Large crowds returned to the *piazza* when the space hosted the city's general market from 1477 to 1869. Festivals and jousts were commonplace, as was the contest of the *Cuccagna*, in which contestants shimmied up a greased pole to win fabulous prizes. These days, the market, selling beautifully crafted porcelain *presepi* (nativity scenes), marzipan fruit, and *Befane* of every size, comes to the *piazza* only from Christmas until Epiphany (Jan. 6). Legitimate portrait artists and less legitimate caricaturists, however, roost here year-round, as do multilingual fortune tellers.

Navona owes much of its existence to a case of pure oneupsmanship. Innocent X, the Pamphilj Pope who came to the papal throne in 1644, was eager to distract the Roman people from the achievements of his predecessor, the ubiquitous Barberini Urban VIII. Innocent cleared out the old stadium (where his family had had a palace for centuries) and set about constructing a new *piazza* and palace to rival those of the Barberini family across town (see **Piazza Barberini,** p. 111). If Innocent were alive today, you can be sure that not only would Piazza Navona have a Planet Hollywood like P. Barberini, but it would be bigger and better.

FOUNTAIN OF THE FOUR RIVERS. The towering, rippling bodies in Bernini's famous Fountain of the Four Rivers *(Fontana dei Quattro Fiumi)* command the center of the *piazza* with the grandeur that Innocent intended. In an effort to sabotage his nemesis, the Pope managed to divert the flow of a previously repaired channel, which had been supplying the Fontana del Tritone in Piazza Barberini. Having stolen old Urban's thunder, Innocent commissioned Bernini to make something impressive out of it, and the artist responded with this impressive work. Each of the river gods represents one of the four continents of the globe (as they were thought of then): the Ganges for Asia, the Danube for Europe, the Nile for Africa (veiled, since the source of the river was unknown), and the Rio de la Plata for the Americas.

According to legend, Bernini designed the Nile and Plata statues to shield their eyes from his arch-rival Borromini's Church of San Agnese in Agone. The rivalry continued when Borromini made his statue of St. Agnes perched on top of the church to look out beyond the *piazza*, not deigning to drop her gaze onto Bernini's work. At least half of the story seems to be a sham, however, since the fountain was finished in 1651, before Borromini had even started work on the church.

OTHER FOUNTAINS. At the southern end of the *piazza*, the **Fontana del Moro** attracts pigeons and small children alike. Originally designed by Giacomo della Porta in the 16th century—Bernini renovated it in 1653 and added Il Moro—the central figure perches precariously on a mollusk while struggling with a fish. The tritons around the edge of the fountain were moved to the Giardino del Lago in the Villa Borghese in 1874 and replaced by copies. Balancing the whole scene is the **Fountain of Neptune,** flowing in the north end of the *piazza*. It too was designed by della Porta and spruced up by Bernini, but was without a central figure until 1878, when Antonio della Bitta added the Neptune.

CHURCH OF SANT'AGNESE IN AGONE. According to legend, in ancient times St. Agnes rebuffed the advances of the lascivious son of a magistrate and was stripped naked in Domitian's stadium as punishment. Miraculously, her hair instantly grew to cover her shameful nudity. Unhappy with this miracle, her persecutors tried to burn her at the stake. When the flames didn't even singe her, the efficient Diocletian decided to cut her head clean off. It worked. The church marks the spot where she was nearly exposed and houses her severed skull (referred to as the *Sacra Testa,* or Holy Head) in its sacristy. Girolomo and Carlo Rainaldi reconstructed the run-down church in 1652, but it was Francesco Borromini who orchestrated the exterior, with its soaring dome embraced by twin bell towers. *(On the western side of P. Navona, opposite the Fontana dei Quattro Fiumi. Open Tu-Sa 4:30-7pm, Su 10am-1pm.)*

PIAZZA SANT'AGOSTINO

The simple Renaissance facade of the **Church of Sant'Agostino** is a sharp contrast to its ornate interior; its 15th-century design was augmented by layers of Baroque and Rococo stucco and frippery. Keep an eye out for Raphael's shiny *Prophet Isaiah,* painted on the 3rd pillar of the left aisle. For L200, you can turn on the lights to see the detail of Caravaggio's shadowy *Madonna of the Pilgrims,* in the first chapel on the left. *(From P. Navona, take V. Agonale north; bear right into P. di S. Apollinare, then immediately left into P. S. Agostino. Open daily 7:45am-noon and 4:30-7:30pm.)* The Rococo **Church of Sant'Antonio dei Portoghesi** is the Portuguese National Church in Rome. Its interior is all shine: electric bulbs highlight the copious clusters of gilt throughout the church. *(From P. S. Agostino, walk up V. dei Pianellari. Open daily 9am-noon and 4-6pm.)*

SANTA MARIA DELLA PACE

CHURCH OF SANTA MARIA DELLA PACE. To enter the church, pass through **Bramante's cloisters** (1504). Originally built in 1480, the church's facade received a facelift from the imaginative Baroque architect da Cortona in 1656, giving it a charming semi-circular porch and making it so popular among Rome's upper crust that the *piazza* became jammed with the carriages of devout patricians. It was only in the 19th century that the *piazza* was expanded, a development so popular that a Latin inscription was put up declaring that no stone in the *piazza* could ever be moved.

The Chigi chapel (first on the right) is decorated by **Raphael**'s *The Sybils*. The painting of the Virgin over the altar supposedly bled when hit by a stone in the 15th century; the church was built in commemoration. *(From P. Navona, take V. di Sant'Agnese in Agone (V. Tor Millina), then turn right on V. della Pace. Open daily 8am-noon and 3:30-7pm.)*

CHURCH OF SANTA MARIA DELL'ANIMA. The unassuming German National Church in Rome hides a fragrant courtyard and a spookily deserted, dark interior. Keep an eye out for the bizarre skull-cherub reliefs everywhere and the smooth imitation of Michelangelo's *Pietà*. *(V. della Pace, 20. Across from S. Maria della Pace. Open M-F 8am-7pm, Sa 8am-6pm, Su 8am-1pm and 3-7pm. Ring the bell to get in.)*

Piazza del Poppolo

VIA DEL GOVERNO VECCHIO

V. del Governo Vecchio runs west from the southern end of P. Navona, and is best known for its art and antique galleries and restaurants (see p. 185). The street, which heads west to the Vatican, used to be a papal thoroughfare, lined with the townhouses of prosperous bankers and merchants.

PIAZZA PASQUINO. Here, at the beginning of the road, a misshapen figure is all that remains of poor Pasquino, an ancient Roman bust that has been used as a a *statua parlante* or "talking statue" (basically a communal bitch-board) ever since Cardinal Caraffa put him here in 1501. Irate citizens are free to cover Pasquino with their complaints about government, the church, or just about anything else. Though in earlier times people wrote directly onto the statue, nowadays signs and posters are taped to it.

Mausoleum of Augustus

PIAZZA DELL'OROLOGIO. Further down the street, Borromini's Baroque clock tower stands guard—when it's not shrouded in scaffolding. Don't miss the beautiful Virgin supported by cherubs carved into the rear corner of the oratory below the clock tower. Beyond P. dell'Orologio, V. del Governo Vecchio becomes V. dei Banchi Nuovi, and ends in P. Banco di Santo Spirito. In the 15th century, the *via* and *piazza* made up a banking district that attracted moguls from all over Italy. Not only did they change and hoard money here, they also acted as bookies, taking bets on anything from sporting events to papal behavior. (The "pope eating a baby" 300 to 1 longshot was never cashed in.) The **Palazzo di Banco di Santo Spirito** was a working mint until 1541, and now functions as a regular bank, despite the fact that its ornate facade is crumbling and sprouting weeds. The dank little **Arco dei Banchi**, on the left down V. di S. Spirito toward the Tiber, houses a Virgin and lamp to which Catholic passers-by say a quick Hail Mary. Just inside the entrance and to the left, the arch shows the height of the 1277 flood.

Villa Mèdici

CHIESA NUOVA

⏵ Bus #64. Seven blocks down C. V. Emanuele II from P. Sant'Andrea della Valle. Church open daily 8am-noon and 4:30-7pm.

Originally founded in the 12th century as Santa Maria in Vallicella, Chiesa Nuova became the home base for Philip Neri's congregation of Counter-Reformation Oratorians. He remodeled the church in 1605, calling it the "new church" (it was further restored in the 19th century). During construction, the future St. Philip had a vision of the Virgin rescuing churchgoers by supporting a collapsing section of the old church; inspection of the beams proved that they were indeed about to fall apart. Pietro da Cortona represented this mini-miracle in a 1644 ceiling painting; da Cortona was also responsible for much of the other art in the interior, excluding the early **Peter Paul Rubens** paintings (1606-1608) above the altar. The chapel on the left holds the remains of St. Philip Neri and is decorated with bronze, marble, mother-of-pearl, and gold.

Next door is the 17th-century **Palazzo dei Filippini,** complete with the Borromini-designed Oratorio dei Fillippini, a mix of convex and concave surfaces for which the geometrically-minded architect is famous.

CAMPO DEI FIORI

Two blocks south of C. V. Emanuele II (on P. della Cancelleria or V. del Paradiso) stands Rome's most schizophrenic *piazza*, **Campo dei Fiori**, a bustling marketplace during the day that turns into a bustling meatmarket of drunken young foreigners when the sun goes down (see p. 204). Until papal rule ended in 1869, the area was the site of countless executions. In the middle of the Campo, a statue commemorates the death its most famous victim: **Giordano Bruno** (1548-1600), who rises above the bustle with his arms folded over a book. Scientifically and philosophically out of sync with his time, Bruno sizzled at the stake in 1600 for taking Copernicus one step further: he argued that the universe had no center at all. Now the only carcasses that litter the *piazza* are those of the fish in the colorful **market.** (Open Sunday 6am-2pm.)

NEAR CAMPO DEI FIORI

PALAZZO DELLA CANCELLERIA. An imposing stone coat of arms marks this early Renaissance *palazzo*. Designed in 1485, it impressed an array of popes and cardinals who affixed their insignia to it. The building's designer remains unknown, but its unprecedented size and style have led the optimistic to suspect Bramante. While Bramante may not have had anything to do with the building itself, his fingerprints are all over the **court-yard,** which is ringed by three stories of *loggie* supported by Doric columns and resembles his restoration of the adjoining **Basilica of San Lorenzo in Damaso.** Today, the Cancelleria is the seat of the three Tribunals of the Vatican and is legally considered part of the Vatican City. *(Just down P. della Cancelleria from the Campo and around the corner to the left on C. Vittorio Emanuele II. Open daily 7am-noon and 5-8:30pm; in winter 7am-noon and 4:30-8pm. No admittance beyond the courtyard.)*

THEATER OF POMPEY. Walk out of Campo dei Fiori on Passetto del Biscione and make your first right at V. di Grotta Pinta, a canyon of curved *palazzi* built over the remains of the semi-circular Theater of Pompey. Pompey the Great, one of the power-hungry generals of the first century BC, competed with his rival Julius Caesar in both war and peace. When Caesar's popular victories in Gaul became too galling, the pompous Pompey built a grandiose theater, the first of its kind in the city. Unfortunately, the prudish Senate had outlawed permanent theaters because they feared they would corrupt public morals. To outwit the censors, Pompey built a small shrine at the top of the stands and called the whole complex a temple. Though Caesar bested Pompey politically, in a certain sense the old general still got the last laugh: it was in Pompey's portico, built to surround his sumptuous theater, that Caesar was assassinated on the Ides of March, 44 BC. A note to archaeology nuts: on the back side of the theater on V. del Biscione, two restaurants, **Ristorante San Pancrazio** and **Ristorante da Costanza,** have basement dining rooms built out of the theater's substructure.

CHURCH OF SAN CARLO AI CATINARI. Built from 1612 to 1620 by Rosato Rosati, its facade draws on the architecture of the Counter Reformation. Its Greek-cross interior was influenced by Domenichino, Lanfranco, and da Cortona. *(Turn right from V. di Grotta Pinta onto V. dei Chiavar and then left on V. dei Giubbonari. Open daily 6:30am-noon and 4:30-7pm.)*

PALAZZO MASSIMO "ALLE COLONNE". Just across C. Vittorio Emanuele II from P. della Cancelleria in P. S. Pantaleo, this *palazzo* was built by Baldassar Peruzzi in 1527 and is home to a family that traces its origins all the way back to the Roman general Fabius Maximus (hence "Massimo") Cunctator, who kept Hannibal from capturing Rome in the late 3rd century B.C. The *palazzo* has a curved exterior because it rests on the foundations of Domitian's ancient Odeon theater. Behind the *palazzo*, a solitary column remains from the ancient edifice. The back wall of the palace preserves a cycle of 16th-century monochrome paintings; most houses in Rome once boasted such intricate decoration, but few have resisted the assaults of wind and rain as well as this one. Also in P. S. Pantaleo, is the 1216 **Church of San Pantaleo.** Giuseppe Valadier added the strange facade in 1806. *(Open for mass M-Sa 7:30am and 7:15pm, Su 7:30 and 11:30am, and 7:15pm.)*

PALAZZO DELLA FARNESINA AI BAULLARI. Just across C. Vittorio Emanuele II from Palazzo Massimo, this little *palazzo*, also known as the **Piccola Farnesina**, holds its own against the Campo's other stunning *palazzi*. Built in 1523 by Antonio da Sangallo the Younger for Thomas Leroy, an English diplomat, it got its name from a case of mistaken identity. Leroy's brilliant career in Rome was rewarded when he was made a nobleman and given special permission to add the lily of France to his coat of arms. The lilies were mistaken for the flowers that represent the Farnese family. The 19th-century interior houses the **Museo Barracco**'s Greek, Roman, Egyptian, and Assyrian art (see p. 158).

PIAZZA FARNESE

PALAZZO FARNESE. One block southwest of Campo dei Fiori on V. dei Baullari, this huge, stately *palazzo* was begun in 1514. Today, it's considered the greatest of Rome's Renaissance *palazzi*. The Farnesi, an obscure noble family from the backwoods of Lazio, parlayed Pope Alexander VI's affair with Giulia Farnese into popehood for her brother Alessandro. He became **Pope Paul III,** set up the Council of Trent, refounded the Inquisition, and commissioned the best architects of his day—da Sangallo, Michelangelo, and della Porta—to design his dream abode. He also continued the trend of papal hijinks, having four children with unknown women and granting legitimacy to three.

Although the facade and entrance passage are remarkable, the most impressive part of the building is **Michelangelo**'s elaborate cornice. Note the band of *fleurs de lis* encircling the building. Since 1635, the French Embassy has rented the *palazzo* for L1 per year in exchange for the Hôtel Galiffet in Paris, home of the Italian Embassy. The Farnese family had two huge tubs (the present-day fountains) dug up from the Baths of Caracalla (see p. 91) to serve as "royal boxes" from which members of the patrician family could view the parties and shows they hosted in the square during the 16th and early 17th centuries.

On the northwest side of the *piazza* stands the **Church of Santa Brigida,** whose portal upstages its *palazzo*. The Swedish St. Bridget lived here until her death in 1373.

PALAZZO SPADA. To the east of Palazzo Farnese, off P. Capo di Ferro, the Baroque **Palazzo Spada** houses the picture collection of the **Galleria Spada** (see p. 155). The *palazzo* is a treasure in itself, recently restored to its original creamy whiteness. Outside, eight ancient Roman kings, generals, and emperors stand proudly under Latin inscriptions describing their achievements. Inside, 18 even less modest Roman gods stand, buck naked, around the court—even the usually prudish Vesta. Bernardino commissioned the elaborate decorations to compensate for the relatively puny size of his palace, but not even naked deities could keep the poor cardinal from feeling boxed in on all sides. To ease his discomfort, Borromini, an architectural illusionist, designed a colonnade beyond the library on the right side of the courtyard. The colonnade seems to stretch far back through a spacious garden, framing a life-size classical statue. In reality, Borromini manipulated perspective by shrinking the columns and pavement dramatically. The colonnade is only a few meters long, the statue stands a meter tall, and the garden is no more than a narrow alley.

VIA GIULIA

As part of his campaign in the early 1500s to clean up Rome after the Babylonian Captivity (when the popes moved to Avignon and the city fell into serious disrepair; see p. 49), Pope Julius II commissioned Bramante to construct a straight road leading to the Vatican. V. Giulia runs parallel to the Tiber northwest from Ponte Sisto to P. d'Oro. Don't be confused by the fact that the odd building numbers begin near Ponte Sisto, while the evens begin at P. d'Oro. This relatively wide road was a contrast to the narrow and winding medieval streets of the day. Throughout the 16th century, the charming road was a fashionable neighborhood, and later architects built its expensive residences in accordance with Bramante's restrained, classical vision. In the 17th century, however, Innocent X built a prison here to slum down the area and make his own P. Navona more important. It didn't work: the tiny neighborhood still attracted popes, nobility, and artists, including Raphael, who lived at #85, while P. Navona attracted 2nd-rate caricaturists and pickpockets. At least the prison drew him some prestige—until it fell out of use in the 18th century, experts called it the "most solid and salubrious" in Europe. Today, V. Giulia remains one of Rome's most exclusive streets, with well-maintained *palazzi*, antique stores, and art galleries.

MICHELANGELO'S FOOTBRIDGE. Perhaps the most striking of the area's sights is the ivy-draped bridge that spans V. Giulia from the back of the **Palazzo Farnese** (p. 103) to the Tiber embankment. Michelangelo designed the bridge, which was originally intended to be the first leg of a much longer bridge that would cross the Tiber. Michelangelo wanted to connect the *palazzo* with the Villa Farnesina on the other side (see **Museums**, p. 154), but funds dried up before its completion. Off the southeast corner of the *palazzo* lurks the **Fontana del Mascherone.** Erected by the Farnesi, its immense marble mask and granite basin are ancient Roman.

CHURCH OF SAN GIOVANNI DEI FIORENTINI. Seated at the center of Rome's Renaissance Florentine community, this church was built by Pope Leo X, a Mèdici from Florence, in hopes of illustrating the glories of his hometown. All the famous artists competed for the privilege of building it; Jacopo Sansovino finally beat out deadbeats like Peruzzi, Raphael, and Michelangelo. He didn't live long enough to finish it, though, so the work was farmed out to da Sangallo and della Porta, and finally wrapped up by Carlo Moderno in 1614. Notice the church's two busts: Bernini's is on the right and a work by his lesser-known father, Pietro, is on the left. *(In P. d'Oro, at the northern end of V. Giulia. Open M-Sa 7am-noon and 4:30-7:30pm, Su and holidays 7:30am-1pm and 4:30-8pm.)*

PALAZZO SACCHETTI. This *palazzo*, down from S. Giovanni dei Fiorentini on the right, at #66, was designed in 1543 by Sangallo the Younger, who built Palazzo Farnese. The courtyard features a relief of a Madonna and Child illuminated by a candle. In the two blocks between V. del Gonfalone and V. del Cefalo, giant stones known as the **Via Giulia sofas** protrude from the buildings on the left. Meant to be the foundation for the never-completed courts of Julius II, they eventually served as bases for Innocent X's prisons. To see the big house, head to **Museo Criminologico** (p. 158). The prison also houses the Ministry of Mercy and Justice. A block north on V. dei Banchi Vecchi is Alexander VI's **Palazzo Sforza Cesarini.**

PALAZZO FALCONIERI. At the southern end of V. Giulia on the river side is the sumptuous Palazzo Falconieri, which was expanded by Borromini and has housed the Hungarian Academy since 1928. The *palazzo*, which looks out over the river, is easily recognizable by the giant falcons with breasts that roost on each corner. Hot stuff.

SANTA MARIA DELL'ORAZIONE E MORTE. This Corinthian column-studded church was revamped by Ferdinando Fuga from 1733 to 1737. It's decorated with a *vanitas* skull motif and belongs to a confraternity founded in 1551 to collect unidentified corpses and give them Christian burials. *(Next to Palazzo Falconieri. Open Su and holidays for 6pm mass.)*

LARGO ARGENTINA

Toward the beginning of C. Vittorio Emanuele II lies Largo di Torre Argentina (referred to as Largo Argentina), a busy cross-street that sees an unhealthy portion of Rome's bus and taxi traffic. The largo, named for the square *Torre Argentina* (silver tower) that dominates its southeastern corner, is filled with medieval towers and narrow old houses.

AREA SACRA DI LARGO ARGENTINA. This sunken area in the center of the largo is a complex of four Republican temples unearthed during Mussolini's project of demolishing the medieval city. Their excavation is as much testament to *il Duce*'s disregard for Rome's medieval heritage as it is a tribute to his reverence for its antiquities. Archaeologists don't know to whom the temples were dedicated, but it is believed that they were connected with the larger complex built around the **Theater of Pompey** (see p. 102). If you're feeling charitable, give a few thousand *lire* to the site's **cat shelter.**

CHURCH OF SANT'ANDREA DELLA VALLE. Begun in 1591 by Grimaldi and completed by Baroque bigwig Carlo Maderno, this church sports a 1665 facade by Rainaldi, which challenged the contemporary style by displaying orderly rows of columns and pediments in place of the usual swirls and curls. The more conventional interior, where Puccini's opera *Tosca* begins, is modeled on **Il Gesù** (see p. 95). The twin wall tombs of the Piccolomini Popes Pius II and III (on either side of the nave right before the dome) are overshadowed by Domenichino's colossal 17th-century frescoes of St. Andrew, crucified on his characteristic X-shaped cross. That's not a real body in the glass case on the right side of the altar; it's a wax sculpture marking the tomb of St. Joseph Tomasi. *(One block down C. Vittorio Emanuele II from Largo Argentina. Open M-Sa 7:30am-noon and 4:30-7:30pm, Su 7:30am-12:45pm and 4:30-7:45pm.)*

Piazza di Siena

JEWISH GHETTO

🏛 *South of Largo Argentina. Bordered by V. Arenula (**tram** #8) on the west and by V. di Teatro di Marcello (**bus** #44, #63, or #170) on the east. The **Service International de Documentation Judeo-Chrétienne**, V. Plebiscito, 112, an information center for Jewish-Christian relations, offers half-day walking tours of the Ghetto on an irregular basis during the school year (☎ 06 6795307; L5000 donation). **Enjoy Rome** (p. 14) offers a very informative tour of the Ghetto and Trastevere.*

Galleria Borghese

> It was dirty, but it was Rome, and to anyone who has long lived in Rome even its dirt has a charm which the neatness of no other place ever had.
> —William Wetmore Story (1862)

Although Dickens declared the area "a miserable place, densely populated, and reeking with bad odours," today's Jewish Ghetto is one of Rome's most charming and eclectic neighborhoods, with family businesses dating back centuries and restaurants serving up some of the tastiest food in the city (see p. 187).

HISTORY. The Jewish community in Rome is the oldest in Europe, and was initially established in 161 BC by Israelite ambassadors petitioning for Roman help against invaders. The community grew, as traders anxious to establish themselves in the Mediterranean's greatest center of commerce swelled its ranks. Romans were initially tolerant of what was for them just another subject people, and one Christianized Jewish family, the Pierleoni, even managed to produce its own pope, the controversial Anacletus II.

Muro Torto

Once the Dark Ages set in, however, discriminatory measures like **Innocent III**'s 13th-century law forcing all Jews to wear yellow circles in public began to appear. The early community was forced from Trastevere (where it had initially established itself) into a controlled area by **Pope Paul IV,** who stated in a 1555 papal bull that it was unthinkable for Jews and Christians to cohabitate. He had a walled ghetto built in what was then a highly undesirable location, due to frequent flooding. The Jewish population was restricted to money-lending and used clothes peddling, and was required to take oaths of submission to the pope each year in ceremonies that took place next to the **Arch of Titus** (p. 81), a monument celebrating the Roman conquest of Jerusalem.

Segregation persisted in Rome until 1870, when the Church lost political control of Rome and the Ghetto was dismantled. During World War II, the vast majority of Jews in Rome were deported to concentration camps. Today, 16,000 of Italy's 40,000 Jews live in Rome. The community has been the target of international terrorism—its synagogue was bombed in 1982—so heavily armed *carabinieri* are a frequent sight.

CHURCH OF SANTA MARIA IN CAMPITELLI. A surprisingly successful project during the Counter-Reformation effort to beautify Rome was relocating an earlier church here to this swanky *piazza*. Carlo Rainaldi designed the church, which exemplifies the theatrics of Baroque architecture. Built in 1662 to give thanks to Mary for delivering the city from plague in 1656, it still houses (above the altar) the statuette believed to have miraculously ended the plague. *(Off of V. di Teatro di Marcello in P. di Campitelli. Open M-Sa 7am-noon and 4-7pm, Su and holidays for mass 7:30 and 10am, noon, and 6:30pm.)*

PALAZZO CENCI. Technically outside the Ghetto, Palazzo Cenci is at the end of V. Catalana, which runs parallel to V. del Portico d'Ottavia. It was the scene of a shocking crime on September 9, 1598, when Beatrice Cenci, aided by her brother and stepmother, murdered her abominable father Francesco Cenci. The whole clan was beheaded a year and two days later at the command of Pope Clement VIII, in spite of the fact that the public sympathized with the group's plea of self-defense against the incestuous and drug-addicted Francesco. Every September 11, a mass for the wronged Beatrice is held in the church at P. Cenci. Beatrice's story has inspired works by Shelley, Dickens, and others. She is also thought to be the subject of Reni's *Portrait of a Young Woman*, which hangs in the **Palazzo Barberini** (p. 153). Palazzo Cenci now houses an art gallery and the Rhode Island School of Design European Honors Program, which sponsors free art exhibitions of student work (in early May and early December).

One block north of the *palazzo* is a clunky modern building has replaced what was once five amalgamated synagogues, one each for the separate populations of Jews: Aragonese, Castilian, Catalan, Sicilian, and Roman.

SANT'ANGELO IN PESCHERIA. This church was built right into the Portico d'Ottavia (see p. 93) in 755 and named after the fish market that once flourished here. You can still see a official plaque requiring that the head and body up to the first fin of any fish longer than the length of the plaque be given to the Conservators of Rome. It was here that the Jews of the Ghetto were forced to attend mass every Sunday from 1584 until the 18th century—an act of forced evangelism that they quietly resisted by stuffing their ears with wax. At V. del Portico d'Ottavia, 28, to the right of the old fish market, a plaque commemorates the 2091 Roman Jews who died in the Holocaust. Several houses on this street date from the early Renaissance; you can see traces of *loggie* in their upper stories. *(Toward the eastern end of V. del Portico d'Ottavia. Open for prayer meetings W 5:30pm and Sa 5pm.)*

CHURCH OF SAN GREGORIO A PONTE QUATTRO CAPI. The facade of this church displays Hebrew and Latin inscriptions urging Jews to convert to Catholicism. *(At the very end of V. del Portico d'Ottavia near the Tiber. Open M-Sa 8-11:30am and 4-7pm.)*

SINAGOGA ASKENAZITA. The heavily guarded synagogue symbolizes the unity of the Jewish people in Rome and proclaims its unique heritage in a city of Catholic iconography. Built between 1874 and 1904, it incorporates Persian and Babylonian architectural devices, attempting to avoid any resemblance to a Christian church. A gray metal dome tops the temple, and, inside, the front is graced with seven massive gold menorahs below the rainbow-colored dome. Orthodox services, to which anyone is welcome, are given entirely in Hebrew. To the left of the gate, a small crater in the sidewalk marks the spot of the 1982 terrorist attack. To protect worshipers, the doors are bolted from the inside during services. The synagogue houses the **Jewish Community Museum** (see p. 159), a visit to which gets you a brief tour of the temple itself. *(At the corner of Lungotevere dei Cenci and V. Catalan, opposite the Theater of Marcellus. ☎06 6875051. Temple open for services only.)*

PIAZZA MATTEI

🔁 *The center of the Ghetto, accessible by walking down toward the river on V. Paganica from V. delle Botteghe Oscure (which runs between V. Arenula and P. Venezia).*

TORTOISE FOUNTAIN. The 16th-century Fontana delle Tartarughe, in which four little boys are portrayed standing on the backs of small dolphins while pushing tortoises into the water, is the center of this hidden *piazza*. Designed by the Florentine Giacomo della Porta, the fountain actually wasn't graced with turtles until Bernini restored it in 1658; in fact, its origins are rather slapdash. According to local legend, Duke Mattei, a notorious gambler, lost everything in one night, and his father-in-law-to-be was so disgusted that he rescinded his approval of Mattei's marriage to his daughter. The Duke, in a bid to pull his name from the mud of scandal, had the fountain built in a single night to show that a Mattei could accomplish anything, even when completely destitute. Apparently, fountain-building for speed was an important skill for a suitor; he got the girl, although she blocked up her window so she would never have to see the fountain that got her married.

RED BRIGADE MURDER. The infamous Red Brigade kidnappers and murderers of former Prime Minister Aldo Moro dumped his body here in P. Mattei in 1978 (see **The 20th Century,** p. 51)—there are occasionally flowers and candles to commemorate the bloody events of that year. Moro's likeness is found at V. Caetani, 9, the street to the right of Palazzo Mattei as you face it.

CHURCH OF SANTA CATERINA DEI FUNARI. Designed in 1554 by Michelangelo's apprentice, Guido Guidetti, the church is a rare late-Renaissance specimen, built on the site of a 10th-century monastery. It was named for the ropemakers who once worked in the neighborhood. *(One block past P. Mattei on V. dei Funari on the left. Closed for renovation.)*

PIAZZA DI SPAGNA AND THE CORSO

see map p. 322

🔁 *M:A-Spagna. Touring the area should take about a half-day.*

If you need directions to the Piazza di Spagna, you're lost. Though today you're likely to see more con artists than fine artists, the *piazza* has attracted many a creative spirit. Stendhal, Balzac, Wagner, and Liszt all lived near here. At **L'Antica Caffè Greco,** the well-known establishment on swanky V. Condotti, Goethe, Gogol, Berlioz, and Baudelaire used to linger over cups of espresso (see p. 196).

Henry James and the Brownings lived, at different times, on V. Bocca di Leone, a small side street in the area, while Peter Paul Rubens and Poussin preferred flats on V. del Babuino. Above V. Frattina, 50, amid the glitter and glamour of chic boutiques, you'll see a plaque commemorating James Joyce's former residence. Another small plaque on the side of the pink house to the right of the Spanish Steps (P. di Spagna, 26) marks the home where John Keats died in 1821. The 2nd floor now houses the Keats-Shelley Memorial Museum (see p. 159).

The Spanish Steps and P. di Spagna were once literally Spanish; the area around the Spanish ambassador's residence, located in the western end of the hourglass-shaped *piazza* since 1622, once held the privilege of extra-territoriality. Wandering foreigners who fell asleep there were liable to wake up the next morning as grunts in the Spanish army. Nowadays, they're likely to wake up with a string tied around their finger and no wallet (see **The String Guys,** at left).

THE STRING GUYS

If you spend more than five minutes in the general vicinity of the Spanish Steps, you will likely be approached by small groups of young men brandishing what appears to be some kind of lanyard or braid. These are the string guys. "My friend," the string guys will say to you "Give me your finger." Two things to keep in mind. The string guys are not your friends, and you really should not be giving your finger to anyone, especially the string guys. They are not performance weavers. They want your wallet. And while pickpocketry is, in a sense, an art form, their ruse is given away by the fact that five to seven of them will approach you at the same time. Simply tell them "No," and allow yourself to enjoy the rest of your trip with all of your valuables.

SPANISH STEPS. Designed by an Italian, paid for by the French, named for the Spaniards, occupied by the British, and currently under the sway of American ambassador-at-large Ronald McDonald, the Spanish Steps *(Scalinata di Spagna)* are a truly international hangout. A stop on just about everyone's itinerary in Rome, the steps are almost always filled with the madding crowd, choked with people from all corners of the earth.

The 137 steps (count 'em) were constructed from 1723 to 1725 to link the *piazza* with important locales above it, including the Pincio and the Villa Mèdici. The beginning of May heralds the world-famous flower show, when the steps are covered with pots of azaleas and postcard photographers.

When the steps first opened, Romans hoping to earn extra *scudi* as artists' models flocked to the steps dressed as the Madonna and Julius Caesar. Posers of a different sort abound today, and dressing like a virgin does not seem to be the main objective. Each night, hordes of testosterone-injected adolescent males, along with tipsy foreigners imitating their Italian counterparts, descend on the *piazza* in search of females, any females. These amateur Romeos are mostly harmless, but prone to making annoying catcalls and gestures. Equal in number, though less irritating, are the scruffy *artistes* who will offer a hair wrap or "write your name on a grain of rice."

FONTANA DELLA BARACCIA. This fountain, which anchors the foot of the steps, was designed by Gian Lorenzo Bernini's less famous father Pietro. The sculptor was inspired to carve the central basin in the shape of a sinking boat after he saw a barge washed up in the *piazza* after a Tiber flood. It was built below ground level to compensate for meager water pressure.

CHURCH OF SANT'ANDREA DELLE FRATTE. Capped by a Borromini bell tower (on which eight delicate angels fold their wings while small faces peek out of the Corinthian columns on the lower ring), this church's strong point is definitely its exterior. If you have time, though, head inside to see, near the altar, the two angels by Bernini that originally decorated the Ponte Sant'Angelo. Their companions can still be seen along the bridge in front of Castel Sant'Angelo (see p. 119). On the right is the leafy and peaceful **Sanctuary Madonna del Miracolo,** built in honor of the alleged appearance of the Madonna to a Roman Jew that caused his immediate conversion to Christianity. Upon his conversion, he became a man of the cloth, later working as a missionary in Palestine. *(V. S. Andrea, 1, off the southern end of P. di Spagna, at the end of V. della Propaganda at V. Mercede. Open daily 6:30am-12:30pm and 4-7pm.)*

OTHER SIGHTS. At the southern end of the *piazza* rises the **Column of the Immaculata,** an 1857 celebration of Pope Pius IX's acceptance of the Immaculate

Conception. On December 8, the Pope kneels at the base of the Madonna-capped shaft, while Roman firemen climb their ladders to place a wreath atop the column. Just south of the column stands the **Collegio di Propaganda Fide,** or, as the Latin inscription above the entrance reads, the *Collegivm Vrbanvm de Propaganda Fide.* Though it sounds like a left-over from the fascist era, the college was actually founded to train missionaries in the 16th century. The facade along V. di Propaganda was designed by Borromini. Just across from Sant'Andrea delle Fratte, at V. della Mercede, 12, a plaque commemorates the building, now full of offices, where **Bernini** died.

NEAR THE STEPS

CHURCH OF SANTA TRINITA' DEI MONTI. Despite its simple design by Carlo Maderno, the church, with its rosy, Neoclassical facade, provides a worthy incentive to climb the steps, not to mention a sweeping view of the city. Built in 1502 under the auspices of French King Charles VIII, it was shortly and unceremoniously pillaged in the infamous 1527 sack of the city by Spanish King Charles V. Maderno. Work was completed on the new building in 1570; the new edifice was consecrated in 1595. This time, the church lasted over 200 years until it was visited and sacked anew in 1798 by armies of Revolutionary France. The church was restored after the fall of Napoleon by the Mazois, and today the only original section of the church is the transept, above the largest altar.

Castel Sant'Angelo

The 3rd chapel on the right and the 2nd chapel on the left contain works by Michelangelo's star pupil, Daniele da Volterra. The last figure on the right of his *Assumption* depicts his cantankerous teacher. Poussin rated Volterra's other painting, *Descent from the Cross,* as one of the three greatest paintings ever. The 4th chapel on the left was frescoed in the 16th century by the Zuccari brothers, who built their *palazzetto* at the corner of the nearby *piazza* on V. Sistina. The obelisk in the center of the church's *piazza* was brought to Rome in the 2nd century; its hieroglyphics were plagiarized from the obelisk in P. del Popolo. *(At the top of the Steps. Open daily 9:30am-12:30pm and 4-7pm; upper half open Tu and Th 4-6pm.)*

Pietà

VILLA MÈDICI. To the left of Santa Trinità, the Villa Mèdici houses the **Accademia di Francia.** Founded in 1666 to give young French artists an opportunity to live in Rome (Berlioz and Debussy were among the scheme's beneficiaries), the organization now keeps the building in mint condition and arranges excellent exhibits, primarily of French art. Behind the villa's severe facade lie a beautiful garden and an elaborate rear facade. The **Pincio,** a park with formal gardens, extends up the hill beyond the villa (see p. 114).

PIAZZA DI TREVI

🚇 M:A-Barberini or A-Spagna. Alternatively, take a bus to P. S. Silvestro or Largo del Tritone.

TREVI FOUNTAIN

Nicolo Salvi's (1697-1751) extravagant and now sparkling clean Fontana di Trevi emerges from the back wall of **Palazzo Poli.**

St. Peter's Basilica

TOO MUCH CAPPUCCINO WILL DO THE SAME TO YOU

The bones of 4000 Capuchin friars (for whom cappuccino is named) decorate the four rooms of the Church of L'Immacolata Concezione's Capuchin Crypt, one of the most bizarre and elaborately macabre settings in Rome. A French monk inaugurated the crypt in 1528, but never saw his brilliant concept brought to its completion because the crypt was not finished until 1870. Angels deck the halls, with hip bones serving as wings. The bodies of more recently dead friars stand, robed and hooded, beneath bone arches. Even the hanging lights are made of bones. Dirt was shipped in especially from Jerusalem to line the floors. The last chapel displays two severed arms with mummy-like skin hanging on the back wall. Also featured in this chapel is a child's skeleton plastered to the ceiling, holding a scale and a reaper, and accompanied by the uplifting inscription: "What you are now we used to be, what we are now you will be."

The fountain was completed in 1762 by Giuseppe Pannini, who may have altered the original design. The fountain may also have been based on designs by Bernini which elaborated on a simpler one by Leon Battista Alberti; the idea for combining the fountain and *palazzo* was based on a project by da Cortona. Regardless of its architectural heritage, Fontana di Trevi simply fascinates crowds with the rumble and spray of its cascading waterscape, and has for centuries. Much of its charm comes from the surprise one has in stumbling on it, after so many narrow streets, and the startling way in which it fills up such a small square.

RELIEFS AND SCULPTURES. The fountain's source is the **Acqua Vergine** aqueduct, which also supplies the spouts in P. Navona and P. di Spagna. The aqueduct bears the name of Trivia, the maiden who allegedly pointed out the spring to thirsty Roman soldiers—she is also immortalized in one of the bas reliefs above the fountain. The opposite relief shows Augustus's right-hand man, Agrippa, giving the go-ahead for the aqueduct in 19 BC. The unfinished stone spans the length of the *palazzo*, cleverly incorporating the building into the fountain's dynamic depiction of the fathoms below. In the foreground, two enormous Tritons guide the winged chariot of Neptune. Flanking the burly mermen are inset statues representing Abundance and Health. From just under the Corsini family arms, the Four Seasons survey the madness. Notice that the **window** on the upper right is not a window at all, but a painting of one. A young Corsini took his own life one day by taking a dive out of that window, and his family bricked it up shortly after.

TOSSING A COIN. Legend has it that the traveler who throws a coin into the fountain will have a speedy return to Rome. Proper form is to put one's back to the fountain and toss over the left shoulder with the right hand. As the funds increase, so do the rewards—the traveler who tosses two coins will fall in love in Rome. The more ambitious visitor can throw three coins to be married in the city. Years of this have taken their toll; the metal eats away at the travertine and stains the pool. Since the restoration, travelers have been advised not to follow the custom—this hasn't stopped many.

TAKING A DIP. The bodacious Anita Ekberg takes a midnight wade in the fountain in Fellini's *La Dolce Vita*. Squads of roving policemen and policewomen armed with whistles and attitude keep others from re-enacting the famous scene. Though we won't say how we came to know this, illicit bathing will cost you upwards of L1,000,000 and a stern talking-to in Italian. Impossibly buxom "model" Anna Nicole Smith tried to do her own Ekberg impression in 1997 and had to cough up the dough.

OTHER SIGHTS

CHURCH OF SAN CRISPINO. While not a church, or even a sight per se, ◪**Gelateria di San Crispino** serves up heaven in a cup, and is, indeed, the best *gelato* in Rome. *(V. della Panetteria, 42. Facing the fountain, turn right onto V. Lavatore, and take your 2nd left. ☎06 6793924. Open M and W-Th noon-12:30am, F-Sa noon-1:30am, Su noon-midnight. Cups L3-10,000.)*

CHURCH OF SANTI VINCENZO AND ANASTASIO, The Baroque Church of Santi Vincenzo and Anastasio, rebuilt in 1630, houses a crypt that preserves the **hearts and lungs of popes** from 1590-1903, which, unfortunately for you anatomy fans, is closed to the public. *(Opposite the Trevi Fountain. Open daily 8am-7:30pm.)*

PIAZZA BARBERINI

Rising from the hum of a busy traffic circle at the end of V. del Tritone, Bernini's **Triton Fountain** spouts a stream of water high into the air over P. Barberini, the fulcrum of Baroque Rome. Traffic, banks, hotels, a cinema, and Planet Hollywood give the *piazza* a distinctly modern feel. On the corner of V. V. Veneto, Bernini's **Fontana delle Api** (Bee Fountain), buzzes with the same motif that graces the Barberini coat of arms.

CHURCH OF L'IMMACOLATA CONCEZIONE. This severe 1626 Counter-Reformation church holds the tomb of Cardinal Antonio Barberini, the church founder. Seemingly the only modest member of the family, his tomb's inscription reads "Here lies dust, ashes, nothing." Head downstairs for the main attraction: the artistically arranged bones of 4000 dead friars in the **Capuchin Crypt** (see **Too Much Cappuccino,** p. 110). Five rooms of methodically arranged bones show off the creative, if morbid, sides of the 18th-century Capuchin friars. *(V. V. Veneto, 27a. Walk up V. V. Veneto away from P. Barberini. Open F-W 9am-noon and 3-6pm. Donation requested.)*

PALAZZO BARBERINI. On the southern side of P. Barberini, up V. delle Quattro Fontane, rises the Palazzo Barberini. Begun by Carlo Maderno in 1624 on commission from Pope Urban VIII, it took Borromini and Bernini a decade to finish the palace. Since 1984, the "under construction" signs have returned to conceal the combined structural style of the three master plasterers. Among the highlights are Bernini's layers of Doric, Ionic, and Corinthian columns and Borromini's spiral stairs, which toyed with the building's perspective so that the upper-level windows look the same size as those on the first floor. The *palazzo* houses the **Galleria Nazionale d'Arte Antica** (see p. 153).

VIA VITTORIO VENETO. Curving north toward the Villa Borghese, this road has seen its *dolce vita* replaced by a flood of embassies and airline offices. At the turn of the 19th century, pushy real-estate developers demolished many of the villas and gardens, including the wooded preserve of the **Villa Ludovisi.** The speculator who bought the Ludovisi built a colossal palace in its place, but soon even he couldn't afford those crazy 19th-century Italian taxes, and the government repossessed the palace. The US embassy now inhabits the immense *palazzo* (currently called the Villa Margherita), which it received in return for tons of war surplus goods in 1945. The rise of the movie industry and tourism in the 1950s marked V. Veneto's most glamorous days. The grand cafes and hotels attracted bigwigs like Roberto Rossellini and Ingrid Bergman, eager paparazzi, and wide-eyed Americans. V. Veneto's prominence has since faded, though the pricey cafes and restaurants prey upon tourists still looking for Sophia Loren.

PIAZZA DEL POPOLO

⚑ M: *A-Flaminio. Exit the station and pass under the city walls to the northern entrance to the piazza. A visit to the sights below should take about an hour.*

The southern end of the square marks the start of three major streets: V. del Corso, which runs to P. Venezia (you can see the gleaming *Vittoriano* at the end); V. di Ripetta on the right, built by Leo X for service to the Vatican; and V. del Babuino on the left, cleared in 1525 by Clement VII to lead to the Spanish Steps. Outside the Porta del Popolo (Bernini designed its southern facade) is an entrance to the **Villa Borghese** (see p. 114).

At Napoleon's request, architect Giuseppe Valadier spruced up the once-scruffy *piazza* in 1814, adding the travertine fountains on the western and eastern sides. To the west, a beefy Neptune splashes in his element with two Tritons. The eastern figures represent Rome flanked by the Aniene and the Tiber. Also present is the she-wolf suckling Romulus and Remus. Walls extending from either side of the fountains form two semi-circles that enclose the square. Each end of the walls displays one of the Four Seasons.

Once upon a time in a grislier era, P. del Popolo was a favorite venue for popes to perform public executions. Today the "people's square" has become a lively gathering place, though executions are infrequent at best, and the Pope just isn't as lively as he used to be. Masked revelers once filled the square for the torch-lit festivities of the Roman carnival, and the *piazza* remains a favorite arena for communal antics. After a soccer victory or government collapse, the *piazza* resounds with music and celebration.

CHURCH OF SANTA MARIA DEL POPOLO

◪ *On the north side of P. del Popolo.* ☎ *06 3610487. Open M-Sa 7am-noon and 4-7pm, Su and holidays 8am-1:30pm and 4:30-7:30pm.*

Don't let the unassuming facade of the church deceive you into passing it by—within its early Renaissance walls are several Renaissance and Baroque masterpieces. The gilded relief above the altar depicts the exorcism that led to the church's foundation. Pope Pascal II chopped down a walnut tree marking the legendary spot of Nero's grave, clearing ground for the church and allowing the terrified neighbors to live free of his ghost. The apse behind the altar (sporadically accessible) was designed by **Bramante**—look for his signature shell pattern on the walls. In the vault of the apse, **Pinturicchio** painted a cycle of the *Coronation of the Virgin*. It is illuminated by 16th-century stained glass windows by Frenchman Guillaume de Marcillat.

DELLA ROVERE CHAPEL. Immediately to the right after the main entrance, this chapel harbors an *Adoration* by Bernardino Betti, better known as Pinturicchio (1454-1513). The fresco and its lunettes depict the life of St. Jerome (turn on the light for a better view). More frescoes by Pinturicchio's pupils are found in the 3rd chapel on the right; note its interesting *trompe l'oeil* benches.

CERASI CHAPEL. The Cerasi Chapel, immediately to the left of the altar, houses two exquisite **Caravaggios.** *Conversion of St. Paul* depicts Paul seconds after being thrown from his horse. Shaken by the fall, his only recourse was to convert to Christianity. Notice the irreverent focus of the painting; the canvas is taken up almost entirely by the horse's rump, while Paul lies suffering in the lower corner. In the *Crucifixion of St. Peter*, three faceless men drag the martyred first pope, still nailed to his upside-down cross. Caravaggio's dramatic style and earthy realism contrast the bland, classical restraint of the *Assumption of the Virgin* by his contemporary rival, Antonio Carracci, which hangs over the chapel's altar.

CHIGI CHAPEL. The Chigi Chapel, 2nd on the left, was designed by **Raphael** for the wealthy Sienese banker Agostino Chigi, reputedly the world's richest man (see **The Era Before Dishwashers,** p. 154). Raphael proved especially ingenious in his designs for the mosaic of the dome. Instead of representing the angels as flat figures, he used clever tricks of perspective and foreshortening to make them seem to stand on top of the chapel, peering down from their gilded empyrean. Raphael designed the statue of Jonah (who stands with one foot in the mouth of the whale that swallowed him) and the tombs, which were inspired by the Pyramid of Gaius Cestius outside the Porta San Paolo in Testaccio (see p. 135). Work on the ornate chapel ceased in 1520, when Raphael and Agostino Chigi died within days of each other. A century later, Bernini completed the chapel for Cardinal Fabio Chigi, the future Pope Alexander VII. Bernini added two medallions of faces to the pyramids and the marble figure of Death in the floor. Outside the chapel, look for more gruesome portraits of Death in the wall tombs and the marble skeleton who hides behind bars beside the doors. *(Open daily 7am-noon and 4-7pm.)*

OTHER SIGHTS

OBELISK OF PHARAOH RAMSES II. Restored in 1984, the obelisk commands the center of the *piazza*. Some 3200 years old, it was already an antique when Augustus brought it back as a souvenir from Egypt in the first century BC. Flanked on four sides by floppy-eared lions spouting water, its foundation provides a fantastic perspective of the city.

SALA DEL BRAMANTE. This little art museum is tucked under the stairs to the right of the Church of S. Maria del Popolo, and hosts frequent temporary exhibitions (see p. 161).

CHURCHES OF SANTA MARIA DI MONTESANTO AND SANTA MARIA DEI MIRACOLI. If you look closely, you'll see that the Baroque "twins" aren't quite identical. S. Maria di Montesano, on the left, with a facade by Bernini, is the older sibling (1662). Santa Maria dei Miracoli was completed by Fontana in 1681. *(At the southern end of P. del Popolo. S. Maria di Montesanto open Apr.-June M-F 5-8pm; Nov.-Mar. M-F 4-7pm. S. Maria dei Miracoli open M-Sa 6am-1pm and 5-7:30pm, Su and holidays 8am-1pm and 5-7:30pm.)*

Piazza Sonino

PIAZZA AUGUSTO IMPERATORE

🚺 **M:**A-Flaminio. Walk down V. di Ripetta from the south side of P. del Popolo. After years of being closed, the **mausoleum** has opened for tours: Tu and F at 9pm in German and 10pm in English. **Admission** L10,000, students L8000, over 60 and under 18 L6000, under 12 free. **Ara Pacis** is closed for renovation until an undisclosed time; it is typically open Tu-Sa 9am-7pm, Su 9am-1pm. **Admission** L3750, students L2500.

The mausoleum, the Ara Pacis, and an obelisk that now stands in P. Montecitorio once fit together into a strategically designed complex whose dimensions and orientation were dictated by celestial and solar phenomena. On the day and hour of the anniversary of Augustus' birth, the shadow of the obelisk would point directly at the center of the Ara Pacis. In the 2000 years that have passed since the construction of the complex, however, only the mausoleum has remained in its original position.

Church of Santa Maria

MAUSOLEUM OF AUGUSTUS

The circular brick mound of the Mausoleum of Augustus once housed the funerary urns of the Imperial family. The oversized tomb was originally crowned by a tumulus of dirt and planted with cypress trees in imitation of archaic Etruscan mound-tombs, and possibly topped by a colossal statue of the emperor. Two obelisks, now relocated to other *piazze*, once guarded the entrance. Later centuries saw the mausoleum converted to a Colonna family fortress, a wooden amphitheater where Goethe watched some bear-baiting in 1787, and even a concert hall, until concerned Italians restored it in 1936.

ARA PACIS

To the right of the mausoleum (coming from P. del Popolo), the glass-encased Ara Pacis stands as a monument to both the grandiosity of Augustan propaganda and the ingenuity of modern-day archaeology. The marble altar, completed in 9 BC, was designed to celebrate Augustus's success in achieving peace after years of civil unrest and war in Gaul and Spain. The

G. G. Belli

reliefs on its front and back include depictions of allegorical figures from Rome's most sacred national myths: a Roman Lupercalia, Aeneas (founder of Rome and Augustus's legendary ancestor) sacrificing a white sow, Tellus the earth goddess, and the goddess Roma. The side panels show the procession in which the altar was consecrated, with realistic portraits of Augustus and his family and various statesmen and priests, all striding off to sacrifice cattle on the new altar to peace. Killing an animal was apparently more than enough to convince the people that Augustus was their man: thanks at least partly to this, he was soon acclaimed as a divine figure.

ARCHAEOLOGY. The altar, which originally stood alongside the ancient **Via Lata** (now the Corso), was discovered in fragments over the course of several centuries and only pieced together in the last century by Mussolini's archaeologists. The final stages of excavation were almost never completed, as it was discovered that the altar, buried some 10m underground, was actually supporting one of Rome's larger *palazzi*. To make matters worse, the water table of the city, having risen with the ground level over the past two millennia, had submerged the monument in over 3m of water. Archaeologists and engineers devised a complicated system of underground supports for the palace and, after freezing the water with carbon dioxide charges, painstakingly removed the precious fragments. Mussolini provided the colossal, aquarium-like display case.

VILLA BORGHESE

see map p. 321

🔼 M:A-Spagna and follow the signs. Alternatively, from the Flaminio(A) stop, take V. Washington under the archway into the Pincio. From P. del Popolo, climb the stairs to the right of Santa Maria del Popolo, cross the street, and climb the small path.

The park of the **Villa Borghese** covers 6km² north of the Spanish Steps and V. Veneto. Its shady paths, overgrown gardens, scenic terraces, and countless fountains and statues are a refreshing break from the fumes and chaos of the city. Many office workers eat their lunches or enjoy siestas on the park benches, ignoring the tourists who tool around in silly bicycle-car contraptions and slurp overpriced Cokes.

In celebration of becoming a cardinal, Scipione Borghese hired architect Flaminio Ponzio and landscaper Domenico Savino da Montepulciano to build a little palace on the hills. They did him proud: the Borghese became the most vast and variegated garden estate in the city and one of the first to follow the Baroque craze of edging ornamental gardens with contrived "wildernesses." Completed by Dutch architect Jan van Santen in 1613, the building remained in the callous hands of the Borghese until 1902, when it and all the works of art inside were purchased by the Italian state.

Abutting the gardens of the Villa Borghese to the southwest is the **Pincio,** first known as the *Collis Hortulorum* (Hill of Gardens) for the monumental gardens the Roman Republican aristocracy built there. The hill is graced with the **Moses Fountain,** which depicts the future spiritual leader as a wee babe in a basket. During the Middle Ages, it served as a necropolis for bodies denied a Christian burial. Claudius's third wife, Messalina, created quite a stir in the nearby **Villa of L. Licinius Lucullus** by murdering the owner. When she later ran off with her lover, her infuriated husband sent his troops to track down and kill her. The Pincio family took possession of the villa in the 4th century. Fleets of Vespas, skippered by surly teenagers, have replaced the Victorian carriages, but the view is still one of the best in Rome.

The elegant terrace of restaurants and cafes in **Casa Valadier,** rising above P. del Popolo, offers an even better view. This locale has fed an unusual clientele of politicians and celebrities, from Gandhi to Chiang Kai-shek. The north and east boundaries of the Pincio are formed by the **Muro Torto,** or "crooked wall," so named for its irregular lines and centuries-old dilapidation. Parts of the wall have seemed ready to collapse since Aurelian built it in the 3rd century. When the Goths failed to break through this precarious pile of rocks in the 6th century, the Romans decided St. Peter must be protecting it and refused to strengthen or fortify it, giving St. Pete a chance to do his job.

Northwest of the Pincio is the rose-planted **Villa Giulia,** home of the resplendent Museo Nazionale Etrusco (see p. 151). Villa Giulia also hosts outdoor classical concerts during the month of July (see **Entertainment,** p. 176).

The park's other major museums are the **Galleria Borghese** (see p. 149), which houses one of Rome's finest sculpture collections as well as an enjoyable gallery of Renaissance paintings, and the **Galleria Nazionale d'Arte Moderna** (see p. 155).

The villa's art is not limited to its museums; in the **Giardino del Lago** (Garden of the Lake), Jacopo della Porta's Tritons look suspiciously like those in Piazza Navona. These are the real thing, moved here in 1984—the ones in Piazza Navona are copies. In the lake itself is the **Temple of Aesculapius.** Get a picturesque close-up from a rowboat. Finally, there's an imitation medieval fortress, now the **Museo Canonica** (see p. 159). The **Bio-Parco,** V. del Giardino Zoologico, 3, is no world-class zoo, but it has plenty of animals, mostly sluggish in the Roman heat. (☎06 3216564. Open daily 9:30am-6pm; in winter 9:30am-5pm. L14,000, 4-12 L10,000, under 4 and over 60 free.)

North of Villa Borghese are the **Santa Priscilla catacombs,** V. Salaria, 430, just before V. Antica crosses V. Ardeatina. The catacombs, along with the gardens of **Villa Ada,** are best reached by bus #57 or #219 from Termini or bus #56 from V. del Tritone. Get off at P. Vescovio and walk down V. di Tor Fiorenza to P. di Priscilla, where you'll find the entrance to the park and the catacombs. (☎06 86206272. Open Tu-Su 8:30am-noon and 2:30-5pm. L10,000.)

VATICAN CITY

🚩 M: A-Ottaviano or A-Cipro/Musei Vaticani. Alternatively, take bus #64 or #492 from Termini or Largo Argentina, #62 from P. Barberini, or #23 from Testaccio.

Perched on the western bank of the Tiber and occupying 108.5 independent acres within Rome, Vatican City is the last foothold of the Catholic Church, once the mightiest power in Europe. Since the Lateran Treaty of 1929 (see **History,** p. 52), the Pope has reigned with full sovereignty over this tiny theocracy, but he must remain neutral in see map p. 320 Roman and Italian politics. As the spiritual leader of millions of Catholics around the world, however, the Pope's influence extends far beyond the walls of his tiny domain. The nation preserves its independence by minting coins (Italian *lire* with the Pope's face), running a separate postal system, and maintaining an army of photogenic Swiss Guards. The Guards, the world's most photographed military men, continue to wear flamboyantly garish uniforms designed, *not* by Michelangelo, as every tour guide will insist, but in 1914 by some nameless seamstress, perhaps inspired by a Raphael painting. Although priests, nuns, and other official visitors are allowed in all areas, tourists are only admitted to the Basilica and the superlative **Vatican Museums** (see p. 140).

What's it like to live in the Vatican? It's certainly no party. More than 95% male, the population must conform to a set of rules even the meanest hostel owner would never dare to enforce. The effective curfew is 10pm, as the last city gates lock up then for the night, and no commercial entertainment is permitted. The 800 inhabitants are nonetheless very well connected: the Vatican's phone per capita ratio is the highest in the world.

ST. PETER'S BASILICA

🚩 *Open* daily April-Sept. 7am-7pm, Oct.-Mar. 7am-6pm. **Dress appropriately** when visiting or you'll be refused entrance—no shorts, miniskirts, sleeveless shirts, or sundresses allowed, though jeans and a t-shirt are fine. **Mass** M-Sa at 9, 10, and 11am, noon, and 5pm; Su 9, 10:30, and 11:30am, and 12:10, 1, 4, and 5:45pm. Multilingual confession available; languages spoken (about 20) are printed outside the confessionals by the main altar. **Plan on spending at least 2 hours in St. Peter's.**

Bernini's elliptical **Piazza San Pietro** serves as the grand entrance to the basilica. The obelisk at its center, originally erected in Alexandria by Augustus, is framed by two fountains. V. della Conciliazione, the main street leading up to the *piazza*, was built in the 1930s by Mussolini to connect the Vatican to the rest of the city. Benito promptly opened up a view of St. Peter's that Bernini never intended; the architect had wanted the marble *piazza* to greet

CHURCH CHAT

St. Peter's interior measures 186m (610.08 ft.) along the nave and 137m (449.36 ft.) along the arms. If you include the walls, the nave is actually 192.76m (632.32 ft.) long and 58m (190.24 ft.) wide. To simplify this, if for some reason the Pope wanted to replace the entire interior with two football fields, he'd have to exclude the end zones, but he could do it. Additionally, if he got a chocolate craving like nobody's business, and wanted to line the Basilica's floor with candy bars, he could pile in roughly 3.96 million Snickers bars. Should parking cars in church become all the rage, 2750 moderately-sized Fiats could be parked within St. Peter's. All of these things the Pope could do but doesn't. Such resolve.

pilgrims as a surprise after their wanderings through the medieval Borgo district. One hundred and forty statues by Bernini's school perch above the colonnade. Those on the basilica represent Christ (at center), John the Baptist, and the Apostles (excluding Peter).

The basilica marks the resting spot of the bones of St. Peter, the church's founder. (For more on church history, see p. 57.) A Christian structure of some kind has stood here since Emperor Constantine made Christianity the state religion in the 4th century. In 1506, with Constantine's original brick basilica aging badly, Pope Julius II called upon Donato Bramante, who designed the new church with a centralized Greek-cross plan—a decision which proved contentious for the next 100 years. When Bramante died before completing his project, Sangallo and Raphael usurped his design and changed St. Peter's to a Latin cross (in which one arm of the church is longer than the others). In 1546, Paul III handed the 72-year-old Michelangelo the job of completing the basilica. Even though he and Bramante reportedly hated each other, Michelangelo reverted to the Greek-cross plan because of his love for symmetry. But Michelangelo, too, was finished before his project. Whether out of spatial necessity or a desire to best the architects who had come before, the final architect, Carlo Maderno, lengthened St. Peter's nave and added three chapels, giving the basilica a Latin-cross layout once and for all.

PORTICO AND ENTRANCE. Near the portico of the basilica, Swiss Guards protect a courtyard where, in the first century, thousands of Christians, probably including St. Peter, were slaughtered. The five large doors in the portico itself all have special themes, including death and good and evil. The Door of Sacraments stands between the larger bronze door that originally stood in the old St. Peter's and the *Porta Sancta* (Holy Door). This last door on the right can only be opened by the Pope, who knocks in its bricked-up center with a silver hammer every 25 years to initiate the Jubilee years of holy celebration.

Along the floor, metal lines mark the dimensions of the world's other major religious structures, proof that this is indeed the world's largest church.

PIETÀ. In the right aisle as you enter the church, Michelangelo's sorrowful marble *Pietà* (1497-1500) lies far back, behind a wall of protective glass. Created when Michelangelo was 25, the sculpture was the artist's second commission in Rome, and the only one he ever signed (on the sash falling diagonally across the Madonna's robe), reputedly after overhearing some onlookers who thought that it was done by a Milanese artist. It is actually displayed incorrectly as it is, frontally, with the Virgin facing us and the Christ in profile. The artist intended it to be seen from the right side, which emphasizes the Virgin's piteous gesture (she extends her hand toward the viewer) and foreshortens the elongated limbs and torso of Christ.

Michelangelo's *Pietà* made the artist and the subject famous, but Michelangelo did not invent the genre of the Madonna cradling the dead Christ. The type originated in 14th-century Germany and was popularized in France; Michelangelo was the first to portray the unwieldy pose with such elegance. His Madonna is unusually youthful—too young to be the mother of a 32-year-old man. For this, Michelangelo was accused of heresy; he defended himself by claiming that Mary's virginity preserved her youth. Michelangelo never again finished a sculpture to this level of refinement: the detail, visible particularly in the draping of the garments, is without parallel.

In 1962, the work was sent to the World's Fair in New York, but it travels no more. In 1972, a hammer-wielding maniac attacked the famous sculpture, smashing the nose and breaking the hand off the Madonna. Since then, it has been restored by meticulous sculptors who examined the 1934 copy of *Pietà* which stands in the Treasury Museum of St. Peter's (see p. 119). If you're frustrated by the crowds of flash-camera-toting tourists and the long distance to the sculpture, you might take a closer look at the replicas in the treasury and just outside the Vatican Museum's Pinacoteca. Further down the right aisle is the **Chapel of the Sacrament.** Entrance is granted only for praying, though there are thin windows through which one can peer into the sanctuary—Bernini's sacrament and gilded bronze angels definitely merit the snoop.

BALDACCHINO. Down the nave on the right, toward the intersection of the two arms of the church, a medieval **bronze of St. Peter,** seated on a marble throne, presides over the crossing, his feet worn smooth by those who stop to kiss or rub them. He is outfitted in full religious regalia on holidays. The dizzying crossvault is anchored by four niches with **Bernini** statues of St. Helena, St. Veronica, St. Andrew, and St. Longinus holding sacred relics. Next to St. Helena is the staircase leading down to the **Vatican Grottoes** (see p. 118). In the center of the crossing, the *baldacchino*, another work by Bernini, rises on spiraling dark columns over the marble altar, reserved for the Pope's use. The canopy, cast in bronze pillaged from the Pantheon, was unveiled on June 28, 1633, by Pope Urban VIII, a member of the wealthy Barberini family. Bees, the symbol of the Barberinis, buzz here and there (as well as on buildings and statues all over Rome), while vines climb up toward Michelangelo's cavernous cupola. Above each of the coats of arms (except the two facing the nave), there is a woman's face contorted in varying expressions of pain and surrounded by various objects of gynecological significance, while on the last pedestal on the right, her face is replaced by that of a smiling baby. Some historians interpret this bizarre detail as a coded (and rather indelicate) offering of thanks by Pope Urban VIII for the survival of a niece who nearly died in childbirth or as an elaborate allegory of the Church as mother of the faithful. It's possible, though, that this is actually Bernini's covert reference to the Pope Joan legend (see p. 58). In front of the *baldacchino*, seventy gilded oil lamps burn, illuminating Maderno's sunken Confession. Two semi-circular marble staircases lead to the Peter's tomb, directly beneath the papal altar. A better view of the tomb is possible from the grottoes.

i ESSENTIAL
INFORMATION

VATICAN INFO

Vatican Online
(www.vatican.va) The official site of the Vatican has information on sights, events, the Vatican museums, and history and news. Yes, you can click on the Pope's head, but nothing will happen.

Pilgrim Tourist Information Office, P. San Pietro (☎06 69884466). To the left as you face the basilica. The Vatican's tourist office and official souvenir shop in one. The office conducts free English tours of the Basilica daily. Phone to arrange tours of the otherwise inaccessible Vatican Gardens. Tour lasts 2hr.; Mar.-Oct. M-Tu and Th-Sa 10am, except during Papal Ceremonies; Nov.-Feb. Sa 10am, except during ceremonies; L20,000. Office open M-Sa 8:30am-7pm.

Papal Audiences Every W, John Paul II himself adresses audiences of 2000-3000 rapt pilgrims, usually at 10am behind the colonnade left of the basilica. For free tickets, stop by the Prefettura della Casa Pontificia (☎06 69883273) the day before the audience you wish to attend. The office is beyond the bronze doors to the right of the basilica (open M-Sa 9am-1pm). Sometimes a Swiss guard will hand out the tickets outside the Prefettura. To secure your tickets in advance, write to the *Prefettura della Casa Pontificia,* 00120 Città del Vaticano, specifying the number of people and the desired and alternate date. Seating is limited, so arrive early. As ever, wear appropriate clothing.

ST. PETER'S DOME. High above the *baldacchino* and the altar rises the dome designed by Michelangelo, built with the same double shell as Brunelleschi's earlier one in Florence, but made much rounder, like the Pantheon (see p. 97). Out of reverence for that ancient architectural wonder, Michelangelo is said to have made this cupola a meter shorter in diameter than the Pantheon's, but the measurements of the dome are still eye-popping. The highest point towers 120m above the floor and the diameter of the dome measures in at 42.5m. At the time of Michelangelo's death in 1564, only the drum of the dome had been completed. Work remained at a standstill for until 1588, when 800 laborers were hired to complete it. Toiling round the clock, they finished the dome on May 21, 1590. Mosaic representations of Matthew, Mark, Luke, and John adorn one level of the dome; angels fill up four more levels surrounding the top, and God sits on top.

CATHEDRAL PETRI AND SURROUNDINGS. At the end of the nave stands **Cathedral Petri,** a Baroque reliquary that houses the throne of St. Peter, a Bernini masterpiece dating from 1666. Peter's original chair supposedly lies inside the massive bronze throne, but the wood in the chair was carbon-14 dated in 1968 (at the request of Pope Paul VI) to an embarrassingly recent AD 300; the Vatican has issued no comment. To the throne's right, the Bernini **tomb** of Pope Urban VIII waves to the sarcophagus of Pope Paul III on the left side of the throne. To the left of the Cathedral Petri, in the left aisle and behind the statue of St. Veronica in the crossing, is Bernini's last work in St. Peter's, the **monument to Alexander VII.** It's enlivened by a bronze skeletal figure of Death, whose face is concealed by a fluid marble drapery. He thrusts an hourglass to the viewer; time was up for Bernini, who died two years after he finished this statue. Nearby, in the **Cappella della Colonna,** there is a monument to St. Leo the Great, surrounded by the tombs of littler St. Leo II and St. Leo III and surmounted by Algardi's famous relief of (the great) Pope Leo meeting with Attila the Hun. On the opposite side of the basilica you'll find **Cappella Clementina,** where a monument to Pius VII (sculpted by Thorvaldsen in 1823) is the only piece of St. Peter's made by non-Catholic hands.

CUPOLA. For not-to-miss views of the interior of St. Peter's and the skyline of Rome, head to the ticket office, located just outside the basilica (on the left as you face the entrance), for the climb to the cupola. You can reach the interior observation level by elevator or make the macho climb up the winding path of 330 stairs—both narrow and wide, brick, marble, metal, and wood. At the top, you'll reach the outdoor ledge around the very top of the dome, 370 ft. above the ground. No elevator can save you from this climb, which will leave even the fittest *Let's Go* reader bordering on cardiac arrest. But it's well worth it. *(Cupola closes 75min. earlier than the Basilica, and when the Pope is inside. Admission on foot L7000, by elevator—though there's still a climb to the very top—L8000.)*

TOMB OF ST. PETER AND PRE-CONSTANTINE NECROPOLIS. On the left side of the Piazza San Pietro is the entrance to the necropolis, one level below the grottoes (see below). A double row of mausoleums dating from the first century is found here. Multilingual guides remind you that the center of the Catholic Church used to be a pagan burial ground and tell of the discovery of St. Peter's tomb. In 1939, workers came across ancient ruins beneath the Vatican, and, unsure of finding anything, the Church set about looking for St. Peter's tomb secretly. Twenty-one years later, the saint's bones were discovered in a small *aedicula* (temple) directly beneath the altars of both the Constantinian and modern basilicas. *(☎06 69885318. Open M-Sa 9am-5pm. Only small, pre-arranged tours may enter. To request a tour, call or write: The Delegate of the Fabbrica di San Pietro, Excavations Office, 00120 Vatican City. L10,000.)*

VATICAN GROTTOES. Below the crossvault and Bernini's St. Helena, steps lead down to the Vatican Grottoes, the final resting place of many Catholic VIPs. The passages are lined with tombs both ancient and modern, and although the space is modernized and well-lit, it's still creepy. Skulking around the grottoes will lead you to various ethnic chapels, a great view of St. Peter's resting place, and statues 'n' tombs galore. In addition to Peter, 11 other popes are buried down here, as well as a handful of emperors and Queen Christina of Sweden. *(Open daily Apr.-Sept. 7am-6pm; Oct.-Mar. 7am-5pm.)*

TREASURY OF SAINT PETER'S. To the left of the Confession, in the first arm of the transept, a door leads into the **Treasury of St. Peter's,** which contains many of the gifts donated to his tomb in past centuries. Among the highlights of the nine-room museum are: the "dalmatic of Charlemagne," an angelic, intricately designed robe that the illiterate Holy Roman Emperor donned for sacred ceremonies; the exact copy of *Pietà* made in 1934; Bernini's clay angel statue; the magnificent bronze tomb of Sixtus IV; and the stone sarcophagus of Junnius Bassius (4th century), which is decorated with ten biblical episodes (from Adam and Eve to the capture of St. Peter). *(Open M-Sa 9am-6:30pm. L8000, children 12 and under L5000.)*

CASTEL SANT'ANGELO

Isola Tiberina

*▶ Down V. di Conciliazione from St. Peter's. To enter the castle, walk along the river with St. Peter's behind you, and the towering castle to your left. Signs will point you to the entrance; descend via ramp or stairs into the former moat. ☎06 6875036. **Open** Tu-F and Su 9am-8pm, Sa 9am-midnight; in winter daily 9am-2pm. **Admission** L10,000, EU citizens under 18 or over 60 free. **Guided tour** with archaeologist L8000, given in summer Tu-F 3pm, Sa-Su 4:30pm; **audio guide** L7000 (in English, French, German, Italian, Japanese, and Spanish).*

The massive Castel Sant'Angelo was built by Emperor Hadrian (AD 117-138) as a mausoleum for himself and his family. Despite its somber purpose, it has since been cannibalized by the popes of Rome for use as a convenient and forbidding fortress, prison, and palace. The towering complex consists of a mausoleum, a suite of palatial Renaissance apartments on top, and concentric rings of fortifications (including the Leonine Wall that extends to the Vatican Palace).

Hadrian, an architect as well as emperor, designed the mausoleum in imitation of his predecessor Augustus's tomb across the river (see p. 113). However, the tomb was used as a mausoleum alone for only 60 years. By 271, Aurelian had incorporated it into the fortified walls of Rome.

Casa di Dante

In 410, Alaric took time off from sacking the rest of Rome to sack Hadrian's tomb, and in 537 a defending garrison found itself smashing the tomb's statues and heaving the fragments over the walls to ward off besieging Goths.

When the plague hit Rome in 590, Pope Gregory the Great is said to have seen the archangel Michael sheathing his sword at the top of the citadel. The plague abated soon thereafter, and the edifice was loudly dedicated to the angel in thanks; at that point it underwent the name-change to "Sant'Angelo." During the Sack of Rome in 1527, Pope Clement VII ran for his life along the covered wall between the Vatican and the fortress, while the imperial invaders took potshots at his streaming white papal robes.

Pope Paul III used the fortress for more leisurely pursuits, building a sumptuous suite of apartments atop the ancient foundations; its "grotesque" ceiling paintings are particularly gorgeous. The lower levels were used as a prison for heretics and other troublemakers, including the revolutionary astronomer Giordano Bruno and thieving artist Benvenuto Cellini (who was once stored for a day in one of the structure's larger vertical ventilation ducts). The colossal fortress now contains a museum of arms and artillery, but the weirdly whimsical papal apartments and the panoramic views of Rome possible

Basilica of Santa Cecilia

from the upper levels are the real reasons to pay a visit. If you'd like more information, the **audio guide** is probably your best bet, as the archeology tours tend toward a little too much minutiae for most people's taste and actually bypass several of the most beautiful rooms. Wandering and poking around its nooks and crannies is definitely the best way to see this mausoleum-cum-fortress-cum-prison.

RAMPARTS AND MAIN CASTLE ROOMS. From the ticket booth, a ramp leads up to the fortress's ramparts and four circular bastions, named for the four evangelists. From the ramparts you can see the massive cement remains of Hadrian's mausoleum and bits of the travertine marble that once completely encased it. A bridge crosses into the base itself, where a wooden ramp (built by Alexander VII) rises steeply over the emperor's tomb. Along the way, the walls hold creepy incendiary urns of the castle, typical of those that held the ashes of many a Roman emperor. All of Hadrian's lineage, ending with Caracalla, were cremated in the mausoleum. The ramp leads outside into **The Court of the Angel,** where Raphael's original *Michael* (sculpted in 1544) stands tall.

This courtyard leads into the **Sala di Apollo,** whose *grotteschi* frescoes were painted in imitation of ancient Roman designs. Two rooms adjoining the Sala di Apollo display 15th- and 16th-century paintings and Renaissance maps of Rome. From the adjacent **Courtyard of Alexander VI,** you can descend into a dank labyrinth of prison cells and storerooms (including endless rows of vats where oil was kept boiling to douse besiegers) or stop to study the enormous crossbows and cannonballs that once served as the castle's defense. Another stairway climbs to a gallery that circles the citadel, decorated at intervals with *grotteschi*, stuccos, *loggie* built by Popes Julius II and Paul III, a bar, and a souvenir stand. The **bathroom of Pope Clement VII** is nearby. Formerly heated by hot furnace air pumped behind the walls, it is still heavily frescoed with flighty grotesques painted for Clement's personal contemplation.

PAPAL APARTMENTS. The extravagant Papal Apartments include the lush Sala Paolina, plastered with paintings of Hadrian and the castle's patron angel. Don't miss the out-of-place black-coated man peeking out from a faux doorway—it's speculated to be a caricature of Raphael, the sometime architect and sculptor of parts of the castle.

OTHER ROOMS. Much of the rest of the castle is relatively unexciting; high points include the **Camera del Perseo, Camera di Amore e Psyche** (frescoed and filled with period furniture), and the **Hall of the Library** (awash with scenes of cavorting sea gods and lined with stucco reliefs). Political prisoners of the popes were kept in the hot little stone cells along the rim of the fortifications as late as the 19th century. Keep climbing through exhibition rooms, which hold temporary exhibits, usually of recent Italian painters or photographers, to reach a broad, circular terrace with excellent views of the city.

TRASTEVERE

see map p. 314–315

Trastevere—a name that is a reference either to its *trans Tevere* (across the Tiber) location or its settlement during the reign of Tiberius—asserts a vibrance that gives it a character and atmosphere unlike that of the city center. The *Trasteverini* claim to be descendants of the purest Roman stock—*Romani dei Roma* (Romans from Rome). Some residents even claim to have never crossed the river.

The legendary founder of Ostia, King Ancus Martius, first settled Trastevere not as a residential spot but as a commercial and military outpost to protect the valuable salt-beds at the base of the Tiber. The hills beyond Trastevere became important outposts for defending the city from pesky Etruscan invasions. During the Empire, sailors in the imperial fleet inhabited the area, building mud and clay huts along the river's banks. The success of a commercial port started by Hadrian lured Syrian and Jewish merchants to the neighborhood, and the maritime business flourished alongside such cottage industries as tanning, carpentry, milling, and prostitution.

By the Middle Ages, Trastevere's commercial activity began to wane and many residents retreated to the other side of the river. In his 1617 edition, guidebook editor

Fynes Moryson warned readers, "because the aire is unwholesome, as the winde that blows here from the South, Trastevere is onely inhabited by Artisans and poore people." The popes took little interest in the neighborhood and rarely extended their wealth to build grandiose churches or monuments here; the community remained wholly self-sufficient. In keeping with its independent spirit, Trastevere backed two revolutions: Mazzini's quest for a Republic in 1849 and Garibaldi's resurgence in 1867 (see p. 51).

Since WWII, Trastevere has been the victim of aggressive foreign-funded gentrification. Today, Trastevere attracts hordes of bitter expatriates, bohemians, and lackluster artists, but thanks to rent control and centuries of fiery patriotism, the area retains its gusto. To keep the spirit of independence alive, **Noantri** ("We others," in dialect) is celebrated during the last two weeks of July. Though a bit tacky, the festival features grand religious processions, some kiddie rides, and a *porchetta* (roast pig) on every corner.

ISOLA TIBERINA

The cleverly named Tiber Island has been inhabited for nearly 3000 years, so, like everything else in Rome, it has a long, drawn-out story to share. According to legend, the island shares its birthday with the Roman Republic—after the Etruscan tyrant Tarquin raped the virtuous Lucretia, her outraged husband killed him and threw his corpse in the river, where muck and silt collected around it, forming a small land mass.

These felonious origins may have deterred Republican Romans from settling the island; it was used as a dumping ground for slaves who had grown too weak to work. Abandoned by their masters, the pitiful slaves prayed to Aesclepius, the Greek god of healing. Legend has it that when the Romans took his statue from the sanctuary at Kos and dragged it up the Tiber in 293 BC, the god appeared to them as a snake and slithered onto the island. The Romans took this event as a sign that this was where he wanted his temple and, with their typical architectural aplomb, encased the island in marble, building its walls in the shape of a boat to commemorate the god's arrival. Traces of the original travertine decoration on the southeast side of the island are still visible—look for the serpent carved in relief near the "prow." The Romans built a large Aesclepius temple with porticoes where the sick could wait for the god to visit them in their dreams and prescribe a cure. Nearby, archaeologists have found pits full of ex voto statuettes of arms, legs, and other body parts offered as thanks. The site has been associated with healing ever since.

FATEBENEFRATELLI HOSPITAL. The Fatebenefratelli monks established a hospital here in 154; it still occupies the northern half of the island. Here, English King Henry I's courtier, Rahere, reputedly fought off malaria, a fatal disease in those pre-quinine days. He was so thankful that he promised to build a church and hospital in gratitude back in England, though how that was supposed to benefit the people of Rome we'll probably never know. (True to his word, he built the structures that still stand in London's Smithfield district.) Expectant Roman mothers consider the hospital the most fashionable place in the city to give birth. That's not surprising since it looks like a huge tropical villa on the outside and a church, replete with statues and open-air *piazze*, on the inside.

BRIDGES. The bridge leading from the east bank of the river is the **Ponte Fabricio** (commonly known as the **Bridge of Four Heads** for its two busts of Janus, two-headed god of beginnings and endings). It's the oldest in the city, built by Lucius Fabricius in 62 BC. From the *lungotevere*, you can see the inscription Lucius carved into the bridge to record his public service. From the bridge, the beleaguered **Ponte Rotto,** one of Rome's less fortunate ancient constructions, is also visible to the south. Built in the 2nd century BC, the poor bridge underwent medieval repair after medieval repair, each time succumbing to the Tiber's relentless floods. Since its last collapse in 1598, it's been slowly disintegrating, suffering a final defeat when it was accidentally blown up during the construction of the current metal bridge just downstream, the Ponte Palatino. Now all that remains is a single marble arch planted squatly, but proudly, midstream.

The **Ponte Cestio** (originally built by Lucius Cestius in 46 BC and rebuilt in 1892) links the island to Trastevere. The little bridge offers a stellar view of the Gianicolo and the

Church of Santa Maria in Cosmedin (see p. 92). Stairs lead down to the bank, where lovers, graffiti artists, and other social derelicts enjoy secluded anonymity.

CHURCH OF SAN BARTOLOMEO. This 10th-century church has been flooded and rebuilt many times, and is now something of a funky architectural melange, with a Baroque facade, a Romanesque bell tower, and 14 ancient columns. *(In P. S. Bartolomeo. Open daily 9am-1pm and 4-6:30pm.)*

CENTRAL TRASTEVERE

From the Ponte Garibaldi, V. di Trastevere opens onto P. G. G. Belli (centered on a statue of the famous dialect poet) and then P. Sonnino, Trastevere's transportation hub (centered on the Golden Arches).

PIAZZA SIDNEY SONNINO

TORRE DEGLI ANGUILLARA. On the left, the 13th-century Torre degli Anguillara stands over a *palazzo* of the same name. The various members of the Anguillara family were notoriously active as priests, magistrates, warlords, criminals, and swindlers. The building now houses the **Casa di Dante,** which hosts readings of the *Divine Comedy* every Sunday from November to March.

CHURCH OF SAN CRISOGNO. A well-known Roman name is perpetuated in an etching on the facade of this church, that of Cardinal Borghese. Although founded in the 5th century, the church has been rebuilt many times. Twenty feet beneath the most recent structure lie the remains of the original. To visit the ruins, walk into the room to the left of the altar; an attendant will lead you down the narrow, wrought-iron staircase. Traces of original wall paintings and some well-preserved sarcophagi and inscriptions are still visible. On the left side of the church you can view a memorial and listen to a parochial explanation of the life and times of Beata Anna Maria Taigi, housewife and saint who did good works while tending her husband, "a difficult, rough character." Wives may wish to use this moment to chastise their husbands for being such lazy pigs. *(Across the street from the Casa di Dante, off P. S. Sonnino. Open daily 8am-1pm and 4-7pm. L2000 donation.)*

CHURCH OF SAN FRANCESCO A RIPA. One of the first Franciscan churches in Rome, it showcases Bernini's *Beata Lodovica Albertoni* in a chapel on its left side. Shown at her death, she lies in a state of euphoria. *(From P. S. Sonnino, go down V. di Trastevere, then turn left on V. di S. Francesco a Ripa. Open M-Sa 7am-noon and 4-7pm, Su 7am-1pm and 4-7:30pm.)*

BASILICA OF SANTA CECILIA IN TRASTEVERE

◪ *From P. S. Sonnino, walk south and go left on V. G. C. Santini, which runs into V. dei Genovesi. From V. Genovesi, go right on V. S. Cecilia. Open daily 8am-12:30pm and 2:30-7pm. Cloister open Tu and Th 10-11:30am, Su 11:3am-noon, donation requested. Admission to crypt L4000.*

During the 3rd century, Cecilia converted to Christianity and also managed to convert her husband Valerian and her brother-in-law. Unfortunately, her husband and brother-in-law were beheaded for their refusal to worship Roman gods. Cecilia inherited a considerable fortune from both of them, becoming one of the richest women in Rome and inciting so much resentment that the prefect of Rome ordered her death in 230. She was locked up in her own steamroom to die, but miraculously survived. Her relations then tried to behead her, but despite three tries, the executioners botched the job and she survived for three more days, slowly bleeding to death. In the meantime, the hemorrhaging evangelist converted over 400 people. She bequeathed her palace to build this beautiful church. Cecilia is known as the patron saint of music because she was found singing after her three-day stint in the steamroom. On November 22, St. Cecilia's day of martyrdom, churches hold a musical service. The National Academy of Music in Rome is also named after her.

INTERIOR. Pope Urban I consecrated the church in her palace, but Pascal I rebuilt it in 821 when, according to one Vatican account, he dreamed that St. Cecilia revealed her true burial grounds in the catacombs of St. Callisto. He had her body exhumed and transferred to the new church. Stefano Maderno's famous **statue of Santa Cecilia** lies under the high altar. The marble sculpture shows what she looked like when exhumed from her tomb in 1599 in Maderno's presence—pretty good for a 1200-year-old corpse.

CLOISTER AND CRYPT. Rococo restorers wreaked untold havoc on the medieval frescoes by Pietro Cavallini that once covered the church. However, fragments of his magnificent 1293 *Last Judgment* remain, in the adjacent **cloister.** Beneath the church are the ruins of Roman buildings and an ancient church, accessible whenever the church is open. The entrance to the ruins is on the left as you enter the church and is marked by the sign *"cripta e scavi."* Cardinal Rampolla, the man responsible for the excavations, is memorialized in a tomb in the last chapel outside.

SANTA MARIA IN TRASTEVERE

🔃 *From P. S. Sonnino, take V. della Lungaretta. Open daily 7:30am-7pm.*

The church has the distinction of being the first in Rome dedicated to the Virgin Mary. Though this structure dates from the 12th century, an earlier basilica was constructed on the site under Calixtus in the 3rd century. The mosaics of the Virgin and the 10 saintly women lining the exterior are only a set-up for what's inside: lots and lots of men. The 12th-century mosaics in the apse and the chancel arch are still in full splendor, depicting Jesus, Mary, and a bevy of saints and popes in rich Byzantine detail.

Palazzo del Quirinale

GIANICOLO

PIAZZA SAN PIETRO IN MONTRORIO

🔃 *From V. della Scala, take V. Garibaldi. Before coming to the first sharp right turn, take the steep staircase on the right up the hill. Church and Tempietto open daily 9:30am-12:30pm and 4-6:30pm.*

Built on the spot once believed to be the site of St. Peter's upside-down crucifixion, the biggest draw of the **Church of S. Pietro in Montorio** is a masterly *Flagellation*, painted on slate by Sebastiano del Piombo from designs by Michelangelo. The church also contains the tombs of Irish noblemen, exiles persecuted by English Protestants. Next door in the center of a small courtyard is the stunning ▨**Tempietto** of Bramante (1499-1502). A combination of Renaissance and classical architecture, it was constructed on the site of Peter's martyrdom and provided the inspiration for the larger dome of St. Peter's. The belvedere before the Tempietto offers quite a view: the Pantheon's dome, Bramante's inspiration, rises straight ahead.

Fontana del Acqua Felice

Just up the hill from P. S. Pietro in Montorio is **P. Giuseppe Garibaldi,** the site of a patriotically over-blown statue-complex crowned by an equestrian likeness of the revolutionary leader himself. Further down is a statue to his daughter Anita Garibaldi, on the back of a rearing horse, brandishing baby in one hand, a pistol in the other. The *piazza* commands a spectacular view of Rome, and marks one of the last places that Garibaldi's ragtag Italian troops tried to hold off Napoleon.

SUMMIT

The ridge of the Janiculan Hill is a vast park commanding the finest view of the city available. On clear days the Alban Hills and the Abruzzi Mountains are visible in the distance. Climb the tortuous V. Garibaldi from V. della Scala, off V. della Lungara in

Church of Santa Susana

Trastevere, or take bus #41 from the Vatican. From Trastevere, bus #44, #75, or #710 will take you to the residential district of Monteverde, a 10-minute walk south of the park.

BOTANICAL GARDENS. Filled with well-labeled specimens of trees and flowers, the gardens remain green and luxuriant even when the rest of Rome is yellow. The impressive, well-maintained assemblage of flora stretches from valleys of ferns through groves of bamboo to a hilltop Japanese garden. Of interest are the **Garden of Rose Evolution,** containing the two founding bushes from which all roses supposedly have sprung, and the **Garden for the Blind,** a star-shaped garden of various tactile and odiferous plants labeled in Braille. *(At the end of V. Corsini, off V. della Lungara, at Largo Cristina di Svezia, 24. Grounds open Apr.-July and Sept. M-Sa 9am-6:30pm; Oct.-Mar. M-Sa 9am-5:30pm. Greenhouse open M-Sa 9am-12:30pm. Closed Aug. L4000, ages 6-11 L2000, under 6 free.)*

TERMINI & SAN LORENZO

NORTH OF TERMINI

PIAZZA DEL QUIRINALE AND VIA XX SETTEMBRE

see map p. 316–317

🔢 *Several blocks south of P. Barberini and northeast of P. Venezia.*

PIAZZA DEL QUIRINALE. This *piazza*, at the southwest end of V. del Quirinale, occupies the summit of the tallest of Rome's original seven hills. From the belvedere, the view takes in a sea of Roman domes, with St. Peter's in the distance. In the middle of the *piazza*, the heroic statues of **Castor and Pollux** (mythical warrior twins whom ancient Romans embraced as their protectors) flank yet another of Rome's many obelisks. The fountain over which they preside was once a cattle trough in the Roman Forum.

PALAZZO DEL QUIRINALE. The President of the Republic officially resides in this imposing *palazzo*, a Baroque collaboration by Bernini, Carlo Maderno, and Domenico Fontana. Maderno designed the front, while Bernini set himself to the *manica lunga* (long sleeve) on V. del Quirinale. Look through the portals on the *piazza* for a glimpse of the white-uniformed, silver-helmeted Republican Guards (each of whom must be at least 2m tall to get his job) and the *palazzo's* lush gardens. The *palazzo* was once the papal summer palace and then a royal residence; since 1947, it has hosted the president. The palazzo is not open to the public. The neighboring white stone **Palazzo della Consulta** houses the constitutional court.

CHURCH OF SANT'ANDREA AL QUIRINALE. One of Bernini's simpler designs, its oval-shaped interior departs from traditional church plans; the altar is on the long wall, making the nave wider than it is long. Note Bernini's theatrical orchestration of the main altar. *(From P. Quirinale, go east on V. Quirinale. Open Sept.-July W-M 8am-noon and 4-7pm; Aug. W-M 8am-noon.)*

CHURCH OF SAN CARLINO. The marvelous facade of this Borromini church, officially **San Carlo alle Quattro Fontane,** provides a sharp contrast to neighboring Sant'Andrea alle Quattro Fontane. Borromini avoided the kind of mixed-media extravaganzas that Bernini perfected, choosing to focus on architecture alone. As a result, San Carlino presents a relatively simple interior, organized by periodic pairs of pilasters. The triangle motif throughout is meant to symbolize the Trinity. The church also has the distinction of being both Borromini's first and last work: though he designed the simple interior early on in his career, he finished the more ornate facade just before his suicide. He also designed the **cloister** next door, which holds the **crypt** where he had hoped in vain to be buried. *(Near the corner of V. Quirinale (V. XX Settembre) and V. Quattro Fontane. Open M-F 9:30am-12:30pm and 4-6pm, Sa 9am-12:30pm; if the interior is closed, ring at the convent next door.)*

VIA XX SETTEMBRE. The intersection of V. del Quirinale and V. delle Quattro Fontane showcases one of Pope Sixtus V's more gracious additions to the city. In an effort to ease traffic and better define the city's regions, the 16th-century pontiff straightened many of Rome's major streets and erected obelisks at important junctions. From the cross-roads here, you can survey the obelisks at P. del Quirinale, at the top of the Spanish Steps, and at Santa Maria Maggiore, as well as (in the distance) Michelangelo's famous *Porta Pia.* Two of the four reclining figures in the fountains represent the two virtues, Strength and Fidelity, and the other two represent Lazio's two rivers, the Tiber and the Aniene. V. del Quirinale becomes V. XX Settembre at this intersection, and after a few more blocks opens into the Baroque **Piazza San Bernardo,** site of Domenico Fontana's colossal **Fontana dell'Acqua Felice,** built in 1587 at the point where the **Acqua Felice aqueduct** enters the city. The beefy and horned statue of Moses is said to have been carved by Prospero Antichi, who nearly died of disappointment after seeing the finished product.

Palazzo del Quirinale

CHURCH OF SANTA MARIA DELLA VITTORIA. This church is named for a miraculous icon of Mary that won a battle near Prague for the Catholics in 1620. In the Cornaro Chapel (last on the left), **Bernini**'s turbulent *Ecstasy of St. Theresa of Avila* depicts the young Spanish saint, reformer of the Carmelite nuns, in a moment of ecstatic revelation, in which she felt an angel pierce her heart with a flaming arrow. *(On the south side of P. S. Bernardo. Open daily 7:30am-12:30pm and 4-6:30pm.)*

CHURCH OF SANTA SUSANNA. On the north side of P. S. Bernardo, the Church of Santa Susanna, the American National Church in Rome, has a distinctive Counter-Reformation facade by Carlo Maderno (1603). Inside, Baldassarre Croce's frescoes of the life of the biblical Susanna cover the walls, and Giovanni Antonio Paracea's four large statues of the prophets stand on pillars dating from the 9th century. St. Susanna, niece of Pope Caius, converted to Christianity as a youth and "sacrificed herself to God, making an offering to him of her virginity." When she refused Emperor Diocletian's orders to marry his son and worship an idol of Jupiter, he had her beheaded in his home.

Piazza San Bernardo

BATHS OF DIOCLETIAN

◗ *P. della Repubblica, at the end of V. Nazionale, just north of Termini.*

Though all that's left now are scattered ruins, from AD 298 to 306, 40,000 Christian slaves were kept busy building these baths, then the grandest community center of Rome. The baths, which could serve 3000 people at once, contained gymnasiums, art galleries, gardens, libraries, and concert halls. Going to the heated public toilet was a social event in itself, as it could accommodate thirty people at a time. The cold pool *(frigidarium)* alone measured 2500m^2, the size of a small lake. The baths were modeled on Trajan's thermal baths, the first to abandon a strict north-south axis to make better use of solar energy; the *calidarium,* or hot bath, faced southwest, thus facing the sun during the warmest parts of the day, and the *frigidarium* faced

Baths of Diocletian

northeast. The complex fell into ruin in 538 when the aqueducts supplying water for the baths were destroyed, perhaps out of jealousy, by Witigis and his dirty Ostrogoths. Damn barbarians.

CHURCH OF SANTA MARIA DEGLI ANGELI. Centuries later, a Sicilian priest had a vision of a swarm of angels rising from the baths and pestered Pius IV to build a church on the dilapidated site. So, in 1561 Pope Pius IV ordered Michelangelo, then 86, to undertake what would be his last architectural work and convert the ruins into a church. Imitating the architecture of the baths, his original design used the remains of the *calidarium* as the church facade. This is how it appears today, although much of his interior plan was changed after he and the Pope died three years later. Despite the departure from Michelangelo's plan and the many years of design revisions, the interior gives a sense of the ancient baths. The church was constructed in the ancient *tepidarium* (lukewarm baths); Michelangelo scavenged material from the baths to construct the red porphyry columns that line the church interior. In the floor leading from the east transept to the altar is a sundial, which provided the standard time for Roman clocks for hundreds of years. The sacristy leads to ruins of the *frigidarium* as well as a small exhibit on the construction of the church. *(Open daily 7:30am-12:30pm and 4-6:30pm.)*

ROTONDA AND BATHS EXHIBIT. Statues from the baths of Diocletian and other imperial baths stand in a ring around this 4th-century rotonda's vaulted octagonal room, which once served as a planetarium. Glass panels in the center and on the edges of the floor allow a view down into the excavations. In the center of the room are two well-preserved bronze statues—a rare sight, due to the medieval propensity to use ancient ruins as quarries for raw materials. *(On the right after exiting S. Maria degli Angeli, in the building on V. Romita between V. Parigi and V. Cernaia. Open M-F 9am-2pm, Sa-Su 9am-1pm. Free.)*

VIA NOMENTANA

◪ *Beginning at the **Porta Pia** (designed by Michelangelo), this breezy road is lined with pleasant villas, embassies, and parks. Hop on bus #36 in front of Termini or head to V. XX Settembre and catch the #60; both traverse the boulevard.*

VILLA TORLONIA. About a kilometer from the Porta Pia is Mussolini's former estate. The house is now abandoned and somewhat dilapidated, but the grounds have become a public park. Walk in through the foreboding gates to see over 50 species of birds and 100 types of trees and shrubs. Don't miss the **Museo della Casina delle Civette** (see p. 160).

CHURCH OF SANT'AGNESE FUORI LE MURA. The courtyard of the church doubles as a boys' center playground and is worth exploring. Inside the basilica, a 7th-century apse shows off the extraordinary Byzantine-style mosaic of St. Agnes with a pair of popes. St. Agnes was a 12-year-old martyred by Diocletian for refusing to marry. Its **catacombs,** perhaps the best preserved and least crowded in Rome, contain the remains of St. Agnes and other early Christians. *(V. Nomentana, 349. ☎06 86205456. Open daily 9am-noon and 4-6pm; closed M afternoons. Catacombs L8000 with Italian tour. English guidebook available.)*

CHURCH OF SANTA COSTANZA. On V. Nomentana, next to Sant'Agnese Fuori le Mura, the original round structure of this church was built by Constantine's daughter Constantinia as a mausoleum for herself. She was cured of leprosy while sleeping on St. Agnes's tomb, leading her to convert to Christianity. In the following centuries, her tomb was transformed into a baptistry, then a church. Note that the 4th-century mosaics are void of Christian symbolism; they predate current Christian iconography.

ESQUILINE HILL

The Esquiline and Caelian (see p. 129) hills, the biggest of Rome's seven original hills, also happen to be home to some of the city's greatest chaos. In ancient times, Nero built his decadent Domus Aurea (see p. 86) between these hills. In the wake of its destruction, many of Rome's early Christian churches were constructed here.

BASILICA OF SANTA MARIA MAGGIORE

From Termini, exit south onto V. Giolitti, and walk down V. Cavour. The back of the basilica will be on your left; walk around to the southeastern side to enter. Open daily 7am-7pm. Dress code enforced.

The Basilica of Santa Maria Maggiore crowns the summit of the Esquiline. Fourth among the seven major basilicas traditionally visited on the pilgrimage to Rome, it is also one of the five churches in Rome granted extraterritoriality, making it officially part of Vatican City. It is the best-preserved paleo-Christian basilica in the city.

According to legend, the Virgin Mary appeared before Pope Liberius in August 352 and requested that he build a church in her honor. The locale was to be the spot on the Esquiline that would be covered in snow the next morning. On the morrow, the Pope discovered that snow had indeed fallen on the hill's crest. Liberius promptly set out to design and build the church, first named Santa Maria della Neve (St. Mary of the Snow). However, it appears that the basilica was actually built 80 years later by Pope Sixtus III, who had noticed that Roman women were still visiting a temple to mother goddess Juno Lucina, built on the hill next to Liberius's small, older church. Sixtus enthusiastically tore both down to build his new basilica, not only substituting a Christian cult for a pagan one, but also celebrating the very recent Council of Ephesus, which had declared Mary to be imbued with a divinity that raised her above general humankind. Most of the beautiful mosaics inside are designed to commemorate her radiant new status.

Maria Maggiore has a deceptive exterior: while the shell Ferdinando Fuga built for it in 1750 is 18th-century Baroque, inside it is one of the best-preserved classical basilicas. Ancient columns divide the rectangular church into a central nave with two side aisles surmounted by clerestory windows. The triumphal arch over the high altar swims in mosaics honoring the Holy Virgin Mary, most excitingly in the 13th-century depiction of her coronation. The rest of the mosaics date from the 5th century, including one on the left which shows details from a story in an apocryphal gospel, in which Mary is featured as a devotee in service of the Jewish temple, spinning a basket of purple wool to make a veil. The coffered ceiling above it all is believed to have been gilded with the first gold sent back from America by Columbus.

In the subterranean *confessio* before the altar, a charming marble Pope Pius IX kneels in front of a relic of the baby **Jesus' crib.** Though now sheathed in globs of silver, the crib is revealed each Christmas morning. A dazzling *baldacchino* looms over the altar, which enshrines the famous *acheiropoieton* picture of the Madonna. To the right of the altar, a simple marble slab marks the **tomb of Gian Lorenzo Bernini.** Outside in the P. di Santa Maria Maggiore, pigeons flock around a statue of the Virgin perched atop a 15m column left over from Constantine's 3rd-century basilica.

The **loggia**'s 14th-century mosaics tell the story of Liberius's snowy dream. A visit to the *loggia* grants access to the one-time private chambers of Pope Paul V and Bernini's stunning, steep, spiral staircase. *(Open daily 9:30am-noon and 2-5:30pm. Buy tickets in the church souvenir shop, L5000.)*

CHURCH OF SANTA CROCE IN GERUSALEMME

M:A-San Giovanni. From P. di Porta S. Giovanni north of the Metro stop, walk east on V. Carlo Felice; the church is on the right. From P. V. Emanuele II, take V. Conte Verde (V. di S. Croce in Gerusalemme). Open M-Sa 9:30am-noon and 3-6pm, Su and holidays 9:30am-noon and 2:30-5:30pm.

This unique church is believed to have been built around 326, but was rebuilt twice—in 1144, when the *campanile* was added, and in 1744, when the facade got a facelift. Its true attraction is the fascist-era **Chapel of the Relics,** containing fragments of the "true cross" found by St. Helena. It also houses a healthier chunk of the cross of Dismas (the Good Thief), thorns from Christ's crown, and a nail used in the crucifixion. Perhaps the eeriest of the chapel's relics is the dismembered finger used by doubting Thomas to probe Christ's wounds. At the end of the right aisle in the church's interior, the **Chapel of St. Helena** contains 15th-century mosaics depicting Christ, Peter, Paul, and Helena. On the left side of the church, next to the main entrance, lies the **Chapel of the Crucifixion,** with a 14th-century Giottist fresco of the scene on Golgotha.

CHURCH OF SANTA PRASSEDE

◪ *From the front of Santa Maria Maggiore, walk up V. Merulana, taking the first right onto tiny V. San Giovanni Gualberto. The church is ahead at the dead-end. Open daily 7am-noon and 4-6:30pm.*

Prassede and Pudenziana, the daughters of the powerful Senator Pudente, reputedly buried the corpses of 3000 persecuted Christians and were converted themselves by St. Peter around AD 50. The Vatican doubted this story enough to remove the girls from the register of saints in 1969. Built in 822, the Church of Santa Prassede houses what may be the most beautiful set of Christian **◪mosaics** in Rome. In the apse is the New Jerusalem, a triumphal lamb, and the two sister saints being presented to Christ, with Peter and Paul encouraging them. In the right aisle is the small but stupendously glittering **Chapel of St. Zeno** (lit by a machine outside the door, L600). The chapel is populated by various saints, while four angels in the vault hold up a Byzantine Christ floating in a sea of gold. Note the Empress Theodora, far above your head, who has a square halo, indicating that she was still alive when the mosaics were made. This chapel also holds part of a column of rare oriental jasper retrieved from Jerusalem in 1228 during the 6th Crusade, reputedly the column to which Christ was strapped and flogged.

CHURCH OF SANTA PUDENZIANA

◪ *From the back of Santa Maria Maggiore, walk down V. A. Depretis, taking a left onto V. Urbana. The church will be on your right. Open Tu-F 7am-7pm, M and Sa 7:30am-5pm.*

Legend has it that this small church was built by Pope Pius I in 145 on the property of the late Senator Pudente, in gratitude to his daughters. The original buildings of the church do in fact date to 145, and they were used as places of meeting and worship for Christians in Rome. The church still has substantial traces of its 2nd-century origins. The original windows, though walled up, are still visible, as are remnants of the original buildings in an area behind the altar. The mosaic of Christ teaching the Apostles in the apsidal vault is the oldest known mosaic in a place of worship in Rome.

PIAZZA VITTORIO EMANUELE II

Down V. Carlo Alberto from the front steps of Santa Maria Maggiore, this large piazza contains a large outdoor market, with piles of fresh fish, fresh fruit, clothes, shoes, and luggage. Its small park houses the curious remains of a 4th-century fountain. The Porta Magica, a few steps away, reveals an alchemist's ancient instructions for turning lead into gold; look for it next to fake Prada bags on nearby streets.

CAMPO VERANO & THE JEWISH CEMETERY

◪ *Bus #492 from Termini to P. Verano. To the right of Basilica S. Lorenzo Fuori le Mura, down V. Tiburtina, in San Lorenzo. A bus runs through the cemetery on Sa and holidays. Campo Verano open daily 8am-6pm. Jewish cemetery open daily Apr.-Sept. 7:30am-6pm; Oct.-Mar. 7:30am-5pm.*

More beautiful than bone-chilling, Campo Verano, Rome's largest public cemetery, features a maze of underground tombs lined with fresh-cut flowers, statuary, and a fetishistic number of photographs of the dead incorporated into tombstones. On November 1 and 2, All Saints' and All Souls' Days, Romans make pilgrimages to the tombs of their relatives, placing chrysanthemums on the stones. The Jewish Cemetery is next door on the far side of the cemetery at Campo Verano.

OPPIAN HILL

CHURCH OF SAN PIETRO IN VINCOLI

◪ *M:B-Cavour. Alternatively, take bus #75 to Largo V. Venosta. Walk southwest on V. Cavour, down toward the Forum. Take the stairs on your left up to P. S. Pietro in Vincoli. Open daily 7am-12:30pm and 3:30-7pm.*

Dating from the 4th century, San Pietro in Vincoli is so-named after the sacred chains by which St. Peter was supposedly bound after having been imprisoned on the Capitoline. The two chains were separated for more than a century in Rome and Constantinople, brought back together in the 5th century, and now lie beneath the altar.

In the right aisle of the church, an unfinished fragment of Michelangelo's *Tomb of Julius II* testifies to the monumental frustration that the artist suffered trying to complete the work. He originally designed an enormous rectangular structure decorated with over 40 statues (among them the unfinished *Captives,* now in Florence's Accademia). Pope Julius II quibbled over the cost, his successor popes stalled out of jealousy, and Michelangelo never found the time or money to finish what he had hoped would be his greatest work. Nevertheless, his central figure, the imposing ■**statue of Moses,** presides regally over the church. The anomalous goat horns protruding from his head come from a medieval misinterpretation of the Hebrew Bible. According to Exodus, when Moses descended from Sinai with the Ten Commandments, "rays" (similar to "horns" in Hebrew) shone from his brow. Flanking the statue are Leah and Rachel, who represent the contemplative and active lives, respectively. Julius wanted this to be the greatest funeral monument ever built. The wish is now moot, as Julius's remains were scattered in the Sack of Rome (1527). For a little extra insight, pick up Freud's fast-paced essay on the statue, *Moses and Michelangelo.*

Triton Fountain

SOUTHERN ROME

CAELIAN HILL

see map p. 322

Just east of the Colosseum, the Caelian, along with the Esquiline (see p. 126), is the biggest of Rome's seven original hills and home to some of the city's greatest chaos. In ancient times, Nero built his decadent Domus Aurea between these hills (see p. 86). In the wake of its destruction, many of Rome's early churches were constructed here.

CHURCH OF SAN CLEMENTE

🔲 *M:B-Colosseo. Turn left out of the station, walk east on V. Fori Imperiali (V. Labicana) away from the Forum, and turn right onto P. S. Clemente. From the Manzoni (A) stop, walk west on V. A. Manzoni (V. Labicana), and turn left onto P. S. Clemente. ☎06 70451018. Open M-Sa 9am-12:30pm and 3-6pm, Su and holidays 10am-12:30pm and 3-6pm. Admission to lower basilica and mithraeum L5000.*

Ecstasy of St. Theresa

Split into three levels, each from a different era, the ■**Church of San Clemente** is one of Rome's most intriguing churches. The complex incorporates centuries of handiwork into three layers: a 12th-century church on top of a 4th-century church, with an ancient mithraeum and sewers at the bottom.

The upper church holds medieval mosaics of the Crucifixion, saints, and apostles. A fresco cycle by Masolino (possibly executed with help from his pupil Masaccio) dating from the 1420s graces the **Chapel of Santa Caterina.** A fresco of St. Christopher, upon which 15th-century hooligan pilgrims scrawled their names, decorates the left wall that supports the arch of the chapel. The marble choir enclosure, dating

Church of l'Immacolata Concezione

from the 6th century, shows off a Romanesque paschal candlestick that originally belonged to the lower church. The 12th-century courtyard to the upper church is the only extant medieval atrium in Rome; in summer, it is sometimes a venue for opera or live music.

The early plan of the sprawling 4th-century lower church has been obscured by piers and walls built to support the upper church. With a little imagination, one can trace the lines of the original nave, aisles, and apse, which retain rare 11th-century frescoes. On this level are a few curiosities, including the tomb of St. Cyril (responsible for the Cyrillic alphabet) and a series of frescoes depicting scenes from the life of St. Clement, the 4th Pope. In one, a Roman general, angry at Clement for converting his wife, sends his men to arrest him. Through divine intervention, they are lead to believe that some marble columns are the wily Pope; their swearing when they cannot drag Clement away is rendered in Italian, the first written use of the language.

A 2nd stair leads further underground to the dank imperial ruins and creepy 2nd-century **mithraeum** (see **Mithraism,** p. 56). A little further lies the *insulae,* a warren of brick and stone rooms where Nero is rumored to have played his lyre in AD 64 while the rest of Rome burned. Below this is a still-operative complex of Republican drains and sewers, some 30m below street level.

CHURCH OF SANTO STEFANO ROTONDO

🚩 *V. di S. Stefano Rotondo, 7. From P. di S. Giovanni, take V. di S. Giovanni. The road forks twice; stay to the left. Open M 3:30-6:30pm, Tu-Sa 9am-1pm and 3:30-6pm; July 1-Sept. 3 Tu-Sa morning only.*

Built in the late 5th century, the Church of Santo Stefano Rotondo is one of the oldest and largest circular churches in existence. Long-needed restoration continues on the church, and much of it is inaccessible; it takes some imagination to picture what the first church must have looked like. It was once structured in three conentric rings, but centuries of decay and remodeling reduced it to the two inner rings by 1450. Partial conclusion of renovations have made the impressive round structure of the church itself and the 17th-century mosaics in the first chapel on the left accessible to visitors.

CHURCH OF SANTI QUATTRO CORONATI

Named after four soldiers of Diocletian who were martyred for refusing to offer sacrifices to pagan deities, this church, though small and inconspicuous, has played a prominent part in Roman ecclesiastical history. Due to its proximity to the Lateran Palace (early seat of the papacy), the church housed a high-raking Catholic official *in loco* for many years.

The position of the church on the Caelian Hill made it a perfect location for a fortified defense for the Lateran area, and during the 13th century the massive western walls were raised. As such, the church became a refuge for Popes under siege, as well as visiting royalty like Charles of Anjou, earning it the moniker, "The Royal Hospice of Rome."

The little **chapel** to the right off the entrance courtyard contains an extraordinary fresco cycle of the life of Constantine painted in 1248 (ring the bell of the convent; the cloistered nuns will send you a key on a lazy susan; L1000). Take a break from your climb to the church to sit on the benches that line the walls of the chapel and gaze on a series of frescoes from the life of Sylvester, including Constantine presenting him with the papal crown.

The 13th-century **cloister** (ring the bell from inside and a sister will let you in) ranks as one of the most beautiful in the city, along with the that of the Basilica San Paolo fuori le Mura (see p. 136). While San Paolo's cloister owes its magnificence to size and splendor, the cloister here strikes the senses with its elegant simplicity and utter peacefulness. The marble arches and columns of artisan Pietro dè Maria surround a 12th-century Romanesque cantarus. The result is beautiful. Sadly, the cloister is one of the most endangered historical sites in Rome. See it while it's still here. *(V. dei S.S. Quattro Coronati, 20. From P. di S. Giovanni, take V. di S. Giovanni, bear left at the first fork, right at the second. Open M-Sa 9:30am-noon and 4:30-6pm, Su 6:45am-12:30pm and 3-5:30pm.)*

SAN GIOVANNI

CHURCH OF SAN GIOVANNI IN LATERANO

🏛 M:A-San Giovanni or bus #16 from Termini. Open daily 7am-7:30pm. Cloister open daily 9am-6pm; L4000. Dress code enforced.

To the west of the *motorino*-filled P. di Porta San Giovanni stands the immense Church of San Giovanni in Laterano, the cathedral of the diocese of Rome and the end of the traditional pilgrimage route from St. Peter's. The church and adjoining Lateran Palace, which possess the same rights of extraterritoriality as Vatican City, was the seat of the popes until their flight to Avignon in the 14th century. The church, founded by Constantine in AD 314, is the oldest Christian basilica in the city. On Corpus Christi, the ninth Sunday after Easter, a triumphal procession including the College of Cardinals, the Swiss Guard, and hundreds of Italian girl scouts, leads the pontiff back to the Vatican after mass. The doors of the main entrance, facing the Porta San Giovanni, were pillaged from the Curia, the Roman senate house in the Forum. Inside, the old basilica plan, notable for its four aisles, has been obscured by Borromini's 17th-century remodel.

Aventine Hill

The stately Gothic *baldacchino* over the altar houses two golden reliquaries containing **the heads of Saints Peter and Paul.** A door to the left of the altar leads to the modest 13th-century **cloister,** home to the church's collection of sacred relics and regalia. The exquisite twisted double columns and inlaid pavement are typical of the Cosmati family, which designed them and many other stone projects in Rome.

A terrorist bomb heavily damaged the basilica in 1993 (a simultaneous blast devastated the Church of San Giorgio in Velabro). The facade received most of the damage and some frescoes nearly collapsed, but the damage has been contained.

Basilica of Santa Maria Maggiore

BAPTISTERY OF SAINT JOHN AND THE LATERAN PALACE. Built by Constantine in the 4th century, the baptistry is part of the original Lateran Palace, now closed to the public. During that era, all Christians were baptized here, and the octagonal building served as the model for its famous cousin in Florence. Try to sneak in to see its wonderful frescoes and mosaics. *(Just west of the church on the south end of P. di S. Giovanni in Laterano. Open only for masses and baptisms, usually on Su.)*

SCALA SANTA

🏛 M:A-San Giovanni or bus #16 from Termini. Across the street from the church. Open Apr.-Sept. 6:15am-7:30pm, Oct.-Mar. 6:15am-6:30pm.

The Scala Santa houses what are believed to be the 28 marble steps used by Jesus outside Pontius Pilate's house in Jerusalem. Pilgrims win indulgence for their sins if they ascend the steps on their knees, while pausing to recite prayers on each step. Martin Luther experienced one of his key early breaks with Catholicism while on pilgrimage here—in the middle of his way up, he realized what he saw as the futility and false piety of what he was doing, stood up, and left. If you too have difficulties with the idea of kneeling your way up to the Sancta Sanctorum, use the secular stairs on either side. In the

Church of San Pietro in Vincoli

sanctuary you'll find, among other relics, the so-called *acheropite* image, a depiction of Christ supposedly not created by human hand (though some research claims it to be of 5th- or 6th-century Roman origin).

AVENTINE HILL

Along with the Parioli district north of the city, the Aventine stands out as one of the most wealthy areas of the city. In contrast to many of the less affluent southern neighborhoods, the tree-lined streets here are lush, flanked by villas and luxury apartments with some of the nicest views south of the Centro Storico.

While mainly residential, the Aventine is also home to several ancient churches, the famous keyhole view of St. Peter's, and a breathtaking rose garden. Its green spaces offer a welcome respite from the intense heat and pollution that blanket Rome in the summer. You can see most of the sights in a few hours, especially if you're near the Palatine or Circus Maximus. Reach the Aventine from the north (via the Circus Maximus Metro (B) stop) or south (via the Piramide (B) stop).

PIAZZA DEI CAVALIERI DI MALTA. This postcard-perfect *piazza* from which you can see St. Peter's Basilica through a keyhole was home to the crusading Knights of Malta. Peek through the keyhole in the large green gate at #3 for a perfectly framed view of the dome of St. Peter's. *(At the end of V. Santa Sabina, past the Church of Santi Bonifacio e Alessio.)*

CHURCH OF SANTA SABINA. First built in the 5th century under Celestine I, it has seen much remodeling over the years. However, the few original remains make a tremendous impression. The carved wooden doors of the basilica depict several notable Biblical scenes, including one of the earliest known representations of the Crucifixion. *(At the southern (uphill) end of Parco Savello, in P. d'Illiria. Open daily 7am-12:30pm and 3:30-7pm.)*

ROSETO COMUNALE. A gardener's dream, the Roseto offers a 10,000m² respite from motorino-choked Rome. Take a leisurely stroll through over 1200 varieties of rose plants and sit at one of the tables under the umbrellas in the lower section to enjoy the view of the Palatine. Each May, the horticultural world descends upon the Roseto to compete for the *Premio Roma*, given to the best new variety of rose. Winners are featured in the lower section. Built in 1954 after the old Roseto was destroyed in WWII, the new version sits atop the site of the old Jewish Cemetery, which was moved to Campo Verano (see p. 137). When asked for the land by the city, the leader of the Jewish community agreed, but requested that the old site be remembered. As a result, steles of the Ten Commandments flank the entrances, and the upper section is shaped like a menorah. *(V. di Valle Murcia, up from P. Ugo la Malfa, across the Circus Maximus from the Palatine Hill. Open daily 8am-7pm.)*

CHURCH OF SANT'ANSELMO. Constructed between 1893 and 1900, it has a peaceful garden courtyard and a weekly Gregorian chant mass. *(P. Cavalieri di Malta 5. Open daily 8:30am-7:15pm; chant mass Su 8:30am.)*

APPIAN WAY

🚩 *Parco dell'Appia Antica info: V. Appia Antica, 42. ☎ 800 2800. Bus #218 from San Giovanni; get off before Domine Quo Vadis. Open daily 9am-5:30pm, hours sometimes vary. See map, p. 323.*

The Appian Way was built in 312 BC and has been called the "queen of roads" ever since. It once traversed the whole peninsula, providing a straight path for legions heading to conquests in the East. It also witnessed the grisly crucifixion of Spartacus's rebellious slave army in 71 BC—bodies lined the road from Rome to Capua. Decades later, St. Peter took the Appian Way on his first trip to Rome with his disciples in AD 42. Since burial inside the city walls was forbidden during ancient times, fashionable Romans made their final resting place along the Appian Way, while early Christians secretly dug the maze-like catacombs under the ashes of their persecutors.

Some of Italy's modern *autostrade* still follow the ancient path, but a sizeable portion of the road remains in its antique state. If you make it far enough south, past the tomb of Cecilia Metella, you will get to a stretch of the road paved with enormous original paving stones, lined with fragments of white tomb statues and cornices, and bordered by horse pastures and views of the valley below. It will also take you past a minor Italian military base; be careful!

Exercise **caution** when walking on V. Appia Antica. As in antiquity, the Appia Antica is a very busy thoroughfare, especially during rush hour, when it is used as a shortcut from the center of town to the major roads in the southeast. Shoulders are virtually non-existent, and you will be walking very near speeding cars. The road is **closed to traffic** on Sundays and holidays from 9:30am to 7pm, making it the ideal time to walk or bike along the ancient road. The road near the catacombs is sometimes closed when all of the catacombs are closed—often on Wednesdays.

Beyond Cecilia's tomb (see below), the Appian Way continues 7km through rural countryside before it meets the GRA. The remains of circular and turreted tombs, commemorative reliefs, and steles line the road between the country villas of Rome's glitterati. The ruins of the large Villa dei Quintilli and the Casal Rotondo are most notable. If you're walking, note that bus #660 stops its service shortly after reaching the catacombs; you'll have to walk back, too.

Catacombs

CATACOMBS

🚺 *M:A-San Giovanni. Take bus #218 from P. di S. Giovanni to the intersection of V. Ardeatina and V. delle Sette Chiese. At least two catacombs are open any given day (see individual listings). Admission to each L8000. In all three, visitors follow a free guided tour in the language of their choice (every 20min.).*

Outside the city proper lie the catacombs, multi-story cellars for the dead that stretch through tunnel after tunnel for up to 25km on as many as five levels. Of the 60 near Rome, five are open to the public; the most notable are those of San Callisto, Santa Domitilla, and San Sebastiano next door to one another in parks on V. Appia Antica.

For the first 200 years of Christianity in Rome, there were no established burial places—the Romans generally preferred cremation. From the 2nd to the 5th centuries, Christians took their burial business outside the city walls, so that, little by little, more underground tombs were carved into the *tufa* (a type of volcanic rock) beneath the property of wealthy Romans. As the number of martyrs increased, the catacombs evolved from burial grounds of relatives to pilgrimage sites. Refugees never used them for shelter or protection, as popular belief has it.

Testaccio

The long-lost mazes were rediscovered in the 16th century, but excavation didn't begin until the 19th century, under Giovanni Battista de Rossi. Early pilgrims filched bones to sell as relics; consequently, all the bones in the parts of the catacombs open to the public were reinterred in Roman churches.

The catacombs are not recommended for people who are claustrophobic or have difficulty walking, nor are they recommended for those with an irrational fear of death.

SAN CALLISTO. The first public Christian cemetery, the catacombs of San Callisto are Rome's largest, with almost 22km of subterranean paths. The four serpentine levels once held 16 popes (nine were buried in what's now called "The Crypt of the Popes" or, more jovially, "The Little Vatican"), seven bishops, St. Cecilia (the patron saint of music—her remains can now be found in the Church of S. Cecilia in

Mausoleum of Cecilia Matella

Trastevere, see p. 122), and some 500,000 other early Christians. While the tombs in San Callisto are among the most impressive in the city, they're also the most crowded. *(V. Appia Antica, 110. Take the private road that runs northeast to the entrance to the catacombs. ☎06 5130151. Open M-Tu and Th-Su 8:30am-5:30pm, in winter Th-Su 8:30am-5pm; closed Feb.)*

SANTA DOMITILLA. Santa Domitilla enjoys acclaim for its paintings—a 3rd-century portrait of Christ and the Apostles remains intact—and for its collection of inscriptions from tombstones and sarcophagi. The tour also includes a visit to an ancient frescoed pagan tomb adjoining the catacombs. This is the least crowded of the catacombs on the V. Appia Antica. *(V. delle Sette Chiese, 282. Facing V. Ardeatina from the exit of San Callisto, cross the street and walk right up V. delle Sette Chiese; the catacombs are on your left. ☎06 5110342. Open W-M 8:30am-5:30pm, in winter W-M 8:30am-5pm; closed Jan.)*

SAN SEBASTIANO. San Sebastiano's claim to fame is being the temporary home for the bodies of Peter and Paul (or so ancient graffiti on its walls suggests). Running 10km along three levels and accommodating 174,000 tombs, its tunnels are decorated with animal mosaics, disintegrating skulls, and fantastic early Christian iconography. Bernini's bust of St. Peter resides in the chapel on the first level. In addition to the Christian tombs, San Sebastiano contains three elaborate pagan tombs. *(V. Appia Antica, 136. From the #218 bus stop near S. Callisto and S. Domitilla, walk down V. delle Sette Chiese to V. Appia Antica and turn right. ☎06 7850350. Open M-Sa 8:30am-5:30pm, in winter M-Sa 8:30am-5pm; closed Nov.)*

OTHER SIGHTS

PORTA SAN SEBASTIANO. Marking the beginning of the Appian Way, this is one of the nine surviving gates of the ancient Aurelian walls and a fine example of an ingenious Roman defense: the killing gate. The gate was left deceptively weak, but when invaders stormed through, they were trapped in an inner court, where archers picked them off like sitting ducks. Inside, the **Museo delle Mura** tells the walls' history. *(V. di Porta S. Sebastiano, 18. Take bus #218 to the intersection of V. delle Mura Latine and V. Appia Antica. ☎06 70475284. Museum open Tu-Su 9am-7pm. L5000, reduced price L3000, under 18 and over 65 free.)*

DOMINE QUO VADIS? (CHURCH OF SANTA MARIA IN PALMIS). St. Peter is said to have had a vision of Christ at this spot as he was fleeing Rome. Upon being asked *"Domine quo vadis?"* ("Lord, where are you going?"), Christ replied that he was going to Rome to be crucified again because St. Peter had abandoned him. Peter instead returned to Rome and suffered his own martyrdom. In the middle of the aisle lie the alleged **footprints of Christ** in a piece of stone set into the floor of the church. *(At the intersection of V. Appia Antica and V. Ardeatina. Bus #218 from P. di S. Giovanni. Open daily 8am-noon and 4-7pm.)*

BASILICA OF SAN SEBASTIANO. Originally built in the 4th century, the basilica is home to some arrows plucked by St. Agnes from the body of the stalwart soldier saint before he was clubbed to death. The archery death squad scene, a popular subject for later paintings, did not actually have fatal consequences for the historical Sebastian—it was necessary to take sterner measures to do away with the stubborn man.

The church holds an even more distinctive and popularly acclaimed relic, however: a set of **Christ's footprints.** When Christ appeared to speak with Peter on the Appian Way, he left footprints behind. In August 1999, thieves broke into the church and stole a healthy chunk of the art adorning the church. However, they missed the holy footprints (guilt?). *(Directly above the catacombs of the same name (see above). Open daily 8am-6pm.)*

MAUSOLEO DELLE FOSSE ARDEATINE. One of the only modern monuments on the Appian Way is at the Fosse Ardeatine, site of a WWII atrocity. In these caves, Nazis slaughtered 335 prisoners (75 Jews) as a reprisal for an attack by Roman partisans that killed 32 German military police. To hide the corpses and cover their tracks, the Nazis demolished those sections of the cave with explosives. The bodies were recovered and placed in a mass grave that is marked by a monument and a sculpture. *(Bus #218 to the intersection of V. Ardeatina and V. delle Sette Chiese. Walk down V. Ardeatina; it's to your right. ☎06 5136742. Open M-Sa 8:15am-5:45pm, Su and holidays 8:15am-5:15pm.)*

VILLA MASSENZIO. The **Villa of Maxentius** lies half-buried in cricket-filled greenery. Emperor Maxentius built the villa in the first decade of the 4th century, but he never got to enjoy it, having been ejected by the newly Christian Constantine at the Battle of Ponte Milvio. The **Tomb of Romulus,** inside a giant brick portico, housed the remains of the emperor's son, named for the city's founder. The circus is the main attraction, measuring over half a kilometer in length. Those watching the races here would have sat on the sloping sides of the structure, had they ever had the chance. The circus was not finished before the death of its owner. *(Bus #218 to the intersection of V. Appia Antica and V. Fosse Ardeatina. Walk 2 km down V. Appia Antica. The villa is on your right as you start up the hill toward the tomb of Cecilia Metella. Open Tu-Su 9am-7pm, in winter Tu-Su 9am-5pm. L5000, reduced price L3000.)*

MAUSOLEUM OF CECILIA METELLA. This towering turret-like structure was built in the 3rd decade BC for the patrician Cecilia. It was preserved by its conversion into a fortress in the Middle Ages, when its famous crenelations were added. Used as a medieval roadblock of sorts, it stopped travelers to "request" a payment for the Caetni family coffers. The medieval complex includes the ruins of a Gothic church (rare in Rome), the Chiesa San Nicola a Capo di Bove. *(Bus #218 to the intersection of the V. Appia Antica and V. Fosse Ardeatina; walk down V. Appia Antica for about 2½ km. Or take bus #660 from the Colli Albani Metro station to the intersection of V. di Cecilia Metella and V. Appia Antica. Open M-F 9am-7pm, Sa-Su and holidays 9am-1pm, in winter M-F 9am-4pm, Sa-Su and holidays 9am-1pm.)*

TESTACCIO

PYRAMID OF GAIUS CESTIUS. The off-white *Il Piramide di Caio Cestio* towers over Testaccio at the foot of the Aventine. Gaius, tribune of the plebes under Augustus, got caught up in the craze for things Egyptian following the defeat of Cleopatra in the late first century BC (see **History**, p. 45) and had his slaves build this marble pyramid to serve as his tomb. Unfortunately, he got his angles wrong: there's nothing Egyptian about this short grey pyramid except its inspiration. It was built in less than 330 days, and the close fit of its marble blocks ensured that it would never be pillaged. For extra protection from the marauding Goths in the 3rd century, Aurelian had the pyramid built into his city walls. Medieval tradition asserts that it stands over Remus's grave. Nowadays, it's a favorite hangout for Rome's transvestite population. *(M:B-Piramide, bus #175 from Termini, or bus #23 from P. Risorgimento.)*

CIMITERO ACATTOLICO PER GLI STRANIERI. The Protestant Cemetery, or, more literally, the Non-Catholic Cemetery for Foreigners, is the only non-ancient burial space in Rome for those who don't belong to the Catholic Church. Crowded tombstones fight for attention with stray teams of meowing cats in the shade of overgrown tamarind trees. In the far left corner, **John Keats** lies beside his friend, Joseph Severn. At his request, the tombstone itself doesn't mention Keats by name. It soberly states to contain "all that was mortal of a Young English Poet," and (after a quick disclaimer written by friends) records the words Keats wished to be inscribed on his grave: "Here lies one whose name was writ in water." On the other side of the small "New Cemetery," **Percy Bysshe Shelley** rests in peace beside his friend Trelawny, under a simple plaque hailing him as *Cor Cordium*, "Heart of Hearts." Also buried here are Goethe's son Julius, Italian thinker Antoni Gramsci, and Richard Henry Dana, author of *Two Years Before the Mast.* Henry James supposedly buried Daisy Miller here after she died of malaria. Good luck finding her grave, though. That Henry James was a dirty liar. *(V. Caio Cestio, 6. From the Piramide station, follow V. R. Persichetti onto V. Marmorata, immediately turning left onto V. Caio Cestio. Ring bell for admission. Donation requested. Open Apr.-Sept. Tu-Su 9am-5:30pm; Oct.-Mar. 9am-4:30pm.)*

PORTA SAN PAOLO. Called *Porta Ostiense* in antiquity, this gate began the famous *Via del Mare*, which linked Rome to its major port at Ostia. Today, this colossal fragment of the city wall keeps watch over the gnarls of traffic converging at Piramide. Inside lies

Museo Della Via Ostiense, an exellent little history museum with impressive models of life on V. del Mare (see p. 160). *(M:B-Piramide: next to the Pyramid of Gaius Cestius.)*

MONTE TESTACCIO. One of the most famous and historically significant landfills around, Monte Testaccio once served as a transfer area for grain, oil, wine, and marble unloaded from river barges. After goods were stored, ancient Roman merchants tossed leftover terra cotta urns into a vacant lot. The pile grew and grew, and today the ancient garbage dump (whose name is derived from *testae,* or pot shards) rises in lush, dark green splendor over the drab surrounding streets. While the park is no longer open to the public, and pilfering pot shards is illegal, V. di Monte Testaccio, home to a disproportionate number of Roman nightclubs, surrounds the base of the hill and affords a good view. *(Follow V. Caio Cestio from V. Marmorata until it ends at V. Nicola Zabaglia. Continue straight onto V. Monte Testaccio; the hill is ahead and to the right.)*

OSTIENSE

South of Testaccio lies Ostiense, a neighborhood largely born of turn-of-the-century urban migrations. The city's only power plant was once in Ostiense, and though the generator houses are now used for less industrial purposes (such as storing artwork during the Capitoline Museums renovation), the area retains its industrial and somewhat bleak character. Ostiense and neighboring Garbatella are poor, and their development according to government housing schemes precluded the appearance of many cultural attractions. A huge wholesale market *(Mercati Generali)* has been held here for years, though it will soon be moved to the eastern part of the city.

BASILICA SAN PAOLO FUORI LE MURA

This renowned and hulking church holds extraterritorial status (along with San Giovanni in Laterano, Santa Maria Maggiore, and St. Peter's). Until the construction of the new St. Peter's, the church was the largest and (by many accounts) the most beautiful in Rome. St. Paul is believed to be buried under the altar (his body, that is; the head is in San Giovanni). Rebuilt after a huge fire in 1823 (which Stendhal called "sad as the music of Mozart"), the present church is the latest in a long series on this spot; the original was built in 324. The mammoth layout is in the Latin cross style (in the shape of a T), with two aisles flanking the nave on each side.

Warmly lit through high agate windows, the church is deserving of its renown. The triumphal arch before the altar is set with original mosaics, reassembled after the fire, depicting an awkward-looking Christ and the apostles. Along the basilica's periphery, portraits of the popes solemnly greet sporadic tour groups. There is only space for eight more portraits, and legend says that when the wall fills up, the world will end. The fire-damaged Porta Santa (to the left of the central doors of the church when viewed from within) dates from 1070, and is still an excellent example of the Byzantine style. For L1500, the ViewMaster-style "History of This Place" (near the entrance) will transport you back to the exciting world of Catholicism in the 1950s. Don't miss the **cloister;** its gorgeous twisting columns and mosaics make it one of the most beautiful in the city. Be sure to buy a bottle of monk-made **benedictine** in the gift shop (L13,000). *(M:B-Basilica San Paolo. Alternatively, take bus #23 or #170 from Testaccio. Open daily 7am-6:30pm, in winter 7am-6pm; cloister open 9am-1pm and 3-6:30pm, in winter 9am-1pm and 3-6pm. Dress code enforced.)*

EUR

South of Ostiense lies what is perhaps the most striking neighborhood in Rome—EUR (AY-oor), an acronym for Universal Exposition of Rome. Walking through EUR is a shocking contrast to the rest of Rome. Instead of ancient *piazze,* Roman ruins, and meandering, narrow streets, EUR is filled with wide, straight boulevards, apartment highrises, and an eerily perfect street grid reminiscent of Brasilia. Built in good fascist style, EUR was to be the site of the 1942 World's Fair that Mussolini intended as a showcase of fascist and imperial Roman achievements. Apparently, the new, modern Rome was to shock and impress the rest of the world with its futuristic ability to build dozens of rectangular buildings that all look the same. World War II meant cancellation of the fair and demands on manpower and material, ensuring that EUR would never complete Mussolini's dream of extending Rome to the sea.

EUR lies near the end of Metro Linea B (EUR-Palasport or EUR-Fermi stops). You can also take bus #714 from Termini or San Giovanni in Laterano to P. Guglielmo Marconi. Walking north from the Metro stops brings you to the enormous P. Guglielmo Marconi, home of a somewhat garish 1939 modernist obelisk and the major EUR museums (see **Museums**, p. 157). To the south, across the artificial lake, looms the dome of the **Palazzo dello Sport,** which is a major venue for large concerts and sporting events.

North on V. Cristoforo Colombo stands the **Palace of the Civilization of Labor,** EUR's definitive symbol. Designed by Marcello Piacentini in 1938, the big white rectangle is an anticipation of postmodern architecture. By wrapping arched windows around the building, Piacentini attempted to evoke Roman ruins and create a "square Colosseum." Nearby, **Piazzale delle Nazioni Unite** embodies EUR's spirit: imposing modern buildings decorated with spare columns meld the ancient empire with Mussolini's.

Pyramid of Gaius Cestius

ABBAZIA DELLE TRE FONTANE. St. Paul is said to have been beheaded at the site of this Trappist abbey. According to legend, his head bounced on the ground three times, creating a fountain with each bounce—hence the name. Viewing the fountains, one can only imagine the velocity at which his skull hit the ground and the elasticity it possessed to travel so far on each bounce. A millennium later, St. Bernard stayed here during his 12th-century visit to Rome. The Trappist monks who live here today sell their own potent eucalyptus liquor (L14-L27,000) and divine chocolate (L9-18,000 for monstrous bars of this wonderful stuff), as well as marmelade, body cream, and shampoo. *(M:B-Laurentina. Walk about half a mile north on V. Laurentina and turn right onto V. di Acque Salve. The abbey is at the bottom of the hill. Alternatively, take bus #761 north from the Laurentina stop; ask when to get off for the intersection of V. Laurentina and V. di Acque Salve. Open M-Sa 11am-5pm, Su noon-5pm.)*

Porta San Sebastiano

LUNEUR PARK. Tired of museums, ruins, and churches? Head to LunEUR, an old-fashioned amusement park where it's possible to have a good time without any cultural strings attached. Eschewing the grandiose megalomania of, say, Disney, Lunapark has old-fashioned rides and games. Enjoy cheap thrills like the "Himalaya Railroad," "Musik Express," and "Gravitron," or, if you're up to it, dare to enter any of four haunted houses. *(V. delle Tre Fontane. ☎06 5925933. From P. G. Marconi, walk north on V. C. Colombo, turning right onto P. dell'Industria. The piazzale dead-ends into V. dell'Industria; turn left and follow it to V. delle Tre Fontane. Turn right; the park will be on your right. Open M-F 5pm-midnight, Sa 5pm-2am, Su 11am-1pm and 4pm-midnight. Pay by the ride, usually L1-5000.)*

LAGO ARTIFICIALE. Remember the episodes of *Star Trek: The Next Generation* where Captain Picard and crew landed on some Utopian garden planet with peace-loving natives? They must have filmed those scenes here. The man-made lake and small adjoining park are a spitting image of them. We swear. Must be that fascist architecture. *(Just south of Metro (B) stops EUR-Palasport and EUR-Fermi.)*

Appian Way

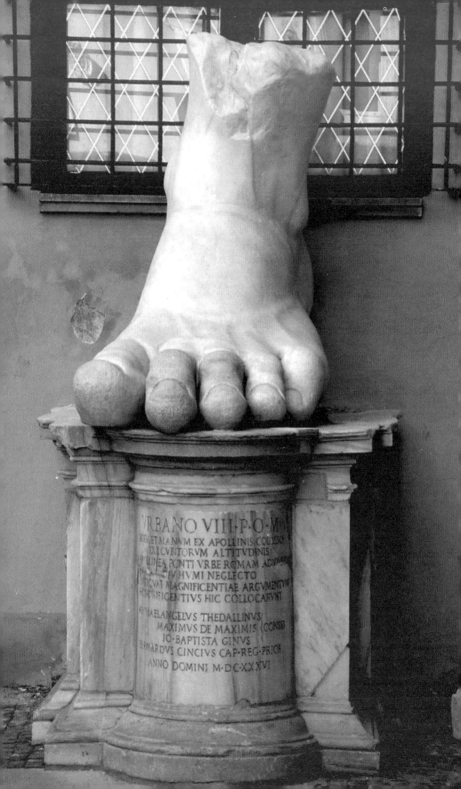

Museums

In a city with so much history that the subway system cannot be expanded for fear of running into yet another underground ruin, one can understand why there's a museum on every block. Etruscans, emperors, popes, and *condottiere* have been busily stuffing Rome's belly full with artwork for several millennia, leaving behind a city teeming with galleries. Ancient, medieval, and Renaissance art are all exceedingly well-represented. To these are added works plundered from Greece, Egypt, and the Orient, as well as modern art obtained in more respectable ways.

Students of art and architecture may be eligible for a special pass, or *tessera*, which allows them to visit certain national museums and monuments for free or at a discount. The bureaucratic bonanza begins at the **Ufficio Centrale Beni Culturali,** Divisione VI, V. di S. Michele, 22, 00153 Roma. Applications should include a letter from your school, two passport photos, and will be processed much more quickly if written in Italian.

Museums are generally closed on Sunday afternoons and all day Monday, as well as major holidays. For up-to-the-minute info on many of Rome's museums, go to www.museionline.it. Museum displays tend toward the haphazard in organization. In exchange for the confusion, however, you'll have the opportunity to tour the *palazzi* which often house these collections, sometimes left just as their 17th- and 18th- century owners decorated them.

PRINCIPAL COLLECTIONS

The museums and galleries described below are the largest and most famous in Rome, and constitute the heart of the city's collections. Most of these museums are wheelchair accessible, but call ahead to request assistance.

◼ ⬚ ⬚ ⬚ 🏛 ⬚ ⬚ ⬚ ⬚ ⬚ ⬚ ⬚ ⬚

VATICAN MUSEUMS

🧭 *Walk north from the right-hand side of P. San Pietro along the wall of the Vatican City about 10 blocks. From the Ottaviano Metro(A) stop, walk south several blocks to the Vatican City Wall, and turn right. ☎ 06 69883333 or 06 69884341. Information and gift shop (with the very useful* **official guidebook***, L12,000) on the ground level past the entrance of the building.* **Currency exchange** *and* **first aid** *stations are near the ticket booths. Valuable* **audio guide** *with information and amusing anecdotes, L8000. All major galleries* **open** *M-Sa 8:45am-1:45pm. Extended hours Mar. 16-Oct. 30: M-F 8:45am-4:30pm, Sa 8:45am-1:45pm. Last entrance 1hr. before closing. Closed on major religious holidays.* **Admission** *L18,000, with ISIC card L12,000, children under 1m tall free.* **Free** *last Su of the month 8:45am-1:45pm. Most of the museum is wheelchair accessible, though less visited parts, such as the upper level of the Etruscan Museum, are not. Various galleries close without explanation; call ahead.* **Snack bar,** *located between the collection of modern religious art and the Sistine Chapel, is open during the summer.* **Plan on spending at least 4-5 hours** *in the Vatican Museums.*

If you have limited time, spend some time plotting your tour before you go—the galleries are so crowded, maze-like, and enormous that aimless wandering will likely leave you frustrated and exhausted. The best known and most noteworthy attractions are Michelangelo's incomparable Sistine Chapel; the Pio-Clementine Museum, with masterpieces of ancient sculpture, mostly first-century Roman copies of 4th-3rd century BC Greek originals; the brilliantly frescoed Raphael Rooms; the beautiful Papal Borgia Apartments, now filled with some of the riches of the modern religious art collection; and the extraordinary Pinacoteca, a collection of 13th- to 18th-century paintings. Surprisingly undervisited, the Vatican's Etruscan collection is among the world's finest. Enjoy Rome offers an excellent Vatican tour that highlights the must-see exhibits (see p. 298).

Other possibilities include: the excellent galleries of Egyptian, Greek, and Roman art; the more esoteric **Pio-Christian Museum** (with early Christian sarcophagi); the exhibition rooms of the Vatican Library; the intermittently open **Missionary-Ethnological Museum** (with mostly African art); and the **Historical Museum** (with furnishings from papal households of the past). The remaining candelabras, Roman and Flemish tapestries, map frescoes, antique globes, reliquaries, carriages, and rare books line the long corridors leading to and from the Sistine Chapel; you'll see them whether you want to or not.

As you wander these treasure troves, don't forget to notice the decoration of the rooms themselves. Practically every floor, however unassuming, is paved with polychrome inlaid marble designs, and the ceilings are brilliant melanges of gilding, fresco, and elaborate stucco relief decoration. From the many large windows you'll glimpse picturesque courtyards, lush gardens, and breathtaking vistas of the Eternal City itself, shimmering across the Tiber.

Most collections sport **English and Italian** labeling of some sort, although the descriptions become frustratingly sparse in certain galleries. There are four theoretical color-coded tour routes of the collections laid out by the management, based on how much time you want to spend; however, unless you buy the official guide (worth the price!), it is almost impossible to follow these paths, as too few colored arrows are visible to direct you. Most rooms have signs to direct you to the Sistine Chapel and nearby collections. The individual gallery coverage that follows is arranged for those who wish to see absolutely everything. Don't try to do this all in a single day! Even if you only wish to see *la Sistina*, it usually takes an hour to 90 minutes simply to navigate all of the crowded galleries that lie between the entrance and that glorious ceiling. However, an early morning run through the halls can land you in the Sistine Chapel before the crowds for the exquisite experience of admiring Michelangelo's masterpieces in silence.

EGYPTIAN MUSEUM

At the top and to the right of the entrance stairs is the **Egyptian Museum,** with ten rooms of Egyptian and pseudo-Egyptian (Roman-made) statuary, paintings, coffins, and mummies. The collection is made up of pieces bought by 18th- and 19th-century popes, brought to Rome during ancient times and unearthed in Roman excavations, and first-century "Egyptian style" Roman sculptures made of Italian marble. Among the most remarkable of the Egyptian antiquities are brilliantly painted polychrome mummy sarcophagi, 3rd-century Coptic (early Egyptian Christian) painted death masks on linen and wood, and a 2100 BC pharaoh bust. The fourth room is filled with colossal fakes: the enormous, mostly black marble first-century Roman emulations of Egyptian antiquities. Many of these statues were excavated from the site of Hadrian's Tivoli villa. Also tucked into the last rooms of the "Egyptian" museum are Mesopotamian seals and ceramics and a large variety of Sumerian and Assyrian bas-reliefs, featuring mythological animal-gods and some of the earliest writing known.

CHIARAMONTI MUSEUM

On the east side of the courtyard, steps lead down to the evocative **Chiaramonti Museum,** a 300m long vaulted corridor designed by Bramante that is little more than a storeroom for the Vatican's muddled collection of over 1000 classical busts, statues, and reliefs, arranged here by Canova in the early 19th century. The **Braccio Nuovo** (New Wing), another gallery of Roman marble copies of classical Greek (4th-3rd century BC) originals, connects to the midpoint of the corridor of the Chiaramonti. This collection of life-size (and larger) statues includes the famous ▨**Augustus of Prima Porta,** a portrait of the emperor at the height of power, and the reclining **Colossus of the Nile,** surrounded by crocodiles, sphinxes, and 16 small boys (representing the 16 cubits of the river's annual flood, of course).

BELVEDERE COURTYARD

Cortile della Pigna (Courtyard of the Pinecone), the uppermost end of Bramante's Belvedere Courtyard, is accessible from the stairway leading into the Chiaramonti as well as from the Braccio Nuovo. It's not hard to see where the name came from; a gigantic bronze pinecone stands flanked by two bronze peacocks on the stone railing of the balcony. The first-century pinecone, formerly the center of a fountain, is actually one of the only works that remains of the original Vatican Museums collection begun by Pope Julius II in 1506. The center of the courtyard features a modern bronze spherical sculpture by a contemporary Italian artist, Gio Pomodoro. The structure atop the end of the building to the right is the **Tower of the Winds.** The sundial inside was used in the 16th century to cast doubt on the Julian calendar. Queen Christina of Sweden briefly lived there after abdicating her throne before insisting on more comfortable apartments.

▨ PIO-CLEMENTINE MUSEUM

Back through the Chiaramonti corridor and up the stairs, a square vestibule leads to the stellar Pio-Clementine Museum, thought to be the Western world's finest collection of antique sculpture. The placid, outdoor **Octagonal Court** opens off the first three small rooms, the birthplace of the Vatican Museums. Julius II filled the court with classical sculpture, thus beginning a rich tradition of papal art collecting.

CABINET OF CANOVA. In the corner of the court on the right stands the Cabinet of Canova, which exhibits the works that Pius bought back from the plundering Napoleon (see **History,** p. 51). These Neo-Classical marbles follow mythological themes: the central group is *Perseus with the Head of Medusa,* flanked by the boxers Kreugas and Damoxenos. After a fight that ended in a draw, the surly Damoxenos, on the right, stabbed his opponent in the stomach and gutted him alive. To the left in the next corner stands the sublime ▨**Apollo Belvedere,** once called "the highest ideal of art" and probably the best-known work of ancient sculpture around. The god's placid features and posture (apparently the sculpture once held a bow in one hand and drew an arrow from its quiver with the other) inspired innumerable Renaissance copies in stone and on canvas. Michelangelo particularly loved this sculpture. Turning clockwise, the next piece is the musculature of the tortured **Laocoön** family, a sculpture that was famous even in ancient times for its vivid grotesqueness. Virgil told the story of Laocoön in his *Aeneid* (and may have modeled his description of the events on the sculpture): the Trojan priest, advising his people against drawing the Trojan Horse into their city, was punished by Athena, protectress of the Greeks, who sent two sea serpents to devour him and his sons. Of course, the Trojans misinterpreted this omen, and happily dragged the "gift" into Troy: *C'est la vie.*

It is thought that the figures of Laocoön and the son to his left were carved from a single piece of marble. Laocoön's raised arm was only discovered and reattached in this century. Many art historians now debate the authenticity of this appendage; if you look closely, the proportions are somewhat off (the arm is puny compared to the original body), and the marble seems slightly off color.

OTHER ROOMS. Two slobbering Molossian hounds guard the entrance to the **Room of the Animals,** a marble menagerie that reveals a lot about the importance of brutality in Roman pastimes. The zoo is adjacent to the **Gallery of Statues**—home to Apollo, Hermes, Ariadne, and others—at the end of which are the stone faces in the **Room of the Busts** (which showcases a thoroughly engaging 1.25m foot and calf muscle). The **Cabinet of the Masks,** also adjacent to the Room of the Animals, houses the **Venus of Cnidos.**

The **Room of the Muses** opens off the animal room and centers around the inscrutable **Belvedere Torso,** a shattered work much beloved in the Renaissance and thought to represent Hercules sitting on the skin of the Nemean lion. Michelangelo's unusually muscled *Last Judgment* Christ in the Sistine Chapel (see p. 147) is modeled after this famous chest. The **Round Room** next door houses colossal Roman statues, including two of Antinous (the ill-fated boy lover of Hadrian), one of the Emperor Claudius in a general's uniform (his reputed obesity and propensity to drool tactfully forgotten), and a breathtakingly gaudy gilded Hercules. In the middle of the Round Room stands a mammoth fountain (measuring 13m in circumference), once thought to be a pterodactyl bath. The **Greek Cross Room,** the last of the gallery, contains the enormous **sarcophagus of St. Helen,** mother of Constantine; directly across from this is the enormous sarcophagus of Constance, daughter of Constantine. On either side of the exit, enormous second-century red-granite sphinxes pose riddles before permitting you to leave. No joke.

ETRUSCAN MUSEUM

The next flight of the Simonetti Stairway climbs to the **Etruscan Museum,** which is filled with artifacts from the necropolis of Tuscany and northern Lazio. This museum is undergoing renovations in parts, but the splendid contents of the **Regolini-Galassi Tomb,** a *tumulus* (burial mound) found intact and treasure-filled outside the necropolis at Cerveteri (see **Daytripping,** p. 230), are always open. In **Room I,** the case on the right holds the extraordinary bronze chariot and bed with which the deceased 7th-century BC couple were supplied for their journey to the other side. **Room III** contains the rare 5th-century BC bronze **Mars of Todi,** while more far-flung rooms keep smaller bronzes, terra cotta figures, red- and black-figure vases (imported from Greece by wealthy Etruscan traders), and jewelry. At the end of the Etruscan Rooms, visit the excellent **Rooms of the Greek Originals,** the **Stairway of the Assyrian Reliefs,** and the **Vase Collection.**

OTHER GALLERIES

GALLERY OF THE CANDELABRA. Back on the landing of the Simonetti Staircase is the usually closed **Room of the Biga,** which holds a first-century marble chariot outfitted with newly sculpted wheels and horses. It once served as an elaborate throne for the bishops of the Church of San Marco. Past the door of the Biga is the Gallery of the Candelabra, named for the mammoth marble candlesticks housed under each archway between its six rooms. More Roman sculptures reside here, including a rather morbid work of a boy strangling a goose in the 4th room, a marble copy of the 3rd-century BC original bronze. It which was immortalized in Pliny's *Natural Histories*. The 5th room contains a statue of Atalanta, the beautiful and rich huntress of mythology. According to legend, Atalanta (perhaps at the prodding of her incestuously interested father) refused to marry any of her many suitors, but promised to espouse any man who could beat her in a footrace. Finally, the crafty young Hippomenes distracted her by tossing golden apples in her path, winning the contest and the lady. Don't miss the 3rd room's extraordinarily detailed fish mosaic, similar to those in Pompeii (see **Daytripping,** p. 213). This room also contains some wonderful detached fresco fragments from the 2nd century.

GALLERY OF THE TAPESTRIES. The Gallery of the Tapestries is next as you exit the Gallery of the Candelabra. Not surprisingly, its walls are hung with massive tapestries, completed by different schools of artistic imitation (Raphael's workshop, etc.). On the left hang Flemish depictions of the life of Christ, including three gory panels on the slaughter of the innocents. On the right, Roman tapestries illustrate exciting stories of obscure Popes and their courtly doings.

GALLERY OF THE MAPS. The next room ahead is a gilded walkway between 40 large frescoes depicting the east and west sides of Italy and the Apennine Mountains. The extensive fresco, stucco, and gold-leaf work on the ceiling is particularly impressive.

APARTMENT OF PIUS V. The Apartment of Pius V comes next, holding yet more tapestries. To the right of the "apartment" there is a shortcut staircase down to the Sistine Chapel. To the left, the longer journey through the museum continues with the Sobieski Room and the Room of the Immaculate Conception.

SOBIESKI ROOM. The Sobieski Room is named for the Polish work that takes up the north wall, "Sobieski Liberates Vienna," in which Sobieski, the king of Poland, defeats the Turks in battle and saves Christendom from takeover by Islamic warriors.

ROOM OF THE IMMACULATE CONCEPTION. The Room of the Immaculate Conception holds hundreds of beautiful and rare books in dozens of languages, all delivering a single statement: Pius IX's 1854 decree announcing the doctrine of Mary's permanent and unsullied virginity. The main fresco on the wall portrays Pope Pius IX proclaiming the controversial dogma.

◪ RAPHAEL ROOMS

From the Room of the Immaculate Conception, a door leads into the first of the four Raphael Rooms (or *stanze*), the papal apartments built by Pope Julius II in the first decade of the 16th century. Julius abandoned the apartments of his predecessor Alexander VI Borgia one story below, saying he couldn't stand to live under the portraits of the nefarious Spanish Pope painted there. He hired the best painters of his day (including Perugino, Peruzzi, and Il Sodoma) to decorate a new suite of rooms and a cozy little *cubiculum* (bedroom) for himself. Although they had already been working for several years, even these geniuses had to make way for the precocious talent of Raphael Sanzio, who painted the astonishing **School of Athens** as a trial piece for Pope Julius. The Pope was so impressed that he immediately fired his other painters, had their frescoes destroyed, and handed the entire suite of rooms over to Raphael. How did Il Sodoma respond to this snub? See p. 155 to find out. The commission marked the beginning of Raphael's brilliant career in Rome. After his death in 1520, Raphael's students completed the decoration of the Holy See's pad from their master's designs.

CONSTANTINE'S ROOM. A detour down an outdoor walkway over the Belvedere Courtyard takes you to Constantine's Room, where the not-so-subtle theme is Christianity's victory over paganism. The tip-off might be the ceiling painting of a pagan god's statue broken on the ground in front of a gleaming gold crucifix on a pedestal. On the entrance wall, Constantine addresses his soldiers and sees the vision of the cross; on the opposite wall is the baptism of Constantine; on the window wall, Constantine donates the city of Rome to Pope Sylvester; on the wall facing the window, Constantine defeats Maxentius at the Battle of the Milvian Bridge.

ROOM OF THE CHIAROSCURI AND THE CHAPEL OF NICHOLAS V. The Room of the Chiaroscuri and the Chapel of Nicholas V lie behind the door in the corner nearest the entrance to the Raphael Rooms. The small chapel forms the oldest section of the palace and was delicately decorated by Fra Angelico between 1447-51, with frescoes depicting events from the lives of St. Stephen and St. Lawrence.

HELIODORUS ROOM. Take the other exit from Constantine's Room to follow the sequence of the Raphael Rooms, which will land you in the **Heliodorus Room** (1512-14), the secret antechamber of the apartments. The room's obscure subjects were chosen by Julius to illustrate the miraculous protection that God afforded to the Church at various times. The right wall tells the Biblical story of Heliodorus. Heliodorus had come to loot the Temple of Jerusalem, but was chucked out by a couple of angels and a horseman. On the entrance wall is the miracle of Bolsena: a priest, who had trouble believing in transubstantiation, came to Mass in Bolsena and saw the wine and bread become blood and flesh. Raphael painted Julius himself in the guise of Pope Urban IV, who, after the miraculous appearance of blood on the altar linen at Bolsena, instituted the feast of Corpus Christi. Note the Swiss Guards, dressed just as festively as they are today, kneeling on the right. On the long wall is Leo I expelling Attila from Rome; on the fourth wall is Raphael's depiction of the miraculous deliverance of St. Peter from the Tullianum Prison on the Capitoline Hill.

STANZA DELLA SEGNATURA. The Stanza della Segnatura (1508-1511), once a library, is considered by some to be Raphael's Vatican masterpiece. The walls represent four branches of learning—theology, law, philosophy, and poetry. Opposite the entrance is the **Disputation of the Holy Sacrament,** in which theologians and celebrated doctors of the Church crowd around a monstrance holding the communion host. On the wall of the entrance is the splendid **School of Athens,** in which ancient philosophers and scientists (many of whom Raphael painted with the features of his friends and fellow artists) stroll through an airy architectural fantasy. In the center, Plato, with the features of Leonardo da Vinci, argues with Aristotle; Euclid, explaining geometry on the ground, has Bramante's face; to the far right of the composition stands Raphael, in three-quarter profile, and his friend and fellow artist, Il Sodoma. In the center, the isolated, brooding figure of Heraclitus is thought to be a portrait of Michelangelo, added as an afterthought when Raphael was given a sneak preview of the Sistine Chapel. Part of what is so remarkable about this fresco is the speed with which it was executed. Raphael supposedly drew up the elaborate cartoons for the frescoes in a matter of days. Furthermore, it appears that Raphael spent as much time working on the face of Heraclitus as the entire left half of the fresco. The remaining scenes depict Mount Parnassus peopled by classical and contemporary Italian poets; opposite are the cardinal and theological virtues, represented by *Gregory IX Approving the Decretals* and *Justinian Publishing the Pandects.*

STANZA DELL'INCENDIO. The final room is the Stanza dell'Incendio (the corner of which you passed through before), containing works by Raphael's pupils, including Giulio Romano. By the time of their painting (1514-17), Pope Leo X Medici had taken up residence in the *stanze*, and portraits of earlier Leos dominate the room. The riotous *Fire in the Borgo* depicts the 847 blaze that was miraculously extinguished when Leo IV made the sign of the cross from the *loggia* of St. Peter's. The painting depicts the facade of the old Constantinian basilica that was pulled down to make way for the new St. Peter's. Other scenes represent the coronation of Charlemagne in 800, the victory of Leo IV over the Saracens at Ostia, and, on the window wall, the oath of Leo III. From here you pass through the precious **Chapel of Urban VIII,** decorated by Pietro da Cortona.

BORGIA APARTMENTS & MUSEUM OF MODERN RELIGIOUS ART

The last stops before the Sistine Chapel are the 55 rooms of the Borgia Apartments and the Museum of Modern Religious Art. The **Borgia Apartments,** named after the infamous Alexander VI Borgia, father of the even more infamous Lucrezia and Cesare, comprise six rooms decorated from 1492-95 by Pinturicchio. Today, the only visible decorations are the lunettes and ceiling vaults, as the walls have been covered by the Vatican's collection of modern religious art, which includes works by Auguste Rodin, Felice Casorati, Barlach, Roualt, and Manzu.

The staircase descends into the **Room of the Sibyls,** named for the 12 lunettes, which depict pairs of classical sibyls and Old Testament prophets, foreshadowing Michelangelo's arrangement of the same subjects on the Sistine ceiling. Legend has it that in this room, the ambitious Cesare Borgia had his brother-in-law Alfonso d'Aragone murdered in order to free up his sister Lucrezia for marriage to Alfonso d'Este, the guy from Browning's *My Last Duchess.* In the room to the left are two remarkable Rodin sculptures and a wall of Matisse drawings of the Madonna and Child.

The other rooms depict members of the Borgia court in the unlikely guises of saints and Biblical figures. The **Room of the Mysteries** (Room VI) showcases the *Resurrection*. The central soldier, kneeling with a lance, may be a depiction of Cesare himself. Above the door leading to the Room of the Mysteries is Pinturicchio's *tondo* of the Madonna and Child, thought to be a portrait of Giulia Farnese, Alexander VI's mistress and mother of Pope Paul III.

Outside the Borgia apartments portion, the **collection of modern religious art** (largely assembled by Pope Paul VI) extends for many more rooms. Dozens of famous modern artists have works exhibited here, not the least of whom are Picasso, Dalì, Matisse (look out for his gorgeous clerical capes, designed for a chapel near Nice despite his avowed atheism), Modigliani, Henry Moore, Morandi, Munch, Diego Rivera, Max Beckmann, Kandinsky, Klee, Gauguin, and Chagall. Also included are the likes of Francis Bacon and Ben Shahn. To be found here are mosaics, sculptures, sketches, ceramics, expressionist paintings, impressionist paintings, cubist paintings, body paintings... everything but the kitchen sink (although there is a Duchamp here).

SISTINE CHAPEL

Called "Sistine" after its founder, Pope Sixtus IV, this chapel has served as the chamber in which the College of Cardinals elects popes since its completion in the 16th century. Its inclusion in the museum tour is somewhat deceiving, since the chapel is really part of St. Peter's Basilica. The barrel vault of the ceiling, some 22m above the floor, gleams with the results of its recent, hotly debated restoration.

WALL FRESCOES

Before craning your neck, prepare yourself by taking in the older, all too often ignored frescoes on the side walls. Facing the *Last Judgment*, the left wall contains six scenes from the life of Moses, paralleling the six scenes from the life of Christ on the right wall. The cycle, frescoed in 1481-83, was completed by a team of artists under the direction of Perugino that included Botticelli, Ghirlandaio, Roselli, Pinturicchio, Signorelli, and della Gatta.

FIRST FRESCOES. Starting with the frescoes nearest the *Last Judgment* altarpiece, we see Moses leaving his father-in-law (in the background) to return to Egypt to free the Israelites from slavery, and an angel confronting him (in the foreground) for neglecting to circumcise his son; on the right, the circumcision takes place. Opposite is the baptism of Christ by John the Baptist, which marked the beginning of Christ's teaching; in the background on the left, Christ preaches; on the right, John does, predicting Christ's coming.

SECOND FRESCOES. From left to right: Moses hears God speaking out of the burning bush, instructing him to free the Israelites from Egyptian slavery; Moses defends and helps Jethro's daughters (he later marries one); and Moses kills an Egyptian who had beaten an Israelite slave. Opposite, in the background, Christ is tempted by the devil, who suggests that he test God by throwing himself from various high places to see if angels save him.

THIRD FRESCOES. These depict the crossing of the Red Sea. The newly freed Israelite people, on the left, have passed safely across the sea, which was lifted to the side, while the pursuing Egyptians, at right, drown with all their troops. Opposite, Christ calls the first apostles, Peter and Andrew, who were fishermen.

FOURTH FRESCOES. At background center, Moses receives the Ten Commandments from God, as the Israelites, at right, immediately break the new laws by worshiping the golden calf they constructed. In the foreground, Moses breaks the tablets in anger, symbolizing the people's breaking of the laws. Opposite, Christ gives the Sermon on the Mount, which contained the famous Beatitudes, among other salient Christian proverbs. In the right foreground, Christ heals a leper.

FIFTH FRESCOES. Datan, Korah, and Abiron are punished for trying to stone Moses. Behind Moses, on the far right, the figure in black is a portrait of Botticelli, the fresco's painter. Opposite, as the stoning of Christ occurs in the right background, Christ hands over the keys to the kingdom (symbolically the power to decide who enters heaven) to Peter, the first Pope, in the foreground.

SIXTH FRESCOES. Moses hands over his staff to his successor, Joshua; in the background, on the right, the angel shows Moses the promised land; on the left is depicted the death of Moses. Opposite, the disciples enjoy the Last Supper. Judas Iscariot, the bad disciple who betrayed Christ with a kiss, is easy to make out: he's sitting across from Christ on the wrong side of the table, and is the only one around without a halo.

The far inferior frescoes on the wall opposite *The Last Judgment* are not original, but were added in the 1570s in the place where Michelangelo was supposed to have painted another full wall masterpiece. Botticelli, Ghirlandaio, and Fra Diamante painted the series of 26 popes who stand in the niches between the high windows. Phew.

SISTINE CEILING

It's said that Bramante, worried that the genius might take over his project (the construction of the new basilica) hinted to Pope Julius that Michelangelo should paint the ceiling instead; the Florentine sculptor and architect had the commission for the Sistine Chapel ceiling foisted upon him unexpectedly. The work is wholly Michelangelo's in design and execution. He had never worked in fresco before and kept his assistants only long enough to learn the technique from them before settling down to a frenzied four years of solitary work. Michelangelo did not paint flat on his back, but standing up and craning backwards, and he never recovered from the strain to his neck and eyes. If you would like to avoid a similar fate, consider bringing a pocket mirror on your visit to the Sistine Chapel; hold the mirror in hand, at chest level, and view the ceiling in reflection.

The painter chose to depict the history of mankind before the coming of Christ, linking the ceiling decoration with the stories of Moses and Christ on the side walls. He divided the vault into a monumental architectural scheme, each section enclosing a scene from Genesis. Contrary to popular belief, however, these panels were completed in reverse order: Michelangelo began working on the ceiling next to the entrance of the chapel, contrary to Church tradition, in which paintings surrounding the altar always came first. These paintings, focussing on the life of Noah, are far more complex, simply because he was at that point still working with numerous assistants, which made more detail possible. The central figures in such scenes as *The Flood* were painted exclusively by Michelangelo, while the marginal characters were almost certainly the duty of the assistants he employed for the first portion of the Ceiling. In 1510-1511, halfway through the ceiling, Michelangelo took a six-month hiatus to seek financing from the Pope. This break may account for the change in style between the Noah story and the Creation scenes, painted later, in which the figures become larger (and thus more suitable for viewing from the far-off floor) and more expressive—attesting to Michelangelo's growth as an artist during these years and his growing confidence in the medium.

ADAM AND EVE. Looking from *The Last Judgment* toward the chapel's rear, the panels begin with *Separation of Light from Darkness; Creation of the Sun, Moon, and Planets;* and *Separation of Land from Water.* In creating the next panel, **Creation of Adam,** Michelangelo revolutionized conceptions of the birth of man; mortal is placed on nearly equal footing with God, as both are depicted in human form. Much scholarly attention has been devoted to the "tension" in the void between the two fingers.

In the central panel, **Creation of Eve,** Eve rests next to the stump of a tree, an allusion to the cross. In *Temptation and Expulsion from Paradise*, the image of the cross is still more obviously cited in the winding form of the serpent.

LIFE OF NOAH. The last three panels (the first three paintings completed) take on the life of Noah—**Sacrifice of Noah** (where Noah thanks God for saving him and his family from the flood), **The Flood,** and the **Drunkenness of Noah** (in which Noah forgets himself after the flood in a bout of shameful and ungodly revelry, thus proving the sinful nature of all mankind, even God's favorites). Michelangelo painted the story out of order due to space limitations, since the pattern demanded a repeating sequence of small panel-large panel. Though Michelangelo could have just ended with the *Flood*, it was theologically important to include the *Drunkenness of Noah* as a reminder that the world began anew under a bad light, underlining the need of mankind for a savior. (This savior is predicted by the life of Moses on the left wall and then produced in the right wall frescoes.) A close look at *The Flood* reveals slight damage to a corner, which occurred as a result of an explosion in the nearby Castel Sant'Angelo in 1508. All of the panels are framed by the famous *ignudi*, contorted naked male youths who cavort among the decorative vaulting. In the four spandrels are depictions of *David and Goliath*, *Judith and Holofernes*, *The Bronze Serpent*, and *The Punishment of Haman*. These are surrounded by monumental figures of Old Testament prophets and classical sibyls, some deep in thought and others holding aloft books of revealed wisdom, all by Michelangelo himself. Pay particular attention to the Libyan sibyl and the prophets Daniel and Jonah.

THE LAST JUDGMENT

Museo Nazionale d'Arte Antica

Michelangelo's turbulent vision of the apocalypse, *The Last Judgment* (on the wall behind the altar), was painted 23 years after the completion of the ceiling. The events of the intervening period, including the sack of Rome and the Protestant Reformation, seem to have left the artist bitter and disillusioned. Many interpreted the turmoil in the Christian world at this time as divine punishment for the corruption spreading throughout Europe. The location of *The Last Judgment* above the altar symbolically places the most sacred part of the church in the mouth of hell. Obvious sources for Michelangelo's iconography are Dante's *The Inferno*, the *Dies Irae*, and biblical texts, particularly the chapters of Ezekiel and Revelation (a.k.a. Apocalypse).

This masterpiece, finished in 1541, was executed during a period of intense political turbulence, as reformers within and outside of the Catholic Church vied to revise its teachings. *The Last Judgment* represents a ploy by Pope Paul III to reassert the political, financial, and spiritual power of the Catholic Church and its pontiff. Using the greatest artist of the time, extremely expensive materials, and images that reminded heretics and enemies of the Church of the inevitable consequences of opposition, the Pope hoped to reclaim wandering souls and strengthen the One True Church. Paul III was satisfied with the results of his commission: upon the unveiling of the altarpiece, he fell to his knees on the cold marble floor, crying, "Lord, charge me not with my sins when Thou shalt come on the day of judgment!" Apparently, he didn't know of the later-declared doctrine of Papal infallibility (see p. 58); he needn't have worried.

Arte Antica

Chaotic swarms of naked mortals encircle the unusually muscular figure of Christ-as-Judge in the upper center; Christ's body is modeled after Michelangelo's beloved ancient sculpture, the Belvedere Torso, his facial features pilfered either from the Laocoön or the Belvedere Apollo, depending on which art historian you believe. This remarkable *Christus Judex* is surrounded by Mary (modestly averting her eyes from the grotesque spectacle) and a saintly entourage. Below Christ on the right sits St. Bartholomew (in actuality, a self-portrait of the 65-year-old artist) on a cloud, holding his skin.

Vatican Museums

On the left, angels pull the lucky souls into heaven, while on the right, demons cast the damned into an abyss. The ferryman Charon carts the unfortunate cast of evildoers across the river and viciously whacks them out with his oar. In the lower right-hand corner, Minos, Master of the Underworld, sports a coiling tail and ass-ears. His face is a portrait of Biagio da Cesena, who, speaking for Pope Paul III, objected to Michelangelo's use of "shameless nudity in a holy space." In fact, after Michelangelo's death, during the conservative Counter-Reformation (see p. 58), many of the shameful nudes had strategically draped, inelegant cloth swatches painted onto them. These additions were largely removed by the recent restoration, but a few of these impromptu loincloths remain. Of the many figures represented in the Last Judgment, only a handful peer out from the painting to the viewer; the most apparent is on the bottom left-hand corner of the work, where a grim skeleton looks directly at the rest of the chapel.

Before, during, and after the renovation of the frescoes, art historians quibbled over whether the restoration improved the works. Regardless, the ceiling was on the verge of collapse from damage wrought by time and weather, and the frescoes were in danger of peeling away from the ceiling and walls. The restorers, whether they removed a crucial layer or not, managed to reattach the frescoes and repair the surfaces. **Refrain from taking flash photos,** even if you see others around you doing it, since the light of the flash damages the frescoes. You can buy much better shots (actually cheaper than using your own film) on postcards in the gift shop.

OTHER MUSEUMS

CHAPEL OF ST. PIUS V. From the exit along the left-hand wall of the Chapel, several corridors return to the Galleries of the Library and back to the Belvedere Courtyard. The corridors pass numerous rooms containing artifacts collected during the reigns of various popes. In the 2nd room, the Chapel of St. Pius V, a reliquary case contains fragments of saints retrieved from the treasury of *Sancta Sanctorum*, including the Reliquary of the Head of St. Praxedes.

ROOM OF THE ALDOBRANDINI MARRIAGE. A short way up on the left, the Room of the Aldobrandini Marriage hides a series of rare ancient Roman frescoes, including the celebrated wedding scene, set in a flowering park filled with animals.

ROOMS OF THE PAPYRUS. The Rooms of the Papyrus contain medieval papyrus sheets with Latin writings dating back to the 16th century. The corridor continues past cases of strikingly bad modern religious art (skip the *Mute Swans of Peace*) and antique globes, bells, and maps. The papal geocentric "universe" globes, midway down on the left-hand side, are worth a glimpse.

THE SISTINE HALL. The Sistine Hall, leading off the main corridor to the right, is used for exhibits from the Vatican Library's superb collection of books and manuscripts. Although most visitors rush through this part of the museum, keep in mind that the "one-way" system prevents you from returning to the corridors once you've gone to another part of the museum. When you reach the end of the corridor, you will find yourself again in the Vestibule of the Four Gates, from which the stairs on the opposite side lead up to the Sistine Chapel. On the left is the **Atrium of the Four Gates** and the **Court of the Pinacoteca,** with an excellent view of St. Peter's.

PINACOTECA

The Pinacoteca, the Vatican's eclectic painting collection that spans the 12th to 18th centuries, was started by Pope Pius VI in 1790, and now boasts more than 460 works, including masterpieces by Giotto, Poussin, da Vinci, Titian, Veronese, and Caravaggio.

ROOMS 1-3. These galleries hold wonderful wood panel tempera (yolk-based, quick-drying paint) paintings from the 12th to 14th centuries, thinly painted in brilliant colors with extraordinary detail and gobs of gold leaf. Here, as elsewhere, nativities, annunciations, and blood-spurting crucifixions predominate, along with a generous sampling of paintings of the lives of saints. **Room 1** houses a curious, keyhole-shaped wood panel of *The Last Judgment* dating from the 12th century, which provides an interesting contrast to Michelangelo's monumental composition of the same subject in the Sistine Chapel. Here, hell possesses different levels, as in Dante's *Inferno*. Ladies, note that the wife who spoke in church is lower than the homicides and the matricides! In **Room 3,** don't miss Fra Angelico's wonderful *Life of St. Nicholas of Bari*, along with his *Madonna and Child*, and Fra Filippo Lippi's *Coronation of the Virgin*.

ROOM 8. Three works by Raphael (from left to right: the *Madonna of Foligno*, the *Transfiguration*, and the *Coronation of the Virgin*) hang here among tapestries copied from the master's cartoons, which once hung on the lower walls of the Sistine Chapel but were plundered during the sack of Rome (only to be returned later).

ROOMS 9-10. This room houses Giovanni Bellini's *Pietà* and a mutilated Leonardo da Vinci panel of St. Jerome. Prior to its discovery, the panel had been cut in two, the bottom half had served as a coffer lid in an antique store, the top part as a stool seat in a shoemaker's shop. **Room 10** contains Titian's massive *Madonna of San Nicoletta dei Frari* (look for Titian's mark on the wall of the painting).

ROOMS 12-15. Room 12 brings you into the devilishly cruel world of Baroque devotional art. Here you can see Caravaggio's sensual *Deposition from the Cross* and Nicholas Poussin's grisly *Martyrdom of St. Erasmus* (who had his intestines rolled out on a winch). **Room 14,** much like Room 12, contains fanciful and largely hideous still lifes of devilish fruit and flowers. In **Room 15,** Pope Benedict XIV glowers down at the bewildered spectator, while Thomas Lawrence's full-length portrait of King George IV, in full coronation robes, seems wildly out of place. There is also a series of astronomical observations showing the various phases of the moon, executed for the observatory at Bologna by Donato Cretti. Gruesome animal portraits populate the final room.

MINOR MUSEUMS

GREGORIAN PROFANE MUSEUM. The Gregorian Profane Museum, on the left as one heads toward the museum entrance, makes a quiet change from the bustle and bombast of the other museums. Look for the statues of Marsyas, the satyr who dared to play Athena's pipes (and was skinned alive for doing so), and the fragmentary *Chiaramonti Niobid*. Niobe, a mother of 14 children, had taunted Leto for having given birth to only two. Unfortunately for Niobe, the two were Apollo and Diana, and the irritated gods avenged their insulted mother by shooting down all 14 of Niobe's kiddies. The gallery also contains reliefs from imperial monuments, many depicting buildings of ancient Rome.

PIO-CHRISTIAN MUSEUM. Next door, the Pio-Christian Museum holds artifacts of a fascinating historical synthesis—the marriage of the Greco-Roman sculptural tradition to the newer iconography of the Christian Church. The sarcophagi and statuary here date from the earliest centuries AD, when the Roman Empire and its artistic vocabulary were still alive and well. Many a small statue of the Good Shepherd stand among the many intricately carved sarcophagi. Nearby, the **Ethnological-Missionary Museum** displays non-Christian religious articles alongside missionary-inspired works from Third-World cultures. The **Carriage Museum** contains comparatively recent papal goodies, including armor, guard uniforms, and carriages.

GALLERIA BORGHESE

🔲 *P. Scipione Borghese, 5. **M:**A-Spagna. Alternatively, take **bus** #910 from Termini to V. Pinciana or follow Villa Borghese exit signs and head left up the road to reach V. del Museo Borghese. Helpful brown signs within the park point the way. ☎06 8548577. **Open** Tu-F 9am-7:30pm, Sa 9am-11pm, Su and holidays 9am-8pm; entrance only on the hr., visits limited to 2hr.; last entrance 30min. before closing. A limited number of people are admitted every hour; **the gallery does sell out. Admission** L14,000, EU nationals ages 18-25 L8000, EU nationals under 18 and over 60 L2000. Tickets include both the ground floor galleries and the Pinacoteca upstairs. The basement of the palace contains: the ticket office, a bookshop selling an informative **guidebook** for your tour (L20,000), a computer info kiosk, an inexpensive snack bar, and restrooms. Tickets may be reserved in advance by phone or in person for an extra L2000.*

The Galleria Borghese is quite simply one of the most important and enjoyable art collections in Rome. After getting a ticket, go back outside and head up the grand staircase to the sculpture-filled **main galleries.** On your way in, don't ignore the spectacular Greek and Roman statuary that litters the porch, including some colossal feet and several figures of Hercules, always recognizable by his lion skin cloak and signature club. For more on the Villa Borghese's history and sights, see p. 114.

GROUND FLOOR

The grand entrance hall sports a splendid ceiling fresco, *trompe l'oeil* medallions, and false architectural supports found throughout the Borghese home. The floor's fourth-century gladiator mosaics are a worthy base for its striking second-century Roman copies of creatures historical and mythological.

ROOM 1. To the right of the entrance, this room features 19th-century neoclassicist Antonio Canova's sexy statue of **Pauline Bonaparte Borghese** as Venus. Supposedly, her husband thought the figure so luscious that he forbade anybody else to see it. Asked by a 19th-century tabloid writer if she felt uncomfortable posing disrobed, Pauline replied, "No, the room was quite warm." The vivid marble figure holds an apple, a reference to the story played out in the ceiling fresco of the beauty contest which launched the Trojan war. According to Greek mythology, a beautiful golden apple appeared one day amid the gods of Olympus, inscribed "For the Fairest." Hera, Athena, and Aphrodite all claimed the epithet and the lovely apple. Unwilling to entangle himself, Zeus brought in a second opinion, that of Paris, the most beautiful man, to resolve the dispute. Each goddess offered Paris wonderful gifts to name her most beautiful: Hera offered unlimited power, Athena unsurpassed knowledge and wisdom, and Aphrodite the love of the most beautiful mortal woman. A true man, Paris picked the last, and happily made off with a certain Helen. And the rest is history.

ROOM 2. Here lies Bernini's magnificent **David,** who crouches in controlled aggression with his slingshot. Sculpted when the artist was only 21 years old, the handsome but grimacing face is supposedly Bernini's own. As will become more than evident, Cardinal Borghese was a big fan of this emerging star, commissioning several of Bernini's greatest achievements, most of which remain in the Galleria Borghese.

ROOM 3. 🖼 **Apollo and Daphne** shows Bernini at it again: two figures, the hunter-god and a wood nymph, are portrayed in an extraordinarily elegant and dynamic pose. The god, enamored of the lovely sprite, is depicted in mid-chase, his limbs and draped garment still flying; meanwhile, the maiden metamorphoses into a laurel tree, her curls sprouting foliage, her toes twisting into gnarled roots. According to Ovid, the chaste nymph was unable to outrun her insistent suitor, and so called on her father, the river god, for aid. He transformed her into a tree to protect her virginity. As Apollo clasped her in his arms, he could still feel Daphne's heart beating beneath the spreading bark. Be sure to examine this sculpture from all angles; it was originally placed so as to be approached from behind Apollo, so that the nymph is only gradually revealed, in mid-transformation, as the viewer circles the group.

ROOM 4. Follow the religiously themed hallway to Room 4, where pagan myth once more takes over in the form Bernini's **Rape of Proserpina.** According to myth, Pluto carried off the young daughter of Ceres (variously Gaia or Demeter), the goddess of harvest, as she picked flowers in a springtime field. Ceres wasn't pleased, and, mourning her lost child, refused to bring about the earth's usual harvest. Zeus told his brother Pluto to return the girl, but Prosperina had already eaten of the food of Hades (three kernels of a pomegranate), and so was eternally bound to her new husband. It was finally agreed that she spend six months a year with her mother on earth, and the rest in Hades, as queen of the underworld. While Prosperina dwells with Ceres, the earth is fruitful, but winter reigns whenever she departs. The menacing Pluto is here flanked by his three-headed guard dog, Cerberus (its privates discretely hidden by a bunch of leaves). Elsewhere in the room, a dignified marble Artemis reaches into her quiver, a second-century copy of a fourth-century BC Greek bronze. Meticulously wrought grotesque mosaics cover the walls between elegant Renaissance columns.

The best way to keep in touch when you're traveling overseas is with **AT&T Direct® Service**. It's the easy way to call your loved ones back home from just about anywhere in the world. Just cut out the wallet guide below and use it wherever your travels take you.

For a list of AT&T Access Numbers, tear out the attached wallet guide.

AT&T

Italy ● 172-1011	Russia (Moscow) ▶▲●755-5042
Luxembourg + ..800-2-0111	(St. Petersbg.)▶▲● ..325-5042
Macedonia● ..99-800-4288	Slovakia ▲ ..00-42-100-101
Malta 0800-890-110	South Africa ..0800-99-0123
Monaco ● 800-90-288	Spain 900-99-00-11
Morocco 002-11-0011	Sweden 020-799-111
Netherlands ● ...0800-022-9111	Switzerland ● 0800-89-0011
Norway 800-190-11	Turkey ● 00-800-12277
Poland ▲● ..00-800-111-1111	Ukraine ▲ ....8♦100-11
Portugal ▲ ʼ...800-800-128	U.A. Emirates ● 800-121
Romania ●......01-800-4288	U.K.............0800-89-0011

FOR EASY CALLING WORLDWIDE
1. Just dial the AT&T Access Number for the country you are calling from.
2. Dial the phone number you're calling.   *3.* Dial your card number.

For access numbers not listed ask any operator for **AT&T Direct®** Service.
In the U.S. call 1-800-331-1140 for a wallet guide listing all worldwide AT&T Access Numbers.

Visit our Web site at: **www.att.com/traveler**

Bold-faced countries permit country-to-country calling outside the U.S.

- ● Public phones require coin or card deposit to place call.
- ▲ May not be available from every phone/payphone.
- ✚ Public phones and select hotels.
- ♦ Await second dial tone.
- ▶ Additional charges apply when calling from outside the city.
- † Outside of Cairo, dial "02" first.
- ✘ Not available from public phones or all areas.
- ✔ Use U.K. access number in N. Ireland.

When placing an international call *from* the U.S., dial 1 800 CALL ATT.

Italy ● 172-1011	Russia (Moscow) ▶▲●755-5042
Luxembourg + ..800-2-0111	(St. Petersbg.)▶▲● ..325-5042
Macedonia● ..99-800-4288	Slovakia ▲ ..00-42-100-101
Malta 0800-890-110	South Africa ..0800-99-0123
Monaco ● 800-90-288	Spain 900-99-00-11
Morocco 002-11-0011	Sweden 020-799-111
Netherlands ● ...0800-022-9111	Switzerland ● 0800-89-0011
Norway 800-190-11	Turkey ● 00-800-12277
Poland ▲● ..00-800-111-1111	Ukraine ▲ ....8♦100-11
Portugal ▲ 800-800-128	U.A. Emirates ● 800-121
Romania ●......01-800-4288	U.K.............0800-89-0011

FOR EASY CALLING WORLDWIDE
1. Just dial the AT&T Access Number for the country you are calling from.
2. Dial the phone number you're calling.   *3.* Dial your card number.

For access numbers not listed ask any operator for **AT&T Direct®** Service.
In the U.S. call 1-800-331-1140 for a wallet guide listing all worldwide AT&T Access Numbers.

Visit our Web site at: **www.att.com/traveler**

Bold-faced countries permit country-to-country calling outside the U.S.

- ● Public phones require coin or card deposit to place call.
- ▲ May not be available from every phone/payphone.
- ✚ Public phones and select hotels.
- ♦ Await second dial tone.
- ▶ Additional charges apply when calling from outside the city.
- † Outside of Cairo, dial "02" first.
- ✘ Not available from public phones or all areas.
- ✔ Use U.K. access number in N. Ireland.

When placing an international call *from* the U.S., dial 1 800 CALL ATT.

EMEA   © 8/00 AT&T

ROOMS 5-6. In Room 5, the enigmatic Hermaphrodite, who reclines in a first-century Roman sculpture with a modern head, holds court. Hermaphrodite is also found in each panel of the ceiling, always wearing red draperies. In Room 6, a weary-looking Aeneas, followed by his son Ascanius, carries his elderly father away from the burning city of Troy in *Aeneas and Anchises*, one of the Bernini's first commissions (executed when he was just 21). Art historians speculate that his sculptor father, Pietro, gave the prodigy considerable help.

ROOMS 7-8. Room 7, the **Egyptian Room,** lives up to its name, showcasing a Roman portrait of the goddess Isis in black marble, two sphinxes, and several fine Roman mosaics. A second-century Roman satyr dances around Room 8, clanging his marble cymbals, but don't let him distract you from the room's real attractions—no fewer than six **Caravaggio** paintings grace the walls, including the world-famous *St. Jerome*, a *Self Portrait as Bacchus* (1605), and the *Madonna of the Palafrenieri*.

PINACOTECA

The Pinacoteca (painting gallery) is accessible from the gardens around back by a winding staircase. Go outside by the door you came in and walk around the building to find the door on the opposite face of the building.

ROOM 9. Don't miss several works by Raphael, especially the **Deposition** and the enigmatic *Signorina con Licorne*, a portrait of a young woman with a unicorn (formerly painted over to look like St. Catherine), in addition to several holy family pictures of Andrea del Sarto. Perugino's exquisite *Madonna and Child* and Pinturicchio's *Crucifixion with St. Jerome* and *St. Christopher* also deserve special attention.

ROOMS 10-13. Room 10 contains gorgeous paintings of Venus by Cranach the Elder and Brescianino, while rooms 11 to 13 hold a variety of smaller, more minor works. Room 11 houses a beautiful Correggio, briefly owned by Queen Christina of Sweden, of Zeus appearing to Danae as a golden thunder cloud raining bright golden sparks toward her pelvis as she reclines on a bed. This unusual romantic encounter, schemed up by Zeus in a vain attempt to circumvent Hera's jealousy, gave rise to an important demigod: Danae gave premature birth to Bacchus, the god of wine, several months later, when the vengeful Hera struck the unlucky mistress down with lightning. *Leda and the Swan*, a copy of a Leonardo da Vinci piece, graces Room 12, as does Il Sodoma's **Pietà.**

ROOMS 14-16. Room 14, the large hall to the left (as one faces the stairway) provides beautiful views of the curlicue French gardens below. Note the *trompe l'oeil* macho men holding up the ceiling. Notable as well are the two small self-portraits by Bernini. The red walls of Room 15 are home to Bassano's sweet *Sheep and Lamb*, juxtaposed (a dark joke by the curators?) with a *Circe* by Dosso Dossi. Directly across in Room 16 is Zucchi's fabulous *Allegory of the Discovery of the New World*. Also look for del Conte's arresting paintings of Cleopatra and Lucrezia.

FINAL ROOMS. The doorway under Cleopatra leads to Room 17 and its excellent 17th-century Dutch and Italian interior paintings, notably Frans Francken's whimsical *Antique Dealer's Gallery* and two views of Rome by **Canaletto.** Room 20 holds several works by Titian, including the quietly lovely *Sacred and Profane Love*.

MUSEO NAZIONALE ETRUSCO DI VILLA GIULIA

◪ *In Villa Borghese at P. Villa Giulia, 9.* **M:***A-Flaminio or* **bus** *#19 from P. Risorgimento or #52 from P. San Silvestro.* ☎ *06 3201951.* **Open** *Tu-F, Su, and holidays 8:30am-7:30pm, Sa 9am-8pm. Extended hours June-Sept. Sa 9am-11pm.* **Admission** *L8000, EU citizens and Southern and Central Australians under 18 and over 60 free; Canadians under 15 free.* **Audioguide** *L8000,* **guidebook** *L20,000, available at the bookstore just outside the museum entrance.* **Plan to spend** *1½-2hr.*

The national Etruscan museum is housed in the Villa Giulia, built in 1552 by Pope Julius III, who was criticized by contemporaries for leading a frivolous life while the Council of Trent erupted around him. Designed by Vignola, with some input from Michelangelo, the home's decorative sculpture was partially scraped away by more conservatives popes, but Vignola's nymphaeum was preserved as a cool and attractive refuge from the heat.

Though every town in the region seems to host an Etruscan museum, Rome's collection is by far the strongest. The 35 rooms of this vast museum are well labeled in English and Italian, with instructive maps and historical and archeological details. Don't miss the ceramic uteruses used as fertility charms (**Room 5,** case 2) or the bronze funerary urn (**Room 6,** case 5) decorated with small modeled figures who, knives brandished, circle round a terrified captive monster. Other highlights include a graceful 6th-century BC terra cotta sarcophagus of a husband and wife (**Room 10)** and an Etruscan *biga* (chariot), along with the petrified skeletons of two horses found beside it **(Room 19).**

Room 20 houses a sparkling collection of hundreds of necklaces, bracelets, rings, pins, and extraordinarily detailed earrings, dating from Pre-Colombian times (1500 BC) to the 16th century. Catch a glimpse of the Etruscan idea of a good time: in **Room 27,** a large jar depicts two men feasting with a nubile female flute player; another shows Eros seated with a naked lass on a panther skin. For an even more personal look at Etruscan life, examine 2000-year-old cylindrical "beauty-cases" and their surprising contents, including bronze mirrors and a small set of dentures **(Room 34).**

Upstairs, archaeologists have put together fragments of the entire facade of an Etruscan temple, complete with terra cotta gargoyles, chips of original paint, and a fresco of the Greek warrior Tydaeus biting into the brain of a still-living adversary while Athena, who had been planning on giving him the gift of immortal life, turns away in disgust.

CAPITOLINE MUSEUMS

⚐ *On top of the Capitoline Hill (behind the Vittorio Emanuele II monument).* ☎ *06 39746221. Open Tu-Su 10am-8pm, holidays 9am-1:30pm. Ticket office closes 30min. before closing. L15,000, with ISIC L11,000, Italian citizens under 18 and over 60 free. Guidebook L30,000; audioguide L7000; daily tours in English L6000. Not wheelchair accessible.* **Plan to spend 2-3hr.**

The Capitoline Museums, founded in 1471 by Pope Sixtus IV, is the world's oldest public museum, and one of Rome's most important repositories of Greek and Roman sculpture. The beautiful *piazza* and the facades of both *palazzi* were designed by Michelangelo. Though certainly worth a careful and patient visit, it is important to know that few works are labeled, random heads and limbs are patched onto bodies, whole sculptures are placed on alien plinths, and priceless collections of inscriptions and reliefs are plastered at random into the walls as decoration.

Artwork often seems to have been grouped by size and color, rather than period or genre, which (a helpful sign informs the befuddled art lover) should be regarded as "charming" and an interesting historical experience, since all museums were this disorganized in the 18th and 19th century. Every room does, however, sport signs about key works in Italian and English. The **Palazzo Nuovo** (to the left as you enter the piazza) contains hundreds of unlabeled statues from the 4th century BC through the 3rd century AD, while the **Palazzo dei Conservatori** (on the right), houses mostly Renaissance art, along with a few of the most famous Hellenistic Roman bronzes.

PALAZZO NUOVO. Inside the Palazzo Nuovo's courtyard, the original 2nd-century gilded bronze statue of philosopher-king **Marcus Aurelius** sits astride his horse behind protective glass. The statue is the only equestrian bronze to survive from ancient Rome; most bronzes were melted down during the Middle Ages. Marcus Aurelius only survived because he was thought to be Constantine, the first Christian emperor. Indoors, the large sculpture room contains such figures as a young Zeus, Hera, a hunting Centaur, a giant Trajan, and a sampling of less noble farmers and drunks. In a smaller room, a ▧**Dying Gaul** heaves through the last moments of his life. Note his intricately carved torso, the "torque" around his neck (a sign of his Gallic heritage), and scrumptious physique. **Satyr Resting** is the "Marble Faun" that inspired Hawthorne's book of the same title. Other rooms are full of busts: Greek philosophers and writers are portrayed here, as well as a variety of Romans, including Augustus, a polychrome bust of Caracalla looking cruel as cruel can be, several bearded soldier-emperors from the 3rd century AD, and an iconic head of Constantine. His mother, St. Helena, reclines coyly in the center of the room.

PALAZZO DEI CONSERVATORI. In the courtyard reside sundry limbs long separated from their owner, the 12m 4th-century **Colossus of Constantine;** this is your chance to get a picture of yourself cradled in the Emperor's muscular forearm. This Constantinian tribute used to stand in the basilica in the Forum, a dedication to his victory over Maxentius and subsequent conversion to Christianity. On a landing before the first floor, four reliefs from a monument to Marcus Aurelius show scenes of the Emperor sacrificing, driving a triumphal chariot, bestowing clemency on captives (with the same gesture as in his equestrian statue), and receiving the ominous and glowing "orb of power."

At the second landing, a door leads to the **Sale dei Conservatori.** Cavaliere d'Arpino frescoed the giant main room with episodes from the reigns of the early kings, telling the typical Italian stories of a little love, a little religion, and a little carnage. On one end of the hall, Pope Urban VIII amorously eyes Pope Innocent X on the other side. In the middle, a boy quietly picks a splinter out of his feet (the Hellenistic bronze, the **Spinario**). In the next room sits the famous **Capitoline She-Wolf,** a 6th- or 5th-century BC Etruscan bronze, perhaps the work of the renowned Vulca of Veii. Antonio Pollaiuolo added Romulus and Remus in the 15th century. On the walls are the *Fasti*, the archival records of the ancient Pontifex Maximus, excavated from the Regia in the forum. **Bernini's** serpentine *Head of Medusa* snakily highlights another room.

PINACOTECA. The Museo del Palazzo dei Conservatori opens up to the left from the landing, a long gallery that showcases disembodied limbs and limbless torsos. Admire the colossal foot and the two pudgy armless boys. At the top of the stairs, the Pinacoteca houses an assortment of 16th- and 17th-century Italian paintings. Much of the collection was pilfered by the Vatican Museums long ago, leaving an awkward array of poorly hung canvases and a sad, empty feeling in the curators' hearts. The paintings are carefully labeled in English, however, and the rooms are well-numbered. Among the masterpieces not purloined by the popes are (in **Room 2**) Bellini's *Portrait of a Young Man* and Titian's *Baptism of Christ*. **Room 4,** the center of the museum, holds a collection of second-rate 14th- and 15th-century paintings. Bypass these large works to see **Caravaggio's** rendition of St. John the Baptist past the porcelain and enamel galleries. Also noteworthy is his recently restored *Gypsy Fortune-Teller*, in a room off the central gallery. You will find it among a collection of ornate 17th-century Baroque paintings including Il Guercino's *St. Matthew and the Angel* and the Persian *Sibyl*. A Rubens, a Velasquez, and a distinctly unthrilling Tintoretto are also on display.

MUSEO NAZIONALE D'ARTE ANTICA

This national collection of 12th- through 18th-century art is split between Palazzo Barberini and Galleria Corsini. The former houses more masterworks, but the latter collection is nothing to sniff at; both galleries deserve a visit.

PALAZZO BARBERINI. The Barberini contains paintings from the medieval through Baroque periods and an impressive central stairway, full of Barberini bees, designed by Bernini. Dubbed by some the "apogee of Baroque splendor," it deserves a visit for its architecture alone. The Barberini family lived here from 1625, when Pope Urban VIII built it to commemorate his accession. Once an hour, on the hour, guards open gates on the upper floor and allow you to wander through the gaudy Rococco apartments originally belonging to Cornelia Costanza Barberini, who married into the family at age 12. Despite hocking the place to the state in 1949, Barberinis lived in these rooms until 1960.

The museum holds a healthy number of masterpieces by del Sarto, Il Sodoma, Tintoretto, Bernini, Holbein, Lippi, Raphael, El Greco, Carracci, Caravaggio, and Poussin. The usual themes predominate: lots of Holy Families, St. Sebastians bristling with arrows, and mystical marriages of St. Catherine to the Christ child (always represented with the chaste Catherine fully adult and Christ as an infant, presumably to avoid any possible sexual implications). *(V. delle Quattro Fontane, 13. M:A-Barberini. ☎06 4814591. **Open** Tu-Sa 9am-7pm, Su 9am-8pm. **Admission** L12000, EU citizens 18-25 L7000, EU citizens under 18 and over 65 and students of art and architecture L2000. **Plan to spend about 2 hrs. in the Palazzo.**)*

THE ERA BEFORE DISH- WASHERS

The Villa Farnesina used to be one of *the* spots where that legendary Roman excess took place. Artists, ambassadors, courtesans, cardinals, and even Pope Leo X were known to enjoy Agostino Chigi's extravagantly lavish parties.

Stories of his largesse are legendary. He once invited the Pope and the entire College of Cardinals to dinner in a gold-brocaded dining hall so imposing that the Pope reproached him for not treating him with greater familiarity. Chigi, an honorable man, ordered the hangings removed and revealed to his astonished guests that they'd actually only been eating in his stables.

At another infamous banquet in his *loggia* overlooking the Tiber, Chigi had his guests pay their tab by tossing his gold and silver dishes into the river after every course. Slyly, the shrewd businessman had already hidden nets under the water to recover his original treasures.

GALLERIA CORSINI. The Corsini houses a collection of mostly 17th- and 18th-century paintings by the Dutch masters Van Dyck and Rubens, Italian virtuosi Fra Angelico, Titian, and Caravaggio, and many others. The palace's cheerily over-the-top Baroque decor is a treat in itself, as are the many classical statues. In **Room II**, note in particular Fra Angelico's ecstatic triptych of the Last Judgment, the Ascension of Christ, and Pentecost. Nicolas Poussin's *Triumph of Ovid* in **Room VI** is also especially remarkable. Try not to miss the bedroom where Queen Christina of Sweden died—it's marked by a plaque of her dying words in Italian and Swedish ("I was born free, I lived free, and I will die free"), as well as a rather jowly portrait of her, painted as the goddess Diana. (*V. della Lungara, 10. Opposite Villa Farnesina in Trastevere.* ☎ *06 68802323 Open Tu-Su 9am-6pm. L8000, EU students L2000. Plan to spend 1½-2hrs.*)

VILLA FARNESINA

🖪 *V. della Lungara, 230. Just across from Palazzo Corsini off Lungotevere Farnesina. Bus #23.* ☎ *06 68801767. Open M-Sa 9am-1pm. L8000, under 18 L6000. Plan to spend 1-1½hrs.*

Thought to be the wealthiest man in Europe in his day, Agostino "il Magnifico" Chigi entertained the stars of the Renaissance papal court in his sumptuously decorated villa and its extensive palm gardens. The interior decoration, with frescoes by Raphael, Peruzzi, Il Sodoma, and Giulio Romano, smacks of the same decadence. After the banker's death in 1520, however, the villa fell into disrepair and was later bought by the Farnese family.

FIRST FLOOR. To the right as one enters the villa lies the fantastical **Sala of Galatea.** The villa's architect, Baldassare Peruzzi, bears most of the responsibility for the frescoes in here. The ceiling is garlanded with symbols of astrological signs, which, taken with the two central panels of Perseus decapitating Medusa and Callisto (in a chariot drawn by oxen), add up to a symbolic plan of the stars in the night sky at 9:30pm, November 29, 1466—the moment of Chigi's birth. But the masterpiece of the room, on the long wall opposite the windows, is Raphael's vibrant fresco, **The Triumph of Galatea,** in which Galatea appears surfing the seas on a conch-shell chariot drawn by two rather nasty-looking dolphins. Galatea was the lover of Polyphemus, the Cyclops whom Odysseus kills in the *Odyssey*. Prior to his Homeric debut, Polyphemus had his mistress stolen by Venus, who took pity on the nymph's love for another—two-eyed—man.

One room over is the lovely **Loggia di Psiche,** where the row of arches facing the garden served as an entrance hall before the Farnese family glassed them in to protect the paint. The 1520 ceiling fresco recreates the adventures of Psyche on Earth, including her love affair with Cupid and the ensuing jealousy of Venus. **Raphael** was commissioned to paint these, and even drew up designs for them, but never actually came through. Rumor has it that he was too obsessed at the time with his new mistress, la Fornarina, to do any work. Instead, they are attributed to Penni, Giovanni da Udine, and Giulio Romano.

SECOND FLOOR. Upstairs you'll find perhaps the most impressive paintings in the palace: two rooms decorated with frescoes to celebrate Chigi's wedding to a young Venetian noblewoman, whom he had abducted and kept cloistered in a convent for several years. The first, the **Sala delle Perspettive,** is a playful room embellished on two ends by Baldassare Peruzzi with views of 16th-century Trastevere (right) and the Borgo (left), framed between *trompe l'oeil* columns. The geometry's not all there, but it's still an amusing work of illusion. Vulcan sits above the fireplace, trying to reach beyond the painting's surface with his iron, and, over the doorways, 11 Olympian gods atop vine-covered arches attempt to crowd their way into the room. The adjacent bedroom, the **Stanza delle Nozze** (Marriage Room), is the real reason for coming. It was frescoed by **Il Sodoma,** who had been busy painting the papal apartments in the Vatican until Raphael showed up and stole the commission. Il Sodoma rebounded well, making this masterful fresco of Alexander the Great's marriage to the beautiful Roxanne in 1509. The side walls show the family of Darius the Persian surrendering to Alexander, and a rather awful depiction of Bellerophon the Pegasus-tamer that was painted by another (unknown) hand.

GALLERIA NAZIONALE D'ARTE MODERNA

⚐ *In Villa Borghese, V. delle Belle Arti, 131. M:A-Flaminio; enter the park and walk up V. George Washington, following the signs.* ☎ *06 322981. Open Tu-Sa 9am-7pm, Su 9am-8pm. L12,000; discounts for art and architecture students. Wheelchair accessible. Plan to spend 2hrs.*

This gargantuan museum with its Corinthian columns may look like yet another Renaissance art showcase or ancient bust warehouse. Inside, though, this airy museum is as modern as it gets. Designed with a dramatic Neoclassical facade by Cesare Bazzani in 1911 and enlarged in 1933, the museum holds a vast collection of mostly Italian 19th- and 20th-century art. Be advised that the museum's 20th-century galleries feature far more significant work than the mediocre 19th-century wings (the only pieces of particular note are two busts by Hiram Powers, a Vermont emigre to Florence, and a marble Canova sculpture group of Hercules and Lica). Skip to the back galleries which feature, on the right, work from 1900 to 1950, and, on the left, work from 1950 to the present. This is no world-class collection, but it does showcase one or two works each by many superstars as well as extensive work by important others.

A few of the 20th-century treasures include Gustav Klimt's *The Three Ages of Man,* several gorgeous still lifes by Felice Casorati, Rodin's bronze *The Age,* and Modigliani's *Portrait of a Lady with a Collar.* Lucio Fontana, Marcel Duchamp, Giorgio de Chirico, and the Neoclassical sculptor Giacomo Manzu are extremely well-represented, as is the Italian Futurist school and its founders, Giacomo Balla, Severini, and Umberto Boccioni. Mathematician and painter Max Bill's enigmatic bronze *Tripartite Unity* is an elegant variation on the Möbius strip, not far from Alberto Burri's sexy charred cellophane creations and melted plastic-on-satin wall sculptures. Other notables include Giacometti, Mondrian, Kandinsky, Moholy-Nagy, Jackson Pollock, and Alexander Calder pieces.

Intriguing multimedia installations by contemporary Italian artists fill several of the rear rooms, and the central *Saloni* feature changing exhibits of contemporary sculpture, photography, and painting. After your tour, take a coffee break on the gorgeous terrace of the **Caffè delle Arti.**

GALLERIA SPADA

⚐ *P. Capo di Ferro, 13, in the elaborate Palazzo Spada. South of Campo dei Fiori. Bus #64.* ☎ *06 328101. Open Tu-Sa 9am-7pm, Su 9am-12:30pm. L10,000, EU citizens under 18 and over 60 free. Call for reservations (L2000 extra). Plan to spend 1hr.*

Seventeenth-century Cardinal Bernardino Spada bought up a grandiose assortment of paintings and sculpture, and, needing to stick them somewhere, bought and opulently renovated this 1549 *palazzo*. Various descendants, most of them cardinals too, added to the stash, which was acquired by the state in 1926. Time and luck have left the palatial apartments nearly intact, and a visit to the gallery offers a glimpse of the luxurious Baroque court life. The gallery is only four rooms of the Palazzo Spada; the rest is government offices. Before entering the gallery, be sure to check out **Borromini's** *Perspective*, on the right side of the courtyard. By distorting angles and lengths, the Baroque master managed to make a tiny space look like an immense hallway.

ROOMS 1-2. In the first of the four rooms, Spada hung three portraits of himself, by Il Guernico, Guido Reni, and Cerini. Reni's portrait of St. Jerome is also to be found here. In the portrait-studded **Room 2**, look for paintings by the Venetians **Tintoretto** and **Titian**, in particular Titian's *Portrait of a Musician*. **Andrea del Sarto's** *Visitation* is also lovely. **Lavinia Fontana,** one of the few women painters whose work has survived from the 16th century, painted the rather silly-looking *Cleopatra*. Above the windows is a frieze painted by del Vaga, originally intended to be placed beneath Michelangelo's far less cherubic *The Last Judgment* in the Sistine Chapel.

ROOMS 3-4. Grandiose **Room 3** houses 17th-century portraits and overblown mythological scenes along its capacious walls. Most overblown is **Il Guercino's** *Death of Dido*, in which the Carthaginian queen scorned by Aeneas manages to throw herself onto her sword and her funeral pyre at once. In the distance, Aeneas's ships set sail for Italy. Opposite *Dido*, **Tornioli's** *Cain Kills Abel* portrays the slaughter of the prostrate younger brother with a vulture strapped about Cain's hulking torso.

In **Room 4**, the father-daughter team of **Orazio and Artemisia Gentileschi** is represented by three outstanding canvases: Orazio's *David*, Artemisia's *Santa Cecilia* (the patron saint of musicians), and *Madonna with Infant Jesus*. The other artists are mostly influenced by Caravaggio, including the French **Valentin**, whose 1841 *Holy Family with St. John* is remarkable.

MUSEI NAZIONALI ROMANI

◢ *A six-day ticket book is good for all three museums, the Colosseum, and the Palatine Hill (L30,000).*

MUSEO NAZIONALE ROMANO PALAZZO MASSIMO. This fascinating museum is devoted to the history of Roman art during the Empire. The *palazzo* is divided into five sections: art during the transition between republic and empire in the first centuries BC and AD; sculpture from the first to 4th centuries AD (including the *Lancellotti Discus Thrower*); painting and mosaic from the first century BC to the end of the Empire (including a mosaic of Nero's); numismatics (coins); and jewelry. Most pieces were excavated from beneath the modern city. *(Largo di Via Peretti, 1. In the left-hand corner of P. dei Cinquecento as you stand with your back to Termini. ☎06 4815576. Open Tu-Su 9am-7pm. L12,000, EU citizens 18-24 L6000, EU citizens under 18 and over 60 free.)*

MUSEO NAZIONALE ROMANO TERME DI DIOCLEZIANO. Open for the first time since 1983, this beautifully renovated complex is partly housed in the huge **Baths of Diocletian** (see p. 125). The two permanent exhibits are devoted to ancient epigraphy (writing) and Latin history through the 6th century BC. Both have an imposing number of artifacts—almost too many to see. A nice break is provided by the *Chiostro Michelangiolesco*, a peaceful cloister decorated with ancient sculpture. Another wing of the museum is dedicated to exhibits on completely different world cultures. The most impressive display space is the **Aula Grande,** inside the baths' vaulted halls. Its frequent temporary exhibitions on Roman history often cost up to L10,000 extra. In the southwestern corner of the baths complex is the **Aula Ottagonale,** which contains 19 sculptures, including two bronzes found in the baths. *(Museum: P. dei Cinquecento, 78. Opposite Termini. ☎06 39967700. Open Tu-Su 9am-7pm. L8000, EU citizens 18-24 L4000, EU citizens under 18 and over 60 free. Audioguide L6000; guided tour with archaeologist L10,000. Aula Ottagonale: V. Romita, 8. ☎06 488 2364. Open Tu-Su 9am-2pm. L6000; EU citizens 18-24 L3000; EU citizens under 18 and over 60 free.)*

MUSEO NAZIONALE ROMANO PALAZZO ALTEMPS. Literally the Renaissance man of the three *musei*, Palazzo Altemps displays ancient Roman sculpture, including the personal collection of Cardinal Altemps, in a beautiful 16th century edifice. Many of the states in the museum have been restored, but their original condition is well documented. The most famous piece is the *Ludovisi Throne*. Sculpted in the 5th century BC for the Temple of Epizephiris, it features a relief of Aphrodite being born from the waves. The goddess of love is also the protagonist in the lewd *Aphrodite Bathing*. Don't miss the *Parthenon Athena*, the *Ludovisi Ares* (believed to be derived from the work of Alexander the Great's personal sculptor, Lysippus), and the *Suicidal Gaul*. *(P. S. Apollinare, 44. Just north of P. Navona. ☎ 06 390871. Open Tu-Su, 9am-7pm. L10,000, EU citizens 18-24 L5000, EU citizens under 18 and over 60 free.)*

EUR MUSEUMS

🖪 *M:B-EUR-Palasport or B-EUR-Fermi. Walk north up V. Cristoforo Colombo, or take bus #714 from Termini. Make your final destination P. Giuglielmo Marconi; the museums are splayed about Mussolini's decidedly phallic obelisk. One morning should be enough to see the musuems.*

If anything good came of Mussolini's bloodthirsty regime, it just might be the extensive collections in that bastion of fascist organization and architecture, EUR.

Laocoön

MUSEO DELLA CIVILTÀ ROMANA. This expansive museum contains excellent and comprehensive exhibits on ancient Rome. The two vast scale models of Republican and Imperial Rome are incredibly intricate. A cast of Trajan's Column is laid out to let you follow the thrill of victory at eye level (see **History,** p. 46), and the life-size model of a Roman library is fascinating. Exhibits on everyday life in Rome even provide a list of household goods converted into 1937 prices for comparison. *(P. Agnelli, 10. Down V. Civiltà Romana. ☎ 06 5926041. Open Tu-Sa 9am-7pm, Su 9am-1:30pm. L5000, under 18 and over 60 free.)*

MUSEO DELL'ALTO MEDIOEVO. Come see how the Longobords overran the remains of the Roman Empire in the smallest of the EUR museums. Check out the large collection of weapons, jewelry, household items, and art from the Middle Ages. A morning with the Longobords and their knives can cure cases of Roman museum malaise if you've had it up to here with decadent Renaissance art. *(V. Lincoln, 3. ☎ 06 54228199. Open M-Sa 9am-2pm, Su 9am-12:30pm. L4000, reduced price L2000, under 18 and over 65 free. Wheelchair accessible.)*

Vatican Museums

MUSEO NAZIONALE DELLE ARTI E TRADIZIONI POPOLARI. As recently as 30 years ago, much of Italy lived much as it did 1000 years ago. The traditions of such rural areas are rapidly disappearing from the world; this museum may be one of their last refuges. Magnificent luxury items such as the gondola made for Queen Margherita sit next to incredible replicas of traditional attire and farming equipment. *(P. G. Marconi, 8. ☎ 06 5910709; www.ips.it/musis/museo_arti. Open Tu-Su 9am-8pm. Closed New Year's, May Day, and Christmas. Call for tours in Italian or Braille. L8000, reduced price L4000, under 18 and over 65 free.)*

MUSEO PREISTORICO ED ETNOGRAFICO LUIGI PIGORINI. Cower in the face of this impressive collection of ethnographic artifacts from Italy and elsewhere (especially Africa and Australia). Contains the skull of the famous Neanderthal Guattari Man, discovered near Circeo. Often hosts visiting exhibitions. *(P. G. Marconi, 14. ☎ 06 549521; for guided tours in Italian, call 06 8412312. Open daily 9am-2pm. L8000, under 18 and over 65 free.)*

Museo Nazionale d'Arte Antica

RECOMMENDED COLLECTIONS

MUSEO CENTRALE TERMOELETTRICA MONTEMARTINI. This museum wins the prize for best presentation in Rome; it's housed in a turn-of-the-century electrical plant, complete with gargantuan cast-iron machinery. The contrast with the fluid lines of the Classical sculpture on display is striking. Many of the works were taken from storage spaces of the Capitoline Museum and the Antiquarium Forense. Highlights include the *Hercules' Presentation at Mount Olympus* group (a huge and amazingly well preserved floor-mosaic of a hunting scene) and busts of just about every Roman emperor. *(V. Ostiense, 106. M:B-Piramide. From P. Ostiense, walk or take bus #702 or #23. ☎06 5748030. Open Tu-Su 10am-6pm. L8000, EU citizens18-24 L4000, EU citizens under 18 and over 60 free.)*

GALLERIA COLONNA. Despite its disorganization and inhospitable opening hours, the Galleria Colonna remains an impressive collection of art. The *palazzo* was designed in the 18th century to show off the Colonna family jewels, among them Tintoretto's *Narcissus*. The dazzling central gallery is covered with gold and mirrors, and lined with ancient statues. Its chaotic ceiling fresco celebrates the victory of Marcantonio Colonna over the Turks at the Battle of Lepanto in 1571. The ebony desk in the next room is adorned with ivory reliefs of Michelangelo's *The Last Judgment*. The throne room preserves a modest portrait of the portly Pope Martin V and the velvet throne he used to sit on. *(V. della Pilotta, 17. Just north of P. Venezia in the Centro Storico. ☎06 6794362. Open Sa 9am-1pm. L10,000, students L8000. Closed Aug.)*

GALLERIA DORIA PAMPHILJ. The Doria Pamphilj family, whose illustrious kin included Pope Innocent X, remain in custody of this stunning private collection, on display in their palatial home. The villa's classical art is quirkily arranged by size and theme. Don't let the Pamphilj's old-style need to fill every space make you overlook the masterpieces, such as Caravaggio's *Rest during the Flight in Egypt*, Raphael's *Double Portrait*, Velasquez's portrait of Innocent X, Bernini's two busts of the Pope, and a few works by Breughel. Be sure to catch the preserved corpse (from the Catacombs) in the small chapel. *(P. del Collegio Romano, 2. From P. Venezia, walk up V. del Corso and take your 2nd left. ☎06 6797323. Open F-W 10am-5pm. L14,000, students and seniors L11,000. Audioguide included. Useful catalogue with a L10,000 deposit. Private apartments (10:30am-12:30pm) L6000.)*

MUSEO BARRACCO. Housed in a small and elegant Renaissance *palazzo* donated to the city in 1902 by Senator Giovanni Barracco, this impeccably arranged and labeled collection holds some Greco-Roman art, but its Egyptian and Assyrian holdings are what you came for. The 2nd floor houses mostly Egyptian and Greek artifacts and some wonderful Sumerian reliefs; the 3rd floor is home to many a sarcophagus and noseless Roman head. Be sure to check out the 16th-century BC *Sphynx of Queen Hatshepsut*. *(C. V. Emanuele II, 166. Take bus #64 from Termini to Largo di Torre Argentina. ☎06 68806848. Open Tu-Sa 9am-7pm, Su 9am-1pm. L3700, with ISIC card L2500.)*

MUSEO NAZIONALE D'ARTE ORIENTALE. This museum sports a wide array of artifacts dating from prehistory up to the 19th century, divided into six main sections: evolution of art in the Near East; Islamic art; Nepalese and Tibetan art; Buddhist art from India; Southeast Asian art; and Chinese history. Highlights include Stone Age fertility dolls and psychedelic paintings of the Buddha. *(V. Merulana, 248. In Palazzo Brancaccio on the Esquiline Hill. ☎06 4874415. Open M, W, and F 9am-2pm, Tu and Th 9am-7pm, Su 9am-1pm. Closed first and 3rd M of the month. L8000, Italian citizens under 18 and over 60 and humanities students free.)*

OTHER INTERESTING COLLECTIONS

LARGER MUSEUMS

MUSEO CRIMINOLOGICO. After overloading on "artwork" and "culture," this museum dedicated to crime and punishment (the only museum in Rome run by the Dipartimento dell'Amministrazione Penitenziaria) is the perfect chaser. Torture devices comprise the majority of the first floor, as well as some olde English etchings, among them *A Smith Has His Brains Beaten Out With a Hammer*. Joining the festivities are three guillotines and executioner's garb. On the 2nd floor, learn all about the phrenology of criminals and the secret language of tattoos. The 3rd floor contains terrorist, spy, and druggie paraphernalia. Children will learn a great deal. *(V. del Gonfalone, 29. Near Ponte Mazzini. ☎ 06 68300234. Open Tu 9am-1pm and 2:30-6:30pm, W 9am-1pm, Th 2:30-6:30pm, F-Sa 9am-1pm. May be closed in Aug. L4000, those under 18 and over 60 L2000.)*

MUSEO DELLE CERE. Billing itself as an "emulation" of London's Madame Tussaud's—it's more like a photocopy of a photocopy—this **wax museum** has the standards (the Queen of England, Elvis), plus a few distinctly Italian (and distinctly bizarre) scenes. Lowlights include the *Last Meeting of the Fascist Grand Council in Piazza Venezia*, featuring a very sickly-looking Mussolini, and a "moving" nativity scene. There are also vaguely realistic representations of the Yalta Conference, an evening at La Scala, and an execution. *(P. S. Apostoli, 67. Two blocks to your left as you stand at the end of V. del Corso facing the Vittorio Emanuele II monument. ☎ 06 6796482. Open M-F 9am-8:30pm, Sa-Su 9am-11:30pm. L8000. Call to arrange discounts for groups over 15.)*

MUSEO NAPOLEONICO. The Primoli family, to whom this *palazzo* belonged, married into the Bonapartes in the 19th century, and established this museum about Napoleon and his family. It contains paintings, statues, letters, and some of the Emperor's not-so-new clothes (apparently from the boys' section of *Le Deparment Store*). *(V. Zanardelli, 1, first Fl. East of Ponte Umberto. ☎ 06 68806286. Open Tu-Sa 9am-7pm, Su 9am-1:30pm. L7000.)*

MUSEO MARIO PRAZ. This eccentric, smallish museum is housed in seven rooms in the last home of Mario Praz (1896-1982), an equally eccentric and smallish professor of English literature and 18th- and 19th-century art collector. Neighbors believed that Praz had supernatural powers; when they saw him, they spat or flipped coins. *(V. Zanardelli, 1, top fl., east of Ponte Umberto. ☎ 06 6861089. Hourly visits in small groups Tu-Su 9am-1pm and 2:30pm-6:30pm. L4000; under 18 and over 60 free.)*

KEATS-SHELLEY MEMORIAL HOUSE. The house where Keats lived until his death in 1821 houses both interesting artifacts and morbid curiosities. On the morbid side are the plaster casts of Keats's face before and after he succumbed to tuberculosis, a lock of his hair, and his deathbed correspondence with his sister. More scholarly exhibits include the impressive library. *(P. di Spagna, 26. M:A-Spagna. Right of the Steps as you face them. ☎ 06 6784235. Open May-Sept. M-F 9am-1pm and 3-6pm; Oct.-Apr. M-F 9am-1pm and 2:30-5:30pm. Closed mid-July to mid-Aug. L5000.)*

JEWISH COMMUNITY MUSEUM. Sinagoga Askenazita's museum houses a small collection of objects that were hidden during the nine-month Nazi occupation of Rome: magnificently decorated torahs, altar cloths, and various ceremonial objects, as well the original plan of the ghetto (see **Jewish Ghetto**, p. 105). The synagogue itself is lavishly decorated in bright and very beautiful nonfigurative designs. Like all Jewish temples in Italy, this is an Orthodox synagogue; services are segregated by gender. *(Lungotevere Cenci, 15. Take bus #23, which runs along the Tiber. ☎ 06 6840061. To see the synagogue interior, you must take a tour. Open July-Sept. M-Th 9am-7:30pm, F and Su 9am-1:30pm. No cameras. L10,000.)*

GALLERIA COMUNALE D'ARTE MODERNA E CONTEMPORANEA DI ROMA. If you come mid-week, there's a good chance you'll find yourself pacing the gallery's seven rooms alone. On display: a couple of Rodins and a lot of works by late 19th- and early 20th-century Italian painters and sculptors you've never heard of. *(V. F. Crispi, 24. M:A-Barberini. Northwest of P. Barberini. ☎ 06 4742848. Open Tu-Sa 9am-6:30pm, Su 9am-1:30pm. L10,000, students L5000, under 18 and over 60 free. Last Su of the month free. Wheelchair accessible.)*

MUSEO CANONICA. The home and studio of artist Pietro Canonica, the museum houses a collection of his sculptures. *(V. Pietro Canonica, 2. ☎ 06 8842279. In Villa Borghese. Open Tu-Sa 9am-7pm, Su 9am-1:30pm. L4000, with student ID L2500, over 60 and under 18 free.)*

MUSEUM OF ZOOLOGY. While the very Italian take on animal reproduction near the entrance is spanking new, the rest of the museum has a distinctly Victorian feeling, betraying a lack of funding. Glass cases display a multitude of birds and mammals stuffed or skeletonized in the 19th and early 20th centuries, with a few reptiles, amphibians, and fish thrown in for variety. *(V. del Giardino Zoologico, 20. ☎06 3216586. Inside the zoo in Villa Borghese. Open Tu-Su 9am-5pm. Admission L5000, in addition to L10,000 zoo admission.)*

SMALLER MUSEUMS

ARTS AND LETTERS. If you come to the **Museo Comunale Birreria Peroni,** V. Cagliari, 29, just off V. Nomentana, looking for beer, you'll be disappointed. If what you want is contemporary Italian painting and sculpture in an ex-brewery, look no further. *(☎06 8844930. Open M-Sa 10am-8pm. L6000.)* The **Museo della Casina delle Civette,** in the Villa Torlonia, and easily reached by bus #36 bus from Termini, is full of art nouveau stained glass. *(☎06 44250072. Open Apr.-Sept. Tu-Su 9am-7pm; Oct.-Mar. Tu-Su 9am-5pm. L5000.)* The **Goethe Museum,** V. del Corso, 18, near P. del Popolo, is located in the writer's former house, and celebrates his life. *(☎06 32650412. Open W-Su 10am-6pm L6000.)*

Booking is required for the **Museo Internazionale del Cinema e dello Spettacolo,** V. Bettoni, 1, across the river from Testaccio *(☎06 3700266.)* The **Museo e Biblioteca Teatrale del Burcardo,** V. del Sudario, 44, contains costumes, scripts, and other artifacts of the stage *(☎06 6819471. Open M, W, and F 9am-1:30pm, Tu, Th 9am-4pm.)*

MARTIAL ARTS. The ancient defenses of Rome are chronicled in the **Museo delle Mura Porta San Sebastiano,** V. di Porta San Sebastiano, 18. Take bus #760 from the Circus Maximus or #218 from San Giovanni. Walk around the Aurelian ramparts! *(☎06 70475284. Open Tu-Su 9am-7pm. L5000.)* The **Sacrario delle Bandiere,** on the left side of the Vittorio Emanuele II monument as you face it, is the only part of the big white wonder open to the public. This curious museum salutes 20th-century Italian war efforts, displaying battle-weary flags and two hulking World War I submarines. *(☎06 647355002. Theoretically open Tu-Su 9am-1pm. L3000.)* The **Museo Storico dell'Arma dei Carabinieri,** P. del Risorgimento, near the Vatican, is dedicated to the glorious history of the machine-gun-toting Italian military police. Full of costumes, guns, swords, and statues, it's a glorious tribute to the extraordinary heroism of the Carabinieri. Please don't laugh at the tiny toy Fiats. *(☎06 6896691. Open Tu-Su 9am-12:30pm. L4000.)*

MATH AND SCIENCE. The **Museo Astronomico Copernicano,** V. del Parco Mellini, 84. It's dedicated to Copernicus and the history of astronomy. *(From the Vatican, take bus #907. ☎06 35347056. Open W and Sa 9am-1pm. L6000.)* The **Museo della Matematica,** P. Aldo Moro, 5, is located in the math department of La Sapienza. *(Take bus #492. ☎06 5833102.)* All manner of medical instruments from the 16th century to the present are contained in the **Museo Storico Nazionale dell'Arte Sanitaria,** Lungotevere Sassia, 3, across Ponte Vittorio Emanuele II on the Vatican bank. *(☎06 68351. Open M, W, and F 9:30am-1:30pm. L3000.)*

PASTA, PRESEPIO, AND PURGATORY. The ◪**Museo Nazionale delle Paste Alimentari,** P. Scanderbeg, 117, is easy to reach (follow the signs) from P. di Trevi. Its greater purpose is ending world hunger with pasta. While they're working on that, though, the museum will be happy to tell you everything you've ever wanted to know about Italy's favorite first course. *(☎06 6991119. Open daily 9:30am-5:30pm. L5000.)* Crêches, 3000 of 'em, are the focus at the **Museo Tipologio Nazionale del Presepio,** V. Tor dei Conti, 31a, near the intersection of V. dei Fori Imperiali and V. Cavour. *(Call 06 6796146 to arrange a visit.)* The ◪**Piccolo Museo delle Anime del Purgatorio,** Lungotevere Prati, 12, near Ponte Cavour inside the Chiesa del Sacro Cuore del Suffragio, is a tiny museum that displays communications from souls trapped in Purgatory. *(Open daily 7:30-11:30am and 4:30-7:30pm.)*

REVOLVING EXHIBITIONS

Rome's museum collections are supplanted by all manner of temporary exhibits. A number of museums listed above host temporary shows. The galleries below are mainly known for their temporary exhibitions. Major exhibitions are usually listed in the English section of *Roma C'è.*

MUSEO NAZIONALE DEL PALAZZO VENEZIA. The museum (an impressive 1455 *palazzo* that once belonged to the embassy of the Venetian Republic) hosts Rome's most prominent exhibitions. These are held in three large rooms, including the *Sala del Mappamondo*, the office where Mussolini used to deviously leave his light on all night, (earning the title "Sleepless One"). An easy way to find out what's showing is to watch the gigantic ads the museum routinely projects onto the facade of the building opposite. There is also an extensive permanent collection, including 13th- through 19th-century painting, Renaissance sculpture, and gold. Don't miss the inner garden, a remarkable oasis of peace next to one of Rome's busiest intersections. *(V. del Plebiscito, 118. On the left-hand side of P. Venezia as you stand with your back to the Vittorio Emanuele II monument. ☎06 67994319. Exhibits usually open Tu-Th, Su 10am-7pm; F and Sa 10am-10pm. Admission varies. Guided tours available. Permanent collection open Tu-Su 9am-2pm. L8000, under 18 and over 60 free.)*

PALAZZO DELLE ESPOSIZIONI. This behemoth has no permanent collection, but hosts a varied and ever-changing array of exhibits and film festivals. Film festival movies are included in museum admission. Recent successes have been an Andy Warhol film festival, an El Greco show, and an exhibit on Pirandello. *(V. Nazionale, 194. Six blocks in search of an author down V. Nazionale from P. della Repubblica. Open W-M 10am-9pm. ☎06 4885465. L12,000, with student ID L6000, four student tickets L20,000.)*

SALA DEL BRAMANTE. A small gallery that unveils temporary art exhibitions, the most recent being a wildly popular Goya show. Other past favorites have been Mark Chagall, Picasso, and Dali exhibitions. *(P. del Popolo. M:A-Flaminio. In the small courtyard to the rear of the Church of Santa Maria del Popolo. ☎06 32600569. Open Tu-Su 10am-7pm. L5000.)*

Shopping

You can buy damn near anything in Rome. Here we list only frivolities, so, if you're look-ing for sustenance, see **Food and Wine,** p. 198. Go now, indulge, you filthy capitalist pig.

CLOTHING & SHOES

Rome is famous for its fashion, and justly so. Though Roman taste can take horrifying turns toward the skintight and garish, Romans usually know how to look good, and you can, too. Some advice before setting out with credit card in hand: sales in Italy happen twice a year, in mid-January and mid-July. Don't be surprised if you're not allowed to try on everything in all stores. Finally, be very clear about exchanges and returns *before* giv-ing a store your money; Europe is not exactly known for its customer service.

These listings are just a teaser; *Roma C'è* publishes a comprehensive shopping guide (in bookstores, about L10,000). For browsing, the areas along V. Cola di Rienzo, Ottavi-ano, Nazionale, Appia Nuova (near San Giovanni), and Europa (in EUR) are great.

While hours change, most stores are open Monday through Saturday from 9am to 7:30pm. Small stores often close for one to three hours beginning at 1pm. Most clothing stores and boutiques accept major credit cards.

BOUTIQUES

Regardless of your place on the political spectrum, you know you've secretly longed to own a Versace jacket or a MaxMara skirt, no matter how ideologically impure it seems. Particularly for those coming to Italy from overseas, Rome is one of the best places in the world to sate these forbidden desires, since prices in the boutiques here are well below those in the US and Australia.

WALK LIKE AN ITALIAN

Italians have an uncanny ability to pick tourists out of a Roman crowd (and an equally remarkable ability to pick *up* tourists from a crowd). Perhaps it's because every American is wearing khaki shorts, a white t-shirt, and a pair of Tevas. Make the leap into Euro-chic by adding this simple starter kit of must-haves to your wardrobe.

Pickwick shirt: It doesn't matter what it says, as long as Pickwick's on it somewhere. Be sure to buy one that is too tight.

Really tight jeans: Dark with untapered leg. Ouch. Or...

Really tight cargo pants: Thus negating the utility factor of all those pockets.

Invicta backpack: Who knew that neon yellow went with neon pink? It's all OK if the word Invicta is plastered across the back in neon blue. Head to Invicta (at right) to find one in the "Invicta Jolly" line. Make sure all of your friends sign your backpack in permanent ink.

Telefonino: You won't get anywhere without a mobile phone. If you can't afford one, no one is stopping you from pretending. Buy a fake from a cigarette lighter salesperson in P. Barberini (or anywhere).

Dolce & Gabbana, P. di Spagna, 82-83 (☎06 6792294). Who wouldn't kill for their suits?

Emporio Armani, V. del Baubino, 140 (☎06 36002197). Houses the less expensive end of the Armani line.

Fendi, V. Borgogna, 36-40 (☎06 6794824).

Genny, P. di Spagna, 27 (☎06 6796074).

Gianni Versace. Men: V. Borgogna, 24-25 (☎06 6795037). Women: V. Bocca di Leone, 26 (☎06 6780521).

Giorgio Armani, V. dei Condotti, 75 (☎06 6991460).

Gucci, V. dei Condotti, 8 (☎06 6789340).

Laura Biagiotti, V. Borgogna, 43-44 (☎06 6795040).

Lacoste, V. Giulia, 18 (☎06 6869590).

Krizia, P. di Spagna, 87 (☎06 6793772).

Missoni, P. di Spagna, 78 (☎06 6792555).

Prada, V. dei Condotti, 92-95 (☎06 6790897).

RoccoBarocco, P. di Spagna, 93 (☎06 6797914).

Salvatore Ferragamo. Men: V. dei Condotti, 66 (☎06 6791017). Women: V. dei Condotti, 73-74 (☎06 6792297).

Valentino, V. dei Condotti, 12 (☎06 6790479).

CHIC FOR LESS

Designer emporiums such as **Cenci,** V. Campo Marzio 1-7 (☎06 6990681), and **David's of Rome** stock many lines of designer clothes at lower prices. Workers won't be as ready to prostrate themselves before you for the contents of your wallet, and you have to buy directly off the rack. These are an especially good deal during the sale months of January and July; look for the *Saldi* sign in the window.

Benetton. They're all over the place. You can't miss them. The sponsor of many controversial advertising campaigns is more within reach of the average *Let's Go* traveler.

Diesel, V. del Corso, 186 (☎06 6783933). Off V. dei Condotti. *The* label in retro fashion is surprisingly high-octane. No one said that being a fashion plate was easy.

Ethic, V. del Corso, 94 and V. delle Carozze, 20. The hip yet less adventurous can find a balance between the avant garde and the tasteful here. Prices won't break the bank.

Invicta, V. del Baubino, 28 (☎06 3600 1737). When the time has come for a garishly colored backpack (as it surely will), run, don't walk, to Invicta. Chartreuse never looked so good on a backpack. Neither did hot pink or neon blue. Though the senses rebel, social conformity says yes.

DEPARTMENT STORES

Finally, clothes on a budget! Even though the following hallowed halls of fashion may not hold the latest styles or top-tier quality, much of the fashion adorning Roman bodies can be found here. These are also excellent places to buy necessities like socks and underwear, should the need ever arise.

La Rinascente, Largo Chigi, 20-21 (☎06 6797691). Just off V. del Corso. The classiest of the bunch, La Rinascente carries many designer lines and offers friendly English help and information. Open M-Sa 9:30am-8pm, Su 11am-8pm.

COIN, V. Cola di Rienzo, 173 (☎06 3380750). The sensible, middle-of-the-road option. Some good deals, especially on cosmetics. Also at P. Appio, 7 (☎06 7080020) and V. Mantova, 1 (☎06 8415884), near Porta Pia. All locations open M-Sa 10am-8pm.

SHOES

Mada, V. della Croce, 57 (☎06 6798660). A very popular women's shoe store, Mada has been called a "must" for Roman women. Open Tu-Sa 9:30am-1pm and 3:30-7:30pm, M 9:30am-1pm.

Brugnoli Calzature, V. Ripetta 26 (☎06 3600 1889). A shoe store selling classic footwear for men and women, along with belts and purses to complete the leather selection. Also at V. S. Giacomo, 25 (☎06 3612325). Open Tu-Sa 9:30am-1pm and 3:30-7:30pm, M 9:30am-1pm.

NON-PRODUCE MARKETS

Expect to bargain, especially on clothing. Often, prices aren't marked in order to allow the vendor to size you up. Be prepared to counter the seller's first offer; you'll get much further if you use Italian. Don't be surprised if a vendor feigns offense—it's all part of the game. Be prepared for a hard sell, and know when to bust out the *"No, grazie"* and walk away. For markets that sell food primarily, see p. 198. Hours are never set in stone—markets begin when everyone gets there and end when they get bored.

▨ Porta Portese, in Trastevere at Porta Portese. Tram #8. A fever dream of a market, where booths selling clothing, shoes, jewelry, bags, and anything else that can be imagined extend beyond the horizon. The biggest in Rome. Su 5am-2pm.

Garage Sale—Rigattieri per Hobby, P. della Marina, 32, Borghetto Flaminio. Near the Olympic Stadium. A market primarily dedicated to hobbies of all sorts; if you want it, chances are you can probably find it. Admission L3000. Open Su 5pm-midnight.

Borgo Parioli, V. Tirso, 14. Mainly dedicated to antiques, jewelry, household wares, and ceramics, the Borgo Parioli has been going strong in one of the most fashionable areas of town for years. You gotta love it. Open Su 10am-8pm.

Via Sannio, near the San Giovanni (A) Metro stop. Clothing and shoe stalls line up to peddle inexpensive new and used wares. Open M-Sa 8:30am-1:30pm.

Mercatino Madonna della Luce, V. Filippi, 57, in EUR. Run by a society that also manages social services for the homeless and marginalized, this is the Italian equivalent of the Salvation Army. Used and recycled clothes, furniture, books, and more at low, low prices. Open usually 9am-12:30pm and 3:30-7pm, on varying days of the week; check *Roma C'e'* for details.

MUSIC

Over-stuffed lovers and undying affection parade through the weird wide world of Italian pop. (If you're ready to face this dark side of humanity, see p. 173.) Those looking for cheap music and willing to take a walk on the wild side may look for pirated CDs and PlayStation games. You can find vendors on the street in well-trafficked areas or in outdoor markets. CDs sell for around L10,000, but you can often bargain. A word of warning before you drool over low-cost rip-offs—there is no guarantee of quality or the content matching what is advertised. Many vendors have CD players with them; listen first, then buy. For a more savory and legal shopping experience, try the following stores.

Disfunzioni Musicali. New music: V. degli Etruschi, 4 (☎06 4461984). Used music and imports: V. dei Marrucini, 1 (☎06 4454263). Both in San Lorenzo. CDs, cassettes, and LPs available, including an excellent selection of rock, avant-garde classical, jazz, and ethnic music. Open M-F 10:30am-7:30pm, Sa 10:30am-4:30pm; in winter M-Sa 10:30am-7:30pm.

Messaggerie Musicali, V. del Corso, 122 (☎06 6798197). This 3-story music store specializes in CDs and electronics; their music collection is strongest on the pop front and often reasonably priced. Portable stereos and electronics on the 2nd floor. Open daily 10am-8pm.

RicordiMedia. Several locations: V. del Corso, 506 (☎06 3612370); V. G. Cesare, 88 (☎06 37351589), in Prati; P. dell'Indipendenza, 25 (☎06 4440706), near Termini; and V. C. Battisti, 120 (☎06 6798022), just off P. Venezia. A chain with an average selection of music. Look for *Prezzi Pazzi* signs for deals on indie music. Check here for concert listings; ticket offices at the V. del Corso and V. G. Cesare locations. Open daily 9:30am-8pm.

BOOKS

Although you already own the only book you'll need during your trip to Rome, sometimes it's nice to read something that's not *so* damn witty and irreverent.

BOOKSTORES

Via di Terme di Diocleziano, connecting Termini with P. della Repubblica, is lined with booksellers full of dirt-cheap used English paperbacks. **Via di Conciliazione,** the broad avenue leading to St. Peter's, has several bookstores selling English-language histories and guidebooks, as well as devotional materials.

▩ **Libreria Feltrinelli International,** V. V. E. Orlando, 84-86 (☎06 4827878). Near P. della Repubblica. A Roman fixture. Excellent selection of books in several languages, dictionaries, and travel guides. Cheaper than most English-language bookstores. Shops at V. del Babuino, 41 (☎06 36001899) and Largo Argentina, 5a (☎06 68803248) have the same hours and carry some English titles, but don't specialize in foreign books. Open daily 9am-7:30pm. AmEx, MC, V.

▩ **Anglo-American Bookshop,** V. della Vite, 102 (☎06 6795222; www.aab.it). South of the Spanish Steps. In case the name didn't give it away, this place specializes in English language books. Fiction, history, and poetry abound in this well-stocked bookshop. The bilingual staff really knows its stuff and is always willing to help. The bulletin board in back lists apartments for rent. *Wanted in Rome* sold here. Summer hours: M-F 9am-1pm and 4-8pm, Sa 9am-1pm.

The Lion Bookshop, V. dei Greci, 33-36 (☎06 32654007). Off V. del Corso, near P. di Popolo. For the Anglophile literature lover. A well-stocked bookstore with poetry, fiction, new releases, and children's books. Small selection of rental videos. Community bulletin board. Open M-F 10am-7:30pm, Sa 10am-1pm; in winter M 3:30-7:30pm, Tu-Sa 10am-7:30pm. AmEx, MC, V.

Economy Book and Video Center, V. Torino, 136 (☎06 4746877; www.booksitaly.com). Off V. Nazionale. Wide range of English language books, as well as books on tape and greeting cards. Expanded gift section lets you spend, spend, spend on those envious of your stay in Rome. Also buys used English paperbacks and rents videos (L10,000 per night with L150,000 deposit or credit card). Bulletin board with various postings; *Wanted in Rome* available. Open June-Aug. M-F 9am-8pm, Sa 9am-2pm; Sept.-May M 3-8pm, Tu-F 9am-8pm, Sa 9am-2pm. AmEx, MC, V.

Corner Bookshop, V. del Moro, 48. (☎06 5836942). In Trastevere. Pick up an English book and get some of what the proprietress calls "the best bread in Rome" at the shop across the street. A handy bulletin board displays ads for rooms and classes. Open M-Sa 10am-1:30pm and 4-8pm, Su 11am-1:30pm and 4-8pm. Closed Su in Aug. In winter closed M morning. AmEx, MC, V.

The English Bookshop, V. di Ripetta, 248 (☎ 06 3203301). Near P. del Popolo. A small bookstore selling English-language books at reasonable prices. Two rooms provide plenty of light reading, as well as travel guides and a large selection of children's books, cookbooks, Italian fiction translated into English, and reference works. Open M-Sa 10am-7:30pm. AmEx, MC, V.

ENGLISH LIBRARIES

Centro Studi Americani, V. M. Caetani, 32, 2nd Fl. (☎06 68806624). Off P. Mattei in a large *palazzo*. Every section of the Dewey Decimal System represented. Check out books with a membership (one-year L30-70,000). Open M-F 9am-7:30pm, Sa 9am-1:30pm. Closed part of Aug.

Santa Susanna Lending Library, V. XX Settembre, 15, 2nd Fl. (☎06 4827510). In the Church of Santa Susanna. About 9000 English volumes. 3mo. membership L20,000; L50,000 yearly. 6mo. family membership L35,000; L60,000 yearly. Open Tu and Th 10am-1pm, W 3-6pm, F 1-4pm, Sa-Su 10am-12:30pm. In July open only Tu, W, and Su; in Aug. open only Su.

SOUVENIRS & RELIGIOUS PARAPHERNALIA

You can't turn around in Rome without seeing a souvenir stand. For sacred objects, look near the Vatican, where countless booths and stores sell everything from mini relics to 3-D Pope postcards. (Seeing is believing.) Feeling hungry? Try a Popesicle. Open that ice-cold beer with your very own Popener. If it's sacred, you'll see it. A word of warning: pay more than L6000 for a t-shirt and you are being ripped off.

Barbiconi, V. Caterina di Siena, 59 (☎06 6794985). Barbiconi sells a lovely array of clerical vestments, including plenty of nun outfits. Become a creature of "habit" and drop by for a fitting. Open M-F 9am-1pm and 3:30-7:30pm. Closed early July-end of Aug. MC, V.

Fabbroni Colombo, P. del Pantheon, 69a (☎06 6790483). A hole in the wall with what must be the largest postcard collection in Rome. Send one to a friend, you ingrate. Open daily 10am-7:30pm.

Comandini, Borgo Pio, 151 (☎06 6875079). Sate your endless desire for popery. A truly vast array of religious accoutrements is on display, from John Paul II ashtrays to calligraphic messages personally blessed by His Holiness. Open daily 9am-7pm.

L'image, V. della Scrofa, 67-68 (☎06 7221121). Posters of every size and shape. Open M-Th 10am-8pm, F-Sa 10am-8pm and 10pm-1am, Su 11:30am-1:30pm and 4-8pm.

Piazza di Spagna

MISCELLANEOUS

HOME FURNISHINGS. If you are planning a long-term stay in Rome, head out to furnish those barren rooms.

Modigliani, V. dei Condotti, 24 (☎06 6991143). Nothing large to be found here, but a large selection of smaller (and quite elegant) housewares to be had. Some of the glassware and ceramic pieces are just gorgeous. Open M 1-7pm, Tu-Sa 10am-7pm.

Linn sui, V. del Boschetto, 79 (☎06 4820761). If a bed isn't your thing, you can still find a place to lay your head on an average-priced futon. Open M-Sa 9:30am-1pm and 3:30-7:30pm.

Centro Storico

Archidomus, V. Leonardo da Vinci, 256 (☎06 547945). In Ostiense. Beds, couches, tables, and other such large objects at discounted prices. Open M 4-8pm, Tu-Sa 9:30am-1pm and 4-8pm.

JEWELERY. Rome boasts a large array of jewelers, and many carry work that is quite original and creative.

Inor, V. della Stelletta, 23 (☎06 6868739). A good selection of silver goods, from expensive to very affordable. Open M-F 9am-6pm.

Alcozer, V. delle Carozze, 48 (☎06 6791388). Near P. di Spagna. Gorgeous jewelry at decent prices. Open M 3:30-7:30pm, Tu-Sa 10am-1:30pm and 3:30-7:30pm.

Window Shopping

Entertainment

Roman entertainment just isn't what it used to be. Back in the day, you could swing by the Colosseum to watch a man viciously clawed to death by a bear. Now, Romans seeking diversion are far more likely to go to the opera, a soccer game, or the latest Hollywood flick. Is this progress? Perhaps. But this is no reason for you, bloodthirsty traveler, to content your restless heart with eating *gelato* next to a monument or people-watching in a *piazza*. Rome is full of more entertaining entertainment options.

   Roma C'è, Time Out, and **TrovaRoma** contain comprehensive lists of events and venues (see p. 28), and *Roma C'è* includes a section in English detailing goings-on of special interest to English speakers. Tourist offices (p. 27) also have lots of information on cultural activities—ask for *Un'Ospite a Roma* and a list of upcoming concerts. Of course, the city's walls are plastered with advertisements for upcoming concerts, plays, operas, parties, and circuses.

MASS MEDIA: AN INTRODUCTION

Rome became my home as soon as I saw it. I was born that moment.
That was my *real* birthday.
   —Federico Fellini

THE SILVER SCREEN

To see Rome's major contribution to the arts in this century, don't go to the museum—go to the movies. Years before Hollywood began producing films, the **Cines** studios thrived in Rome. Constructed in 1905-6, Cines created the so-called Italian "super-spectacle"—extravagant, larger-than-life recreations of momentous historical events. **Enrico Guzzani**'s

SPAGHETTI WESTERN

In attempting to jump-start the export of Italian film to America, Italian movie-makers decided to use Rome's Cinecittà studios to make American Westerns. Producers carefully sprinkled token, tow-headed Americans among the extras, and encouraged actors and directors to think up pseudonyms for their spaghetti Western output. Sergio Leone (whose emotion-driven camera work gave the world *The Good, the Bad, and the Ugly* (1966) and *A Fistful of Dollars* (1964)) went as "Bob Robertson."

The spaghetti Western flourished between 1961 and 1973, providing revenue to fund the art-house dreams of directors like Fellini. By the end of the '60s, many other Italian filmmakers had eagerly jumped into the odd but lucrative cross-breed genre. Some of these young talents, inspired by the flavor of the times, began making explicitly Marxist films that built on the Mexican setting of the Western to become what some called "the Zapata-Spaghetti plot." Unfortunately, few of these more revolutionary bandit and cowherd-gringo flicks ever made it across the ocean to that mother lode of capitalism, distribution, and profits, the United States.

incredible *Quo Vadis*, enjoyed international success as the first "blockbuster" hit in film history.

Recognizing the power of popular cinema, Mussolini created the *Centro Sperimentale della Cinematografia*, a national film school, and the gargantuan **Cinecittà studios.** The famous director and covert Marxist **Luigi Chiarini** attracted many students—including **Roberto Rosselini** and **Michelangelo Antonioni,** both of whom rose to enormous and well-deserved directorial fame after the war. Mussolini avoided most aesthetic questions of film but instituted a few "imperial edicts," one of which forbade laughing at the Marx Brothers' *Duck Soup*.

When Fascism fell, a generation of young filmmakers enjoyed new freedom, sparking the explosion of **neorealist cinema.** Neorealists first gained attention in Italy with **Luchino Visconti**'s 1942 *Ossessione* and Rosselini's widely acclaimed *Roma, Città Aperta (Rome, Open City)*, a 1946 movie about a Resistance leader trying to escape the Gestapo that was filmed mostly on the streets of Rome during the Fascist occupation.

FELLINI. Fellini rejected the Neorealists' use of plots and characters to portray a world of moments and witnesses. Rome figures largely in the director's work. In *Nights of Cabiria* (1957), his wife Giulietta Masina gives a heartbreakingly beautiful performance as a Roman prostitute. *8½* (1963), the quintessential study of writer's block, childhood, sexuality, and religion, is one of the most critically acclaimed films of all time. In Fellini's autobiographical *Roma* (1972), a gorgeous stand-in for the director encounters another bizarre set of characters. The film focuses on the city itself, exploring how Rome of the imagination (and the director's nostalgia) clashes sharply with reality.

La Dolce Vita (1960), banned by the pope but widely regarded as *the* representative Italian film, scrutinizes the unscrupulously stylish Rome of the 1950s. In the movie, buxom blonde Anita Ekberg jumps into the Trevi Fountain (p. 109), prompting such a widespread fad that the Italian government had to enact laws prohibiting wading in the water.

ANTONIONI. Fellini's colleague Michelangelo Antonioni was even more radical in his refusal to comply with the artificiality of a traditional plot line, conflict, and resolution. His films frustrated movie-goers' trained reflexes by following internal rhythms of the story rather than the stylized sequential cause-and-effect plots, gaining instead a weird purity and mesmeric beauty. His first three major works form a conceptual trilogy. *L'Avventura* (1960) examined the hollow lives of the upper classes, focusing on the repercussions of a woman's disappearance on her friends. *La Notte* (1960) continued his exploration of moral emptiness in a masterful study of a couple failing to communicate. *L'Eclisse* (1962) portrays a series of relationships damned by materialism. *Blow-Up* (1967), filmed in English, is ostensibly the story of a photographer in swinging London who accidentally films a murder, reconceptualizing the way in which film makes use of sound and image.

PASOLINI. Pier Paolo Pasolini—who spent as much time on trial for his politics as he did making films—remains Italy's most controversial director. For Pasolini, Rome was not only a birthplace but also a major source of inspiration. An ardent Marxist, he set his first films in the Roman underworld of poverty and prostitution. An early film titled *Mamma Roma* (1962) chronicles the allegorical downfall of a passionate and motherly whore who repeatedly tries to prevent her son from joining a band of criminal louts. He moved on from his neorealist roots to a cinema more oriented toward myth and ideology, making film adaptations of *Oedipus Rex* (1967), the *Decameron* (1970), and the *Thousand and One Nights* (1974). His austere ✍*Gospel of St. Matthew* (1964), made without professional actors, has been praised as the greatest film made of the life of Christ. Pasolini's final film, *Salo* (1975), was an extremely controversial adaptation of the Marquis de Sade's *The 120 Days of Sodom.* Often held to be the most obscene film ever, *Salo* is still banned in Australia. Pasolini set de Sade's novel in Italy during World War II: the nihilistic violence has been interpreted as indicting Italian compliance with fascism and capitalism. Pasolini's radical politics, homosexuality, and alleged pedophilia made him decidedly unpopular with right-wing groups. He was murdered by a male hustler in Ostia in 1975; the youth was later released from prison.

Stardust

BERTOLUCCI. Much less controversial, though decidedly leftist, are the films of Bernardo Bertolucci. His 1970 masterpiece *The Conformist* studies the affect of fascism on a weakwilled man. ✍*Last Tango in Paris* (1972) features what is arguably Marlon Brando's greatest performance as he plays an expatriate involved in a doomed love affair. Once seen as controversial for its anonymous sex, it now seems tame. The Italian film industry ostracized him in response to what they saw as the pornography and excessive internationalism of his onscreen aesthetics. This boycott forced him to look abroad for funding, eventually directing such Hollywood epics as the wonderful *The Last Emperor* (1987), a version of Paul Bowles's *The Sheltering Sky* (1990), and the muddled *Little Buddha* (1993). After a 20-year exile, Bertolucci returned to Italy to film *Stealing Beauty* (1996) and *L'Assedio* (1998).

Roman Forum

COMMEDIA DELLA CINEMA. Unlike Bertolucci, Italian comedy makers have tended to find much support and success at home. Directors like **Nanni Moretti,** creator of the *Caro Diario* (*Dear Diary,* 1994), and **Lina Wertmüller,** maker of such complex and explosively funny films as *Seven Beauties* (1976) and 1993's popular *Ciao, Professore!* have managed to sustain a viable contemporary alternative to Hollywood. Perhaps the best-known of their number, the charmingly funny actor and director **Roberto Benigni** (also the star of *Ciao, Professore!*) romped victorious through the 1999 Academy Awards and the 1999 French *César* (among others) for his controversial Holocaust-based comedy *Life is Beautiful.* Benigni has also been in more interesting films in the past, including his hilarious *Johnny Stecchino* (*Johnny Toothpick,* 1991) and Jim Jarmusch's *Down by Law* (1986).

Festa de l'Unite

THE BOOB TUBE

If you thought American TV was sexist, you haven't seen Italian television. Game shows, news commentary, and even children's programs are populated by buxom (often top-less), leggy bombshells in flashy clothes. *O tempora, O mores!*

Italian television comes in two varieties—the three vaguely educational, state-owned **RAI** channels and the often shamelessly insipid networks owned by former prime minis-ter Silvio Berlusconi. Italia Uno, Rete 4, and Canale 5 transmit all your favorite American trash, including "Beverly Hills, 90210," "Baywatch," and "Saved by the Bell," as well as a few indigenous crimes against human intelligence. The Italian music television channel is **Magic,** bringing you videos for pop music you never knew existed and sometimes never wanted to know existed. Late-night TV brings lots of dubbed movies and fairly explicit 30-minute advertisements for phone sex.

Eight-year-old girls and adolescent boys rush home every day at 2pm to watch **Non È La RAI,** a variety show featuring scantily clad high-school-age girls dancing and lip-syncing to all their favorite tunes. You can even catch a glimpse of Ambra, the hostess and singer of the popular song "Aspettavo Te," outside the studios near San Giovanni in Laterano (p. 131). Those brushing up on Italian pop culture can watch and learn from countless game shows like **La Ruota della Fortuna** and **OK: Il Prezzo È Giusto,** on which Italians make fools of themselves for cash. One quiz show, **Il Vinca È Migliore,** polls the audience with multiple choice questions and then embarrasses the people who get them wrong.

MUSIC

The Italians have always been slaves to a pretty tune, as anyone who has studied the piano, belonged to a school band, or slaved over a cello can attest. The *piano, cre-scendo,* and *allegro* are there for a reason: Italians, with help from the French, invented the system for musical notation still used today. Before there was Julie Andrews, there was Guido D'Arezzo, who came up with *solfege,* the "do, re, mi" syllable system of expressing the musical scale. A 16th-century Venetian printed the first musical scores with movable type. Cremona offered violins by Stradivarius and Guarneri; the piano (actually the *pianoforte,* which means "soft-loud") is an Italian invention. For Italians, vocal music has always occupied the position of highest glory. **Madrigals,** free-flowing secular songs for three to six voices, grew in popularity, leading into a still-popular genre. One of the greatest contributors to Italian madrigals and sacred music was **Gio-vanni Pierluigi Palestrina.** Born and bred in Lazio, he served as a choirboy at the Church of Santa Maria Maggiore (see p. 127) and went on to direct choirs at S. Maria Maggiore, San Giovanni in Laterano (see p. 131), and St. Peter's (see p. 115).

OPERA. Born in 16th-century Florence, nurtured in Venice, and revered in Milan, the opera is the greatest musical innovation in Italian history. Invented by the **Camerata,** an artsy clique of Florentine poets, noblemen, authors, and musicians, opera began as an attempt to recreate the dramas of ancient Greece by setting the lengthy poems to music. As opera spread from Florence to Venice, Milan, and Rome, the styles and forms of the genre also grew more distinct. Contemporaneous with the birth of opera was the emer-gence of the **oratorio.** Introduced by Roman priest **St. Philip Neri,** the oratorio set biblical text to dramatic choral and instrumental accompaniment.

In opera, Baroque ostentation yielded to classical standards of moderation. To today's opera buffs, Italian opera means Rossini, Bellini, Donizetti, Verdi, and Puccini—all com-posers of the 19th and early 20th centuries. Giuseppe **Verdi** had become a national icon by mid-life, writing such masterworks as the tragic, triumphal *Aïda* and *La Traviata.* Another great composer of the era, **Gioacchino Rossini,** boasted that he could produce music faster than copyists could reproduce it, but he proved such an infamous procras-tinator that his agents resorted to locking him in a room with a single plate of spaghetti until he completed his compositions. Apparently, it was good spaghetti, and his *Barber of Seville* remains a favorite with modern audiences. Finally, **Giacomo Puccini,** composer of *Madama Butterfly,* deserves a nod for his kick-ass female characters.

INSTRUMENTAL MUSIC. Instrumental music began to establish itself as a legitimate genre in 17th-century Rome. During the Baroque period, **Corelli** developed the *concerto* form with its contrasting moods and tempos that added drama to technical expertise. **Antonio Vivaldi** wrote over 400 *concerti* while teaching at an orphanage in Venice. His *Four Seasons* remains one of the best-known Baroque orchestral works.

In the mid-17th-century, operatic overtures began to be performed separately, resulting in the creation of a new genre. The *sinfonia* (symphony) was modeled after the melody of operatic overtures and simply detached from their setting. At the same time, the composer Domenico **Scarlatti** wrote over 500 sonatas for the harpsichord.

Italy's chokehold on the musical world continued into the 19th century. Relying on devilish pyrotechnical virtuosity and a personal style marked by mystery and scandal, violinist **Nicolò Paganini** brought Europe to its knees. One of the first musicians to make highly publicized concert tours, he inspired **Franz Lizst** to become a virtuoso pianist; the pair was the 19th century equivalent of rock stars, complete with groupies.

TWENTIETH CENTURY. Italian classical **music** continued to grow in the 20th century. **Ottorino Respighi,** composer of the popular *Pines of Rome* and *Fountains of Rome*, experimented with orchestral textures. Known for his work with meta-languages, **Luciano Berio** defied traditional instrumentation with his *Sequenza V* for solo trombone and mime and other works for voice and solo wind instrument. Needless to say, among performers, **Luciano Pavarotti** retains followers, despite the loss of his voice; his 1990 concert with Placido Domingo and José Carreras, "The Three Tenors," drew a full-capacity crowd to the Baths of Caracalla (p. 91). A 1997 repeat filled the stadium of Modena, and the 1998 reunion during the World Cup in Paris reportedly drew one million people.

POP, ROCK, AND RAP(?). Once upon a time, Italian pop had its own unique and indigenous character that blended Italian folk songs and Mediterranean rhythms with pop beats. Pino Daniele, Lucio Battisti, **Vasco Rossi,** and others used to perform their folk-inspired ballads for captive audiences of university students. Since the 1980s, however, traditional Italian pop has slowly been assimilated into the global hegemony of the American/British pop scene. Some have faded from the scene; others, like Rossi, have adapted to the times and become very successful and popular once again. There are a still good number of native pop talents, though many locals would be loath to admit it, among them Renato Zero, Gianna Nannini, **Laura Pausini,** and **883** *(Otto otto tre)*. The aging Renato keeps churning out the hits, and the Romans love him for it: in the summer of '99, he ws able to fill the Foro Italico six nights in a row. Nini's "Lupi Solitari" expresses the angst felt by all 15-year-olds, while 883's ballad "Come Mai" was suggested by some as the new Italian national anthem. After Laura Pausini conquered Italy, she has begun to try, with mixed success, for international stardom.

Italian rock acts are even better than their pop comrades. **Zucchero,** who has played stadiums with the likes of Sting and Pavarotti, is the tried-and-true warhorse of Italian rock, with a solid international fan base as well. The aforementioned Vasco Rossi has turned from folk to rock; his "Rewind" was an anthemic hit 1999. **Litfiba,** with their U2-esque stylings and the impressive cheekbones of lead singer Pelù, are perennially popular, though some claim they have sold out and left their socially conscious roots behind.

Though many would be hard-pressed to believe it, Italian rap exists, and it's not bad. The ultra-left wing and super-socially conscious **99 Posse**'s reggae-and-rap hybrid music was featured in the controversial film *Sud*, while the charismatically curly-haired **Jovanotti** has risen from TV-variety-show pop star to rapper. **Articolo 31,** though it's more pop/rock than rap, puts in a good showing—its name derives from the Italian law that bans pot smoking, in case you were wondering. Rome's contributions to Italian-language rap include local boy **Er Piotta,** whose "SuperCafone '99" ignited dance floors and *coatti* everywhere, the pseudo-gangster-rap **Flaminio Maphia,** and **Colle der Fomento,** whose "Il Cielo su Roma" explains all you need to know about why living in Rome is so damn cool.

THEATER & CINEMA

THEATER

The Roman theater scene is host to a number of quality productions, ranging from mainstream musicals to black box experimental theater, mostly in Italian. For theater listings, check with a tourist office or the major venues listed below. In summer, many plays spring up in open-air theaters, some of them free to the public. The city's two major festivals improve the pickings considerably with international productions: **Festival Roma-Europa** in summer and early fall; and **Festival d'Autunno** in fall. Check newspapers for listings. For information on plays and musicals in English, check tourist offices or the English section of *Roma C'è*. Useful websites include www.musical.it and www.comune.rome.it.

Teatro Argentina, Largo di Torre Argentina, 52 (☎06 68804601 or 06 6875445). Bus #64 from Termini. Considered to be the most important theater in Rome, Argentina hosts plays (in Italian), concerts, and ballets. Teatro Argentina is also the head of many drama/music festivals taking place throughout the year around Rome. Call for specific information. Box office open M-F 10am-2pm and 3-7pm, Sa 10am-2pm. AmEx, DC, MC, V.

Teatro Colosseo, V. Capo d'Africa, 5a (☎06 7004932 or 06 4441375). M:B-Colosseo. Walk away from the station with the Colosseum to your right for one block. This theater offers a selection of new alternative plays (Italian or translated into Italian), but also produces an English-speaking theater night (M in summer), featuring new works from American and British playwrights. Box office open Tu-Sa 8-10pm. Tickets L10-25,000. Student discount around L5000.

Teatro Ghione, V. delle Fornaci, 37 (☎/fax 06 6372294). See p. 176.

Teatro Nazionale, V. del Viminale, 51 (☎06 47825140, 06 485498, or 06 4870614). From P. della Repubblica, walk one block toward Termini. Offers mostly original Italian plays; produces some translations of international works. Box office open daily 10am-7pm. Tickets L35-50,000.

Teatro Sistina, V. Sistina, 129 (☎06 4826841 or 06 4200711). M:A-Barberini. One of the biggies in mainstream musical theater. Recent productions include *Can-Can, Rugantino, L'Anatra all'Arancia,* an exclusive engagement of *Sister Act* (in English), and The Who's *Tommy* (in Italian). Box office open daily 10am-1pm and 3:30-7pm. Tickets L35-200,000. AmEx, DC, MC, V.

Teatro Valle, V. del Teatro Valle, 23a (☎06 68803794). Near C. V. Emanuele II. A pretty little theater with an excellent repertoire. Box office open Tu-Sa 10am-7pm, Su 10am-1pm.

CINEMA

Italy, much to the horror of cineastes foreign and native, insists on dubbing all the film and video it imports. Unless you know Italian well and get a kick out of hearing Woody Allen speak it, this idiosyncracy poses a definite obstacle to your Roman cinematic enjoyment. Undubbed English-language films are hard to find, especially more recent releases. Luckily, a few valorous Cineclubs show foreign films, old goodies, and an assortment of favorites in the original language. Check newspapers or *Roma C'è* for listings. A v.o. or l.o. in any listing means **versione originale** or *lingua originale* (i.e., not dubbed, usually with Italian subtitles). All first-run theaters offer lower priced tickets for the first two screenings of the day from Monday to Friday (around 4:30 pm and 6:30pm), as well as all day Wednesday.

Though popular Italian film of late has tended towards the banal, it's definitely worth checking out as well, particularly Nanni Moretti's (p. 171) thoughtful and humorous work. The antics of Roberto Benigni are amusing even without understanding dialogue.

In summer, especially July, huge screens come up in *piazze* around the city for **outdoor film festivals.** These night shows can be a lot of fun, especially if you remember to bring insect repellent. One of the most popular is the **San Lorenzo sotto le Stelle** film festival at Villa Mercede, V. Tiburtina 113, with shows at 9 and 11pm (tickets L10-15,000). In addition, films are usually shown outdoors on the southern tip of Tiber Island.

Festa de l'Unite

Visit the **I Love Rome** website (www.alfanet.it/welcomeItaly/roma/default.html) for an excellent searchable database of films, theaters, and showtimes. While *Roma C'è* isn't as comprehensive, it does a fairly good job of indexing films, even indexing by director.

▓ **Il Pasquino,** V. del Piede, 19 (☎06 5833310 or 06 5803622). Off P. S. Maria in Trastevere. Rome's biggest English-language movie theater. Program changes daily, so call for the schedule or stop by and pick one up. L12,000. Theaters 2 and 3 are a film club: instead of the normal fee, pay L2000 for a two-month membership and L10,000 for the ticket.

Alcazar, V. Merry del Val, 14 (☎06 5880099). In Trastevere. M brings films in the original (with Italian subtitles). Tickets L13,000, matinee and W L8000.

Giulio Cesare, V. G. Cesare, 259 (☎06 39720975). M:A-Ottaviano. M films in the original. Tickets L12,000, matinee and W L8000.

Greenwich, V. Bodoni, 59 (☎06 5745825). In Testaccio, near bus lines #75, 673, and 719. Films frequently in the original with Italian subtitles. Tickets L13,000, matinee and W L8000.

Baths of Caracalla

Nuovo Sacher, Largo Ascianghi, 1 (☎06 5818116). M films in the original. L13,000, matinee and W L8000.

LIVE MUSIC & DANCE

CLASSICAL MUSIC & OPERA

The spectacular stage of the Baths of Caracalla (see p. 91) used to host summertime opera performances, but this lively tradition was halted once it was discovered that performers' barreling voices were bringing the ancient house down—literally. The live elephants that were brought on stage for productions of *Aïda* also did little to fortify the structure. There are still smaller classical music concerts that sporadically pop up in the crazy emperor's baths; or at least there will be until Renzo Piano's immense new auditorium, which has been in the works for several years now, is built.

Stardust

There are many opportunities to see solid musical performances. *Telecom Italia* hosts a classical music series at the Teatro dell'Opera (see p. 176). At 9am on concert days, unsold tickets are given out for free at the box office. Be prepared to get in line early; tickets go on a first come, first served basis. Local churches often host free choral concerts—check newspapers or tourist offices for details. Finally, and perhaps most interestingly, the *carabinieri* frequently give rousing concerts of various Italian composers in P. di San Ignazio and other outdoor forums free of charge. Other venues occasionally offer special discounts, so keep your eyes peeled.

PRINCIPAL VENUES

Accademia Nazionale di Santa Cecilia (main ☎ 06 3611064, info ☎ 06 6780742). This conservatory, named for the martyred patron saint of music (see p. 122 for the full story), was founded by Palestrina in the 16th century, and is home to Rome's official symphony orchestra. Orchestra and chamber concerts are held at the **Auditorio Pio,** V. di Conciliazione, 4 (☎ 06 68801044), near the Vatican, while the Academy's grand new concert hall is being built. The regular season runs Oct.-June, covering the classics, as well as occasional special presentations, such as piano-playing jazz god Keith Jarrett, Jimi Hendrix played by a string quartet, or Ennio Morricone, the composer of classic soundtracks like that of *The Good, the Bad, and the Ugly.* From late June-late July, the company moves outdoors to the *nymphaeum* in Villa Giulia; see **Summer Events,** below. Auditorio Pio box office open Th-Tu 10:20am-1:30pm and 3-6pm, and until showtime on concert days. Tickets L15-50,000. Auditorio Pio's acoustics are notoriously bad, so you might want to splurge on expensive seats to hear more.

Auditorium del Foro Italico, P. Lauro de Bosis, (☎ 06 36865625). Near P. Mancini. Home of Rome's RAI Orchestra, this auditorium hosts various classical music concerts. Season runs Oct.-June. Tickets L20-50,000.

Teatro Ghione, V. delle Fornaci, 37 (☎ 06 6372294). Near the Vatican. This red velvet theater hosts Euromusica's classical concerts and other musical guests throughout its season. Season runs Oct.-Apr. Box office open Tu-Su 10:30am-1pm and 4-8pm. Tickets from L15,000.

Teatro Olimpico, P. Gentile da Fabriano, 17 (☎ 06 3265991). This newer auditorium with good acoustics is home to many different classical music, theater, and dance events. Season runs Oct.-May. Box office open daily 11am-7pm.

Teatro dell'Opera di Roma, V. Firenze, 72 (main ☎ 06 481601, info ☎ 800 016665; www.the-mix.it). Summer performances take place in P. di Siena in Villa Borghese. The theater also runs seasonal concerts at Stadio di Olimpico and the Baths of Caracalla (primarily in the summer). Also be on the lookout for occasional performances during the year at the Teatro Valle, the Teatro Manzoni, and the Loggia della Villa Medici. Box office open Tu-Su 10:30am-5pm.

SUMMER EVENTS

The classical scene in Rome goes wild in summer. The smaller festivals that run from mid-May to August are just parts of the larger Roma Estate festival (for full information about the summer's events, consult www.romaestate.com). Also popular is the Opera-festival di Roma (☎ 06 5691493), held in the Teatro dell'Opera di SRoma. It all starts with the Festa Europea della Musica, a weekend of non-stop music at the end of June—most concerts are free. A hop, skip, and jump from Rome is the summer Spoleto Festival in Umbria. This world-renowned music and art fest takes place in June and July. Visit the festival's Rome office at V. Beccaria, 18, for more information. (☎ 06 3210288.) For tickets to summer events, try one of the following venues:

Villa Giulia/Santa Cecilia ticket office, P. della Villa Giulia, 9 (☎ 06 3611064 or 063611833, credit card reservations ☎ 06 68801044), in Villa Borghese, is the summer home of the Accademia Nazionale di Santa Cecilia. Open Tu-Sa 10am-2pm, Su 10am-1pm, and on performance days until showtime. You can also buy tickets at Villa Giulia's Etruscan Museum (see p. 151).

Theater of Marcellus, V. del Teatro di Marcello, 44, hosts evening concerts organized by the Associazione Il Tempietto (see below). Tickets L30,000.

MUSIC ASSOCIATIONS

The following associations organize and host concerts and recitals—contact them directly for a full schedule of events, or check newspapers for weekly listings.

Amici di Castel Sant'Angelo (☎06 8456192). Livens up Hadrian's Mausoleum with free concerts Sa nights at 9pm in a relaxed atmosphere. The casual concerts are aimed at those simply strolling by the Castel. Look for occasional concerts by the Accademia Filarmonica Romana and the Coro Polifonico Romano.

Associazione Il Tempietto, V. in Selci, 47 (☎06 4814800). Organizes frequent small concerts in churches and, in summer, at the **Theater of Marcellus.** Tickets L30,000, though some concerts held in church venues are free.

JAZZ

Rome is no New Orleans. It's no Chicago. It's not even Paris. Rome is Rome (*Roma C'è*, as newsstands will tell you). Even so, jazz swings on within the confines of the eternally hip city. Listings are in *Roma C'è* and *Time Out;* the latter does a slightly better job with jazz, though *Roma C'è* tends to translate most of their jazz listings into English. During the summer, Alexanderplatz (see below) organizes the popular **Jazz & Image** festival, in the **Villa Celimontana,** the ruin-filled park that stretches from the Colosseum to the Baths of Caracalla. For tickets, call **ORBIS** (☎06 5897807). From mid-June to mid-August, films about jazz show on a huge outdoor screen at 9pm. Entrance is usually around L15,000, though the price may be hiked up significantly (L40,000) for bigger names. In past years, the festival has hosted the Manhattan Transfer, Branford Marsalis, Herbie Hancock, Ray Brown, and Cedar Walton. The world-renowned **Umbria Jazz Festival** in July takes place in Perugia, only a few hours away by train. Past performers include Joao Gilberto, B. B. King, Joe Henderson, and Sonny Rollins (call 075 5733363 for information).

PRINCIPAL VENUES

The streets of Trastevere are the best romping grounds for those in search of a good jazz joint. Wander the winding streets, listening for sax riffs and vocalists doing a damn good job with mostly English lyrics, or try some of our favorites:

Alexanderplatz Jazz Club, V. Ostia, 9 (☎06 39742171). M:A-Ottaviano. Near Vatican City. From the station, head west on V. G. Cesare, take the 2nd right onto V. Leone IV and the first left onto V. Ostia. Night buses to P. Venezia and Termini leave from P. Clodio. Known by some as Europe's best jazz club, it's stuffy, smoky atmosphere conveys the mythical feeling of the '40s jazz joint, while sparkling walls and a funky bar suggest a modern side. Read messages left on the walls by the greats who have played here, from old pros like Art Farmer and Cedar Walton to young stars like Steve Coleman and Josh Redman. Cocktails L12,000. Guests must buy a *tessera* (L12,000), good for 2 months. Open Sept.-June daily 9pm-2am. Shows start at 10:30pm.

Big Mama, V. S. Francesco a Ripa, 18 (☎06 5812551). Off V. di Trastevere on the left as you face the river. Blues, blues, and more blues. A *tessera* (L20,000) is valid for a year and allows you into the club's many free concerts. Occasional L10,000 cover for big-name groups. Open Oct.-June daily 9pm-1:30am (sometimes closed Su and M; call ahead).

Stardust, V. dei Rienzi, 4 (☎06 58320875). Take a right off V. Lungaretta onto V. del Moro right before P. S. Maria in Trastevere; V. dei Renzi is the 2nd street on the left. This classy cocktail bar is a great place to chill and listen to live jazz. When's the next time you're going to get to do it while eating crepes? Open daily 7pm-4am; in winter M-F 1:30pm-3am, Sa-Su 11am-2am.

Selarum, V. dei Fienaroli, 12 (☎06 5819130). Off V. di Fratte di Trastevere. More jazz-while-you-eat, as well as South American and blues acts. Treat yourself to some dessert wines (L8-13,000). A gourmet dessert mecca; try the scrumptious *mandorlita* (chocolate, amaretto, and whipped cream; L15,000). Open May-Oct. daily 9pm-2am. Music usually starts around 10:30pm.

Berimbau, V. dei Fienaroli, 30b (☎06 5813249). Rome's premier location for Brazilian music. Live music is followed by a raging disco of salsa, merengue, and a variety of other Latin music. Cover L10-25,000, includes a drink. Open W-Su 10:30pm-3:30am.

ROCK & POP

Big-name shows (which usually play at the **Palazzo dello Sport** in EUR or at the **Foro Italico** north of Flaminio) will also invariably have massive poster campaigns. If you still feel inadequately in touch with what the cool kids are up to, ticket agencies and tourist offices have information on big upcoming shows. In summer, the city's pop and rock music scene explodes with outdoor concerts and festivals lasting late into the night.

Ticket agencies (see p. 298 for a list of them) can arrange reservations and provide more information about major rock concerts. Tickets and info for many concerts are also available at the RicordiMedia (see p. 166) shops scattered throughout the city.

The more popular festivals and performances include:

Roma Live, at the Stadio Olimpico. Concerts by the likes of Deep Purple, the Backstreet Boys, Ziggy Marley, Lou Reed, and Joan Baez, among others.

Testaccio Village, V. di Monte Testaccio, 16 (☎06 57287661). Live, mostly local music of all kinds from mid-June to mid-Sept. every night around 9pm.

Roma Incontra il Mondo (☎06 4180369 or 06 58201564), a festival of world music and "musica etnica," livens up the lake in Villa Ada at V. di Ponte Salario. Performers have included the late Nusrat Fateh Ali Khan, Ruben Gonzales, and Blonde Redhead. Late June-early Sept. 6pm-whenever.

Fiesta, Ippodrome di Capannelle, V. Appia, 1243 (☎06 71299855; www.fiesta.it), is an extremely popular festival running all summer, featuring all things Latin American. Performers have included Cesaria Evora, Jose Feliciano, and Burning Spear. Don't know how to salsa? Don't worry, you too will be assimilated. Attendance can swell to over 30,000 on weekends.

DANCE

The **Rome Opera Ballet,** affiliated with the **Teatro dell'Opera,** shares its ticket office, info line, and, sometimes, its stage. The ballet company stages joint performances with the opera company in the summer at P. di Siena in Villa Borghese. During the rest of the year, the company performs at the ex-Aquarium, in P. Fanti, south of Termini. (☎06 481601, toll-free info ☎800 016665.) Another tiny venue, a bit further out, is **Argilia Teatri,** at V. dell'Argilia, 18. It can help when you've got to have ethnic dancing, and you've got to have it now. (☎06 6381058.) In summer, there is also a festival of dance, art, and culture called **RomaEuropa,** with venues throughout the city. Call 06 4742319 or 06 4742286 for information or pick up a program at the **Museo degli Strumenti Musicali** in P. San Croce in Gerusalemme, one of the performance locations. The theaters listed above may also host dance performances.

SPECTATOR SPORTS

While other spectator sports may exist in Rome (and the key word is "may"), the only one that matters is **calcio** (soccer). Rome has two teams in Italy's Serie A, the most prestigious league in the world: **A.S. Roma** and **S.S. Lazio.** Traditionally, Lazio's fans come from the suburbs and countryside around Rome, while Roma fans are from the city itself, especially the Centro Storico, Trastevere, Testaccio, and the Jewish Ghetto. Lazio, which is literally owned by the man from Del Monte, has lately spent close to a hundred billion *lire* on a revolving cast of expensive players, while Roma relies on the genius of superstar Italian playmaker Francesco Totti, protagonist of the 2000 European national championship, and legendary Argentine striker Gabriel Batistuta. Games at the **Stadio Olimpico,** in the Foro Italico, are as close to the spectacles that used to happen in the Colosseum as you're going to find these days: *tifosi,* as the hardcore fans are called, show up hours before the games to drink, sing team songs, and taunt rivals. During the thrilling games, fans chant, stomp, and sing their teams on to victory, or at least an honorable defeat. Unfortunately, the cheering sometimes turns ugly, as evidenced by several incidences of Lazio fans displaying racist banners and booing minority players during the last season. For the most part, though, the celebrations are cheerful and melodious: flags are waved madly to the strains of the "Macarena," while Queen's "We Are the Champions" blends imperceptibly into the inspiring sound of fight songs being sung to the tune of the "Battle Hymn of the Republic" by tens of thousands of fans in unison. League matches are held almost every Sunday (sometimes Saturdays) from September to June, with European cup matches often played mid-week. The can't miss appointments of the season are the two Roma-Lazio *derby* matches, which often prove decisive in the race for the championship. While each team has close to 50,000 season ticket holders, they also sell single-game tickets, which typically start at L30,000. Tickets can be bought at the stadium box office before games (although the lines are long and tickets often run out), and also at the team's stores: **A.S. Roma Store,** P. Colonna, 360 (☎ 06 6786514), just off V. del Corso; and **Lazio Point,** V. Farini, 24 (☎ 06 4826688).

The ultra-trendy, world class **Concorso Ippico Internazionale** (International Horse Show) is held at P. di Siena in the Villa Borghese in May. For information, check *Roma C'è* or call CSIO. (☎ 06 3279939.) The beginning of May also sees the holding of the **Italian Open Tennis Championship,** a warm-up event for the French Open which draws many of the world's top players. For more information, call the Italian Tennis Federation. (☎ 06 3233807.) Tickets for many sporting events can be bought at the **Orbis Agency,** P. dell'Esquilino, 37. (☎ 06 4827403.)

Food & Wine

In ancient Rome, dinners were lavish, festive affairs lasting as long as ten hours, with entertainment considered as vital as the food. Roman writers such as Petronius and Juvenal reported the erotica, exotica, and excess found upon the Imperial dinner table—peacocks, flamingos, and herons were served with their full plumage meticulously replaced after cooking. Acrobats and fire-eaters distracted guests between courses of dormice and camels' feet. Food orgies went on *ad nauseam*, literally—after gorging themselves, guests would retreat to a special room called the *vomitorium*, throw it all up, and return to the party to eat still more.

These days, however, Roman food rituals are considerably tamer. Breakfast, if you're lucky enough to get it, is usually just a gulp of cappuccino and a pastry. Lunch is traditionally the day's main meal, though some Romans now eat lunch on the go during the week, *all'americana*. Keep in mind that restaurants tend to close from 3pm to 7:30pm.

THE ITALIAN MEAL

A full meal begins with **antipasti,** or appetizers. It is acceptable to order *antipasti* alone for lunch, but it is considered gauche at dinner.

Next, the **primo piatto** (first course, a.k.a. *primi*) arrives: usually some sort of pasta, risotto, or soup. Especially on Thursdays, many restaurants serve up homemade *gnocchi*, dense dumplings of potato or semolina flour, frequently in a gorgonzola or four-cheese sauce. While *lasagna al forno* (baked lasagna) may be tempting, know that it's often prepared well in advance and will probably not be particularly fresh.

The **secondo piatto** (second course, a.k.a. *secondi*) usually consists of meat or fish. Innards and other odd parts of the cow or pig are often a particularly important part of Roman cuisine. Seafood is common: *calamari* is very good here, especially when grilled.

USE YOUR NOODLE

Selecting the correct pasta for the dish and cooking it right (*al dente*—literally "to the teeth" and slightly chewy) is as close to Italian hearts as the Madonna herself. *Lasagne* come in at least two forms: flat or *ricce* (one edge crimped). The familiar *spaghetti* has larger, hollow cousins, such as *bucatini* and *maccheroni*, as well as smaller, more delicate relatives like *capellini*. Flat pastas include the familiar *linguine* and *fettuccine*, with *taglierini* and *tagliatelle* filling in the size gaps. Short, roughly two-inch pasta tubes include *ziti*, *penne* (cut diagonally and occasionally *rigate*, or ribbed), *sedani* (curved), *rigatoni* (bigger), and *cannelloni* (biggest and usually stuffed). More excitingly shaped pastas include *fusilli* (corkscrews), *farfalle* (butterflies or bow-ties), and *ruote* (wheels). Don't be alarmed if you see pastry displays with the label *pasta;* the Italian word refers to anything made of dough and vaguely edible.

There are numerous **contorni** or side dishes, mostly vegetable specialties, which are generally served with the main course. Even the most single-minded carnivores will enjoy dishes like *fagiolini* (early-picked, tender string beans) or *pomodori* (fresh tomatoes in olive oil with salt and fresh basil). Roman mixed salads *(insalata mista)* are usually full of veggies, and, interestingly enough, anise.

Dolce, desserts, are typically accompanied by the essential espresso. Freshly made *tiramisù* (sponge cake soaked in espresso and rum, layered with sweet mascarpone cheese, and dusted with cocoa powder) can be wonderful. *Profiteroles*, delicate rolled pastries with chocolate and cream filling, are also popular. *Panna cotta* is a delicious cream custard, covered in chocolate sauce or *frutti di bosco* (blackberries and raspberries). And if *gelato* just isn't rich enough for you, try *tartufo*, truffly ice cream usually served in the *bianco* (vanilla) and *nero* (chocolate) versions, sometimes served in *espresso*.

For your after-dinner drink **(digestivo),** try *grappa*, a potent, doubly distilled clear liqueur made from old grape pressings. Another option is *sambuca con le mosche* (anise liquor "with flies"—that is, flaming with coffee beans floating on top).

The billing at Roman restaurants can be a bit confusing. Bottled water is usually automatically served and charged to your bill: ask for *frizzante* (fizzy) or *naturale* (still), but don't even think of asking for tap water—it's just not done. Many restaurants add a cover or bread charge of L1500 per person. Service charges *(servizio)*, if not included in food prices, may be added to the bill, to the tune of 10-15%. Be sure to check your bill, as restaurateurs have been known to make "errors" when dealing with tourists.

RESTAURANT TYPES

Ristorantes are the most elegant eateries, with dolled-up waiters, linen tablecloths, and expensive (though not necessarily better) cuisine. A **trattoria** has a more casual atmosphere and lower prices. If you find an original **osteria** or **hostaria,** you'll see old locals sitting around a table, chewing the fat, playing cards, and downing bottles of wine. Another cheap option is the **tavola calda** or **rosticceria,** where you buy platefuls of pastas, cooked vegetables, and well-seasoned meats to eat on the spot or wrap up for a picnic elsewhere.

There are two kinds of **pizzerias.** At a *pizzeria forno a legno,* you sit down to your own plate-sized pizza. A well-prepared Roman-style crust is light, crispy, and blackened a little around the edges, unlike the famous Neapolitan pizzas, which are thicker and made from tastier dough. In a pizzeria *rustica* or *a taglio,* order a slice or particular weight of any of the pizzas displayed at the counter.

MENU READER

ANTIPASTI

antipasto rusto	assortment of cold appetizers
bruschetta	crisp baked slices of bread with tomatoes or other toppings
prosciutto e melone	cured ham and honeydew melon

PRIMI

pasta aglio e olio	garlic and olive oil
pasta all'amatriciana	in a tangy tomato sauce with onions and bacon
pasta all'arabbiata	in a spicy tomato sauce
pasta alla bolognese	in a meat sauce
pasta alla boscaiola	in a sauce of cream, peas, and bacon
pasta cacio e pepe	with pepper and pecorino cheese
pasta ai funghi porcini	with a sauce of large wood mushrooms
pasta al pomodoro	in tomato sauce
pasta alla carbonara	in a creamy sauce with egg, cured bacon, and cheese
pasta alle cozze	in a tomato sauce with mussels
pasta alla pizzaiola	tomato based sauce with olive oil and red peppers
pasta alla pescatore	with several kinds of clams and mussels, and sometimes with squid
pasta alla puttanesca	in a tomato sauce with olives and capers
pasta al tartufo	with a truffle sauce
pasta alle vongole	in a clam sauce; *bianco* for white, *rosso* for red
gnocchi	dumpling-like pasta made from potatoes
polenta	deep fried cornmeal
risotto	rice dish (comes with nearly as many sauces as pasta)

PIZZA

ai carciofi	with artichokes
ai fiori di zucca	with zucchini blossoms
ai funghi	with mushrooms
alla capriciosa	with ham, egg, artichoke, and olives
con alici	with anchovies
con bresaola	with cured beef
con melanzana	with eggplant
con prosciutto	with ham
con prosciutto crudo	with cured ham (also called simply *crudo*)
con rucola (rughetta)	with arugala (rocket for the Brits)
margherita	plain ol' tomato, mozzarella, and basil
napoletana	with anchovies, tomato, and cheese
peperoncini	chillies
polpette	meatballs
quattro formaggi	with four cheeses
quattro stagioni	four seasons; a different topping for each quarter of the pizza, usually mushrooms, *crudo*, artichoke, and tomato

SECONDI

animelle alla griglia	grilled sweetbreads
calamari alla grigliata	grilled squid
carciofi alla giudia	fried artichokes
coda alla vaccinara	stewed oxtail with herbs and tomatoes
filetto di baccalà	fried cod
fiori di zucca	zucchini flowers; filled with cheese, battered, and lightly fried
involtini al sugo	veal cutlets filled with ham, celery, and cheese, topped with tomato sauce
melanzane parmigiana	eggplant parmesan
osso buco	braised veal shank
pasta e ceci	pasta with chick peas
saltimbocca	slices of veal and ham cooked together and topped with cheese
scamorza grigliata	a type of grilled cheese
supplì	fried rice ball filled with tomato, meat, and cheese
trippa	tripe; chopped, sautéed cow intestines, usually in a tomato sauce

CONTORNI

broccoletti	broccoli florets
cicoria	chicory
fagioli	beans (usually white)
fagiolini	green beans
funghi	mushrooms
insalata caprese	tomatoes with mozzarella cheese and basil, drizzled with olive oil
insalata mista	mixed green salad
melanzana	eggplant
piselli	peas
spinaci	spinach

PREPARATION

cruda/o	raw
al sangue	rare
non troppo cotta/o	medium-rare
ben cotta	well-done
al dente	firm to the bite
fresca/o	fresh
frittura	fried
griglia	grilled
marinata/o	marinated
stracotta	overcooked
poco cotta	undercooked
raffermo	stale
ripieno	stuffed
condita/o	seasoned
scottata	scorched
secca	dry
aromatica/o, piccante	spicy
stracetti	strips (of beef, usually)
surgelato	frozen
al vino	in wine sauce
resentin	coffee in a grappa-rinsed mug

RESTAURANTS BY LOCATION

ANCIENT CITY

The area around the Forum and the Colosseum is home to some of Italy's finest tourist-traps, replete with L25,000 *menù turistici*. The snack carts lining the streets will serve you no better; expect to pay L4000 for water and L7000 for a questionably appetizing sandwich. If you forgot to pack a lunch and the stroll down V. dei Fori Imperiali seems too long in the blazing heat, there are a few places that offer tasty meals at fair prices.

see map p. 77

Taverna dei Quaranta, V. Claudia, 24 (☎06 7000550), off P. del Colosseo. Shaded by the trees of the Celian Park, outdoor dining at this corner *taverna* is a must. Not at all touristy. The menu changes daily, and in summer often features delights such as *fiori di zucca* (L8500) and *ravioli all'Amalfitana* (L11,000). 0.5L of house wine L5000. Cover L3000. Open daily noon-3:30pm and 7:45pm-midnight. AmEx, DC, MC, V.

I Buoni Amici, V. Aleardo Aleardi, 4 (☎06 70491993). From the Colosseum, take V.Labicana to V. Merulana. Turn right, then left on V. A. Aleardi. It's a long walk, but the cheap and excellent food is worth it. Choices include the *linguine all'astice* (linguini with crayfish sauce; L10,000) *risotto con i funghi* (L8000), and *penne alla vodka* (L8000). Cover L2500. Open M-Sa noon-3pm and 7-11:30pm. AmEx, DC, MC, V.

Hostaria da Nerone, V. delle Terme di Tito, 96 (☎06 4745207). Take the stairs to the right (with your back to the Colosseum) of the Colosseo(B) Metro stop, and walk up to V. delle Terme di Tito. Outdoor dining with views of the Colosseum and Baths of Titus through the trees. Traditional specialties like *tegamino di cervello burro e funghi* (brains with butter and mushrooms; L15,000). Pasta L10-12,000. Also try **Cafe dello Studente,** next door, for lunch. Cover L2500. 10% service. Open M-Sa noon-3pm and 7-11pm. MC, V.

CENTRO STORICO

PIAZZA NAVONA

There are plenty of delicious, inexpensive *trattorie* and pizzerias near P. Navona, but it often takes a short stroll to reach them. A walk down V. del Governo Vecchio reveals some of the best restaurants in the city, often charging less than their more convenient neighbors in the *piazza*. If you're really lucky, you'll happen upon one of the smaller *enoteche* and *trattorie*, some of which advertise themselves with no more than a beaded curtain guarding an open doorway—Romans who know will tell you that these places offer a constantly changing menu at unbeatable prices. No matter where you eat, you can expect to be subjected to numerous performances by street performers.

see map p. 314–315

■ **Pizzeria Pentola,** V. Metastasio, 21 (☎06 68802607). Off P. di Campo Marzio. A short walk north from the Pantheon is long enough to escape the tourist traps that define dining in the area. Ignore the regular menu: the delicious *pizze* (L8-16,000) are where it's at. Try the *Pizza dello chef* (spinach and parmesan; L13,000) or the daily specials. Open daily noon-11pm. MC, V.

■ **Pizzeria Baffetto,** V. del Governo Vecchio, 114 (☎06 6861617). At V. Sora. Once a meeting place for 60s radicals, Baffetto now overflows with Romans of the hungry persuasion. It's gotten famous, so you might have to wait a while for a table outdoors (as well as for your delicious *pizza* once you've sat down). Always crowded. *Pizze* L8-14,000. Cover L1000. Open M-F noon-3pm and 7:30pm-1am, Sa-Su noon-3pm and 7:30pm-2am.

Pizzeria Corallo, V. del Corallo 10-11 (☎06 68307703). Off V. del Governo Vecchio near P. del Fico. For those who refuse to eat anywhere that doesn't have outdoor tables with red-checkered tablecloths and a metal palm tree, this local favorite might be the only option. Lasso a pizza for L8-15,000. Excellent *primi* options like *Tagliolini ai fiori di zucca* (with zucchini blossoms; 13,000). Open Tu-Su 7pm-1am. Reservations accepted. AmEx, MC, V.

Piedra del Sol, V. Rosini, 6 (☎06 6873641). Off V. di Campo Marzio across from P. del Parlamente. Tucked away in a tiny cul de sac, del Sol offers a distinctly Italian take on Mexican cooking. Decor from Aztec to Zapata. Try their *Chimichangas del Sol* (L12,000) and get a liter of margaritas for L35,000. Chips and salsa L3000 per person. *Cerveza* L6000 and up. Open Sept.-July daily 12:30-3pm and 7:30pm-2am. AmEx, MC, V.

Trattoria Gino e Pietro, V. del Governo Vecchio, 106 (☎06 6861576). At V. Savelli. Don't come here if you want to eat bad Roman food; they serve only the good stuff here, like *Gnocchi verdi al Gorgonzola* (L12,000) and *Saltimbocca alla Romana* (veal with *prosciutto* and sage; L16,000). Reservations accepted. Open F-W 12:30-3pm and 6:30-11pm. Closed late July to mid-Aug.

CAMPO DEI FIORI

If you're not in a rush, take the time to navigate the labyrinth of crooked streets and alleyways that surround Campo dei Fiori. While you might get yourself horribly lost, you will certainly find several exceptional *ristoranti* that can provide sustenance until the search party arrives. If your friends still can't find you after dinner, screw 'em: just go pubbing in the Campo and make some new ones (see p. 204).

■ **Trattoria da Sergio,** V. delle Grotte, 27 (☎06 6546669). Take V. dei Giubbonari and take your 1st right. Just far enough away from the Campo to keep away the tourists, Sergio offers honest-to-God Roman ambience and hearty portions of great food. Try the *Spaghetti all'Amatriciana* (with spicy tomato sauce; L9000) and the *Straccetti* (shredded beef with tomatoes; L13,000) Open M-Sa 12:30-3pm and 7pm-12:30am.

the BIG $plurge

Osteria dell'Ingegno, P. di Pietra (☎06 6780662). Between the Trevi Fountain and the Pantheon. Dell'Ingegno serves up a refreshingly modern take on timeless Italian cuisine in a comfortable, upscale setting. They do the classics of the Boot right, and are also quite successful in their attempts at more pan-Mediterranean fare. Try the superb *risotto matecato alle punte di asparagi* (risotto with asparagus tips, saffron, and parmesan; L20,000); you also won't regret the daring *crema fredda di melanzane e cerfoglio allo yogurt* (cold eggplant soup with mint and yogurt; L16,000). *Secondi* (L20-30,000) include a delicious *tartara di salmone e spigola* (tartar of fresh salmon and sea bass; L24,000). Meal-size salads L16-20,000. Open M-Sa noon-3pm and 7:30pm-midnight. Service not included. AmEx, DC, MC, V.

Ristorante Quattro Fiumi, P. Navona 37-38 (☎06 68801435), in the northwestern corner of the *piazza*. Delicious food and classy outdoor atmosphere in the heart of the *piazza*. Enjoy traditional cuisine like *Pollo alla Romana* (roast chicken with red peppers; L24,000). *Primi* L17-18,000. Service 12%. Open F-W noon-3:30pm and 7pm-midnight. AmEx, MC, V.

Trattoria Da Luigi, P. S. Cesarini 24 (☎06 6865946) Near Chiesa Nuova, four blocks down C. V. Emanuele II from Campo dei Fiori. Enjoy inventive cuisine such as *tagliolini* with shrimp, asparagus, and tomato (L13,000), as well as simple dishes like *Vitello con funghi* (veal with mushrooms; L15,000). Great *antipasti* buffet. Bread L2000. Open Tu-Su 7pm-midnight.

La Pollarola, P. Pollarola, 24-25 (☎06 6880 1654). Off V. del Biscione on the way into Campo dei Fiori. As the Romans say, *"si mangia bene e si spende giusto"* ("one eats well and pays a fair price"). Enjoy typical Roman dishes like *Spaghetti alla Carbonara* (with egg and *pancetta* ham; L10,000). Open M-Sa noon-3:30pm and 7:30pm-midnight. No service charge. AmEx, MC, V.

Hostaria Grappolo d'Oro, P. della Cancelleria, 80-81 (☎06 6864118). Between C. V. Emanuele II and the Campo. This increasingly upscale *hostaria* is running out of space in their front window to plaster all the awards they've won over the years. The small menu, which changes daily, offers homestyle dishes like *Fregnacce al Casaro* (home-made pasta with ricotta and tomato; L14,000) and innovative creations such as *Controfiletto di manzo* (steak with herbs and goat-cheese; L20,000). Top it all off with a creative dessert like *Arancia caramellata* (caramel orange; L7000). Cover L2000. Open M-Sa noon-3:30pm and 7-11pm. AmEx, DC, MC, V.

L'Insalata Ricca, Largo di Chiavari, 85 (☎06 68803656). Off C. Vittorio Emanuele II near P. S. Andrea della Valle. You like salads, damn it, so come here. What kind of salad would you like? They have *all of them* (L10-16,000). If you don't like this location, there are six others around town: P. Pasquino, 72; V. del Gazometro, 62; P. Albania, 3; V. Polesine, 16; P. Risorgimento, 5; and V. F. Grinaldi, 52. Open daily 12:30-3:15pm and 6:45-11:15pm. MC, V.

Giardino del Melograno, V. dei Chiodaroli, 16-18 (☎06 68803423). Off V. dei Chiavari near Campo dei Fiori. A highly renowned Chinese restaurant. The vast menu includes a fine dumpling appetizer (L5000). Tourist *menù* (appetizer, entree, and drink) L13,000. Open Th-Tu noon-3pm and 7-11:30pm. AmEx, MC, V.

Trattoria Arnaldo ai Satiri, V. di Grotta Pinta, 8 (☎06 6861915). Take Largo dei Chiavari off C. Vittorio Emanuele II and turn right on V. di Grotta Pinta. Unusual dishes include spicy *Fusili con melanzane* (pasta with eggplant; L12,000) and the house specialty, *Rigatoni alla crema di cavoli* (pasta with cream of cabbage sauce; L11,000). Glowing with red lightbulbs and candles, the interior seems like a cross between a bordello and a darkroom. Outdoor dining in summer. Open W-M 12:30-3pm and 7:30pm-1am. AmEx, MC, V.

Trattoria La Moretta, V. Monserrato, 158 (☎06 6861900). From Campo dei Fiori, take V. dei Pellegrino to the *piazza* where it turns into V. dei Banchi Vecchi. On a small *piazza* with a lovely view of the river, La Moretta serves pasta and pizza to lost tourists and hungry locals. *Primi* include *Penne alle melanzane* (with eggplant; L10,000) and *Spaghetti alle vongole* (with clams; L13,000). Open M-Sa noon-3:30pm and 7pm-midnight.

Ristorante Bacco, V. dei Pettinari, 94-95 (☎06 68805349). Near Ponte Sisto. Take V. dei Giubbonari from the Campo and turn right on V. delle Monte (V. dei Pettinari). Hail Bacchus, God of Wine, grant us a pleasant yet affordable *ristorante* within walking distance of Campo dei Fiori. One in which *Risotto alla pescatora* (with seafood) costs L12,000 and in which there is fresh fish daily (from L18,000). Open daily 10am-midnight. AmEx, MC, V.

JEWISH GHETTO

On the other side of V. Arenula from Campo dei Fiori, the former Jewish Ghetto has patiently endured centuries of modernization, anti-Semitism, and tourism to remain a proud community. In terms of restaurants, there is plenty to be proud of. Quiet, cozy *trattorie* line the streets of this neighborhood, each serving traditional Roman-Jewish dishes, like *carciofi alla giudia* (fried artichokes) and *fiori di zucca* (zucchini blossoms filled with cheese and anchovies, battered, and lightly fried).

Vino!

Ristorante da Giggetto, V. del Portico d'Ottavio, 21-22 (☎06 6861105). Rightfully famous but increasingly pricey, Giggetto serves up some of the finest Roman cooking known to man. Their *Carciofi alla Giudia* (L10,000) are legendary, but be daring and go for the fried brains with mushrooms and zucchini (L20,000). If your food isn't spicy, pepper it with peppers picked from the potted pepper plants (free). Cover L3000. Open Tu-Su 12:30-3pm and 7:30-11pm. AmEx, MC, V.

Al 16, V. del Portico d'Ottavio, 16 (☎06 6874722). Around the corner from the Teatro di Marcello. A neighborhood favorite run by neighborhood guys, Al 16 offers traditional dishes alongside delicious house specialties like *Pennette al 16* (with eggplant, sausage, and tomato; L13,000), all at reasonable prices. Be fearless and try the *Coda alla Vaccinara* (oxtail stew; L16,000). Cover L2500. Open W-M 12:30-3pm and 7:30-11pm. AmEx, MC, V.

PIAZZA DI SPAGNA

see map p. 322

Though the Spanish Steps area may seem very different from the less affluent environs of Termini, there is one big similarity—lots and lots of bad, bad food. The irony of it all is that while a crappy restaurant at Termini might set you back 15,000 *lire*, the same awful food here will be twice as much. The best food in the area tends to be toward the Ara Pacis, across the V. del Corso, and away from the crush and press of tourists.

Formaggio!

▨ **Pizza Re,** V. di Ripetta, 14 (☎06 3211468). A block from P. del Popolo on the left. Even though it's a chain, Pizza Re serves some of the best Neopolitan pizza (L12-18,000) in town. Especially tasty is the (go figure) *Pizza Re* (L17,500), with mozzarella di bufala and fresh cherry tomatoes. Service is fast and courteous, and the A/C feels sooooo good. Save around L3000 if you order in person and take it out. Open M-Sa 12:45-3:30pm and 7:30pm-12:30am, Su 7:30pm-12:30am. Closed for 2 weeks in mid-Aug. AmEx, DC, MC, V.

Trattoria da Settimio all'Arancio, V. dell'Arancio, 50-52 (☎06 6876119). Take V. dei Condotti from P. di Spagna; take the 1st right after V. del Corso, then the 1st left. Arrive early to avoid the throngs of natives who come for the great service and tasty seafood. Excellent grilled *calamari* L18,000. Fresh fish Tu and F. Cover L2000. Open M-Sa 12:30-3pm and 7:30-11:30pm. Reservations accepted. AmEx, DC, MC, V.

Gelato!

the BIG $plurge

'Gusto, P. Augusto Imperatore, 9 (☎06 3226273). Facing the Mausoleum of Augustus. Already a trendy locale for Roman diners, 'Gusto offers "contemporary Italian/fusion" cuisine. Both a pizzeria and a restaurant, the non-pizza side of the establishment experiments with wok dishes and couscous, in addition to more traditional fare. The pizzeria is much more simple (tasty *pizze* L12-16,000). Meals average L25,000 at the pizzeria and L50,000 at the restaurant. Brunch served Su. Open daily noon-2pm and 8:30pm-midnight. AmEx, V, MC.

Ristorante Alla Rampa, P. Mignanelli, 18 (☎06 6782621). Facing the bottom of the Steps, head right and make your first left. Eat among those who have just finished their Armani shopping in this super-elegant eatery near the über-fashionable shopping district. At lunch, you can make a meal out of a large plate from their excellent *antipasti* buffet (L16,000), one of Rome's most imaginative and expensive. *Primi* L10-18,000; *secondi* from L18,000. Cover L2000. Open Tu-Su 11am-3pm and 7pm-midnight. AmEx, DC, MC, V.

Centro Macrobiotico Italiano-Naturist Club, V. della Vite, 14, 4th Fl. (☎06 6792509). Just off V. del Corso. The Naturist Club offers up extremely fresh, well-seasoned macrobiotic fare at low prices in its breezy attic restaurant. Probably the only restaurant in Rome where they offer you ground sesame seeds with your salad. Buffet only in the afternoon, but evening brings a full restaurant, where you can eat tasty vegetarian entrees and fresh fish to the sound of the Sugar Plum Fairy Waltz. Health food store downstairs. *Primi* L10-12,000; *secondi* L12-18,000. Open M-F noon-3:30pm and 7:30-11pm. MC, V.

Pizzeria al Leoncino, V. del Leoncino, 28 (☎06 6876306). Take V. Condotti from P. di Spagna, then the 1st right after V. del Corso. A solid pizzeria with reasonable prices. *Pizze* L9-15000, *bruschette* L3000. Sweet, sweet Nastro Azzuro on tap. Open M-Tu and Th-F 1-3pm and 7pm-midnight, Sa-Su 7pm-midnight. Closed Aug.

Il Brillo Parlante, V. Fontanella, 12 (☎06 3243334). Near P. del Popolo. The wood-burning pizza oven, fresh ingredients, and excellent wine attract many lunching Italians. Sophisticated food and shady outdoor tables available—as long as you don't mind the occasional *motorino* eruption on this narrow side-street. *Pizze* L10-15,000. Restaurant open Tu-Su noon-3pm and 7pm-1am; *enoteca* (wine bar) open Tu-Su 11am-2am. MC, V.

Birreria Peroni, V. S. Marcello, 19 (☎06 679 5310). Near P di Trevi. You never thought you'd find an entire establishment dedicated to Peroni? Think again. Though the food is definitely nothing to write home about, it is quite inexpensive (*bruschetta* L2500; *wurstel* L8-11,000), the beer is abundant and cheap in all of its forms—from small cups (L3500) to liter glasses (L12,000). Best of all, you can drop by later in the evening and just munch on something light over some beers—the very relaxed staff would hardly notice. Cover L2000. Open M-W 12:30-11:30pm, T and F 12:30pm-midnight, Sa 7pm-midnight.

Sogo Asahi, V. di Propaganda, 22 (☎06 6786093). Japanese locals and tourists alike come to eat excellent sushi, noodles, and more in this stylish little Japanese restaurant. The miso soup is particularly good, as are the *iniri* (sweet tofu), *unaga* (eel), and *sake* (salmon) sushi. *Nigiri* sushi L4-19,000, 13-piece plate L33,000, 6-piece *maki* plates L12-15,000. Entrees L15-25,000. Open M-Sa noon-2:30pm and 7-10:30pm. AmEx, MC, V.

Margutta Vegetariano RistorArte, V. Margutta 118 (☎06 32650577). Off V. del Babuino, near P. del Popolo. All vegetarian, all the time. While the food is not always fantastic, it is green, and the service is excellent. By no means formal or expensive, but you might feel silly walking in shorts and a t-shirt. Lunch buffet L20,000; all-you-can-eat brunch Su L30,000. Open M-Sa 1-3:30pm and 7:40-11:40pm, Su 11am-3pm. Closed Aug. AmEx, MC, V.

McDonald's, P. di Spagna, 46-47 (☎06 69922400). You swore you'd never come here in Italy. But you know you're curious. You've heard about the fountains, the statues, the powerfully refreshing A/C, and those hot, crispy fries that had Gorbachev saying *perestroika*. Why resist? Micky D's even offers free maps that will get you lost in no time. Over 30 other locations scattered about the city. Value meals vary from location to location; usually L7800-10,000.

Al Piccolo Arancio, V. Scanderbeg, 112 (☎06 6786139). Facing the Trevi Fountain, make a right on V. del Lavatore; V. Scanderbeg is on the right. Close to but surprisingly removed from the thick crowds of the Trevi Fountain. *Ravioli all'arancia* (ravioli of ricotta and oranges; L10,000). Cover L2000. Open Tu-Su noon-3pm and 7-11pm. Closed Aug. AmEx, DC, MC, V.

BORGO & PRATI (NEAR VATICAN CITY)

The streets near the Vatican are paved with bars and *pizzerie* that serve mediocre sandwiches at hiked-up prices. For far better and much cheaper food, head to the residential district a few blocks north and east of the Vatican Museums, home to specialty shops with fresh bread and pastries and small family-run *osterie*. For picnic supplies, try the immense indoor market on V. Cola di Rienzo.

see map p. 320

🖾 **Franchi,** V. Cola di Rienzo, 200-204 (☎06 6874651). Franchi ("Frankie") has been serving the happy citizens of Prati superb *tavola calda*, prepared sandwiches, and other luxurious picnic supplies for nearly 50 years, and not an unsatisfied customer yet. Delicacies include *supplì* (fried balls of veggies, mozzarella, and rice or potato, L1800 each), marinated munchies (anchovies, peppers, olives, and salmon, all sold by the kilo), and pastas like vegetarian lasagna and *cannellini* stuffed with ricotta and beef (L8800 per generous portion). More expensive than buying bread and cheese for a midday snack, but certainly cheaper and better than most Vatican area restaurants and snack bars. Open M-Sa 8:15am-9pm.

🖾 **Pizza Re,** V. Oslavia, 39 (☎06 3721173). Called by many the best pizza in Rome, this chain serves Neopolitan (thick crust) pizzas with every topping imaginable in cheerful yellow surroundings. Try it with *alicis* (marinated uncooked anchovies, L14,000). Wonderful desserts, from mousse to tiramisu. Lunch specials L11-13,000. Dinner L7-18,000. Pizzas are L3-5500 less if you take them out. Long lines form outside at dinnertime, so get there early. Open M-Sa noon-3:30pm, daily 7:30-11pm. AmEx, MC, V.

Ristorante Max, P. dell'Unita, 26-27 (☎06 3223113). East of P. del Risorgimento at V. dei Gracchi and V. C. Mario. The pink neon MAX lights up the street, beckoning you to come and enjoy a bite. Advertises *"Cucina classica"* and a small menu of scrumptious pizzas and pastas. *Fiori di zucca* (deep fried zucchini flowers) are particularly tasty here, as are the daily specials. Big ol' pizzas L8-15,000. Delicious *bruschetta con tapenade* (olive spread) L2500. Open W-M noon-3pm and 7-11pm. AmEx, DC, MC, V.

Il Barcone di Vacanze Romane (☎06 3240128), on the Lungotevere Mellini at Ponte Cavour. Make your way down the worn stone steps of the Tiber bank to this floating blue *ristorante*. You'll be treated to a creative reinterpretation of Roman dishes, including curried *risotto* (L15,000), *farfalle* with shrimp and garlic (L15,000), and *gnocchi al pomodoro* (L13,000). No tourists here, only relaxed Italians and some delicious pastas. Service is decidedly leisurely and the Tiber's mosquitoes are ravenous; bring insect repellent and a good book. *Let's Go* does not recommend the pizza. *Primi* around L15,000; *secondi* L13-20,000. Open Tu-Su noon-4pm and 7-11pm.

TRASTEVERE

You can't say you've been to Rome without having savored a pizza and swilled some tasty Nastro Azzuro in one of the rowdy outdoor pizzerias in Trastevere. Trastevere is home to raucous pubs, hopping pizza joints, and a loud bohemian population. By day, the cobblestone streets rumble only with the sounds of children and Vespas, but when night falls, P. di Santa Maria di Trastevere is packed with expatriate hippies and their dogs, howling along with out-of-tune guitars.

see map p. 314–315

🖾 **Pizzeria San Calisto,** P. S. Calisto, 9a (☎06 5818256). Right off P. S. Maria in Trastevere. Massive *pizze* (L9-15,000) roam free at this busy neighborhood pizzeria. The *bruschetta* (L3-4000) alone is worth a postcard home. Management shoos the rose-sellers away for a meal taken in peace. Open Tu-Su 7pm-midnight. MC, V.

the BIG $plurge

Da Cesare, V. Crescenzio, 13 (☎06 6861912). **Near the Vatican.** This upscale classic Tuscan restaurant features a wonderful Tuscan "tasting menu" (L50,000, all inclusive), including choices such as seafood risotto, tagliatelle with spicy greens, garlic, and olive oil, thick fish soup, all manner of fresh seafood, and a famous white *tartufo* for dessert. A la carte options are a bit more expensive and will probably run to about L75,000 per person. Good wine cellar. Open Tu-Sa noon-3pm and 7-11pm, Su noon-3pm. AmEx, DC, MC, V.

Augusto, P. de' Rienzi, 15 (☎06 5803798). North of P. S. Maria in Trastevere. Enjoy the daily pasta specials at lunch (around L8000), and the *pollo arrosto con patate* (L10,500). The homemade desserts are out of this world. Dinner is chaotic and crowded; lunch tends to feature laid-back discussions between waiters and their clientele. Either way, you have to be pushy to get service. Open M-F 12:30-3pm and 8-11pm, S 12:30-3pm. Closed Aug.

Ristorante al Fontanone, P. Trilussa, 46 (☎06 5817312). North of P. S. Maria in Trastevere. Small restaurant serving up traditional Roman cuisine, including *rigatoni con pajata* (L13,000). The menu board outside tells you what's fresh even before you step inside. The *carciofi alla giudia* (L13,000) are stupendous, as is anything with fresh porcini mushrooms. Open W-Su noon-2pm and 7-11pm. Closed mid-Aug.-early Sept. MC, V.

Pizzeria Ivo, V. di S. Francesco a Ripa, 158 (☎06 5817082). Take a right on V. delle Fratte di Trastevere off V. Trastevere and another right on V. S. Francesco a Ripa. A long-standing favorite in Trastevere, Ivo rests on its laurels somewhat, but still serves up a good pizza. Long waits, high prices (*pizze* L8-16,000). *Gigante* pizza only slightly larger than standard pizzas elsewhere. Open W-M 5pm-2am. Closed Aug. MC, V.

Il Tulipano Nero, V. Roma Libera, 15 (☎06 5818309). Take V. de Trastevere; turn right on V. E. Morosini. Some of the more innovative pizzas in Rome. Almost removed from the nighttime chaos of P. S. Maria in Trastevere, this pizzeria is smack in the middle of the nighttime chaos of P. Cosimato. Iron palates can attempt the *pennette all'elettroshock* (L12,000). All plates served in large or gigantic portions. Open Tu-Su 6pm-2am.

Osteria der Belli, P. Sant'Apollonia, 11 (☎06 5803782). Off V. della Lungaretta near P. S. Maria in Trastevere. A bustling *trattoria* specializing in Sardinian cooking, especially seafood. Nice outdoor seating area. *Ravioli sardi* (in tomato cream sauce) L12,000. Excellent grilled *calimari* L20,000. Cover L2000. Open Tu-Su 11:30am-2:30pm and 7:30-10:30pm.

Pizzeria Panattoni, V. Trastevere, 53-59 (☎06 5800919). Waiters in matching t-shirts race around an entire block of tables. Crispy pizzas L8-13,000, appetizers L5-9000. Try the multi-veggied "fabulous fancy salad" (L9800). Open Th-Tu 6pm-2:30am.

see map p. 316–317

TERMINI & SAN LORENZO

NORTH OF TERMINI

You're near the train station, hungry, and in a hurry. This is no reason to subject yourself to the gastronomic nightmare of a shady tourist establishment offering a L10,000 "quick lunch." The following provide good service and food for a largely local clientele.

▧ **La Cantinola da Livio,** V. Calabria, 26 (☎06 4282 0519). From P. della Repubblica, walk down V. V. E. Orlando, turn right on V. XX Settembre, take the 5th left onto V. Piave, and then the 4th left onto V. Calabria. This lively, pink-walled establishment specializes in seafood: the *Spaghetti alla Cantinola* (with seafood, caviar, tomato, and cream; L12,000) is transcendent. Follow it up with grilled fresh snapper, sole, sea bass, or flounder (L16-18,000). If it's a special night, one of the nervous-looking live lobsters can be yours for a whopping L120,000. Cover L1500. Open M-Sa 12:30-3pm and 7:20-11:30pm. Closed first 3 weeks of Aug. AmEx, MC, V.

▧ **Africa,** V. Gaeta, 26-28 (☎06 4941077). Near P. Independenza. Decked out in yellow and black, Africa continues its 20-year tradition of serving excellent Eritrean/Ethiopian food. The meat-filled *sambusas* (L4500) are a flavorful starter; both the *zighini beghi* (roasted lamb in a spicy sauce; L12,000) and the *misto vegetariano* (mixed veggie dishes; L11,000) make fantastic entrees. Act out those repressed childhood fantasies of eating with your hands with their spongy Ethiopian flatbread, known as *injera*. Cover L1500. Open M-Sa 8pm-midnight. MC, V.

▧ **Trattoria da Bruno,** V. Varese, 29 (☎06 490403). From V. Marsala, next to the train station, walk three blocks down V. Milazzo and turn right onto V. Varese. A neighborhood favorite with daily specials. Start with the *Tortellini con panna e funghi* (with cream and mushrooms; L10,000) or the tasty homemade *gnocchi* (L10,000) and continue with the delicious *Ossobuco* (L13,000). Bruno, the owner, makes créches, and he's very good at what he does: note the picture of him shaking hands with the Pope, upon presentation of one of his little masterworks. Open daily noon-3:30pm and 7-10:15pm. Closed Aug. AmEx, V.

Pizzeria da Giggetto, V. Alessandria, 43 (☎06 8543490). From Porta Pia, turn right onto C. Italia and right onto V. Alessandria. Giggetto has crowned himself *"Il Re della Pizza,"* and it's hard to argue with that. The popular *bruschetta* with salmon (L6000) is just a prelude to the pizza (L8-16,000). Should you have a hunger fit for a king, try the *pizze giganti* (L10,500-30,000). Be sure to give the automatic sliding door to the bathroom a whirl. Expect a wait on weekends. Open M and W-Sa 7pm-1am. Closed in Aug. AmEx, MC, V.

Hostaria La Capitale, V. Goito, 50 (☎06 486793). From V. XX Settembre, walk 2½ blocks down V. Goito. Perfect for those times when your *lire* just can't stretch any further. A cozy place, run by a kindly Italian gentleman who will advise you on what to eat. Enjoy typical Roman dishes like *Penne all'Amatriciana* (with spicy tomato sauce; L8000) and *Lombata di vitello* (veal steak; L12,000). Pizze L7-13,000. Bread L2000. Four *menù* of four courses in four languages, L15-20,000. Open Tu-Su 9am-4pm and 6pm-midnight. AmEx, MC, V.

Hostaria Il Varesino, V. Varese, 5b. (☎06 491191) From V. Marsala, walk three blocks down V. Milazzo and turn right. The closest meeting point of you, Stazione Termini, and horse-steak (*Bistecche di cavallo* L14,000). For your less carnivorous dinner companion, there's excellent *Ravioli con ricotta e spinaci* (L7000). Open Su-F noon-3pm and 6:30-10:30pm. MC, V.

SOUTH OF TERMINI (ESQUILINO)

Eateries closest to Termini aren't exactly known for their high quality and low prices, but a five- to 10-minute walk from the station will get you to some good eatin'.

Ristorante da Lisa, V. Foscolo, 16-18 (☎06 730027). South of P. V. Emanuele II. A homey kosher restaurant with an eclectic selection of the owner's favorite art. The food provides a twist on standard Italian fare and is cooked by the owner and his wife on demand. Try *burik con patate* (potatoes, cinnamon, and parsley wrapped in a crepe, L3000), *sciksciuka* (L10,000), *minestrone* (L10,000), or *kuskus bianco* (L5000). Open Su-F 1-3pm and 7-11pm.

Ristorante Due Colonne, V. dei Serpenti, 91 (☎06 4880852). On the left, down from P. della Repubblica on V. Nazionale, after the Palazzo delle Esposizioni. By day, Romans on lunch break fill the tables. By night, tourists struggle with the surprisingly broad menu. Excellent pizzas (L8-14,000). *Pasta e fagioli* (L9000), *linguine alla pescatora* (L13,000). Tourist *menù* L18-26,000. Open M-Sa 9am-3:30pm and 6:30pm-12:30am. AmEx, DC, MC, V.

Osteria da Luciano, V. Giovanni Amendola, 73/75 (☎06 4881640). Head south on V. Cavour from Termini and turn left after one block onto V. G. Amendola. For those in a hurry, this *osteria* is better than most within a stone's throw of Termini. Heaping plates of pasta (L4000-5500) will stop your travel-induced hunger pangs in no time. *Insalata di mare* L7000. Wine L4500 per liter. Cover L1000. Service 10%. Open M-Sa 11:30am-9pm. AmEx, MC, V.

SAN LORENZO

Though *Let's Go* doesn't recommend communist watching, this would be the place to do it if we did (wink wink). San Lorenzo is Rome's university district, and thank god; a discriminating student palate, combined with student financial resources, have ensured that just about every restaurant here is good and cheap. Definitely a place that travelers should dine if they're spending more than a few days in Rome, although women may find the areas nearest the train station a little uncomfortable if they're alone at night. From Termini, walk south on V. Pretoriano to P. Tiburtino, or take bus #492 to P. Verano (at the other end of V. Tiburtina from P. Tiburtino).

Il Pulcino Ballerino, V. degli Equi, 66-68 (☎06 4941255). Off V. Tiburtina. An artsy atmosphere with cuisine to match. The cook stirs up an ever-changing menu of imaginative dishes like *Tagliolini al limone* (pasta in a lemon cream sauce, L12,000) and *risotto* (various types, L10-12,000). You can also skip the chef altogether and prepare your own meal on a warm stone at the table. Very romantic. Cover L1000. Open M-Sa 1-3:30pm and 8pm-midnight. Closed first week of Aug. AmEx, MC, V.

Arancia Blu, V. dei Latini, 65 (☎06 4454105). Off V. Tiburtina. This elegant little vegetarian restaurant is technically a cultural association, so you'll have to write out a free membership card before you get your food. Don't worry, though—once some of the excellent, creative food on the menu arrives, it'll be worth all the paperwork. Enjoy elaborate dishes like *Tonnarelli con pecorino romano e tartufo* (pasta with sheep cheese and truffles; L12,000), *Lasagnette con cipolle rosse, funghi porcini, zucchine e zenzero* (pasta with red onions, mushrooms, zucchini, and ginger; L14,000). Extensive wine list. Open M-F noon-3pm and 7-11pm, Sa-Su 7-11pm.

Pizzeria la Pappardella, V. degli Equi, 56 (☎06 4469349). This popular *pizzeria* offers authentic Roman cuisine and quiet outdoor dining. A meal with appetizer, *primo*, *secondo*, and wine is about L30,000. *Pappardelle con funghi porcini* (pasta with mushrooms; L10,000) is the house special. *Pizze* L7-L13,000. Open Tu-Su 12:30-3pm and 7:30pm-midnight. AmEx, MC, V.

Il Capellaio Matto, V. dei Marsi, 25. From V. Tiburtina, take the 4th right off V. degli Equi. Vegetarians, rejoice! This offbeat place (named for the Mad Hatter) offers pasta and rice dishes like *Risotto al pepe verde* (with green peppercorn; L9000), imaginative salads like *Insalata di rughetta, pere, e parmigiano* (arugula, pears, and parmesan; L7000), and a variety of crepes (L7-9000). Plenty of meat dishes, too. Cover L1500. Open W-M 8pm-midnight.

Armando, P. Tiburtino, 5 (☎06 4959270). Lots of locals and outdoor seating, although there's often a wait for the outdoor tables. A great place to go with choosy eaters; the menu contains everything from *Fettucine al nero di seppia* (with squid ink; L15,000) to *Penne agli asparagi* (with asparagus; L12,000). Bread L4000. Service L1000 per person. Open Th-Tu 12:30-3:30pm and 7:30pm-2am. Reservations accepted.

La Pantera Rosa, P. Verano, 84-85 (☎06 4456391). At the eastern end of V. Tiburtina. The house specialty is the delicious pink salmon and caviar pizza (L13,000). There's also a variety of excellent *primi* like *Bucatini all'Amatriciana* (thick spaghetti with spicy tomato sauce; L9000). Open Th-Tu noon-3pm and 6:30pm-12:30am. MC, V.

Pizzeria Il Maratoneta, V. dei Sardi, 20 (☎06 490027). Off V. Tiburtina. Four young marathoners bake pizza on the run (L7-12,000). Tomatoes and marinated seafood cover half of their excellent *Pizza mari e monti* (surf and turf pizza; L12,000), while mozzarella and assorted veggies bury the other half. Pizza to go comes (or rather, goes) with everything from octopi to fried eggs. Cheerfully crowded. Open M-Th 9:30am-12:30am, F-Sa 9:30am-1am.

TESTACCIO

see map p. 322

In the shadow of the affluent Aventine lies working-class Testaccio. Once home to a giant slaughterhouse *(il Mattatoio)*, the neighborhood is the seat of many excellent restaurants serving traditional Roman fare and is the center of Roman nightlife. True to their roots, Testaccio eateries offer food made of just about every animal part imaginable. The gastronomically adventurous can sample local delicacies such as *pagliate* (calf intestines with curdled milk), *animelle alla griglia* (grilled sweetbreads), and *fegato* (liver).

Luna Piena, V. Luca della Robbia, 15-17 (☎06 5750279). Tastefully decorated with wood paneling and elegant paintings. Savor the stupendous *carpaccio di salmone* appetizer (L10,000), the excellent *rigatoni con pagliata* (L10,000), and the hearty *straccetti con carciofi* (L13,000). Open Th-Tu noon-3pm and 7:30-11:30pm. AmEx, DC, MC, V.

Non Solo Pizza, V. Benjamino Franklin, 11 (☎06 5685031). Not only pizza, but kebab! Order at the counter. Very popular with area students. Open 6:30pm-12:30am, in winter also noon-4:30pm.

Pizzeria il Cantinone, P. Testaccio, 31-32. Follow V. Luca della Robbia to P. Testaccio. A cavernous locale where you can sit inside and cool off or watch the market wind down outside over lunch. Try the hearty *tonarelli cacio e pepe* (tonarelli with cheese and pepper, L9000) or the *magro di vitello* (L18,000). Pizzas L9-14,000, but served only in the evening. Open noon-3pm and 7pm-2am. MC, V.

Don Pachino, V. Galvani, 24 (☎06 57283840). Look for the caricature of a tomato with glasses. Salient facts about this cheap and tasty pizzeria: first, waitresses with crazy remote control things wander the restaurant unimpeded. It's bat-shit insane in there. Second, a window opens onto the interior of the Monte Testaccio. *Pizze* L8-15,000. Try the *tartufo bianco* (white truffle; L5000) or the *pizza Don Pachino* (*pachino* tomatoes, mozzarella, basil; L12,000). Good for warming up before clubbing. Open daily 7:30pm-1am. MC, V.

Caffè Greco

Trattoria da Bucatino, V. Luca della Robbia, 84-86 (☎06 5746886). Take V. Luigi Vanvitelli off V. Marmorata, then the first left. A friendly neighborhood *trattoria* serving a variety of dishes involving animal entrails, as well as pasta (around L8000), pasta (only in the evenings; L7-14,000), and seafood, including *cosse alla marinara* (L10,000), more mussels than anyone in their right mind could hope to eat. Cover L2000. Open Tu-Su 12:30-3:30pm and 6:30-11:30pm. Closed Aug. DC, MC, V.

DESSERT

Though translated as "ice cream," *gelato* is in a league of its own. Unfortunately, shops catering to stupid tourists may sell you commercially made, disgusting imitations of true *gelato:* to avoid this sad fate, try our recommended *gelaterie*, or at least look for shops advertising *gelato artigianale* or *propria produzione*, which means they make it themselves. If the *gelato* flavors are grayish and barely distinguishable, instead of an artificially colored rainbow, it's a good sign that you're getting the good stuff. Saying *"con panna"* when you order will add a mound of fresh whipped cream to your serving for free. Most *gelaterie* require you to pay before you eat, so first head for the *cassa* (cash register) and then present your receipt to the scooper when you order.

Filetti di Baccalà

Some flavorful vocabulary: *mela* (apple), *ananas* (pineapple), *mirtillo* (blueberry), *stracciatella* (chocolate chip), *cannella* (cinnamon), *cocco* (coconut), *nocciola* (hazelnut), *miele* (honey), *pompelmo* (grapefruit), *menta*/after eight (mint, often with chocolate chips), *latte/panna/crema* (cream), *cocomero* (watermelon), *nutella* (streaks of hazelnut chocolate spread in vanilla), *meringa* (meringue, often with hazelnuts or chocolate chips added), *limone* (lemon), *amareno* (sour cherry), *liquirizia* (black licorice), *frutti di bosco* (mixed berries), *arancia* (orange), *pesca* (peach), *lampone* (raspberry), *fragola* (strawberry), *baci* (chocolate and hazelnut), *amaretto* (sweet and nutty like the alcohol, and yourself),

Tazza d'Oro

on the cheap

Gold Bar, P. del Viminale, 1 (☎06 4819227). In **Esquilino,** just off V. A. Depretis. Packed with Romans on their lunch breaks, this *tavola calda* serves excellent lunch fare at very reasonable prices. Don't expect to find a seat during peak hours, though; competition for empty space is fierce. Don't be surprised if the busy staffers get a little surly at your bad Italian. Good *panini* about L3500; entrees around L4-5000 per plate. *Poi, caro?* Open M-F noon-3pm.

Pizzeria Ficini, V. Luca della Robbia, 23 (☎06 5743017). In **Testaccio:** Take V. Luigi Vanvitelli off V. Marmorata, then take your first left. A no-frills pizzeria befitting this working-class community. They don't even hand you a menu; they just assume you've looked outside and know what you want. Pizzas (L6-8000) are delicious and dirt cheap. *Calzone* L8000. Wine L6000 per liter. Open Sept.-July Tu-Su 6-11:30pm.

cassata (fruity ice cream with nuts and candied fruits), *riso* (rice pudding), and *tiramisù*.

Another option is a slushy flavored ice treat called **granita.** Three common flavors are *limone* (lemon), *amareno* (sour cherry), and *caffè* (slushy frozen espresso). Alternately, try visiting a **grattachecce** stand. At these little booths (usually around parks and busier streets), muscled vendors will scrape shavings off a block of ice for you on the spot with a metal shovel, then spike your drink with any of the flavoured syrups they have on hand. The Roman specialty in *grattachecce* is a combo flavor called **lemon-cocco,** a yummy mix of lemon and coconut flavors with bits of fresh coconut fruit mixed in.

San Crispino, V. della Panetteria, 42 (☎06 6793924). Very near the Trevi Fountain. Facing the fountain, turn right onto V. Lavatore and take your 2nd left; the *gelato* temple is on the right. Positively the best *gelato* in the world. Don't miss their exquisite meringue, armagnac (similar to cognac), and grapefruit flavors. No cones; the proprietors claim that they "interfere with the purity of the product." Cups L3-10,000. Also at V. Acaia, 56 (☎06 70450412), south of the center in Appio. Both locations open M and W-Th noon-12:30am, F-Sa noon-1:30am, Su noon-midnight.

Tre Scalini, P. Navona, 30 (☎06 6880 1996). This chic, old-fashioned spot is famous for its *tartufo*, a hunk of truffled chocolate ice cream rolled in chocolate shavings (L5000 at the bar, L11,000 sitting). A touristed location has brought high prices, but *tartufo* is not to be missed. Bar open Th-Tu 9am-1:30am; pricey restaurant open Th-Tu 12:30-3:30pm and 7:30-9pm.

Giolitti, V. degli Uffici del Vicario, 40 (☎06 6991243). From the Pantheon, follow V. del Pantheon (at the northern end of the *piazza*) to its end and then take V. della Maddelena to its end; V. degli Uffici del Vicario is on the right. An old-fashioned ice cream shoppe, Giolitti makes wonderful *gelato* in dozens of flavors, both to take-out or eat-in. Fashionably surly service people don't have much patience with *turisti,* so be sure to pay and get a receipt first, and choose your flavors before you step up to the bar. Very festive and crowded at night. Cones L3-5000. Open daily 9am-1am. Nov.-Apr. closed M. AmEx, DC, MC, V.

Da Quinto, V. di Tor Millina, 15 (☎06 686 56 57). West of P. Navona. Eccentric interior decoration, huge queues, and icy, lighter gelato. The fruit flavors are especially good, as are the house specialty banana splits (L8000). Enormous *macedonia* of fruit (with yogurt, *gelato,* or whipped cream topping), L12,000. Open daily noon-2am. In winter closed W.

Palazzo del Freddo Giovanni Fassi, V. Principe Eugenio, 65-67 (☎06 4464740). Off P. V. Emanuele II, southeast of Termini. This century-old *gelato* factory is famous throughout Rome for its superb, creamy ice cream. Try *riso* (rice), try *coco* (coconut), try them all. Its most famous flavor is *la caterinetta,* a delicate honey and vanilla concoction. Cones L3-7000. *Frulatti* L3-5000. Also at V. Vespasiano, 57, near the Vatican. Open Tu-F noon-midnight, Sa noon-1am, Su 10am-midnight. In summer, also open M noon-midnight.

Il Fornaio, V. dei Baullari, 5-7 (☎06 6880 3947). Across from P. San Pantaleo, south of P. Navona. Wonderful, fresh-baked cakes, pies, and cookies. *Torta di mele* (L3000 per big slice), delicious *biscotti* (L1800 per *etto*), melting *cornetti* (L1500). Open daily 7am-8:30pm.

Yogufruit, P. G. Tavani Arquati, 118 (☎06 587972). Off V. della Lungaretta near P. S. Sonnino. No tradition here; it's filled with the young and the fruitful. Tart frozen yogurt blended with just about anything: fruit, M&Ms, even cornflakes. Cups or cones L3-5000. Open M-Sa noon-2am.

CAFFÈ

Italian coffee is the world's best, and coffee itself is the perfect solution to early hostel lockouts, hangovers, and too-many-museums-itis. It's also incredibly cheap and easily found absolutely everywhere. What to order? **Caffè** or **espresso** is a small cup of very strong coffee. A **cappuccino** is *espresso* with steamed milk and foam, often with a sprinkle of *cacao* on top; Italians only drink it for breakfast, but you can get it anytime you like. A **caffè latte** is a shot of *espresso* with an entire glass of hot milk. **Caffè macchiato** is *espresso* with a spot of milk. **Caffè ristretto** (or **alto**) is *espresso* with less water than usual. A **caffè lungo** has more water than normal, for non-Italian nervous systems. **Caffè corretto** is a black *espresso* "corrected" with a spot of liqueur. **Caffè americano** may be either filtered coffee or a *caffè lungo*. **Decaffeinato** coffee is available and may be made into any of the above delicacies. Better than decaf, though, is **caffè orzo,** a coffee-like drink made from barley—it tastes better than decaf and contains no trace caffeine.

Note that in most *caffès* and bars, you pay one price to stand at the bar, and a much higher price (as much as double) to sit down. There is usually a menu on the wall of the bar listing the prices *al bar* or *al banco* (standing up) and *a tavola* (at a table). The streets around Campo dei Fiori and Trastevere hide some of the best *caffès*. The bars around the Spanish Steps cater to rich tourists and are often packed and over-priced. Take the few extra steps toward the river, around V. della Scrofa, or across the bridge to the neighborhood around P. Cavour. Avoid the numerous bars near the Vatican; the prices are some of the highest in Rome, and the quality tends to be poor. Wander a few blocks north to V. Cola di Rienzo to find more authentic *caffès*. **Internet cafes** (p. 30) have become the trendy place to relax and unwind. Some places let you "sip and surf," charging a special price for a cup of coffee and an hour in front of a computer.

Forno del Ghetto, V. Portico d'Ottavia, 1 (☎06 6878637). Not really a cafe, this is a take-out only pastry bakery deep in the Jewish Ghetto. No advertising, no sign even, but long queues of locals who line up for fabulous blueberry pies, heavy fruitcake-like bars of dough and figs, buttery cookies, and chocolate and pudding concoctions, all sold by weight at excellent prices. Buy a big wedge of pie, make yourself a thermos of coffee, and head to a park or P. Mattei for a delightful picnic. Open Su-Th 8am-8pm, F 8am-5:30pm. Closed Jewish holidays.

Tazza d'Oro, V. degli Orfani, 84-86 (☎06 6792768). Standing with your back to the Pantheon's portico, you'll see the yellow-lettered sign on your right. Look for the bas relief (or check out the photo on p. 188) of the woman throwing coffee beans out of...her skirt ? No seating, but the best coffee in Rome at great prices (*caffè* L1200, *cappuccino* L1500). Extensive tea, coffee, and coffee bean selection. Superlative *granita di caffè* with mounds of fresh whipped cream (L2500), perhaps Rome's best. Open M-Sa 7am-8:20pm.

Antica Pasticceria Bella Napoli, C. V. Emanuele II, 246 (☎06 6877048). Good coffee and fantastic Neapolitan pastries. Try the *sfogliatelle ricce,* an orgasmic ricotta-stuffed pastry flavored with orange peel and cinnamon, or the rum soaked *baba* cakes. Available for take-out or eat-in. Pastries L1500-9500. Open Su-F 7:30am-9pm.

Dagnino, Galleria Esedra, V. V. E. Orlando, 75 (☎06 4818660). Conveniently snuggled between Termini and P. Repubblica, this wonderful find serves fabulous Sicilian pastries, *gelato* in special sweet pastry cups, marzipan wonders, almond drinks, and exquisite, never-soggy ricotta *cannoli siciliani.* Don't miss the splendid, sticky *cassata,* a heavy mix of candied orange and lemon peel, green icing, almond paste, and sweet, moist ricotta.

Sant'Eustachio, Il Caffè, P. S. Eustachio, 82 (☎06 6861309). Take a right on via Palombella behind the Pantheon on the right as you face it. Rome's "coffee empire." Perpetually jam-packed with Romans and Italian celebrities, this cafe was once a favorite haunt of Stendhal and other literary expatriates. Excellent coffee at rather inflated prices. Cool blue industrial decor under office lighting enhances the atmosphere. Try a *granita di caffè* with all the works (L8000, at the bar L6000), or their very own *gran caffè speciale* (L5000, at the bar L3000). If you don't want your espresso heavily sugared, here you must specify "*caffe amaro.*" Open Tu-F and Su 8:30am-1am, Sa 8:30am-1:30am.

Caffè della Pace, V. della Pace, 3-7 (☎06 6861216). Off P. Navona. Great people-watching, very hip, very expensive. The ivy-covered walls are a must for those of us who are a little too cool to be seen by others. *Cappuccino:* daytime L3000 at bar, L5000 at table; nighttime L4000 at bar, L8000 at table. Red wine L7000 at bar, L10,000 at table. Open daily 9am-8pm.

L'Antico Caffè Greco, V. Condotti, 86 (☎06 6791700). Off P. di Spagna. One of the oldest and most famous *caffès* in the world, this posh house, founded in 1760, has entertained the likes of European kings, Goethe, Wagner, Baudelaire, Byron, Shelley, movie stars, John F. Kennedy, and others wishing to spend far too much on a normal cuppa java. *Cappuccino* L2800. Pot of tea L3200. Hot chocolate with cream L4500. Open M-Sa 8am-8pm.

Sala da Te Trastè, V. della Lungaretta, 76 (☎06 5894430). Crepes, desserts, salads (L7-10,000). Lots of tea (L5000 a pot), herbal and otherwise. Try the coconut. Great atmosphere, groovy low couches and tables, and a friendly owner who will allow you to relax as long as you like over your tea. Open Tu-Su 5pm-midnight.

Bar San Calisto, P. S. Calisto, 4 (☎06 5835869). Join Trasteverean youth and Roman elders as they engage in heated debates over truly incredible, yet inexpensive *cappuccino* (L1200 sitting or standing) and *granita di limone* (L2000). Also plenty of Romans in their 20s and 30s sipping Peroni. Open M-Sa 6am-1:30am, Su 4pm-1:30am. In winter closed Su.

WINE

The god Bacchus is credited with having first brought "the vine" to the Aegean from India. The beverage caught on, and Italians became supreme wine-makers. In the highly efficient Roman Republic, wine was so widely produced that vineyards were occasionally demolished in order to check the problem of over-production. Unlike the popularized *Asti Spumante* and *Chianti* from the North or *Marsala* from Sicily, Lazio's harvest never travels far from the wine-maker's own dinner table. While those on a tight budget may not get to sample the choicest brands, there are numerous inexpensive good local wines that will have you seeing Bacchus in no time.

Lazio is primarily known for its white wine, which, chilled, is a pleasant antidote to the Roman heat. **Frascati,** the most famous local white, is fruity and dry. Look for Frascati Superiores, particularly Fontana Candida's *Santa Teresa* Frascati, Cantine San Marco, Villa Simone, Colle Picchioni, or Castel De Paolis. Est! Est!! Est!!! is the famous white wine of Montefiascone (see **Est! Est!! Est!!! (in Peace),** p. 198). **Colli Albani** wines, from the nearby foothills, are pale gold and delicate. **Cerveteri** wines include full-bodied reds and a slightly bitter white. **Zagarola,** a white wine, was all the rage in the Renaissance. House wine, though cheap, is usually downright terrible. Except in wine bars, it is difficult to find decent wine by the glass. Useful wine terminology: **vecchio** means "old" and **stravecchio** means "very old." **Secco** means "dry," and **abboccato** or **dolce** means "sweet."

ENOTECHE (WINE SHOPS)

Enoteche (or *bottiglierie*), traditional wine and olive oil shops, have become an economical and more authentic lunchtime alternative to pricey *trattorie*. Originally these shops did not serve the tasty fare for which they are known today. This tradition began in the days when shop proprietors had the common decency to feed the men who delivered barrels of the local harvest. Eventually word got out, and the wine shops had to install card tables, put up signs "*vino e cucina,*" and turn family members into waiters. In the 60s and 70s, students, hippies, and political activists gathered in such places to discuss Marx and Marcuse. Today, anyone looking for tasty, inexpensive food in an informal, personable setting will enjoy the cuisine and company in these neighborhood establishments. Most are open only on weekdays during lunchtime (approximately noon-3pm).

VINO E CUCINA

Bar Da Benito, V. dei Falegnami, 14 (☎06 6861508). Off P. Mattei in the Jewish Ghetto. You can't get more authentic than this: a tiny shop lined with bottles and hordes of hungry workmen. One hot pasta is prepared each day (L6000), along with delicious *secondi* like *prosciutto* with vegetables (L8000) or smoked salmon with potatoes and vegetables (L8000). Always packed, noisy, and incredibly hectic; excellent, if harried, staff. Open M-Sa 6am-8pm; lunch noon-3:30pm. Closed Aug.

Enoteca Constantini, P. Cavour, 16 (☎06 3211502). A big, beautiful wine shop with restaurant and bar, dripping inside and out with grapes. Wines L3-16,000 per glass, although true connoisseurs should stay for dinner, and have a bit of caviar (L18,000) or a sampling of some 80 different cheeses with their *vino*. Open daily 11:30am-3pm and 6:30pm-midnight. Closed for 20 days in Aug.

Al Parlamento, V. dei Prefetti, 15 (☎06 6873446). Take V. di Campo Marzio from the Corso. Have your morning *chianti* here; they open bright and early. Cognac dating back to 1865. Open M-F 9:30am-1:30pm and 4:30-8:15pm, Sa 9am-1:30pm. Sept.-Apr. closed M mornings.

Enotecantica, V. della Croce, 76b (☎06 6790896). Off P. di Spagna. Relax at the elegant semicircular bar after a draining day at Cartier. Sip wine (L4-8000 per glass) in a soothing atmosphere. *Melanzane alla parmigiana* (eggplant parmesan) L13,000, salads L8-16,000. Open M-Sa 11am-1am. AmEx, MC, V.

Curia di Bacco, V. del Biscione, 79 (☎06 6893893). Off Campo dei Fiori. If you took every bottle of wine in this *enoteche* and lined them up end to end, it would probably make the owners very unhappy. Choose from over 200 selections (L10-130,000). Also offers an extensive imported beer list, and over 20 different salads. Order the L12,000 lunch *menù* and receive a *pizza margherita,* salad, and *bruschetta.* If that's not enough, rumor has it that the remains of Julius Caesar himself lie underneath the foundation. Open daily 7am-5am. AmEx, MC, V.

WINE SHOPS

Some shops still sell just bottles of wine (but damn good wine at damn good prices).

Trimani, V. Goito, 20 (☎06 4469661). Near Termini. Founded in 1821, Trimani is indisputably Rome's best wine shop. Vast selection of wines, which range from the very affordable to way-beyond-your-credit-card-limit. Expert staff will be happy to advise you in selecting a bottle to fit your palate and wallet. Don't forget to have a snack at the incomparable Trimani Wine Bar, around the corner on V. Cernaia. Open M-Sa 8:30am-1:30pm and 3:30-8pm, Su 10am-1pm and 4-7:30pm. AmEx, DC, MC, V.

Gaudenzi Isola, V. Due Macelli, 111 (☎06 6795722). Near the Trevi Fountain. Excellent selection of wines, both cheap and expensive, and a vast array of domestic and imported liqueurs. Try the lovely French Chartreuse, in its yellow or more famous green varieties (L45,000) or a more Italian bottle of Campari, limoncello, or one of the myriad *grappas* in stock. Also a nicely stocked *fruiteria,* with those hard-to-find limes for your gin and tonics. Open M-Sa 10am-8pm.

WINE BARS

Wine bars are rather different than *vino e cucina* shops, though equally lovely. These bars offer more upscale, elegant foods and settings. Here you'll find not home cooking but smoked fish, imported cheese, delicate desserts in multicolored exotic syrups, cigar-smoking businessmen, and besuited waiters. No worries: the extensive, inexpensive lists of wines by the glass are still the same.

Trimani Wine Bar, V. Cernaia, 37b (☎06 4469630). Near Termini, perpendicular to V. Volturno (V. Marsala). Excellent food at good prices. Pastas (L12,000), filling quiches (try the spiny lobster and leek quiche; L9000), smoked fish, impressive cheese board, and desserts worth writing home about (L9-12,000). The ricotta pie with orange sauce is particularly heavenly (L10,000). Wines from L3500 a glass. Reservations recommended for dinner. Their shop is around the corner at V. Goito, 20. Open M-Sa 11am-3:30pm and 6pm-12:30am. AmEx, MC, V.

La Bottega del Vino da Anacleto Bleve, V. S. Maria del Pianto, 9a-11 (☎06 6865970). Wonderful light lunches and dinners of pasta (L9-12,000) and a range of French and Italian cheeses,

EST! EST!! EST!!! (IN PEACE)

One of the finest golden wines of the region, grown on the slopes of Montefiascone, near Viterbo (p. 221), owes its name, *Est! Est!! Est!!!*, to a German cardinal, Johan Defuk, who was traveling through the district. He sent his valet ahead of him to sample the local wines and chalk "Est" (short for *"est bonum vinum,"* or "it's good wine) on the doors of inns with satisfactory offerings, and "Est Est" if it was particularly good. When the valet reached Montefiascone, he was so enraptured with the harvest that he wrote "Est Est Est," a great piece of publicity for the wine which has since assumed the name. The cardinal himself unintentionally spent the last, very happy days of his life in Montefascione. He stayed at the inn for several days and drank such vast quantities of the wine that he died a sudden, if giddy, death. His grave, 20km north of Viterbo in Montefiascone, bears the inscription, "Est Est Est."

smoked fish, cured meats, and creative salads. Superlative wine list. Wine by the glass begins at L4000. Open for food Tu and Sa 12:45-3pm, W-F 12:45-3pm and 8-10pm. AmEx, DC, MC, V.

Cul de Sac, P. Pasquino, 73 (☎06 6880 1094). Off P. Navona. Everything a wine bar should be and more. Come here for a huge selection of great, decently priced wines, outdoor tables, and excellent food. Scrumptious *escargot alla bourguigonne* L12,000; hefty Greek salad L9000. Wonderful soups. Open M 6:30pm-12:30am, Tu-Su 12:30-3pm and 6:30pm-12:30am.

Enoteca Buccone, V. Ripetta, 19 (☎06 3612154). Two blocks south of P. del Popolo on the left. Choose from hundreds of wines by the bottle, dozens by the glass, or head into the back room for elegant light fare. Eloquent quiches (L4500), tiny *tartini* (L1500), and good cold pasta salads (L8500). *Secondi* L12-22,000. Wines by the glass (L3500-14,000). Try the marvelous Sardinian dry white (L4500). Lunch served noon-3:30pm. Open M-Sa 9am-8:30pm, Su 10am-7:30pm.

Il Piccolo, V. del Governo Vecchio, 75 (☎06 68801746). Off the southwest corner of P. Navona. Sophisticated but simple food and gentle 20s and 30s jazz floating out to street-side tables make this an indulgent and sunny haven. Glasses of wine from L2000. Salads and pasta for lunch (L5-12,000) and assorted *antipasti* at night (L4-8000). Open daily 11:30am-4pm and 6pm-2am.

La Vineria (a.k.a. Da Giorgio), Campo dei Fiori, 15 (☎06 6880 3268). One of the more lively wine bars, caught between the orbits of the Drunken Ship and Sloppy Sam's (see p. 204). Full of ex-pats during the day; at night, throngs of young Italians and tourists mingle over surprisingly cheap wines and harder drinks. White table wine L2000 per glass; gin and tonic L8000. *Tartine* (L2000) make a tasty addition to the wine. Open M-Sa 10am-2pm and 6pm-2am.

SHOPPING FOR FOOD

ALIMENTARI. These small stores, sprinkled about the city, are your best bet for standard groceries, stocking dairy, dry goods, and deli items. For specialty cheeses, fresh bread, and meats, head to a **panificio** or a **salumeria.** These shops can fix you a sandwich or simply sell you the ingredients; an **etto** (100g) of anything is usually enough for a sandwich. For produce, open-air markets are the best for freshness and price. Otherwise seek out small **frutta e verdure** shops and stands. Food stores tend to be open Monday to Wednesday and Friday 8am to 1pm and 4 to 8pm, Thursday and Saturday 8am to 1pm.

OPEN-AIR MARKETS. The cheapest eats in the city are at Rome's open-air markets, which carry a fresh and varied array of produce, dairy, and meat products...big fish, big watermelons, big octopi. Note

Here's your ticket to freedom, baby!

**Wherever you want to go...
priceline.com can get you there for less.**

- Save up to 40% or more off the lowest published airfares every day!

- Major airlines serving virtually every corner of the globe.

- Special fares to Europe!

If you haven't already tried priceline.com, you're missing out on the best way to save. **Visit us online today at www.priceline.com.**

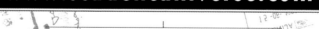

that dairy products are generally cheaper in supermarkets, but fish, meat, and produce are far cheaper in markets. Most are open Monday to Saturday from 6am to 2pm. Major food and produce markets include:

Mercato di Campo dei Fiori. Flowers, fruits, veggies, cheese, fish. Weekdays only.

Mercato di Piazza Vittorio Emanuele II, near Termini. The usual produce and mayhem, this time with lots of clothes.

Mercato di Piazza Navona, on V. della Pace, off V. di Governo Vecchio. Primarily a fruit market.

Mercato di Piazza San Cosimato, in Trastevere. A raging produce market. Walk up V. di Trastevere away from the river, turn right on V. Fratte di Trastevere, and left on V. S. Cosimato.

Mercato Trionfale, V. delle Milizie. Near the Vatican Museums entrance.

Mercato di Via del Lavatore, near the Trevi Fountain.

Mercato di Via Milazzo, north of Termini, between V. Varese and V. Palestro. 7am-2pm.

Mercato di Via Tomacelli, near the Spanish Steps, halfway down V. Tomacelli between the Trevi Fountain and V. dell'Arancio.

Produce Market, P. Testaccio, on V. Luca della Robbia. M:B-Piramide. Come here for juicy fodder. Excellent selection and prices on fish.

SUPERMARKETS. Besides markets, supermarkets are generally the cheapest source of everything. They're also quieter, air-conditioned, and open longer. Produce, however, is much less fresh, and there's usually a poor selection. Furthermore, Rome's supermarkets tend to be inconveniently far away from tourist-land. See the Service Directory, p. 297, for listings of major supermarkets in Rome.

Nightlife

When you're most frustrated about the random afternoon closing times of restaurants, museums, and just about everything else in the Eternal City, remember this simple fact of Roman life: everyone is sleeping now, so they don't have to after dark. The following lists the best places in Rome to drink, grind, and go bump in the night.

AFTER-DINNER WALKING TOUR

⏱ *From grub to pub: Spanish Steps to Campo dei Fiori. Begin at P. di Spagna (M:A-Spagna). 1½-2½hr.*

As you've no doubt noticed by now, meals in Rome are a serious affair. You'll want to digest, cool off, then gear up before you hit the nightlife—and this after-dinner tour is the perfect way to do such. After a meal at one of Rome's countless *trattorie* (see **Food**, p. 181, for suggestions), take in the vibrant atmosphere of the Spanish Steps (p. 107), where tourists go to sit and watch Bernini's **Barcaccia** fountain and Italians go to *rimorchiarli* (hit on them). Either sit around and ponder the fact that the Spanish Steps were actually paid for by French King Louis XV, or head to **Via Condotti** and **Via Borgognona**, Rome's most exclusive retail space. Either while away the time window-shopping or pick out what you're going to come and buy tomorrow (yeah, right).

In P. di Spagna, head past the column in adjoining P. Mignanelli and bear right along V. di Propaganda (V. San Andrea delle Fratte). Bear left onto V. Nazarena, taking time to notice the **ruins of the Vergine Aqueduct** on the right, which once fed Bernini's fountain. Cross V. del Tritone onto V. della Panetteria.

About three-quarters of the way down on the left, you'll find the best *gelato* in Rome at ☑**Gelateria San Crispino** (p. 194), with more than 20 delicious flavors (cups L3-6000). *Gelato* in hand, turn right onto V. del Lavatore (before the ramp up to the Quirinale) and you'll hit the **Trevi Fountain** (p. 109). Feel free to ensure your own return to Rome.

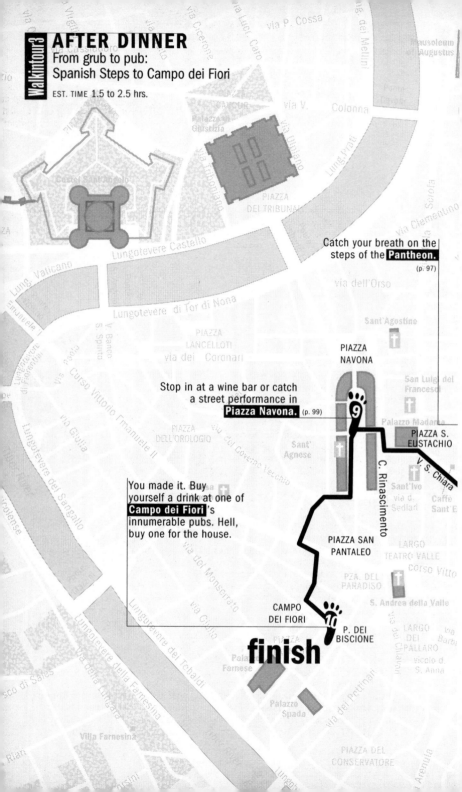

AFTER DINNER
From grub to pub:
Spanish Steps to Campo dei Fiori

EST. TIME 1.5 to 2.5 hrs.

Catch your breath on the steps of the **Pantheon.**
(p. 97)

Stop in at a wine bar or catch a street performance in **Piazza Navona.** (p. 99)

You made it. Buy yourself a drink at one of **Campo dei Fiori**'s innumerable pubs. Hell, buy one for the house.

finish

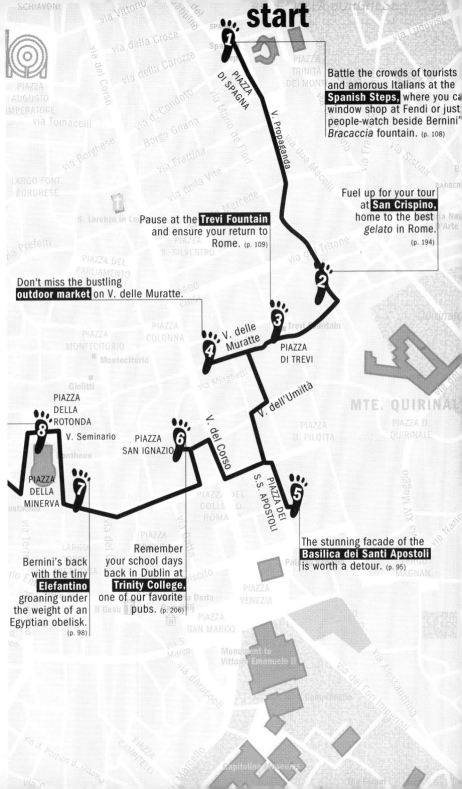

start

Battle the crowds of tourists and amorous Italians at the **Spanish Steps,** where you ca window shop at Fendi or just people-watch beside Bernini' *Bracaccia* fountain. (p. 108)

Fuel up for your tour at **San Crispino,** home to the best *gelato* in Rome. (p. 194)

Pause at the **Trevi Fountain** and ensure your return to Rome. (p. 109)

Don't miss the bustling **outdoor market** on V. delle Muratte.

The stunning facade of the **Basilica dei Santi Apostoli** is worth a detour. (p. 95)

Bernini's back with the tiny **Elefantino** groaning under the weight of an Egyptian obelisk. (p. 98)

Remember your school days back in Dublin at **Trinity College,** one of our favorite pubs. (p. 206)

Leaving the fountain, walk out onto V. delle Muratte and make a left onto V. delle Vergini. (A little farther down V. delle Muratte, skilled artisans sell their wares outdoors.) Make a right onto V. dell'Umiltà and a quick left onto V. San Marcello. If you're thirsty for some Italian beer, try **Birreria Peroni** (p. 188), on the right, a neighborhood favorite affiliated with the Peroni brewery (L3500-12,000).

Continue down V. S. Marcello and take a quick right onto V. Santi Apostoli. (Continuing straight on Via S. Marcello leads you to the **Basilica dei Santi Apostoli** (see p. 95). It has a beautifully ornate facade and a portico full of sculptures.)

When you arrive at V. del Corso, turn right, and take a look back down the street at the **Vittorio Emanuele II monument** (p. 94), which is majestically illuminated at night. After passing the **Church of San Marcello al Corso** on your right, cross V. del Corso and make your first left down V. A. Specchi. On the right at the end of the block is ☒**Trinity College** pub (p. 206), a quintessential Roman Irish pub with much Guinness and Harp paraphernalia and many distinctly non-Irish Italians (pint L6-9000).

Stumbling out of the pub, turn left down V. del Collegio Romano (V. Pie' di Marmo) and bear right on V. S. Caterina da Siena into P. della Minerva. The **Church of Santa Maria sopra Minerva** was built on top of an ancient temple, but the real eye-catcher is the so-called "Pulcin della Minerva" (p. 98), a cute 18th-century Bernini sculpture of a baby elephant beneath a 6th-century B.C. Egyptian obelisk. With your back to the church, bear right to P. della Rotonda, site of the ancient Roman masterpiece, the **Pantheon** (p. 97). The temple is closed at night, but there are crowds, musicians, and pricey cafes. Exit the *piazza* on Salita de' Crescenzi, and take your first left to P. S. Eustachio. If your spirits are flagging, stop and get your caffeine fix (*caffè* L1600) at **Il Caffè Sant'Eustachio** (p. 195).

Walk out of P. S. Eustachio on V. Staderari and turn right onto C. Rinascimento. Cross the street and take your first left into **Piazza Navona** (p. 99), where street performers, musicians, and portrait painters do their best to entertain. Keep an eye on your wallet and remember that the biggest crowds don't always indicate the best shows.

Walk down to the southern end of the *piazza* and turn right to get to P. del Pasquino, where you'll find **Cul de Sac** (p. 198), a classy little wine bar where you can drink tasty *vini* by the glass (L5000 and up) and enjoy fancy appetizers.

From P. del Pasquino, head down V. dei Leutari and turn left on C. Vittorio Emanuele II. Take your first right onto P. della Cancelleria to get to **Campo de' Fiori,** where you can finally become serious about getting your drink on (see **Pubs,** below).

PUBS

Exactly why the Irish pub should have become the *de facto* form of Roman nightlife is unclear, but that's the way it is. Rome has more pubs than Dublin, and more on the way. Not all of Rome's pubs are Irish: some claim to be English, Scottish, American, or Brazilian, and many are distinctly Roman concoctions. Nationality is in the eye of the drinker.

Many Roman pubs feature live music, dancing, and entertainment. The tradition of staying *all'aperto* is alive and well in Rome's pubs—most have substantial outdoor seating areas for your enjoyment in the hot summer months. The more traditional drinking experience lives on in the slightly more upscale **wine bars** (see p. 197), where you can drink without the darkness, smoke, and pick-up scene of the bars.

Listed below are some of our favorites for your pub-crawling pleasure. Of course, *Let's Go* researchers are not allowed to drink while on duty, which, ramble they be gin to ?drinking much merry, vodka be good.

CENTRO STORICO

🔲 *The area is well served at night by Bus #45N on C. Vittorio Emanuele II.*

CAMPO DEI FIORI

see map p. 314–315

The statue of Giordano Bruno looks down on the nightly insanity taking place in the Campo with an expression of dismay. During the summer, all hell breaks loose on a nightly basis at Campo dei Fiori. Have a drink at one of the hordes of pubs and bars, grab a slice of watermelon from a street vendor, and count the pairs of Capri pants within eyeshot.

The Drunken Ship, Campo dei Fiori, 20-21 (☎06 68300535). Because you're tired of meeting Italians. Because you have an earnest desire to commune with others in the hosteling set. Because you feel the need to have an emotion-free fling with a kindred spirit. Because you're proud to be an American, dammit. A brew will set you back L8000. Happy hour daily 5-9pm, all night Tu. W 9-10pm is power hour—all the beer you can drink (L10,000). Ask about the student discount on Heineken. Takeout window. Open 5pm-2am.

Sloppy Sam's, Campo dei Fiori, 9-10 (☎06 68802637). Run by the Drunken Ship people and strangely indistinguishable from it. Do note that once at home wistful stories about that special someone you "befriended" at Sloppy Sam's will probably be laughed at. Going home with someone you met at the Drunken Ship, though—now that's something to be proud of!

Caipirinha Pub-Café, V. del Gallo, 10 (☎06 6892561). This fun Brazilian bar serves up tropical drinks and plays Brazilian music for your dancing enjoyment. Cocktails around L10,000. Bud L4000, Guinness L6000. Panini L4000. Open daily 7pm-2am.

Taverna del Campo, Campo dei Fiori, 16 (☎06 6874402). Is it a pub? Is it a wine bar? Goodness me, it's both. And it has damn tasty food to boot. More elegant than the typical pub-crawler's digs. Open Tu-Su 8pm-2am.

Artu

Campo degli Elfi, P. della Cancelleria, 87 (☎06 68308888). More a place for intimate conversation than hard drinkin', this Campo is full of Italian 20-somethings and elves. Very popular among both demographics. Open daily 10pm-2am.

La Taverna di Orusdir, V. dei Cappellari, 130 (☎06 68804654). Celtic environment with a heavy metal crowd. Do be careful. 1.5L beer L5000. Cocktails L6000. Open daily 8pm-2am.

PIAZZA NAVONA

Also a nightly three-ring circus is elegant P. Navona, which transforms within hours from tourist-packed destination by day to tourist-packed destination by night. Fend off the rose vendors, who become more aggressive as the night (and their bouquets) fades. The more touristed pubs are generally toward C. V. Emanuele II, but there are some fantastic cocktail bars in the area, especially in the winding streets by V. del Governo Vecchio, though these tend toward the wine-bar feel.

Jonathan's Angels

⬛ Jonathan's Angels, V. della Fossa, 16 (☎06 6893426). West of P. Navona. Take V. del Governo Vecchio from Campo dei Fiori, turn left at the Abbey Theatre onto V. Parione, and then a left toward the lights. Not since Pope Julius II has there been a case of Roman megalomania as severe as that of Jonathan. Michelangelo's accomplishments pale before the bathroom at Jonathan's Angels, the finest ⬛ bathroom in Rome, nay, Italy. Medium beer on tap L10,000, cocktails/long drinks L15,000. Open daily 4pm-2am.

⬛ Abbey Theatre, V. del Governo Vecchio, 51-53 (☎06 6861341). One of the only establishments in Rome where you can drop in for a 10am Guinness (L10,000). Stay for lunch (a lot of vaguely Irish dishes), watch MTV, and admire the rather touching painting of a druggy-looking Yeats. Before you know it, it'll be time for happy hour (daily 3-7pm). Should you have the staying power, dinner's also available. Open M-Th 10am-2am, F-Sa 10am-3am, Su 2:30pm-2am. MC, V.

The John Bull Pub, C. V. Emanuele II, 107a (☎06 6871537). Why anyone would want to go to an English pub when there are plenty of fine Irish pubs available is unclear, but that's Rome for you. Often full of pub-crawling kiddies. Food available. Open Tu-Sa 9pm-3am. V.

Drunken Ship

the BIG $plurge

Bar del Fico, P. del Fico, 26-28 (☎06 6865205). Off V. del Governo Vecchio. A place to see and be seen with Romans, Fico is almost always mobbed with locals at night. Lounge under the heated, ivy-covered awning or have your drink inside in one of the three oh-so-chic sitting rooms. Wide range of drinks, but pricey: 0.5L beer L12,000. Open daily 8am-2am.

Bar della Pace, V. della Pace, 4-5-7 (☎06 6861216). Off V. del Governo Vecchio. Its proper name is Antico Caffe della Pace, but you won't hear it called that very often. One of *the* places to be for celebrity-watching in the Eternal City by night, this locale is upscale and it knows it. Sit outside or in one of the two gorgeous rooms, which are tastefully appointed with wood furniture and cushy armchairs. The waitresses seem to have been picked out of a beauty contest, and you know why. Prices are out of sight, but that's why you're here. Open daily 9am-2am.

ELSEWHERE IN CENTRO STORICO

▪ **Trinity College,** V. del Collegio Romano, 6 (☎06 6786472). Off V. del Corso near P. Venezia. Offers degrees in such diverse curricula as Guinness, Harp, and Heineken. Tuition L6-9000. Pub food served for lunch and dinner. Classes held every day noon-3am.

Night and Day, V. dell'Oca, 50 (☎06 3202300). Off V. di Ripetta near P. del Popolo. Don't even think of coming until the rest of the bars close. At 2am, Italians who don't let dawn stop their fun stream in. Buy a membership card (L10,000) for discounts on drinks. Beer L5000-7000, Guinness L8000. Happy hour until midnight. Open daily 7pm-6am. Closed part of Aug.

Bartaruga, P. Mattei, 9 (☎06 6892299), in the Jewish Ghetto. Named after the tortoise-shaped fountain in this secluded *piazza,* Bartaruga provides a surreal drinking experience in a myriad of Murano glass, light blue and pink sofas, and tassled drapery. On weekends it overflows with Italians in tight clothes. Wide variety of cocktails available; beer L8000. Open Tu-Su 10pm-2am.

Victoria House, V. di Gesù e Maria, 18 (☎06 3201698), near P. del Popolo. If this place were any more British, all the Irish pubs would be pissed. Pretty much everything inside was shipped from Sheffield. Shepherd and venison pies, jacket potatoes, and other lovelies served along with several kinds of beer. Happy hour M-F 6-9pm, Sa and Su 6-8pm. Pints L8000. Open M-Th 6pm-12:30am, F-Sa 5:30pm-1am, Su 5pm-12:30am.

The Nag's Head, V. IV Novembre, 138b (☎06 6794620). Off P. Venezia toward Termini. Pier the bartender, who is straight out of *Cocktail* (and advertises himself as a master of *"flair estremo"*), makes this place worth a visit. After the bottle-twirling and other excesses, you almost don't seem to mind the L1000 he tacks on to your bill as a "tip." Dance floor inside; sometimes hosts live music. Guinness L10,000. Open daily 10am-3am. V.

Rock Castle Café, V. B. Cenci, 8 (☎06 68807999). In the old days, people would wish that there was a discopub with a frat-house atmosphere in the Jewish Ghetto. And they would wish that they could find Red Dog somewhere in the Eternal City. With the advent of the Rock Castle Café there's nothing left to wish for. Resist the urge to drink Budweiser; the Beamish (L7000) is much better for you. Cover L10,000 (includes a drink).

see map p. 320

BORGO, PRATI, & VATICAN CITY

The area around the Vatican is largely residential and full of clergy, making for quiet nights, but a couple of establishments keep the liquor flowing and the music pumping. Pray for us sinners now and in the hour of our death, Amen.

The Proud Lion Pub, Borgo Pio, 36 (☎06 6832841). A block north and a block east of P. San Pietro. The outside of the pub says "Rome, Borgo Pio," but the inside says "hey, I don't forget my Highland roots." Beers on tap include Red Stripe and Caffrey's Ale. Affiliated with the Italian Dart Club; call and ask about upcoming tournaments. Open Su-Th 8:30pm-1am, F-Sa 8:30pm-2am.

Morrison's, V. E. Q. Visconti, 88 (☎06 3222265). Two blocks north of P. Cavour. Quite an elegant place. Harp, Kilkenny, and Guinness on tap, an excellent selection of Irish and Scotch whiskey and whisky, and pseudo-Gaelic slogans on the wall. Theme nights include the ever-popular Beach Party. How can you go wrong? Open Tu-Su 7pm-2am.

TRASTEVERE

Follow the crowds wandering the little streets: you're bound to find something. But if wandering time is wasted drinking time, make a beeline for one of the following:

Artu Cafe', Largo Fumasoni Biondi, 5 (☎06 5880398). In P. San Egidio, one block north of Santa Maria in Trastevere. Artu offers a random melange of people fresh from partying in Trastevere. Good selection of drinks; beautiful location. Making Star Wars jokes about the name will get you kicked out. Open Tu-Su 6pm-2am.

see map p. 314–315

Royal Ceres Pub, V. G. Mameli, 5 (☎06 5882060). Take tram #8 from Largo Argentina or bus #75 from Termini to V. Morosini. Still the only place in Rome to drink a Ceres. A veritable hodgepodge of Danish beer, English pub, movies, bikers, and that most horrifying of concoctions, Roman-style Tex-Mex. Surreality factor: high. Very high. Open Tu-Su 8pm-2am. V, MC.

Mediterraneo, V. del Cinque, 15 (☎06 5803630). Behind Santa Maria in Trastevere. *Tapas* and salsa dancing. Very Mediterranean. Open M and W-Sa 8:30pm-2:30am, Su 8:30pm-3am.

La Scala, P. della Scala, 60 (☎06 5803763). On the left on V. della Scala behind Santa Maria in Trastevere. Manages to be fun and feel like a cheesy American franchise at the same time. Painfully kitschy knick-knacks don't keep away the teeming masses, even on weeknights. Live music frequently. Cocktails L11,000. Open Th-Tu 7:30pm-2am. AmEx, DC, M, V.

TERMINI & SAN LORENZO

NORTH OF TERMINI

The Termini area has few pubs oriented to the backpacker crowds that otherwise hold the area in thrall. These pubs do make for an easy stumble home to your hotel, though:

Julius Caesar, V. Castelfidardo, 49 (☎06 4461565). Just north of Termini near P. dell'Indipendenza, on the corner of V. Solferino. Always packed with backpackers and locals, here for live music, cheap drinks, and good times. Upstairs features beer on tap (L6-8000) amid Roman decor while the downstairs is filled with blaring live music most nights. Happy Hour (beer and sandwich L10,000) 9-10pm. Pitchers L15,000, cocktails L10,000, wine L20,000 per bottle. Inquire about the *Let's Go* discount. Open daily 8:30pm-2am.

see map p. 316–317

Bandana Republic, V. Alessandria, 44-46 (☎06 44249751). Dumb name, good pub. Despite being English, it has the good sense to serve Guinness, Harp, and Kilkenny (pints L8000, ha'-pints L5000). The classy crowd enjoys the reasonably priced food, laid-back ambience, and occasional live music. Open Su-Th 7:30pm-2am; F-Sa 7pm-3am.

SOUTH OF TERMINI (ESQUILINO)

Druid's Den, V. S. Martino ai Monti, 28 (☎06 48904781). Traveling south on V. Merulana from V. S. Maria Maggiore, take your 2nd right. One of the 1st Irish pubs in Rome, this is an Irish hangout where Romans get to be tourists. Good place to watch a soccer match. Guinness and Strong Bow on tap (L7500). Open daily 5pm-12:30am.

SAN LORENZO

Being the university district, San Lorenzo is home to one of the best pub scenes in Rome. Tourists rarely venture into San Lorenzo, but that shouldn't stop you from enjoying the nightlife: it's only a 15 minute walk from Termini (or take bus #492).

Pub Hallo'Ween, P. Tiburtino, 31 (☎06 4440705), at the corner of V. Tiburtina and V. Marsala. Abandon all hope of not having fun, ye who enter here. The plastic skulls and fake spiders and spiderwebs confirm your suspicions that this is indeed a gateway to the darkest pits of Hell. Draft beer L6-8000, bottles L7-10,000. Cocktails L8-9000. Enjoy delicious sandwiches such as the Freddy (salami and mozzarella), the Candyman (nutella), or the Frankenstein (double cheeseburger). Happy hour (free appetizers) 8:30-10pm. Open daily 8:30pm-2:30am. Closed in Aug.

Down Town, V. dei Marsi, 17 (☎06 4456270). Irish with non-Irish decor. Live music F-Su. Their "apple pie" (apple and papaya juice, coffee, and gin; L8000) is more like grandma's than you'd care to admit. Happy hour 1-3am. Open daily 9pm-2am; in winter 8pm-3am. Closed part of July and Aug.

Pigmalione, V. di Porta Labicana, 29 (☎06 4457740). Mellow rock and blues play under the watchful gaze of a massive one-eyed Buddha painted on the wall. An eclectic mix of Indian, Egyptian, and astrological decor. It's a bit cheaper than its Irish counterparts, and there's a horoscope machine. Medium beer L6-7000. Open daily 7pm-2am.

Lancelot, V. dei Volsci, 77a (☎06 4454675). A cavernous, smoky underground labyrinth of drinkers and wayward knights. At times there is a bit of a wait to get in. Open 8pm-2am.

Legend Pub, V. dei Latini (☎06 4463881). Just what you always wanted, a sports bar in Rome! Watch soccer and get plastered. Sweet. Do note that it refers to itself as a "steakhouse pub." Make of that what you will. Open Tu-Su 7pm-3am. AmEx, DC, MC, V.

Lupo Alberto, V. degli Equi, 22 (☎0347 2216878) A little beer joint with a cartoon wolf chilling on the door. Happy hour brings you a sandwich, beer, and coffee for L8-13,0000. Open Su-Th 4pm-3am, F and Sa 4pm-6am.

Dalhu' Pub, V. degli Equi, 38 (☎06 4457369). This quiet Irish pub attracts something of an older crowd. Open 7pm-2am.

Drome, V. dei Latini, 49-51 (☎06 4461492). A small cocktail bar with live ethnic music of various sorts. Open M-Sa 7pm-3am.

Nirvana, V. degli Equi, 57 (☎06 5902287). Hosts live music, usually of the rock 'n' roll variety. A newcomer to the scene, it's quickly become extremely popular. Open daily 9pm until it closes.

TESTACCIO & OSTIENSE

see map p. 322

Testaccio and Ostiense are nightlife-central. Their clubs truly shine, and the pubs aren't too shabby. Bus #20N heads up V. Ostiense, stopping by the pyramid every half-hour.

Il Barone Rosso, V. Libetta, 13 (☎06 5783562). M:B-Garbatella. Left on V. Ostiense, then left at V. Libetta. The closest thing to a German beer garden in Rome. Plenty of room on the two floors and outdoor patio, plenty of snacks, and plenty of beer. Attracts a *telefonini*-toting crowd of young Romans. Beamish and König Pilsener on tap (L7000). Open Tu-Su 7pm-3am.

Aldebaran, V. Galvani, 54 (☎06 5746013). A cocktail bar spanning two cave-like rooms with world music and a sedate, older crowd. Cocktails L10,000. Open 10pm-2:30am.

Four XXXX Pub, V. Galvani, 29 (☎06 5757296). From Piramide, turn left at the pyramid on to V. Marmorata, then left on V. Galvani. Four XXXX serves up its namesake beer (L10,000) every night and live jazzzz, folkkkk, and soullll in its lower level Th-Sa 10pm (cover L5000). Local and Latin American food. Open daily 7:30pm-2am. AmEx, DC, MC, V.

CLUBS

Tourists and foreigners rarely club in Rome, largely because the DJs and the music they spin are almost invariably terrible and almost invariably all the same. This has its advantages. Despite the music, die-hard dancers may enjoy a few nights grinding with hordes of beautiful, Lycra-coated, sweaty young Romans. As a tourist, you may get strange looks at the door of many clubs, but unless you show up late on a weekend, they should let you in. Many of Rome's clubs require a *tessera*, or pass, usually costing around L10,000 and valid for two weeks to a year of (usually free) access.

Rome's club scene changes frequently: Check *Roma C'è* or *Time Out* (see p. 28) to see what's new and exciting. All of Rome's clubs used to shut down for the summer and move to the beaches of Ostia and Fregene, but A/C has recently made its long-heralded debut in Rome, so more clubs stay open.

ANCIENT CITY

see map p. 77

Ciak Dance, V. S. Saba, 11a (☎06 5782022). Head for the Aventine Hill, but don't go all the way to up to Santa Prisca. Blown-up stills from films such as *Superman, Basic Instinct,* and *The Blues Brothers* line the walls and shake to hip-hop, house, disco, and, yes, sweet electro. Drinks L10,000. Cover L30,000, Th L15,000 (includes a drink). Open Tu-Su 11:30pm-4am. In summer, moves to Ciak Estate, V. dell'Artigianato, 34 (☎06 5740093), near LunEUR (p. 137). AmEx.

CENTRO STORICO

see map p. 314–315

Dub Club, V. dei Funari, 21a (☎06 68805024). In the Jewish Ghetto. Bask in the blue light of its subterranean, circular dance floor. Spins techno, funk, acid jazz, and exotica. Cover L10-20,000. Open Tu-F 11pm-4am, Sa-Su 11pm-6am. Things get rolling at 2am. Closed most of summer.

Groove, V. Savelli, 10 (☎06 6872427). Head down V. del Governo Vecchio from P. Pasquino and take the 2nd left. Look for the black door and unlit neon sign. Lose it to acid jazz, funk, soul, and disco. F and Sa 1-drink minimum (L10,000). Open Tu-Su 10pm-2am. Closed most of Aug.

TERMINI AND SAN LORENZO

see map p. 316–317

NORTH OF TERMINI

Alien, V. Velletri, 13-19 (☎06 8412212). One of the biggest discos in Rome attracts a well-dressed crowd and plays the house you know and love. As of this writing, the comfy chill-out room had not yet reached 1987. Cover L10-30,000 (includes a drink). Occasional theme nights. Open Tu-Sa 11pm-4am. Moves to Fregene during the summer.

Piper, V. Tagliamento, 9 (☎06 8414459). From V. XX Settembre, take V. Piave (V. Salaria). Take a right on V. Po (V. Tagliamento). Alternatively, take bus #319 from Termini to Tagliamento. A popular club that occasionally hosts gay nights in collaboration with Hangar (p. 211). 70s, rock, disco, as well as the standard house and underground. Very gay friendly all the time. Cover L15-35,000 (includes a drink). Open Sa-Su 11pm-3am; in summer Su 11pm-3am.

Club 52, V. Montebello, 102b (☎06 4441331). Take V. Volturno away from Termini; turn right on V. Montebello. Club 52 is the closest disco to Termini and has style to burn. Not yet popular with the backpacker crowd; you can make it happen. One drink minimum. Open daily 10pm-3:30am.

SOUTH OF TERMINI (ESQUILINO)

🔲**Qube,** V. Portonaccio, 212 (☎06 4381005). From P. di Porta Maggiore, take V. Prenestina east; turn left on V. Portonaccio. Seedy neighborhood; plan to take a cab home. A warehouse-style disco, and one of Rome's biggest. Three packed dance floors. "Transmania," on Su, is one of Rome's most popular gay nights. Open Th-Su 11pm-4am. Cover L10-20,000.

Black Out, V. Saturnia, 18 (☎06 70496791). From the Colosseum, take V. Claudia (V. della Navicella/V. Gallia) southeast; turn right on V. Saturnia. Punk and Britpop. Occasional bands. Cover L10-15,000. Open Th-Sa 10:30pm-4am. Closed mid-June to August.

SAN LORENZO

Il Giardini di Adone, V. dei Reti, 38a (☎06 4454382). Though it fancies itself a "spaghettipub," the happy students who frequent this little place would remind you that tables are properly used for dancing, not for eating linguini. Cover L10,000 (includes a drink). Open Tu-Sun 8pm-3am.

TESTACCIO

see map p. 322

Roman clubs are most concentrated here in the easiest clubbing area to reach without resorting to taxis. V. di Monte Testaccio (the road that circles the hill of pot shards) is a strip of clubs; if you're looking to dance, you're bound to find something you like here.

Radio Londra Caffè, V. di Monte Testaccio, 65b (☎06 5750444). Admit it: you've always fantasized about watching Italian bands cover rock classics badly. Always packed with an energetic, good-looking, mostly straight young crowd. Pint of Carlsberg L7000. Pizza, *panini*, and hamburgers (L8-12,000). Monthly *tessera* L10,000. Open Su-F 9pm-3am, Sa 9pm-4am.

Il Santo, V. Galvani, 46-48 (☎06 5747945). Two packed floors: one's heaven, and one's hell. Cover L20-30,000 (includes a drink). Open Tu-Su 10:30pm-4am. Closed summer.

Charro Cafe, V. di Monte Testaccio, 73 (☎06 5783064). So you wanted to go to Tijuana, but got stuck in Rome. Weep no more, *mis amigos:* make a run for Charro, home of the Museo del Tequila (L5000 per shot). Photos of John Paul II and Paul VI wearing sombreros pontificate over a case of rather dubious relics from the Mexican Revolution. Italians guzzling a good selection of beer (L7000) and strong Mexican-themed mixed drinks (L10,000) dance themselves silly to pop and house. Cover L10,000 (includes a drink). Open M-Sa 8:30pm-3:30am.

C.S.I.O.A. Villaggio Globale, Lungotevere Testaccio (☎06 57300329). Take bus #27 from Termini, get off before it crosses the river, and head left down the river. Women probably don't want to travel alone on the Lungotevere at night. One of the best-known *centri sociali* in Rome—your one-stop shop for all things countercultural. Housed in a huge Testaccio slaughterhouse, it hosts live music, films, art exhibits, and more. Hours and cover vary.

Vecchio Mattatoio, V. di Monte Testaccio, 23 (☎06 491508). Also in, as the name suggests, the old slaughterhouse. A welcome respite from the Testaccio strip, Vecchio Mattatoio plays a variety of intelligent (or at least more cerebral) dance music. Cover L5-20,000. Open sporadically; call ahead or look for posters.

Heaven, V. di Porte Ardeatina, 118a (☎06 5743772). From the Piramide Metro stop, follow the city walls to the right. Spacious, with a rather young crowd. House and disco, with occasional 70s and 80s nights. Cover L15-25,000. Open Th-Sa 11pm-4am. Closed summer. AmEx, DC, MC, V.

Caruso, V. di Monte Testaccio, 36 (☎06 5745019). No opera here: Caruso is a reliable venue for live salsa, DJed hip hop, and "music black" (rap and R&B). Five rooms of tropical decor and writhing Latino wannabes. Monthly *tessera* L15,000. Open Tu and Th-Su 11:30pm-3am.

Picasso, V. di Monte Testaccio, 63 (☎06 5732975). Next door to Radio Londra. Adequate cover bands and DJs play mostly R&B and soul to a yuppie crowd. On weekends, show up early for the L20,000 meal/cover combo; otherwise L15,000 (includes a drink). Open Tu-Su 8pm-3:30am.

Jungle, V. di Monte Testaccio, 95 (☎0338 2240556). A small disco bar full of well-dressed Italians furiously getting freaky to Latin music. Live music and great DJs F and S. Softdrinks L5000, beer L10,000, cocktails L15,000. Monthly *tessera* L10,000. Open Tu-Su 11pm-3am.

OSTIENSE

see map p. 322

Goa, V. Libetta, 13 (☎06 5748277), a block west of the Garbatella Metro stop (Linea B). While the jet set claims that the crazy club scene in Goa, India has seen better daze, Goa in Roma happily packs 'em in, with occasional gay nights Th. Cover L15-30,000. Open Tu-Sa 11pm-3am. Closed in summer.

Alpheus, V. del Commercio, 36 (☎06 5747826). Off V. Ostiense. Three huge dance floors and a couple of chillout rooms. Rome's most popular gay night, "Mucassassina," (literally, cow killer) F. Other nights find live jazz, rock, folk, cabaret and comedy. Cover L10-L20,000. Students free Th. Open Tu-Su 10pm-4:30am.

Ex-Magazzini, V. dei Magazzini Generali, 8b (☎06 5758040). An interesting club/bar/gallery combo. Two floors feature avant-garde drinking, dancing, music, and art. Mostly mixed by good DJs, and live bands have been known to play. Rock Th; electric F; drum 'n' bass, big bass, electro-funk, and trip-hop Sa; lounge Su. Carlsberg and Moretti on tap. Cover L10,000. Open Th-Sa 10:30pm-4am, Su 6:30-11pm. Closed July and Aug.

Speedy Gonzales, V. G. Libetta, 13 (☎06 57287338). Popular Mexican disco themed after your other favorite cartoon mouse. Hip-hop, pop, house, rap, funk, a bit of Latin, and what the Italians charmingly refer to as trash. Wash down greasy TexMex food with daiquiris and various tequilas. Cover F and Sa L15,000 (includes drink). Open Tu-Su 8:30pm-3am. Other location in Trastevere: **Speedy Tre,** V. degli Orti Di Cesare, 7 (☎06 58333494).

GAY & LESBIAN NIGHTLIFE

Aldebaron

Rome has fewer gay bars and clubs than most cities its size, but those it does have are solid and keep late hours. Many of the following establishments require an **ARCI-GAY pass** (L10,000 per year), available from **Circolo di Cultura Omosessuale Mario Mieli** (☎06 5413985). Of the above clubs, **Alpheus, Goa, Piper,** and **Qube** host gay nights. *Time Out* has coverage of gay clubs and events. For more info on gay life in Rome, see p. 264.

Hangar, V. in Selci, 69 (☎06 4881397). M:B-Cavour. Near Termini; off V. Cavour. Friendly John from Philly runs this small bar, once the home of Nero's wife. Hangar is considered the hotspot for gay night-lifers in Rome, attracting mostly 20-something men. Though usually packed, the atmosphere is cool, neon blue, and laid back. Women are welcome (except M, dirty movie night), but may feel out-of-place. Some of the cheapest drinks in Rome (L3-10,000). Open W-M 10:30pm-2am. Closed three weeks in Aug. ARCI-GAY pass required.

L'Alibi, V. Monte di Testaccio, 39-44 (☎06 5743448). In Testaccio. Bus #30N. Large, elegant, and diverse, the club's rooms spread over three levels, including an expansive rooftop terrace. Especially in summer, this is *the* gay club in Rome. Underground, house, and retro prevail. Mostly gay, though lesbians and straights are welcome. Open W-Su 11pm-4:30am. Cover L15-20,000; Th and Su free.

Abbey Theater

New Joli Coeur, V. Sirte, 5 (☎06 86215827). Off V. Eritrea. Rome's primary lesbian dance club is a little out of the city center, east of Villa Ada. Kind of seedy neighborhood; women often go together or split the cab fare. Kitsch decor and retro underground music, with the occasional live cabaret show or girl group. Women only. 1-drink minimum (L15-20,000). Open Sa 11pm-3am, may be open Su.

Angelo Azzuro, V. Cardinal Merry del Val, 13 (☎06 5800472). Off V. di Trastevere. Subterranean bar with a big, crowded dance floor and *gelato*. Black lights highlight a vast collection of trippy statu-ettes, nouveau art, mirrors,. House music. F women only. Cover F and Su L10,000, Sa L20,000. Open F-Su 11pm-4am.

Skyline Club, V. degli Aurunci, 26-28 (☎06 4440817). In San Lorenzo. This elegant leather bar is one of the newest entries on the Roman gay scene. Films Su. Open Tu-F 10:30pm-2am, Sa 10:30pm-3am, Su 5:30pm-2am (Oct.-June) and 10:30pm-2am (July-Sept.).

Jonathan's Angels

Daytripping

In Rome you long for the country; in the country—oh inconstant!—you praise the distant city to the stars.
—Horace

How much a dunce that has been sent to roam
Excels a dunce that has been kept at home!
—William Cowper

LAZIO

When the speeding *motorini* and the tourist-choked morass of Rome are too much, seek sanctuary nearby in rural Lazio. The cradle of Roman civilization, Lazio was originally known to the Romans as *Latium*, Latin for "wide land." Today, the standard translation of Lazio for most Romans is "Winner of the 2000 Italian soccer cup." Stretching from the Tyrrhenian coastline through volcanic mountains to the foothills of the Abruzzese Apennines, Lazio encompasses ancient metropoloi, imperial Roman villas, exquisite Baroque estates, beautiful, sandy beaches, tranquil lakeside resorts, and cool, shady woodlands.

Known as *Ager Romanus*, Lazio has always been a rich land. Volcanic soil feeds its farms and vineyards, and travertine marble quarried from its hills was used to build the Colosseum, St. Peter's, and many buildings in between. The territory attracted the Etruscan Empire's notice in the 9th century BC, when it colonized Tarquinia and Cerveteri. The less advanced Latin tribes near Lake Albano spread to the south. While Rome was just a few mud huts on the Palatine, Etruscan and Latin towns enjoyed relative sophistication.

After a grueling stint in Rome, take a day and run for the hills (or the forest or the sea). The time required is minimal—most trips are no more than 90 min. by train or bus.

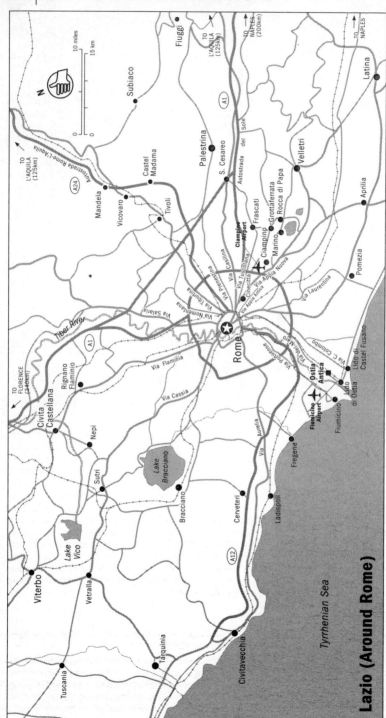

Lazio (Around Rome)

Central Italy

BEACHES

The lovely Mediterranean sunshine, clear waters, and a national predilection for dark tans make Italian beaches a popular destination. While most beaches get crowded on weekends, they don't really become overcrowded until August. The farther from the city you go, the better your prospects for sunning and swimming in relative peace. Many of Rome's most popular discos close during the summer months and reappear at the beaches of **Ostia** and **Fregene** (see **Nightlife,** p. 201), although you may need a car to get back late at night. *Rome C'è* lists what's going on and where on the beach scene.

Great stretches of the Lazio beaches lie under the thumb of nefarious *stabilimenti balneari*—private companies that fence off the choicest bits of beach and charge admission (usually L10-15,000), which includes the use of a changing cabin. Beach chair and umbrella rentals, as well as hot showers, are extra. A little polite inquiry, however, will usually get you to a *spiaggia libera* (public beach).

NETTUNO

🚩 *Take the regionale train from Termini to Nettuno (about 1hr.; outbound 6:50am-9:30pm, return 5am-9:50pm; L5600). Nettuno is the last stop, about 1min. after Anzio.*

The broad arc of beach stretching south of Rome is a natural extension of the Lido di Ostia, but the President of the Republic's vast seaside compound at Castel Fusano has effectively isolated the southern half of the shoreline. Bustling **Nettuno** sprawls along the coastline. If you're coming from Anzio, take the orange local bus from P. Cesare Battisti (L1500). There is a **Pro Loco tourist office** at the marina. (☎ 06 9803335. Open M-F 8am-noon.) Below the gaudy Palazzo Municipale, a busy marina teems with boats; the **public beach** lies to the left. But there's more to Nettuno than just surf, sun, and sand. The little town managed to preserve more of its ancient foundations than Anzio did, including a tourist-riffic walled medieval quarter: to the right of the marina, the walls of the **Borgo Medioevale** preserve a picturesque scene of vaulted passageways, narrow *piazze*, and a handful of not-so-medieval nightspots. A few blocks up toward Anzio, at P. S. Francesco, stands the **Fortezza Sangallo,** an early 16th-century fortress that houses the **Museo dello Sbarco Alleato,** which is devoted to the Allied landing. (Fortress open Tu-Sa, 9am-noon and 4-7pm. Museum open M, W, and F 8am-2pm, Tu and Th 8am-7pm. Free.)

Nettuno has done its best to forget its war-torn past, but one reminder remains: the **Sicily-Rome American Cemetery** stretches over 77 acres of beautiful parkland donated to the US by Italy. (Turn right coming out of the train station and then right again onto V. Santa Maria.) The solemn and beautiful grounds hold the graves of 7861 Americans (as well as a memorial to the 3695 missing) who died during the 1943-44 Italian campaign, which began with the invasion of Sicily and ended with the liberation of Rome. The memorial at the top of the park contains a chapel, as well as extensive maps and descriptions of the Allied drive up the peninsula. An American custodian remains on duty to provide information and help locate graves. (Open daily 8:30am-5:30pm.)

ANZIO

Anzio, 3km. north of Nettuno, was the site of the Allied invasion on January 22, 1944, and was mostly destroyed by the fighting. It is consequently fairly modern and not terribly interesting independent of the beaches (unless you're a big fan of the fishing and ship-building industries). From the train station, walk down V. Palombi to reach P. C. Battisti (where the bus stops); two blocks down and to the left is the **IAT tourist office,** with maps and hotel and transportation information. (☎0669 845147. Open M-Sa 9am-1pm.) Anzio is a point of departure for the **Pontine Islands** (see p. 227). Almost all of the prime sand in Anzio is controlled by *stabilimenti*, but, if you walk all the way down Riviera Zanardelli you'll find a fairly appealing swath of public coastline. A few miles up the coast from Anzio is **Lavinio,** where legend has it Aeneas first set foot in Italy.

SPERLONGA

When the beaches near Rome start to feel overcrowded and dirty, head south to **Sperlonga** for soft sands, clear blue waves, and plenty of elbow room. From Termini, take a Naples train (1¼hr.; every 15min.-1hr., 6:10am-10:30pm; L8000). It's well worth the trip.

OSTIA ANTICA

◪ *M:B-Piramide. Exit the station and walk left past the bar to the Lido trains. Get off at the Ostia Antica stop. You can use the same ticket you used on the Metro. Cross the overpass, take the road until it ends, cross the street, and walk down the parking lot past the bar. Take a left when the parking lot dead-ends into the lot for the ruins, and follow the signs to the entrance. ☎06 56358099. Open daily 9am-7pm; in winter daily 9am-5pm; last entrance 1hr. before closing. Admission L8000. Guided tours Su mornings, except in Aug., L7000. For info, call 06 21803030.*

The ruins of Ostia offer a closer, cheaper alternative to the more famous ruins at Pompeii and Herculaneum (p. 232 and p. 234). Though not quite as intact as the cities buried by Vesuvius, the ruins of the old port are much closer to Rome and sparsely visited—and still quite well preserved. The sea breeze keeps temperatures reasonable in the summer months, as well. The site is large and requires the better part of a day to explore, so bring some food and water to keep you going.

The city, named for the *ostium* (mouth) of the Tiber, was founded around 335 BC as the first Roman colony. Ostia grew alongside its mother city from a mere fortified camp established to guard the salt fields of the Tiber delta into a port and naval base during the 3rd and 2nd centuries BC. After Rome won control of the seas in the Punic Wars, almost all imports to Rome passed through Ostia. The great bakeries that supplied Rome with much of its bread were here, near the Egyptian grain docks. Rebellious and criminal slaves were often sentenced to labor in these bakeries, pounding grain and shoveling

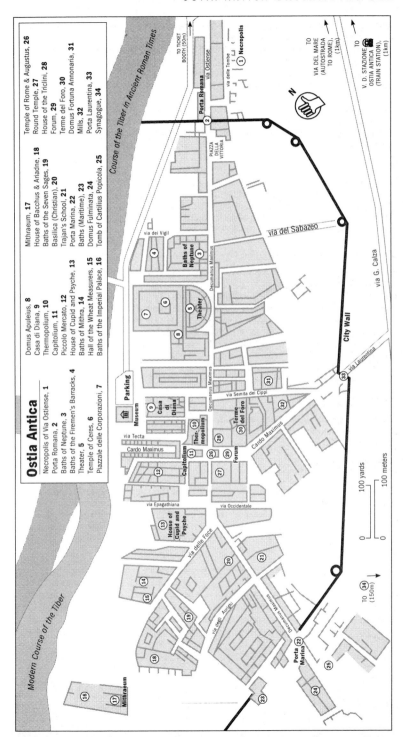

Ostia Antica

Necropolis of Via Ostiense, **1**
Porta Romana, **2**
Baths of Neptune, **3**
Baths of the Firemen's Barracks, **4**
Theater, **5**
Temple of Ceres, **6**
Piazzale delle Corporazioni, **7**

Domus Apuleius, **8**
Casa di Diana, **9**
Thermopolium, **10**
Capitolium, **11**
Piccolo Mercato, **12**
House of Cupid and Psyche, **13**
Baths of Mithra, **14**
Hall of the Wheat Measurers, **15**
Baths of the Imperial Palace, **16**

Mithraeum, **17**
House of Bacchus & Ariadne, **18**
Baths of the Seven Sages, **19**
Basilica (Christian), **20**
Trajan's School, **21**
Porta Marina, **22**
Baths (Maritime), **23**
Domus Fulminata, **24**
Tomb of Cartilius Popicola, **25**

Temple of Rome & Augustus, **26**
Round Temple, **27**
House of the Triclini, **28**
Forum, **29**
Terme del Foro, **30**
Domus Fortuna Annonaria, **31**
Mills, **32**
Porta Laurentina, **33**
Synagogue, **34**

waste into enormous brick ovens. The work was considered second in unpleasantness only to being chained to an oar in a galley.

The late Republican and early Imperial periods saw the construction of the most grandiose (and the most well-preserved) structures in the port. By AD 45, the wharves lining the river had reached their capacity, and the port had begun to be blocked with sand deposits, prompting Claudius to dredge an artificial harbor to the northwest (fragments of which have been found near Fiumicino airport).

The port fell into disuse during the onslaught of the Goths, and the silty Tiber slowly moved the coastline a mile or so west. After the city was sacked by the Goths in the 9th century, Pope Gregory IV built a new fortified town up the road from the present-day entrance gate, and the ancient city receded into malarial swampdom. Fortunately, the mud acted to preserve the ruins. Like the Roman Forum, Ostia was plundered for marble during the Middle Ages—much of it was processed into lime in crude furnaces still present in the city—but many brick buildings survived and much marble was missed.

From the entrance gate, **Via Ostiense** (the same highway that now leads out of Rome), leads to a **necropolis** of brick and marble tombs. The road passes through the low remains of the **Porta Romana**—one of the city's three gates, it's framed by Sulla's 1st-century BC walls—and becomes the city's main street, the **Decumanus Maximus.** To the immediate left are a square and the remains of a fountain where *cisiarii* (cart drivers) who ran between Rome and Ostia parked their vehicles.

SITE MUSEUM. At the north of Ostia, the park museum displays the more interesting statues recovered at Ostia and a diverse collection of artifacts monumental and mundane. Among the treasures are a colossal statue of Trajan, bas reliefs of various trades and businesses, a statue of Mithras slaying the sacred bull (Room 3), several sarcophagi (Room 9), and a spectacular set of 4th- and 5th-century marble panels of Jesus (Room 11). Those with a pressing interest in male anatomy may gawk at the *Hero in Repose* (Room 8). *(Open Tu-Su 9am-6pm. Free with park ticket.)*

THEATER. Built in 12 BC, the Ostian theater is almost completely intact thanks to a restoration effort that has left it in usable condition. The large central entrance still has fragments of stucco work added in AD 196. The building once housed several small stores in its bottom levels. A vaulted passage leads underneath the stands to the semicircular *cavea.* The stage itself was backed by a wall several stories high, decorated with columns, arches, niches, and statuary; only the low wall of its foundation survives. Seating around 3500, the theater once hosted aquatic shows by flooding the orchestra section with water stored in two pools visible just off the Decumanus Maximus in front of the theater. In summer, the theater hosts plays and concerts. *(For events info, check Roma C'è or call the Teatro Roman Scavi Archeologici di Ostia Antica at 06 5683712 or 06 56352830.)*

PIAZZALE DELLE CORPORAZIONI. Just north of the theater are the remains of this expansive and beautiful center for shipping agents stationed in Rome. The sidewalk around the central forum is lined with mosaic inscriptions, each telling the trade and origin of the merchant. They are accompanied by amazingly intact mosaic pictograms. In the center of the *piazzale*, a small staircase and a few columns are all that remain of a temple to Ceres, the goddess of grain, the heart of Ostia's trade.

THERMOPOLIUM. Ancestor to the modern coffee/snack bars that adorn the streets of modern Italy, this place offered the Ostian a chance to walk in for a drink and a bite to eat. An elegant marble counter greeted customers from the street; here they could order hot beverages out of the sunken clay jars or cold wine from the cellars. A still life in the central room depicts what are possibly popular foods of the time.

BATHS OF NEPTUNE. The large baths rise on the right a few hundred yards down the road from the entrance gate. Walk up the stairs to the viewing area for a view of the 18 by 12m entrance hall mosaic, in which Neptune drives his chariot. The room to the north contains a smaller mosaic of Amphitrite. A quick walk up V. dei Vigili allows a glimpse of a room heated by pipes set inside the walls *(laconicum)* and a standard *calidarium.*

FULLONICA. Off the Decumanus to the left of the baths, the **Via della Fontana,** a well-preserved street lined with stores and apartment houses, leads back to a Fullonica, or ancient cleaning shop. Its deep pits were filled with clothing and fresh urine, which contains bleaching agents; slaves had to jump in and splash around to agitate the wash.

FORUM. Occupying a wide rectangular space to the west of the Thermopolium is the Forum of Ostia, anchored by the imposing **Temple to Jupiter, Juno, and Minerva** (called the **Capitolium**), which was used in lieu of the Forum on rainy days. During the 1700s, however, it was used as a sheepfold, dubbed "the red house" by shepherds. The largest baths at Ostia, the **Terme del Foro** complex sits just southeast of the Forum. Note the remains of the complex heating system in the subterranean passage and the exquisite veined marble columns rising in the *frigidarium*.

HOUSE OF CUPID AND PSYCHE. At the fork in the Decumanus, V. della Foce leads right to this elaborate, marble-paneled dwelling, where the statue of the two lovers (now in the museum) was found. Down from the house and to the right on V. di Terme del Mitra, a staircase descends to a shadowy *mithraeum* (see **Mithraism,** p. 56) and the beginning of the maze of sewers and cisterns that sprawls beneath the city.

SCHOLA OF TRAJAN. A marbled *exedra* greets the visitor to the Schola of Trajan, believed to be owned by a corporation of shipbuilders. The first-century BC *domus* contains beautiful and rare mosaics; the interior court and fountain are striking.

ANCIENT SYNAGOGUE. South of the city through the **Porta Marina,** through which disembarking sailors entered the city, is a large synagogue. Two architraves with Jewish symbols led to the discovery that these ruins, which include an oven and a podium for religious services, were a Jewish temple. The entrance is marked by two steps that lead into a vestibule. On the right lies the *mikvah*, or ritual bath. The tabernacle contains two columns that once held corbels resembling seven-branched candelabra.

CASA DI DIANA. East of the Theater off V. dei Molini lies the Casa di Diana (named for the terra-cotta relief of Diana in the main courtyard), the best preserved Roman house at Ostia and among the most complete in the world. At the time of its construction, the edifice reached a height of almost 18m, encompassing three or four floors. Buildings like this, known as *insulae*, once filled most Imperial Roman cities. Unlike the large, single-family villas at Pompeii (see p. 232), an *insula* was a collection of three-story apartments where several dozen people lived together, sharing the courtyard and kitchen facilities. The ground floor housed *tabernae* (shops), which opened onto the street. The grooves in the thresholds show where sliding wooden screens served as doors. At the back of the ground floor, a dark, windowless room holds a **mithraeum.**

TIVOLI

Water is the inspiration and the chief attraction of the city of Tivoli, a hilltop town perched 120m above the Aniene River, only an hour from Termini. The poets Horace, Catullus, and Propertius once vacationed in villas lining the rocks overhanging the river. Modern Tivoli stretches beyond the original narrow strip, providing dramatic views of Rome from its hilly streets and gardens. Three distinct villas are its principal sights.

Take the Metro (B) to Rebibbia (15 min. from Termini); exit the station and follow signs for Tivoli through an underpass to reach the other side of V. Tiburtina. Find the marker for the blue ACOTRAL bus to Tivoli (25 min.). The **L3000 ticket** can be purchased in the bar next door or in the subway station. Once the bus has climbed up to Tivoli, get off slightly past the green P. Garibaldi at P. delle Nazioni Unite (the bus back to Rome leaves from P. Garibaldi). On the street leading from P. Garibaldi, the **tourist office,** a round shack with a big "I" in front, is loaded with historical information, restaurant and hotel maps, and bus schedules. (☎ 0774 311249. Open M-Sa 9:45am-3pm.) Tivoli is best visited as a daytrip from Rome, where cheaper accommodations are available.

HADRIAN'S VILLA (VILLA ADRIANA)

To get to the Villa, take orange bus #4x 5km from P. Garibaldi. Tickets are L1400, available at the news kiosk. The bus will let you off right in front of a long path down to Hadrian's Villa. The return bus stop is halfway down the street to the right, diagonally from the gelateria with the clover leaf outside of it. ☎0774 530203. Open daily 9am-1½hr. before sunset. L8000.

In the valley below Tivoli, Emperor Hadrian, a fairly sophisticated patron of art and architecture, built this enormous complex according to his own unique design. The largest and costliest villa ever constructed in Ancient Rome, Hadrian's Villa has some of the best-preserved imperial architecture near Rome, now scattered in fields of olive trees and purple thistles. Though his predecessor, Trajan, expanded the borders of the empire to their furthest reaches, Hadrian, who came to power in 117, was a homebody. As long as the citizens were kept happy, this "emperor of the arts" was satisfied with enlightening himself through building projects. Each section of the estate was built in the style of a monument Hadrian had seen during his travels in Greece and Egypt.

Just through the gate, there is a bar on the right, equipped with public bathrooms, **tour maps,** and a sizeable model of the villa. From there, the path leads to the **Pecile,** a great, once-colonnaded court built to recall the famous Painted Porch *(Poikile)* in Athens where Hadrian's heroes, the Greek Stoic philosophers, met to debate. The large pool of the Pecile is now home to ducks and some very hostile swans. At the northeast corner of the Pecile, the Philosopher's Hall (its seven niches that probably held the seven Greek sages' tomes) leads to the circular **Maritime Theater.** This was the emperor's private study and bedroom, cloistered inside a courtyard and protected by a still extant green moat.

Beneath the broad **Court of the Libraries** (south of the Maritime Theater), a shadowy **cryptoporticus,** one of several in the villa, hid the emperor's army of slaves from view as they ran the enormous complex. The rest of the palace lies nearby in heavily labeled enclaves. South of the Pecile, beyond the main buildings, the **Canopus,** a green expanse of water surrounded by plasters of original Egyptian sculptures (including some very lifelike crocodiles) and broken columns, replicates a famous canal near Alexandria.

The **Serapeum,** a semicircular Baroque-like dining hall modeled after the Alexandria's Temple of Serapis, anchors the far end of the canal. Here the emperor and his guests dined on a platform completely surrounded by water cascading down from the fountains at rear. On the walk back to the entrance, note the small and great **thermae** (baths) crumbling beneath the remnants of a large dome, suspiciously like that of the Pantheon.

VILLA D'ESTE

From P. Garibaldi, weave your way through the gauntlet of souvenir stands through P. Trento down the path to the Villa d'Este. ☎0774 312070. Open daily May-Aug. 9am-6:45pm; Sept.-April 9am-1hr. before sunset. On Sundays, the villa closes 1½hr. earlier. L8000, EU citizens under 18 and over 60 free.

Villa d'Este was laid out by Cardinal Ercole d'Este (son of Lucrezia Borgia) and his architect Pirro Ligorio in 1550 to combine the feel of ancient Roman *nymphaea* and pleasure palaces with that modern *je ne sais quoi* of the cutloose 1550s. The palace is decorated with amusing grotesque frescoes, shell-studded grottoes, and large picture windows. The gardens are built along the slope of the hill; cleverly constructed terraces above them offer views of the greenery and the distant countryside. The fountains (which are the real attractions) and the park are an ideal setting for a picnic or some casual frolicking, preferably in the company of small children spitting mouthfuls of water.

Immediately below the terrace is the **Fontana del Bicchierone,** a shell-shaped goblet of Bernini's design. To the left (with your back toward the villa), a path leads down to the **Grotto of Diana,** which contains mythological scenes in its shiny mosaic nooks. Another path (on the right) leads to the **Rometta,** or Little Rome, a series of fountains including one representing the Tiber (the boat with the obelisk is the Tiber Island) as well as stuccoed miniatures of principal temples and a statue of Roma herself, accompanied by the suckling Romulus and Remus. The **Viale delle Cento Fontane** runs the width of the garden, endlessly spurting water from grimacing masks into its narrow basins. At the other end from the Rometta, the **Fontana dell'Ovato,** designed by Pirro Ligorio, spurts a great sheet of water 5m into the air. Down the semi-circular steps from the center of the Viale delle

Cento Fontane is the **Fontana dei Draghi,** a round pool from which four dragons with moss-covered heads protrude. Nearby, the **Fountain of the Ephesian Goddess** spouts curved streams of water from each of her 18 round breasts. To the left of the pond stand the **Fontana di Proserpina** and the **Fontana della Civetta e degli Uccelli,** which is said to emit the chirps of birdsong. (Not to ruin the magic and mystery, but there are actually unseen pipes inside the fountain creating the peeps.) Across the ponds, is the behemoth **Fontana dell'Organo Idraulico,** which once used water pressure to power a hydraulic organ. It's connected to the fishponds below by the **Fountain of Neptune.**

VILLA GREGORIANA

🚺 *Follow the signs to the northern end of the city, along the bend in river, then cross the bridge. Open June-Aug. Tu-Su 9:30m-7:30pm; Sept.-May Tu-Su 9:30am-1hr. before sunset. L3500, under 12 L1000.*

The **Villa Gregoriana** is a park designed around a man-made waterfall by Pope Gregory XVI in 1835. There are several waterfalls and grottoes, but the star of the show is the Great Cascade, a thundering 160m waterfall. For the best view, bear right at the entrance. If you want more, follow the signs to **Grotta delle Sirene** and the **Grotta della Sibilla,** two natural grottoes carved out by the falls. Enjoy the long walk down (through some non-descript ruins) and try not to think about the taxing climb back up. The west exit leads you past the 2nd-century BC **Temple of Vesta** and the **Temple of Tiburnus.**

VITERBO

The quiet streets of Viterbo wind unexpectedly into quirky *piazze* and hidden stairwells, visible references to a medieval past. This city of 60,000 is perched high in the hills north of Rome, and is a cool refuge from the city's heat. Imposing walls still surround Viterbo, and even though the area near the train station looks like something out of a subtropical retirement subdivision, the walls shelter relics of its medieval grandeur. The city began as an Etruscan center but earned fame as the papal refuge from Frederick Barbarossa's siege of Rome in the 12th century. When Viterbo became a Guelph stronghold in the aristocrats' civil war, the (literally) torturous process of papal elections first took shape. The *capitano* (city dictator) locked the cardinals in their palace, threatening to cut off food deliveries and remove the roof from the conference room (so that cold could creep in), until they chose a new one. Today Viterbo serves as an induction point for Italian military draftees; the streets brim with more than their share of boys in uniform.

There aren't many tourists in Viterbo, but it still draws some curious (and perhaps ailing) sightseers to its sulphurous **Bulicane hot spring** (3km from the center), famous for its curative powers. During the winter, the soothing waters are used to fill a large public swimming pool. The city's cathedral and medieval remnants are also prime attractions.

GETTING THERE. The easiest way to get to Viterbo from Rome is to take the **train** from San Pietro station, the *capolinea* of bus #64 near the Vatican (hourly 5am-9pm each way; 1¾hr.; L6500). Viterbo's two stations are **Porta Romana** (near the historical district) and Porta Fiorentina (to the north). **Romana** is located two blocks north of Porta Romana on V. Romiti. The **bus station** is located just outside the northeast corner, on the Tangenziale Ovest near V. A. Volta. **Bus tickets** can be purchased at the *bigletteria* to the left of the bar in the parking lot of the bus station. (Open 7am-7pm.) Buses depart for Orvieto (1½hr., L6000), Civitavecchia (1¾hr., L6000), and Tarquinia (1hr., L5000).

ORIENTATION AND PRACTICAL INFORMATION. The neighborhoods of San Francesco and Santa Rosa are in the northern region (right inside **Porta Fiorentina**), San Sisto and San Pellegrino (the historical center) are in the southeast, and San Lorenzo is west of the center. **Piazza dei Caduti** is just north of **Piazza del Plebiscito** in the center of town. The **APT tourist office** is at P. San Carluccio, three blocks down V. San Lorenzo from the Cathedral. (☎0761 304795. Open M-F 9am-noon and 1pm-4pm, Sa 9am-1pm.)

FOOD. Local specialties include *lombriche* (a type of pasta) and a chestnut soup known as *zuppa di mosciarelle.* While these may sound innocuous, Viterbo's potables have a sinister bent. *Sambuca,* a sweet anise-flavored liqueur, is native to the city. Light it on fire, but blow it out before drinking. Also dangerously tasty is the local wine that goes by the name of *Est! Est!! Est!!!;* one happy German cardinal actually tippled himself to death on it (see p. 198 for the juicy details). Pope Martin IV experienced doom of a different sort—Dante postmarked him for purgatory—for his weakness for another local dish, the tasty roasted eel from Lake Bolsena.

For those with a taste for danger, *alimentari* can be found along V. dell'Orologio Vecchio, up one block up from P. del Plebiscito on C. Italia and right, and at the huge **outdoor market** in P. Martiri d'Ungheria, up V. Ascenzi from P. del Plebiscito. (Open Sa 7am-2pm.) Restaurants in the city are cheap and plentiful. **Trattoria L'Archetto,** V. San Cristoforo, 1, off V. A. Saffi and P. delle Erbe, makes local Italian delights that you can enjoy outside under a medieval arch. (☎0761 325769. *Primi* L7-10,000. Open M-Sa 10am-4pm and 7-9:30pm.) In the medieval neighborhood, tasty pizzas (L6-13,000) and a lively atmosphere are to be found at **Taverna del Padrino,** V.della Cava, 22. (Open daily 6:30pm-2am.)

SIGHTS. Viterbo's most interesting sight is the aforementioned 1267 **Palazzo dei Papi,** the site of three drawn-out papal conclaves. It is west of the center of town and there are plenty of signs for it. On the right side of the edifice is the impressive *loggia*, which has excellent views of the city. Inside is the **Museo d'Arte Sacra,** which contains 16th- and 17th-century religious paintings and sculptures. (Palazzo open M-Sa 10am-12:30pm. Museum open daily 9:45am-1pm. Free.) Next door looms the 13th-century (the facade is from 1570) **San Lorenzo Cathedral,** its *faux*-Sienese bell tower dominating the *piazza.*

Just inside the Porta Fiorentina and on the right is the imposing 14th-century **Rocca Albornoz,** home to the **Museo Archeologico Nazionale.** The museum spans the history of the area from Neolithic times to the Middle Ages, with particular emphasis on Etruscan settlements of the 6th and 7th centuries BC. (☎0761 325929. Open Tu-Su 9am-7pm. L4000.)

Beginning at P. Carlucci, two blocks down from the Cathedral, picturesque **V. San Pellegrino,** once the principal axis of medieval Viterbo. It's the parade route for the festival of Viterbo's patron saint, Santa Rosa, who is honored every September 3rd at 9pm, when 100 burly citizens carry the **Macchina di Santa Rosa,** a 30m illuminated tower of iron, wood, and paper-mâché, through the streets. The bearers lug the construction around town, then sprint uphill to the **Church of Santa Rosa,** in the northeast part of town, where the saint's 700-year-old body is preserved in a glass urn. (Open Th and Su 8:30am-12:30pm and 4-5:30pm.) In 1814, the *macchina* fell on the bearers, and in 1967 it had to be abandoned in the street because it was too heavy. The frenzied celebrations that accompany this event are well documented in the **Museo della Macchina di Santa Rosa,** V. S. Pellegrino, 60. (Open W-Su 10am-noon and 4-7pm. L3000.)

The medieval quarter's administrative center, **P. del Plebiscito,** occupies the southern end of town. The medallion-bedecked building with the tall clock tower is the **Palazzo del Popolo,** across from the **Palazzo della Prefettura.** Both are guarded by large, decidedly unfierce stone lions, symbols of Viterbo. Between them stands the **Palazzo Comunale.** The odd frescoes in its Sala Regia (painted in 1592) depict the history of Viterbo, mixing in Etruscan, classical, Christian, and medieval legends. Peek into the **Capella dei Priori** (because all they let you do is peek) on the right at the top of the stairs for Sebastiano del Piombo's compelling *Flagellation of Christ* and *Pietà.* Visit the *loggia* for a dazzling view of the community garden and the **Chiesa della Trinità.** (Open 8am-2pm. Free.)

Outside, across from the clock tower, the facade of the **Church of Sant'Angelo** incorporates a late Roman sarcophagus containing the body of the beautiful and virtuous Galiana. (Open daily 8am-noon and 4-6:30pm.) South of P. del Plebiscito, off V. San Lorenzo, is the 11th-century **Church of Santa Maria Nuova,** from the pulpit of which St. Thomas Aquinas once delivered a sermon. (Open M-Sa 10am-1pm and 4-7:30pm.)

Just a stone's throw down V. Cavour from P. del Plebiscito is **P. Fontana Grande,** which features (you guessed it) a big fountain dating from the beginning of the 13th century. Further down V. Garibaldi is the **Church of San Sisto,** which is built right into the medieval wall, on the site of a 9th-century pagan cult.

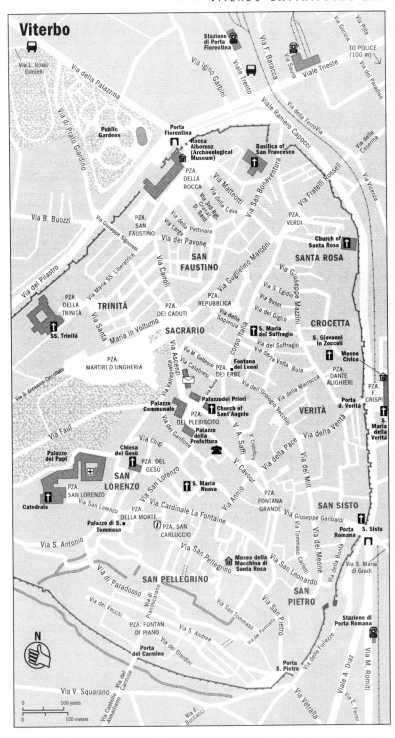

Viterbo

Via L. Rossi
Danielli

Via della Palazzina

Via di Prato Giardino

Public Gardens

Stazione di Porta Fiorentina

Via Igino Garbini

Viale Trento

Via F. Baracca

Via Sauro

Via Gonzia

Via Pola

Viale Trieste

Via del Paradiso

TO POLICE (100 m)

Viale Raniero Capocci

Via della Ferrovia

Porta Fiorentina

Rocca Albornoz (Archaeological Museum)

Basilica of San Francesco

Via della Caserma

PZA. DELLA ROCCA

Via Matteotti

Via San Bonaventura

Via Fratelli Rosselli

Via Vicenza

Via B. Buozzi

Via Giuseppe Signorelli

PZA. SAN FAUSTINO

Via della Cava

Via 3rd Reg. Granat. D. Sard.

Via della Pettinara

Via Tarqu

Via dei Pavone

PZA. VERDI

Church of Santa Rosa

Via del Pilastro

Via Maria SS. Liberatrice

Via Caroli

SAN FAUSTINO

Via Guglielmo Marconi

SANTA ROSA

Via Giuseppe Mazzini

PZA. DELLA TRINITÀ

TRINITÀ

PZA. DEI CADUTI

PZA. REPUBBLICA

Via S. Egidio

Via Bussi

Via dei Giglio

CROCETTA

SS. Trinitá

Via Santa Maria in Volturno

SACRARIO

Via della Sapienza

Corso Italia

S. Maria del Suffragio

Via del Suffragio

S. Giovanni in Zoccoli

PZA. MARTIRI D'UNGHERIA

Via S. Giovanni Decollato

Via M Gattesco

Via Ascenzi

Via Calabresi

PZA. DEI ERBE

Fontana dei Leoni

Via della Volta Buia

Museo Civico

PZA. DANTE ALIGHIERI

PZA. F. CRISPI

Via Faul

Via Roma

Palazzodei Priori

Via dell'Orologio Vecchio

Via della Marrocca

S. Maria della Verità

Palazzo Communale

Church of Sant'Angelo

VERITÀ

PZA. DEL PLEBISCITO

Palazzo della Prefettura

V. A. Saffi

V. Cristoforo

Via della Venta

Porta d. Verità

S. Maria della Verità

Palazzo dei Papi

Chiesa del Gesù

Via Chigi

Via del Ganfione

PZA. DEL GESÙ

V. Cavour

Via della Pace

Via del Mili

Catedrale

PZA. SAN LORENZO

SAN LORENZO

Via San Lorenzo

S. Maria Nuova

Via Annio

SAN SISTO

Via San Lorenzo

Via Cardinale La Fontaine

PZA. FONTANA GRANDE

Via Giuseppe Garibaldi

Porta Romana

S. Sisto

Palazzo di S. Tommaso

PZA. DELLA MORTE

PZA. SAN CARLUCCIO

Via S. Antonio

Via San Pellegrino

Museo della Macchina di Santa Rosa

Via Tommaso Calisiti

Via del Meone

Via della Bonta

Via S. Maria di Gradi

Via di Paradosso

SAN PELLEGRINO

Via di Pianoscarano

Via San Leonardo

SAN PIETRO

Via dei Vecchi

Via San Pietro

Via San Tommaso

Via San Pietro

Via del Ponticello

Stazione di Porta Romana

PZA. FONTAN DI PIANO

Via S. Andrea

Via dei Giardini

Via A. Diaz

Via M. Romiti

N

Porta del Carmine

Porta S. Pietro

Via della Fortezze

Viale A. Diaz

Via del Carmine

Via V. Squarano

Via F. Boccacci

Via Vetralla

Via E. Fermi

Via Castello Almadiano

0   100 yards
0   100 meters

the BIG $plurge

Hotel Chiaia di Luna (☎0771 80113; fax 0771 809821). Above the beach bearing the same name. The views and service here are worth the extra cost; many rooms overlook the awe-inspiring Chiaia di Luna. All quarters with private bath, TV, phone, and elegant hardwood furniture; some have balconies. Also enjoy the large swimming pool and terrace below. Breakfast included; half board available. Van service to and from the port at arrival/departure and every morning. Rooms L90-180,000 per person per night, depending on the season; single rooms pay 50% surcharge.

Ristorante Acqua Pazza, P. Carlo Pisacane, 10 (☎0771 80643). Pass a truly unforgettable evening under the awnings of Acqua Pazza. Savor the excellent seafood on beautiful blue and yellow place settings overlooking the harbor. Quite possibly one of the best restuarants on the island, though the bill reflects this fact. Booked solid almost every night in high season; reserve in advance. *Primi* L15-25,000 (including great *linguini ai scampi e gamberi*, L22,000), *secondi* are bought by the *etto*: L7-8000 for most whole fish, L20,000 per fillets; expect a whole fish to cost L35-L40,000. Pane L3000; servizio 10%. Open daily 8pm-"until we finish." AmEx, MC, V.

CASTELLI ROMANI

◪ *Blue COTRAL buses from Anagnina Station at the end of Metro Linea A run to Frascati (every 30 min. 5:30am-10:30pm, on weekends every 1½hr.; L2400) and Albani (every 30min., L2000). Trains from Termini connect Rome to Frascati and Albano (departures throughout the day; L3200), but take longer than the bus. For bus travel between the Castelli Romani, ask at the tourist offices in the region's towns.*

Overlooking Rome from the Alban hills, the Castelli Romani are famed for their Renaissance villas and their white wine. Fortunately, the pace of life has slowed since the good old days, when feuding families built foreboding forts and slung insults across the hills.

FRASCATI

◪ *The bus driver will let you off at the bus depot in P. Marconi, the town center and train station. The tourist office, P. Marconi, 1 (☎06 9420331), is across the street, next to the town hall. Open M-F 8am-2pm and 4-7pm, Sa 8am-2pm; in winter M-F 8am-2pm and 3:30-6:30pm.*

From its lofty position on an ancient volcanic ridge, Frascati has attracted fugitives from the summer heat for centuries. Frascati's patrician villas and famed fruity, dry white wines remain two of the town's finest attractions. Those lucky enough to be in Frascati in October or November can get caught up in the fevered dipsomania of the annual **vendemmia**, the celebration of the grape harvest.

The 1598 **Villa Aldobrandini** dominates the hill over town. Up V. Catone from P. Marconi, hang a right onto V. G. Massaia, which leads to the Renaissance *villa* and its sculpture-filled gardens, Bernini fountains, and panoramic views of town. (Open M-F 9am-1pm and 3:30-6pm; winter M-F 9am-1pm. Ask for a free pass in the tourist office.)

About 1km uphill from the *villa* on G. Massaia is the tiny **Chiesa dei Cappuccini,** which houses the unique **Ethiopian Museum,** built in honor of Cardinal Massaia, who spent 35 years as a missionary in Ethiopia. The museum houses a collection of weapons, handmade crafts, and the cardinal's personal paraphernalia, including his death mask. (☎06 9420400. Open daily 9am-noon and 3-6pm. Free.) Frascati also has a 17th-century **duomo,** which was reconstructed due to extensive war damage, and the **Chiesa del Gesù,** an intricately decorated church worth a brief exterior look.

From the entrance of the Villa Aldobrandini, turn right onto V. Tuscolo, which climbs 5km over winding country roads to reach the ruins of **Tusculum,** an ancient resort that hosted such Roman luminaries as Cato and Cicero. The town was destroyed in 1191 during a feud between its residents and the Romans, but the ruins and view make the ghost town worth the climb. Check at the tourist office in Frascati to see if tours are being given; if not, ask for a map. The **citadel** of Tusculum, marked by an iron cross at the hill's summit, affords a 360° view of southern Lazio, with Rome to the right, the Tyrrhenian Sea in front, and the extinct volcano Monte Cavo to the left.

Ethiopians and churches not withstanding, the main attraction here is still wine. Pick up a bottle and other picnic supplies at the market at P. del Mercato, off P. del Duomo (open M-Sa 9am-noon), or try **Trattoria Sora Irma,** V. S.S. Filippo e Giacomo, 12. The restaurant is situated above the center of Frascati. From P. Marconi, take a left up the steps of V. Pietro Campana; V. S.S. Filippo e Giacomo is on your left. The local specialty is *porchetta*, a greasy, sliced, fried pork dish said to complement the fine Frascati vintages perfectly. (Open W-Su 11am-3pm and 7-11pm.) Another place to soak up the local culture—and wine—is at the **Cantina Il Pergolato,** V. del Castello, 20, off P. del Mercato. It serves homemade wine, pizza, and other fare in a cave-like dining room. (☎ 06 9420464. Open daily 12:30-2:30pm and 3:30-6:30pm.) **Zaraza,** V. R. Margherita, 2, is another *trattoria* with simple, good food for low prices. (Open Tu-Su noon-3pm and 7:30-11pm.)

LAKE ALBANO & LAKE NEMI

🚌 *From Frascati, take a bus marked "Albano" from P. Marconi (hourly, 6:35am-8:35pm). The bus should let you off in P. Mazzini, the center of Albano. Free map from tourist office, V. Risorgimento, 1 (☎ 06 9324082; fax 06 9320040) is north of the piazza. Open M-F 9am-1pm and 4-7pm, Sa 9am-noon.*

A few kilometers across the hills from Frascati, the other Castelli Romani cling to the sides of an extinct volcanic crater, now filled with the shimmering blue waters of **Lago Albano,** one of Lazio's cleanest and chilliest swimming spots. Crisp wines, clear mountain views, and a taste of Italian country life are the main attractions among these *castelli*. An outdoor market in P. Luigi Sabatini (down C. Matteoti and up the stairs from P. Mazzini), sells the region's fruits, vegetables, and gigantic fish. (Open M-Sa 7am-2pm.)

North of the P. Mazzini, artifacts and pictorial reconstructions of the Paleolithic through Renaissance ages gathered in Albano and surrounding areas are housed in the **Museo Civico,** V. Risorgimento, 3, next to the tourist office. (☎ 06 9323490. Open daily 8:30am-noon, W-Th 4-7pm. L4000, over 60 L3000.)

CASTEL GANDOLFO. North of Albano, tiny **Castel Gandolfo** owes its fame to the Pope, who occupies its volcanic ridge in the summer. He likes to stop by when the Vatican gets too stifling to enjoy his famed gardens, which spread down the outer rim of the crater toward the sea. The palace is topped by a modern dome, the center of the old Vatican Observatory. The town's public street and one tiny *piazza*, dominated by Maderno's early Baroque papal palace, offer glimpses of the lake and mountain scenery which have drawn pontiffs here for centuries. The *piazza* also houses the **Church of San Tommaso di Villanova,** an early work by Bernini, along with a Bernini fountain. A lake road opens out to several belvederes, from which you can catch better views of Lake Albano. A winding road leads down to a public beach (about 2km), where you can rent sailboats. Buses go to the beach from Castel Gandolfo and Albano (every 1-1½hr., L1200).

ARICCIA. South of Albano, the same lake road passes a spacious park (open Apr.-Sept. 8am-7pm; Oct.-May 8am-5pm) and the curious **Tomb of the Horatii and Curiatii,** a Republican-age funeral monument believed to mark the graves of the famous triplets whose duel secured Rome's supremacy over ancient Alba Longa. Ariccia, 1km east of Albano on the same road, isn't noted for much other than the soaring viaduct that brings you into town. Its *piazza* is graced by the remains of a Republican temple, the medieval **Palazzo Chigi** (spruced up by Bernini in the 17th century), and—for the obsessive Bernini fan—another minor Bernini original, the round **Santa Maria dell'Assunzione.**

NEMI. From Ariccia, the road continues south to Lake Nemi, another flooded crater. Ancient Romans, marveling at Nemi's placid blue waters, called the lake "the Mirror of Diana" and graced its sloping shores with a **temple** to the goddess. Surrounded by a sacred grove, the temple was presided over by a eunuch priest who got his job by killing his predecessor and plucking a golden bough off one of the grove's trees. At Genzano, take the COTRAL bus across the lake to secluded Nemi (L1500), where life is a little more tranquil than in other, more touristed *castelli*. The village boasts more staircases

CULT OF SAN SILVERIO

Prominently displayed near the cash registers and by the corners and crossroads of much of Ponza is San Silverio, aged graybeard and martyr of choice in the Pontine archipelago. Who is this saintly man, you ask? Ah. Silverio was a minor deacon when a web of intrigue propelled by the Ostrogothic king Theoda had him elected as pope in 536 to keep the Goths in charge. The angry empress Theodora sent her husband Justinian's general to convince him to stand down. When Silverio refused, forged letters of plots between the pope and the Goths were suddenly brought to light. Poor Silverio was summarily degraded to the rank of monk, deposed in a hasty trial, forced to sign an abdication by his successor pope, and sent into exile on the island of Pomarola, just off the coast of Ponza, where he soon died of starvation and the hearty island life. His grave quickly became a center of miracles and cures for the faithful *Pontinesi*, who encouraged the Vatican to have him elevated to sainthood in the 11th century. His image is still enthusiastically plastered about the islands; his somewhat dubious memory is celebrated on June 20th and February 2nd.

than streets, but miniature strawberries *(fragoline di Nemi)*, grown along the lake's shores, are its real glory. A bowl filled with the tiny fruits, soaked in lemon juice, and topped with a dollop of fresh *panna* (cream) is a specialty at bars lining the belvedere overlooking the lake. In late June and early July, the town hosts a strawberry festival.

The **Nemi Museum of Ships** is 15 minutes down the road from Nemi. The museum was built to house two Roman barges that were dredged from the lake, but the ships were torched by the Nazis as they retreated from Italy, so the museum displays two scale models and the few bits of lead and bronze that weren't melted in the blaze. (Open Tu-Su 9am-2pm. L8000, EU citizens under 12 free.)

ROCCA DI PAPA. The lake road continues north to the summit of Monte Cavo, where Rocca di Papa, the highest of the Castelli Romani, glowers over Lake Albano. The town doesn't offer much in the way of architecture, but the views of the lake are the reason for the hike. On the other side of Monte Cavo, Marino closes the circle of *castelli* to the north. If you're in town on the first Sunday in October, you'll see the town's fountains flowing with wine during the annual Sagra dell'Uva; otherwise, Marino's a good place to make COTRAL bus connections back to Rome (L2000).

PONTINE ISLANDS

One of the most beautiful destinations in Lazio, the Pontine Islands are literally legendary. The largest island in the volcanic archipelago, Ponza, was the Homeric isle of Eea, home of the sorceress Circe and of the temporarily porcine crew of Odysseus. To the east, smaller Ventotene was reputedly the Isle of the Sirens.

You can understand the pull of the Sirens' call as soon as you catch sight of the islands, which can take your breath away. The Pontines contain stunning, cliff-sheltered beaches connected by rugged Mediterranean coastline knifing into the clean, turquoise-blue water of the Tyrrhenian. Coves, natural harbors, and beautiful grottoes cut from the volcanic stone appear around every turn of the tortuously winding roads.

The *Pontinesi* know that the fastest way to your heart is through your stomach. Following in the grand tradition of the generations of fishermen inhabiting the isles, you can feast famously on fresh seafood. After a long day taking in the sun and surf, there is nothing better than a dinner overlooking the water.

Though the 60-mile boat trip here will be somewhat pricey, it is an excellent alternative to Capri and Ischia, as it is less crowded, less expensive, and just as pretty. On the other hand, an actual daytrip is not recommended; stay at least one night to make the time and money spent getting here worthwhile.

GETTING THERE. Several companies run *aliscafi* (hydrofoils) and the slower, cheaper *traghetti* (larger car ferries) to the Pontine Islands. **From Rome,** the best option is taking the train from Termini to Anzio (L5100) and then the **CAREMAR** ferry. The ticket office is in the white booth on the quay. (Anzio ☎ 06 98600083, Ponza ☎ 0771 80565; caremar.gestelnet.it; L42,200 roundtrip). **Linee Vetor** only uses *aliscafi* and has offices on the Anzio quay (Anzio ☎ 06 9845083, Ponza ☎ 0771 80549; www.vetor.it; L35,000 one-way). Both companies also offer many options from **Formia.**

Anzio-Ponza: CAREMAR ferries from Anzio during the summertime, Th-Tu 8:10am and 2pm, W 8:10am; ferries from Ponza, M-Tu, Th-Su 11:00am and 5pm, W 5pm only; 2½hr. Linee Vetor hydrofoils year-round; from June-Sept. M-F 3 per day, Sa-Su 5 per day, 8:30am-5:30pm; 75min.

Ponza-Ventotene: CAREMARE hydrofoil from Ponza, daily (except Su Oct.-Apr.) 6:10am; from Ventotene, 4pm (daily, except Su Oct-Apr.; Apr. 15-Oct. 15 also 7:10pm); 35min.; L20,000.

PONZA

The craggy cliffs of this paradisical island were created in the late Tertiary, when volcanic activity thrust the precipices up out of the water over the course of three million years. Imperial Romans built a port and fortifications on this island, known as Circide or Enotria. The collapse of Roman order severely depopulated the islands, and until the arrival of the Bourbons in 1734, the island was in the hands of pirates, who used its few inhabitants as chattel when they could catch them. Mussolini used Ponza as a depository for dissenters, and in a beautiful piece of historical irony, was imprisoned here himself for two weeks in summer 1943. The island sustains a yearly invasion of tourists and, at times, Italian celebrities looking for fun in the sun. The pace of life is still slow, however, and you won't feel as overrun by daytripping tourists from Naples as you might in Capri.

PRACTICAL INFORMATION

In Ponza, the laid-back island lifestyle has resulted in a happy disregard for street signs, addresses, or maps. There are only a handful of streets and addresses you'll ever need to know: **Via Dante,** which runs along the docks; **Corso Pisacane,** which runs along the port above them; **Via Molo Musco,** the road jutting into the port where the Vetor hydrofoils arrive; and **Piazza Carlo Pisacane,** where V. Molo Muscolo meets C. Pisacane. Everything you might ever want is on the docks or close to them, and the locals are friendly and more than helpful in showing you the way, even if they don't know English. For a surfeit of information, pick up a free copy of *Ponza e le Altre Isole* at most any locale on the island. *Isole Pontine*, a comprehensive guide to the islands is L12,000 at newsstands.

Buses: Autolinee Ponzesi, leaving from V. Dante. Follow C. Pisacane until it becomes V. Dante (past the tunnel); stop is to your left. Buses circuit the island every 15-20min. until 1am (buy tickets from the driver, L1750). The buses stop by request, so be sure to flag them down at stops.

Taxis: Private taxis are available for speedier transport; look for one near the main bus stand or pick up a list of phone numbers at the tourist office. Water taxis go to beaches and harbors around the island (from L6000 roundtrip); find them near the docks. Be sure to set a pick-up time with the driver.

Tourist Office: Pro Loco, V. Molo Musco (☎ 0771 80031; email prolocoponza@libero.it), at the far right of the port, next to the lighthouse, in the long red building. Offers "alternative" tours of the island's many Roman and Bourbon-era archaeological sites; call or write ahead for information. Open daily M-Sa 9am-12:50pm and 4-7:30pm, Su 9am-1pm.

Banks: Banco di Napoli, P. Pisacane (☎ 0771 80106). Open M-F 9am-1pm. **ATMs** accepting credit cards and Cirrus at **Banco di Napoli** and **Monte Paschi di Siena,** C. Pisacane, 85.

Luggage Storage: Isotur, C. Pisacane, 18. Reasonable prices.

Emergencies: ☎ 113.

Police station: V. Molo Musco (☎ 0771 80130).

Pharmacy: Farmacia Mazzella, P. Piscane (☎0771 80708). Open M-Sa 9am-8:30pm. **Farmacia Tagliamonte** (☎0771 80633). On V. Dante, near tunnel. Open Tu-Su 8am-1pm and 5pm-9pm.

First Aid: Località Tre Venti (☎0771 80687). Emergency care available at **Ospedale Poliambulatorio,** V. Tre Venti (☎0771 80687).

Post Office: P. Pisacane (☎0771 80672). Open M-F 8:15am-1:30pm, Sa 8:15am-noon. **Postal code:** 04027.

ACCOMMODATIONS & FOOD

Though sleeping on the beach is tempting, camping on Ponza is illegal. A room in a private home is the cheapest option (as low as L45,000 per person per night in the high season), since hotel rooms tend to be a bit more expensive than a typical *pensione* in Rome. The tourist office has a list of over ten helpful agencies that can assist you in finding a room; or try **Agenzia Immobiliare "Arcipelago Pontino,"** C. Pisacane, 49. (☎0771 80678. Open daily 9am-1pm and 4:30-8:30pm.)

Hotels are cheapest near the port, though rooms with a view on the top of the island's many mountains may be worth the splurge. Reserve a room well in advance during the high season. To get to **Pensione-Ristorante Arcobaleno,** V. Scotti D. Basso, 6, go straight up the ramp, follow the street until it ends, then veer right until you pass the Bellavista Hotel. Turn left and follow the signs up, up, up. When you reach the summit, you'll understand why you came: wonderful people, immaculate rooms with televisions and bath, a lovely garden terrace, and some of the best views in Ponza. Reservations may save you the aforementioned ascent: Arcobaleno offers a free car service up the hill for guests. Half-board mandatory, but the food is excellent. (☎0771 80315. L100,000 per person; July-Aug. L120,000. V.) The islands are known and loved for their lentil soup, fish, and spiny lobster. Restaurants and bars line the port and are also scattered around the little highway that circles the island; eat some seafood! You're not going to find it any fresher unless you go out and net it yourself. For grocery and fruit stores, take a stroll along any road.

SIGHTS

Excellent beaches are everywhere on Ponza. Cala dello Schiavone and Cala Cecata (on the bus line) are excellent spots. Water taxis (L6000) are available to the beach of Frontone on the east side of the island, as well as such unspoiled beaches as Core, Arco Naturale, and Punta della Madonna. Set a pick-up time with the driver. Additionally, the tourist office offers tours of the sites on the island.

You can rent kayaks, paddle-boats, motorized rafts, scuba gear, and more almost anywhere along the port. **Ponza Mare,** V. Banchina Nuova (☎0771 80679; www.giglio.net/Ponza) offers an especially large variety of rentals. **Scuola Sub "Nautilus"** (☎0771 808701) at Piscine Naturali gives scuba lessons.

PALMAROLA. Palmarola is an uninhabited islet perched off the northeast coast of the island and is accessible only by boat. Either rent one (from L65,000 per day) or sign up for a guided boat tour (about L45,000 per person). At the port, look for one of the innumerable offices offering *una gita* (JEE-tah) *a Palmarola*. The clear, turquoise water, irregular volcanic rock formations, and steep white cliffs (tinted red by iron deposits and yellow by sulphur) of the island are incredible. As you approach Palmarola, you will see Dala Brigantina, a natural amphitheater of limestone. Also visible are houses built directly into the mountainside, in sites inhabited by people since prehistoric times. Most excursions also visit the Pilatus Caves at Ponza, a breeding ground for fish.

ZANNONE. Another great boat destination is Zannone, a nature and wildlife preserve and part of the National Park of Circeo. Tours will usually take you around the coast and lead you on walks through the *lecci* forests to the large monastery of S. Spirito, and through areas populated by *mufloni*. The opportunity to see a Mediterranean island in its natural state is rare and a refreshing break from sunbathing, especially if you are a nature-lover.

ONSHORE DESTINATIONS. Superlative onshore destinations include **Chiaia di Luna.** Take a 10-minute walk from the port to this spectacular beach and its dramatic, audibly eroding cliffs. Go down C. Pisacane and turn left before reaching the tunnel. Soon, a path to the left will lead you under the road and through a series of tunnels to the beach. A sheer wall of *tufo* rises 20 feet from the water's edge. The rocky beach still provides ample room for sunbathing, though it does get crowded. Showers, L2000.

Don't miss **Piscine Naturali,** perhaps the most beautiful swimming spot on the island. (Take the bus to Le Forna and ask to be let off at the Piscine. Cross the street and make a long descent down a steep path.) Though not quite as visually striking from afar as Chiaia di Luna, the Piscine's steep cliffs plunge directly into the ocean, creating a series of deep, crystal-clear natural pools separated by a smooth rocky outcropping perfect for sunbathing. Rumor has it that there are spots for cliff-diving in the area, though Let's Go does not officially recommend throwing yourself off of a 15m cliff. Locals know the right spots; jump at your own risk. One word of **caution:** spiny sea urchins line the rocks.

Pompeii

Inside Pompeii

Pottery

VENTOTENE

i ***Tourist office,*** *Centro Servizio Ventotene, Località Porto Romano (☎0771 85273; fax 0771 854107; open daily 9am-1pm and 4:30-7pm, in winter generally 4-7pm) is at the port (follow the "i" signs), and managed by an affable English-speaking staff. You'll be happier if you reserve in advance during July and August. In the port, motor* ***boat rentals*** *run from L60,000, rowboats from L20,000.*

Far less accessible than Ponza (and freer of the summer vacationing hordes) Ventotene is more striking, too. Here, the island lifestyle is untainted even by the roar of engines—cars and *motorini* are forbidden; the only flourishing homage to internal combustion is the outboard motor. In the past it's been the legendary home of the Sirens, a Roman port, a refuge for pirates, and a place of exile for Fascist-era political prisoners; today Ventotene awaits you with the last vestiges of untouristed peace near Rome.

The **Archaeological Museum** of Ventotene covers everything from Roman ruins and underwater archaeology techniques to the prison Mussolini built here for "enemies of the state." (Call the Comune di Ventotene to arrange a visit at 0771 85193. L4000.) The tourist office also arranges Italian-language tours of archaeological sites, including the **Villa Giulia** (a well-preserved villa where Augustus exiled his daughter, Giulia, for crimes of indecency, L6-8000), the prehistoric **Necropoli** (L6-8000), and the **Carcere of Santo Stefano,** the citadel where Mussolini enjoyed locking up anti-fascists (about L18,000, includes roundtrip boat ride). Splendid beaches flank the port.

ETRURIA

Welcome to Etruscanland, former home of a mythologized tribe that has fascinated scholars and artists from Herodotus to D. H. Lawrence. The Etruscans, who dominated north-central Italy from the 9th to the first century BC, gave Rome much of its early art and architecture. Since the Etruscans' buildings were wood, only their carved-out tufa tombs survive. Tomb paintings (at Tarquinia) celebrate life, love, eating, drinking, and sport in the hilly countryside. Tombs are visible in Cerveteri and Tarquinia, although most of the artifacts found therein are in the **Villa Giulia** (see p. 151) and other museums.

CERVETERI

▓ Blue **COTRAL** buses run to Cerveteri from Lepanto (**M**:A-Lepanto or bus #70) in Rome (every 30min.-1hr., L4900). Last bus to Rome leaves 8:05pm; ask at the station. Fewer buses run on Sundays. From the village, it's 1.5km to the necropolis along a country road; follow the signs downhill and then to the right. Whenever you see a fork in the road without a sign to guide you, choose the fork on the right, but don't follow the "Da Paolo Vino" sign at the final fork. **Tourist office**, V. della Necropoli, 2, will answer any queries. (☎06 9952304. Open Tu-Su 9:30am-12:30pm and 6-7:30pm.)

Kysry, the Etruscan town once located here, was a port that conducted a lively trade business throughout the Mediterranean from the 7th to 5th century BC. The town was much larger than is visible from the excavated area; archeologists estimate that Kysry was about 20 times larger than modern Cerveteri.

The bulbous earthen tombs of the **Banditaccia Necropolis** slumber in the tufa bedrock. The simple chambers are carved to resemble the wooden huts in which Etruscans once resided. Archaeologists have removed the objects of daily life (chariots, weapons, cooking implements) with which the dead were equipped, but the carved tufa columns and couches remain. Small rooms off each tomb's antechamber were the resting places of slaves and lesser household members; the central room held the bodies of the rest of the family, and the small chambers off the back were reserved for the most prominent men and women. A triangular headboard on a couch marks a woman's grave, a circular one indicates a man's. Only some 50 of an estimated 5000 tombs have been excavated, mostly in a cluster of narrow streets at the heart of this city of the dead. Don't miss the **Tomb of the Shields and the Chairs,** the smaller **Tomb of the Alcove** (with a carved-out matrimonial bed), and the row houses where less well-to-do Etruscans rested in peace. Look for the colored stucco reliefs in the **Tomba dei Rilievi.** (☎06 9940001. Open May-Sept. Tu-Su 9am-7:30pm; Oct.-Apr. Tu-Sa 9am-4pm. L8000.)

Also worthwhile is the **Museo Nazionale di Caerite,** on the P. Santa Maria Maggiore, in **Ruspoli Castle,** a fairy-tale edifice of ancient walls and crenellations, next to the bus stop in town. The museum displays such Etruscan artifacts as painted vases and funerary statues that have been dug from the necropolis in the last 10 years (most of the rest reside in the Etruscan museums of the Villa Giulia and the Vatican). (☎06 9941354. Open May-Sept. Tu-Su 9am-7pm; Oct.-Apr. Tu-Sa 9am-4pm. Free.)

TARQUINIA

▓ **Trains** leave from Termini (1hr., 11 per day; last train leaves Tarquinia at 10:12pm, L10,200). **Buses** run from the train station to the beach (L1100) and to the city center (L1500) about every 30min. until 9:30pm. Buses also link the town with Viterbo (1hr., L6000). For bus schedules and info on southern Etruria, try the **tourist office** in P. Cavour, near the medieval walls. (☎0766 856384. Open M-Sa 8am-2pm and 4-7pm.)

When Rome was naught but a village of mud huts on the Palatine Hill, Tarquin kings held the fledgling metropolis under their sway. Although little remains today of the once-thriving Etruscan city, a subterranean **necropolis** of tombs lined with vibrant frescoes tells the tale of this city's ancient history.

Buses stop just outside the medieval ramparts. Just inside P. Cavour is the majestic **Museo Nazionale,** one of the most comprehensive collections of Etruscan art outside of Rome. It houses a superb collection of Etruscan sarcophagi (some with bright paintings still visible), votive statues, and an enormous range of Etruscan and (occasionally sexy) Greek vases. Look for the famous 4th-century BC terra cotta **Winged Horses** upstairs (☎0766 856036. Museum open Tu-Su 9am-7pm. L12000.)

The museum ticket will admit you to the **necropolis.** Take the bus marked "Cimitero" from just outside the gate or walk (15min.) from the museum. Head up C. V. Emanuele from P. Cavour and turn right on V. Porta Tarquinia (V. delle Tombe Etruschi). Because of the tombs' sensitivity to air and moisture, only nine are open to the public. Nevertheless, the visit is worth it for the fascinating and realistic paintings, sketched in warm red, yellow, and green pigments with beautiful twisting lines. D. H. Lawrence's section on Tarquinia in *Etruscan Places* will give you a picture of the tombs before they were museumified. (☎ 0766 856308. Open 9am-1hr. before sunset.)

Tarquinia's medieval churches also merit a look. Don't miss **San Pancrazio,** with its spiny-egg tower, or **San Martino,** with its simple interior and Romanesque arches. The most interesting church, the crumbling **Santa Maria del Castello,** must be reached by the old city bastions overgrown with climbing honeysuckle. The asymmetrical facade is due to the fact that the 12th-century church was built over the foundations of an earlier edifice. The white marble flooring, inscribed with cabalistic pictures, can still be seen at the edges of the later multi-colored mosaic. Ask the custodian to unlock the church doors—she lives to the left of the church.

Most restaurants here are expensive and tourist-oriented. One exception is the excellent **Le Due Orfanelle,** V. Breve, 4, near the Church of San Francesco. (☎ 0766 856307. Open W-M noon-3pm and 7:30-11pm.)

LAKE BRACCIANO

⚑ *By train, Anguillara and Bracciano are accessible by the Rome-Viterbo line (every hr.; from Rome's San Pietro station 5:35am-9:45pm, last train to Rome 10:14pm; L5300).*

Lake Bracciano provides Rome with its nearest freshwater beach, about an hour away by bus. Despite recent pollution, a meager shore and volcanic, gravelly sand that may hurt your rear, this huge body of water is still well worth a visit. Fresh air, cool water, and a lush and hilly surrounding landscape compensate for its minor flaws. An impressive medieval castle dominates the town, whose many *trattorie* cook up mounds of fresh lake fish and eel (the local specialty), though siestas often go a little overboard, and hours of operation are inconsistent. Down at the beach, a ferry ride across the lake to nearby Anguillara or Trevignano offers more spectacular scenery.

To get to Bracciano's main attraction, the **Orsini-Odescalchi Castle,** take V. A. Fausti from P. Roma to V. Umberto and turn right. The castle was built in the late 15th century for the Orsini, an ancient, independent-minded Roman family who managed to provoke (and withstand) the jealous rages of a succession of autocratic Renaissance popes. Even Cesare Borgia, Alexander VI's Machiavellian son and commander-in-chief, never breached the castle's towers (the castle only succumbed in the 1670s, when the Odescalchi family tried a more powerful weapon—cash). Inside, a series of salons and chambers wraps around two medieval courtyards, their walls and ceilings frescoed with the Orsini arms and with a few stellar cycles by Antoniazzo Romano (a pupil of Pinturicchio), Taddeo, and Federico Zuccari. The rooms also house an impressive collection of arms and armor and a **furry collection** of stuffed wild boars. (☎ 06 99804348. Open Apr.-Sept. Tu-F 10am-noon and 3-6pm; Oct.-Mar. Tu-F 10am-noon and 3-5pm, Sa 10am-12:30pm and 3-5:30pm, Su 10am-12:40pm and 3-5:40pm. Tours every hour. L11,000, children under 12 and military L9000.) In the summer, **classical music concerts** are hosted inside the castle.

To get to the lake from the castle (about 1km), head down V. Umberto and turn right, following the signs. Take the path on the right when the fork in the road comes up, and follow it down until it makes a left. To the right, there should be a small steep footpath down a dusty hill. The lake is visible from the base of this footpath. Rough sand stretches in both directions, and stands rent **canoes** (L10-20,000 per hr.) and umbrellas (L5000).

Numerous lakeside restaurants serve generally adequate pastas and tasty lake fish for reasonable prices. *Gelaterias* and a video arcade also tempt those bored by sunburning their skin off, a little further down along the coast.

CAMPANIA

The fertile crescent of Campania, in the shadow of Mt. Vesuvius, cradles the Bay of Naples and the larger Gulf of Salerno. The fiery fields of Hades to the west and the ruins of Pompeii hiding beneath the crater captivate visitors year after year.

POMPEII (POMPEI)

🗹 *The easiest way to get to Pompeii is to take one of many Rome-based bus tours.* **Enjoy Rome**'s self-guided tour (p. 14) is a deal at L70,000 per person. On your own from Termini, take the train to Naples (every 15min.-1hr., 6:10am-10:30pm, L18,600-39,500). From there, take the Circumvesuviana train (☎081 7722111), getting off at "Pompeii Scavi/Villa dei Misteri" (ignore "Pompeii Santuario"). Eurailpasses are not valid. Stop by the **tourist office**, V. Sacra, 1, for a free map. (☎081 8507255. Open M-F 8am-3:30pm, Sa 8am-2pm.) Store your pack for free at the entrance to the ruins. There is a **police station** at the entrance to the ancient site, but the main station is at P. Schettini, 1 (☎081 8506164), in the modern town, on the corner of P. B. Longo, at the end of V. Roma. Food at the ruins cafeteria is horribly expensive, so bring a lunch. Of the few restaurants and fruit stands that cluster outside the excavation entrances, the best is **La Vinicola**, V. Roma, 29 (☎081 863 12 44; cover L1500; open daily 9am-11pm). Site **open** 9am-1hr. before sunset: in summer around 7pm; in winter around 3pm. **Admission** L16,000. **Guidebooks** from L8000. Useful **audioguide** recommended. A comprehensive exploration of Pompeii will probably take all day.

On August 24, AD 79, life in the prosperous Roman city of Pompeii suddenly halted. A fit of towering flames, suffocating black clouds, and seething lava from Mt. Vesuvius buried the city—temples, villas, theaters, and all—under more than 7m of volcanic ash. Except for the few lucky ones who dropped everything and ran at the first tremors of catastrophe, the inhabitants of Pompeii suffered a live burial. Perhaps the most ghastly and evocative relics of the town's untimely death are the "frozen people," ash casts made of the victims' bodies, preserving their last contortions and expressions of horror. These amazing exhibits are visible (in glass cases) all over the ancient site. The excavation of Pompeii is ongoing, so many sights are poorly labeled. (Hey, it could be worse— you could be trapped under molten lava for 2000 years.) Since the first unearthings in 1748, every decade has brought new discoveries to light, slowly creating a vivid picture of life in the ancient Roman era.

▨ **FORUM.** To the right of the Porta Marina entrance, the **basilica** (law court) walls are decorated with stucco made to look like marble. Walk farther down V. D. Marina to reach the Forum, which is surrounded by a colonnade. Once dotted with statues of emperors and gods, this site was the commercial, civic, and religious center of the city. Cases along the near side display some of the gruesome body-casts of the volcano's victims. At the upper end rises the **Temple of Jupiter**, mostly destroyed by an earthquake that struck 17 years before the city's bad luck got worse. To the left, the **Temple of Apollo** contains statues of Apollo and Diana (the originals are in Naples's Museo Archeologico Nazionale) and a column topped by a sundial. On the opposite long side of the forum, the **Temple of Vespatian** houses a delicate frieze depicting preparation for a sacrifice. To the right, the **Building of Eumachia** has a carved door frame of animals and insects hiding in acanthus scrolls.

▨ **VILLA OF THE MYSTERIES.** To reach the Villa of the Mysteries, go to the far west end of V. della Fortuna, turn right on V. Consolare, and walk all the way up Porta Ercolano. The best preserved of Pompeii's villas, it includes the Dionysiac Frieze (perhaps the largest painting from the ancient world), which depicts the initiation of a bride into the cult of Dionysus. Head through the door in the Porta for a great view of the entire city.

ANCIENT ROMAN HOUSES. Exit the Forum through the upper end, by the cafeteria, and enter the **Forum Baths** on the left. Chipping away parts of the bodycasts here has revealed teeth and bones beneath. A right on V. della Fortuna leads to the ▨**House of the Faun,** where a bronze dancing faun and the spectacular Alexander Mosaic were found. Before the door, a floor mosaic proclaims *Vale* (welcome). The sheer size and opulence of this building has led archaeologists to believe that it was the private dwelling of one of the wealthiest men in town. Continuing on V. della Fortuna and turning left on V. dei Vettii will bring you to the ▨**House of the Vettii,** on the left, decorated with the most vivid

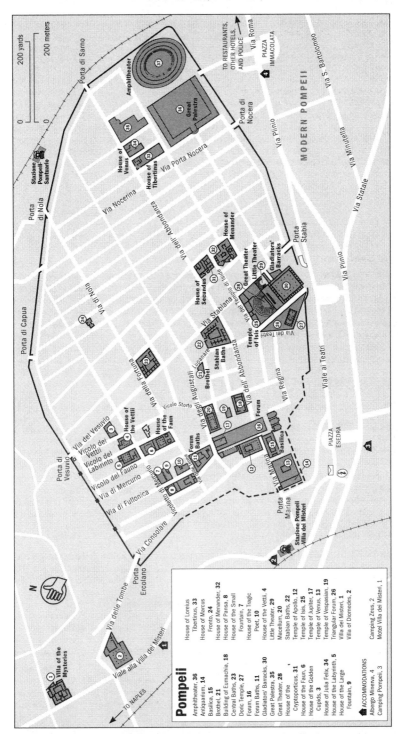

200 yards
200 meters

Porta di Sarno

TO RESTAURANTS,
OTHER HOTELS,
AND POLICE.

Via Roma

PIAZZA
IMMACOLATA

Porta di
Nocera

Via S. Bartolomeo

MODERN POMPEII

Via Plinio

Via Minutella

Via Statale

Stazione
Pompeii
Santuario

Porta
di Nola

Via Nocerina

Via Porta Nocera

House of
Venus

House of
Tibertinus

Amphitheater

Great
Palestra

Via dell'Abbondanza

House of
Menander

Porta
Stabia

Via Plinio

House of
Secundus

Great Theater

Little Theater

Gladiators'
Barracks

Via Stabiana

Via del Tempio di Iside

Temple
of Isis

Via dei Teatri

Via di Nola

Stabian
Baths

Via dell'Abbondanza

Via della Fortuna

Brothel

Vicolo Storto

Via degli Augustali

Via del Lupanare

Porta di Capua

House of
the Vettii

House of
the Faun

Via del Vesuvio

Vicolo dei
Vettii

Vicolo del
Labirinto

Vicolo del Fauno

Via di Mercurio

Forum
Baths

Forum

Basilica

Via Regina

Via Marina

Via di Fullonica

Porta di
Vesuvio

Via Consolare

Porta
Marina

Stazione Pompeii
Villa del Misteri

PIAZZA
ESEDRA

Viale ai Teatri

Viale al Teatri

Porta
Ercolano

Via delle Tombe

N

Villa of the
Mysteries

TO NAPLES

Viale alla Villa dei Misteri

Pompeii

Amphitheater, **36**
Antiquarium, **14**
Basilica, **15**
Brothel, **21**
Building of Eumachia, **18**
Central Baths, **23**
Doric Temple, **27**
Forum, **16**
Forum Baths, **11**
Gladiators' Barracks, **30**
Great Palestra, **35**
Great Theater, **28**
House of the
Cryptoporticus, **31**
House of the Faun, **6**
House of the Golden
Cupids, **3**
House of Julia Felix, **34**
House of the Labyrinth, **5**
House of the Large
Fountain, **9**

House of Loreius
Tibertius, **33**
House of Marcus
Fronto, **24**
House of Menander, **32**
House of Pansa, **8**
House of the Small
Fountain, **7**
House of the Tragic
Poet, **10**
House of the Vettii, **4**
Little Theater, **29**
Macellum, **20**
Stabian Baths, **22**
Temple of Apollo, **12**
Temple of Isis, **25**
Temple of Jupiter, **17**
Temple of Venus, **13**
Temple of Vespasian, **19**
Triangular Forum, **26**
Villa dei Misteri, **1**
Villa of Diomedes, **2**

ACCOMMODATIONS
Albergo Minerva, **4**
Camping Pompeii, **3**

Camping Zeus, **2**
Motel Villa dei Misteri, **1**

frescoes in Pompeii. In the vestibule, a depiction of Priapus, the god of fertility, displays his colossal member. In ancient times, phalli were believed to scare off evil spirits.

VIA DELL'ABBONDANZA AND ENVIRONS. Back down V. dei Vetti, cross V. della Fortuna over to V. Storto, then turn left on V. degli Augustali, which displays deep wagon ruts on either side; the Romans who were repaving this path when the volcano struck left their task incomplete. A quick right leads to a **brothel** (the *Lupenar*) containing several bedstalls. Above each stall, a pornographic painting depicts with unabashed precision the specialty of its occupant. (Even after 2000 years, this is still the most popular place in town; you may have to wait in line.) The street continues down to the main drag, V. dell'Abbondanza, on which red writing glares from the walls, expressing everything from political slogans to love declarations. Popular favorites include "Albanus is a bugger," "Restitutus has decieved many girls many times," and the lyrical "Lovers, like bees, lead a honey-sweet life." To the left of the street lie the **Stabian Baths,** which were privately owned and therefore fancier than the Forum Baths. The men's and women's sides each include dressing rooms, cold baths (*frigidaria*), warm baths (*tepidaria*), and steam baths (*caldaria*). At the end of the street rest the **House of Tiburtinus** and the **House of Venus,** huge complexes with gardens replanted according to modern knowledge of ancient horticulture. The nearby **amphitheater** (80 BC), the oldest standing in the world, held 12,000 spectators. When battles occurred, crowds decided whether a defeated gladiator would live or die with a casual thumbs up or thumbs down.

VIA DEI TEATRI. V. dei Teatri, across the street, leads to a huge complex consisting of the **Great Theater,** constructed in the 1st half of the 2nd century BC, and the **Little Theater,** built later for music and dance concerts. North of the theaters stands the **Temple of Isis,** Pompeii's monument to the Egyptian fertility goddess. Through the exit on the right, the road passes two fine houses, the **House of Secundus** and the **House of Menander.** At the end of the street, a left turn will return you to the main road. The Romans believed that crossroads were particularly vulnerable to evil spirits, so they built altars (like the one here) designed to ward them off.

HERCULANEUM (ERCOLANO)

*Take the **Circumvesuviana train** from Naples's central train station toward "Sorrento," to the "Ercol-ano" stop (20min., L2300). Walk 500m downhill to the ticket office, passing the **Municipal Tourist Office,** V. IV Novembre, 84, on the way. (☎081 7881243. Open M, W-F 9am-1pm, Tu 4-6:30pm.) **Open** daily 9am to 1hr. before sunset. **Admission** L16,000; illustrated guidebooks (L10-15,000) available at any of the shops at the entrance. Tourist office tours only worth it if you're traveling in a large group.*

Neatly excavated and impressively intact, the remains of the prosperous Roman town of Herculaneum (modern Ercolano) hardly deserve the term "ruins." Indeed, exploring the 2000-year-old houses—complete with frescoes, furniture, mosaics, small sculptures, and even wooden doors—feels like an invasion of privacy. Herculaneum does not evoke the tragedy of Pompeii; all but a handful of its inhabitants escaped the ravages of Vesuvius. Only a small part of the southeastern quarter of the city has been excavated. Between 15 and 20 houses are open to the public.

ANCIENT HOUSES. One of the more alluring houses is the **House of Deer** (named for the statues of deer in the courtyard), which displays *Satyr with a Wineskin* and a statue of Hercules in a drunken stupor trying to relieve himself. The **baths,** with their largely intact warm and hot rooms and vaulted swimming pool, conjure up images of ancient opulence. The **House of the Mosaic of Neptune and Amphitrite** belonged to a rich shop owner, and the front of the house has a well preserved wine shop. A mock colonnade made of stucco distinguishes the **Samnise House.** Down the street, the **House of the Wooden Partition** still has a preserved door in its elegant courtyard, and an ancient clothes press around the corner. Cardo IV shows you what a Roman street must have looked like.

NEARBY SITES. Outside the site, 250m to the left on the main road, is the **theater,** perfectly preserved underground. (Occasionally open for visits; call 081 7390963 for more info.) The **Villa dei Papiri,** 500m west of the site but not frequently open to the public, recently caused a stir when it was thought that a trove of ancient scrolls in the library included works by Cicero, Virgil, and Horace.

MT. VESUVIUS. The only active volcano on mainland Europe hasn't erupted since March 31, 1944, and scientists say that the hike (20-30min.) is safe. Hikers can take the orange city bus #5 (L1800) from V. IV Novembre to the base of the mountain and climb from there. Otherwise, Trasporti Vesuviani buses (L6000 round-trip) run from the Ercolano Circumvesuviana station up to the crater (buy tickets on the bus and not at the bus stop that is part way up the crater). *(Admission to area around the crater L9000.)*

PAESTUM

◪ *From Termini, take the **train** to Naples (every 15min.-1hr., 6:10am-10:30pm, L18,600-39,500), then take the train to Paestum (1¼hr., 9 per day 5:30am-10pm, L8200) via Salerno (35min., L4700).* **CTSP buses** *from Salerno (1hr., every hr. 7am-7pm, L4700) stop at Via Magna Graecia, the main modern road. The tourist office in Salerno provides a helpful list of all return buses from Paestum. The **AAST Information Office**, V. Magna Graecia, 155, is next to the museum. (☎082 811016; fax 082 8722322. Open July-Sept. 15 M-Sa 8am-2pm and 3:30-7:30pm, Su 9am-noon; Sept. 16-June M-Sa 8am-2pm.) The pleasant beachside **Ostello "La Lanterna" (HI)**, V. Lanterna, 8, in Agropoli, is the nearest budget accommodation. (☎/fax 0974 838364. 56 beds. Sheets and shower included. Dorms L17,000; quads L68,000.) To get to Agropoli, take the CTSP buses from Paestum (10min., 1 per hr. 7am-7pm, L2000) or from Salerno (1hr., L4700). Agropoli is also connected by train to Paestum (10min., L2200); Salerno (45min., L4700); and Naples (1½hr., L8200). Temples **open** daily 9am-1hr. before sunset; closed 1st and 3rd Monday of each month; last admittance 2hr. before sunset. **Admission** L8000, EU citizens over 60 and under 18 free.*

Not far from the Roman ruins of Pompeii and Herculaneum, the three Doric Greek temples of Paestum are among the best preserved in the world, even rivaling those of Sicily and Athens. They rank among the best preserved in the world. Originally built without any mortar or cement (they were simply covered by roofs of terra-cotta tiles supported by wooden beams) the temples remained standing even after the great earthquake of AD 69 reduced Pompeii's streets to a pile of rubble. When excavators first uncovered the three temples, they misidentified (and thus misnamed) them, and the names have stuck.

Misnomers have been Paestum's M.O. from the beginning. Greek colonists from Sybaris founded Paestum as Poseidonia in the 7th century BC, and it quickly became a flourishing commercial and trade center. After a period of native Italian control in the 5th and 4th centuries BC, Poseidonia fell to the Romans in 273 BC, was renamed Paestum, and remained a Roman town until the deforestation of nearby hills turned the town into a swampy mush. Plagued by malaria and syphilitic pirates, Paestum's ruins lay relatively untouched until they were rediscovered in the 18th century.

Because Paestum is not urbanized, you may think that you missed your stop as you step off the train and nervously scan the sky for vultures. Fear not the dearth of modern urban squalor; the ruins alone are a must-see. Sporadic restoration work on the temples occasionally leaves them fenced off or obscured by scaffolding, but they are especially magnificent when the *Sovrintendenza Archeologica* lets visitors walk around on the temples (sometimes they are fenced off).

TEMPLE OF CERES AND ENVIRONS. There are three entrances to Paestum's ruins. The northernmost entrance leads to the Temple of Ceres. Built around 500 BC, this temple became a church in the early Middle Ages but was abandoned in the 9th century. The ancient Greeks built Paestum on a north-south axis, marked by the paved V. Sacra. Farther south on V. Sacra is the Roman **forum,** which is even larger than the one at Pompeii (p. 232). The Romans leveled most of the older structures in the city's center to build this proto-piazza, the commercial and political arena of Paestum. To the left, a pit marks the pool of an ancient **gymnasium.** East of the gymnasium lies the Roman **amphitheater.**

TEMPLE(S?) OF POSEIDON. South of the forum lies the 5th-century BC Temple of Poseidon (actually dedicated to Hera), which incorporates many of the optical refinements that characterize the Parthenon in Athens. Small lions' heads serve as gargoyles on the temple roof. The southernmost temple, known as the **basilica,** is the oldest, dating to the 6th century BC. Its unusual plan, with a main interior section split by a row of columns down the middle, has inspired the theory that the temple was dedicated to two gods, Zeus and Hera, rather than one. A **museum** on the other side of V. Magna Graecia houses an extraordinary collection of pottery, paintings, and artifacts taken primarily from Paestum's tombs, with outstanding bilingual descriptions and essays on site. It also includes samples of 2500-year-old honey and paintings from the famous **Tomb of the Diver,**

dating to 475 BC. *(Museum open daily 9am-6:30pm. Ticket office open daily 9am-5:30pm; closed 1st and 3rd Monday of each month. L8000, EU citizens over 60 and under 18 free.)*

UMBRIA

Umbria has long enjoyed renown for its rivers, valleys, and wooded hills. Over the centuries, ravenous barbarian hordes, aggressive Romans, and the meddlesome papacy eventually trampled the vast empires of Umbrii here. The region still draws countless pilgrims each year, particularly for the artistic legacy left by Rome and the papal states.

ASSISI

For it is in giving that we receive; it is in pardoning that we are pardoned; and it is in dying that we are born to eternal life.
—St. Francis of Assisi

Assisi's serenity is the lasting legacy of St. Francis, a 12th-century monk who generated a revolution in the Catholic church. He founded the Franciscan order, devoted to the then-unusual combination of asceticism, poverty, and chastity. Young Franciscan nuns and monks still fill the city, dressed in their brown *cappucci* robes, carrying on his legacy with spiritual vigor. Assisi is an important pilgrimage site, especially among Italian youth, who converge here for conferences, festivals, and other religious activities.

Fervent religiosity is not a prerequisite for adoring Assisi. Giotto's frescoes adorning the basilica merit a pilgrimage on their own. The Basilica of St. Francis is perhaps the most visited sight in all Umbria, containing the saint's relics and Giotto's renowned fresco series of St. Francis' life, as well as works by Cimabue, Jacopo Torriti and Filipo Rusuti, Simone Martini and Pietro Lorenzetti. The influence of such masters infuse the streets, *piazze*, and *palazzi* of the town as well as its numerous places of worship. Assisi also has monuments to its Etruscan and Roman roots in the ruins throughout the town. Grand palaces and majestic *rocce* (castles) from a later era tower above the orange roofs. The rose-colored town is beautifully preserved, its accommodations are terrific, and its restaurants are among the best in Umbria. Earthquakes in the fall of 1997 devastated much of the city, but renovations have restored much of the damage.

GETTING THERE & GETTING AROUND

Trains: Below the town near the Basilica of Santa Maria degli Angeli. Assisi lies on the Foligno-Terontola line. Trains to **Rome** (1 per day, more frequent service via Foligno; L25,500); and **Ancona** (from 20,200). Ticket office open 6am-8pm. **Luggage Storage:** L5000 for 12hr. at the newsstand. Open daily 6:30am-6:30pm. **Bike rental** also available at the newsstand (☎033 93724592).

Buses: ASP buses leave from P. Matteoti. To **Florence** (2½hr., 1 per day) and **Rome** (3hr., 1 per day). To reach the bus stop from P. del Comune, walk up V. San Rufino to P. San Rufino and take V. del Torrione (to the left of the church) to P. Matteotti.

Public Transportation: Local buses (2 per hr., L1200) run from the train station to the town's bus stop at P. Unità d'Italia (near the basilica), Largo Properzio (near the church of St. Claire), and P. Matteotti (above P. del Comune).

Taxis: in P. del Comune (☎075 813193), in P. San Chiara (☎075 812600), in P. Unità d'Italia (☎075 812378), and at the train station (☎075 8040275).

Car Rental: Agenzia Assisiorganizza, Borgo Aretino, 11a (☎075 815280). Cars from L90,000 per day; L500,000 per week. Minimum age 21.

ORIENTATION & PRACTICAL INFORMATION

Towering above the city to the north, the **Rocca Maggiore** can help you reorient yourself should you become lost among Assisi's winding streets. The center of town is **Piazza del Comune.** To reach it from **Piazza Matteotti,** where buses drop off, take V. del Torrione to

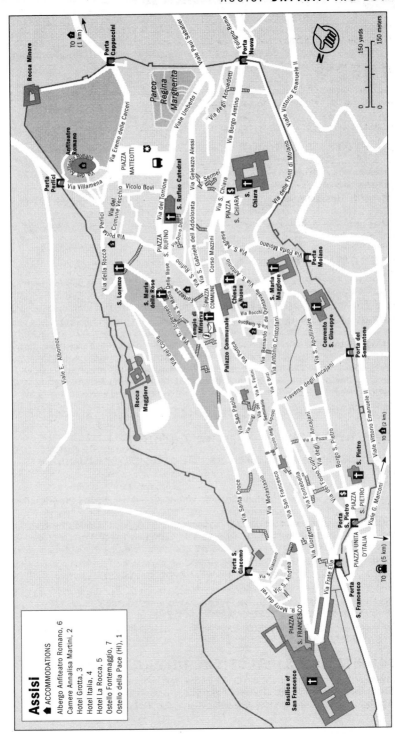

Assisi

▲ ACCOMMODATIONS

Albergo Anfiteatro Romano, 6
Camere Annalisa Martini, 2
Hotel Grotta, 3
Hotel Italia, 4
Hotel La Rocca, 5
Ostello Fontemaggio, 7
Ostello della Pace (HI), 1

Piazza San Rufino, bear left in the piazza, and take **Via San Rufino** until it hits the bustling town center. **Via Portica** (which intersects V. Fortini, V. Seminario, and finally **Via San Francesco**) connects P. del Commune to the **Basilica di San Francesco.** Heading in the opposite direction, **Corso Mazzini** leads to the **Chiesa di Santa Chiara.**

Tourist Office: P. del Comune (☎075 812534; fax 075 813727). Head down V. Mazzini and duck down a doorway on the right. Knowledgeable staff. Free, decent map. Sells the **Assisicard,** good for discounts throughout the city. Train and bus schedules posted outside. Open M-F 8am-2pm and 3:30-6:30pm, Sa 9am-1pm and 3:30-6:30pm, Su and holidays 9am-1pm.

Banks: Exchange traveler's checks (L2000 for sums up to L100,000; L5000 for larger sums) at the post office, or try **Banca Toscana,** P. S. Pietro; **Cassa di Risparmio di Perugia,** on P. del Comune; and **Banca Popolare di Spoleto,** on P. S. Chiara. Banks open 8:20am-1:20pm and 2:15-3:15pm. **ATMs** are outside the banks.

Emergencies: ☎113. **Police: Carabinieri,** P. Matteotti, 3 (☎075 812239).

Hospital: Ospedale di Assisi (☎075 812824), on the outskirts of town. Take the "Linea A" bus from P. del Comune. **Guardia Medica Turistica:** ☎075 8043616.

Post Office: Largo Properzio, 4. Open M-F 8:10am-6:25pm, Sa 8:10am-1pm. Postal Code: 06081.

ACCOMMODATIONS

Reservations are crucial around Easter and Christmas and are strongly recommended for the *Festa di Calendimaggio* in early May. Also consider booking ahead of time in August. The tourist office has a list of *affittacamere* (rooms for rent).

■ **Ostello della Pace (HI),** V. di Valecchi, 177 (☎/fax 075 816767). Turn right as you exit the train station and then left at the intersection onto V. di Valecchi (30min.), or take the bus to P. S. Pietro and walk 50m down the main road to the small path marked by the hostel sign. The hostel is 10min. away. Large, 4-bed rooms and spotless bathrooms. Breakfast included. Generous home-cooked dinner L14,000. Washer L6500. Communal areas locked by 11:30pm. Check-out 9:30am. Dorms L22,000, with private bath L27,000. Open daily 7-9:15am and 3:30-11:30pm. Reserve ahead if possible (even if you're just calling from the train station in Assisi). V, MC.

■ **Camere Annalisa Martini,** V. S. Gregorio, 6 (☎075 81 35 36). The lovely Annalisa offers *affittacamere* at excellent prices. In the medieval core of Assisi, this peaceful refuge is tucked away in a sunny garden. Outdoor picnic seating, washer, telephone, and fax available. If she doesn't have room, Annalisa can point you toward the rooms of one of her friends. Laundry L5-10,000. Singles L38,000, with bath L40,000; doubles L60,000/L65,000; triples L90-L100,000.

FOOD

Assisi will tempt you with a sinful array of nut breads and sweets. *Bricciata umbria,* a strudel-like pastry with a hint of cherries, and *brustengolo,* packed with raisins, apples, and walnuts, are divine. **Pasticceria Santa Monica,** at V. Portica, 4, right off P. del Comune, sells these and other treats at low prices with extremely friendly service (open daily 9am-8pm). On Saturday mornings, there's a market in P. Matteotti; on weekdays, head over to V. S. Gabriele for fresh fruits and vegetables.

Pizzeria Otello, V. San Antonio, 1 (☎075 812415), on a side street off P. del Comune and across from St. Francis's home. No-nonsense, family-run pizzeria. Summer dining in the garden. Hearty portions. Pizza L7500-11,000. Focaccia sandwiches and large salads L8500-10,000. *Primi* L7500-11,000; *secondi* L8500-14,500. Cover L2000. 10% discount with Assisicard. Open daily Jul.-Aug. for pizza by the slice 7:30am-noon, main restaurant noon-4pm and 7-11pm. In off-season, M-Sa 7:30am-noon by the slice, restaurant noon-4pm. V, MC, AmEx.

Il Duomo Pizzeria, V. Porta Perlici, 11 (☎075 816326). The large pizza oven is the focal point of this medieval lair/pizzeria. In addition to pizza, they offer a varied and well-priced menu. Ravioli *duomo* L11,000. Open daily noon-2:30pm and 6:30pm-1am.

Trattoria da Ermini, V. Monte Cavallo, 19 (☎075 81 25 06), off V. Porta Perlici. Enjoy *Tagliatelle capricciose* (L10,000) or *bistecca di pollo alla brace* (grilled chicken; L13,000) beneath a tremendous vaulted dome. *Menù* L26,000. Open F-W noon-2:30pm and 7-9pm. V, MC.

SIGHTS

At age 19, St. Francis (b. 1182) abandoned military and social ambitions, rejected his father's wealth, and embraced asceticism. His renouncement of the church's worldliness, his love of nature, and his devoted humility earned him a huge following throughout Europe, posing an unprecedented challenge to the decadent papacy and corrupt monastic orders. St. Francis continued to preach chastity and poverty until his death in 1226, when, ironically enough, the order he founded was gradually subsumed into the Catholic hierarchy that it had criticized.

📰 BASILICA DI SAN FRANCESCO

🔛 ☎ *075 8190084. Basilica* **open** *Easter-Nov. M-Sa 6:30am-7pm; Su and holidays 6:30am-7:30pm (but no tourist visits allowed during the morning, on Su, or on holidays); off-season open daily 6:30am-6pm. Closed on Holy Days. Tours 9am-noon and 2-5:30pm.* **Sala Norsa** *open M-Sa 9am-12:30pm and 3-6pm, Su 3-6pm.* **Museum** *open M-Sa 9:30am-noon and 2-6pm. L3000.* **Tours** *convene outside the basilica; call the basilica's tourist information office to arrange one. Free tours also given by young, enthusiastic Franciscan monks—usually in perfect English.* **Dress code** *strictly enforced: cover knees and shoulders, and no miniskirts or short shorts. No* **photography** *of the interior of the churches permitted.*

When construction of the Basilica di San Francesco began in the mid-13th century, the Franciscan order protested—the elaborate church seemed an impious monument to the wealth that St. Francis had scorned. As a solution, Brother Elia, the vicar of the order, insisted that a double church be erected, the lower level to be built around the saint's crypt, the upper level to be used as a church for services. The subdued art in the lower church commemorates Francis's modest life, while the upper church pays tribute to his sainthood and consecration. This two-fold structure inspired a new type of Franciscan architecture. The Basilica was badly damaged by an earthquake in 1997, although the furious restoration efforts to prepare for the Jubilee Year of 2000 are now complete.

UPPER LEVEL. The walls of the upper church are covered with Giotto's renowned *Life of St. Francis* fresco cycle, dramatically lit from the windows above. A comprehensive introduction to the frescoes is offered in the **Sala Norsa** across from the basilica. Full appreciation necessitates much neck-craning and creative maneuvering. The story begins on the right wall near the altar and runs clockwise, beginning with a teenage Francis in courtly dress surprised by a prophecy of his future greatness. The cycle closes with an image of the saint passing through the agony of the "Dark Night." Paralleling St. Francis's pictorial path of holy deeds is the equally linear story of Jesus. Most frescoes and sculptures in the basilica come complete with "History Tell" machines, which charge L1000 for a sketchy (one refers to Francis as "a sissy" rather than "of Assisi") oral history of each work.

Cimabue's magnificent *Madonna and Child, Angels,* and *St. Francis* grace the right transept. Tragically, most of Cimabue's frescoes in the transepts and apse have so deteriorated that they now look like photographic negatives. Pietro Lorenzetti decorated the left transept with his outstanding *Crucifixion, Last Supper,* and *Madonna and Saints.* Stunning also are Simone Martini's frescoes in the first chapel off the left wall, which revolve around the life of St. Martin. Descend through a door in the right side of the apse to enter the room which houses St. Francis's tunic, sandals, and sundries.

LOWER LEVEL (ST. FRANCIS'S TOMB). The inspiration for the entire edifice lies below the lower church. The coffin itself was hidden in the 15th century, out of fear that the war-mongering Perugians would desecrate it, and not rediscovered until 1818. The original tomb was Neoclassical, but was disliked by so many friars that a simplified version was constructed in 1935. The stone coffin sits above the altar in the crypt, surrounded by the sarcophagi of four of the saint's dearest friends. The attached library houses the remarkable **Museo Tesoro della Basilica.** Particularly impressive are rare illuminated manuscripts, the graceful 13th-century French ivory *Madonna and Child,* 17th-century Murano glass work, and a fragment of the Holy Cross.

OTHER SIGHTS

DUOMO. V. S. Rufino climbs steeply up from P. del Comune between closely packed old houses, opening onto P. S. Rufino to reveal the squat *duomo* with its massive bell tower. The restored interior is quite spartan and will probably come as a disappointment when compared to the decorative facade. *(Open daily 10am-noon and 3-6pm.)*

BASILICA DI SANTA CHIARA. The pink and white Basilica di Santa Chiara honors St. Clare. It stands at the opposite end of Assisi on the site where St. Francis attended school. The church shelters not only the tomb (and hair) of St. Clare, but also the tunic and shoes worn by St. Francis and the crucifix that revealed God's message to him. The nuns in this convent are sworn to seclusion. *(☎ 075 812282. Open daily 7am-noon and 2-7pm. Mass 11:30am and 5:30pm.)*

OTHER SIGHTS. From the Basilica di San Francesco, V. S. Francesco snakes between medieval buildings and their 16th-century additions. The colorfully frescoed **Oratorio del Pelegrino** (Pilgrim Oratory) is especially noteworthy. At the end of the street, P. del Comune sits upon the old **Foro Romano** (☎ 075 813053). Among the impressive buildings in the square is the appealing **Chiesa Nuova** (☎ 075 812339), with slightly crumbling exterior columns and a frescoed interior. *(Both the forum and the Pinacoteca open daily Mar. 16-Oct. 15 10am-1pm and 3-7pm; Oct. 16-Mar. 15 10am-1pm and 2-5pm. L4000 per sight. Biglietto cumulativo (entry into the forum and the Pinacoteca) L10,000, students L7000. Chiesa Nuova open 6:30am-noon and 2:30pm-6pm.)*

ENTERTAINMENT

All of Assisi's religious festivals involve feasts and processions. An especially long, dramatic performance marks **Easter Week.** On Holy Thursday, a mystery play depicts the Deposition from the Cross. Traditional processions trail through town on Good Friday and Easter Sunday. Assisi welcomes spring with the **Festa di Calendimaggio** (the first Thursday, Friday, and Saturday of May). A queen is chosen and dubbed *Primavera* (Spring), while the lower and upper quarters of the city compete in a clamorous musical tournament. Ladies and Knights overtake the streets bellowing amorous notes in celebration of the young St. Francis, who wandered the streets of Assisi singing serenades at night. It was on one such night that he encountered a vision of the *Madonna della Povertà* (Lady of Poverty). Classical concerts and organ recitals occur once or twice each week from April to October in the various churches. October 4 marks the **Festival of St. Francis.** Each year a different region of Italy offers oil for the cathedral's votive lamp and the traditional dances and songs of that region are performed.

On any given evening in Assisi, youth groups flood P. del Comune to croon international folk songs (including "Kumbaya" and "La Macarena") with guitar-strumming monks. There is little late-night carousing in pious Assisi, so don't expect too much Bacchanalian revelry. The most hoppin' bars in P. Commune close around 2am. If you're itching to disco, head down to **Hermitage,** V. degli Aromatari, 1 (☎ 075 816671, closed Jul.-Aug.) or **Il Tropicana,** V. Madonna delle Grazie, 11 (☎ 075 804385, closed Th), in nearby S. Maria degli Angeli (the village where the train station is located).

NEAR ASSISI

⛰ EREMO DELLE CARCERI. A pleasant, steep, hour-long hike through the forest above the town leads to the inspiring Eremo delle Carceri (Hermitage of Cells), in the woods of Mt. Subasio. This oasis of peace and tranquility, to which St. Francis used to retreat, conveys the saint's true spirit more successfully than the opulent basilica. At the hermitage, you can view the small cell where St. Francis slept and the altar where he preached. Beyond the hermitage, **Mt. Subasio** has a number of trails; ask at the tourist office for a map to explore this natural treasure. (Pass through the Porta S. Francesco below the basilica and follow V. Marconi. At the crossroads, take the left road and pass the Seminario Regionale Umbro. *(Open daily Easter-Oct. 6:30am-7:15pm; Nov.-Easter 6:30am-5:30pm.)* On the road up the mountain, the delightful **Le Carcerelle,** V. San Rufino Campagna, 15, has refreshing fruit drinks (L3000), cocktails and beer (L3500-5000), and delicious home-made meals like *polenta con salcicce* (L8000), *parmigiane con melanzone* (L9000), or *torta al testo* (L4500). (☎075 816286. Open daily 7:30am-11pm.)

BASILICA DI SANTA MARIA DEGLI ANGELI. The train to Assisi passes the huge Basil-ica di Santa Maria degli Angeli, a church inside a church. The impressive basilica, with its majestic purple dome, shelters the tiny **Porziuncola,** historically the first center of the Franciscan order. Benedictines own the building, and the Franciscans pay them a basket of carp every year as rent. In order to overcome temptation, St. Francis supposedly flung himself on thorny rosebushes in the garden just outside the basilica, thus eternally stain-ing the leaves red. Today, in deference to the saint, the bushes no longer produce thorns. This site gained popularity with St. Francis's institution of the annual **Festa del Perdono** (Aug. 2), during which indulgences were offered to all who visited the church. The adja-cent **Cappella del Transito,** was the site of St. Francis's death. *(Open daily 8am-noon and 2:30-7pm; closes earlier in winter.)*

ORVIETO

Orvieto sits, as it has for the past 3000 years, above an incredible volcanic plateau rising from the rolling farmlands of southern Umbria. In the 7th century BC, Etruscans began to burrow under the city for *tufo* (a volcanic stone out of which most of the medieval quarter is built), creating the subterranean "city" beneath Orvieto's surface. Five centu-ries later, the Romans sacked and reoccupied the plateau, calling their "new" city *urbs ventus* ("old city"), from which the name Orvieto is derived. In medieval times, the city again became a center of worship. In the 13th century, as Thomas Aquinas lectured in the local academies and fervent Christians planned their crusades, countless churches sprang up along the winding city streets. In the 14th and 15th centuries, the Masters of Orvieto, alongside those of Siena, Assisi, and Perugia, formed a highly influential school of painters. Today, Orvieto is a popular tourist destination; visitors are drawn to the stunning 13th-century *duomo* (and the city's renowned Orvieto Classico wine), discov-ering the city's steeples, streets, and underground chambers. Did we mention wine?

ORIENTATION & PRACTICAL INFORMATION

Orvieto lies midway along the Rome-Florence train line. From the train station, cross the street and take the funicular (every 15min., L1300; with shuttle L1600) up the hill to **Piazza Cahen,** where ATC buses stop. A shuttle leads from P. Cahen to **Piazza del Duomo.** If you choose to walk, you can follow **Corso Cavour** to its intersection with **Via Duomo.** The left branch leads to the *duomo* and surrounding museums; the right, to the **Piazza del Popolo.** Sprinkled between V. Duomo and the **Piazza della Repubblica** along C. Cavour are most of the city's restaurants, hotels, and shops. Past P. della Repubblica is the medieval section of town, housing the city's oldest buildings and roads.

Trains: To **Rome** (1½hr., every 1-2 hr. 4:25am-10:27pm, L12,500) and **Florence** (2hr., every 1-2hr. 7:29am-11:32pm, L17,700) via **Cortona** (45min.). **Luggage Storage:** L5000 per bag for 12hr. Open 6:30am-8pm.

Buses: COTRAL (☎0761 266592) runs 1 daily bus from the train station to P. Cahen and to sur-rounding towns. Buy tickets at the *tabacchi* in the train station. To **Viterbo** (7 per day 6:25am-3:45pm, L5400).

Tourist Office: P. del Duomo, 24 (☎0763 341772; fax 0763 344433). Sells special deals on underground tours of Orvieto, as well as the **Orvieto Unica card** (L20,000, students L17,000), which includes an underground tour, a round-trip ticket for the funicular-minibus, entrance to the Museo "Claudio Faina," the Torre del Moro, and the Cappella della Madonna di San Brizio. Open M-F 8:15am-1:50pm and 4-7pm, Sa 10am-1pm and 4-7pm, Su 10am-noon and 4-6pm. The **Tourist Information Point,** Borgo Largo Barzini, 7 (☎0763 342 297), just off V. Duomo, will help you find a place to stay for free. They also **exchange traveler's checks and currency** for 5% com-mission. Open M-F 8am-1pm and 4-6pm, Sa 8am-1pm.

Emergencies: ☎113. **Police:** (☎0763 40088), in P. della Repubblica. **Hospital:** (☎0763 3091), off P. del Duomo.

ACCOMMODATIONS & CAMPING

▉**Hotel Duomo,** V. Maurizio, 7 (☎0763 341887), off V. Duomo, the first right as you leave the *piazza*. Steps away from the cathedral. Light and airy rooms have delicate lace curtains; some with excellent views. Breakfast in the garden L9000. Singles L40,000; doubles L78,000, with bath L85,000; triples L80,000.

Posta, V. Luca Signorelli, 18 (☎076 3341909). Small grapevine-covered *piazza* in back, beautiful rooms with gilded mirrors, tiled floors, and a Venetian glass chandelier. Breakfast L10,000. Lockout midnight. Singles L60,000, with bath L70,000; doubles L75-80,000/L100,000.

FOOD (AND WINE)

Amidst a crowd of pricey *ristoranti*, there are plenty of reasonable opportunities to treat your stomach well in Orvieto. Tellingly, one of the ancient names of Orvieto was Oinarea (the city where wine flows). Today it still flows (hic!) to the beautiful tune of L6-9000 per bottle. Don't leave Orvieto without sampling its world-renowned wine, *Orvieto Classico*. **Alimentari** with local treats dot the city; one is below P. della Repubblica at V. Filippeschi, 29. Bottles of Orvieto Classico start at L5000. (Open M-Tu and Th-Sa 7:30am-noon and 5-8:30pm, W 7:45am-2pm).

▉**Al Pozzo Etrusco Ristorante,** Piazza de' Ranieri, 1/A (☎0763 44456). Follow V. Garibaldi from P. della Repubblica and walk diagonally left across P. de' Ranieri. *Al Pozzo Etrusco* means "the Etruscan well," and, believe it or not, they've got one. If you missed the underground city, you can catch up on your studies over delicious regional fare. *Pasta fresco* L7-9000. *Secondi* L9-15,000. AmEx, MC, V.

Asino D'oro, Vicolo del Popolo I, 9 (☎0763 343302), in a little *piazza* between C. Cavour and P. del Popolo. At the intersection of V. Duomo and C. Cavour, head towards P. della Repubblica and duck down the first alley to your right. Innovative menu changes daily. Casual cafe environment with exquisite and reasonably priced food. *Primi* and *secondi* L6-12,000. Open Tu-Su 12:30pm-midnight. Wheelchair accessible.

Internet@caffe, V. Cavour, 25 (☎0763 34 12 61). Enjoy delectable pastries (L2-3000) that are regional specialties while you check email (L6000 for 30min.). Open Oct.-Mar. daily 7am-midnight; Nov.-Apr.; closed W.

SIGHTS

▉**DUOMO.** Even a quick glance at Orvieto's pride and joy will shock you. Its fanciful facade, designed around 1290 by Lorenzo Maitani, dazzles the admirer with intertwining spires, mosaics, and sculptures. Initially envisioned as a smaller Romanesque chapel, the *duomo* was later enlarged with a transept and nave. The bottom level features exquisitely carved bas reliefs of the Creation and Old Testament prophecies as well as the final panel of Maitani's realistic *Last Judgment*. Set in niches surrounding the rose window by Andrea Orcagna (1325-1364), bronze and marble sculptures emphasize the Christian canon. Thirty-three architects, 90 mosaic artisans, 152 sculptors, and 68 painters worked for over 600 years to bring the *duomo* to this point, and the work continues—the bronze doors were only installed in 1970. Visitors in the spring of 2001 should find newly restored frescoes by Ugolino dé Prete Ilario behind the altar.

The **Cappella della Madonna di San Brizio** (sometimes called the **Cappella Nuova**), off the right transept, includes Luca Signorelli's dramatic Apocalypse frescoes, considered to be his finest works. On the right wall, skeletons and muscular humans pull themselves out of the earth while ghoulish apparitions of the damned swarm about in the unsettling *Resurrection of the Dead*. Beside it hangs the *Inferno*, with a depiction of Signorelli (a blue devil) embracing his mistress. Rumor has it that the Whore of Babylon, carried on the back of a devil above the masses, was modeled after an Orvieto woman who rejected Signorelli's advances. Begun by Fra Angelico in 1447, the frescoes were supposed to be completed by Perugino, but the city grew tired of waiting and enlisted Signorelli to finish the project. His vigorous draftsmanship, mastery of human anatomy, and dramatic compositions were inspirations for Michelangelo (whose vision of the Inferno, *The Last Judgment*, is just as frightening—see p. 147). The Cappella also holds the gold-encrusted **Reliquario del Corporale** (chalice-cloth), to which the entire structure is dedicated. The cloth inside the box caught Christ's blood, which dripped from a consecrated host in Bolsena in 1263. *(Duomo open 8:30am-12:45pm; afternoon hours vary monthly—2:30-7:15pm is a safe bet. Su and Holidays 2:30-5:45pm. Duomo free; Capella Nuova L3000, before 10am free. Purchase tickets at the tourist office across the street. No shorts or short skirts permitted.)*

PALAZZO DEI PAPI. From this austere, 13th-century "Palace of the Popes," Pope Clement VII rejected King Henry VIII's petition to annul his marriage to Catherine of Aragon, condemning both Catherine and English Catholicism to a bleak fate. Set back in the *palazzo* is the **Museo Archeologico Nazionale,** where you can examine Etruscan artifacts from the area and walk into a full-sized tomb. *(Right of the* duomo. *Open M-Sa 9am-7pm, Su 9am-1pm. L4000, over 60 and under 18 free.)*

UNDERGROUND CITY. For the most complete tour of Etruscan Orvieto, consider the **Underground City Excursions,** which will lead you through the endless dark and twisted bowels of the city. During its 3000 years of history, while the city rose upward, a companion "city" burrowed into the soft *tufa* of the cliff below. Although the ancient Etruscan city of Velzna (which stood where modern Orvieto now sits) was sacked by Romans, its history is still preserved below the earth. Cisterns, underground mills, pottery workshops, quarries, wine cellars, and burial sites weave an impressive web beneath the city. *(☎0763 344891. 1hr. tours leave from the tourist office at 11am and 4pm. L10,000, groups or those with tickets to Pozzo della Cava L8000, students L6000.)*

MUSEO CIVICO AND MUSEO FAINA. These *musei* hold an extensive collection of Etruscan artifacts found in excavations of local necropoloi. Its exhibits include coins, bronze urns, red- and black-figure vases from the 6th century BC, and ornaments from Roman times. *(Opposite the* duomo. *Open daily 10am-1pm and 2-6pm; Sept.-Mar. closed Mondays. L8000, students and seniors L5000.)*

CHIESA DI SANT'ANDREA. This church marks the beginning of Orvieto's medieval quarter. The church, built upon the ruins of an Etruscan temple, served as a meeting place, or *comune*, in medieval Orvieto. Inside, the crypt (at the beginning of the right aisle) contains recently excavated remains from the underground Etruscan temple. *(In P. della Repubblica, 500m down C. Cavour from P. Cahen.)*

CHIESA DI SAN GIOVENALE. The city's oldest church was dedicated to the first bishop of Orvieto; there's a fresco of him on the left wall as you enter the church. Directly next to the doors on the left is a 14th-century "Tree of Life"—a family tree of the church's founders. The soils of the verdant slope below P. San Giovanni are filled with the graves of thousands who perished in the Black Death of 1348. Walk back from San Giovanni on V. Ripa di Serancia, the city's oldest road. It ends at the **Chiesa di San Giovanni.** Just inside the ancient city walls, this church offers a stunning view of the countryside below. *(From P. della Repubblica, follow V. Filippeschi, which turns into V. Malabranca.)*

ENTERTAINMENT

Orvieto wants to party all the time. In the spring there is the **Palio dell'Oca,** a medieval game of skill on horseback. On Pentecost (49 days after Easter), Orvieto celebrates the **Festa della Palombella.** Small wooden boxes filled with fireworks are set up in front of the *duomo* and the Chiesa di San Francesco. At the stroke of noon, the San Francesco fireworks are set off, and a white metal dove descends across the wire to ignite the explosives. In June, the historic **Procession of Corpus Domini** celebrates the Miracle of Bolsena. Ladies and flag wavers dance in the streets to period music, followed by medieval banquets. From December 29 to January 5, **Umbria Jazz Winter** swings in Orvieto's theaters, churches, and *palazzi* (with the finale in the *duomo*). For specific festival information, contact **Servizio Turistico Territoriale IAT dell'Orvietano,** P. Duomo, 24 (☎0763 341911 or 0763 343658), or **Informazioni Turistiche** (☎0763 341772; fax 0763 344433) at the same address.

For less formal fun, try **Zeppelin,** V. Garibaldi, 28. This classy old-fashioned bar, Orvieto's best nightlife, is a popular place to enjoy live music and drinks. (☎0763 341447. Open W-M 7:30pm-1am. MC, V.) Otherwise, follow signs from P. Duomo for **Engel Keller's Tavern,** on V. Beato Angelico. (Open Th-Tu 7pm-3am.)

Planning Your Trip

DOCUMENTS & FORMALITIES

All applications should be filed several weeks or months before departure. Demand for passports is highest between January and August, so try to apply as early as possible.

ENTRANCE REQUIREMENTS

Passport (p. 246). Required for all citizens of Australia, Canada, Ireland, New Zealand, the UK, and the US.
Visa (p. 247). Required for South Africans and for stays longer than three months.
Work Permit (p. 247). Required for non-EU citizens planning to work in Italy.
Driving Permit (p. 26). Necessary to drive for more than one month.

ITALIAN CONSULAR SERVICES ABROAD

Address questions concerning visas and passports to consulates, not embassies. For consular services in Rome, see **Service Directory**, p. 294.

Australia: Embassy, 12 Grey St., **Deakin, Canberra** ACT 2600 (☎ (02) 6273 3333; fax 6273 4223; email embassy@ambitalia.org.au; www.ambitalia.org.au). Open 9am-12:30pm; 2-4pm. **Consulates:** Level 14 AMP Place, 10 Eagle St., **Brisbane** QLD 4000 (☎ (07) 3229 8944; fax 3229 8643; email italcons.brisbane@bigpond.com). Open M-F 9am-1pm; Th 9am-3pm; 509 St. Kilda Rd., **Melbourne** VIC 3004 (☎ (03) 9867 5744; fax 9866 3932; email itconmel@netlink.com.au); Level 45, The Gateway, 1 Macquarie Pl., **Sydney** NSW 2000 (☎ (02) 9392 7900; fax ☎9252 4830; email itconsyd@itconsyd.com). All consular information is available through the embassy website.

Canada: Embassy, 275 Slater St., 21st fl., **Ottawa,** ON K1P 5H9 (☎ (613) 232-2401; fax 233-1484; email ambital@italyincanada.com; www.italyincanada.com). **Consulate,** 3489 Drummond St., **Montréal,** QC H3G 1X6 (☎ (514) 849-8351; fax 499-9471; email cgi@italconsul.mont-real.qc.ca).

Ireland: Embassy, 63 Northumberland Rd., **Dublin** (☎ (3531) 660 1744; fax 668 2759; email italianembassy@tinet.ie; homepage.eircom.net/~italianembassy). Open M-F 10am-12:30pm.

New Zealand: Embassy, 34 Grant Rd., **Wellington** (☎ (04) 473 5339; fax 472 7255; email ambwell@xtra.co.nz).

South Africa: Embassy, 796 George Ave., Arcadia 0083, **Pretoria** (☎(012) 43 55 41; fax 43 55 47; email ambital@iafrica.com; www.ambital.org.za). **Consulates:** 2 Grey's Pass, Gardens 8001, **Cape Town** (☎(021) 424 1256; fax 424 0146; email italcons@mweb.co.za); Corner 2nd Ave., Houghton 2198, **Johannesburg** (☎(011) 728 13 92; fax 728 38 34); PO Box 46306, Orange Grove 2119.

UK: Embassy, 14 Three Kings Yard, **London** W1Y 2EH (☎ (020) 7312 2200; fax 7499 2283; email emblondon@embitaly.org.uk; www.embitaly.org.uk). **Consulates:** 38 Eaton Pl., **London** SW1X 8AN (☎ (0171) 235 9371; fax 823 1609); Rodwell Tower, 111 Piccadilly, **Manchester** M1 2HY (☎ (0161) 236 9024; fax 236 5574; email passaporti@italconsulman.demon.co.uk); 32 Melville St., **Edinburgh** EH3 7HA (☎(0131) 226 3631; fax 226 6260; email consedimb@consedimb.demon.co.uk).

US: Embassy, 1601 Fuller St. NW, **Washington, D.C.** 20009 (☎ (202) 328-5500; fax 462-3605; email itapress@ix.netcom.com; www.italyemb.org). **Consulates:** 100 Boylston St., #900, **Boston,** MA 02116 (☎ (617) 542-0483; fax 542-3998; email postmaster@italconsboston.org; www.italconsboston.org); 500 N. Michigan Ave. #1850, **Chicago,** IL 60611 (☎ (312) 467-1550; fax 467-1335; email consul@consitchicago.org; www.italconschicago.org); 12400 Wilshire Blvd. #300, **Los Angeles,** CA 90025 (☎ (310) 820-0622; fax 820-0727; email Centralino@conlang.com; www.conlang.com); 690 Park Ave. (visas 54 E. 69th St.), **New York,** NY 10021 (☎ (212) 737-9100; fax 249-4945; email italconsny@aol.com; www.italconsulnyc.org).

PASSPORTS

REQUIREMENTS. Citizens of Australia, Canada, Ireland, New Zealand, South Africa, the UK, and the US need valid passports to enter Italy and to re-enter their own country.

PHOTOCOPIES. Be sure to photocopy the page of your passport with your photo, passport number, and other identifying information, as well as any visas, travel insurance policies, plane tickets, or traveler's check serial numbers. Carry one set of copies in a safe place, apart from the originals, and leave another set at home. Consulates also recommend that you carry an expired passport or an official copy of your birth certificate in a part of your baggage separate from other documents.

LOST PASSPORTS. If you lose your passport, immediately notify the local police and the nearest embassy or consulate of your home government. To expedite replacement, you will need to know your passport info (number, etc.) and show ID and proof of citizenship. In some cases, a replacement may take weeks to process, and it may be valid only for a limited time. Any visas stamped in your old passport will be irretrievably lost. In an emergency, ask for temporary traveling papers that will permit you to re-enter your home country. Your passport is a public document belonging to your nation's government. You may have to surrender it to a foreign government official, but if you don't get it back in a reasonable amount of time, inform the nearest mission of your home country.

NEW PASSPORTS. Contact your nearest passport and/or post office to obtain a passport. File new passport or renewal applications well in advance of your departure date. Most passport offices offer rush services for a steep fee. Citizens living abroad who need a passport or renewal should contact the nearest consular service of their home country.

VISAS & WORK PERMITS

VISAS. A visa—a passport stamp, sticker, or insert specifying the purpose of your travel and the permitted duration of your stay—can be purchased at your home country's consulate. **British, Irish,** and **EU** citizens need only carry a valid passport to enter Italy, and they may stay in the country for as long as they like. Citizens of **Australia, Canada, New Zealand,** and the **US** do not need visas for stays of up to three months. US citizens can take advantage of the **Center for International Business and Travel (CIBT; ☎** (800) 925-2428), which, for a service charge, secures visas for travel to almost any country.

Within eight days of arrival, all foreign nationals staying with friends or relatives or uptaking private residence must register with the local police office and receive a *permesso di soggiorno* (permit of stay) for L20,000. If you are staying in a hotel or hostel, the officials will fulfill registration requirements for you and the fee is waived. Those wishing to stay in Italy for more than three months for the sole purpose of tourism must apply for an extention at a local *questura* at least one month before the original permit expires. Extensions are granted at the discretion of the local authorities.

As of August 2000, citizens of **South Africa** need a visa in addition to a valid passport for entrance to Italy. Any visa granted by Italy will be respected by the following countries: Austria, Belgium, France, Germany, Greece, Luxembourg, Portugal, Spain, and The Netherlands. The extensive requirements for this visa include: passport (valid for 10 months from departure), recent passport photo, application form, itinerary including border of entry and duration of stay in each country, proof of sufficient funds, proof of insurance, return airline ticket, proof of accommodations, or if residing with friends or relatives, a letter of invitation certified by Italian Police Authorities. The duration of one stay or a succession of stays may not exceed 90 days per six months. The cost of a Schengen visa varies with duration and number of entries; one entry with the maximum 90-day stay costs 198 SAR.

Be sure to double-check entrance requirements at the nearest embassy or consulate of Italy for up-to-date info before departure. US citizens can also consult www.pueblo.gsa.gov/cic_text/travel/foreign/foreignentryreqs.html.

WORK PERMITS. EU citizens do not need permission to work in Italy. Non-EU citizens seeking work must apply for an Italian work permit before entering the country. For more information on working in Italy, see **Living in Rome,** p. 281.

IDENTIFICATION

Always carry at least two forms of identification, including a photo ID. A passport and driver's license or birth certificate usually serve as adequate proof of identity and citizenship, which you'll need for transactions such as cashing traveler's checks. To prevent disaster in case of theft or loss, never carry all your ID in one place. Bring several extra passport photos to attach to the sundry IDs or passes you'll acquire. For extended stays, register your passport with local consular services (see **Service Directory,** p. 293).

ONE EUROPE

The idea of European unity has come a long way since 1958, when the European Economic Community (EEC) was created in order to promote solidarity among its six founding states. The EEC is now the European Union (EU), with political, legal, and economic institutions spanning 15 member states: Austria, Belgium, Denmark, Finland, France, Germany, Greece, Ireland, Italy, Luxembourg, the Netherlands, Portugal, Spain, Sweden, and the UK.

What does this have to do with the average non-EU tourist? Well, 1999 established **freedom of movement** across 14 European countries—the EU minus Denmark, Ireland, and the UK, but including Iceland and Norway. This means that border controls between participating countries have been abolished, and visa policies harmonized. While you're still required to carry a passport (or government-issued ID card for EU citizens) when crossing an internal border, once you've been admitted into one country, you're free to travel to all participating states. Britain and Ireland have also formed a **common travel area,** abolishing passport controls between the UK and the Republic of Ireland, meaning that the only times you'll see a border guard within the EU are traveling between the British Isles and the Continent and in and out of Denmark.

For more important consequences of the EU for travelers, see **The Euro** (see p. 251) and **Customs** (see p. 248).

STUDENT AND TEACHER IDENTIFICATION. The **International Student Identity Card (ISIC),** the most widely accepted form of student ID, provides discounts on sights, accommodations, food, and transport. The ISIC is preferable to a school-specific card because it is more likely to be honored abroad. Cardholders have access to a 24hr. emergency helpline for medical, legal, and financial emergencies (US collect +1 (715) 345-0505), and US cardholders are also eligible for insurance benefits (see **Insurance,** p. 255). ISICs are issued by Council Travel (www.counciltravel.com/idcards/default.asp) and many other student travel agencies (see p. 257). The card is valid from September of one year to December of the following year and costs AUS$15, CDN$15, or US$22. Applicants must be degree-seeking students of a secondary or post-secondary school and must be at least 12 years of age. Because of the proliferation of fake ISICs, some services (particularly airlines) require additional proof of student identity, such as a school ID or a signed letter of introduction stamped with your school seal. The **International Teacher Identity Card (ITIC)** offers the same insurance coverage as well as limited discounts. The fee is AUS$13, UK£5, or US$22. For more info, contact the **International Student Travel Confederation (ISTC),** Herengracht 479, 1017 BS Amsterdam, Netherlands (☎+31 (20) 421 28 00; fax 421 28 10; email istcinfo@istc.org; www.istc.org).

YOUTH IDENTIFICATION. The ISTC issues a discount card to non-students 25 or younger: the **International Youth Travel Card (IYTC;** formerly **GO 25**) offers many of the same benefits as the ISIC, and is usually sold at the same locations (US$22 per year).

CUSTOMS & VAT

ARRIVING IN ITALY. Upon entering Italy, you must declare certain items from abroad and pay a duty on the value of those articles that exceeds the allowance established by the Italian customs service. Note that goods and gifts purchased at **duty-free** shops abroad are not exempt from duty or sales tax at your point of return and thus must be declared as well; "duty-free" merely means that you need not pay a tax in the country of purchase. Duty-free allowances were abolished for travel between EU member states on July 1, 1999, but still exist for those arriving from outside the EU.

Italy allows duty-free importation of the following for non-EU citizens: 200 cigarettes or 100 small cigars or 50 cigars or 250g of loose tobacco, 750 ml of spirits over 22% or 2L of wine; 50cc of perfume and 500g of coffee or 100 grams of tea. EU citizens may bring in the above items in larger quantities: 800 cigarettes or 400 small cigars or 200 cigars or 1kg of tobacco, 90L of wine, 10L of spirits over 22%, 110L of beer. In addition to personal effects, non-EU tourists may also bring in two cameras, a reasonable amount of film, a video camera, one radio, one television, one tape recorder, one bicycle, one boat (with or without motor), two pairs of skis, two tennis rackets, one canoe, and one surf board.

RETURNING HOME. Upon returning home, you must declare all articles acquired abroad and pay a duty on the value of articles in excess of your home country's allowance. In order to expedite your return, make a list of any valuables brought from home and register them with customs before traveling abroad. Be sure to keep receipts for all goods acquired abroad. Upon departure from the EU, non-EU citizens can claim a refund for the value added tax (VAT or IVA) paid on major purchases. For specific customs requirements, contact the nearest customs office.

VALUE-ADDED TAX. The **Value-Added Tax** (**VAT,** in Italian, *imposto sul valore aggiunta,* or IVA) is a sales tax levied in the European Union. VAT (ranging from 12-35%) is usually part of the price paid for goods and services. Upon departure from the EU, non-EU citizens can get a refund of the VAT for purchases over L650,000. The receipt, purchases, and purchaser's passport must be presented at the Customs Office as you leave the EU, and the refund will be mailed to you. "Tax-Free Shopping for Tourists" at some stores enables you to get your refund in cash when at the airport or a border crossing.

MONEY

If you stay in hostels and prepare your own food, expect to spend approximately L100,000 per person per day in Rome. **Accommodations** start at about L30,000 per night for a dorm, L60,000 for a single, and L90,000 for a double. A basic sit-down meal costs about L30,000. Carrying cash, even in a money belt, is risky but still necessary, though Mastercard and Visa are widely accepted in the city (establishments that accept credit cards are noted in the book), many shops and restaurants are still cash-only.

TIPS FOR STAYING ON A BUDGET. Considering that saving just a few dollars a day over the course of your trip might pay for days or weeks of additional travel, the art of penny-pinching is well worth learning. Museums are often free once a month, and Rome often hosts free open-air concerts and cultural events. Do your **laundry** in the sink (unless you're explicitly prohibited from doing so). You can split **accommodations** costs (in hotels and some hostels) with trustworthy fellow travelers; multi-bed rooms almost always work out cheaper per person than singles. The same principle will also work for cutting down on the cost of **restaurant** meals. You can also buy food in supermarkets instead of eating out. That said, don't go overboard with your budget obsession. Never penny-pinch at the expense of your sanity or health.

CURRENCY & EXCHANGE

The Italian currency unit is the *lira* (pl. *lire*). Coins are minted in L50, L100, L200, and L500 denominations. The most common bills are L1000, L2000, L5000, L10,000, L50,000, and L100,000. The currency chart below is based on August 2000 exchange rates. Check a large newspaper or the web (www.letsgo.com/Thumb, finance.yahoo.com, or www.bloomberg.com) for the latest exchange rates.

EUR€1 = L1936 (FIXED)	L1000 =EUR€ 0.52
US$1 = L2119	L1000 = US $0.47
CDN$1 =L1425	L1000= CDN $0.70
UK£1 = L3158	L1000 = UK £0.32
IR£1 = L2459	L1000 = IR £0.41
AUS$1 = L1226	L1000 = AUS $0.82
NZ$1 = L961	L1000 = NZ $1.04
SAR1= L302	L1000 = SAR3.32

As a general rule, it's cheaper to convert money in Italy than at home. However, you should bring enough foreign currency to last for the first 24 to 72 hours of a trip in case you should arrive after bank hours or on a holiday. Travelers from the US can get foreign currency from the comfort of home: **International Currency Express** (☎ (888) 278-6628) delivers foreign currency or traveler's checks overnight (US$15) or 2nd-day (US$12) at competitive exchange rates.

Often, the cheapest way to obtain *lire* is from ATM machines. When changing cash, look for *cambio* signs and shop around. Banks usually have the best rates; never use an establishment that has more than a 5% margin between its buy and sell prices. Since you lose money with each transaction, **convert large sums** (unless the currency is depreciating rapidly), but no more than you'll need.

TRAVELER'S CHECKS

Traveler's checks (**American Express** and **Visa** are the most recognized) are one of the safest and least troublesome means of carrying funds. Several agencies and banks sell them for a small commission. Each agency provides refunds if your checks are lost or stolen, and many provide additional services, such as toll-free refund hotlines abroad, emergency message services, and stolen credit card assistance.

Money From Home In Minutes.

If you're stuck for cash on your travels, don't panic. Millions of people trust Western Union to transfer money in minutes to 176 countries and over 78,000 locations worldwide. Our record of safety and reliability is second to none. For more information, call Western Union: USA 1-800-325-6000, Canada 1-800-235-0000. Wherever you are, you're never far from home.

www.westernunion.com

WESTERN UNION | MONEY TRANSFER®

The fastest way to send money worldwide.

While traveling, keep check receipts and records separate from the checks themselves. Leave a list of check numbers with someone at home. Never countersign checks until you're ready to cash them, and always bring your passport with you to cash them. If your checks are lost or stolen, immediately contact your check company's refund center to be reimbursed (for locations in Rome, see **Service Directory,** p. 295); they may require a police report verifying the loss or theft. Ask about toll-free refund hotlines and the location of refund centers when purchasing checks, and always carry emergency cash.

American Express: In Australia, call (800) 251 902; in New Zealand (0800) 441 068; in the UK (0800) 521 313; in the US and Canada (800) 221-7282. In Italy call (800) 872000. Elsewhere call US collect +1 (801) 964-6665; www.aexp.com. Traveler's checks are available in *lire* at 1-4% commission at AmEx offices and banks, commission-free at AAA offices. *Cheques for Two* can be signed by either of 2 people traveling together.

Thomas Cook MasterCard: In the US and Canada, call (800) 223-7373; in the UK call (0800) 62 21 01; elsewhere call UK collect +44 (1733) 31 89 50. Checks available in 13 currencies at 2% commission. Thomas Cook offices cash checks commission-free.

Visa: In the US call (800) 227-6811; in the UK (0800) 895 078; elsewhere call UK collect +44 (1733) 318 949.

CREDIT CARDS

Credit cards offer excellent exchange rates—up to 5% better than the retail rate used by banks and other money changers. Credit cards may also offer services such as insurance or emergency help, and are sometimes required to reserve hotel rooms or rental cars. **MasterCard** (a.k.a. EuroCard or Access in Europe) and **Visa** are the most welcomed; **American Express** cards work at some ATMs and at AmEx offices and major airports.

Credit cards are also useful for **cash advances,** which allow you to withdraw *lire* from banks and ATMs (called Bancomats) throughout Italy (see **Cash Cards,** below). However, transaction fees for all credit card advances (up to US$10 per advance, plus 2-3% extra on foreign transactions after conversion) tend to make credit cards a more costly way of withdrawing cash than ATMs or traveler's checks. To be eligible for an advance, you'll need to get a **Personal Identification Number (PIN)** from your credit card company.

CREDIT CARD COMPANIES. Visa (US ☎ (800) 336-8472) and **MasterCard** (US ☎ (800) 307-7309) are issued in cooperation with banks and other organizations. **American Express** (US ☎ (800) 843-2273) has an annual fee of up to US$55. AmEx cardholders may cash personal checks at AmEx offices abroad, access an emergency medical and legal assistance hotline (24hr.; in North America call (800) 554-2639, elsewhere call US collect +1 (202) 554-2639), and enjoy American Express Travel Service benefits, including plane, hotel, and car rental reservation changes, baggage loss and flight insurance, mailgram and international cable services, and held mail.

THE EURO

On January 1, 1999, 11 countries of the European Union, including Italy, officially adopted the Euro as their common currency. Euro notes and coins will not be issued until January, 1, 2002, and until that time the Euro will exist only in electronic transactions and traveler's checks. On June 1, 2002, the *lira* will be withdrawn from circulation and the Euro will become the only legal currency in Italy. Let's Go lists all prices in Italian *lire*, as these will still be most relevant in 2001. However, all Italian businesses must quote prices in both *lire* and Euros.

Travelers who will be passing through more than one nation in the Euro-zone should note that exchange rates between the 11 national currencies were irrevocably fixed on January 1, 1999. Henceforth, *cambiari* will be obliged to change Euro-zone currencies at the official rate with **no commission,** though they may still charge a nominal service fee. Euro-denominated traveler's checks may also be used throughout the Euro-zone, and can be exchanged commission-free in any of the 11 Euro nations.

CASH CARDS (ATMS)

Twenty-four-hour cash machines (ATMs) are widespread in Italy. Depending on the system that your home bank uses, you can most likely access your personal bank account from abroad. ATMs get the same wholesale exchange rate as credit cards, but there is often a limit on the amount of money you can withdraw per day (around US$500), and unfortunately computer networks sometimes fail. There is typically also a surcharge of US$1-5 per withdrawal.

In Rome, ATMs are dubbed *Bancomats*. The banks with the most reliable ATMs accepting Visa and Mastercard are Banca Nazionale del Lavoro and Banca di Roma (see **Service Directory**, p. 293). **Credit card ATMs** abound on V. Arenula, V. del Tritone, V. del Corso, and near the Pantheon. The five-block radius surrounding Termini is chock full of banks and machines, as is the 10-block radius surrounding St. Peter's Basilica. The ATM at the AmEx office at the Spanish Steps accepts **AmEx** cards, as does the Banca Popolare di Milano. Some machines shut down after midnight. In case of serious problems with ATMs, contact the Smarrimento Bancom (☎ (800) 822056).

The two major international money networks are **Cirrus** (US ☎ (800) 424-7787) and **PLUS** (US ☎ (800) 843-7587). For ATMs around the world, call the above numbers, or consult www.visa.com/pd/atm or www.mastercard.com/atm.

Visa TravelMoney (for customer assistance in Italy, call (800) 819 014) allows you to use any Visa ATM. To activate a card from the US, call (877) 394-2247. You deposit an amount before you travel (plus a small fee), and you can withdraw up to that sum at Visa's favorable exchange rates. Check with your local bank to see if it issues Travel-Money cards.

GETTING MONEY FROM HOME

AMERICAN EXPRESS. Cardholders can withdraw cash from their checking accounts at any of AmEx's offices (up to US$1000 every 21 days; no service charge, no interest). AmEx "Express Cash" withdrawals from any AmEx ATM in Italy are automatically debited from the cardholder's checking account or line of credit. Green card holders may withdraw up to US$1000 in any seven-day period (2% transaction fee; min. US$2.50, max. US$20). To enroll in Express Cash, call (800) 227-4669 in the US; elsewhere call the US collect +1 (336) 668-5041. The AmEx national number in Italy is 06 72282.

WESTERN UNION. Westerm Union can wire money abroad from the US, Canada, or the UK. In the US, call (800) 325-6000; in Canada, (800) 235-0000; in the UK, (0800) 833 833; in Italy, (800) 220055. To wire money from within the US using a credit card (Visa, MasterCard, Discover), call (800) CALL-CASH (225-5227). The rates for sending cash are generally US$10-11 cheaper than with a credit card. Transfers usually take an hour or less. There are dozens of Western Union locations in Rome; consult www.western-nunion.com.

US STATE DEPARTMENT (US CITIZENS ONLY). In dire emergencies, the US State Department will forward money within hours to the nearest consular office, which will then disburse it according to instructions for a US$15 fee. Contact the Overseas Citizens Service, American Citizens Services, Consular Affairs, Room 4811, US Department of State, Washington, D.C. 20520 (☎ (202) 647-5225; nights, Sundays, and holidays 647-4000; http://travel.state.gov).

HEALTH & SAFETY

PERSONAL SAFETY

BLENDING IN. In Rome, as in any city, tourists are particularly vulnerable to crime for two reasons: they often carry large amounts of cash and they are not as street savvy as locals. Try to blend in as much as possible. Dress inconspicuously: the gawking camera-toter is a more obvious target than the low-profile traveler, and wearing a fanny-pack is tantamount to sporting a bullseye. Walking into a cafe or shop to check a map beats checking it on the street corner. Muggings are more often impromptu than planned; nervous, over-the-shoulder glances can be a tip that you have something valuable to protect.

EXPLORING. Even late at night, hordes of Italians and tourists traverse the streets around the popular sights. However exercise caution in the outlying parts of the city, as well as in Esquilino, the area south of Termini. Whenever applicable, *Let's Go* warns of unsafe areas, but exercise your own judgment about your environs; buildings in disrepair, vacant lots, and unpopulated areas are all bad signs. Ask around about unsafe areas before venturing out at night. When walking at night, stick to busy, well-lit streets and avoid dark alleyways, parks, and other deserted areas. If you are traveling alone, be sure that someone at home knows your itinerary. Never say that you're traveling alone. The **emergency phone number** in Rome is 113 (police) or 112 (carabinieri).

SELF DEFENSE. There is no sure-fire way to avoid all the threatening situations you might encounter when you travel, but a good self-defense course will give you concrete ways to react to unwanted advances. **Impact, Prepare, and Model Mugging** can refer you to local self-defense courses in the US (☎ (800) 345-5425) and Vancouver (☎ (604) 878-3838). Workshops (2-3hr.) start at US$50; full courses run US$350-500.

DRUGS AND ALCOHOL. Travelers should avoid drugs altogether. All foreigners in Italy are subject to Italian law. Drugs (including marijuana) are illegal in Italy, although arrests are much less common than in the United States. Your home country is essentially powerless to interfere in a foreign court. Even if you don't use drugs, beware of any person who asks you to carry a package or drive a car across the border. Label prescription drug bottles clearly and carry copies of the prescriptions with your important documents. While Italians are known to enjoy a good drink, **public drunkeness** is not tolerated, and nothing will ruin your trip more than a night in a Roman *prigione*.

FINANCIAL SECURITY

CON ARTISTS. Few cities boast con artists of the caliber found in Rome. Tourists should be wary of those in business near the bigger tourist attractions, particularly around the Colosseum and on the #64 bus. Con artists and hustlers often work in groups, and children are among the most effective. Hucksters possess an innumerable range of ruses. Be aware of certain classics: sob stories that require money, rolls of bills "found" on the street, mustard spilled (or saliva spit) onto your shoulder distracting you for enough time to snatch your bag. Do not respond or make eye contact, walk quickly away, and keep a solid grip on your belongings. Call the police if a hustler is insistent or aggressive.

PICKPOCKETS. Don't put a wallet with money in your back pocket. Never count your money in public and carry as little as possible. If you carry a purse, buy a sturdy one, and carry it crosswise on the side, away from the street with the clasp against you. Secure day-packs with small combination padlocks which slip through the two zippers. (Even these precautions do not always suffice: moped riders who snatch bags sometimes tote knives to cut the straps.) Some tourists enjoy the thrill of a **money belt,** the safest and most stylish way to carry cash. A **neck pouch** is equally safe, although far less accessible and far less stylish. Be particularly careful on **crowded buses and subways** (for example, hold your backpack in front of you where you can see it). Pickpockets are amazingly deft at their craft. If someone stands uncomfortably close, move to another car and hold your bags tightly. Also, be alert in public telephone booths. If you must say your calling-card number, do so very quietly.

THIEVES. Thieves thrive on trains; professionals wait for tourists to fall asleep and then carry off everything they can. When traveling in pairs, sleep in alternating shifts; when alone, use good judgment in selecting a train compartment: never stay in an empty one, and use a lock to secure your pack to the luggage rack. Keep important documents and other valuables on your person and try to sleep on top bunks with your luggage stored above you (if not in bed with you). *Never* trust anyone to "watch your bag for a second."

HEALTH

For information on long-term health care and insurance in Rome, see **Living in Rome,** p. 281. For lists of doctors, hospitals, and pharmacies, see **Service Directory,** p. 293.

BEFORE YOU GO

Preparation can help minimize the likelihood of contracting a disease and maximize the chances of receiving effective health care in the event of an emergency.

In your **passport,** write the names of emergency contacts, and also list any allergies or medical conditions of which you would want doctors to be aware. Matching a prescription to a foreign equivalent is not always easy, safe, or possible. Carry up-to-date, legible prescriptions or a statement from your doctor stating the medication's trade name, manufacturer, chemical name, and dosage. While traveling, be sure to keep all medication with you in your carry-on luggage. Also consider carrying a small **first-aid kit.**

While no special immunizations are needed for travel to Italy, a good resource for concerns is the **US Centers for Disease Control and Prevention** (☎ (877) FYI-TRIP; www.cdc.gov/travel).

CHRONIC MEDICAL CONDITIONS. Travelers with chronic medical conditions (e.g. diabetes, allergies to antibiotics, epilepsy, heart conditions) should consult their physicians before leaving. Bring any medication you may need, and a copy of the prescription and/or a statement from your doctor, especially if you will be bringing insulin, syringes, or any narcotics to Rome, as some drugs legal at home may not be legal there. Travelers should also consider obtaining a medic alert bracelet to alert paramedics of their condition.

People with **asthma** or **allergies** should be aware that Rome has visibly high levels of air pollution, particularly during the summer. As elsewhere in Europe, "non-smoking" areas are almost nonexistent.

ONCE THERE

Common sense is the simplest prescription for health while you travel. To prevent minor illnesses and injuries, drink lots of fluids and wear sturdy, broken-in shoes.

In general, English-speaking health care services in Rome are reliable and readily available, but if you are concerned about accessing medical support while traveling, there are special support services you may employ. The *MedPass* from **Global Emergency Medical Services (GEMS),** 2001 Westside Dr. #120, Alpharetta, GA 30004 (☎ (800) 860-1111; fax (770) 475-0058; www.globalems.com), provides 24hr. international medical assistance, support, and medical evacuation resources. If your regular **insurance** policy does not cover travel abroad, you may wish to purchase additional coverage (see p. 255).

AIDS, HIV, STDS. Italy has one of the highest HIV rates in Europe. The easiest mode of HIV transmission is through direct blood-to-blood contact with an HIV-positive person; *never* share intravenous needles of any sort. The most common mode of transmission is sexual intercourse. Health professionals recommend the use of latex condoms. Italian condoms are not the highest quality, so you may want to bring a supply from home. AIDS (*SIDA* in Italian) education, however is becoming more prevalent, and you won't have any problems finding condoms *(preservativi)* at any pharmacy.

There are no restrictions on HIV-positive travelers or travelers with STDs *(malattia venerea)* entering Rome. Italians are generally very sensible about medical treatment, and medical professionals will not pry if you get tested. Tests can be performed at any clinic (see **Clinics,** p. 294) such as **Analisi Cliniche** (a private lab which handles all sorts of tests, from allergies to pregnancy); always confirm that your test is confidential and anonymous. At the clinic, simply ask for the "AIDS test" (AH-eeds) or "HIV test" (A-kah-EE-VOO). Go in the morning for a *prelievo* (withdrawal) and call or pick up the results in the afternoon. For detailed information on **AIDS** in Italy, call the **US Centers for Disease Control's** 24hr. hotline at (800) 342-2437.

WOMEN'S HEALTH. Women taking **birth control pills** should bring a copy of their prescription, as many different forms are available. Women considering an **abortion** abroad should contact the **International Planned Parenthood Federation (IPPF),** Regent's College, Inner Circle, Regent's Park, London NW1 4NS (☎ (020) 7487 7900; www.ippf.org), for more info. First trimester abortion is legal in Italy, but there is considerable objection among health care providers to performing abortions.

PHARMACIES. All pharmacies post the names, addresses, and hours of neighboring pharmacies and all-night pharmacies. *La Repubblica* and *Il Messaggero* newspapers publish a list of pharmacies open in August, and *Roma C'è* lists 24-hour pharmacies in the English language section. You can usually get foreign prescriptions at a pharmacy and condoms are also available, not to mention suspicious looks from the pharmacist. The following are your best bet during the wee hours, but call ahead to make sure they are open, since night service often rotates:

INSURANCE

Travel insurance generally covers four basic areas: medical/health problems, property loss, trip cancellation/interruption, and emergency evacuation. Although your regular insurance policies may extend to travel-related accidents, you may consider purchasing travel insurance if the cost of potential trip cancellation/interruption or emergency medical evacuation is greater than you can afford. Travel insurance generally runs about US$50 per week for full coverage, while trip cancellation/interruption coverage may be purchased separately at a rate of about US$5.50 per US$100 of coverage.

MEDICAL INSURANCE. Medical insurance (especially university policies) often covers costs incurred abroad. **US Medicare** does not cover foreign travel. **Canadians** are protected by their province's health insurance plan for up to 90 days after leaving the country; check with the provincial Ministry of Health or Health Plan Headquarters for details. **Australians** traveling in Italy are entitled to many of the services that they would receive at home as part of the Reciprocal Health Care Agreement. EU citizens traveling to Italy should ask their insurer for an E111 form, which covers EU citizens for emergency medical care in other EU countries. **Homeowners' insurance** often covers theft during travel and loss of travel documents (passport, plane ticket, railpass, etc.) up to US$500.

CARD-CARRYING BENEFITS. ISIC and **ITIC** (see p. 248) provide basic benefits, including US$100 per day of in-hospital sickness for up to 60 days, US$3000 of accident-related medical reimbursement, and US$25,000 for emergency medical transport. Cardholders have access to a toll-free 24hr. helpline for medical, legal, and financial emergencies overseas (US and Canada☎ (877) 370-4742, elsewhere call US collect +1 (713) 342-4104). **AmEx** (US ☎ (800) 528-4800) grants most cardmembers car rental insurance (collision and theft, but not liability) and ground travel accident coverage of US$100,000 when airfare is paid with the card.

CAR INSURANCE. Most credit cards also cover standard car insurance. If you rent, lease, or borrow a car, you will need a green card, or International Insurance Certificate, to prove that you have liability insurance. Obtain it through the car rental agency; most include coverage in their prices. Some travel agents offer the card. Verify whether your auto insurance applies abroad; even if it does, you will still need a green card to certify this to foreign officials. If you have a collision while in Rome, the accident will show up on your domestic records if you report it to your insurance company. Rental agencies may require you to purchase theft insurance, since Italy is seen as a high-risk country.

INSURANCE PROVIDERS. Council and STA (see p. 257) offer a range of plans that can supplement your basic coverage. Other private insurance providers in the US and Canada include: Access America (☎ (800) 284-8300); Berkely Group/Carefree Travel Insurance (☎ (800) 323-3149; www.berkely.com); Globalcare Travel Insurance (☎ (800) 821-2488; www.globalcare-cocco.com); and Travel Assistance International (☎ (800) 821-2828; www.worldwide-assistance.com). Providers in the UK include Campus Travel (☎ (01865) 258 000) and Columbus Travel Insurance (☎ (020) 7375 0011). In Australia, try CIC Insurance (☎9202 8000).

PACKING

If you want to get away from it all, don't take it with you. Set out everything you think you'll need, then pack half the clothes and twice the money. Remember, you have to carry everything you take. Almost all supplies are readily available in Rome.

LUGGAGE. Whatever you choose to bring—whether a large backpack or three trunks—be sure to have a light **daypack** for sightseeing and a **moneybelt** or **neck pouch** to protect your money, passport, railpass, and other important articles. Label every piece of luggage inside and out.

CLOTHING AND LAUNDRY. No nation outdresses Italy, but you should try. Do your best. Most importantly, be sure to bring clothes **appropriate for visits to cathedrals and churches,** since shorts, short skirts, and sleeveless shirts are usually forbidden (a drape or scarf to cover shoulders is a good idea for women). Shorts, university t-shirts, and running shoes brand you as a tourist and may be the cause of undesirable attention in Italy. **For women,** a long sundress or light cotton pants are the most appropriate summer travelwear. **For men,** cotton pants will be more comfortable than jeans. However, most Romans wear jeans, even in July and August. Shorts are more acceptable on men than on women, but are considered rude in cathedrals. If all else fails, head to **Diesel** (p. 164).

Laundry facilities are expensive in Rome: bring non-wrinkling, quick-drying clothes that you can wash in a sink. Nonetheless, there comes a time in every life when washing machines are necessary. When this time comes, consult **Service Directory,** p. 296, for some above-average laundromats.

ELECTRICAL CURRENT. The majority of all electric outlets in Rome spew out 220V; your favorite electrical appliances may require a converter to change the voltage. Check to see what voltage your appliance requires before plugging in or you could zap your electric friend into oblivion. Since Italy's prongs are not flat but round (2 prongs), US, Canadian, and Australian gadgets need an adapter (unless appliance instructions explicitly state otherwise, as with some portable computers), available in any hardware store in Rome or from most travel or hardware stores elsewhere.

MISCELLANEOUS. Film is available but expensive in Rome. Bring lots with you and develop it at home; it's cheaper. Consider bringing a **disposable camera** or two rather than an expensive permanent one. Whatever kind of camera you use, be aware that, despite disclaimers, airport security X-rays *can* fog film. To protect it, either buy a lead-lined pouch from a camera store or ask the security personnel to hand inspect your film. Be sure to pack it in your carry-on luggage, since higher-intensity X-rays are used on checked bags.

Travelers who heat disinfect their **contact lenses** should either buy a small current converter for their machine (US$20) or take their own chemicals to use in Rome. In any case, bring a backup pair of glasses.

Also valuable are insect repellent, an alarm clock, plastic bags that seal shut (for damp clothes, soap, food), a sun hat, sunscreen, a sewing kit, a **sleepsack** (required in some hostels; make one by folding a full-size sheet in half the long way and sewing up the sides), sunglasses, a pocketknife, a water bottle, a padlock, a towel, and a first-aid kit.

A **basic first-aid kit** includes: bandages, aspirin or other painkiller, antibiotic cream, a Swiss Army knife, tweezers, moleskin, decongestant, motion-sickness remedy, stomach medication (Pepto Bismol or Imodium), an antihistamine, and burn ointment.

GETTING THERE

BY PLANE

When it comes to airfare, a little effort can save you a bundle. If your plans are flexible enough to deal with the restrictions, courier fares are the cheapest. Tickets bought from consolidators and standby seating are also good deals, but last-minute specials, airfare wars, and charter flights often beat these fares. The key is to hunt around, to be flexible, and to persistently ask about discounts. Students, seniors, and those under 26 should never pay full price for a ticket. For info on airports in Rome, see **When in Rome,** p. 17.

Airfares to Italy peak between mid-June and early Sept.; holidays are also expensive times to travel. Midweek (M-Th morning) flights run US$40-50 cheaper than weekend flights, but the latter are generally less crowded and more likely to permit frequent-flier upgrades. Return-date flexibility is usually not an option for the budget traveler; traveling with an "open return" ticket can be pricier than fixing a return date when buying the ticket and paying later to change it.

Round-trip flights are by far the cheapest; "open-jaw" (arriving in and departing from different cities) and round-the-world, or RTW, flights are pricier but reasonable alternatives. Patching one-way flights together is the least economical way to travel. Flights between capital cities or regional hubs will offer the most competitive fares.

BUDGET AND STUDENT TRAVEL AGENCIES

While agents specializing in flights to Italy can make your life easy and help you save, they may not spend the time to find you the lowest possible fare—they get paid on commission. Students and under-26ers holding **ISIC** or **IYTC** cards (see p. 248) qualify for big discounts from student travel agencies. Most flights from budget agencies are on major airlines, but in peak season some may sell seats on less reliable chartered aircraft.

usit world (www.usitworld.com). Over 50 **usit campus** branches in the UK (www.usitcampus.co.uk), including 52 Grosvenor Gardens, **London** SW1W 0AG (☎ (0870) 240 1010); **Manchester** (☎ (0161) 273 1721); and **Edinburgh** (☎ (0131) 668 3303). Nearly 20 **usit now** offices in Ireland, including 19-21 Aston Quay, O'Connell Bridge, **Dublin** 2 (☎ (01) 602 1600; www.usitnow.ie), and **Belfast** (☎ (02890) 327 111; www.usitnow.com). Offices also in Auckland and Johannesburg, among other cities.

Council Travel (www.counciltravel.com). US offices include: Emory Village, 1561 N. Decatur Rd., **Atlanta,** GA 30307 (☎ (404) 377-9997); 273 Newbury St., **Boston,** MA 02116 (☎ (617) 266-1926); 1160 N. State St., **Chicago,** IL 60610 (☎ (312) 951-0585); 931 Westwood Blvd., Westwood, **Los Angeles,** CA 90024 (☎ (310) 208-3551); 254 Greene St., **New York,** NY 10003 (☎ (212) 254-2525); 530 Bush St., **San Francisco,** CA 94108 (☎ (415) 566-6222); 424 Broadway Ave E., **Seattle,** WA 98102 (☎ (206) 329-4567); 3301 M St. NW, **Washington, D.C.** 20007 (☎ (202) 337-6464). **For US cities not listed,** call (800) 2-COUNCIL (226-8624). In the UK, 28A Poland St. (Oxford Circus), **London** W1V 3DB (☎ (020) 7437 7767).

CTS Travel, 44 Goodge St., **London** W1 (☎ (020) 7636 0031; fax 7637 5328; email ctsinfo@ctstravel.com.uk).

STA Travel, 6560 Scottsdale Rd. #F100, Scottsdale, AZ 85253 (☎ (800) 777-0112; fax (602) 922-0793; www.sta-travel.com). A student and youth travel organization with over 150 offices worldwide (check the website). Tickets, insurance, railpasses, and more. In the UK, 11 Goodge St., **London** WIP 1FE (☎ (020) 7436 7779 for North American travel). In New Zealand, 10 High St., **Auckland** (☎ (09) 309 0458). In Australia, 366 Lygon St., **Melbourne,** Vic 3053 (☎ (03) 9349 4344).

Travel CUTS (Canadian Universities Travel Services Limited), 187 College St., **Toronto,** ON M5T 1P7 (☎ (416) 979-2406; fax 979-8167; www.travelcuts.com). 40 offices across Canada. Also in the UK, 295-A Regent St., **London** W1R 7YA (☎ (020) 7255 1944).

Wasteels, Platform 2, Victoria Station, London SW1V 1JT (☎ (020) 7834 7066; fax 7630 7628; www.wasteels.dk/uk). A huge chain in Europe, with 203 locations. Sells the Wasteels BIJ tickets, which are discounted (30-45% off regular fare), 2nd-class international point-to-point train tickets with unlimited stopovers for those under 26 (sold only in Europe).

COMMERCIAL AIRLINES

The commercial airlines' lowest regular offer is the **APEX** (Advance Purchase Excursion) fare, which provides confirmed reservations and allows "open-jaw" tickets. Generally, reservations must be made seven to 21 days in advance, with seven- to 14-day minimum and up to 90-day maximum stay limits, and hefty cancellation and change penalties (fees rise in summer). Book peak-season APEX fares early, since by May you will have a hard time getting the departure date you want.

FROM NORTH AMERICA

Basic round-trip fares to Italy range from roughly US$200-700. Large commercial carriers like American (☎ (800) 433-7300; www.aa.com) and United (☎ (800) 241-6522; www.ual.com) will probably offer the most convenient flights, but they may not be the cheapest, unless you manage to grab a special promotion or airfare war ticket. You might find flying one of the following airlines a better deal.

Alitalia (US ☎ (800) 223-5730) offers roundtrip tickets to most locations in Italy. Senior and student discounts available.

Delta Airlines (☎ (800) 241-4141; Canada (800) 221-1212) offers round-trip flights to Rome. Senior and student discounts available for as low as $400 during the fall season for seniors, $540 for students. Website (www.delta-air.com) contains more info.

Lufthansa Airlines (US ☎ (800) 645-3880; www.lufthansa.com/ehome.htm) offers round-trip flights to Rome. Call 3 weeks in advance. Senior citizen and student discounts up to 10%.

FROM THE UK AND IRELAND

Because of the myriad carriers flying from the British Isles to the continent, we only include discount airlines or those with cheap specials here. The **Air Travel Advisory Bureau** in London (☎ (020) 7636 5000; www.atab.co.uk) provides referrals to travel agencies and consolidators that offer discounted airfares out of the UK.

FLIGHT PLANNING ON THE INTERNET

The Web is a great place to look for travel bargains—it's fast, it's convenient, and you can spend as long as you like exploring options without driving your travel agent insane.

Many airline sites offer special last-minute deals on the Web. For fares, see Alitalia (www.alitalia.it), Air-One (www.air-one.it/airone.htm), and Gandalf Air (www.gandalfair.com). For a great set of links to practically every airline in every country, see www.travelpage.com/air/airlines. Other sites do the legwork and compile the deals for you—try www.bestfares.com, www.onetravel.com, www.lowestfare.com, and www.travelzoo.com.

STA (www.sta-travel.com) and **Council** (www.counciltravel.com) provide quotes on student tickets, while **Expedia** (msn.expedia.com) and **Travelocity** (www.travelocity.com) offer full travel services.

Priceline (www.priceline.com) allows you to specify a price, and obligates you to buy any ticket that meets or beats it; be prepared for antisocial hours and odd routes. **Skyauction** (www.skyauction.com) allows you to bid on both last-minute and advance-purchase tickets.

Just one last note—to protect yourself, make sure that the site uses a secure server before handing over any credit card details. Happy hunting!

Aer Lingus: Ireland (☎ (01) 886 8888; www.aerlingus.ie). Return tickets from Dublin, Cork, Galway, Kerry, and Shannon to Rome (IR£102-244).

Go-Fly Limited: UK (☎ (0845) 605 43 21), elsewhere call UK +44 (1279) 66 6388; www.go-fly.com. A subsidiary of British Airways. London to Rome (return UK£53-180).

KLM: UK (☎ (0870) 507 40 74; www.klmuk.com.) Cheap return tickets from London and elsewhere to Rome.

Ryanair: Ireland (☎ (01) 812 1212), UK (☎ (0870) 156 9569). www.ryanair.ie. From Dublin, London, and Glasgow to destinations in Italy. From London to Venice UK£33. Deals from as low as UK£9 on limited weekend specials.

FROM AUSTRALIA AND NEW ZEALAND

Air New Zealand: New Zealand (☎ (0800) 352 266; www.airnz.co.nz). Auckland to Rome.

Qantas Air: Australia (☎13 13 13), New Zealand (☎ (0800) 808 767). www.qantas.com.au. Flights from Australia and New Zealand to Rome.

FROM SOUTH AFRICA

Air France: ☎(011) 880 80 40; www.airfrance.com. Johannesburg to Paris; connections to Rome and the rest of the world.

British Airways: ☎(0860) 011 747; www.british-airways.com/regional/sa. Cape Town and Johannesburg to the UK and the rest of Europe from SAR3400.

Lufthansa: ☎(011) 484 4711; www.lufthansa.co.za. From Cape Town, Durban, and Johannesburg to Germany and elsewhere.

AIR COURIER FLIGHTS

Couriers help transport cargo on international flights by guaranteeing delivery of the baggage claim slips from the company to a representative overseas. Generally, couriers must travel light (carry-ons only) and deal with complex restrictions on their flight. Most flights are round-trip only with short fixed-length stays (usually one week) and a limit of a single ticket per issue. Most of these flights also operate only out of the biggest cities, like New York. Generally, you must be over 21 (in some cases 18), have a valid passport, and procure your own visa, if necessary. For more information, consult *Air Courier Bargains* by Kelly Monaghan (The Intrepid Traveler, US$15) or the *Courier Air Travel Handbook* by Mark Field (Perpetual Press, US$10).

FROM NORTH AMERICA. Round-trip courier fares from the US to Italy run about US$200-500. Most flights leave from New York, Los Angeles, San Francisco, or Miami in the US; and from Montreal, Toronto, or Vancouver in Canada. These organizations provide members with lists of opportunities and brokers worldwide for an annual fee:

Air Courier Association, 15000 W. 6th Ave. #203, Golden, CO 80401 (☎ (800) 282-1202; elsewhere call US +1 (303) 215-9000; www.aircourier.org). Ten departure cities throughout the US and Canada to Rome (high-season US$150-360). One-year US$64.

International Association of Air Travel Couriers (IAATC), 220 S. Dixie Hwy. #3, PO Box 1349, Lake Worth, FL 33460 (☎ (561) 582-8320; fax 582-1581; www.courier.org). From 9 North American cities to Rome. One-year US$45-50.

Global Courier Travel, P.O. Box 3051, Nederland, CO 80466 (www.globalcouriertravel.com). Searchable online database. Six departure points in the US and Canada to Rome. One-year US$40, 2 people US$55.

FROM THE UK AND IRELAND. Although courier traffic is heaviest from North America, there are limited courier flights in other areas. The minimum age for couriers from the **UK** is usually 18. **Brave New World Enterprises,** P.O. Box 22212, London SE5 8WB (email guideinfo@nry.co.uk; www.nry.co.uk/bnw) publishes a directory of companies offering courier flights in the UK (UK£10, in electronic form UK£8). **Global Courier Travel** (see above) also offers flights from London and Dublin to continental Europe.

OTHER AIR TRAVEL OPTIONS

STANDBY FLIGHTS. Traveling standby requires flexibility in arrival and departure dates and cities. Companies dealing in standby flights sell vouchers rather than tickets, along with the promise to get to (or near) your destination within a certain window of time (typically 1-5 days). You call in before your specific window of time to hear your flight options and the probability that you will be able to board each flight. You can then decide which flights you want to try to make, show up at the appropriate airport at the appropriate time, present your voucher, and board if space is available. Vouchers can usually be bought for both one-way and round-trip travel. You may receive a monetary refund only if every available flight within your date range is full; if you opt not to take an available (but perhaps less convenient) flight, you can only get credit toward future travel. Carefully read agreements with any company offering standby flights as tricky fine print can leave you in a lurch. To check on a company's service record in the US, call the Better Business Bureau (☎ (212) 533-6200). It is difficult to receive refunds, and clients' vouchers will not be honored when an airline fails to receive payment in time. One established standby company in the US is **Airhitch**, 2641 Broadway, 3rd Fl., New York, NY 10025 (☎ (800) 326-2009; fax 864-5489; www.airhitch.org) and Los Angeles, CA (☎ (888) 247-4482), which offers one-way flights to Europe from the Northeast (US$159), West Coast and Northwest (US$239), Midwest (US$209), and Southeast (US$189). Intracontinental connecting flights within the US or Europe cost US$79-139. Airhitch's head European office is in Paris (☎ +33 01 47 00 16 30); there's also one in Amsterdam (☎ +31 (20) 626 3220).

TICKET CONSOLIDATORS. Ticket consolidators, or **"bucket shops,"** buy unsold tickets in bulk from airlines and sell them at discounted rates. The best place to look is for tiny ads in the travel section of any major newspaper. Call quickly, as availability is typically extremely limited. Not all bucket shops are reliable, so insist on a receipt that gives full details of restrictions, refunds, and tickets, and pay by credit card so you can stop payment if you never receive your tickets. For more information, see www.travel-library.com/air-travel/consolidators.html or pick up Kelly Monaghan's *Air Travel's Bargain Basement* (Intrepid Traveler, US$8).

In the US, **Travel Avenue** (☎ (800) 333-3335; www.travelavenue.com), works with several consolidators and will search for cheap flights from anywhere for a fee. **NOW Voyager,** 74 Varick St. #307, New York, NY 10013 (☎ (212) 431-1616; fax 219-1793; www.nowvoyagertravel.com) arranges flights, mostly from New York. Other consolidators worth trying are: **Pennsylvania Travel** (☎ (800) 331-0947); **Rebel** (☎ (800) 227-3235; email travel@rebeltours.com; www.rebeltours.com); **Cheap Tickets** (☎ (800) 377-1000; www.cheaptickets.com); and **Travac** (☎ (800) 872-8800; fax (212) 714-9063; www.travac.com). Web consolidators include **Internet Travel Network** (www.itn.com); **Surplus-Travel.com** (www.surplustravel.com); **Travel Information Services** (www.tiss.com); **TravelHUB** (www.travelhub.com); and **The Travel Site** (www.thetravelsite.com). Keep in mind that these are just suggestions to get you started in your research; *Let's Go* does not endorse any of these agencies. Be cautious, and research companies before you hand over your credit card number.

In London, the **Air Travel Advisory Bureau** (☎ (020) 7636 5000; www.atab.co.uk) can provide names of reliable consolidators. In Australia and New Zealand, look for ads in the travel section of the *Sydney Morning Herald* and other papers.

CHARTER FLIGHTS. Charters are flights a tour operator contracts with an airline to fly extra loads of passengers during peak season. Charter flights fly less frequently than major airlines, make refunds particularly difficult, and are almost always fully booked. Schedules and itineraries may also change or be cancelled at the last moment (as late as 48 hours before the trip, and without a full refund), and check-in, boarding, and baggage claim are often much slower. Most charter flights to Rome fly into Ciampino airport (see p. 18) rather than Fiumicino.

Discount clubs and **fare brokers** offer members savings on last-minute charter and tour deals. Study contracts closely; you don't want to end up with an unwanted overnight layover. **Travelers Advantage,** Stamford, CT (☎ (800) 548-1116; www.travelersadvantage.com; US$60 annual fee includes discounts, newsletters, and cheap flight directories) specializes in European travel and tour packages.

BY TRAIN

Most major Italian cities and European hubs lie on a direct line to Rome or can reach it with a single change. **Tickets** can be bought and **reservations** made in any train station and at many travel agencies (see **Tourist Offices,** p. 266). Reservations are mandatory for **Eurostar** trains and some express trains (usually less than L10,000). Machines opposite the ticket counter at Termini station provide instructions in English and handle most transactions, accepting bills up to L50,000, ATM, Diner's Club, Matercard, and Visa.

While the economical, efficient, and romantic trains are the first choice of many budget travelers, they are not always safe. While passengers sleep, they may be robbed. Sleep wearing your money belt or neck pouch, and if you are traveling with a companion, try to sleep in shifts. See **Personal Safety,** p. 252, for more information. For information on **service within Italy,** contact **Ferrovie dello Stato (FS),** the Italian state railway (☎ 1478 88088; www.fs-on-line.com). For more information on service from outside Italy, contact Rail Europe (US ☎ (800) 438-245; www.raileurope.com).

The following are rates and times for second-class seats, one-way to Rome from: **Florence** (2-3hr., L40,900); **Venice** (5hr., L66,000); **Milan** (4½-8hr., L50,500); **Vienna** (13hr., US$102); **Prague** (16½hr., US$154); **Paris** (14½hr., US$158).

DOMESTIC. FS offers **Cartaverde** people aged 12 to 26. The card (L40,000) is valid for one year, and entitles you to a 20% and 30% discount on first- and second-class seats, respectively. If you're under 26 and plan to travel extensively, it should be your *first* purchase upon arrival. Families of four or more and groups of up to five adults traveling together qualify for discounts on Italian railways. Persons over 60 get a 20% discount on train tickets with purchase of a **Carta d'argento** (L40,000 per year).

MULTI-COUNTRY. For extended or extensive travel, a variety of passes are available. Contact Rail Europe (US ☎ (800) 438-245; www.raileurope.com) for more information.

TRAIN STATIONS. Termini, the transportation hub of Rome, is the focal point of most train lines and Rome's subway. Services including hotel reservations (across from track #20), ATMs, luggage storage (at track #1), and police (at track #13, or call 112) are available in the station. Not to be missed are ◼**Termini's bathrooms,** a blacklit wonderland off track #1 (L1000). Be warned, they become a way of life.

The various other stations on the fringe of town—**Tiburtina, Trastevere, Ostiense, San Lorenzo, Roma Nord, Prenestina**—are connected by bus and/or subway to Termini. Trains that arrive in Rome after midnight and before 5am or so usually arrive at Tiburtina or Ostiense, which are connected to Termini during these hours by the 40N and 20N-21N buses respectively. Be particularly wary of pickpockets and con artists in and around the stations. For more tips on how to avoid theft, see **Personal Safety,** p. 252.

BY BUS

An often cheaper alternative to rail passes for travelers visiting many cities is an **international bus pass,** which allows unlimited travel between major cities on a hop-on, hop-off basis. Buses are most popular among non-American backpackers.

Busabout, 258 Vauxhall Bridge Rd., London SW1V 1BS (☎ (171) 950 1661; fax 950 1662; www.busabout.com). Offers 5 interconnecting bus circuits covering 60 cities and towns in Europe; rolls into Rome twice daily. Consecutive Day Passes and FlexiPasses both available. Consecutive Day Standard/student passes are valid for 15 days (US$229/207), 21 days (US$324/295), 1 month (US$428/384), 2 months (US$666/592), 3 months (US$740/894), or for the season (US$977/873).

Eurolines, 52 Grosvenor Gardens, London SWIW OAG (☎ (1582) 404 511; www.eurolines.com). Unlimited 30-day (UK£229, under 26 and over 60 UK£199) or 60-day (UK£279/249) travel between 30 major European cities in 16 countries.

Pack the Wallet Guide
and save 25% or more* on calls home to the U.S.

It's lightweight and carries heavy savings of 25% or more*
over AT&T USA Direct and MCI WorldPhone rates. So take this
YOU wallet guide and carry it wherever you go.

To save with YOU:
- Dial the access number of the country you're in (see reverse)
- Dial 04 or follow the English voice prompts
- Enter your credit card info for easy billing

Service provided by Sprint

Hmm, call home or eat lunch?
With **YOU**^{SM}
you can do both.

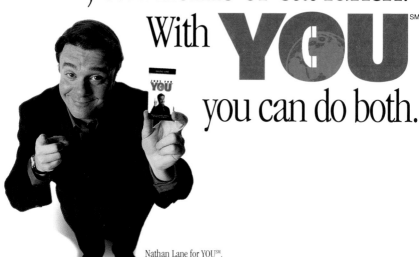

Nathan Lane for YOU^{SM}.

No doubt, traveling on a budget is tough. So tear out this wallet guide and keep it with you during your travels. With YOU, calling home from overseas is affordable and easy.

If the wallet guide is missing, call collect 913-624-5336 or visit www.youcallhome.com for YOU country numbers.

SPECIAL CONCERNS

TRAVELING ALONE

Traveling alone gives you greater independence and challenges, as well as more opportunities to meet and interact with locals. Without distraction, you can write a great travelogue (or at least some interesting letters) in the grand tradition of Henry James, Ernest Hemingway, or St. Paul. You may also be a more visible target for robbery and harassment. Lone travelers need to be well organized and look confident at all times. Try not to stand out as a tourist. **If questioned, never admit that you are traveling alone.** Maintain regular contact with someone at home who knows your itinerary. A number of organizations can find travel companions for solo travelers who desire them.

For more tips, pick up *Traveling Solo* by Eleanor Berman (Globe Pequot, US$17) or subscribe to **Connecting: Solo Travel Network,** P.O. Box 29088, Delamont RPO, Vancouver, BC V6J 5C2 (☎/fax (604) 737-7791; www.cstn.org; membership US$25-35) or *Travel Companions,* a newsletter for single travelers seeking company published by **Travel Companion Exchange,** P.O. Box 833, Amityville, NY 11701 (☎ (631) 454-0880 or (800) 392-1256; www.whytravelalone.com; US$48).

WOMEN TRAVELERS

Italy has long been viewed as a particularly difficult area for female travelers, largely due to the amount of unsought attention they routinely, constantly, and universally receive from Italian men. In general, harasssment does not go beyond honking, whistling, obnoxious hissing noises, and raucous "compliments."

To minimize harassment, adopt the attitude of Roman women: walk like you know where you are going, avoid eye contact—**sunglasses** are indispensable—and meet all advances with dignity, silence, and an impassive gaze. Try not to show too much skin if you aren't comfortable attracting attention. Wearing touristy attire (college shirts, sneakers, Tevas, or Birkenstocks) can also attract unwanted attention.

If you are physically harassed on the bus or in some public place, don't talk to the person directly (this often encourages him). Most Italians are embarrassed by the treatment that foreign women receive in Italy and will be supportive and helpful if they see that you are being bothered. Don't travel alone at night, if you can help it.

All travelers to Italy should be aware that the Italian conception of **personal space** might be different from that to which they are accustomed. The guy crowded next to you on the bus or the woman gesticulating madly in your face is not necessarily threatening you or being rude; it is fairly normal in Italian culture to stand close to the person you're addressing and to gesture wildly. Beyond this, if you feel at all uncomfortable, don't hesitate to seek out a police officer or passerby. Memorize the **emergency numbers** in Italy (113 and 112). Always carry a phone card for the phone and enough extra money for a bus or taxi. Self-defense courses suggest carrying a whistle on your keychain.

When choosing a train compartment, look for other women, couples, or, better yet, nuns. Nuns, both on and off trains, rival the police, guard dogs, and the most state-of-the-art personal protection devices in their effectiveness in warding off potential danger. **Never sit in an empty train compartment.** Be especially careful on overnight trains; many women have had the unpleasant surprise of waking up to find themselves being pawed by a lecherous stranger. A simple but loud *"non mi toccare"* ("don't touch me") will alert the other riders that you're being bothered and may humiliate your harasser enough to make him leave. Some travelers recommend wearing a fake (or real, if you've got one) wedding or engagement ring and even carrying pictures of their "children," who are back at the "hotel" with their "husband." Blondes and redheads will probably be harassed more than others with calls of *"Pssssst, biondina"* and other, less flattering phrases, but even brunettes and native Romans have to deal with harassment fairly regularly.

OLDER TRAVELERS

Older travelers in Italy are generally treated with considerable respect, and senior travelers are often entitled to travel-related discounts. Always ask about them, and be prepared to show proof of age (you probably look younger than you are). Agencies for senior group travel are growing in enrollment and popularity.

For more info, check out: *No Problem! Worldwise Tips for Mature Adventurers*, by Janice Kenyon (Orca Book Publishers, US$16); *A Senior's Guide to Healthy Travel*, by Donald L. Sullivan (Career Press, US$15); *Unbelievably Good Deals and Great Adventures That You Absolutely Can't Get Unless You're Over 50*, by Joan Rattner Heilman (Contemporary Books, US$13).

BISEXUAL, GAY, AND LESBIAN TRAVELERS

While Rome does not have a thriving gay and lesbian community like those to be found in many northern Italian cities, the gay scene is slowly but surely expanding. Italian society is, unfortunately, not the most gay-friendly in the world. Straight Roman men and women are open in showing affection for members of the same sex; embracing, holding hands or walking arm-in-arm is common; sadly, however, this homosocial ease hasn't translated into tolerance for men or women who want to express a *different* kind of affection for one another.

However concealed public gay life may be, the scene is on the rise. In 2000, Rome hosted World Pride 2000, drawing thousands of men and women from around the world. Sexual acts between members of the same sex have been legal for those above the age of consent (16) since 1889—more than many Anglo-Saxon countries can say.

The national organization for gay men, **Arci-Gay**, has its headquarters in Bologna, P. di Porta Saragozza, 2, 40123 (☎051 6447054; www.malox.com/arcigay/link.htm). Arci-Gay (www.gay.it/arcigay/roma) and **Arci-Lesbica** (www.women.it/~arciles/roma) share two offices in Rome: V. Orvinio, 2 (☎06 86385112) and V. Lariana, 8. (☎06 8555522). Both groups hold group discussions, dances, and many special events. It might be a good idea to buy an Arci-Gay membership card (L20,000 annually), which gives admission to many gay clubs all over Italy.

Rome's Arci-Gay office publishes the monthly newsletter *Pegaso*. In addition, the monthly *Babilonia* (published by Babilonia Edizioni, V. Ebro, 11, 20141 Milan; ☎02 5696468) and the annual *Guida Gay Italia* (available at most newsstands) confront gay issues and list events. Finally, the **Italian Gay and Lesbian Yellow Pages** (www.gay.it/guida/italia/info.htm) includes listings of gay bars, hotels, and shops. Other useful websites include www.women.it and www.gay.it.

In Rome, the **Circolo Mario Mieli di Cultura Omosessuale,** V. Corinto, 5, provides loads of info about gay life in Rome. Take Metro Linea B to San Paolo, walk one block to largo Beato Placido Riccardi, hang a left, and walk a block and a half to V. Corinto to find gay-related brochures, pamphlets, and a bulletin board with announcements and special events. The staff offers group discussions, social events, a welcome group every Friday at 7pm, and info sessions on topics such as gay health concerns. (☎06 5413985; fax 06 5413971; www.mariomieli.it. Open M-F 9am-1pm and 2-6pm; closed Aug.)

Unfortunately, there isn't much organized lesbian activity for the traveler in Rome. The best source of info is the **Coordinamento Lesbico Italiano,** V. S. Francesco di Sales, 1a (☎06 6864201), off V. della Lungara in Trastevere. Rome's one and only gay bookstore, **Libreria Babele,** V. dei Banchi Vecchi, is across the bridge from Castel Sant'Angelo. (☎06 6876628. Open M.-Sa. 10am-7:30pm.) It is also one of the only places that sells the *Gay and Lesbian Map of Rome* (L12,000).

During the day, gay and lesbian Romans crowd the **gay beach** *Il Buco* at Lido di Ostia. The dunes along the beach hide an amusing pick-up scene, with many middle-aged Italians standing gopher-like atop mounds of sand; the beach itself accommodates a more relaxed, younger crowd. Take the train from Piramide or Magliana (Metro Linea A) to Lido di Ostia, then bus #7 to the *capolinea;* from there, walk 2km south along the beach.

For information on **gay nighlife,** see p. 211. For **general travel concerns,** check out **Out and About** (www.planetout.com), which offers a bi-weekly newsletter addressing travel concerns. Also contact the **International Gay and Lesbian Travel Association,** 4331 N. Federal Hwy. #304, Fort Lauderdale, FL 33308, an organization of over 1350 companies serving gay and lesbian travelers worldwide. (☎ (954) 776-2626; www.iglta.com.)

MINORITY TRAVELERS

Until recently, the Roman population was relatively homogeneous. Immigration in the latter half of the 20th century from Eastern Europe, North Africa, the Philippines, and former Italian colonies like Somalia and Ethiopia has changed the make-up of the city. Many Romans have not quite gotten used to these newcomers and blame them for—among other things—the rise in crime and social unrest. Although immigrants of color do experience discrimination, tourists of color from the West, who are easily distinguishable by western clothes and language, are not the usual targets of racism. Women of Asian heritage may be referred to as *giapponese*. Women from India may be called *Indiana*. African-American women may find that Italian men can't get past *bellissima*.

Let's Go does not list known discriminatory establishments. If, in your travels, you encounter discriminatory treatment, let us know so that we can check out the establishment and warn other travelers. If you have any trouble, contact your country's embassy or consulate in Rome (many of them are listed in the **Service Directory,** p. 293).

DIETARY CONCERNS

Vegetarians should have no problems in Italian restaurants, since the majority of first courses (primi, the pasta course) are meatless, and most restaurants will also supply you a mixed plate of their vegetable side dishes upon request—ask for verdure miste (mixed vegetables). *Let's Go: Rome* includes some vegetarian restaurants (see the **Index,** under vegetarian) and you can always ask for a dish *senza carne.* If you aren't sure of the contents of a particular dish, ask *"c'è carne?"* Be wary, since Italians don't believe that fish is meat, and many seemingly veggie treats may hide meat. Soups are never vegetarian: they're all made with a meat base, even if no meat is added.

Since many Italian dishes count pork as their principal ingredient, and lots of the rest consist of little other than meat and cheese, those who keep kosher may have to turn vegetarian to satisfy their dietary requirements. Travelers who keep **kosher** should contact the synagogue of Rome in the Jewish Ghetto (☎ 06 6875051) for information on kosher restaurants (also see the **Index,** under kosher).

TRAVELERS WITH DISABILITIES

Romans are making an increased effort to meet the needs of people with disabilities. Still, many of the sights (like the Ancient City) can be difficult to navigate in a wheelchair, and in general, establishments are not wheelchair accessible unless stated otherwise. The **Italian Government Travel Office (ENIT)** (see p. 266) will let you know which hotels and buildings are wheelchair accessible. When making arrangements with airlines or hotels, specify exactly what you need and allow time for preparation and confirmation of arrangements. Many of the larger **Ferrovie dello Stato (FS)** trains are marked wheelchair accessible; they suggest that you call ahead to reserve a space (☎ (800) 888088). For more info, call the **Italian State Railway Representative** in New York (☎ (212) 730-2121). If you plan to bring a **seeing-eye dog** to Italy, contact your vet and the nearest Italian consulate. You'll need import documents and records certifying your dog's health. For additional info, try **Global Access** (www.geocities.com/Paris/1502/disabilitylinks.html), which has several great links for disabled travelers in Italy.

TRAVELING WITH CHILDREN

In cities like Rome, where long bus rides and longer walks are usually required to see just about anything, traveling with children can be quite challenging. Your children will almost certainly find historical sites far less interesting than you will. On the other hand, they will find all sorts of unexpected things interesting, especially if you take the time to explain things to them.

Rome also boasts a bountiful supply of *gelaterias*, candy stores, and free water fountains, which are surprisingly helpful in keeping a kid's morale up. Don't forget to schedule an afternoon nap for *everyone*, which will nicely correspond with the siesta planned right into Roman business hours anyway.

If you're going beyond Rome, note that while car rental is convenient, train travel might be more fun for the kids, and certainly cheaper. **Discount Eurailpasses** are available for groups, families, and children. Make sure that your children have some sort of ID (including your hotel info) on their person in case they get lost.

Caffè della Palma (near the Pantheon) and **Jolly Pop candy stores** (in P. Navona and in the entrance of Termini Station) are always good for a rest stop or a bribe. The **Villa Borghese** park is a cool respite from ancient monuments and churches, and you can rent bicycles or a rowboat to paddle in the small lake (see p. 114). There are **boat rides** down the Tiber and **horse-drawn carriage rides** around the city, originating from P. di Spagna.

Children also love the **caricatures** and portraits done in P. Navona—either watching or posing. There are puppet shows in English on Saturday and Sunday at **Teatro dei Satiri**, V. di Grotta Pinta, 19, off Campo dei Fiori. (☎06 68806244.) Check out the genuine Sicilian puppet shows at the **Teatro Crisogono**, V. S. Gallicano, 8, off viale di Trastevere. **LUNEUR** park (see p. 137) is an old-fashioned amusement park, with a hokey wax museum, roller coaster, and carnival attractions.

Apart from the obvious, manufactured fun, most kids enjoy the **Colosseum** (see p. 82), **Trevi Fountain** (see p. 109), **St. Peter's dome** (see p. 118), the Tiber, and those crazy monkeys at the **BioParco** (see p. 115). A visit to the **Museo Crimonologico** (p. 158) is both educational and fun. Then there's the **Baby Park**, on V. Tiburtina across from #46, and **Pizzeria L'Economica,** which offers a food all children know and love. Take bus #492 to Tiburtina and turn right. Your kids won't even know they're away from home unless they can read the communist graffiti nearby. They can enjoy their own culture with a jungle gym, merry-go-round, and a playground. For more ideas, try *Take Your Kids to Europe*, by Cynthia W. Harriman (Globe Pequot, US$17) or *Have Kid, Will Travel: 101 Survival Strategies for Vacationing With Babies and Young Children*, by Claire and Lucille Tristram (Andrews and McMeel, US$9).

OTHER TRAVEL RESOURCES

TOURIST OFFICES

The privately owned **Enjoy Rome** (p. 27) and the official **EPT** (p. 28) and **PIT** (p. 27) are the best places to turn when you have questions about Rome and your trip to the Eternal City. Other places to turn are:

Italian Government Tourist Board (ENIT), 630 Fifth Ave. Ste. 1565, **New York,** NY 10111 (☎ (212) 245-5618; fax (212) 586-9249; www.enit.it). Write or call their travel brochure hotline (☎ (212) 245-4822) to receive a free copy of their guide *Italia: General Information for Travelers to Italy* (containing train and ferry schedules). **Branch offices:** 1 Princess St., **London** WIR 9AY (☎ (020) 7408 1254; fax (020) 7493 6695); 12400 Wilshire Blvd. #550, **Los Angeles,** CA 90025 (☎ (310) 820-1898 or (310) 820-1959; fax (310) 820-6357); 1 Pl. Ville Marie #1914, **Montréal,** QC H3B 2C3 (☎ (514) 866-7667; fax 392-1429).

Italian Cultural Institute, 686 Park Ave., New York, NY 10021 (☎ (212) 879-4242; fax (212) 861-4018; italcultny.org). Often more prompt and helpful than ENIT. Great website for independent travelers looking for less-touristed spots in Italy.

TRAVEL ORGANIZATIONS

Council on International Educational Exchange (CIEE), 205 E. 42nd St., New York, NY 10017-5706 (☎ (888) 268-6245; fax (212) 822-2699; www.ciee.org). A private, nonprofit organization, the council administers work, volunteer, academic, internship, and professional programs around the world. They also offer identity cards (including the ISIC and the IYTC), and a range of publications, among them the useful magazine *Student Travels* (free).

Federation of International Youth Travel Organizations (FIYTO), Bredgade 25H, DK-1260 Copenhagen K, Denmark (☎ (45) 33 33 96 00; fax 33 93 96 76; email mailbox@fiyto.org; www.fiyto.org), is an organization that promotes educational, cultural, and social travel for youth. Affiliates include language schools, educational travel companies, national tourist boards, and other suppliers of travel services to youth and students. FIYTO sponsors the IYTC card; for more info, see p. 248.

USEFUL PUBLICATIONS

Forsyth Travel Library, Inc., 1750 E. 131st St., P.O. Box 480800, Kansas City, MO 64148 (☎ (800) 367-7984; fax (816) 942-6969; www.forsyth.com). A mail-order service that stocks a wide range of maps and guides for rail and ferry travel in Europe; also sells rail tickets and passes, and offers reservation services. Sells the *Thomas Cook European Timetable* for trains, a complete guide to European train departures and arrivals (US$28, with full map of European train routes $39; postage $4.50 for priority shipping). Free catalogue.

Hippocrene Books, Inc., 171 Madison Ave., New York, NY 10016 (☎ (212) 685-4371, orders (718) 454-2366; fax (718) 454-1391; www.netcom.com/~hippocre). Free catalogue. Publishes travel reference books, travel guides, foreign language dictionaries, and language learning guides that cover over 100 languages.

INTERNET RESOURCES

GENERAL TRAVEL SITES

Let's Go: www.letsgo.com. Besides carrying our newsletter and ordering information for the entire series, our site features a travel forum, links to help you find everything you could ever want to know about Rome, currency converters, and other useful tools.

CIA World Factbook: www.odci.gov/cia/publications/factbook/index.html. This top-secret site has tons of vital statistics on Italy. Check it out for an overview of the economy, or an attempt at an explanation of their system of government.

Foreign Language for Travelers: www.travlang.com. Can help you brush up on your Italian with its downloadable pronunciation sound files. If nothing else, you can amuse yourself by having it chirp *"Dov'é il bagno?"* at you.

Shoestring Travel: www.stratpub.com. Budget travel e-zine featuring listings of home exchanges, copious links, and accommodations information.

TravelHUB: www.travelhub.com. A great site for cheap travel deals.

ROME SITES

A.S. Roma and **S.S. Lazio:** www.asromacalcio.it and www.sslazio.it. Rome's two soccer teams. Deciding which you like better before you go will make your time in Rome far less confusing.

Comune di Roma: www.comune.roma.it. An intimidating Roman site with up-to-the-minute events information and metric tons more.

I Love Rome: www.alfanet.it/welcomeItaly/roma/default.html. Don't we all, though? The cool thing about this site is that you can search all the movie theaters in the city for the time and place of any show you want to see.

InformaRoma: www.informaroma.it. From the Comune di Roma, the site has information on just about anything a tourist could desire. English version available.

Romeguide: www.romeguide.it. An amazingly complete site; particularly strong in the area of accommodations, transportation, and cultural events.

Accommodations

"Everyone sooner or later comes round by Rome," wrote poet Robert Browning. Chances are they're coming at the same time you are and have the reservations you wanted. Roman hotels were underwhelmed by low numbers of visitors in 2000 (most people, aside from pilgrims, feared either the Jubilee crowds or the end of the world), but a surge is expected in 2001; make reservations well in advance.

BOOKING A ROOM

Many hotels now let you book directly over the Internet, which is significantly cheaper than calling or sending a fax from abroad. English may not be spoken at some smaller places, but this shouldn't dissuade a non-Italian speaker from calling; most Useful phrases for making a room reservation in Italian are on p. 32, but most *pensione* owners are used to calls from travelers. Useful phrases for making a room reservation in Italian are included in **Let's Speak Italian, p. 32.**

When you check in, the proprietor will ask for your passport to register you with the police, as required by Italian law. They should only need it to write down the number—be sure to retrieve it. If the hotel asks for a deposit, send a bank draft (unless a credit card is required). Prices vary widely according to season. You'll pay the most during high season, June and July.

LATE RESERVATIONS. If you arrive in Rome without reservations, it is usually possible to find a place to stay, although you may not like it very much and may have to pay more than you ought to for it. Termini is full of officials ready to direct you to a hotel. Some of them are the real thing and have photo IDs issued by the tourist office. Some, however, are sneaky impostors who issue themselves fake badges and cards, and they may well direct you to a sketchy location charging a ridiculous rate, particularly if you arrive late at night. Private tourist agencies like Enjoy Rome (see p. 27) are also a good resource.

APT (AZIENDA DI PROMOZIONE TURISTICA). The APT classifies all Italian hotels on a five-star system. An official rate card is then put on the inside of the door of each room. Prices are set each October, which explains why you may sometimes encounter rates slightly above those listed in *Let's Go: Rome 2001*, which was researched during the summer of 2000. No hotel can legally charge more than the maximum permitted by the inspector, but be warned that some proprietors increase their prices up to double at the sound of a foreign voice. If you find that your hotel is charging more than the maximum posted rate, complain by calling APT at 06 488991 or visiting any tourist office. Illegal *pensioni* and hostels abound in the area around Termini. While some of these establishments are cheap and may suit your needs, be aware that they have no price controls, and often have no insurance. If you have a problem at these establishments, complaints to the officials at APT will get you nowhere. All establishments listed in *Let's Go: Rome 2001* are registered with APT.

RATES. Rates tend to be lower per person in a shared room; it will be less expensive for you to share a triple with two friends than to get a single on your own. A single (which will often be quite small) is called a *camera singola*, a double with separate beds is a *camera doppia*, and a double with one big bed is a *camera matrimoniale*. A triple *(camera tripla)* will occasionally be a large double with an extra bed. This is almost always the case with quads *(camera quadrupla)* and larger rooms (with the exception of hostels). Note that **children are not allowed in most dorm rooms.** Many rooms, even those without private bathrooms, have sinks and bidets—good for chilling wine, washing clothes, and soaking tired feet. As noted above, low season rates are anywhere from L10,000 lower to less than half the price in the high season.

ROOM ETIQUETTE. By Italian law, you are not allowed to have unregistered visitors in your room, so don't be surprised or upset if the proprietor isn't keen on letting you invite your new Italian friend in for a nightcap (or more). Equally illegal is hanging laundry out the window or on a balcony to dry, so don't try it. We list laundromats in the **Service Directory** (p. 296) anyway, so suck it up, budgeteer, and haul your dirty clothes to one of those establishments. Most hotels will let you leave your luggage there before you check in and after you check out, but do not assume that that will be the case, or that it will be free of charge. Always ask any questions you have about your hotel, however trivial they may seem, in advance.

ACCOMMODATIONS BY PRICE

The accommodations listed below are grouped according to prices as they are posted in the high season (June and July in the Eternal City). Low season prices tend to be anywhere from L10,000 cheaper than the high season price to half the high season price. The price listed below is for the cheapest single room, dorm room, or equivalent space available (accurate as of August 2000), without any extra amenities such as A/C or bath (suck it up, budgeteer!). The following key to the neighborhoods of Rome (roughly equivalent to the neighborhood breakdown of the rest of the book) will help you to decipher the neighborhood codes listed directly across from the accommodation name.

L30,000 AND UNDER		**L70,000 AND UNDER**	
Associazione Cattolica Int'l (279)	ESQ	Pensione Monaco (276)	TSL
⚱ Colors (273)	BP	⚱ Pensione Panda (272)	PS
Hotel Il Castello (277)	ESQ	Pensione Piave (276)	TSL
Ostello dei Foro Italico (HI)	BP	Pensione Tizi (275)	TSL
⚱ Pensione Fawlty Towers (274)	TSL	Hotels Castelfidardo & Lazzari (275)	TSL
⚱ Pensione Ottaviano (273)	VC	Hotel Cervia (277)	TSL
⚱ Pensione Sandy (278)	WT	⚱ Hotel Des Artistes (275)	TSL
		Hotel Giu' Giu' (278)	ESQ
L50,000 AND UNDER		Hotel Pensione Cathrine (275)	TSL
Hotel Bolognese (275)	TSL	Hotel Ventura (277)	TSL
⚱ Pensione Papa Germano (275)	TSL	YWCA Foyer di Roma (279)	BP

BP Borgo and Prati (273) **CS** Centro Storico (271) **ESQ** Esquilino–south of Termini (277) **VC** Near Vatican City (273)
PS Piazza di Spagna (272) **TSL** Termini and San Lorenzo (274) **TRV** Trastevere (274) **WT** West of Termini (278)

L80,000 AND UNDER		L110,000 AND UNDER	
Hotel Boccaccio (273)	PS	Albergo Abruzzi (271)	CS
Hotel Lachea (275)	TSL	Albergo del Sole (272)	CS
Hotel Orlanda (277)	ESQ	◪ Hotel Kennedy (277)	ESQ
Hotel Roxena (277)	TSL	Hotel Mimosa (272)	CS
◪ Hotel San Paolo (278)	WT	Hotel Pensione Joli (273)	BP
◪ Pensione di Rienzo (277)	ESQ		
Pensione Katty (277)	TSL	**L120,000 AND UNDER**	
		Hotel Florida (273)	BP
L90,000 AND UNDER		Hotel Lady (273)	BPV
Albergo della Lunetta (271)	CS	Hotel Trastevere (274)	TRV
Hotel Baltic (276)	TSL		
Hotel Dolomiti (275)	TSL		
Hotel Fenicia (276)	TSL	**L140,000 AND UNDER**	
Hotel Magic (276)	TSL	Hotel Adventure (275)	TSL
Hotel Marini (277)	TSL	Hotel Navona (272)	CS
Hotel Pensione Stella (277)	TSL	Hotel Pensione Suisse S.A.S. (273)	PS
Hotel Selene (278)	ESQ	Hotel Teti (278)	ESQ
L100,000 AND UNDER			
Albergo Pomezia (271)	CS	**OVER L140,000**	
Hotel Carmel (274)	TRV	Hotel Canada (274)	TSL
Hotel Galli (276)	TSL	Hotel Cisterna (274)	TRV
Hotel Piccolo (272)	CS	Hotel/Pensione Parlamento (272)	PS
Hotel Sweet Home (278)	ESQ	Hotel Serena (276)	ESQ
◪ Pensione Cortorillo (277)	ESQ	Residenza dei Quiriti (272)	VC
Pensione Ester (276)	TSL		
Pensione Jonella (272)	PS		

BP Borgo and Prati (273) **CS** Centro Storico (271) **ESQ** Esquilino—south of Termini (277) **VC** Near Vatican City (273)
PS Piazza di Spagna (272) **TSL** Termini and San Lorenzo (274) **TRV** Trastevere (274) **WT** West of Termini (278)

ACCOMMODATIONS BY NEIGHBORHOOD

Unless explicitly stated (AmEx, D, DC, MC, V), the following budget accommodations do not accept credit cards. Remember that **price increases,** though regrettable, are inevitable at most establishments. When prices are listed as a range, lower prices are for low season and higher for high season.

CENTRO STORICO

The *Centro Storico* is the ideal, if increasingly expensive, base for living as the Romans do. Most sights are within walking distance, and the market at nearby Campo dei Fiori yields cheap, fresh nourishment. You can expect to pay a 10-15% premium for the classical Roman charm lacking in Termini-area accommodations.

see map p. 314–315

Albergo Pomezia, V. dei Chiavari, 12 (☎/fax 06 6861371). Off C. V. Emanuele II behind Sant'Andrea della Valle. The rooms on the first and 2nd floors have been renovated and are nicer than those on the 3rd; all of the redone rooms have baths. Clean, quiet rooms with phones, fans, and heat in the winter. You haven't had too much to drink—the managers really are twins. Breakfast in the pleasant dining room included (8-11am). Singles L70-100,000, with bath L100-170,000; doubles L100-170,000/L130-220,000; extra bed 35% surcharge. AmEx, MC, V.

Albergo della Lunetta, P. del Paradiso, 68 (☎06 6861080; fax 06 6892028). The first right off V. Chiavari. Clean, well-lit rooms with phones; some around a small, fern-filled courtyard. Fairly good value in a great location (between Campo dei Fiori and P. Navona). Singles L90,000, with bath L110,000; doubles L140,000/L190,000; triples L190,000/L240,000; quads L240,000/ 300,000. Reservations with credit card or check (at least two weeks in advance). MC, V.

Albergo Abruzzi, P. della Rotonda, 69 (☎06 6792021). Location, location, location! 200ft. from the Pantheon, these are indeed rooms with a view. The facilities abetting your viewing are old-fashioned but clean. Hall bathrooms are the only option here, but every room comes equipped with a sink. Singles L75-105,000; doubles L120-150,000; triples L200,000.

the BIG $plurge

Hotel/Pensione Parlamento, V. delle Convertite, 5 (☎/fax 06 6792082). **Near the Spanish Steps:** off V. del Corso. The rooms are very well-apportioned, with comfortable mattresses, each with bath, safe, hair dryer, A/C, telephone, and TV, as well as high ceilings, plush velvet chairs, and static-free CNN. Giorgio, the receptionist, speaks English, French, Spanish, and German. Singles L160-180,000; doubles L180-200,000; triples L235-255,000; quads L300-320,000. Ample breakfast included; in the summer you can eat outside on the glamorous terrace. Reservations recommended. AmEx, MC, V.

Residenza dei Quiriti, V. Germanico, 198, 4th fl. (☎06 3600 5389; fax 06 3679 0487). **Near the Vatican:** in same building as Hotel Lady. While a bit more expensive than other area lodgings, the brand new Quiriti is a big step up in comfort and style—definitely worth the splurge. Ten snug, beautiful yellow rooms with private baths and elegant furnishings (Versace lampshades!) offer all the crucial details: A/C, mini fridges, hair dryers, satellite TV, daily maid service, and several even have bathtubs! The friendly staff speaks good English. Singles L160,000, doubles L240,000, triples L280,000; prices drop to L120,000, L160,000, and L180,000 in late July, Aug. and March. AmEx, MC, V.

Hotel Piccolo, V. dei Chiavari, 32 (☎06 6892330). Off C. Vittorio Emanuele II behind Sant'Andrea della Valle. Recently renovated, family-run establishment next to a bustling grocery store. All rooms have fans and telephones. No elevator. English spoken. Curfew 1am. Checkout noon. Breakfast L7000. Singles L100,000, with bath L120,000; doubles L120,000, with bath L160,000; triples with bath L170,000; quads with bath L180,000. AmEx, MC, V.

Hotel Navona, V. dei Sediari, 8, first fl. (☎06 6864203; fax 06 68211392, call before faxing). Take V. dei Canestrari from P. Navona, cross C. del Rinascimento, and go straight. This 16th-century Borromini building has been used as a *pensione* for over 150 years, counting among its guests Keats, Shelley, and the University of Alabama chapter of the ΑΠΘ fraternity. Checkout 10am. Breakfast included. Singles L140,000; doubles with bath L190,000, with A/C L220,000; triples with bath L260,000.

Albergo del Sole, V. del Biscione, 76 (☎06 68806873; fax 06 6893787). Off Campo dei Fiori. Allegedly the oldest *pensione* in Rome. 61 comfortable modern rooms with phone, fan, TV, and fantastic antique furniture. Some rooms look out on the rowdy street, while others ring a pleasant courtyard garden. Parking garage (L30-40,000). Singles L110,000, with bath L130-160,000; doubles L150-170,000/L190-230,000.

Hotel Mimosa, V. Santa Chiara, 61, 2nd fl. (☎06 68801753; fax 06 6833557). Off P. della Minerva behind the Pantheon. Spacious rooms and central location offset cramped bathrooms. No elevator. Drunkenness not tolerated. Curfew 1am, but keys are available. Singles L110,000; doubles L150,000, with bath L170,000; extra bed L70,000. 10% less in winter.

NEAR PIAZZA DI SPAGNA

see map p. 322

The accommodations in this area might run you a few thousand more *lire* per day, but can you really put a price tag on living but a few steps from Prada? John Keats couldn't.

Pensione Panda, V. della Croce, 35 (☎06 6780179; fax 06 69942151; www.webeco.it/hotelpanda). Between P. di Spagna and V. del Corso. Lovely clean rooms, arched ceilings, and neo-Roman reliefs in some of the hallways. Enjoy the painted vaulted ceilings in the bathrooms. 11am checkout. Reservations almost a necessity. In high season, singles L70,000, with bath L100,000; doubles L120,000/L180,000; triples L180,000/L210,000; quads L240,000/L320,000. AmEx, MC, V.

Pensione Jonella, V. della Croce, 41 (☎06 6797966; email jonella@lodgingitaly.com). Between P. di Spagna and V. del Corso. Run by the guys behind Hotel des Artistes (see p. 275), this *pensione* offers four beautiful rooms with a view. Quiet, roomy, and cool even in summer. No reception: call ahead to arrange for someone to meet you when you arrive. Singles L100,000; doubles L120,000. Cash only.

Hotel Pensione Suisse S.A.S., V. Gregoriana, 54 (☎06 6783649; fax 06 6781258). Turn right at the top of the Spanish Steps. Sleek, old-fashioned furniture, comfortable beds, and phone and fan in every room. Close to the wisteria-hung heights of the Steps, but away from the hubbub; at night you'll think you're in another city. Curfew 2am. In-room breakfast included. Singles L135,000, with bath L155,000; doubles L165,000/L225,000; triples L285,000; quads L340,000. Half the bill may be paid by credit card. MC, V.

Hotel Boccaccio, V. del Boccaccio, 25 (☎06 4885962; www.webeco.it/boccaccio). M:A-Barberini. Off V. del Tritone. This well-situated hotel offers elegantly furnished surroundings for a reasonable price. Boccaccio offers seven rooms within walking distance of many sights. Wood floors welcome you to a rather elegant decor and friendly staff. Singles L80,000; doubles L110,000, with bath L150,000; triples L140,000/L180,000. AmEx, DC, MC, V.

BORGO AND PRATI (NEAR VATICAN CITY)

The *pensioni* on the other side of the Tiber aren't the cheapest in Rome, but they tend to be comfortable, spotless, and fairly quiet (which might appeal to families looking to get plenty of rest). It's convenient to the Vatican but a hike from many central sights. Bus #64 from Termini ends near St. Peter's; nearby Metro (A) stops are Lepanto and Ottaviano. Late night buses are infrequent.

see map p. 320 ◪**Colors,** V. Boezio, 31 (☎/fax 06 6874030). M:A-Ottaviano, or take a bus to Piazza Risorgimento. Take V. Cola di Rienzo to V. Terenzio. Sporting lots of amenities and a super-cool English-speaking staff, Colors offers 20 beds in clean rooms in the elegant Prati area. Kitchen, satellite TV, hair dryers, Internet (L2000 per 15min.), laundry service (L8000 per load, the best deal in town). Beautiful terrace open until 11:30pm. Dorm beds L30,000; doubles L110-140,000; triples L130-170,000. Credit card needed for reservations; payment in cash only.

◪ **Pensione Ottaviano,** V. Ottaviano, 6 (☎06 39737253; email gi.costantini@agora.stm.it), just north of P. del Risorgimento, a few blocks from the Metro stop of the same name and a few steps away from St. Peter's. This comfortable hostel has been open since 1956, and just keeps getting better. Dorm rooms hold 3 to 6 beds per room. Amenities include satellite TV, individual lockers, fridges, a microwave, hot showers, free linens, and free email access for guests. Friendly Aussie and British staff and a lively backpacking clientele. No curfew. Lock-out 11am-2pm. Dorm-style rooms L30,000, L25,000 in the winter. Doubles L90,000/L60,000. One triple L120,000.

Hotel Pensione Joli, V. Cola di Rienzo, 243, 6th fl. (☎06 3241854; fax 06 3241893), at V. Tibullo, *scala* A. Winding blue-striped walls and low ceilings make you feel a little like Alice in Wonderland, if Wonderland were a *pensione* with nice beds and gorgeous views of the Vatican. All rooms with bath and telephone. Singles L110,000; doubles L160,000; triples L215,000; quads L270,000. Breakfast included. MC, V.

Hotel Florida, V. Cola di Rienzo, 243 (☎06 3241872 or 06 3241608; fax 06 3241857), on the 2nd and 3rd floors. Floral carpets, floral bedspreads, floral wall decorations. If only we knew the theme here. Very comfortable, with kind, English-speaking staff. Ceiling fans, TVs, phones, and hair dryers in each room. Bathrooms are delightfully clean. Singles with sink L120,000; with bath L140,000; doubles with bath L180,000; triples with bath L240,000; quads with bath L280,000. Call ahead to reserve and ask about discounts. AmEx, MC, V.

Hotel Lady, V. Germanico, 198, 4th fl. (☎06 3242112; fax 06 3243446), between V. Fabbio Massimo and V. Paolo Emilio. A boisterous, non-English-speaking Roman couple has been running this small, peaceful *pensione* for 30 years. Telephones in rooms. Common room sports well-loved, comfortable couches. However, the hotel is a bit on the dark and dusty side of average. Singles L120,000; doubles L160,000, with bath L180,000.

the BIG $plurge

Hotel Canada, V. Vicenza, 58 (☎06 4457770; fax 064450749; email info@hotel-canadaroma.com). From the middle concourse of Termini, exit right, turn left onto V. Marsala and right onto V. Vicenza. This luxurious behemoth near the train station will provide you with almost everything you could ask for in a hotel. Large rooms are elegantly decorated with antique furniture and boast sumptuous bathrooms, satellite TV, telephone, and A/C. Even odder than it's name is its Best Western affiliation. An excellent breakfast in the bright sitting room is included. Singles (doubles occupied by one person) L180-190,000; doubles L220-260,000; deluxe doubles L260-290,000. Extra bed L50,000. Check-out 11am. AmEx, MC, V.

Hotel Cisterna, V. della Cisterna, 7-8-9 (☎06 5817212, fax 06 5810091). Off P. S. Callisto. Right in the heart of Trastevere, yet somewhat secluded from the noise, this elegant three-star hotel has well-furnished rooms with A/C, recently remodeled baths, TV, and phone. Take in some sun on the quiet, green terrace. Breakfast included. Singles L180,000; doubles L210,000; triples L270,000; quads L300,000. AmEx, DC, MC, V.

TRASTEVERE

see map p. 316–317

Trastevere is a beautiful old Roman neighborhood famous for its separatism, medieval streets, and pretty-far-from-the-tourist-crowd charm. Hotels here are few and far between, but it's a nice area to stay in, especially if you'd like to be near the Vatican and great nightlife.

Hotel Trastevere, V. Luciano Manara, 25 (☎06 5814713, fax 06 5881016). Take a right off V. di Trastevere onto V. delle Fratte di Trastevere. Formerly Pensione Manara, this homey establishment overlooks colorful P. S. Cosimato in the heart of Trastevere. Nine quiet rooms with graceful furniture, bath, TV, phone. English spoken. Breakfast L10,000. Singles L120,000; doubles L150,000; triples L180,000; quads L200,000. Short-term apartments for 2-4 persons with neat little kitchens and loft beds available. AmEx, DC, MC, V.

Hotel Carmel, V. G. Mameli, 11 (☎06 5809921, fax 06 5818853, email hotelcarmel@hotmail.com). Take a right on V. E. Morosini (V. G. Mameli) off V. di Trastevere. Though a good walk from the heart of Trastevere, this simple hotel offers nine no-frills rooms for reasonable prices. There is a nice terrace on the top floor. All rooms with bath. Breakfast included. Singles L100,000; doubles L150,000; triples L190,000; quads L220,000.

TERMINI AND SAN LORENZO

see map p. 316–317

NORTH OF TERMINI

Although the area right next to the train station has its fair share of tourist traps, there are many comfortable, reasonably priced *pensioni* and hotels. This area has recently experienced a revival and consequent influx of reasonably-priced lodgings, making it a haven for budget travelers. It's also cheaper than the historic center and safer than the sometimes seedy Esquilino area.

🔳 **Pensione Fawlty Towers,** V. Magenta, 39 (☎/fax 06 4450374; www.enjoyrome.it/ftytwhtl.htm). Exit Termini to the right from the middle concourse, cross V. Marsala onto V. Marghera, and turn right onto V. Magenta. An extremely popular 15-room hotel/hostel, Fawlty Towers never fails to satisfy its customers. The flower-filled communal terrace provides a peaceful respite from the panic of Termini. Common room with satellite TV, library, refrigerator, microwave, and free Internet access. Check-out 9am for dorm rooms and 10am for private rooms. Frequently full, but the reception will do their utmost to find you a place. Dormitory-style quads L30-35,000 per person (no children); singles L70-85,000; doubles L100,000, with shower L110,000, with bath L130,000; triples with shower L140,000, with bath L155,000.

🏠 **Hotel Des Artistes,** V. Villafranca, 20 (☎06 4454365; fax 06 4462368; email info@hoteldesartistes.com; www.hoteldesartistes.com). From the middle concourse of Termini, exit right, turn left onto V. Marsala, right onto V. Vicenza, and then left onto the 5th cross-street. 3-star, 40-room hotel with a room for every budget. Clean, elegant rooms with bathrooms, safes, refrigerators, and TVs. Amenities include a lovely rooftop terrace and the lounge with satellite TV, a small library, breakfast (L8000), and Internet access (L10,000 per hour). 24hr. reception. Check-out 11am. Singles L70,000; doubles L110,000/L170,000; triples L130,000/L210,000; dorms (in rooms with four to six beds) L35,000. Winter discounts 20-30%. AmEx, MC, V.

🏠 **Pensione Papa Germano,** V. Calatafimi, 14a (☎06 486919; fax 06 47881281; www.hotelpapagermano.it). From the middle concourse of Termini, exit right, and turn left onto V. Marsala, which shortly becomes V. Volturno; V. Calatafimi is the 4th cross-street on your right. Clean, affordable rooms (all with TV and telephone) and outstanding service of friendly owners Gino and Pina. Gino organizes tours of the Vatican and ancient Rome. Heck, he'll even help you find a place to stay if he's all booked up. Internet access. 15 rooms. Singles L45-60,000; doubles L70-100,000, with bath L90-130,000; triples with bath L100-150,000. Check-out 11am. MC, V.

Hotel Dolomiti and **Hotel Lachea,** V. S. Martino della Battaglia, 11 (☎06 4957256; fax 06 4454665; email dolomiti@hotel-dolomiti.it; www.hotel-dolomiti.it). From the middle concourse of Termini, exit right, turn left onto V. Marsala and right onto V. Solferino (V. S. Martino della Battaglia). Aging 19th-century *palazzo* houses sparkling new hotels, offering a bar, breakfast room, and Internet access (L10,000). Rooms in three-star Hotel Dolomiti have satellite TV, telephones, minibars, safes, and A/C. Hotel Lachea offers the same excellent service in a simpler hotel (for lower prices). Some rooms with a balcony. Breakfast L10,000. Check-out 11am. **Lachea:** singles L75-85,000; doubles L85-100,000/L110-130,000; triples 110-130,000/L150-170,000; quads L140-160,000/L160-210,000. Five-person rooms available at negotiable price. **Dolomiti:** singles L90-120,000; doubles L130-180,000; triples L160-210,000; quads L200-230,000. A/C L20,000 per night. MC, V.

Pensione Tizi, V. Collina, 48 (☎06 4820128; fax 06 4743266). A 10 min. walk from the station. Take V. Goito from P. dell'Indipendenza, cross V. XX Settembre onto V. Piave, then go left on V. Flavia, which leads to V. Collina. Or take bus #319 or 270 from Termini. The nice people at Tizi have served student travelers in this peaceful neighborhood for years. Marble floors and inlaid ceilings adorn the spacious and recently renovated rooms. Breakfast L9000. Check-out 11am. Singles L70,000, with bath L90,000; doubles L90,000/L110,000; triples L120,000/L148,000; quads L160,000/L180,000.

Hotel Castelfidardo and **Hotel Lazzari,** V. Castelfidardo, 31 (☎06 4464638; fax 06 4941378). Two blocks off V. XX Settmebre. Both run by the same friendly family. Renovated rooms with spanking clean floors, all done up in peach and gray color schemes. Three floors of modern, shiny comfort and bodacious bathroom space. Hall bathrooms shared by three rooms at most. Check-out 11am. Singles L70,000; doubles L95,000, with bath L120,000; triples L120,000/L150,000; quads available on request (price negotiable). AmEx, MC, V.

Hotel Pensione Cathrine, V. Volturno, 27 (☎06 483634). From the middle concourse of Termini, exit right, and turn left onto V. Marsala (V. Volturno). Comfortable *pensione* run by friendly southern Italian woman. Two uncommonly clean common bathrooms serve the spacious singles and doubles that only have a sink. More rooms at V. XX Settembre, 58a. Breakfast L10,000. Let's Go discount L10,000. Singles L75,000, with bath L100,000; doubles L100,000/L120,000; triples with bath L160,000.

Hotel Adventure, V. Palestro, 88 (☎06 4469026; fax 06 4460084; www.hoteladventure.com; email hotel.adventure@flashnet.it). From the middle concourse of Termini, exit right, cross V. Marsala onto V. Marghera, and take the 4th right onto V. Palestro. Much more pleasant and relaxed than the name suggests. Recently renovated rooms (all with bath, satellite TV, telephone, and safe) at excellent rates. Breakfast included. Check-out 11am. Doubles L140,000; triples L200,000. Extra bed L35,000. A/C L30,000. AmEx, MC, V.

Hotel Bolognese, V. Palestro, 15 (☎/fax 06 490045). In a land of run-of-the-mill *pensioni*, this place is spruced up by the artist-owner who provides extra amenities here and there: some of the 14 bedrooms have attached sitting rooms, some feature bathtubs, and still others have terraces. Check-out 11am. Curfew 2am. Singles L50,000, with bath L70-L80,000; doubles L80,000/L120,000; triples L120,000/L150,000.

the BIG $plurge

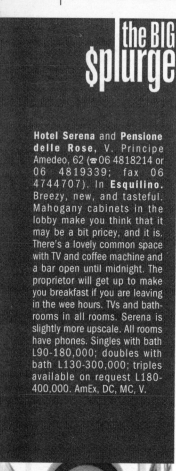

Hotel Serena and **Pensione delle Rose**, V. Principe Amedeo, 62 (☎06 4818214 or 06 4819339; fax 06 4744707). In **Esquilino**. Breezy, new, and tasteful. Mahogany cabinets in the lobby make you think that it may be a bit pricey, and it is. There's a lovely common space with TV and coffee machine and a bar open until midnight. The proprietor will get up to make you breakfast if you are leaving in the wee hours. TVs and bathrooms in all rooms. Serena is slightly more upscale. All rooms have phones. Singles with bath L90-180,000; doubles with bath L130-300,000; triples available on request L180-400,000. AmEx, DC, MC, V.

Hotel Magic, V. Milazzo, 20 (☎/fax 064959880). Alacazam! The owners of Hotel Magic will make a clean, modern room and a beautiful bar appear before your very eyes. Almost all rooms include private baths, TVs, and in-room safes. Singles L90,000; doubles L130,000; triples L180,000; quads L200-220,000. A/C L20,000. MC, V.

Hotel Baltic, V. XX Settembre, 89 (☎06 4814775; fax 06 485509). Just past the intersection with V. Palestro. Espresso machine in the lobby and splendid views onto V. XX Settembre and Michelangelo's nearby Porta Pia. Bar, TV room, beautiful marble foyer. 23 modern, comfortable rooms with bath, TV, and telephone. Breakfast L8000. Check-out 11am. Singles 90,000; doubles L120,000; triples L150,000; quads L195,000. Traveler's checks accepted. AmEx, MC, V.

Pensione Monaco, V. Flavia, 84 (☎/fax 0642014180). From V. XX Settembre, turn left onto V. Quinto Sellia and right onto V. Flavia. Friendly Italian woman and English-speaking children keep these 11 sunlit rooms clean. Comfortable mattresses. Washing machines available. Check-out 9am. Student discount prices: singles L55,000, with bath L70,000; doubles L80,000, with bath L100,000; triples and quads L40,000 per person. Prices about 10% lower in the winter.

Pensione Piave, V. Piave, 14 (☎06 4743447; fax 06 4873360). Off V. XX Settembre to the left. All 12 rooms are well lit and have telephones and carpeted floors. Singles have double beds and one room even has a fireplace. The cozy bathrooms shouldn't bother anyone who doesn't mind showering less than a foot away from the sink and toilet. Check-in 11:30am. Check-out 11am. Singles L65,000, with bath L95,000; doubles with bath L120,000; triples with bath L150,000; quads with bath L160-180,000. AmEx, MC, V.

Hotel Galli, V. Milazzo, 20 (☎06 4456859; fax 06 4468501). Off V. Marsala. Clean and modern. Many a green plant in the white hallways invite you to stay a little longer. All 12 rooms have bath, TV, mini-bar, and safe. Breakfast included. Singles L100,000; doubles L130,000; triples L180,000; quads L210,000. 10-15% lower in winter. A/C L20,000. AmEx, MC, V.

Hotel Fenicia, V. Milazzo, 20 (☎/fax 06490342; www.fenicia-web-page.net; email hotel.fenicia@tiscalinet.it). 11 sparkling, modern rooms close to Termini, all with bath and TV. Singles L85,000; doubles L130,000. Extra beds L45,000. A/C L20,000.

Pensione Ester, V. del Castro Pretorio, 25 (☎06 4957123). From the middle concourse of Termini, exit right, turn right onto V. Marsala and left onto V. del Castro Pretorio. Go through the archway to the courtyard and enter the door on the right marked "C." Avoid the often institutional atmosphere of area hotels in one of these five old-fashioned, airy rooms overlooking a lovely courtyard. Check-out 9am. Curfew 1am. Max. stay 10 days. Doubles L100,000; triples L135,000.

Hotel Cervia, V. Palestro, 55 (☎06 491057; fax 06 491056; email hotelcervia@wnt.it). The TV room, breakfast room with bar, and handmade wool comforters (crafted in Lazio's mountains) are nice, but guests stay on for the friendly atmosphere. Rooms with bath include breakfast; otherwise, it's L5000. 24hr. reception. Check-out noon. Singles L70,000; doubles L90,000, with bath L140,000; triples L135,000/L210,000. AmEx, MC, V.

Hotel Marini, V. Palestro, 35 (☎06 4440058). This 10-room *pensione* practically glows with the proprietress's hospitality. Extremely clean with lovely high ceilings and pictures of her family lining the walls. All rooms have showers. Chek-out 10am. Doubles L80-90,000.

Pensione Katty, V. Palestro, 35 (☎06 4441216). The 23 rooms are plain but large, and you can ask for one with a beautiful mosaic floor. The nicer rooms (some with A/C) are upstairs. Lounge with espresso machine. Check-out 11am. Singles L75,000, with bath L90,000; doubles L90,000/L130,000; triples L120,000/L150,000; quads L140,000/L160,000. Big discounts Nov.-Mar. L2000 key deposit. Traveler's checks accepted. MC, V.

Hotel Ventura, V. Palestro, 88 (☎06 4451951). In a building with many other hotels, Ventura distinguishes itself by rooms with TVs, telephones, and a truly inordinate number of pictures covering their walls. A good option for those not looking to spend a lot. Breakfast L10,000. Doubles L70,000, with bath L80,000; triples L90,000/L105,000. AmEx, MC, V.

Hotel Pensione Stella, V. Castelfidardo, 51 (☎06 4441078; fax 06 4450270). Near the intersection with V. Gaeta. Nineteen newly renovated rooms have it all: TV, phone, luxurious bathroom, and warm teak furniture. Why would you ever leave? Breakfast L10,000. Check-out 11am. Singles with bath L90,000; doubles L140,000; triples L170,000. AmEx, MC, V.

Hotel Roxena, V. Marghera, 13 (☎06 4456823; fax 06 4452629). A little drab, but you could trip on your way out of Termini and be here. Breakfast L10,000. Curfew 1am. 12 rooms: doubles L80,000, with bath L110,000; triples L105,000/L130,000; quads L140,000. MC, V.

SOUTH OF TERMINI (ESQUILINO)

While not the most posh part of town, it has decent rooms at good prices and is still close to many of the major sights. Don't be afraid to haggle for prices.

▨ **Pensione di Rienzo,** V. Principe Amedeo, 79a (☎06 4467131 or 06 4466980). A tranquil, family-run retreat with spacious, newly renovated rooms. Large windows overlook a courtyard. Extremely friendly, helpful staff. It's plain, it's cheap, and it's good. Fifteen rooms, some with balconies and baths. Breakfast L15,000. Check-out 10am. Singles L35-80,000, with bath up to L90,000; doubles L40-90,000, with bath up to L110,000. MC, V.

▨ **Pensione Cortorillo,** V. Principe Amedeo, 79a, 5th fl. (☎06 4466934; fax 06 4454769). A family runs this small and friendly *pensione*. TV and full bath in all rooms. Cheap lobby pay phone. English spoken well. Breakfast included. Check-out 10am. Singles L100,000; doubles L70-100,000; triples 210,000; quads L280,000. AmEx, DC, MC, V.

▨ **Hotel Kennedy,** V. Filippo Turati, 62-64 (☎06 4465373; fax 06 4465417; email hotelkennedy@micanet.it). Ask not what you can do for Hotel Kennedy, ask what Hotel Kennedy can do for you. Classical music in the bar, leather couches, a library, and a large color TV in the lounge. Private bath, satellite TV, phone, and A/C. Hearty all-you-can-eat breakfast in three pleasant breakfast rooms included. English, French, and Spanish spoken. Check-out 11am. Reservations by fax only. Singles L105,000; doubles L169-179,000; triples L299,000. 10% discount to *Let's Go* travelers. AmEx, DC, MC, V.

Hotel Il Castello, V. Vittorio Amedeo II, 9 (☎06 77204036; fax 06 70490068; www.ilcastello.com). M:A-Manzoni. Far beyond Termini, but far within the backpacker's budget. Walk down V. San Quintino and take the first left. Housed in a castle with smallish white rooms and eager serving knaves (mostly native English speakers). Spot damsels in distress from the quaint balcony outside four of the rooms. Come knightfall, enjoy a kitchen with bar and round tables under a TV. Continental breakfast L5000. Check-out 10:30am. Dorm room beds L30,000; singles L50-60,000; doubles L70-80,000, with bath L120-130,000; triples L105,000. MC, V.

Hotel Orlanda, V. Principe Amedeo, 76, 3rd fl. (☎06 4880124; fax 06 4880183). At V. Gioberti. Take the stairs on the right in the vestibule. All 23 rooms have sinks, even if they don't have a bathroom; some have hair dryers. English spoken. Breakfast included. 24hr. reception. Check-out 10am. Singles L45-80,000, with bath L50-120,000; doubles L70-120,000, with bath L90-

180,000; triples L90-150,000, with bath L120-220,000; quads L120-180,000, with bath L160-280,000. A/C L20,000 extra. AmEx, DC, MC, V.

Hotel Giu' Giu', V. del Viminale, 8 (☎06 4827734; fax 06 48912616). Two blocks south of Termini, in an elegant but fading *palazzo*. Pleasant breakfast area, 12 large, quiet rooms, and a friendly family running the place. Breakfast L10,000. Check-out 10am. Singles L65,000; doubles L100,000, with bath L110,000; triples with bath L150,000; quads with bath L195,000.

Hotel Selene, V. del Viminale, 8 (☎06 4824460; fax 06 4782 1977). Two blocks south of Termini. The parrot behind the reception desk speaks flawless Italian and will continue to do so even if you inform him that you don't understand. 27 clean rooms with bath, TV, and telephone. Renovations planned for winter 2001 may drive prices up; call ahead. Breakfast included. Singles L90,000; doubles L140,000; triples L190,000. AmEx, MC, V.

Hotel Sweet Home, V. Principe Amedeo, 47 (☎/fax 06 4880954). At V. D. Manin. Welcome to the Hotel California...oh wait, that's downstairs. Enjoy Home Sweet Home's soothing green decor or watch the goldfish swim in the lobby's small tank. Either way, the setting is tranquil and the proprietors are very welcoming. Such a lovely place... Checkout 11am. Singles L80-100,000, with bath L100-120,000; doubles L120-150,000/L150-180,000; triples 120-150,000/L180-210,000. AmEx, DC, MC, V.

Hotel Teti, V. Principe Amedeo, 76 (☎/fax 06 48904088; email hotelteti@iol.it). Take the stairs at the end of the courtyard. Photographs of 1890s Italy adorn the white walls of Teti. Spacious rooms, but costly for the neighborhood. Satellite TV, shower, and telephone in all rooms. English spoken. Breakfast L8000. Check-out 11am. Reservations available over email. Singles L90-140,000; doubles L120-200,000; triples L150-240,000; quads L160-290,000. 10-15% discount for students. AmEx, DC, MC, V.

WEST OF TERMINI

Just steps west from all the hustle and bustle of beloved Termini, the neighborhood becoming less decrepit and has more sights and stores. It is also home to the city's two women-only establishments (see **Alternative Accomodations,** p. 279). Streets here are busier than those north of Termini and not nearly as grid-like.

Hotel San Paolo, V. Panisperna, 95 (☎06 4745213; fax 06 4745218; email hsanpaolo@tin.it). Exiting from the front of the train station, turn left onto V. Cavour. After you pass Santa Maria Maggiore (on the left), bear right onto V. di Santa Maria Maggiore (V. Panisperna). 10 min. from Termini, San Paolo's 23 rooms are housed in a bright little *palazzo* with tranquil, whimsically decorated rooms. Hall baths are clean and private. Public stereo in the cafe. Breakfast L10,000. Check-out 10:30am. Singles L75,000; doubles L100,000, with bath L140,000; triples L135,000. Large 6-10 person suite L50,000 per person. AmEx, MC, V.

Pensione Sandy, V. Cavour, 136 (☎06 4884585; www.sandyhostel.com). Past Santa Maria Maggiore. No sign; look for the Hotel Valle next door. 4th floor, no elevator (ouch). Under the same ownership as Fawlty Towers and run by Slim, a Roman who is proud to say he learned his English from MTV. Free Internet access and individual lockers in each room. Simple, hostel-style rooms, usually for 2-4 people, in a central location. L30,000 in summer, L25,000 in the winter.

ALTERNATIVE ACCOMMODATIONS

BED AND BREAKFASTS. The phenomenon of the bed and breakfast has finally arrived in Rome. Two services have sprung up to meet the demands of B&Bers everywhere. **Bed and Go,** V. S. Tommaso d'Aquino, 47, offers rooms and apartments of all types, ranging from ultra-budget (L45,000) to chi-chi (L200,000). (☎06 39750907 or 06 39746484; fax 06 39760553; email bedandgo@tin.it. Open M-F 9am-1pm and 2-6pm.) **Bed & Breakfast Association of Rome,** P. del Teatro Pompeo, 2, is another reservation service. (☎/fax 06 6877348; email info@b-b.rm.it; www.b-b.rm.it. Singles in good locations L70-90,000.)

INSTITUTIONAL ACCOMMODATIONS. Rome's only HI-affiliated hostel is certainly not the cream of the crop; you should only consider this very, very inconveniently located hostel if central Rome's many hostels are completely filled.

Ostello del Foro Italico (HI), V. delle Olimpiadi, 61 (☎06 3236267 or 06 3236279; fax 06 3242613). M:A-Ottaviano. Exit onto V. Barletta and take bus #32 to Cadorna (get off when you see pink Foro Italico buildings and an obelisk). 350 beds, in 6-12 person single-sex rooms. No family rooms. Huge, free lockers (bring a lock). Reception 2pm-midnight. Check-out 7-9am. Lock-out 9am-2pm. Strictly enforced curfew midnight. Sizeable lunch and dinner available. Small continental breakfast and hot showers included. Close to the "Big Gym," Rome's largest public sports complex. Bar downstairs open 7am-10:30pm, restaurant open 6pm-10pm. Wheelchair accessible. L25,000 with HI card (buy one at the desk for L30,000), L30,000 without.

STUDENT HOUSING. Student residences throughout Italy are inexpensive and theoretically open to foreign students whenever there is room. The **Centro Turistico Studentesco** (see p. 298) is the Italian student and youth travel organization, which helps people find rooms in *pensioni* or dormitories. They are typically at a loss to actually find anyone a dormitory room, but do post a list of rooms for rent at the main office. The London, Paris, and Athens offices can reserve a room for you in Italy for the first few nights.

RELIGIOUS HOUSING. Certain convents and monasteries host guests (for a fee hovering around L40,000 or more per night) who come with letters of introduction from their local diocese. Contact your home parish for details. Most religious accommodations involve single-sex housing, early curfews, services, and light chores.

CAMPING. In August, when most Italians go on vacation, arrive early (well before 11am) to secure a spot. Rates average L10,000 per person and another L8000 per car. The **Touring Club Italiano** publishes an annual directory of all camping sites in Italy, *Campeggi in Italia*, available in bookstores throughout Italy. Camping on beaches, roads, and inconspicuous plots is illegal.

Seven Hills Village, V. Cassia, 1216 (☎06 303310826; fax 06 303310039). 8km north of Rome. Take bus #907 from the Cipro-Musei Vaticani Metro(A), or bus #201 from P. Mancini. Ask where to get off—it's 3-4km past the GRA (the big highway that circles the city). From the stop, follow the country road about 1km until you see the sign. Spend a lazy poolside afternoon and dance the night away in the disco. It houses a bar, market, restaurant, and *pizzeria*. No *lire* allowed: buy a Seven Hills card for use all over the campground. Doctor on hand during the day. Daily Vatican shuttles leave at 8 and 9:30am, round-trip L6000. Check-in 7am-11pm. L15,000 per person, L9000 per tent, L9000 per car. Camper L16,000. Bungalow L90-150,000. Open late Mar. to late Oct.

WOMEN'S HOUSING. Beware the strict curfews and guest policies.

YWCA Foyer di Roma, V. C. Balbo, 4 (☎06 4880460; fax 06 4871028). From P. dei Cinque-cento (in front of Termini), walk down V. del Viminale, turn left onto V. Torino and right onto V. C. Balbo. The YWCA (pronounced EEV-kah) is a pretty and extremely clean hostel offering a study with leather chairs, a small kitchen with refrigerator, cheery tiled floors, and some very healthy houseplants. Reception open 7am-midnight. Curfew midnight. Check-out 10am. Singles L70,000, with bath L90,000; doubles L120,000, with bath L140,000; triples and quads L50,000 per person. Breakfast included, M-Sa 8am-9am. Tell reception by 10am the same day if you want lunch (1pm-2pm, L20,000).

Associazione Cattolica Internazionale al Servizio della Giovane, V. Urbana, 158 (☎ 06 4880056). From P. Esquilino (in front of Santa Maria Maggiore), walk down V. de Pretis and turn left. Church-run establishment makes living arrangements for women (25 and younger) of any religion. The garden will make you weep. Curfew 10pm. Dorm rooms with 5 beds, L30,000 per person; 8 beds, L24,000 per person. Singles L38,000; doubles L66,000. Open M-Sa 6:30am-10pm, Su 7am-10pm. Closed part of Aug.

Living in Rome

So you long for the romantic life of the writer, artist, student, or loafer in Rome. You long to run off and join the ranks of Keats, Shelley, Goethe, Hemingway, and countless former *Let's Go* researchers. Before you jump on that plane, however, you might want to think just a bit about what you're going to do about immigration, your living situation, daily necessaries, and that biggest pain in most of our collective asses, making money.

USEFUL RESOURCES

Enjoy Rome, the tourist and travel agency, also offers help in finding short-term apartments, and offers access to many community resources. See p. 27.

Roma Online: www.roma-online.com. Helps the longer-term visitor by including information on moving to Rome, as well as an online map and street database.

Welcome Home Relocation Services, V. Barbarano Romano, 15 (☎06 3036 6936; fax 06 3036 1706; email welcome.home@slashnet.it). All kinds of housing plus assistance in documentation (permits, visas, licenses) and orientation. English spoken. Open M-F 9am-6pm.

Transitions Abroad, P.O. Box 1300, 18 Hulst Rd., Amherst, MA 01004-1300 (☎ (800) 293-0373; fax (800) 256-0373; www.transabroad.com). Publishes a bi-monthly magazine listing opportunities and printed resources for those seeking to study, work, or travel abroad. The possibilities are almost endless. They also publish *The Alternative Travel Directory,* an exhaustive listing of information, and *Work Abroad,* a comprehensive guide to finding and preparing for a job overseas. For subscriptions (in US US$20 for 6 issues, in Canada US$30, in other countries US$42), write to them at the address listed above.

VISAS & PERMITS

Italy, in keeping with the predominant European model of large, social welfare government, will throw loads of confusing paperwork at you before you can take part in the utopia that is European living. Not surprisingly—Italy being Italy—the big bureaucracy in Rome is not as well-oiled as its counterparts in Paris, Brussels, or London; be prepared for frustration. Many of the organizations listed throughout this chapter can provide advice on how to cut through the red tape. The City of Rome even realizes the confusion documentation can cause, and publishes *Roma per te*, a guide to obtaining permits and other documents, with the phonebook. Private companies such as the **Center for International Business and Travel**, 25 W. 23rd St. #1420, New York, NY 10036 (☎ (800) 925-2428), can obtain documentation for a fee.

LONG-TERM VISAS

All non-EU citizens are required to obtain a visa for any stay longer than 3 months, even if they are staying only as tourists. For information and applications, contact the Italian Embassy or Consulate in your country (see p. 245).

PERMIT TO STAY. All Non-EU citizens are also required to obtain a *Permesso di Soggiorno* (Permit to Stay) within eight days of arrival in Italy. If you are staying in a hotel or hostel, this requirement is waived, but if you are living on your own, you must apply at a police station or the foreigners office at the main police station *(Quaestra Centrale)*, V. Genoa, 2. (☎06 46861. Open M-F 9am-12:30pm.) EU citizens must apply for a *Permesso di Soggiorno* within three months.

RESIDENCY. Once you find a place to stay, bring your Permit to Stay (it must have at least one year's validity) to a records office *(circoscrizione;* for the nearest location, look up *Come di Roma: Circoscrizione* in the phone book). This certificate, which confirms your registered address, will expedite such procedures as clearing goods from abroad through customs and making large purchases (such as automobiles).

TAX CODE. Anybody who works in Italy must carry a *Codice Fiscale* card, which is often required for procedures such as opening bank accounts and receiving medical coverage. Applications require a passport and Permit to Stay, and should be submitted to the *Ufficio delle Entrate*, V. Ippolito Nuevo, 36, in Trastevere. (☎06 583191. Open M, W, and F 9am-1pm, Tu and Th 9am-1pm and 2:50-4:50pm.)

WORK PERMITS

EU passport holders do not require a visa to work in Italy. Non-EU citizens seeking work in Italy must apply for an Italian work permit *(Autorizzazione al lavoro in Italia)* before entering the country. The employer must receive a work permit from the Provincial Employment Office where the foreigner will be working. The Employment Office, upon determining that there are no Italian workers willing or able to fill the position, may issue a permit. The employer proceeds with the permit to the appropriate *questura* for necessary approval. Next, the employer must send the work permit to the prospective employee in her home country, where she presents the document along with a valid passport in order to obtain a work visa.

STUDY VISAS

EU citizens do not need a visa to study in Italy. Non-EU citizens wishing to study in Italy must obtain a study visa *(permisso di studio)* prior to departure from their nearest embassy or consulate. To obtain a visa, you will need to provide proof of enrollment from your home institution or the school in Italy. US citizens also require a notarized statement that the student has adequate financial means, and that the student will purchase an Italian health insurance policy in Italy as a supplement to American health insurance. The visa fee for US citizens is $32.43 (payable in money order only) and for

Australian citizens is AUS$51. Upon arrival in Italy, students must register with the Foreigners' Bureau (*Ufficio degli Stranieri*) of the local *questura* in order to receive their permit of stay.

WORK & VOLUNTEER

Many years ago, Romulus and Remus, after their long journey up the Tiber, landed on the shores of what we now know to be modern-day Rome. Unfortunately, as unnaturalized immigrants without work permits and the proper tax information, they found themselves ineligible for most employment opportunities and were forced to wait tables at 3rd-rate *trattorie*.

Jewish Ghetto

And just as unfortunately for their modern-day progeny, unemployment is high in central and southern Italy, making job searches in Rome difficult and sometimes fruitless. Italian law requires employers to pony up substantial sums of money for pensions and benefits even for short-term employees, making new hires very substantial investments.

In such a situation, firms are inclined to prefer naturalized Italian labor to your foreign sweat and blood. Work with Italian companies is almost impossible to find if you are not an EU citizen; your best bet is either a position in a foreign firm from an English-speaking country (preferably your own), or under-the-table jobs in the tourism sector. However, it's not easy in this sector, either. Openings are coveted by herds of would-be expats, so competition is fierce.

Officially, you must have a **work permit** (p. 282) to work in Italy. Your prospective employer must apply for this document, usually by demonstrating that you have skills that locals lack. You will also need a **working visa,** available from an Italian consulate. EU citizens can work in Italy without working papers. Students can check with their university's foreign language department, which may have access to jobs abroad.

Piazza Farnese

Unofficially, there is the cash-based, untaxable **underground economy** (*economia sommersa* or *economia nera*). Many permitless agricultural workers go untroubled by local authorities, who recognize the need for seasonal labor. Many foreigners go unnoticed through this route, too, though rarely through the back-breaking and thankless labor of the migrant farm worker. Many expats, for instance, find work (cash-based and official) with well-to-do families as nannies-*cum*-English teachers. Again, your best resource for these jobs is community bulletin boards and magazines such as *Wanted in Rome*, or placement organizations such as those listed below.

GENERAL WORK RESOURCES

◪ **Wanted in Rome** (www.wantedinrome.com). This bi-weekly magazine (L1500) offers cultural information and a wealth of classified advertisements, all delivered in a very British tone. Available at most newsstands, English-language bookstores, and from their main office. V. dei Delfini, 17 (☎06 6790190; fax 06 6783798).

Vacation Work Publications, 9 Park End St., Oxford OX1 1HJ, UK (☎ (01865) 24 19 78; fax 79 08 85; www.vacationwork.co.uk). Publishes a variety of directories with job listings and info for the working traveler. Opportunities for summer or full-time work in numerous countries.

Centro Storico

OPTIONS FOR WORK

TOURISM INDUSTRY

The Roman tourism industry is primarily targeted at the English-speaker, and with some persistence, you may be able to find a position there, albeit with little financial security. Many tourist offices look for tour guides over the summer. These jobs are usually not salaried; you work for a commission by convincing people to come to expensive tours given by the agency. Often, this entails giving free "teaser" tours all day in the hot sun at Roman ruins, working for tips, and begging your fellow countrymen to come to paid events and say that you sent them there. It's not for the faint of heart nor quiet of mouth, but it just might be enough to pay the bills. Besides tour guides, English-speaking hotel and hostel personnel are always in high demand, especially during the summer months. Due to the sometimes unofficial nature of the jobs, often the best course of action is to call establishments directly.

TEACHING ENGLISH

Assuming you lack the stamina to till the fields, consider that teaching English, one of the few long-term job possibilities, can be particularly lucrative. No more than minimal Italian is necessary to teach conversation, though many language institutes require a college degree and/or some sort of TEFL or RSA certificate (or completion of a shorter training course on teaching English as foreign language).

There are numerous English-language institutes in Rome that offer jobs through ads in *Wanted in Rome* (available at most newsstands; see p. 283) and in Rome's daily newspaper *Il Messagero*. Some schools simply post signs in stores, hair salons, or cafes. Many people poster their services around universities and on community bulletin boards. A common method is to set up a small class of four to six students for which the going rate, depending on the size of the class, is about L15-35,000 per hour.

Language schools are listed under *Scuole di Lingua* in the Italian yellow pages and are also listed in the English yellow pages. **International House Academia Britannica,** V. Manzoni, 22, one block from the Manzoni (A) Metro stop, which offers TEFLA and EFL courses, has a good bulletin board and advertises teaching jobs throughout Italy. (☎06 70476894; fax 06 70497842. Open M-F 9am-1pm and 3-7:30pm.) Also try:

International Schools Services, Educational Staffing Program, P.O. Box 5910, Princeton, NJ 08543 (☎ (609) 452-0990; fax (609) 452-2690; www.iss.edu). Recruits teachers and administrators for American and English schools in Italy. All instruction in English. Applicants must have a bachelor's degree and two years of relevant experience. Nonrefundable US$100 application fee. Publishes *The ISS Directory of Overseas Schools* (US$35).

PROFESSIONAL TEACHING

You may be able to secure a teaching position with an American school in Italy through the **Office of Overseas Schools,** Room H328, SA-1, Dept. of State, Washington, DC 20522. (☎ (202) 261-8200; fax (202) 261-8224; www.state.gov.) **International Schools Services,** Educational Staffing Program, 15 Roszel Rd., P.O. Box 5910, Princeton, NJ 08543, can also assist in finding a teaching job. (☎ (609) 452-0990; fax 452-2690; www.iss.edu.) Another short-term option, albeit horrifying, is to be a substitute teacher at one of the American or British schools; generally, you need a college degree, nerves of steel, and a *Codice Fiscale* (tax code).

INTERNSHIPS

The best bet for finding an above-board job that will take care of all documentation requirements is to look for internships with large domestic and multinational firms with offices in Rome. It is probably also your best bet to find professional work as a foreigner without substantial experience and complete fluency in Italian. Most companies post job descriptions and human resources contact information on their websites. Some Embassies offer internships throughout the year; contact your government for more information, or contact your embassy in Rome (see **Service Directory,** p. 294).

ARCHAELOGICAL DIGS

The Archaeological Institute of America, 656 Beacon St., Boston, MA 02215-2010 (☎ (617) 353-9361; fax (617) 353-6550; www.archaeological.org), puts out the *Archaeological Fieldwork Opportunities Bulletin* (US$16 for non-members), which lists over 250 field sites throughout the world. The bulletin can also be purchased from Kendall/Hunt Publishing, 4050 Westmark Dr., Dubuque, Iowa 52002 (☎ (800) 228-0810). For info on anthropology, archaeological digs, and art history in Italy, write to the **Centro Comune di Studi Preistorici,** 25044 Capo di Ponte, Brescia (☎0364 42091; fax 0364 42572; globalnet.it/ccsp/ccsp.htm), a research center involved with the management of cultural property and the organization of congresses, research projects, and exhibitions. They publish *BCSP*, the world journal of prehistoric and tribal art, and offer volunteer work, grants, and research assistant positions for prehistoric art.

Local colleges and universities in your home country are another excellent source of information on archaeological digs in Rome and elsewhere. Check with the departments of the classics, archaeology, anthropology, fine arts, and/or other relevant area studies at your local university or college; many excavations send information and applications directly to individual professors or departments rather than to the general public.

AU PAIR

Accord Cultural Exchange, 750 La Playa, San Francisco, CA 94121 (☎ (415) 386-6203); fax 386-0240; www.cognitext.com/accord), offers *au pair* jobs to people aged 18-29 in Italy. Au pairs work 5-6hr. per day, 30hr. per week, plus 2 evenings of babysitting. Light housekeeping and childcare in exchange for room and board plus US$250-400 per month salary. Program fees US$750 for the summer, US$1200 for the academic year. US$40 Application fee.

Childcare International, Ltd., Trafalgar House, Grenville Place, London NW7 3SA (☎ (020) 8906 3116; fax (020) 8906 3461; www.childint.demon.co.uk) offers *au pair* positions in Italy. The organization prefers long-term placements but does arrange summer work. Member of the International Au Pair Association. UK£80 application fee.

InterExchange, 161 Sixth Ave., New York, NY 10013 (☎ (212) 924-0446; fax 924-0575; www.interexchange.org) provides information on international work, *au pair* programs, and *au pair* positions in Italy and other European countries.

VOLUNTEER

Volunteering is a good way to immerse yourself in a foreign culture without all the bother of being paid for your services. You may receive room and board, and the work can be fascinating. The high application fees charged by the organizations that arrange placement can sometimes be avoided by contacting the individual workcamps directly; check with the organizations. The extensive listings found in Vacation Work Publications' (see **General Work Resources,** *p. 283*) *International Directory of Voluntary Work* (UK£10; postage UK£2.50, within UK £1.50) can be especially helpful. Also try:

Council's Voluntary Services Dept., 205 E. 42nd St., New York, NY 10017 (☎ (888) 268-6245); fax (212) 822-2699; www.ciee.org), offers 1-2 week construction and environmental projects July-Sept. Minimum US$300 placement fee.

Service Civil International Voluntary Service (SCI-VS), 814 NE 40th St., Seattle, WA 98105 (☎/fax (206) 545-6585; email sciivsusa@igc.apc.org). Arranges placement in workcamps in Italy for those age 18 and over. Local organizations sponsor groups for physical or social work. Registration fees US$50-250, depending on the camp location.

STUDY

Full-time university programs will often offer assistance in terms of living and documentation. Language schools, which tend to be less formal, with a smaller time and financial commitment, aim toward providing the foreigner with basic speaking and living skills.

GENERAL STUDY RESOURCES

Institute of International Education (IIE), 809 United Nations Plaza, New York, NY 10017 (☎ (212) 984-5413; fax 984-5358). For book orders: IIE Books, Institute of International Education, P.O. Box 371, Annapolis Junction, MD 20701 (☎ (800) 445-0443; fax (301) 953-2838; email iie-boks@iie.org). A nonprofit, international and cultural exchange agency. Publishes *Academic Year Abroad* (US$43, postage US$4) and *Vacation Study Abroad* (US$37, postage US$5). Write for a complete list of publications.

Peterson's, P.O. Box 2123, Princeton, NJ 08543 (☎ (800) 338-3282; fax (609) 243-9150; www.petersons.com). Their comprehensive, annual study-abroad guide lists programs in countries all over the world and provides essential information on the study abroad experience in general. Find a copy at your local bookstore (US$27), call their toll-free number in the US, or order through their online bookstore.

The College Connection, Inc., 1295 Prospect St., Ste. B, La Jolla, CA 92037 (☎ (619) 551-9770; fax (619) 551-9987; www.eurailpass.com). Publishes *The Passport,* a booklet listing hints about every aspect of traveling and studying abroad. This booklet is free to *Let's Go* readers; send your request by email or fax only. The College Rail Connection, a division of the College Connection, sells railpasses with student discounts.

American Field Service (AFS), 310 SW 4th Avenue, Suite 630, Portland, OR 97204 (☎ (800) AFS-INFO (237-4636); fax (503) 241-1653; email afsinfo@afs.org; www.afs.org/usa). AFS offers summer, semester, and year-long homestay exchange programs in Italy for high school students and graduating high school seniors. Financial aid available.

Centro Turistico Studentesco e Giovanile (CTS) provides info on study in Italy (see p. 298).

Council Travel sponsors over 40 study abroad programs worldwide (see p. 286).

Youth For Understanding International Exchange (YFU), 3501 Newark St. NW, Washington, D.C. 20016 (☎ (800) TEENAGE (833-6243); fax 895-1104; www.yfu.org). Places US high school students worldwide for a year, semester, or summer.

UNIVERSITIES

If you're fluent in Italian, consider enrolling directly in an Italian university. Alternatively, there are several American universities in Italy. Universities are crowded, but you'll probably have a blast and get a real feel for the culture. For further advice, contact **Ufficio Centrale Studenti Esteri in Italia (UCSEI),** Lungotevere dei Vallati 14, 00186 Roma (☎06 8804062; fax 06 8804063), a national organization for foreign students who have already started their course of study in Italy. Remember that student visas are required for study abroad (see **Visas,** p. 282).

La Sapienza, one of the main universities in Rome. M:B-Policlinico. From the Metro station, walk up V. Regina Margherita/Elena past the hospital and Blockbuster to V. Università. For application info, write to the nearest Italian consulate (see p. 245). In Rome, contact the **Segretaria Stranieri,** Città Universitaria, P. Aldo Moro 5, 00185 Roma (switchboard ☎06 49911; fax 06 4452824; direct ☎06 49912707; www.uniroma1.it. Open M, W, and F 8:30am-1pm). Though the university does not offer any week- or month-long classes, the range of activities on campus is as good as any major university; theatrical, musical, and dance productions, debates, and sports—all in Italian, of course.

John Cabot University, V. della Lungara, 233, 00165 Roma (☎06 6819121; fax 06 6832088). US office at 339 South Main St., Sebastopol, CA 95472 (☎ (707) 824-9800; fax (707) 824-0198; www.johncabot.edu; email jcu@johncabot.edu.) This American international university in Trastevere offers undergraduate degrees in art history, business, English literature, and international affairs. Foreign students can enroll for summer, semester ($5500), and year-long ($10,600) sessions. Students are aided in finding internships in their fields of study. Like any college named after a confused British navigator who stumbled upon Canada, John Cabot has a number of conferences, lectures, and dramatic productions that are open to the public.

LANGUAGE SCHOOLS

If you are planning to be in Rome for two weeks or more and desire to learn the language that everybody around you seems to speak all the time (or at least learn how to say something else besides *"Buon giorno, principessa!"* and other choice phrases from Italian import movies),

Italidea, P. della Cancelleria, 85, 00186 Roma (☎06 68307620; fax 06 6892997; www.italiaidea.com). Offers every level of Italian study from an intensive short-term course to more advanced, semester-long courses meeting once or twice per week. Intensive groups meet 3hr. per day M-F for 4 weeks, at a total price of L780,000 and a L30,000 registration fee. The less intensive group meets 3hr. per day twice a week for 4 weeks, at the same price. Private lessons are also available at higher prices. Flexible scheduling. College credit courses offered through some US college and university programs in Italy. Homestays with Italian families are also available.

Centro STorico

DILIT-ih, V. Marghera, 22, 00185 Roma (☎06 4462592 or 06 4462593; fax 06 4440888; www.dilit.it). Near Termini. Resources include a language lab, video and listening center, a computer, and reading room. Intensive courses of 3, 4, or 6hr. per day (min. 2 weeks). 6hr. per day 2-week program L780,000 (plus L50,000 enrollment fee). Individual courses also available. Students of all levels of Italian are accommodated according to a placement exam. Private and home-stay lodgings available. Open summer daily 8:30am-8pm.

Istituto Italiano Centro di Lingua e Cultura, V. Macchiavelli 33, 00185 Roma (☎06 70452138; fax 06 70085122; email istital@uni.net). Near the Manzoni Metro stop on Linea A. Courses offered for students who want a slower pace or for those who seek an intensive setting. Or for people who just want to learn how to say the school's name 3 times quickly. 4-week intensive course (22½hr. per week) L1,020,000. The less intensive 4-week program (15hr. per week) is L760,000. Groups size 3-12. 1 month of accommodations with a family (L760,000) or a student flat with a kitchen (L620,000) are available through the office. Office open M-F 8:30am-7pm. AmEx, MC, V.

Roman Forum

Torre di Babele, V. Bixio 74, 00185 Roma (☎06 7008434; fax 06 70497150; www.torredibabele.it). Small groups of students (max. 12) enjoy personal attention from the instructor in non-intensive or intensive courses for an even number of weeks (min. 2 weeks). 2-week intensive program (4hr. per day) L540,000; 4-week intensive program (4hr. per day) L1,000,000. Additional weeks L250,000 apiece. Students can find lodging through the school. MC, V.

LONG-TERM ACCOMMODATIONS

Finding a long-term apartment rental in Rome can be downright painful, since many potential landlords are wary of renting out properties because of convoluted Italian laws that can make the process of evicting a tenant take up to 20 years. Not wanting to have a squatter on their hands, many apartment owners prefer to keep their properties empty. Short-term rentals are comparatively easier: the months with the most vacancies are July, August, and December, when vacationing

Trastevere

CIAO MEOW

One of the most important things you should know about living in Rome is that there are cats. Lots of them. Everywhere.

After living in the city for a while, you may come to think that you own the place—think again. That honor has long been conferred upon the eternal feline inhabitants of the Eternal City. In fact, Italian composer Ottorino Respighi was so struck by the presence of cats in the city that he named the third piece in his *Rome* trilogy for orchestra *Cats of Rome* (after *Pines of Rome* and *Hills of Rome*).

The cats in Rome live the good life (unlike dogs, many of whom are abandoned when their owners skip town for *Ferragosto*). Thanks to a bizarre 1988 law, Rome's stray cats are granted the right to live where they are born. This has led to the proliferation of an estimated 10,000 cat colonies throughout the city, many of which are cared for by the city (as well as Italians who feed them leftover pasta). Look for the felines among the ruins, especially near Largo di Torre Argentina.

times set in, and homeowners are willing to lease out their places. During the rest of the year, the real estate market is extremely tight. In the last decade, prices for even the most simple pad have skyrocketed; expect to pay no less than L1,300,000 per month for a one-bedroom in the Centro Storico. The longer you stay, the better your chances of finding a cheap rent. In general, the cheaper areas include the Nomentana neighborhood, the area around Piazza Bologna, and San Lorenzo. Utilities are inordinately expensive in Rome; they can augment your rent by up to 25%. Check the English classified ads in *Wanted in Rome* (see p. 283) and Italian ads in *Porta Portese*. Community **bulletin boards** often carry advertisements for roommates—check the English-language ones in bookstores (see p. 166) or the Pasquino movie theater (see p. 175). **Real estate agencies** can help, but many charge fees; definitely avoid agencies that charge a non-refundable fee.

You can also prowl around a particular neighborhood you'd like to live in and look for "*affitasi*" ("for rent") signs. Check with **foreign university programs** as well; they often rent out apartments for their students which are vacant in summer. The best way to find a pad is through connections.

ACCOMMODATIONS AGENCIES

The following real estate agents specialize in finding apartments for foreigners. They may be out of your price range, but they're often willing to give advice. Calling well ahead of time will greatly increase your chances of securing a place on time. Once you've finally found a place and need to furnish it, see **Shopping** (p. 167) for some of our favorite home furnishing stores. When all else fails, head to IKEA.

Romeguide (www.romeguide.it). A great web site to use while searching for an apartment.

Property Center, V. di Gesù è Maria, 25 (☎06 3212341). Near P. del Popolo. Arranges short- and long-term apartment and villa rentals in various price ranges; specializes in Centro Storico and Trastevere. English spoken. Open M-F 9:30am-6:30pm, Sa 10am-2pm.

Welcome Home Relocation Services, V. Barbarano Romano, 15 (☎06 3036 6936; fax 06 30361706; email welcome.home@slashnet.it). All kinds of housing placement services plus assistance in documentation (permits, visas, licenses) and orientation. English spoken. Open M-F 9am-6pm.

Homes International, V. L. Bissolati, 20 (☎06 4881800; fax 06 4881808; email homesenint@tin.it). Arranges short- and long-term rentals for apartments and villas; can also locate cheaper places in the outskirts of Rome. Open M-F 9am-7pm, Sa 9am-noon.

MONEY MATTERS

Anyone who's ever tried to change a few *lire* will attest to the horrors of the Roman banking administration: employees are snippy, computers crash frequently, and the amount of paperwork required is enough to give any Greenpeace member a coronary. Opening a bank account is no exception. In order to open a bank account in Rome you must present the following: *certificato di residenza* (a certificate of residence, which you receive from the *comune* when you register as a resident) or your *permesso di soggiorno;* a passport or photo ID; and a *Codice Fiscale*, equivalent to an American Social Security number, which you also get from the *commune*. Sound simple? Think again. Getting a *Codice Fiscale* is next to impossible. Check with the institution with which you hope to do business or the international desk of your local bank for requirements and other information. For banks in Rome, see **Service Directory,** p. 293.

COMMUNITY RESOURCES

Even though there are upwards of 200,000 registered foreigners living in Rome (and probably many unofficial residents on top of that), the life of an expat can be daunting and lonely, especially at first. Even the establishments listed throughout this book, which often serve a tourist and backpacker crowd, may not provide you with the social network you need to acclimate yourself to your new home. To fill the gap, **Welcome Neighbor** organizes events and support groups for English-speaking expats in Rome. (☎ 06 3036 6936.) For gay and lesbian resources, and other special concerns, see p. 263.

HEALTH & FITNESS

For emergency rooms, clinics, hospitals, and dentists, see **Service Directory,** p. 294.

INSURANCE

Non-EU citizens should first contact their home health insurance provider to see what coverage options are available for long-term stays in Italy. Coverage under the Italian state system costs around L1.2 million per year, and involves significant co-payments for prescriptions, laboratory work, specialist visits, and hospital stays. Family planning services are covered, but non-emergency dentistry is not. To register for coverage, bring your visa, passport, and any other documentation to the nearest INPS (Italian state insurance board).

EU citizens, on the other hand, are eligible for state health care in Italy. Before leaving your home country, pick up an E111 form, and bring it to a hospital in Rome. If you don't have the form, bring your passport, permit to stay, and tax forms instead.

HEALTH CLUBS

Though American-style athletic clubs are few and far between, exercise opportunities present themselves in the form of gargantuan fitness complexes. Consult *Roma C'è* for a more extensive listing. Even if you don't have a membership, you can still use the recreational facilities at Rome's **YMCA** (EEM-kah), V. dell'Oceano Pacifico, 13 (pool), in EUR, and V. Libomo, 68 (gym). For L40,000 you can use the Y's pool, gym, and tennis courts for an entire day (you must be under 45 years old). Call 06 5225247 for more info.

Big Gym (☎ 06 3208666; www.biggym.it). In the Stadio dei Marmi at the Foro Italico . Bus #32, 232, or 280. An open air fitness extravaganza that is everything its name suggests. Under the watchful gaze of the numerous uncomfortably naked statues that line the stadium, customers can choose from weights, aerobics, basketball, fun ball (a game that seems to be the result of a tennis hybridization experiment gone horribly awry), *calcetto* (five-on-five small-field soccer), thunderball, free climbing, and an aggressive in-line course complete with half-pipe. Open Jun. 1-Aug. 5 daily 9am-2am. L7000 before 6pm, L12,000 after 6pm. L3000 discount with stamped bus ticket.

Roman Sport Center, V. del Galoppatoio, 33 (☎06 3201667 or 06 3218096). M:A-Spagna. In Villa Borghese. This large gym offers non-members a day of sweating (aerobics, squash, pool, sauna, Turkish baths, weight room) for L50,000. Open M-Sa 9am-10pm and Su 9am-3pm.

Associazione Sportiva Augustea (A.S.A.), V. Luciani, 57 (☎06 23235112). M:A-Cinecittà. In Cinecittà. Alternatively, take bus #558 or 54. Indoor pool (L10,000 for a day's swim), gym, and tennis courts (L15,000). Open daily 10am-7pm.

Body Image, V. E. Fermi, 142 (☎06 5573356). For women only, this club boasts a weight room, aerobics, and a sauna. L80,000 per month. Open daily 9:30am-9pm. Closed Aug.

Navona Health Center, V. dei Banchi Nuovi, 39 (☎06 6896104). In the Centro Storico. Small gym with weights, 2 fitness rooms, and a sauna. L15,000 per day, L100,000 per month. Open M-F 9am-9pm, Sa 11am-8pm. Closed Aug.

PARTICIPANT SPORTS

JOGGGING. Rome has some spectacular parks, providing the perfect spot for jogging. A note of **caution:** if the air is particularly polluted, stay indoors. Rome suffers from extremely high levels of smog which can at times be dangerous. On clear days, you can head up to **Villa Borghese** for a run. **Villa Ada** also has places to run, along with an exercise course through the park, as does **Villa Doria Pamphilj,** the largest park in the city. Using real running tracks entails declaring yourself a member of **Fidal,** followed by a long bureaucratic process of submitting money, pictures, and proof of health. Head down to the Stadio delle Terme di Caracalla, V. G. Bacelli, 5 (☎06 5780602), if you're up to the challenge of all those steps.

SWIMMING. For chlorinated relief from the Roman heat, ask at a tourist office for locations of public pools or check out the yellow pages under *piscine.* Entertainment magazines often list pools. Many major hotels in Rome open their pools to the public, but often charge a large fee. At **Piscina della Rosa,** V. America, 20 in EUR, the pool is a short walk from the Metro (B) EUR-Palasport stop. (☎06 5926717. Open June-Sept. daily 9am-7pm. Full-day swim in the outdoor pool L20,000, half-day L15,000, 1-4pm L6000.) The **Centro Sportivo Italiano,** Lungotevere Flaminio, 59, accessible by bus #926 or tram #19 or #225, is just north of the city along the Tiber. (☎06 3234732. Open June-Sept. daily 10:45am-10:30pm; one-time membership fee L10,000; full day L22,000, half-day L15,000.)

ICE SKATING. If you prefer water in the solid state and have a car, head for the skating rink **Palaghiaccio di Marino,** on V. Appia Nuova, km 19, which has 1½hr. skating sessions. (☎06 9309480. Open late Aug.-Apr. Rentals M-F 5, 9, and 11pm; Sa-Su 3, 5, 7, 9, and 11pm; Su also 11am. Rentals of skates and pads L10,000, on weekends L11,000.)

BOWLING. "Do you have 12-pound balls?" If you really miss bowling (pronounced *bool-ing* in Italy, thank you very much), head for **Bowling Roma,** V. R. Margherita, 181, off V. Nomentana past the Porta Pia (accessible by bus #62), an A/C time warp to the 1960s. (☎06 8551184. Open M-Sa 10am-11:30pm, Su 5pm-midnight. L3000 per game per person, shoes included, after 9pm L6000.) Or *bool* on over to **Bowling Brunswick,** Lungotevere dell'Acqua Acetosa, 10. Take bus #4 or #230. Three nights a week, this unassuming bowling alley is transformed into the home of "Cosmic Bowling." Lanes and pins glow, accompanied by music and lights of the stroboscopic variety. (☎06 8086147. Open Su-Th 10-2am, F-Sa 10-4am. L3300 per game per person, after 8pm L5300, shoes L1000.)

TENNIS. One club in particular is very friendly to foreigners, open to non-members, and affordable. **Circolo della Stampa** is in P. Mancini and owned by the Italian Journalist's Association. (☎06 3232452. Open M-F 8am-11pm, Sa-Su 8am-8pm. L16,000 per court per hour. Lights L6,000.)

YOGA. Yoga has not yet become a very widespread practice in Rome, but it is growing, and there are a few places in the city where you can find instruction and community. The **Accademia Yoga,** V. XX Settembre, 58a (☎06 4885967), north of P. della Repubblica, offers courses in mental and physical yoga exercise, concentrating mainly on the raja yoga technique of Patanjali, which is theoretically best-suited to the western mind. It has links with various yoga schools in India and frequently brings over visiting teachers. Courses in Hindi and Sanskrit are also available. Contact the **Federazione Italiana Yoga,** V. Belisario, 7, off V. Piave near V. XX Settembre, for further assistance in finding a teacher specially suited to your needs. (☎ 06 4287 0191.) Other listings are available in *Roma C'è's* guide *La Città Invisibile.*

Service Directory

ACCOMMODATIONS

See also Tourist Services, p. 298.

Welcome Home Relocation Services, V. Barbarano Romano, 15 (☎06 3036 6936; fax 06 30361706; email welcome.home@slash-net.it). English spoken. Open M-F 9am-6pm.

Property Center, V. di Gesù è Maria, 25 (☎06 3212341). English spoken. Open M-F 9:30am-6:30pm, Sa 10am-2pm.

Homes International, V. L. Bissolati, 20 (☎06 4881800; fax 06 4881808; email homesenint@tin.it). Open M-F 9am-7pm, Sa 9am-noon.

Italian Youth Hostels Association (HI-IYHF), V. Cavour, 44 (☎06 4871152; fax 06 4880492). Open M-Th 8am-5pm, F 8am-3pm, Sa 8am-noon.

Associazione Cattolica Internazionale al Servizio della Giovane, V. Urbana, 158 (☎ 06 4880056). Open M-Sa 6:30am-10pm, Su 7am-10pm. Closed part of Aug.

Bed and Go, V. S. Tommaso d'Aquino, 47 (☎06 39750907 or 06 39746484; fax 06 39760553; email bedandgo@tin.it). Open M-F 9am-1pm and 2-6pm

Bed & Breakfast Association of Rome, P. del Teatro Pompeo, 2 (☎/fax 06 6877348; www.b-b.rm.it; email info@b-b.rm.it).

AIRPORTS

Ciampino Airport (☎06 794941).

Fiumicino Airport (☎06 65951), also known as Leonardo da Vinci International.

BANKS

Banca Popolare di Milano, P. Flamina.

Banca Nazionale del Lavoro, V. Marsala, 6; V. della Rosetta, 1; P. Venezia, 6; and V. Veneto, 111. Cirrus and PLUS.

Banco di Roma, V. del Banco di Santo Spirito, 31 (☎06 68809710; fax 06 68808651). Open M-F 8:30am-1:30pm and 2:30-4pm. Also at V. Tiburtina, P. Barberini, V. dei Monti Tiburtini, V. del Corso, and others. Cirrus and PLUS.

Istituto Bancario San Paolo di Torino, Termini. Cirrus.

BIKE & MOPED RENTAL

Happy Rent, V. Farini, 3 (☎06 4818185). Take a bus to V. Cavour. Motorbikes L50,000 per day; 600cc bikes L120,000 per day. Open daily 9am-7pm. AmEx, MC, V.

Romarent, V. dei Bovari, 7a (☎06 6896555). Bikes L15,000 per day, L75,000 per week; motorbikes L35,000 per day. AmEx, DC, MC.

Rent-a-Scooter, V. F. Turati, 50 (☎06 4469222). Mopeds from L50,000 per day. Lock, helmet, insurance, and free souvenir included. Open daily 9am-7pm.

Scooters for Rent, V. della Purificazione, 84 (☎06 4885485), off P. Barberini. Bicycles L20,000 per day, L100,000 per week; mopeds L50,000 per day, L250,000 per week. Open daily in summer 9am-7pm. AmEx, MC, V.

I Bike Rome, V. Veneto, 156 (☎06 3225240). In the Villa Borghese parking garage. Bikes L5-8000 per hr., L10,000 per day, L40,000 per week. Mopeds L40,000 for 4 hours, L60,000 per day, L250,000 per week. Open daily 8:30am-7pm.

BUSES

See **Transportation**, p. 299.

CAR RENTAL

Avis (☎06 41998; www.avis.com).

Maggiore (☎06 2291530; www.maggiore.it).

Hertz (☎06 4740389; www.hertz.com).

Europcar (☎06 4882854; www.europcar.it).

CLINICS

See also **Hospitals** (p. 295) and **Emergency Services** (p. 295).

Ospedale San Camillo in Monteverde, Circonvallazione Gianicolense, 87 (☎06 58701). In Gianicolo. Pregnancy tests, STD tests, gynecological exams, and pap smears. Open for info daily 8am-7pm; call for appointment.

Unione Sanitaria Internazionale, V. Machiavelli, 22 (☎06 70453544). M:A-Vittorio Emanuele. Open for info daily 7am-7pm; tests daily 7-11am.

Analisi Cliniche Luisa, V. Padova, 96a (☎06 44291406). M:B-P. Bologna. Pregnancy, STD, and HIV tests (L20,000-90,000). Open M-F 7:30am-8pm, Sa 8am-noon.

Studio Polispecialistico Nomentano, V. Nomentana, 550/552 (☎06 86895611). HIV tests L85,000. Open daily 7am-12:30pm and 3-10pm.

Circolo di Cultura Omosessuale Mario Mieli. See p. 294.

COMMUNITY RESOURCES

See also **Gay & Lesbian Resources** (p. 295).

Welcome Neighbor (☎06 30366936). Events and support groups for English speakers.

CONSULATES & EMBASSIES

Australia, V. Alessandria, 215 (☎06 852721, emergency 800 877790; fax 06 85272300). Consular and passport services around the corner at C. Trieste, 25. Open M-Th 9am-5pm, F 9am-12:30pm.

Canada, Consulate, V. Zara, 30 (☎06 44598421; fax 06 44598912). Consular and passport services open M-F 10am-noon and 2-4pm. Embassy, V. G.B. De Rossi, 27 (☎06 445981).

Ireland, Consulate, P. Campitelli, 3 (☎06 6979121). Passport services open M-F 10am-12:30pm and 3-4:30pm.

New Zealand, V. Zara, 28 (☎06 4417171; fax 06 4402984). Consular and passport services open M-F 9:30am-noon. Embassy services M-F 8:30am-12:45pm and 1:45-5pm.

South Africa, V. Tanaro, 14 (☎06 852541 ; fax 06 85254300). Take bus #86 from Termini to P. Buenos Aires. Open M-F 9am-noon.

UK, V. XX Settembre, 80/A (☎06 4825441; fax 06 42202334; consulate ☎06 42202600). Near V. Palestro. Consular and passport services open M-F 9:15am-1:30pm.

United States, V. Veneto, 119/A (☎06 46741; fax 06 46742217). Passport and consular services open M-F 8:30-noon and 1:30-3:30pm. Visas M-F 8:30-10:30am; IRS M-F 9am-noon in person, 1:30-3:30pm by phone. Closed on U.S. and Italian holidays.

CRISIS LINES

Centro Anti-Violenza, V. di Torrespaccata, 157 (☎06 23269049 or 06 23269053). For victims of sexual violence. Branch offices for legal and psychological consultation throughout the city. 24hr.

Telefono Rosa, V. Tor di Nona, 43 (☎06 6832675; fax 06 6833748). For victims of sexual abuse or harassment. Open M-F 10am-1pm and 4pm-7pm.

Samaritans, V. San Giovanni in Laterano, 250 (☎06 70454444). Native English speakers. Anonymous or face-to-face counseling available. Open for calls and visits (call ahead) daily 1-10pm.

Alcoholics Anonymous (☎06 6636620).

CURRENCY SERVICES

See also **Banks** (p. 293).

American Express, P. di Spagna, 38 (☎06 67641; lost or stolen cards and/or checks ☎06 72281; fax 06 67642499). Open Sept.-July: M-F 9am-7:30pm, Sa 9am-3pm. Open Aug.: M-F 9am-6pm, Sa 9am-12:30pm. Mailing address: P. di Spagna, 38; 00187 Roma.

Thomas Cook, P. Barberini, 21a (☎06 4828082). Open M-Sa 9am-8pm, Su 9:30am-5pm. **Other branches:** V. della Conciliazione, 23-25 (☎06 68300435; open M-Sa 8:30am-6pm, Su 9am-5pm); V. del Corso, 23 (☎06 3230067; open M-Sa 9am-8pm, Su 9am-1:30pm); P. della Repubblica, 65 (☎06 486495; open M-F 9am-5pm with 1hr. lunch break, Sa 9am-1pm).

Western Union, P. di Spagna, 92 (toll-free ☎06 6484583). Open M-F 9am-7pm.

EMBASSIES

See **Consulates & Embassies,** p. 293.

EMERGENCY SERVICES

See also **Police** (p. 297) and **Hospitals** (p. 295).

Carabinieri: ☎112.

Police/Fire/Ambulance: ☎113.

Medical Emergencies: ☎118.

Fire Service: ☎115.

Policlinico Umberto I, V.le di Policlinico, 155 (emergency ☎06 49971, non emergency 06 49971). M:B-Policlinico or #9 bus. Free first aid (pronto soccorso). Open 24hr.

Nuovo Regina Margherita, V. Trastevere, 72 (☎06 58441). Walk-in first aid. Open 24hr.

Condomeria, V. de Prefetti, 25. Open M-Sa 10am-1pm and 4-7:30pm.

Accademia Yoga, V. XX Settembre, 58a (☎06 4885967).

Federazione Italiana Yoga, V. Belisario, 7, (☎06 4287 0191).

ENTERTAINMENT

See **Tickets,** p. 298.

GAY & LESBIAN RESOURCES

Circolo Mario Mieli di Cultura Omosessuale, V. Corinto, 5 (☎06 5413985; fax 06 5413971; www.mariomieli.it). M:B-San Paolo. Open M-F 9am-1pm and 2-6pm; closed Aug.

Arci-Gay, V. Orvinio, 2 (☎06 86385112; www.gay.it/arcigay/roma). Also at V. Lariana, 8 (☎06 8555522).

Arci-Lesbica (www.women.it/~arciles/roma), in the Same offices as Arci-Gay.

Libreria Babele (☎06 6876628), V. dei Banchi Vecchi, across the bridge from Castel Sant'Angelo. Rome's only gay and lesbian bookstore. Gay and Lesbian Map of Rome L12,000. Open M.-Sa. 10am-7:30pm.

Italian Gay and Lesbian Yellow Pages (www.gay.it/guida/italia/info.htm).

Coordinamento Lesbico Italiano, V. S. Francesco di Sales, 1a (☎06 6864201).

GROCERS

See **Supermarkets,** p. 297

HEALTH CLUBS

Big Gym, Stadio dei Marmi at the Foro Italico (☎06 3208666; www.biggym.it). L7000 before 6pm, L12,000 after 6pm. L3000 discount with stamped bus ticket. Open Jun. 1-Aug. 5 daily 9am-2am.

Roman Sport Center, V. del Galoppatoio, 33 (☎06 3201667 or 06 3218096). M:A-Spagna. 1-day membership L50,000. Open M-Sa 9am-10pm and Su 9am-3pm.

Associazione Sportiva Augustea (A.S.A.), V. Luciani, 57 (☎06 23235112). M:A-Cinecittà. Open daily 10am-7pm.

Body Image, V. E. Fermi, 142 (☎06 5573356). Women only. L80,000 per month. Open daily 9:30am-9pm. Closed Aug.

Navona Health Center, V. dei Banchi Nuovi, 39 (☎06 6896104). L15,000 per day, L100,000 per month. Open M-F 9am-9pm, Sa 11am-8pm. Closed Aug.

HOSPITALS

See also **Emergency Services (p. 295)** and **Clinics (p. 294).**

International Medical Center, V. G. Amendola, 7 (☎06 4882371; nights and Su 06 4884051). Call them first. Prescriptions filled, paramedic crew on call, referral service to English-speaking doctors. General visit L130,000. Open M-Sa 8:30am-8pm; on-call 24hr.

Rome-American Hospital, V. E. Longoni, 69 (☎06 22551; fax 06 2285062). Private emergency and laboratory services, HIV tests, and pregnancy tests. No emergency room. On call 24hr.

HOTLINES

See **Crisis Lines,** p. 294.

INTERNET ACCESS

Marco's Bar, V. Varese, 54 (☎06 44703591). L5000 per hr. with *Let's Go.* Open daily 5:30am-2am.

Trevi Tourist Service: Trevi Internet, V. dei Lucchesi, 31-32 (☎/fax 06 6920 0799). L5000 for 30 min., L10,000 for 90 min. Open daily 9am-10pm.

Internet Café, V. dei Marrucini, 12 (☎/fax 06 4454953; www.Internetcafe.it; email info@Internetcafe.it.) 30min. L5000, 1hr. L8000; after 9pm 30min. L6000, 1 hr. L10,000. Open M-F 9am-2am, Sa-Su 5pm-2am.

Bolle Blu (p. 296). Laundromat with Internet accesss (L7000 per hr.).

Freedom Traveller, V. Gaeta, 25 (☎06 4782 3682; www.freedom-traveller.it). L10,000 per hr., students L8000 Open M-Sa 9am-midnight.

Internet Café, V. Cavour, 213 (☎06 4782 3051). L10,000 per hr. Open daily 9am-1am.

The Netgate Internet Point, P. Firenze, 25 (☎06 6893445). W and S free access 8pm-8:30pm; otherwise L10,000 per hr.

X-plore, V. dei Gracchi, 83-85 (☎06 50797474; www.xplore.it). L10,000 per hr. Open M-Th 10-1am, F-Sa 10-3am.

LAUNDROMATS

OndaBlu, V. La Mora, 7 (info ☎800 861346). Other locations throughout Rome. Wash L6000 per 6.5kg load; dry L6000 per 6.5kg load; soap L1500. Open daily 8am-10pm.

Bolle Blu, V. Palestro, 59/61 (☎06 4465804), and V. Milazzo, 20b. Wash L6000 per 6.5kg load; dry L6000 per 6.5kg load; special L10,000 for 16kg; soap L1500. Open daily 8am-midnight.

Acqua & Sapone Lavanderia, V. Montebello, 66 (☎06 4883209). Wash L6000 per 6-8kg; dry L6000 per 6-8kg. Open daily 8am-10pm.

LIBRARIES

Biblioteca Alessandrina, P. Aldo Moro, 5 (☎06 4474021). La Sapienza's inefficient but public library. Open M-F 8:30am-7:45pm, Sa 8:30am-1:30pm.

Biblioteca Nazionale, V. Castro Pretorio, 105 (☎06 49891 or 06 4989249; fax 06 4457635). M-F 8:30am-7pm, Sa 8:30am-1:30pm. Closed mid-Aug.

Centro Studi Americani, V. M. Caetani, 32, 2nd fl. (☎06 68806624). Open M-F 9am-7:30pm, Sa 9am-1:30pm. Closed part of Aug.

Santa Susanna Lending Library, V. XX Settembre, 15, 2nd fl. (☎06 4827510). Open Tu and Th 10am-1pm, W 3-6pm, F 1-4pm, Sa-Su 10am-12:30pm. In July open only Tu, W, and Su; in Aug. open only Su.

LOST PROPERTY

See also **Police** *(p. 297).*

Oggetti Smarriti, V. Nicolo Bettoni, 1 (☎06 5816040); items lost on trains ☎06 47306682). Open Tu and F 8:30am-1pm, M, W 8:30am-1pm and 2:30-6pm, Th 8:30am-6pm.

Termini, in the glass booth in the main passageway. Open daily 7am-11pm.

MARKETS

See also **Supermarkets** *(p. 297). For outdoor markets, see p. 165.*

MOPED RENTAL

See **Bike & Moped Rental** *(p. 294).*

POSTAL SERVICES

Main Post Office (Posta Centrale), P. San Silvestro, 19 (☎06 679 8495; fax 06 6786618). Open M-F 9am-6pm, Sa 9am-2pm. Another **branch,** V. delle Terme di Diocleziano, 30 (☎06 4745602; fax 06 4743536), near Termini. Same hours as San Silvestro branch.

Vatican Post Office (☎06 69883406), two locations in P. San Pietro. No *Fermo Posta.* Open M-F 8:30am-7pm, Sa 8:30am-6pm. **Branch office** 2nd fl. of Vatican Museum. Open museum hours.

FedEx, V. Barberini, 115-119 (☎800 123800). Open M-F 9am-1pm and 2-6pm. AmEx, MC, V.

UPS, V. del Traforo, 136. (☎800 877877). Just next to the tunnel that connects V. del Tritone and V. Nazionale. Open M-F 9am-1pm and 3-7pm. AmEx, MC, V.

PHARMACIES

Most **Hospitals** *(p. 295) also have pharmacies.*

Farmacia Internazionale, P. Barberini, 49 (☎06 4871195). Open daily 24hr. MC, V.

Farmacia Piram, V. Nazionale, 228 (☎06 4880754). Open daily 24hr. MC, V.

Farmacia Arenula, V. Arenula, 73 (☎06 68803278). Call to check hours.

Farmacia Grieco, P. della Repubblica, 67 (☎06 4880410). Open daily 24hr.

Farmacia Di Stazione Notturna, P. del Cinquecento, 51 (☎06 4880019). Call for hours.

PHONE SERVICES

See **Telehone Services,** p. 297.

POLICE

Police: Foreigner's Office (Ufficio Stranieri), V. Genova, 2 (☎06 46862876). Open daily 24hr.

Police Headquarters (Questura Centrale), V. San Vitale, 15 (☎06 46861).

Railway Police (☎06 47306959), track #1 and facing track #2 in Termini. Open 24hr.

RADIO TAXIS

See **Taxis & Radio Taxis,** p. 298.

RELIGIOUS SERVICES

All Saints Church (Anglican), V. del Babuino, 153 (☎06 36001881). English services, usually Su 8:30 and 10:30am and 6:30pm. Prayers M-Tu and Th-F 8am and noon. Eucharists M-Tu and Th-F 6pm.

Rome Baptist Church, P. di San Lorenzo in Lucrina, 35 (☎06 6876652). Sunday service 10am; Bible study 11am. Confession M-W 10am-1pm, F 6-8pm.

Confessionals (Catholic) are in St. Peter's (p. 115), Santa Maria Maggiore (p. 127), San Giovanni in Laterano (p. 131), San Paolo fuori le Mura (p. 136), Il Gesù (p. 95), Santa Maria sopra Minerva (p. 98), Sant'Anselmo (p. 132), and Santa Sabina (p. 132). Languages spoken by the priest are noted on door.

San Silvestro (Catholic), P. San Silvestro, 1 (☎06 6797775). Masses in English Su 10am and 5:30pm.

Santa Susanna (Catholic), V. XX Settembre, 15 (☎06 4882748). Mass in English M-Sa 6pm, Su 9 and 10:30am.

San Paolo fuori le Mura (Episcopalian), V. Napoli, 58 (☎06 4883339). English services Su 8:30 and 10:30am.

Comunita Israelitica di Roma (Jewish), Lungotevere Cenci (☎06 6840061). Hebrew services M-F 7:45am and sunset, Sa 8:30am.

Ponte Sant'Angelo Church (Methodist), P. Ponte Sant'Angelo (☎06 6868314). Su service 10:30am. Communion first Su of every month.

La Moschea di Roma (Muslim), V. della Moschea (☎06 8082258). Prayers in Arabic daily 3:22am, noon, 1:15, 5:13, 8:50, and 10:20pm. Services W and Su 9-11:30am.

St. Andrew's Church (Presbyterian), V. XX Settembre, 7 (☎06 4827627). Services in English Su 11am. Another congregation holds Korean services in the same building daily 6am, W 7pm, and Su noon.

SPORTS FACILITIES

See also **Health Clubs,** p. 295.

Accademia Yoga, V. XX Settembre, 58a (☎06 4885967).

▓ **Bowling Brunswick,** Lungotevere dell'Acqua Acetosa, 10 (☎06 8086147). Cosmic bowling! L3300 per game per person, after 8pm L5300, shoes L1000. Open Su-Th 10-2am, F-Sa 10-4am.

Bowling Roma, V. R. Margherita, 181 (☎06 8551184). L3000 per game per person, shoes included; after 9pm L6000. Open M-Sa 10am-11:30pm, Su 5pm-midnight.

Centro Sportivo Italiano, Lungotevere Flaminio, 59 (☎06 3234732). Swimming pool. One-time membership fee L10,000; full day L22,000, half-day L15,000. Open June-Sept. daily 10:45am-10:30pm.

Circolo della Stampa, P. Mancini (☎06 3232452). Tennis. L16,000 per court per hour. Lights L6,000. Open M-F 8am-11pm, Sa-Su 8am-8pm.

Federazione Italiana Yoga, V. Belisario, 7, (☎06 4287 0191).

Palaghiaccio di Marino, V. Appia Nuova, km 19 (☎06 9309480). Ice skating. 1½hr. skating sessions. Rentals of skates and pads L10,000, on weekends L11,000. Rentals M-F 5, 9, and 11pm; Sa-Su 3, 5, 7, 9, and 11pm; Su also 11am. Open late Aug.-Apr.

Piscina della Rosa, V. America, 20 (☎06 5926717). Full-day swim in the outdoor pool L20,000, half-day L15,000, 1-4pm L6000. Open June-Sept. daily 9am-7pm.

SC Ostiense, V. del Mare, 128 (☎06 5915540). Tennis. L16,000 per singles match per hour, L24,000 per doubles match per hour. Lights L10,000. Open daily 9am-6:30pm. Closed Aug.

SUPERMARKETS

STANDA (☎800 358758). V. Cola di Rienzo, 173 (in Prati, near the Vatican), V. di Trastevere, 62, and other locations.

Alimentari Coreani (Korean Grocery Store), V. Cavour, 84. Near P. di Santa Maria Maggiore. Open M-Sa 9am-1pm and 4-8pm.

Billo, V. S. Ambrogio, 7 (☎06 687 79 66). Off V. Portico, in the Jewish Ghetto. Kosher.

Castroni, V. Cola di Rienzo, 196-198 (☎06 6874383). Coffee bar and phenomenal foreign foods market. Other locations include V. Ottaviano, 55 (☎06 39723279) and V. delle Quattro Fontane, 38 (☎06 44824 35).

TAXIS & RADIO TAXIS

Radiotaxi (☎06 3570).
Radiotevere (☎06 4157).
Prontotaxi (☎06 6645).
Cosmo la Capitale (☎06 4994).

TELEPHONE SERVICES

AT&T (☎1721011).
MCI (☎1721022).
Sprint (☎1721877).
Bell Canada Direct (☎1721001).
British Telecom Direct (☎1720044).
Telecom Éireann Direct (☎1720353).
Telstra Australia Direct (☎1721161).
Telecom New Zealand (☎1721064).
Telkom South Africa (☎1721027).

TICKETS

■**Teatro Argentina Box Office,** Largo di Torre Argentina, 52 (☎06 68804601 or 06 6875445). Tickets for any and all goings-on in Rome. Open M-F 10am-2pm and 3-7pm, Sa 10am-2pm.

Interclub, P. Ippolito Nievo, 3 (☎06 5880564), in Trastevere, covers just about everything going on in the city.

Orbis, P. Esquilino, 37. (☎06 4827403). Rock/pop and sporting events. Open M-Sa 9:30am-1pm and 4-7:30pm.

RicordiMedia, two locations: V. del Corso, 506 (☎06 3612370), and V. G. Cesare, 88 (☎06 37351589). Rock/Pop concerts. Both open daily 9:30am-8pm.

Auditorio Pio Box Office, V. di Conciliazione, 4 (☎06 68801044). Classical music. Open Th-Tu 10:20am-1:30pm and 3-6pm, and until showtime on concert days.

Villa Giulia/Santa Cecilia ticket office, P. della Villa Giulia, 9 (☎06 3611064 or 063611833, credit card reservations ☎06 68801044). Summer classical music. Open Tu-Sa 10am-2pm, Su 10am-1pm, and until showtime on performance days.

TOURIST SERVICES

■**Enjoy Rome,** V. Marghera, 8a (☎06 4451843 or 06 4456890; fax 06 4450734; www.enjoyrome.com). **Branch** office, V. Varese, 39. Open M-F 8:30am-2pm and 3:30-6:30pm, Sa 8:30am-2pm.

PIT (Tourist Information Point) (☎06 48906300), track #4 in Termini. **Kiosks:**

Castel Sant'Angelo (P. Pia; ☎06 68809707); Fori Imperiali (V. del Tempio della Pace; ☎06 69924307); P. di Spagna (Largo Goldoni; ☎06 68136061); P. Navona (P. delle Cinque Lune; ☎06 68809240); Trastevere (P. Sonnino; ☎06 58333457); San Giovanni (P. S. Giovanni in Laterano; ☎06 77203535); Santa Maria Maggiore (V. dell'Olmata); ☎06 47880294); V. del Corso (V. Minghetti; ☎06 6782988); V. Nazionale (Palazzo delle Espozioni; ☎06 47824525); Termini (P. dei Cinquecento; ☎06 47825194); Fiumicino (international arrivals area; ☎06 65956074). All kiosks except Fiumicino open daily 9am-6pm. Fiumicino open daily 8:15am-7:15pm.

Call Center Comune di Roma (☎06 36004399). Open daily 9am-7pm.

Centro Turistico Studentesco (CTS), V. Genova, 16 (☎06 4620431; general info ☎06 441111; fax 06 4679207; www.cts.it). Open M-F 9am-1pm, 2-6pm. Branch offices: V. degli Ausoni, 5 (☎06 4450141); V. Appia Nuova, 434 (☎06 7857906); C. Vittorio Emanuele II, 297 (☎06 6872672); Terminal Ostiense (☎06 5747950); P. Irnerio 43 (☎06 6628597).

EPT (Rome Tourist Authority), V. Parigi, 5 (☎06 48899255 or 06 48899253; fax 06 48899228). Open M-F 8:15am-7:15pm, Sa 8:15am-1:45pm. **Termini branch** (☎06 65956074). Open daily 8:15am-7pm.

Italian Youth Hostels Association (HI-IYHF), see p. 293.

APT (Azienda di Promozione Turistica), ☎06 488991.

Transalpino, P. dell'Esquilino, 8a (☎06 4870870; fax 06 4883094). Open M-F 9am-6:30pm. **Booth** (☎06 4880536) at track #22 in Termini. Open M-Sa 8am-8:30pm, in summer also Su 8:30am-5:30pm.

TOURS

■ **Enjoy Rome: Walk Through the Centuries,** V. Varese, 39 (☎06 4451843; www.enjoyrome.com). Four three-hour English tours (all L25,000 for those under 26; L30,000 for those 26 and over): The Ancient and Old Rome; the Vatican City; Trastevere and the Jewish Ghetto; and night tour of the Ancient City and the Centro Storico **Bike tour** from Villa Borghese to the Circus Maximus (L35,000). "Hollywood on the Tiber," a bus tour (with film clips) of Rome's famous cinematic areas (L50,000). Day-long Pompeii bus trips L70,000. Tickets at the Enjoy Rome office (p. 298), Pensione Fawlty Towers (p. 274),

Hotel Colors (p. 273), Pensione Sandy (p. 278), or Pensione Ottaviano (p. 273).

Appian Line, P. dell'Esquilino, 6 (☎06 4878 6601; fax 06 4742214; www.appianline.it). To the left as you face the Churhc of Santa Maria Maggiore. 11 different bus tours of the city, including Ancient Rome (L53,000), Papal Blessing (L60,000), Tivoli, Florence, Pompeii, and others (L130-215,000); tours within Rome (L25-77,000) include all expenses. Free pick-up from hotel. English, French, Spanish, and German spoken. Open daily 6:30am-8pm. AmEx, MC, V.

American Express, P. di Spagna, 38 (☎06 6764 2413; fax 06 6794953). All expenses paid 4hr. bus-and-walking tours of Vatican City (L75,000), the Ancient City (L70,000), and Tivoli (L80,000) daily (except Su and winter holidays) at 9:30am and 2:30pm. Daytrips to Florence, Pompeii, Capri, Assisi, and Sorrento (L125-210,000). English spoken. Open M-F 9am-5:30pm, Sa 9am-12:30pm. AmEx.

Associazione Culturale dell'Italia, V. Trionfale, 148 (☎06 3972 8186; fax 06 3972 8187). Guided tours of the city in English, French, Spanish, and German. 12,000 per person, 15-20 people L150,000. 2hr. of whatever sights you want to see. Closed Aug.

ATAC 110 City Tour (☎06 4695 2256). City transit authority. 2hr. bus tour along bus #110 line , both leaving from Termini (L15,000). Sightseeing Tour (2½hrs.; daily departures at 10:30am and 2, 3, 5, and 6pm) and Basilicas Tour (3hrs.; daily departures at 10am and 2:30pm). Buy tickets at the information booth inside the train station. English spoken. Reservations possible.

TRANSPORTATION

See also **Airports** *(p. 293),* **Bike & Moped Rental** *(p. 294),* **Car Rental** *(p. 294),* **Taxis & Radio Taxis** *(p. 295).*

Aziende Tramvie Autobus Communali (ATAC) (☎800 555666). Open 8am-8pm.

COTRAL (☎06 5915551).

Ferrovie dello Stato (FS) (☎1478 88088; www.fs-on-line.com).

VESPA RENTAL

See **Bike & Moped Rental,** *p. 294.*

Liberty, Justice, and Globe-trotting for all.

Sip espresso in Paris. Cheer the bulls in Barcelona. Learn the waltz in Saltzburg. 85 years after the Wright brothers discovered flying was easier than walking, wings are available to all. When you Name Your Own Price℠ on airline tickets at priceline.com, the world becomes your playground, the skies your road-less-traveled. You can save up to 40% or more, and you'll fly on top-quality, time-trusted airlines to the destinations of your dreams. You no longer need a trust fund to travel the globe, just a passion for adventure! So next time you need an escape, log onto priceline.com for your passport to the skies.

priceline.com℠
Name Your Own Price℠

Index

V

U

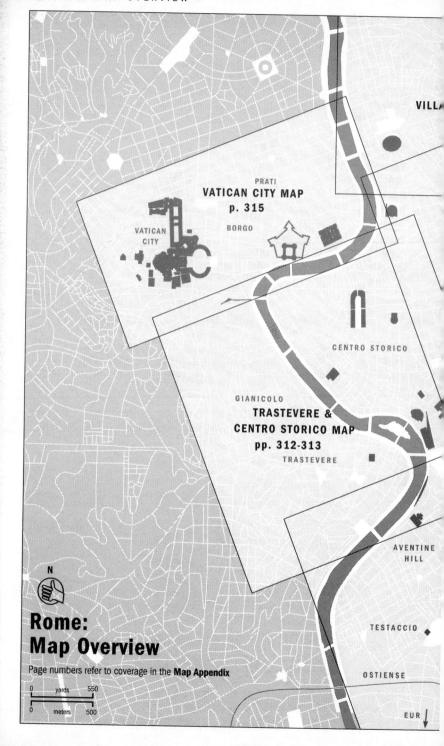

VILLA

PRATI
VATICAN CITY MAP
p. 315

VATICAN
CITY

BORGO

CENTRO STORICO

GIANICOLO
**TRASTEVERE &
CENTRO STORICO MAP
pp. 312-313**
TRASTEVERE

AVENTINE
HILL

TESTACCIO

OSTIENSE

N

Rome:
Map Overview

Page numbers refer to coverage in the **Map Appendix**

| 0 | yards | 550 |
| 0 | meters | 500 |

EUR

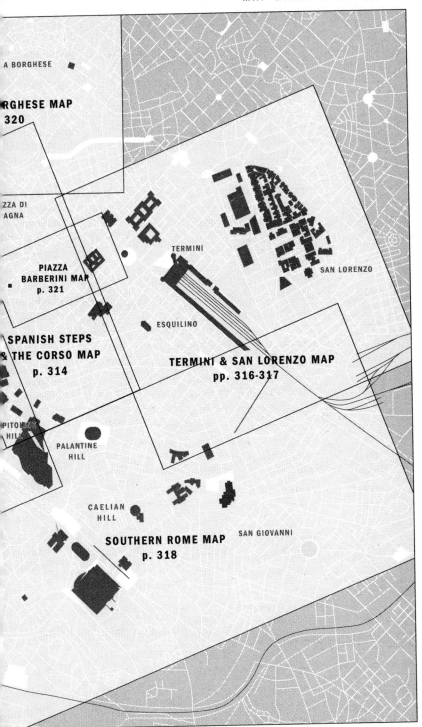

A BORGHESE

RGHESE MAP
320

ZZA DI
AGNA

PIAZZA
BARBERINI MAP
p. 321

TERMINI

SAN LORENZO

SPANISH STEPS
& THE CORSO MAP
p. 314

ESQUILINO

TERMINI & SAN LORENZO MAP
pp. 316-317

PITOLINE
HILL

PALANTINE
HILL

CAELIAN
HILL

SAN GIOVANNI

SOUTHERN ROME MAP
p. 318

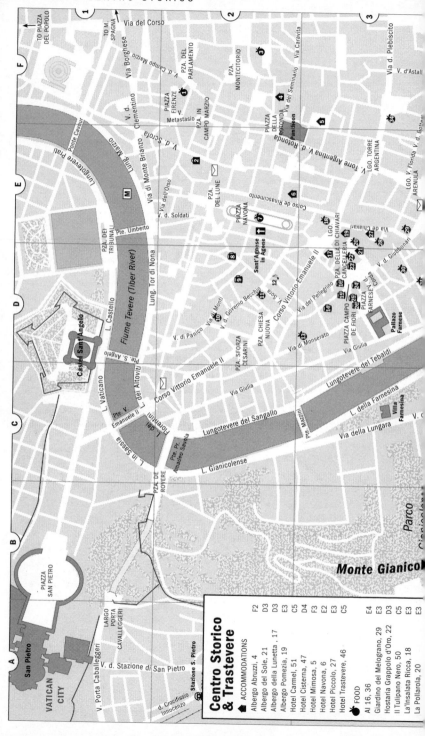

Centro Storico & Trastevere

▲ ACCOMMODATIONS

Albergo Abruzzi, 4	F2
Albergo del Sole, 21	D3
Albergo della Lunetta, 17	D3
Albergo Pomezia, 19	E3
Hotel Carmel, 51	C5
Hotel Cisterna, 47	D4
Hotel Mimosa, 5	F3
Hotel Navona, 6	E2
Hotel Piccolo, 27	E3
Hotel Trastevere, 46	C5

● FOOD

Al 16, 36	E4
Giardino del Melograno, 29	E3
Hostaria Grappolo d'Oro, 22	D3
Il Tulipano Nero, 50	C5
L'Insalata Ricca, 18	E3
La Pollarola, 20	E3

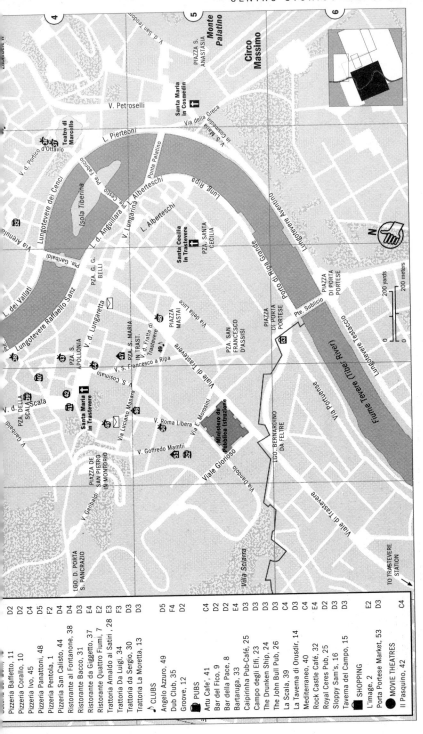

Pizzeria Baffetto, 11 — D2
Pizzeria Corallo, 10 — D2
Pizzeria Ivo, 45 — C4
Pizzeria Panattoni, 48 — D5
Pizzeria Pentola, 1 — F2
Pizzeria San Calisto, 44 — D4
Ristorante al Fontanone, 38 — D4
Ristorante Bacco, 31 — D3
Ristorante da Giggetto, 37 — E4
Ristorante Quattro Fiumi, 7 — E2
Trattoria Amaldo ai Satiri , 28 — E3
Trattoria Da Luigi, 34 — F3
Trattoria da Sergio, 30 — D3
Trattoria La Moretta, 13 — D3

♪ CLUBS
Angelo Azzuro, 49 — D5
Dub Club, 35 — F4
Groove, 12 — D2

🍺 PUBS
Artu Cafe', 41 — C4
Bar del Fico, 9 — D2
Bar della Pace, 8 — D2
Bartaruga, 33 — E4
Caipirinha Pub-Café, 25 — D3
Campo degli Elfi, 23 — D3
The Drunken Ship, 24 — D3
The John Bull Pub, 26 — D3
La Scala, 39 — C4
La Taverna di Orusdir, 14 — D3
Mediterraneo, 40 — C4
Rock Castle Café, 32 — E4
Royal Ceres Pub, 25 — D2
Sloppy Sam's, 16 — D3
Taverna del Campo, 15 — D3

🛍 SHOPPING
L'image, 2 — E2
Porta Portese Market, 53 — D3

● MOVIE THEATRES
Il Pasquino, 42 — C4

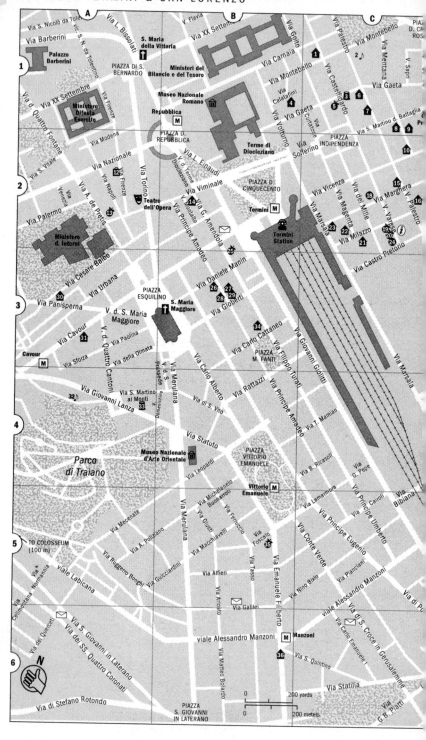

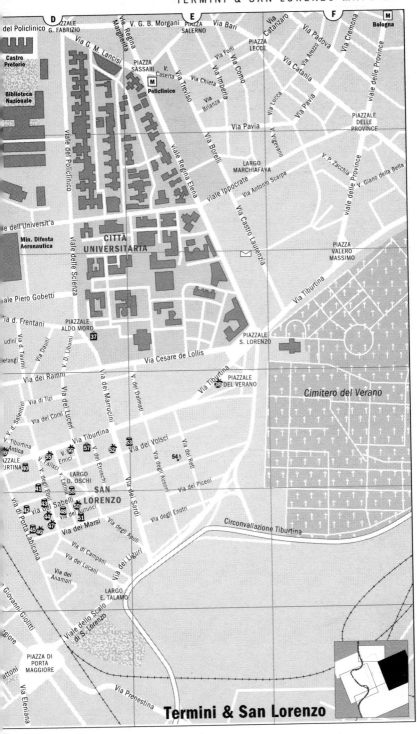

Termini & San Lorenzo

Termini & San Lorenzo

🛏 ACCOMMODATIONS

Hotel Adventure, 16	C2
Hotel Canada, 10	C2
Hotel Castelfidardo and Hotel Lazzari, 1	C1
Hotel Cervia, 15	C2
Hotel Des Artistes, 9	C1
Hotel Dolomiti and Hotel Lachea, 8	C1
Hotel Fenicia, 21	C2
Hotel Galli, 21	C2
Hotel Giu' Giu', 14	B2
Hotel Il Castello, 36	B6
Hotel Kennedy, 34	B3
Hotel Magic, 21	C2
Hotel Marini, 7	C1
Hotel Orlanda, 28	B3
Hotel Pensione Stella, 6	C1
Hotel Roxena, 23	C2
Hotel San Paolo, 30	A3
Hotel Selene, 14	B2
Hotel Serena and Pensione delle Rose, 27	B3
Hotel Sweet Home, 26	B3
Hotel Teti, 28	B3
Hotel Ventura, 16	C2
Pensione Cortorillo, 29	B3
Pensione di Rienzo, 26	B3
Pensione Ester, 17	C2
Pensione Fawlty Towers, 22	C2
Pensione Katty, 7	C1
Pensione Papa Germano, 4	B1
Pensione Sandy, 6	C1

🛍 SHOPPING

Disfunzioni Musicali, 37, 57	D3, D4
Economy Book and Video Center, 12	A2

⚫ SERVICES

Enjoy Rome, 18, 24	C2

🍎 FOOD

Africa, 5	C1
Arancia Blu, 50	D5
Armando, 39	D4
Gold Bar, 13	A2
Hostaria Il Varesino, 19	C2
Il Capellaio Matto, 46	D5
Il Pulcino Ballerino, 47	D5
La Pantera Rosa, 38	E4
Osteria da Luciano, 25	B2
Pizzeria Il Maratoneta, 52	D4
Pizzeria l'Economica, 55	D4
Pizzeria la Pappardella, 44	D5
Ristorante da Lisa, 35	B5
Trattoria Colli Emiliani, 56	D4
Trattoria da Bruno, 20	C2

🍺 PUBS

Dalhu' Pub, 43	D5
Down Town, 45	D5
Drome, 58	D4
Druid's Den, 33	A4
Julius Caesar, 3	C1
Lancelot, 53	E4
Legend Pub, 58	D4
Lupo Alberto, 41	D4
Nirvana, 48	D5
Pigmalione, 42	D5
Pub Hallo'Ween, 40	D4
Skyline Club, 51	D5

♪ CLUBS

Hangar, 32	A4
Club 52, 2	C1
Il Giardini di Adone, 54	E4

Piazza di Spagna & the Corso

🛏 ACCOMMODATIONS

Hotel Pensione Suisse S.A.S., 10
Pensione Jonella, 4
Pensione Panda, 4

🍎 FOOD

Al Piccolo Arancio, 11
Birreria Peroni, 12
Centro Macrobiotico Italiano-Naturist Club, 6
Hostaria da Nerone, 15
McDonald's, 9
Pizzeria al Leoncino, 2
Sogo Asahi, 8
Taverna dei Quaranta, 16
Trattoria da Settimio all'Arancio, 1

🛍 SHOPPING

Messaggerie Musicali, 5
Anglo-American Bookshop, 7
Mada, 3

🍺 PUBS

The Nag's Head, 14
Trinity College, 13

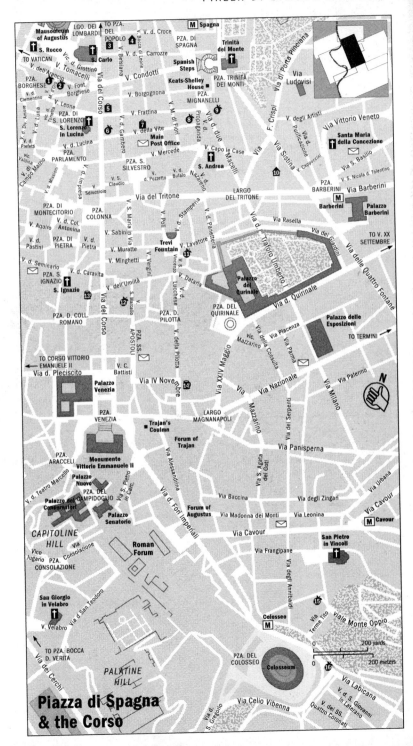

Piazza di Spagna
& the Corso

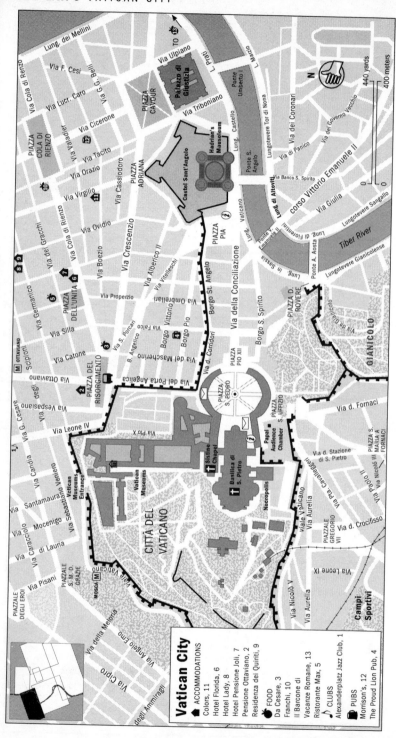

Vatican City

▲ ACCOMMODATIONS
Colors, 11
Hotel Florida, 6
Hotel Lady, 8
Hotel Pensione Joli, 7
Pensione Ottaviano, 2
Residenza dei Quiriti, 9

♦ FOOD
Da Cesare, 3
Franchi, 10
Il Barcone di
Vacanze Romane, 13
Ristorante Max, 5

♪ CLUBS
Alexanderplatz Jazz Club, 1

■ PUBS
Morrison's, 12
The Proud Lion Pub, 4

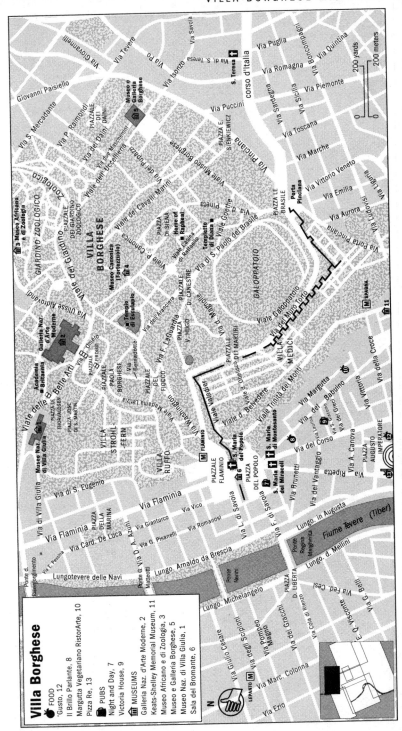

Villa Borghese

◆ FOOD
'Gusto, 12
Il Brillo Parlante, 8
Margutta Vegetariano RistorArte, 10
Pizza Re, 13

🍺 PUBS
Night and Day, 7
Victoria House, 9

🏛 MUSEUMS
Galleria Naz. d'Arte Moderne, 2
Keats-Shelley Memorial Museum, 11
Museo Africano e di Zoologia, 3
Museo e Galleria Borghese, 5
Museo Naz. di Villa Giulia, 1
Sala del Bromante, 6

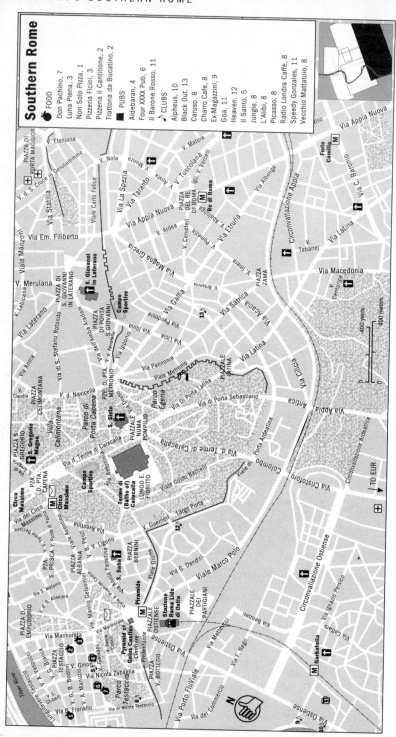

Southern Rome

🍴 FOOD
Don Pachino, 7
Luna Piena, 3
Non Solo Pizza, 1
Pizzeria Ficini, 3
Pizzeria il Cantinone, 2
Trattoria da Bucatino, 2

■ PUBS
Aldebaran, 4
Four XXXX Pub, 6
Il Barone Rosso, 11

♪ CLUBS
Alpheus, 10
Black Out, 13
Caruso, 8
Charro Cafe, 8
Ex-Magazzini, 9
Goa, 11
Heaven, 12
Il Santo, 5
Jungle, 8
L'Alibi, 8
Picasso, 8
Radio Londra Caffè, 8
Speedy Gonzales, 11
Vecchio Mattatoio, 8

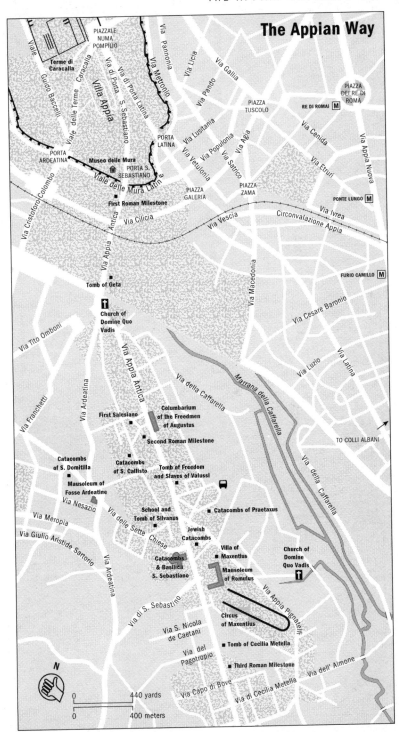

The Appian Way

PIAZZALE NUMA POMPILIO

Via Pannonia

Via Metronio

Via Licia

Via Gallia

Via Pando

Terme di Caracalla

Villa Appia

Viale delle Terme Caracalla

Via di Porta Latina

Via di Porta S. Sebastiano

Guido Baccelli

Viale

PIAZZA TUSCOLO

PIAZZA DEI RE DI ROMA

RE DI ROMA M

Via Cenida

Via Appia Nuova

Via Etrufi

PORTA LATINA

Via Lusitania

Via Vetulonia

Via Populonia

Via Satrico

Via Agia

PIAZZA ZAMA

PORTA ARDEATINA

Museo delle Mura

PORTA S. SEBASTIANO

Viale delle Mura Latine

First Roman Milestone

PIAZZA GALERIA

PONTE LUNGO M

Via Ivrea

Circonvalazione Appia

Via Cristoforo Colombo

Via Appia Antica

Via Cilicia

Via Vescia

Tomb of Geta

FURIO CAMILLO M

Via Cesare Baronio

Church of Domine Quo Vadis

Via Tito Omboni

Via Appia Antica

Via Luzio

Via Latina

Via della Caffarella

Marrana della Caffarella

Via Ardeatina

Via Franchetti

First Salesiano

Columbarium of the Freedmen of Augustus

Second Roman Milestone

TO COLLI ALBANI

Via della Caffarella

Catacombs of S. Domitilla

Catacombs of S. Callisto

Tomb of Freedom and Slaves of Valussi

Mausoleum of Fosse Ardeatine

Via Nesazio

Via delle Sette Chiese

School and Tomb of Silvanus

Catacombs of Praetaxus

Via Meropia

Jewish Catacombs

Via Giulio Aristide Sartorio

Catacombs & Basilica S. Sebastiano

Villa of Maxentius

Church of Domine Quo Vadis

Via Ardeatina

Mausoleum of Romulus

Via di S. Sebastino

Via S. Nicola de Caetani

Circus of Maxentius

Via Appia Pignatelli

Via del Pagotropio

Tomb of Cecilia Metella

Third Roman Milestone

Via dell' Almone

N

Via Capo di Bove

Via di Cecilia Metella

0 ———— 440 yards

0 ———— 400 meters

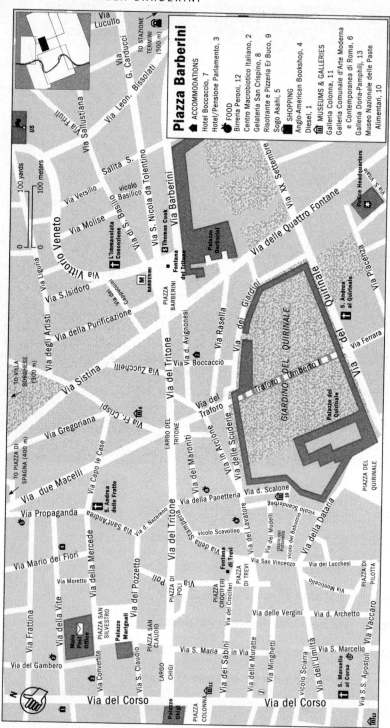

Piazza Barberini

⌂ ACCOMMODATIONS
Hotel Boccaccio, 7
Hotel/Pensione Parlamento, 3

🍴 FOOD
Birreria Peroni, 12
Centro Macrobiotico Italiano, 2
Gelateria San Crispino, 8
Risotrante e Pizzeria Er Buco, 9
Sogo Asahi, 5

🛍 SHOPPING
Anglo-American Bookshop, 4
Diesel, 1

🏛 MUSEUMS & GALLERIES
Galleria Colonna, 11
Galleria Comunale d'Arte Moderna
e Contemporanea di Roma, 6
Galleria Doria-Pamphilj, 13
Museo Nazionale delle Paste
Alimentari, 10

Will you have enough stories to tell your grandchildren?

Yahoo! Travel

Do You YAHOO!?

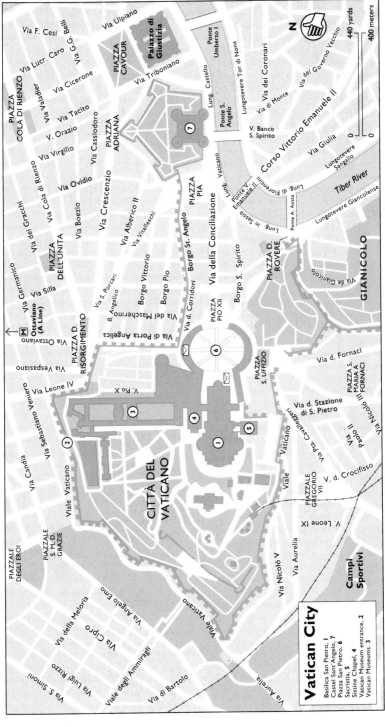

Vatican City

Basilica San Pietro, **1**
Castel Sant'Angelo, **7**
Piazza San Pietro, **6**
Sacristia, **5**
Sistine Chapel, **4**
Vatican Museum entrance, **2**
Vatican Museums, **3**

PIAZZA GIUSEPPE MAZZINI

Lungo. delle Armi

L. delle Navi

L'Amado da Brescia

Via Flaminia

Viale Medaglio d'Oro

Circonvallaz. Trionfale

Via Trionfale

Via della Giuliana

Viale Angelico

Via G. Ferrari

Via Lepanto

Via Marcant. Colonna

L. Michelangelo

Ld. Mellini in Augusta

PIAZZA DEL POPOLO

Via di Ripetta

Via del

Via del Corso

Viale delle Milizie

Via Barletta

Viale Giulio Cesare

Via Citerone

Via Ottaviano

Via Germanico

Via Leone IV

Via Candia

Via Cola di Rienzo

PIAZZA CAVOUR

Via Cipro

Via Crescenzio

PIAZZA AUGUSTO IMPERIALE

Via Angelo Emo

Vatican Museums

CITTÀ DEL VATICANO

Castel Sant' Angelo

L. Prati

Vatican Wall

L. Castello

L. Marianzo

Saint Peter's Basilica

Tiber

Via Aurelia

Viale Vaticano

L.di Tor di Nona

V. s Maria Mediatrice

Via Staz. di S. Pietro

Viale dei Coronari

Corso d. Rinascimento

Via Gregorio VII

L. Gianicolense

Corso Vittorio Emanuele II

PIAZZA NAVONA

Pantheon

Via Giulia

Via d. Cava Aurelia

V. Orti d'Alibert

Palazzo Farnese

Viale delle Mura Aurelia

V. di S. F. di Sales

L. d. Farnesina

L. Arenula

MONTE DEL GIANICOLO

L. dei Vallati

L. dei Cenci

V. Garibaldi

L. Sansio

Isola Tiberina

L. dei Anguillara

Ponte Palatino

Via Aurelia Antica

S. Maria in Trastevere

Villa Doria Pamphili

TRASTEVERE

Via di S. Pancrazio

V. Nicola Fabrizi

Via Glorioso

V. di S. Michele

Via Giacinto Carini

Via Dandolo

Pta. Portese (flea market)

Ponte Sublicio

Lungotevere

Via Marmorata

Via di Villa Pamphili

Via Fontelana

Via di Trastevere

Lungotevere Testaccio

Via Vitte sia

Viale Zambarelli

Via dei Quattro Venti

Via Alessandro Poeria

Via Portuense

V. Giovanni Branca

Via Nicola Galvani

Via Federico Ozanam

Via di Donna Olimpia

V. Cavalcani

Ponte Testaccio

Parco Testaccio

N

0 yards 550

0 meters 500

TESTACCIO

Rome Overview

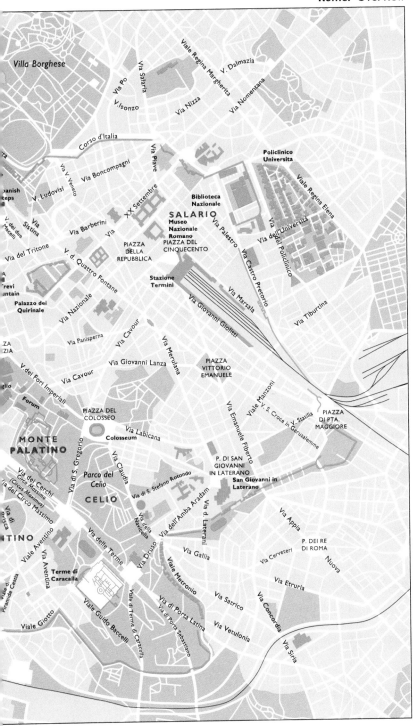

Rome Transport

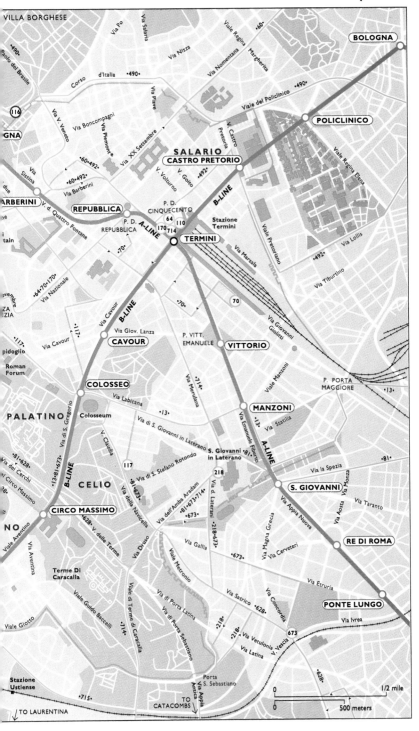

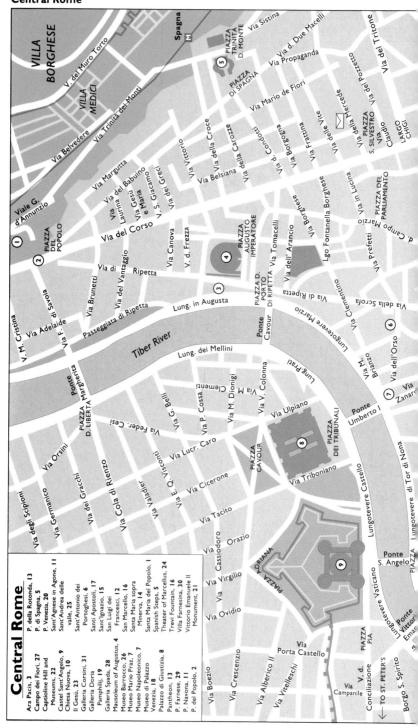

Central Rome

Ara Pacis, 3
Campo dei Fiori, 27
Capitoline Hill and Museums, 22
Castel Sant'Angelo, 9
Chiesa Nuova, 10
Il Gesù, 23
Galleria Corsini, 31
Galleria Doria Pamphilij, 19
Galleria Spada, 28
Mausoleum of Augustus, 4
Museo Barrocco, 26
Museo Mario Praz, 7
Museo Napoleonico, 7
Museo di Palazzo Venezia, 18
Palazzo di Giustizia, 8
Pantheon, 13
P. Farnese, 29
P. Navona, 11
P. del Popolo, 2
P. della Rotonda, 13
P. di Spagna, 5
P. Venezia, 20
Sant'Agnese in Agone, 11
Sant'Andrea delle valle, 25
Sant'Antonio dei Portoghesi, 6
Santi Apostoli, 17
Sant'Ignazio, 15
San Luigi dei Francesci, 12
San Marcello, 16
Santa Maria sopra Minerva, 14
Santa Maria del Popolo, 1
Spanish Steps, 5
Theater of Marcellus, 24
Trevi Fountain, 16
Villa Farnesina, 30
Vittorio Emanuele II Monument, 21

VILLA BORGHESE

VILLA MEDICI

Spagna

Tiber River

Via Lucchesi

PIAZZA D. PILOTTA

(17) PIAZZA DEI S.S. APOSTOLI

S.S. Apostoli

Via del Corso

Via dell'Umiltà

Via V. Minghetti

(20)

TO THE FORUM AND THE PALATINE

(21)

(22)

MONTE CAPITOLINO

Via del Consolazione

Via del Plebiscito

(18)

(19)

Via Gatta

PZA. DEI V. Pie di COLLEGIO Marmo ROMANO

PIAZZA GRAZIOLI

PIAZZA SAN MARCO

V.S. Marco

Via d'Aracoeli

Via Petroselli

Via del Teatro di Marcello

(15)

Via del Gesù

(23) PIAZZA D. GESÙ

PIAZZA CAMPITELLI

(24)

Via V. M. Caetani

V. Colonelle

V. Pastini

V. Seminario

(14)

LARGO DI TORRE ARGENTINA

Corso Vittorio Emanuele II

V. d. Botteghe Oscuro

V. d. Funari

Lung. di Pierleoni

Via Portico d. Ottavia

Via Catalana

Porte Fabricio

V. dell'elena

PIAZZA DELLA ROTONDA

(13)

V. Santa Chiara

V. dl Torre Argentina

V. Paganica

V. Falegnami

PIAZZA CENCI

Lung. dei Cenci

ISOLA TIBERINA

Via Giustiniani

PIAZZA S. EUSTACCHIO

V. Santa

V. Monterone

LARGO ARENULA

V. d. Barbieri

Vic. d. Chiodaroli

Via d. Conservatorio

Via Arenula

V. Dogana

(12)

LARGO TEATRO VALLE

(25)

V. Monte Farina

LARGO DEI LIBRARI

Via dei Chiavari

Via d. Giubbonari

V. d. Zoccolette

Lungotevere dei Vallati

Ponte Garibaldi

PIAZZA G. G. BELLI

Corso del Rinascimento

(11) PIAZZA NAVONA

PIAZZA SAN PANTALEO

PZA. DEL PARADISO

(26)

LARGO DEI PALLARO

Via dei Pettinari

PIAZZA V: PALLOTTI

Lungotevere Sanzio

V. dell'Anima

V. Leutari

(27)

(28)

V. Polverone

Ponte Sisto

Lungotevere dei Vallati

Lungotevere del Moro

Via del Moro

Via Vetrina

Via d. Parione

V. Savelli

Via Sora

(29)

V. Mascherone

Via del Farnesi

Tiber River

PIAZZA DI SANT' EGIDIO

Via del Governo Vecchio

Via del Pellegrino

Via Cappellari

Via del Monserrato

V. d. Armata

Via S. Dorotea

Via della Scala

TO PZA. DI S.M. IN TRASTEVERE

(10)

Via Giulia

Via S. Eligio

Lungotevere dei Tebaldi

Via d. Mattonato

Via Garibaldi

Corso Vittorio Emanuele II

V. dei Banchi Vecchi

Via d. Gonfalone

Via Schina

LARGO PEROSI

Via Mazzini

Lungotevere della Farnesina

Ponte Mazzini

(30)

(31)

Via della Lungara

Vic. di Penitenza

Via di Riari

Via Corsini

CORONARI

Lungotevere Sangallo

Tiber River

Lungotevere Gianicolense

Lungotevere di Fiorentini

Ponte Principe Amadeo

PIAZZA D. ROVERE

Lu...

...dei ...tenzieri

Via di Orti di Albert

Via delle Mantellate

Via di S. Francesco di Sales

PARCO GIANICOLENSE

N

300 yards

300 meters

0

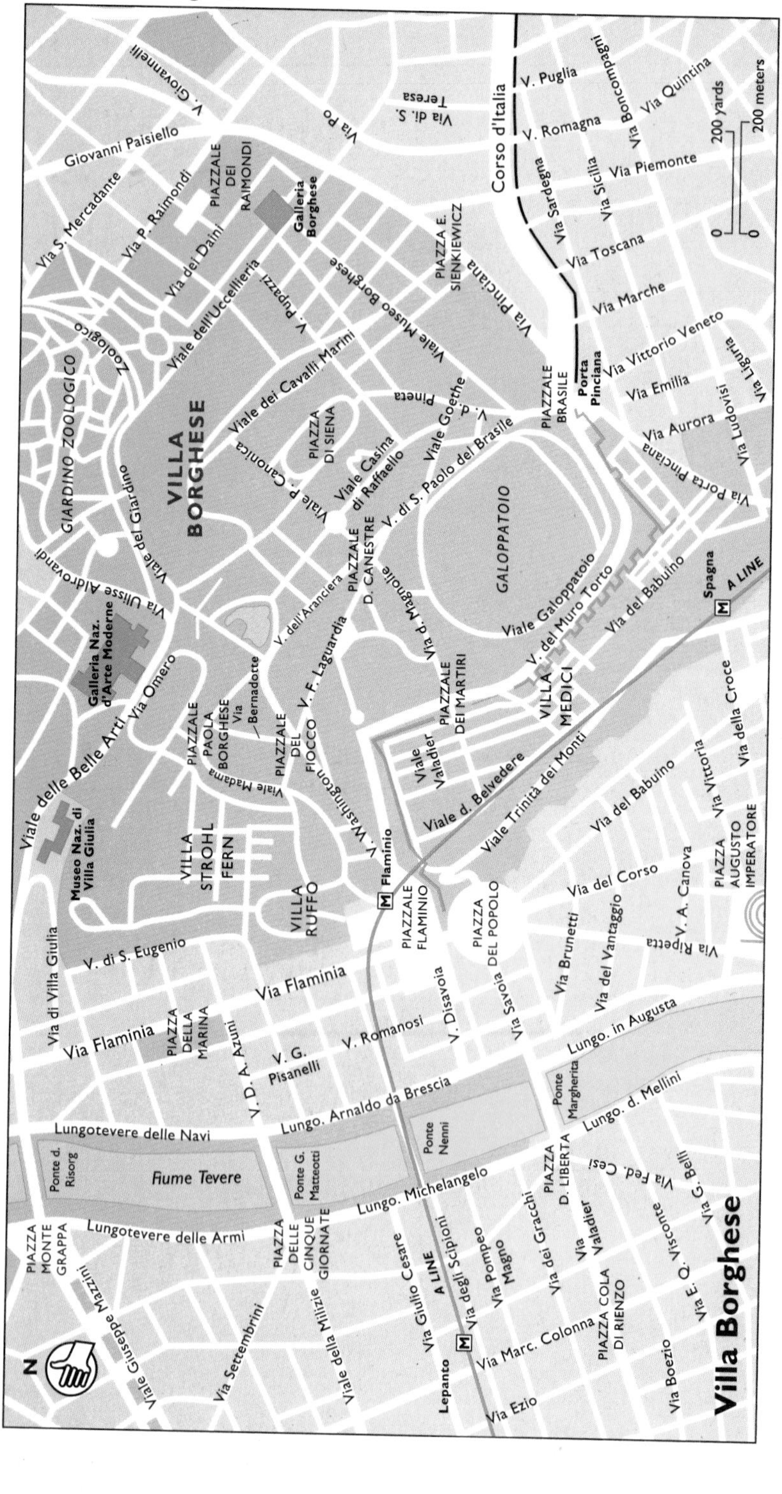
Villa Borghese
VILLA BORGHESE
GIARDINO ZOOLOGICO
Zoologico
Galleria Borghese
PIAZZALE DEI RAIMONDI
Galleria Naz. d'Arte Moderne
Museo Naz. di Villa Giulia
VILLA STROHL FERN
VILLA RUFFO
VILLA MEDICI
GALOPPATOIO
PIAZZA DI SIENA
PIAZZALE D. CANESTRE
PIAZZALE PAOLA BORGHESE
PIAZZALE DEL FIOCCO
PIAZZALE DEI MARTIRI
PIAZZALE BRASILE
PIAZZA E. SIENKIEWICZ
PIAZZALE FLAMINIO
PIAZZA DEL POPOLO
PIAZZA DELLA MARINA
PIAZZA AUGUSTO IMPERATORE
PIAZZA D. LIBERTA
PIAZZA COLA DI RIENZO
PIAZZA DELLE CINQUE GIORNATE
PIAZZA MONTE GRAPPA
Porta Pinciana
Flaminio
Spagna
Lepanto
A LINE
Fiume Tevere
Ponte d. Risorg
Ponte G. Matteotti
Ponte Nenni
Ponte Margherita
Lungotevere delle Navi
Lungotevere delle Armi
Lungo. Arnaldo da Brescia
Lungo. Michelangelo
Lungo. in Augusta
Lungo. d. Mellini
Corso d'Italia
Via Po
Via di. S. Teresa
V. Giovannelli
Giovanni Paisiello
Via S. Mercadante
Via P. Raimondi
Via dei Daini
Viale dell'Uccellieria
V. Pinciana
Viale Museo Borghese
Viale dei Cavalli Marini
V. d. Pineta
Viale Goethe
Viale P. Canonica
Viale Casina di Raffaello
V. di S. Paolo del Brasile
Viale del Giardino
Via Ulisse Aldrovandi
V. dell'Aranciera
V. F. Laguardia
Via d. Magnolie
Viale Galoppatoio
V. del Muro Torto
Via Bernadotte
Viale Madama
V. Washington
Via Omero
Viale delle Belle Arti
Viale Valadier
Viale d. Belvedere
Viale Trinità dei Monti
Via del Babuino
Via della Croce
Via Vittoria
Via del Corso
Via A. Canova
Via Ripetta
Via Brunetti
Via del Vantaggio
V. di S. Eugenio
Via di Villa Giulia
Via Flaminia
V. D. A. Azuni
V. G. Pisanelli
V. Romanosi
V. Disavoia
Via Savoia
V. Puglia
V. Romagna
Via Boncompagni
Via Quintina
Via Piemonte
Via Sicilia
Via Sardegna
Via Toscana
Via Marche
Via Vittorio Veneto
Via Emilia
Via Liguria
Via Aurora
Via Ludovisi
Via Porta Pinciana
Via Fed. Cesi
Via G. Belli
Via Q. Visconte
Via E.
Via Boezio
Via Valadier
Via dei Gracchi
Via Pompeo Magno
Via degli Scipioni
Via Giulio Cesare
Via Marc. Colonna
Via Ezio
Viale della Milizie
Via Settembrini
Viale Giuseppe Mazzini
200 yards
200 meters
N